3

P9-DEQ-434

READER'S DIGEST

How to Increase Your Word Power

*Prepared in Association
with Stuart B. Flexner*

*Published by Writer's Digest Books
with permission of The Reader's Digest Association, Inc.*

ACKNOWLEDGMENT

The editors of the Reader's Digest gratefully acknowledge the assistance of Donald Berwick, professor of English, Hofstra University, in preparing and reviewing the manuscript of HOW TO INCREASE YOUR WORD POWER.

© 1971 The Reader's Digest Association, Inc.
© 1971 The Reader's Digest Association [Canada] Ltd.
Reproduction in any manner, in whole or in part, in English or in other languages, is prohibited.
All rights are reserved
Published in 1987 by Writer's Digest Books, an imprint of F&W Publications, Inc., 1507 Dana Ave., Cincinnati, OH 45207, with permission of The Reader's Digest Association, Inc.
Library of Congress Catalog Card Number: 76-134316
Printed in the United States of America

ISBN 0-89879-292-4

CONTENTS

Introduction   1

How to Use the Pronunciation Key   6

PART ONE: THREE KEYS TO GREATER WORD POWER

1. Roots—Your First Key to Word Power   10
2. Prefixes—Your Second Key to Word Power   183
3. Suffixes—Your Third Key to Word Power   266

Fun With Words:

SHORT WORDS 17; SOME BIG A'S 27; REVIEW OF ROOTS 33; MORE KEY
ROOTS 47; REVIEW OF ROOTS 53; WHICH ROOTS DO YOU KNOW? 66;
COMMON ROOTS 73; REVIEW OF ROOTS 78; REVIEW OF ROOTS 90;
TOUGHER ROOTS 101; STORIES BEHIND THE WORDS 108; REVIEW OF
ROOTS 120; VOCABULARY BUILDING 130; REVIEW OF ROOTS 144; SPOT
THE SPECIALISTS 151; STUMP YOUR FRIENDS 158; REVIEW OF ROOTS 182;
FROM A TO AB 191; PREFIX AD- AND ITS DISGUISES 195; TOGETHERNESS
WORDS 208; PREFIX DE- 212; PREFIX DIS- 216; PREFIX EX- AND ITS
DISGUISES 219; PREFIXES MAL-, MALE-, MIS 231; ALL, AROUND, AND
BESIDE 240; PREFIXES PRO- AND PRE- 246; PREFIX SUB- 254; COLORFUL
ADJECTIVES 269.

Quickie Quizzes:

DESCRIPTIONS, PLEASE 15; ANYONE YOU KNOW? 29; RECOGNIZING ROOTS 38;
COLORS 56; WORD BUILDING 71; WORD BUILDING 81; WORD BUILDING 96;
SOME FAMILIAR ROOTS 106; WORD BUILDING 124; WORD BUILDING 140; TEN
MORE WORD BUILDING BLOCKS 167; PREFIX AB-, ABS- 187; PREFIX COM- 205;
"NOT" WORDS 223; "IN" WORDS 227; BACK AGAIN 249; SUPER-WORDS 256;
DOCTORS AND THEIR SPECIALTIES 261; MORE "NOT" WORDS 263; -OLOGIES
271.

Exploring Words:

THE ANIMAL KINGDOM 23; PEOPLE WHO BECAME WORDS 41; ELEVEN
WORDS TAKEN FROM PLACE NAMES 61; IS THERE A DOCTOR IN THE
HOUSE? 85; FROM THE ART WORLD 117; WHAT KIND OF PERSON IS
THAT? 135; MORE PEOPLE WHO BECAME WORDS 162; HOW WELL DO
YOU KNOW THE BIBLE? 197; HOW MANY LANGUAGES DO YOU SPEAK?
225; CHEERS, OLD CHAP 243; NUMBERING, COUNTING, AND MEASURING
265; SOME WORD MINIATURES 280.

PART TWO: SPELL IT RIGHT

Spelling—A Skill That Can Be Learned   282
1. The Most Frequently Misspelled Words   284
2. Saying It and Spelling It   292
3. Which Is It: -ABLE or -IBLE?   294
4. Which Is It: -AL, -EL, or -LE?   299
5. Which Is It: -ANT or -ENT? -ANCE or -ENCE? -ANCY or -ENCY?   300
6. Which Is It: -AR, -ER, or -OR? or even -RE or -OUR?   307
7. Which Is It: -ARY or -ERY?   314
8. Which Is It: C or CK?   318
9. Which Is It: C, S, or SC?   319
10. Which Is It: -CEDE, -CEED, or -SEDE?   321
11. Which Is It: -CY or -SY?   323
12. The Final-E Rule   325
13. Which Is It: -EFY or -IFY?   329
14. There Is No dg in Privilege   330
15. I Before E Except After C   331
16. Which Is It: -ISE, -IZE, or -YZE?   336
17. Which Is It: -LY or -ALLY?   338
18. Which Is It: -OUS or -US?   338
19. When Is a Final Y Changed to I?   340

Fun With Words:
-ABLE AND -IBLE 298; WORDS ENDING IN -AL, -EL, AND -LE 301; -ANT AND -ENT 305; WORDS ENDING IN -ANCE AND -ENCE 306; WORDS ENDING IN -AR, -ER, AND -OR 313; WORDS ENDING IN -ARY AND -ERY 317; REVIEW: -ARY, -ERY, -CEDE, -SEDE 322; WORDS ENDING IN -CY OR -SY 324; IE AND EI 335; WORDS ENDING IN -OUS OR -US 342; A ROUNDUP 345; A SECOND ROUNDUP 346.

Quickie Quizzes:
EASY 286; MEDIUM 289; HARD 291; SPELLING AND PRONUNCIATION 293; STUMP YOUR FRIENDS 297; STUMP YOUR FRIENDS 319; C, S, OR SC? 320; IE OR EI? 333; -LY OR -ALLY? 339.

Spelling Tests:
FOURTEEN -ABLE, -IBLE SPELLING MISTAKES 297; -AL, -EL, OR -LE? 300; -ANT, -ANCE, -ANCY, OR -ENT, -ENCE, -ENCY 304; -AR, -ER, -OR, OR -RE 311; -ARY OR -ERY? 315; -CEDE, -CEED, OR -SEDE? 321; -CY OR -SY? 323; THE FINAL-E RULE 328; -EFY OR -IFY? 330; -EGE OR -EDGE? 331; IE OR EI? 334; -YZE, -ISE, OR -IZE? 337; Y OR I? 344.

PART THREE: SAY IT RIGHT

Pronunciation—Part Of Your Word Power   348
1. Speak for Yourself   349
2. "Correct Pronunciation"   356
3. Don't Leave Out Letters or Sounds   359
4. Don't Add Letters or Sounds   364
5. Is CH Pronounced CH, SH, or K?   368
6. The Hard G, the Soft G, and Some Other G's   369
7. -ATE, -ILE, and S   373
8. The Shifty Accent   376
9. Where Are You?   381
10. Don't Let Foreign Words Confuse You   384

Fun With Words:
FOURTEEN PRONUNCIATION DEMONS 355; COLORFUL ADJECTIVES 358; SILENT LETTERS 367; C, CH, OR K CHALLENGES 370; THE SHIFTY ACCENT 380; FROM THE FRENCH 387.

Quickie Quizzes:
DEMONS AND DOUBLE DEMONS 352; TEN KEY PUZZLERS 363; GETTING THE GIST OF G'S 372; -ILE AND S SOUNDS 375; IT'S A GREAT PLACE TO VISIT, BUT . . . 383.

PART FOUR: PUNCTUATE IT RIGHT

Punctuation Marks—Clues To Clearer Meaning   392
1. Capitalization   394
2. The Period   402
3. The Question Mark   404
4. The Exclamation Point   405
5. The Comma   408
6. The Colon   412
7. The Semicolon   415
8. The Dash   419
9. Quotation Marks and Italics   421
10. Parentheses and Brackets   425
11. The Apostrophe   427
12. The Hyphen   433

Fun With Words:
MORE FOREIGN WORDS 403; MORE SHORTIES 414; ONE-SYLLABLE WORDS 418; REVIEW OF PREFIX PRE- 432.

Punctuation Tests:
>   CAPITAL LETTERS 401; PERIODS, EXCLAMATION POINTS, AND QUESTION MARKS 407; COMMAS, SEMICOLONS, AND COLONS 417; THE APOSTROPHE 431; THE HYPHEN 437; A HARD FINAL EXAMINATION 438.

PART FIVE: PRACTICAL GRAMMAR

Putting Grammar To Work	442
1. Wrong Pronouns	443
2. Singular and Plural Forms	447
3. Wrong Pronouns	449
4. Misplaced Modifiers	451
5. Wrong Verb Form	454
6. Confusion of Adjectives and Adverbs	462
7. The Double Negative	466

Fun With Words:
>   MORE -ABLE, -IBLE WORDS 446; INTERESTING VERBS 461.

Grammar Tests:
>   I OR ME? SHE OR HER? HE OR HIM? WE OR US? THEY OR THEM? 445; THE NUMBERS GAME 450; JUST FOR FUN 453; CORRECT VERB FORMS 459; WELL OR GOOD? BAD OR BADLY? SLOW OR SLOWLY? 465

PART SIX: USING YOUR WORD POWER

Use Your Word Power Right	470
1. Wrong Usage	472
2. Pairs That Snare	479
3. Confused Words	499
4. Linked Words	513
5. Six Key Questions About Usage and Grammar	515

Fun With Words:
>   REVIEWING THE SPECIALISTS 520.

Quickie Quizzes:
>   PAIRS THAT SNARE 484; REVIEW OF PAIRS THAT SNARE 491; MORE PAIRS THAT SNARE 498; CONFUSED WORDS 505; REVIEW OF CONFUSED WORDS 512; LINKED WORDS 514.

Usage Test: AVOIDING POOR USAGE	478
INDEX	521

INTRODUCTION

The purpose of this book is very simple: to help you master the English language quickly, easily, and thoroughly. If you are a poor speaker or writer, this book will help you become a good one. If you are a good speaker and writer, it will help you become a better one. It will help you to increase that vital asset: your word power.

Starting with the very first chapter, How To INCREASE YOUR WORD POWER teaches you thousands of words to add to your vocabulary and gives you all the clear explanations, simple rules, and professional tips for vocabulary building, perfect spelling, correct pronunciation, proper punctuation, correct usage, and good grammar.

Actual tests have shown that a person's success in any field is closely related to his or her vocabulary and language skills. Such tests show that successful executives, students, scientists, secretaries, housewives, doctors—successful people in all walks of life—all have in common a mastery of words. That is why How To INCREASE YOUR WORD POWER can be important to you. It can teach you to use your language far more easily, correctly, and effectively than you now do. It offers you the kind of self-training that can make you a confident, persuasive speaker and writer.

What This Book Contains

To do all these things, this book offers a complete self-teaching and review of vocabulary building and good English.

The six parts of the book are *Three Keys to Greater Word Power, Spell It Right, Say It Right, Punctuate It Right, Practical Grammar*, and *Using Your Word Power*. Each contains step-by-step chapters that give you important vocabulary words and all the facts and easy-to-remember rules, hints, and tips you need to know. Each teaches you vocabulary building and the do's and don't's of good English. Each is complete, authoritative, and full of information, word lists, and entertaining special features. These special features include over 100 tests, quizzes, and word games. Scattered throughout the entire book, these features include Fun With Words to test your vocabulary, Quickie Quizzes for speedy review, Exploring Words to tell you the fascinating stories behind many of the words we use every day, and spelling, pronunciation, punctuation, usage, and grammar exercises to sharpen your skills. (The correct answers immediately follow all vocabulary tests, review quizzes, and exercises so that you can check yourself quickly.)

Every chapter of the book gives you concise, easy-to-remember explanations of one basic group of vocabulary words or of one basic problem in English. Most chapters contain lists of words to add to your vocabulary or of spelling, pronunciation, or usage demons for you to learn or review. And finally, of course, many chapters end with an entertaining vocabulary test, review quiz, or even a word game to stump your family and friends.

Remember that just because this book is divided into six parts does not mean that you should separate vocabulary building, spelling, pronunciation, punctuation, usage, and grammar in your own mind. The divisions are intended only to make learning easy by letting you concentrate fully on a single vocabulary list or language problem at a time. Even though each part is a unit by itself, all six have been thoroughly integrated into the overall plan of How To Increase Your Word Power. Here's what you will find in each of them.

THREE KEYS TO GREATER WORD POWER   This is the longest and one of the most important parts of the book, because a large, useful vocabulary is the basis of word power. It takes up the three keys to vocabulary building by teaching you to recognize the basic building blocks of words, while at the same time teaching you thousands of words using these building blocks. Every chapter in this part explains one or more basic word elements or building blocks and then lists, defines, and teaches the most useful, typical, and interesting core words based on them. Since the lists of vocabulary words taught in each chapter are grouped together and related in meaning, spelling, and pronunciation, they are easy to learn and remember. This part of the book also lists further related words to study. Many chapters are followed by vocabulary tests and drills.

SPELL IT RIGHT   Step by step this part of the book teaches you all the facts, rules, tricks, and tips you need to spell perfectly—*and* it actually lists and tells you how to spell all of the most commonly misspelled words. It includes spelling lists from high schools and colleges, business firms, and government agencies. Almost every chapter in this section takes up one basic spelling problem, such as double letters; *-able* or *-ible; -ie* or *-ei; -ceed, -cede,* or *-sede; -ance* or *-ence,* and tells you how to solve the problem. Helpful lists of all the most troublesome words in a specific problem category make it easier for you to learn all the related facts, rules, and tips.

SAY IT RIGHT This part teaches you to pronounce words properly. Almost every chapter in this part deals with one common pronunciation problem, such as avoiding slovenly speech, accenting the right syllable, long and short *a* sounds, silent letters, tricky *c* and *k* sounds, what words end in the confusing *-ate* or *-it* sounds and in the *-ile* or *-il* sounds. Each of these chapters contains lists of pronunciation demons, telling you exactly how to pronounce the words properly, and gives you rules and tips on pronouncing new words as you encounter them.

PUNCTUATE IT RIGHT This part of the book gives simple but complete explanations of all the punctuation marks and how, why, and where to use each—*plus* hundreds of examples for you to study or refer to at any time. Separate chapters cover the use of every punctuation mark and formality, including capital letters, the period, the comma, the semicolon, quotation marks, question marks, exclamation points, and parentheses. There are punctuation exercises and drills to give you practice and the Fun With Words vocabulary tests, quizzes, and word games that appear throughout the book.

PRACTICAL GRAMMAR This part of the book does *not* teach grammatical theory but only practical grammar, the grammar you must know and use to speak and write well. It tells what good grammar is and how to know and use it easily and quickly. It takes up only the most common mistakes and problems in grammar and tells you how to recognize and avoid them. There are complete, up-to-date discussions of such old puzzlers as *It is I* or *It is Me, Who* or *Whom,* split infinitives, ending sentences with prepositions, and many others. There are many examples, showing you exactly what to do and how to do it.

USING YOUR WORD POWER This part explains the various levels of speech and writing (formal and informal, slang, nonstandard) and when and how to use or avoid them. Most of the chapters in this section list the most commonly confused, misused, and abused words in the English language, point out the pitfalls of each, tell you how to avoid embarrassing mistakes, and show you how to use the proper word in the proper place.

Thus, the six parts that make up HOW TO INCREASE YOUR WORD POWER can increase your vocabulary by thousands of words and teach you perfect spelling, correct pronunciation, perfect punctuation, correct usage, and good grammar. They will increase your word power and help you master English.

How This Book Was Written

HOW TO INCREASE YOUR WORD POWER combines the "tried-and-true" methods of teaching with modern methods of vocabulary building and English instruction. All of the text, all the words taught and examples given, and all the tests, quizzes, exercises, and word games have been carefully selected to help you master a large vocabulary and the rules of good English.

In order that this book be complete, it teaches you both the most effective and the most troublesome words in the English language, as shown by thousands of actual tests and major word lists. For example, spelling word lists from grade-school tests, high-school tests, Regents and college-entrance exams, remedial-reading courses, college-board and placement exams, secretarial and business schools, large business firms, government agencies, and research bureaus have been checked to ensure that all the most important, useful spelling words, rules, and tips are given in this book. The same care has been taken with all the other sections to ensure that the word lists, rules, tips, and tests given in the vocabulary, spelling, pronunciation, punctuation, usage, and grammar sections include all the most important, practical, easy-to-use information, all the demon words, and all the answers to the questions and problems you may have.

How To Use This Book

How much time you should spend on building your vocabulary and your mastery of good English depends on your present level of skill and your own need and desire to learn. Fifteen minutes a day may be enough to achieve what you want, or you may want to put in as much as an hour a day if you need to make more rapid progress. You can learn the material in HOW TO INCREASE YOUR WORD POWER in thirty days or you can enjoy learning from it at your leisure over a period of several months.

4

To get the most out of this book be sure to master the simple rules, easy tips, and problem words from each chapter before starting the next. Do all the tests, quizzes, and word games, too—they are fun and you will learn something from all of them. In other words, don't just let your eyes passively read this book—get your mind actively involved in it, chapter by chapter and quiz by quiz. Concentrate on your own language problems. If you already know and use a word properly or don't have a problem with this or that spelling, pronunciation, punctuation, usage, or grammar rule, then just review the chapter that covers it and spend more time on the words and chapters that you need to work on.

However much time you take to study, read, browse in, or refer to this book, remember one thing: you'll be mastering the English language—there aren't many more profitable or satisfying ways to spend your time.

HOW TO USE THE PRONUNCIATION KEY

One problem of teaching proper pronunciation in a book is that the reader *sees* the printed words but cannot *hear* them. All dictionaries and language books, including this one, overcome this problem in a very simple way: We "respell" the words within brackets or parentheses so that they are written exactly as they should sound. For example, if the word *cat* were a pronunciation demon that we wanted to show you how to pronounce, we would respell it [kat].

Why is such respelling necessary to show correct pronunciation? First, because English uses over forty-five basic sounds but has only twenty-six letters to represent them. Thus, some letters must do double duty and stand for more than one sound (all vowels, *a,e,i,o,* and *u,* do double duty as does *y,* which is both a consonant and a vowel). Second, because our normal, correct spelling does not always indicate the way words are pronounced today.

Thus, the letter *c* can be represented by a *k* to show that *cat* is pronounced [kat] or it can be represented by an *s* to show that the word *city* is pronounced [sit′ē]. This is simple for all the letters except the vowels *a, e, i, o,* and *u* and the letter *g* when it is pronounced [j] in such words as *gentleman, gem, gelatin,* and *genius.* Each vowel can be pronounced in two or more ways (the letter *o* can be pronounced in at least seven different ways!). So to show you exactly how an *a, e, i,* or *u* should be pronounced in any given word, certain simple marks (called diacritical marks) may be placed over the letter. For example, if a vowel in any word should be pronounceed like the *a* in *ace,* then that vowel is represented by ā. Thus, if the word *age* were a pronunciation demon we would respell it for you as [āj].

You never really have to memorize the letters and symbols used in such respellings. You already know exactly what *k* and *s* sound like; so that, if *cat* is respelled [kat] and *city* is respelled [sit′ē], you just pronounce them exactly as you see them. But suppose you don't know how the ē in the respelling [sit′ē] should be pronounced? It's simple. You turn to the Pronunciation Key (a list of all the letters, symbols, and marks used to indicate pronunciation) and find that the *e* is pronounced as the first *e* in *even* or the *ee* in *tree.* Thus, by already knowing how to pronounce the letters in a respelled word or by looking up any unusual symbols, combinations, or marks (such as an *a, e, i, o,* or *u* with diacritical marks) in the Pronunciation Key, you can pronounce the word properly—because it has been respelled for you exactly as it sounds.

6

Are there any other letters or marks used in respelling words so that they read the same way they sound? Yes, three easy ones. A primary stress mark (′) is placed after the group of letters forming a syllable that should be "stressed" or said loudest. Thus, *city* is respelled [sit′ē] and the primary stress mark shows that it is stressed or accented on the first syllable, said as SITe rather than as sitE. Some longer words will have both a primary stress mark (′) over the syllable to have the greatest emphasis and a secondary stress mark (′) over the syllable to have slightly less emphasis. Thus, the word *commendation* is respelled as [kom′en·dā′shen], which shows you that the first syllable, kom, has less emphasis and the third syllable, dā, has slightly greater emphasis. So the primary stress mark (′) and the secondary stress mark (′) are two marks you should remember to help you pronounce the respelled words properly.

The third unusual mark or symbol you will see in respelled words looks like this: ə. Linguists call this ə symbol the "schwa" and it merely indicates the very common "uh" sound in English. So when you see the symbol ə in a respelled word, it is pronounced "uh." Amazingly enough, all five of our English vowels, *a, e, i, o,* and *u,* are often pronounced as ə or "uh." For example:

> the *a* in *above* respelled [ə·buv′]
> the *e* in *sicken* respelled [sik′ən]
> the *i* in *clarity* respelled [klar′ə·tē]
> the *o* in *melon* respelled [mel′ən]
> the *u* in *focus* respelled [fō′kəs]

That's all you need to know about how words are respelled in this book when it is necessary to show you how they are actually pronounced. The respelling system is simple: it uses common letters like *k* to respell *cat* [kat] and a few special combinations and marks to respell the *a,e,i,o,* and *u* vowel sounds, like the *e* sound in *city* [sit′ē], or like the combined *th* sound in *this* [this]. It also uses primary (′) and secondary (′) stress marks and the ə symbol to represent the common "uh" sound.

On the following page is a complete Pronunciation Key for you to refer to whenever you see a word respelled to indicate its proper pronunciation and aren't sure what the letters, symbols, or marks stand for. (This pronunciation key is based on that used in the Reader's Digest GREAT ENCYCLOPEDIC DICTIONARY.)

PRONUNCIATION KEY

The primary stress mark (′) is placed after the syllable having the heavier stress; the secondary stress mark (′) follows a syllable having a somewhat lighter stress, as in **com·men·da·tion** (kom′ən·dā′shən).

a	add, map	m	move, seem	u	up, done
ā	ace, rate	n	nice, tin	û(r)	urn, term
â(r)	care, air	ng	ring, song	yōō	use, few
ä	palm, father				
b	bat, rub	o	odd, hot	v	vain, eve
		ō	open, so	w	win, away
ch	check, catch	ô	order, jaw	y	yet, yearn
d	dog, rod	oi	oil, boy	z	zest, muse
e	end, pet	ou	out, now	zh	vision, pleasure
ē	even, tree	ōō	pool, food		
f	fit, half	ŏŏ	took, full	ə	the schwa, an un-
g	go, log				stressed vowel
h	hope, hate	p	pit, stop		representing the
		r	run, poor		"uh" sound spelled
i	it, give	s	see, pass		*a* in *above*
ī	ice, write	sh	sure, rush		*e* in *sicken*
j	joy, ledge	t	talk, sit		*i* in *clarity*
k	cool, take	th	thin, both		*o* in *melon*
l	look, rule	th	this, bathe		*u* in *focus*

FOREIGN SOUNDS

à   as in French *ami, patte*. This is a vowel midway in quality between [a] and [ä].

œ   as in French *peu*, German *schön*. Round the lips for [ō] and pronounce [ā].

ü   as in French *vue*, German *grün*. Round the lips for [ōō] and pronounce [ā]

ᴋh   as in German *ach*, Scottish *loch*. Pronounce a strongly aspirated [h] with the tongue in position for [k] as in *cool* or *keep*.

ṅ   This symbol indicates that the preceding vowel is nasal. The nasal vowels in French are œṅ [*brun*], àṅ [*main*], äṅ [*chambre*], ôṅ [*dont*].

,   This symbol indicates that a preceding (l) or (r) is voiceless, as in French *fin-de-siècle* [faṅ·de·sye′kl'] or *fiacre* [fyà′-kr']; that a preceding [y] is pronounced consonantly in a separate syllable followed by a slight schwa sound, as in French *fille* [fē′y']; or that a consonant preceding a [y] is palatalized, as in Russian *oblast* [ô′bləsty'].

8

PART ONE

Three Keys To Greater Word Power

1 ROOTS—YOUR FIRST KEY
TO WORD POWER

The quickest, most useful, and easiest way to increase your word power is to analyze and understand how words are put together. Once you learn to recognize the building blocks with which words are made, many previously unfamiliar words become meaningful and useful. You will see that many words are actually made up of related or identical parts that you already know. For example, most people use the word *salary* and its plural form, *salaries*. They also recognize the word *salaried*, meaning "paying a salary"—*He has a salaried job at the orphanage*—or "receiving a salary"—*How many salaried salesclerks does the firm employ?*

Now here is something interesting. The word *salary* is based on the Latin root *sal-* meaning "salt" (Roman soldiers were given a special allowance to buy their own salt). Now you understand why the expression "He's not worth his salt" means "He's not worth his pay."

Let's have some fun with this root *sal-*. What do we put salt on? SALads. What is a highly salted, spiced meat? SALami. What do chemists call water, soil, or a solution containing salt? They call it SALine. So, if you learn one basic word or one basic root, you can instantly increase your vocabulary.

English has hundreds of thousands of words built up from two or more distinct parts taken mostly from Latin or Greek. It would be impossible to learn and remember them all individually. But the parts, or building blocks, are limited in number and simple in meaning. With them you can analyze, understand, and use thousands of words almost on sight. These simple units are often not words themselves but are combined with other elements to form words.

You've seen a few words derived from the root *sal-*. Here's another example of how words are built. Notice what the following words have in common:

revive	vitamin	viviparous
vital	vivacious	vivid

Although you may not know the meaning of every word on this list, you can easily see that they all have something in common: each of them is built on the building block of *vit-* or *viv-* meaning "life" or "to live." This part is called a root.

10

A root is the part of any word that reveals its essential meaning, a meaning that never changes, even though other letters or word parts may be added at the beginning or end. Note in the above list that roots are used in combination with other word-building blocks such as prefixes, which come at the beginning of a word (*re-* meaning "again" in the first word *revive*), and suffixes, which come at the end of a word (*-al, -amin,* and *-acious* as in the words *vital, vitamin,* and *vivacious*). Many roots will vary slightly in spelling, as do *viv-* and *vit-*. In each word the root is the foundation, the basic building block.

The root *vit-* comes from a Latin noun meaning "life," and its variant spelling *viv-* comes from a Latin verb meaning "to live." Let us analyze the words formed from the root *viv-* or *vit-* to see how they are all built up from the basic meaning "life" or "to live."

revive comes from the prefix *re-* meaning "again" and the Latin root *viv-* meaning "to live." Thus, *revive* means "to live again or make live again; to bring back to life, strength, health, or consciousness."

> *The lifeguard revived the man by artificial respiration.*
> *After a hard day's work, a hot meal revived him.*
> *The stock company has revived several old plays.*

vital is formed from the Latin root *vit-* meaning "life" and the suffix *-al* meaning "pertaining to" or "full of." Thus, *vital* means (1) pertaining to (or necessary for) life; (2) full of life.

> *Oxygen is vital for all animals.*
> *She is a happy, vital person.*
> *Vital statistics relate to births, deaths, marriages, etc.*

vitamin is formed from the Latin root *vit-* meaning "life" and the suffix *-amin* meaning "amine" (an organic chemical compound). Thus, *vitamin* means "an organic substance found in most foodstuffs that is necessary for normal life functions in man and animals."

> *Vitamin C, found in citrus fruits, prevents scurvy.*

vivacious comes from the Latin root *viv-* meaning "to live" and the suffix *-acious* meaning "abounding in; given to." Thus, *vivacious* means "full of life; lively; active."

> *The young kitten was vivacious.*
> *Nick and Sue engaged in a vivacious, witty conversation.*

11

INCREASE YOUR WORD POWER

vivid stems from the Latin root *viv-* meaning "to live" and the suffix *-id* meaning "having a certain quality." Thus, *vivid* means "having the quality of life; lifelike; lively; not dull."

> *The boy had a vivid imagination.*
> *She loved to paint with vivid colors.*
> *Dickens' novels are full of vivid characterizations.*

viviparous derives from the Latin root *viv-* meaning "to live" and another Latin root *par-* meaning "to bring forth" plus the suffix *-ous* meaning "given to; characterized by." Thus, the scientific word *viviparous* means "characterized by giving birth to live offspring" (as opposed to laying and hatching eggs).

> *Most mammals are viviparous.*
> *Chickens are not viviparous.*

Once you know a root and some of the words built on it, you can keep building. For example, you can take *revive* and build *revival* meaning "the act of reviving; recovery" and *revivify*, which has much the same meaning as *revive*. From *vital* you can build *vitality*, which means "vigor; energy." *Survive* will give you *survivor* and *survival*. And you can also figure out that the phrase *vital organs* and the word *vitals*, which has the same meaning, refer to parts of the body that are necessary to sustain life.

This section of HOW TO INCREASE YOUR WORD POWER gives you seventy-two roots that are most basic to the English language and shows how to base words upon them. From these words in the text you can learn to recognize, analyze, build, and use many related words easily and quickly.

One of the most effective and enjoyable ways to increase your word power is to take the vocabulary tests, called Fun With Words, and the shorter tests, called Quickie Quizzes, that appear throughout the section dealing with roots. You will notice that a few of the tests do not relate directly to roots you may have just learned in the pages that precede them; however, they will help you to a better understanding of the function of roots as building blocks toward a greater vocabulary. In addition, the tests will introduce you to hundreds of new words. You will no doubt recognize a large number of these words but feel that you are unsure of the exact meanings of some of them. Take the tests several times if necessary to fix the definitions firmly and permanently in your mind.

ROOT: ACU-, ACR-

The Latin root *acu-* or *acr-* means "sharp." You should sharpen your vocabulary with the five core words in which the root *acu-* or *acr-* appears: *acrid, acrimony, acuity, acumen, acute.*

acrid comes from *acr-* meaning "sharp" and the Latin suffix *-id* meaning "having a particular quality." Thus, *acrid* means "having a sharp quality in taste or smell; bitter or burning to the senses."

The acrid smoke hurt our eyes.

A word based on *acrid* is *acridity,* meaning "the state or quality of being acrid; acridness."

The acridity of the smoke made our eyes water.

acrimony comes from *acr-* meaning "sharp" and the Latin suffix *-mony* which means "quality of being." Specifically, *acrimony* means "sharpness of speech or temper."

Our quarrel was full of acrimony.

A word based on *acrimony* is *acrimonious,* meaning "full of bitterness; sharp; sarcastic."

Their discussion turned into an acrimonious debate.

acuity is made up of *acu-* meaning "sharp" and the Latin suffix *-ity* which means "the state, condition, or quality of being." Thus, *acuity* means "the state or condition of being sharp," but it is applied to sharpness or acuteness of the mind or senses.

The professor has great mental acuity.

acumen comes directly from a Latin word meaning "sharpness of mind; intelligence."

Johnny has shown great acumen in his schoolwork.

acute stems from a Latin word meaning "to sharpen." *Acute* means "sharp" or "coming to a sharp point," and thus it has also come to mean "reaching a crisis; critical; keen; intense; violent." Note carefully these various meanings in the following sentences:

An acute angle is an angle of less than 90 degrees.

He is suffering from acute appendicitis.
The food shortage in India is becoming acute.
The boy has a quick, acute mind.
His toothache was causing acute pain.

A word based on *acute* is *acutely,* meaning "intensely; extremely; keenly; highly."

He was acutely conscious of their disapproval.

REMEMBER: When you see *acu-* or *acr-* it means "sharp."

ROOT: AG-, ACT-

The Latin *ag-* or *act-* means "to do; drive." This root forms some of the most frequently used words in the English language. You already know some common words based on it, such as *act* and *action.* Here are seven more core words based on the root *ag-* or *act-* that you should know: *agenda, agent, agile, active, actor, actual, enact.*

agenda comes directly from a Latin word based on *ag-* meaning "to do" and means "a list of things to be done; a list of things to be discussed or decided upon."

There were three items on the agenda for the business meeting.

agent comes from *ag-* meaning "to do" plus the Latin suffix *-ent* which means "a person who." Thus, *agent* means "a person who does something." This word is applied to someone who does a specific action or job, or who works for or represents an individual, company, or government bureau.

He is an FBI agent.
Does the actor have a press agent?
Does that company have a sales agent in our town?

A word based on *agent* is *agency,* meaning "a company, department, or bureau that does a specific job or that represents other people or companies."

She works for an employment agency.

QUICKIEQUIZQUICKIEQUIZQUICKIEQUIZQUICKIEQUIZQUICKIEQUIZQUICKIEQUIZQUICKIEQUIZQUICKIE

90-SECOND QUICKIE QUIZ
DESCRIPTIONS, PLEASE

These words are sometimes used to describe people. Can you match the word with its definition? Answers follow.

1. winsome	(a) gracefully slender or slight
2. pulchritudinous	(b) modest, reserved, coy
3. demure	(c) social; fond of good company
4. troglodytic	(d) not blatant, immodest, or overly aggressive
5. unobtrusive	(e) very great; notable
6. convivial	(f) charmingly or shyly pleasing
7. sublime	(g) caustic, bitter, angry
8. acrimonious	(h) full of nervous energy; fidgety
9. gracile	(i) beautiful; having physical beauty
10. feisty	(j) coarse, brutal, or degraded in nature

ANSWERS:
1. **winsome**—(f) charmingly or shyly pleasing. 2. **pulchritudinous**—(i) beautiful; having physical beauty. 3. **demure**—(b) modest, reserved, coy. 4. **troglodytic**—(j) coarse, brutal, or degraded in nature. 5. **unobtrusive**—(d) not blatant, immodest, or overly aggressive. 6. **convivial**—(c) social; fond of good company. 7. **sublime**—(e) very great; notable. 8. **acrimonious**—(g) caustic, bitter, angry. 9. **gracile**—(a) gracefully slender or slight. 10. **feisty**—(h) full of nervous energy; fidgety.

QUICKIEQUIZQUICKIEQUIZQUICKIEQUIZQUICKIEQUIZQUICKIEQUIZQUICKIEQUIZQUICKIEQUIZQUICKIE

agile is made up of *ag-* meaning "to do" and the Latin suffix *-ile* which means "pertaining to; like; having the character or quality of." Thus, *agile* means "having the quality of doing or acting" or "able to do or move quickly and easily; nimble."

Charles is agile and athletic.

A word based on *agile* is *agility,* meaning "the ability to move quickly and easily."

The quarterback had remarkable agility.

active comes from *act-* meaning "to do" plus the Latin suffix *-ive* meaning "inclined to; tending to; having the character or quality of." Thus, *active* means "inclined to action; working; busy; lively."

She leads an active social life.
This is an active volcano.

Two words based on *active* are *activity* and *activate*. *Activity* means

15

(1) the state of being active; (2) a particular action. *Activate* means "to make active or make capable of action."

> *There was little activity on the stock market today.*
> *Can you activate this machine?*

actor is formed from *act-* meaning "to do" and the Latin suffix *-or* meaning "a person who or a thing that performs an action." An *actor* is thus "a person who does something," or "a person who acts."

> *My son was an actor in the struggle, not an onlooker.*
> *He was an actor in the play.*

A word related to *actor* is its female form, *actress*.

actual comes from the Latin word *actus*, "a doing," which is based on *act-* meaning "to do," and the Latin suffix *-al* which means "pertaining to; characterized by." *Actual* means "pertaining to something that is in action or in existence now"; thus, it means "existing; real."

> *What were his actual words?*

Two words based on *actual* are *actually*, meaning "really" or "truly," and *actuality*, which means "reality; truth; fact."

> *What did he actually say?*
> *Our dream of reaching the moon has become an actuality.*

enact stems from the Latin prefix *en-* meaning "to make; cause to be" plus the Latin root *act-* meaning "to do." Thus, *enact* means "to cause to be done" or, specifically, "to make into a law."

> *The Senate enacted a bill against air pollution.*

A word based on *enact* is *enactment*, meaning "the passing of a law" or "a law that has been passed."

> *The Senate's enactment of the air-pollution bill goes into effect today.*

◊ Look up the following words in your dictionary. Does knowing the meaning of the root *act-* help you to understand their dictionary meanings?

inactive	transact	interact	react

What other words are based on these words? Can you think of any besides *transaction* and *reaction?*

Fun With Words

SHORT WORDS

The various tests throughout this book will not only review material covered in the text, but will introduce you to many new words. Below is a vocabulary test on short words. Check the word or phrase you believe is closest in meaning to the key word. Answers follow.

1. **aura** [ôr′ə]—(a) oppressive heat. (b) a characteristic atmosphere. (c) pertaining to the sense of hearing. (d) by word of mouth.
2. **avid** [av′id]—(a) stingy. (b) rapid. (c) greedy. (d) bitter.
3. **aver** [ə·vûr′]—(a) to postpone. (b) to turn aside. (c) to declare positively. (d) to dismiss.
4. **avow** [ə·vou′]—(a) to deny. (b) to curse. (c) to swear allegiance to. (d) to declare openly.
5. **allay** [ə·lā′]—(a) to spread out flat. (b) to procrastinate. (c) to connect with. (d) to lessen.
6. **averse** [ə·vûrs′]—(a) unpleasant. (b) opposed. (c) unfortunate. (d) in the opposite order.
7. **arch** [ärch]—(a) playfully sly or roguish. (b) incriminating. (c) patriotic. (d) wandering.
8. **bask** [bask]—(a) any large receptacle. (b) a native of Spain. (c) to luxuriate in pleasant warmth. (d) to swim slowly.

9. **crass** [kras]—(a) irritating. (b) vulgarly stupid. (c) bitter. (d) noisy.
10. **carp** [kärp]—(a) to be boisterous. (b) to wander about. (c) to find fault unreasonably. (d) to insult.
11. **coy** [koi]—(a) shy or coquettish. (b) vain. (c) quiet. (d) authentic.
12. **cull** [kul]—(a) to strip the leaves off. (b) to explain. (c) to select or pick out. (d) to gather.
13. **chide** [chīd]—(a) to scold or admonish. (b) to insult. (c) to scream. (d) to compensate for.
14. **chic** [shēk]—(a) stylish. (b) impudent. (c) youthful. (d) merry.
15. **crux** [kruks]—(a) a laboratory report. (b) cleavage. (c) a problem. (d) the pivotal point.
16. **dire** [dīr]—(a) very poor. (b) cold and damp. (c) angry. (d) dreadful or calamitous.

ANSWERS:

1. **aura**—(b) a characteristic atmosphere. 2. **avid**—(c) greedy. 3. **aver**—(c) to declare positively. 4. **avow**—(d) to declare openly. 5. **allay**—(d) to lessen. 6. **averse**—(b) opposed. 7. **arch**—(a) playfully sly or roguish. 8. **bask** —(c) to luxuriate in pleasant warmth. 9. **crass**—(b) vulgarly stupid. 10. **carp**—(c) to find fault unreasonably. 11. **coy**—(a) shy or coquettish. 12. **cull**—(c) to select or pick out. 13. **chide**—(a) to scold or admonish. 14. **chic** —(a) stylish. 15. **crux**—(d) the pivotal point. 16. **dire**—(d) dreadful or calamitous.

ROOT: AM-

The Latin *am-* means "to love." You should learn these six core vocabulary words that are built on the root *am-: amateur, amatory, amiable, amicable, amorous, enamored.*

amateur comes from *am-* meaning "to love" and the French suffix *-ateur* which means "a person who." Thus, an *amateur* is "a person who does something for the love of it rather than for money; a person who practices an art, sport, or science for pleasure, rather than as a profession."

> *The painter was a gifted amateur.*
> *Some amateur golfers are as good as professionals.*

Two words based on *amateur* are *amateurish* and *amateurishly*. BEWARE: If you say people are *amateurs*, you do not necessarily mean that they are poor or unskillful in what they do. You are merely saying they do it for love or pleasure, not to earn a living. They may be very talented. But when you learn the words based on *amateur*, notice that these related words have a different meaning. Thus, if you call people *amateurish* or say they do something *amateurishly*, you are being critical of them or of what they do. You mean that they lack skills or that what they have done is not as good as it should be.

amatory comes from a Latin word based on the root *am-* meaning "to love" and the Latin suffix *-ory* meaning "related to; like; resembling." Thus, *amatory* means "relating to love; expressing love."

> *The lovers exchanged amatory glances.*

amiable derives from *am-* meaning "to love" plus the Latin suffix *-able* meaning "able to; capable of; worthy of." *Amiable* means "able to love; capable of kindness or friendliness"; hence, it means "kindly; friendly."

> *He is an amiable person.*
> *The two friends had an amiable disagreement.*

A word based on *amiable* is *amiability* meaning "the quality or state of being amiable; friendliness."

> *The amiability of their rivalry impressed us.*

18

amicable comes from the same Latin word as *amiable* and contains the same root and suffix, although the spelling is different. *Amicable* also means "friendly," but it is used in a slightly different way. It means "peaceable."

The lawyer arranged an amicable settlement of the lawsuit.

Two words based on *amicable* are *amicably*, meaning "in a friendly, peaceable manner," and *amicability*, meaning "the quality or state of being amicable; friendliness; peaceableness."

They ended their partnership amicably.
The amicability of their parting was remarkable.

amorous is a combination of *am-* meaning "to love" and the Latin suffix *-ous* meaning "full of, given to, having, or like." *Amorous* thus means "tending to fall in love; showing love; in love."

He has a very amorous nature.
The girl gave him an amorous glance.

Either *amatory* or *amorous* may be used in the second example above, since both words can mean "showing or expressing love."

enamored comes from the Latin prefix *en-* meaning "to make; cause to be" plus the root *am-* meaning "to love" and the suffix *-ed* meaning that the word is a past participle. To be *enamored* means "to be in love; to be fascinated or enchanted."

The boy is enamored of the girl next door.

ROOT: ANIM-

The Latin root *anim-* means "life; mind; soul; spirit." This root appears in several very important words. Learn the following six core vocabulary words based on *anim-: animal, animate, animosity, equanimity, magnanimity, unanimous.*

animal comes from *anim-* meaning "life" plus the Latin suffix *-al* meaning "pertaining to; characterized by." *Animal* means "that which is characterized by life; a living being." Of course, this meaning has been enlarged so that *animal* has other connotations, too, such as "any creature that's not human" or even "creature that's not human, bird, fish, or insect."

Is it animal, vegetable, or mineral?
How many animals are in the zoo?
Both people and dogs are animals.

Two words based on *animal* are *animality* and *animalistic*. *Animality* means "animal nature; the nature and qualities of an animal." *Animalistic* means "resembling an animal; like an animal."

People should subdue the animality in their natures.
They ate in a manner more animalistic than human.

animate comes from *anim-* meaning "life" plus the Latin suffix *-ate,* which means "having; being." Pronounced one way, *animate* means "to give life to; to make alive." Pronounced a different way, it means "having life; living; full of life."

He tried to animate [an'ə-māt] *the conversation by telling jokes.*
Microbes are animate [an'ə-mit] *beings.*

Three words based on *animate* are *animated, animation,* and *inanimate*. *Animated* means "full of life; moving or seeming to move as if alive." *Animation* means "vivacity or liveliness." *Inanimate* means "lifeless."

She was a happy, animated person.
The children enjoy animated cartoons.
She spoke with animation.
A desk is an inanimate object.

animosity is formed from the root *anim-* meaning "mind; spirit" and the Latin suffix *-ity* meaning "the state, condition, or quality of." *Animosity* originally meant "the condition of having a high spirit," but now it is restricted to one specific meaning, "hatred."

There is a great deal of animosity between us.

equanimity comes from the Latin root *equ-* meaning "equal; even" and the root *anim-* meaning "mind" plus the Latin suffix *-ity* meaning "the state, condition, or quality of." Thus, *equanimity* means "evenness of mind; calmness; composure, especially steadiness under stress or trying circumstances."

The mayor listened to their insults with equanimity.
The equanimity of the condemned man was remarkable.

A word based on *equanimity* is *equanimous,* meaning "even-tempered."

The judge was a good-natured, equanimous man.

magnanimity is made up of the Latin root *magn-* meaning "great" and the root *anim-* meaning "mind; spirit" plus *-ity* meaning "the state, condition, or quality of." Thus, *magnanimity* means "greatness of mind or spirit; the quality of being high-minded."

He shows magnanimity in forgiving his enemies.

A word based on *magnanimity* is *magnanimous,* meaning "high-minded; generous in forgiving."

After the war, the victors were magnanimous, not revengeful.

unanimous comes from the Latin root *un-* meaning "one" and the root *anim-* meaning "mind" plus the Latin suffix *-ous* which means "having; being." Thus, *unanimous* means "being of one mind; sharing the same views; showing the assent of all concerned."

There was a unanimous vote in favor of adjourning the meeting.
The committee was unanimous in favoring adjournment.

A word based on *unanimous* is *unanimity,* meaning "the state of being unanimous; complete agreement."

The jury reached unanimity on the question of his guilt.

ROOT: ANNU-, ENNI-

The Latin root *annu-* or *enni-* means "year." Five common core vocabulary words are formed from this root. They are: *annals, annual, perennial, centennial, annuity.*

annals comes from the root *annu-* meaning "year" and the Latin suffix *-al* meaning "of; pertaining to." Basically, *annals* means "yearly

21

records," but its use has expanded to mean "records in general," and especially "historical records."

Mr. Johnson compiles the annals of the Historical Society.
The professor has read all the annals of early American history.

annual also comes from *annu-* meaning "year" and the Latin suffix *-al* meaning "of; pertaining to." *Annual* means "of one year; yearly; occurring every year." As a noun *annual* means "a book or pamphlet issued once a year." In agriculture and gardening, it means "lasting only one year," and is applied to a plant living for only one year or growing season and not blooming again.

We have an annual vacation of two weeks.
Here is a picture of Tom in his high-school annual.
Beans and corn are annuals; you have to plant a new crop every year.

perennial derives from the Latin prefix *per-* meaning "through" plus *enni-* meaning "year." *Perennial* means "continuing or lasting through the year," but its use has expanded to mean "lasting through the years; everlasting." In agriculture and gardening, it means "a plant that lives for three or more years, usually blooming each year."

I'm tired of your perennial nagging!
These flowers are perennials; you don't have to plant new seeds every year.

centennial is formed from the Latin root *cent-* meaning "one hundred" and *enni-* meaning "year." Thus, *centennial* means (1) lasting for a hundred years; (2) marking a period of a hundred years; (3) happening once every hundred years.

This is the centennial anniversary of the founding of our town.
The centennial of the end of the Civil War occurred in 1965.

annuity comes from *annu-* meaning "year" and the Latin suffix *-ity* meaning "the state, condition, or quality of being." *Annuity* means "a yearly allowance or income."

How much is the annuity from this life insurance?

◊ Another word based on the root *annu-* or *enni-* is *biennial.* Look up the word in your dictionary. What does it mean? What does the prefix *bi-* mean? You'll learn more about the prefix *bi-* later on in this section.

22

EXPLORING WORDS

THE ANIMAL KINGDOM

Did you know that you are a viviparous mammalian biped? The following fourteen words describe some of the major types of animal that inhabit the earth, characterizing them according to the class they belong to, their physical make-up, their habits, or the way they bring forth young.

amphibian (1) in popular use: an animal that can or seems to live both in the water and on land, as a crocodile, seal, etc. (2) in scientific use: a class of animal that lives in the water at one stage of its life and on land at another, as the land-living frog, which starts life as a water-living tadpole.

aquatic living in or near water, as fish, whales, ducks, etc.

arboreal living in trees, as most birds, monkeys, etc.

biped an animal having only two feet, as people, apes, and birds.

carnivorous describing an animal that feeds chiefly or exclusively on meat, as dogs, wolves, lions, tigers, etc.

diurnal more active during the day than at night, as people, apes, birds, grazing animals, etc.

herbivorous describing an animal that feeds mainly on vegetable matter; plant-eating.

mammalian describing an animal that suckles its young with milk from breasts.

marsupial a member of an order of mammals whose females nourish and protect their newborn in a pouch in the abdomen, as kangaroos and opossums.

monotreme a member of the lowest order of mammals whose females lay and hatch eggs, as the duck-billed platypus.

nocturnal more active during the night than in the daytime, as bats, certain insects, some cats, etc.

oviparous belonging to a class of animals whose females lay and hatch eggs, as birds, most fishes, and reptiles.

pachyderm any of certain thick-skinned, nonruminant, hoofed animals, as the elephant, hippopotamus, and rhinoceros.

prehensile capable of or adapted for grasping or holding, as the hands or paws of people and some apes, monkeys, bears, opossums, etc., and the tails of certain monkeys.

ROOT: ANTHROP-, ANTHROPO-

The Greek root *anthrop-* or *anthropo-* means "man; human." This root appears in the following three core vocabulary words: *anthropology, philanthropist, misanthrope.*

anthropology comes from *anthropo-* meaning "man; human" plus the Greek root *-logy* meaning "the science or study of." Thus, *anthropology* is literally "the science or study of humans" or, "the science of the physical, social, and cultural development of the human race."

> *In college Steve majored in anthropology and sociology.*

A word based on *anthropology* is *anthropologist,* meaning "a person whose profession or study is anthropology."

philanthropist comes from the Greek root *phil-* meaning "love" and *anthrop-* meaning "man; human" plus the Greek suffix *-ist* meaning "a person who believes in; a person engaged in." Thus, a *philanthropist* is "a person who loves people; especially, a person who is engaged in promoting happiness or social progress of humanity by supporting charities, making donations to colleges, etc."

> *The philanthropist gave a million dollars for the building of a public library.*

Two words based on or related to *philanthropist* are *philanthropy* and *philanthropic. Philanthropy* means "love of mankind; especially, a deed or deeds of charity for mankind." *Philanthropic* means "showing love for mankind, especially by supporting charities, making donations, etc."

misanthrope [mis′ən·thrōp] is made up of the Greek root *mis-* meaning "hate; hatred" and *anthrop-* meaning "man; human." Thus, a *misanthrope* is "a person who hates people."

> *It is impossible for a misanthrope to be a philanthropist.*

Three words based on or related to *misanthrope* are *misanthropist* [mis·an′thrə·pist], which means exactly the same thing (a person who hates people); *misanthropic,* meaning "feeling or showing hatred for people; and *misanthropy,* which means "hatred of the human race."

ROOTS: ARCHEO-, ARCHI-, -ARCH, -ARCHY

Several common words are built on the roots *arche(o)*-, *arch(i)*-, *-arch*, and *-archy*. These roots look alike but are actually quite different. Let's take up each one in order.

The Greek root *arche-* or *archeo-* means "ancient." The most common word that it appears in is *archeology*.

archeology [är′kē·ol′ə·jē] comes from *archeo-* meaning "ancient" and the Greek suffix *-logy*, which means "the science or study of." Thus, *archeology* is "the study of history from the remains of ancient human cultures."

> *The discovery of the buried city of Troy was a great event in archeology.*

Two words based on *archeology* are *archeological*, meaning "of or pertaining to archeology," and *archeologist*, meaning "a person whose profession or specialty is archeology."

The second Greek root, *arch-* or *archi-*, means "chief; principal." (Note that there is no *e* in this root.) Many of the words in which *arch-* or *archi-* appear should be familiar to you, but be sure you know the meaning of the following four core words: *archangel*, *archbishop*, *archenemy*, *architect*.

archangel [ärk′ān′jəl] is made up of the Greek root *arch-* meaning "chief; principal" and the word *angel*. An *archangel* is "a chief or principal angel."

> *Gabriel is an archangel.*

archbishop [ärch′bish′əp] comes from the Greek root *arch-* meaning "chief; principal" and the word *bishop*. An *archbishop* is "the chief bishop of a province."

> *The bishop was elevated to archbishop.*

archenemy [ärch′en′ə·mē] is formed from the Greek root *arch-* meaning "chief; principal" and the word *enemy*. An *archenemy* is "a chief enemy."

> *Satan is often called the archenemy of humanity.*

architect comes from the Greek root *archi-* meaning "chief; principal" and the Greek root *tekt-* meaning "worker." An *architect* is literally "the chief worker; the person who designs and draws up plans for buildings and supervises their construction."

We will require the services of an experienced architect.

A word based on *architect* is *architecture*, which means "the design and construction of buildings; the style of a building."

Have you seen much colonial American architecture?
John took evening courses in architecture.

The final two roots, *-arch* and *-archy*, can be treated together. These roots appear at or toward the end of words and thus resemble suffixes. The Greek root *-arch* means "a ruler; a person who rules." The Greek root *-archy* means "a particular kind of rule or government." The roots *-arch* and *-archy* appear in the following four core words: *monarch, monarchy, matriarch, matriarchy.*

monarch comes from the Greek root *mon-* meaning "one; single" plus *-arch* meaning "a ruler." Thus, a *monarch* is "a person who rules alone; a king or sovereign."

Both kings and queens are called monarchs.

monarchy derives from the Greek root *mon-* meaning "one; single" and *-archy* meaning "rule; government." Thus, *monarchy* means (1) rule or government by a monarch; (2) a land ruled by a monarch.

France was once a monarchy.

matriarch comes from the Latin root *matri-* meaning "mother" and *-arch* meaning "a ruler." A *matriarch* is "a woman who rules or leads a large family or tribe by hereditary right."

Matriarchs ruled in some ancient societies.

matriarchy stems from the Latin root *matri-* meaning "mother" plus *-archy* meaning "rule; government." A *matriarchy* is "a society or culture ruled by a woman."

Some ancient societies were matriarchies.

The Latin root *patri-* means "father." What, then, is the meaning of the word *patriarchy?*

SOME BIG A's

Here are fourteen words beginning with the first letter of the alphabet. Check the word or phrase you believe is closest in meaning to the key word. Answers follow.

1. **allusion** [ə·lōō'zhən]—(a) a false mental image. (b) an indirect reference. (c) a claim. (d) a temptation.

2. **apprehension** [ap'rə·hen'shən]— (a) approval. (b) fear of the past. (c) information. (d) dread of the future.

3. **affinity** [ə·fin'ə·tē]—(a) daintiness. (b) on and on without an end. (c) close relationship (d) strength.

4. **appropriate** [ə·prō'prē·āt]—(a) to take for one's own use. (b) to make fitting and suitable. (c) to express a favorable opinion. (d) to give away.

5. **adaptation** [ad'əp·tā'shən]—(a) imitation. (b) act of fitting into an environment. (c) surrender or yielding. (d) act of taking for one's own.

6. **abridge** [ə·brij']—(a) to shorten or cut off. (b) to delay. (c) to express resentment. (d) to bind together.

7. **append** [ə·pend']—(a) to shorten. (b) to judge. (c) to add to or attach. (d) to scold.

8. **affix** [ə·fiks']—(a) to spread about. (b) to interfere with. (c) to make temporary. (d) to fasten on or attach.

9. **accentuate** [ak·sen'chōō·āt]— (a) to emphasize or intensify. (b) to speak in a dialect. (c) to collect. (d) to increase the cost of.

10. **aspiration** [as'pə·rā'shən]—(a) breathing. (b) discouragement. (c) facial expression. (d) ambition or lofty aim.

11. **align** [ə·līn']—(a) to join with others in a cause. (b) to accuse or slander. (c) to measure. (d) to defame.

12. **appurtenance** [ə·pûr'tə·nəns]— (a) nasty remark. (b) accessory. (c) unnecessary detail. (d) projecting corner.

13. **admonitory** [ad·mon'ə·tôr'ē]— (a) gloomy. (b) death-dealing. (c) terrifying. (d) warning.

14. **appreciable** [ə·prē'shē·ə·bəl]— (a) perceptible. (b) grateful. (c) pleasant. (d) very small.

ANSWERS:

1. **allusion**—(b) an indirect reference. 2. **apprehension**—(d) dread of the future. 3. **affinity**—(c) close relationship. 4. **appropriate**—(a) to take for one's own use. 5. **adaptation**—(b) act of fitting into an environment. 6. **abridge**—(a) to shorten or cut off. 7. **append**—(c) to add to or attach. 8. **affix**—(d) to fasten on or attach. 9. **accentuate**—(a) to emphasize or intensify. 10. **aspiration**—(d) ambition or lofty aim. 11. **align**—(a) to join with others in a cause. 12. **appurtenance**—(b) accessory. 13. **admonitory**—(d) warning. 14. **appreciable**—(a) perceptible.

ROOT: AUD-, AUDIT-

The Latin root *aud-* or *audit-* means "to hear." *Audit-* is a root that we use by itself to form a word, *audit*. An *audit* is "an examination of something, especially of financial records or accounts." It originally meant "a hearing" but later came to mean "any examination or inspection." (In universities, a student who attends a course of lectures but does not take tests or receive a grade is said to *audit* the course—to give it a hearing.)

Numerous other words are based on *aud-* or *audit-*. Learn the following six important core words in which this root appears: *audible, audience, audio, audition, auditor, auditorium.*

audible comes from the root *aud-* meaning "to hear" and the Latin suffix *-ible* meaning "able; capable of." Thus, *audible* means "capable of being heard; loud enough to be heard."

> *The teacher's voice was barely audible.*

Two words based on *audible* are *audibility*, which means "the ability to be heard," and *inaudible*, which means "not loud enough to be heard."

> *The audibility of the speaker's voice was poor.*
> *The speaker's voice was inaudible.*

audience derives from *aud-* meaning "to hear" and the Latin suffix *-ience* meaning "the state or condition of." *Audience* originally meant "a hearing with someone else"; that is, "an interview or conference." Now it also means "the people assembled to hear something."

> *The ambassador had an audience with the Pope.*
> *The audience applauded the musicians.*

audio comes directly from the Latin root *aud-* meaning "to hear." *Audio* means "pertaining to hearing or to sound waves." In some modern uses, it means "electronically broadcast or reproduced sound."

> *I bought my stereo receiver in the audio department of the store.*
> *My television set has a good picture but weak audio.*

Audio is also often used in combination with other words. Make

90-SECOND QUICKIE QUIZ
ANYONE YOU KNOW?

These words are names for different types of people. Can you match the word with its definition? Answers follow.

1. curmudgeon	(a)	one who persists or repeats
2. paramour	(b)	shamelessly immoral person
3. partisan	(c)	illicit lover
4. prima donna	(d)	a gruff, irritable old man
5. recidivist	(e)	a model of excellence or perfection
6. panegyrist	(f)	one to whom secrets are entrusted
7. confidant	(g)	one who lauds or eulogizes
8. paragon	(h)	strict moral or religious person
9. precisian	(i)	person who can't work on a team
10. profligate	(j)	a zealous advocate

ANSWERS:

1. **curmudgeon**—(d) a gruff, irritable old man. 2. **paramour**—(c) illicit lover. 3. **partisan**—(j) a zealous advocate. 4. **prima donna**—(i) person who can't work on a team. 5. **recidivist**—(a) one who persists or repeats. 6. **panegyrist**—(g) one who lauds or eulogizes. 7. **confidant**—(f) one to whom secrets are entrusted. 8. **paragon**—(e) a model of excellence or perfection. 9. **precisian**—(h) strict moral or religious person. 10. **profligate**—(b) shamelessly immoral person.

vocabulary building a lifetime habit. Look up the following words in your dictionary. Do you see how they are all based on the word *audio?*

audiology	audio-visual
audiometer	audiophile

audition is made up of *audit-* meaning "to hear" and the Latin suffix *-ion* meaning "the act of, state of, or result of." Thus, *audition* means "the act of hearing something or someone," and especially "a hearing that serves as a test or trial, as of a singer or any actor trying out for a part."

The actress was late for her audition.
The tenor auditioned for a role in the opera.

29

auditor is made up of *audit-* meaning "to hear" and the Latin suffix *-or* meaning "one who or that which does something." An *auditor* is "one who hears; a hearer or listener."

He was an attentive auditor at the lecture.

Auditor also has the meaning of "one who examines accounts, verifies balance sheets, and the like." In this sense, an *auditor* inspects (that is, gives a hearing to) statements of account.

Mr. James was an auditor for an accounting firm.

auditorium comes from *audit-* meaning "to hear" and the Latin suffix *-orium* meaning "a place for." Thus, an *auditorium* is "a place for hearing; a building or room for concerts, plays, public meetings, etc."

The play was presented in the high-school auditorium.

ROOT: AUT-, AUTO-

The Greek root *aut-* or *auto-* means "self." This root appears in a large number of English words. Its basic meaning is always "self," although sometimes you may have to analyze the entire word carefully to see how the meaning "self" enters into it. Four of the common core *auto-*words are given below: *autocrat, autograph, automatic, automobile.* Be sure that you learn these and the words based on them.

autocrat comes from the Greek roots *auto-* meaning "self" and *-crat* meaning "rule; power." An *autocrat* is "a ruler with unrestricted power"; hence, "any arrogant, dictatorial person."

Grandfather was quite an autocrat at the dinner table.

A word based on *autocrat* is *autocracy*, meaning (1) rule by an autocrat; (2) a state ruled by an autocrat.

Under Hadrian, Rome was an autocracy.

autograph derives from *auto-* meaning "self" and the Greek root *-graph* meaning "a writing." An *autograph* is "the signature or handwriting of a particular person"; that is, "the handwriting of the per-

30

son himself." To *autograph* something is "to sign one's own signature to it" or "to write it in one's own handwriting."

She stood in line to get the singer's autograph.
The singer autographed the program for her.

A word based on *autograph* is *autography* [ô·tog'rə·fē], meaning "the writing of a document in one's own handwriting."

automatic comes from *auto-* meaning "self" plus the Greek root *matic-* meaning "acting; moving." Thus, *automatic* means "acting by itself; self-moving; self-regulating, like a machine."

The clothes dryer is automatic.

Two words related to *automatic* are *automat,* meaning "a restaurant in which food is made available automatically from a receptacle," and *automation,* meaning "an automatic operation or automatic production, as in a factory in which labor is performed by machines."

With increased automation, workers will need to work fewer hours.

automobile comes from *auto-* meaning "self" and the Latin word *mobile* meaning "moving." An *automobile* is literally "a self-propelled or self-moving vehicle."

ROOTS: BENE-, BENIGN-

These two Latin roots look alike and are closely related in meaning. They can be learned together. The Latin root *bene-* means "well; good." Here are six core vocabulary words in which *bene-* appears: *benefactor, benefit, benevolent, benediction, beneficial, beneficiary.*

benefactor comes from *bene-* meaning "well; good" plus the Latin word *factor* meaning "a person who does." Thus, a *benefactor* is "a person who does good; a patron; a backer."

Mr. Smith, the banker, is a benefactor of the museum.

31

benefit derives from *bene-* meaning "well; good" and *-fit* which comes from the Latin root *fac-* meaning "to do." Thus, a *benefit* is "a good deed; an act of kindness" or it may be "that which does someone good; an advantage." To *benefit* is "to help or profit."

The club gave the dance as a benefit to raise money for charity.
What are the benefits of learning new words?
I benefited from your advice.

benevolent is made up of *bene-* meaning "well; good" and the Latin *volent-* meaning "wishing; willing." Thus, *benevolent* means "well-wishing; disposed to do good; kindly."

The townspeople formed a local Benevolent Aid Society.
The teacher has a benevolent attitude toward the students.

benediction comes from *bene-* meaning "well; good" and the Latin root *dic-* meaning "to say" plus the suffix *-ion* meaning "the act of." Thus, *benediction* means "the act of blessing, as at the close of religious worship; the calling down of divine favor on a person."

The priest gave the people his benediction.

beneficial comes from *bene-* meaning "well; good" and the Latin root *fic-* meaning "to do; make" plus the suffix *-ial* meaning "of; pertaining to." Thus, *beneficial* means "of or pertaining to that which does good; helpful; advantageous."

Sleep and proper food are beneficial to health.

beneficiary is formed from *bene-* meaning "well; good" and the Latin root *fic-* meaning "to do; make" plus the suffix *-ary* meaning "a person connected with." Thus, *beneficiary* means "a person connected with benefits"; that is, "a person who receives benefits or advantages from something."

He was the beneficiary of his father's life-insurance policy.

The Latin root *benign-* is a combination of *bene-* meaning "well" and the root *gen-* meaning "born." In English, *benign* is a word in itself, meaning "kind; kindly; gentle; mild; favorable." Hence, those who are *benign* are "well-born" in the sense of being kind and gentle in their treatment of others. A *benign* tumor is "mild" or "favorable" in the sense of being curable.

The benign old gentleman reminded her of her grandfather.

Fun With Words

REVIEW OF ROOTS

The best way to remember what you have learned is by review tests and actual practice. You have already learned all the roots and key words listed below. How well can you score on this review test? Choose the answer which is closest in meaning to each of the key words. Answers follow.

1. **inactive** [in·ak'tiv]—(a) passed into law. (b) containing charcoal. (c) not engaged in activity; idle. (d) in action; working.
2. **enact** [in·akt']—(a) to be in action, to work. (b) to perform between two acts of a play. (c) to make into a law. (d) to do or perform again.
3. **interact** [in'ter·akt']—(a) to act on each other. (b) to perform between two acts of a play. (c) to interrupt. (d) to be angry.
4. **react** [rē·akt']—(a) to give off atomic rays. (b) to explode. (c) to be startled or surprised. (d) to act in response to something.
5. **transact** [trans·akt' or tranz·akt'] —(a) to carry through; accomplish. (b) to sin. (c) to give or carry to someone else. (d) to move from one place to another quickly.
6. **matriarchy** [mā'trē·är'kē]—(a) a country, tribe, or family ruled by a man or by male heirs. (b) a country, tribe, or family ruled by a woman or by female heirs. (c) lawless confusion and political disorder. (d) patriotic feelings.
7. **patriarchy** [pā'trē·är'kē]—(a) a country, tribe, or family ruled by a male or by male heirs. (b) a country, tribe, or family ruled by an elderly person. (c) lawless confusion and political disorder. (d) patriotic feelings.
8. **acuity** [ə·kyōō'ə·tē]—(a) bitterness; sharpness of taste. (b) an overabundance. (c) a lack or deficit. (d) acuteness, sharpness.
9. **acumen** [ə·kyōō'mən or ak'yōō·mən]—(a) bitterness; sharp in taste. (b) quickness of insight; keenness of intellect. (c) an overabundance. (d) a lack or deficit.
10. **enamored** [in·am'ərd]—(a) wearing protective armor. (b) inflamed with love; charmed. (c) conceited. (d) shy; modest.

ANSWERS:

1. **inactive**—(c) not engaged in activity; idle. 2. **enact**—(c) to make into a law. 3. **interact**—(a) to act on each other. 4. **react**—(d) to act in response to something. 5. **transact**—(a) to carry through; accomplish. 6. **matriarchy** —(b) a country, tribe, or family ruled by a woman or by female heirs. 7. **patriarchy**—(a) a country, tribe, or family ruled by a male or male heirs. 8. **acuity**—(d) acuteness, sharpness. 9. **acumen**—(b) quickness of insight; keenness of intellect. 10. **enamored**—(b) inflamed with love; charmed.

ROOT: BIO-

The Greek root *bio-* means "life." Learn the following three core vocabulary words based on *bio-: biochemistry, biography, biology.*

biochemistry comes from *bio-* meaning "life" and the word *chemistry.* Thus, *biochemistry* means "the branch of chemistry relating to the processes and physical properties of living organisms."

> *We plan to study biochemistry at college.*

A word based on *biochemistry* is *biochemist,* meaning "a specialist in biochemistry."

biography is made up of *bio-* meaning "life" and the Greek suffix *-graphy* meaning "a writing." Thus, *biography* means "a writing about a life; a written account of a person's life."

> *This biography of President Kennedy was a best seller.*

Three words based on *biography* are *autobiography,* meaning "a biography of a person written by the person himself," *biographer,* meaning "a writer of biography," and *biographical,* meaning "of or concerning a person's life."

> *Benjamin Franklin wrote a famous autobiography in which he describes his struggles to rise in the world.*
> *The teacher gave a brief biographical account of the author we were studying.*

biology comes from *bio-* meaning "life" and the Greek suffix *-logy* meaning "the science or study of." Thus, *biology* means "the science of life in all its manifestations, and of the origin, structure, reproduction, growth, and development of living organisms."

> *Zoology (the study of animals) and botany (the study of plants) are the main divisions of biology.*

Two words based on *biology* are *biological* and *biologist. Biological* means (1) of or pertaining to biology; (2) used for or produced by biological research. *Biologist* means "a specialist in biology."

> *Biological warfare makes use of germs or bacteria that destroy life.*
> *My uncle is a biologist at the state university.*

ROOT: CAD-, CID-, CAS-

The Latin root *cad-*, *cid-*, or *cas-* means "to fall; befall; happen by chance." Even though it has three spellings, this is one root. This root is used to form several basic words in English. Learn the following six core vocabulary words and the words based on them: *accident, casual, decadent, incident, occident, occasion.*

accident is the most obvious *cid-* word. It comes from the Latin prefix *ad-* or *ac-* meaning "to; upon" and the root *cid-* meaning "to fall; befall; happen by chance" plus the Latin suffix *-ent*, which is the same as the English suffix *-ing*. Thus, *accident* means "something that happens to someone by chance; an unexpected happening without a cause or plan; a chance; a mishap."

> *He was hurt in the automobile accident.*
> *Our meeting wasn't planned; it was just an accident.*

casual comes from *cas-* meaning "to fall; befall; happen by chance" and the suffix *-al* meaning "of; like; pertaining to." Thus, *casual* means "like that which happens by chance; offhand; informal; not planned or serious."

> *He has a relaxed, casual manner.*
> *He was just a casual acquaintance.*
> *He wore casual clothing.*

A word based on *casual* is *casualty*, meaning (1) a person or thing that is hurt or destroyed by chance, as in an accident; (2) an accident.

> *How many highway casualties were there last weekend?*

decadent derives from the Latin prefix *de-* meaning "down" and the root *cad-* meaning "to fall" plus the suffix *-ent*, which is the same as the English suffix *-ing*. Thus, *decadent* means "falling into ruin; falling down morally; declining; decaying."

> *Roman society became decadent before the fall of the Empire.*

A word related to *decadent* is *decay*, meaning (1) a falling into ruin; (2) to decline, rot, or decompose.

> *There is decay in this tooth.*
> *The tooth had decayed badly before Sam saw his dentist.*

incident comes from the Latin prefix *in-* meaning "on; upon" and *cid-* meaning "to fall; happen by chance" plus the suffix *-ent,* which is the same as the English suffix *-ing.* Thus, *incident* means "something that happened (fell on a particular person or happened at a particular time); an event or occurrence."

> *The old man told about an interesting incident in his past.*
> *An incident at the border of the two countries led to war.*

Three words based on *incident* are *incidence, incidental,* and *incidentally. Incidence* means "the degree of occurrence; the frequency with which something happens." *Incidental* means "occurring in the course of something else; secondary; casual." *Incidentally* means "by the way."

> *There is a high incidence of crime here.*
> *You will have incidental expenses besides your plane fare.*
> *Incidentally, how old are you?*

occident comes from the Latin prefix *oc-* meaning "toward" and the root *cid-* meaning "to fall" plus the suffix *-ent,* which is the same as the English *-ing.* Thus, *occident* means "that which is toward the falling (or setting) sun"; hence, "the West; the Western Hemisphere." (For the use of capital letters in these words, see the section on punctuation in this book.)

> *The Occident is the opposite of the Orient.*

A word based on *occident* is *occidental,* which means "of or belonging to the West; belonging to the countries in the Western Hemisphere." It may also mean "a person born or living in a Western country."

> *Europe and America are Occidental continents.*
> *Marco Polo was an Occidental who visited the Orient.*

occasion is made up of the Latin prefix *oc-* meaning "toward" and *cas-* meaning "to fall." *Occasion* originally meant "a falling toward, as an opportunity"; it now means "a favorable time, the time of an event, the event itself, or the reason for it."

> *This seems like a good occasion for a get-together.*
> *She was happy on the occasion of her marriage.*
> *The wedding was quite an occasion.*
> *What, sir, is the occasion for this visit?* (This is *very* formal English.)

A word based on *occasion* is *occasional,* which means (1) happening irregularly or now and then; (2) suiting a particular occasion; (3) small and not part of a set.

> *He made an occasional trip abroad.*
> *He wrote an occasional poem in honor of the queen's birthday.*
> *This is my favorite occasional chair.*

ROOT: CAP-, CAPT-, CIP-, CEPT-, CEIV-

The Latin root *cap-, capt-, cip-, cept-,* or *ceiv-* means "to take; seize." All these various spellings make up just one root. The differing spellings are the result of linguistic history. For example, the spelling *ceiv-* is different from the others because it came into English through French, instead of directly from Latin. Thus, whenever you see a word with *ceiv-* in it, see if you can relate it to a similar word with *cip-* or *cept-*.

Below are six core vocabulary words based on this root: *capable, capture, deceive, except, incipient, receive.* Learn them all, along with the many other words related to them.

capable comes from *cap-* meaning "to take" and the Latin suffix *-able,* which means "able." Thus, *capable* literally means "able to take." Hence, it means "having ability; having the qualities needed for something."

> *Are you capable of solving this problem?*
> *Dr. Smith is a capable dentist.*

Three words based on *capable* are *capability,* meaning "ability; competence"; *capably,* meaning "in a capable manner; skillfully"; and *incapable,* which means "unable or incompetent."

> *No one doubts his capability as a dentist.*
> *The doctor performed the operation capably.*
> *He is incapable of solving the problem.*

capture is made up of *capt-* meaning "to take; seize" and the Latin suffix -*ure* meaning "the act or result of." Thus, *capture* means "the act or result of seizing; a seizure." It also means "to gain, win, or take by force."

The capture of the enemy town was a great victory.
The police captured the thief.
The contestants all tried hard to capture the prize.

QUICKIEQUIZQUICKIEQUIZQUICKIEQUIZQUICKIEQUIZQUICKIEQUIZQUICKIEQUIZQUICKIEQUIZQUICKIE

90-SECOND QUICKIE QUIZ
RECOGNIZING ROOTS

Knowing the meanings of roots can help you to understand many words. Can you match these basic word elements with their meanings? Answers follow.

1. **pyro-** as in pyromaniac [pī′rə·mā′nē·ak]	(a) father
2. **patri-** as in patriarch [pā′trē·ärk]	(b) sleep
3. **pod-** as in podium [pō′dē·əm]	(c) fire
4. **socio-** as in sociology [sō′sē·ol′ə·jē]	(d) cut
5. **psycho-** as in psychoanalysis [sī′kō·ə·nal′ə·sis]	(e) foot
6. **phono-** as in phonograph [fō′nə·graf]	(f) false
7. **toxico-** as in toxicology [tok′sə·kol′ə·jē]	(g) mind
8. **somni-** as in somniferous [som·nif′ər·əs]	(h) sound
9. **-sect** as in bisect [bī′sekt]	(i) poison
10. **pseudo-** as in pseudonym [sōō′də·nim]	(j) society

ANSWERS:

1. **pyro-** —(c) fire. A pyromaniac is a person who feels a compulsion to set things on fire.
2. **patri-** —(a) father. A patriarch is the fatherlike leader of a family, tribe, or race.
3. **pod-** —(e) foot. A podium is a small platform on which a speaker stands.
4. **socio-** —(j) society. Sociology is the science that studies human society.
5. **psycho-** —(g) mind. Psychoanalysis is concerned with the study of mental states.
6. **phono-** —(h) sound. A phonograph reproduces sound from a record.
7. **toxico-** —(i) poison. Toxicology is the science that treats of the detection, nature, and properties of poisons.
8. **somni-** —(b) sleep. Somniferous means tending to produce sleep, as certain drugs.
9. **-sect**—(d) cut. Bisect means to cut in two.
10. **pseudo-** —(f) false. A pseudonym is a fictitious name.

QUICKIEQUIZQUICKIEQUIZQUICKIEQUIZQUICKIEQUIZQUICKIEQUIZQUICKIEQUIZQUICKIE

Four words related to or based on *capture* are *captor, captive, captivity,* and *captivate.* A *captor* is "a person who takes a captive." *Captive* means (1) a person who is captured; (2) taken or held prisoner. *Captivity* is "the state of being held captive." *Captivate* means "to capture by means of charm; fascinate."

> *The prisoner was freed by his captors.*
> *The captive escaped.*
> *The doctor was held captive by the kidnapers.*
> *The circus owned the largest elephant in captivity.*
> *Harvey was captivated by Rhoda's smile.*

deceive comes from the Latin prefix *de-* meaning "away; down" and *ceiv-* meaning "to take." Thus, *deceive* means "to take away from the truth"; that is, "to mislead; trick; lead astray."

> *He was deceived by the friendliness of the thief.*

Four of the many words related to or based on *deceive* are *deceit, deceitful, deception,* and *deceptive. Deceit* means (1) the act of deceiving; (2) a trick; (3) falseness. *Deceitful* means "given to deceiving; treacherous; lying." *Deception* means "deceit." *Deceptive* means "having a tendency to deceive."

> *He was the victim of his friend's deceit.*
> *I have never been tricked by a more deceitful person.*
> *The magician fooled us with his quick deception.*
> *The surface of a highway can be deceptive in the rain.*

except is formed from the Latin prefix *ex-* meaning "out" and *cept-* meaning "to take." Thus, *except* means "taking out"; that is, "leaving out; omitting."

> *Everyone is going except me.*

Three words based on *except* are *exception, exceptional,* and *exceptionally. Exception* means (1) something excluded from a general rule or agreement; (2) an objection or criticism. *Exceptional* means "unusually good." *Exceptionally* means "uncommonly; extremely."

> *Your brothers are lazy, but you're an exception.*
> *He took exception to the announced plans.*
> *John is an exceptional student.*
> *This is an exceptionally cold day.*

39

incipient comes from the Latin prefix *in-* meaning "in" and *cip-* meaning "to take" plus the suffix *-ent,* which is the same as the English *-ing.* Thus, *incipient* means "taking into existence"; that is, "coming into existence; just beginning to be or to appear."

He has incipient influenza.

Two words based on *incipient* are *incipience,* which means "in the early state or beginning of something," and *inception,* meaning "the beginning or start."

The incipience of our trouble dates back to World War II.
He has worked for the company since its inception.

receive derives from the Latin prefix *re-* meaning "back" and *ceiv-* meaning "to take." Thus, *receive* means "to take back toward oneself; take into one's possession; get."

I received a letter from Wayne.
The Giants will kick off and the Cowboys will receive.

Six of the very many words related to or based on *receive* are *receiver, receipt, reception, receptionist, receptacle,* and *receptive. Receiver* means "a person or thing that receives." A *receipt* is "a written acknowledgment of something received." *Reception* means (1) the act or manner of receiving; (2) a formal social entertainment of guests. A *receptionist* is "a person who receives callers in an office." A *receptacle* is "something that contains (or receives) something else." *Receptive* means "able to or inclined to receive."

He acted as a receiver of stolen goods.
Here is the receipt for your money.
Were you given a cordial reception?
We have an efficient receptionist in the front office.
Put the garbage in the trash receptacle.
He is receptive to new ideas.

◊ There are still other words based on the root *cap-, capt-, cip-, cept-,* or *ceiv-.* Look up the following words in your dictionary. Notice how the root always means "to take or seize." Learn the meanings of these words and check their definitions against their etymologies in the dictionary. Can you see the relationship between the way these words are built and what they mean?

| accept | conceive | concept | conception |

EXPLORING WORDS
PEOPLE WHO BECAME WORDS

For better or for worse, people have given their names to many common words. Sometimes the reasons are scientific or practical, and sometimes not so serious. Here are nine words that grew from personal names, some famous and some forgotten.

August the eighth month of the year. Named after Augustus Caesar.

bloomers women's loose, baggy trousers drawn close at the ankles and worn under a short skirt, or a woman's undergarment resembling these. Bloomers were named after Mrs. Amelia Jenks Bloomer (1818–94), an American champion of women's rights.

bobby a British policeman. This word, the familiar form of Robert, came into use after Sir Robert Peel set up the police system in London early in the nineteenth century. These London policemen were first called "Bobby's men" and later just "bobbies."

bowdlerize to censor any kind of writing in a prudish manner. The word immortalizes an English editor, Dr. Thomas Bowdler, who produced a "family" edition (1818) of the works of Shakespeare by removing every word or passage that offended his sense of propriety.

boycott to refuse, as a group, to buy from or have any dealings with a person or organization, in order to reduce prices or bring about some change; also, an instance of this. The word comes from C. C. Boycott, a British army officer and landlord's agent in Ireland in the nineteenth century, who was the first victim of boycotting because of his unpopularity among tenants from whom he collected rents.

chauvinism belief that women are inferior. Militant glorification of one's country; vain patriotism. After Nicholas Chauvin, a devoted soldier and overzealous supporter of Napoleon Bonaparte.

dahlia a flower that takes its name from Anders Dahl, the eighteenth-century Swedish botanist who developed it.

epicure a person given to discriminating luxury; a fastidious devotee of good food and drink; a gourmet. After the Greek philosopher Epicurus, who taught that peace of mind, cultural interests, and a discriminating temperance in sensual pleasure lead to the good life.

guillotine a machine used for beheading a person by means of a heavy knife that drops between two posts. It was named after J. I. Guillotin, a French physician, who developed it. It was used especially on victims of the French Revolution.

41

ROOT: CED-, CEDE-, CEED-, CESS-

The Latin root *ced-*, *cede-*, *ceed-*, or *cess-* means "to go; yield." This root is used in many common and important English words. When you learn that words having *ced-*, *cede-*, *ceed-*, or *cess-* in them are closely related in meaning, you will be able to expand your vocabulary quickly. Here are nine core *ced-*, *cede-*, *ceed-*, or *cess-* words: *antecedent, concede, exceed, excess, precede, proceed, process, recede, recess.*

antecedent comes from the Latin prefix *ante-* meaning "before" and *ced-* meaning "to go" plus the Latin suffix *-ent,* which is the same as the English suffix *-ing.* Thus, *antecedent* means "going before" or "someone or something that goes before or precedes."

> *Henry IV was antecedent to Henry V.*
> *The Wright brothers' airplane was the antecedent of modern airplanes.*
> *A pronoun often has a noun as an antecedent.*

concede is formed from the Latin prefix *con-* meaning "thoroughly" and *cede-* meaning "to go; yield." Thus, *concede* means "to yield completely; give up." It also means "to grant; admit; acknowledge as true."

> *He was so far ahead in the chess game that his opponent conceded.*
> *Mary conceded that Susan had been right.*

A word based on *concede* is *concession,* meaning (1) the act of conceding; (2) something granted or admitted as true; (3) the right to operate a subsidiary business on certain premises, or the business so operated.

> *Both sides made concessions in order to reach an agreement.*
> *The tobacco store in the lobby is a concession.*

exceed comes from the Latin prefix *ex-* meaning "beyond" and *ceed-* meaning "to go." Thus, *exceed* means "to go beyond; surpass."

> *Your spending should not exceed your income.*

A word based on *exceed* is *exceedingly,* meaning "extremely."

> *This is an exceedingly good steak.*

excess is made up of *ex-* meaning "beyond" and *cess-* meaning "to go." Thus, *excess* means (1) a going beyond what is necessary or proper; (2) an immoderate amount; (3) a surplus. It also means "surplus; extra; excessive."

Avoid excess in all things.
The government imposed an excess-profits tax.
You must get rid of that excess weight.

A word based on *excess* is *excessive,* meaning "too much or too great; extreme; inordinate."

There was an excessive amount of traffic last weekend.

precede comes from the Latin prefix *pre-* meaning "before" and *cede-* meaning "to go." Thus, *precede* means "to go before or in front of."

A precedes B in the alphabet.
Soldiers preceded the President in the parade.
The nineteenth century preceded the twentieth.

Two words based on *precede* are *precedence,* which means "the act or right of going before; priority"; and *precedent,* meaning "a past act or instance that can be used as a guide for future actions."

Work takes precedence over play.
The rulings of the Supreme Court often establish legal precedents.

proceed comes from the Latin prefix *pro-* meaning "forward" and *ceed-* meaning "to go." Thus, *proceed* means "to go on or go forward, especially after a stop; continue." It also means "to begin and carry on an action."

If there are no further questions, I shall proceed with the lecture.
The lawyer proceeded to cross-examine the witness.

Five words based on *proceed* are *proceeding, proceedings, proceeds, procedure,* and *procedural. Proceeding* means "a course of continuing action." *Proceedings* are "the records or minutes of the activities of a meeting; courtroom activities." *Proceeds* [prō'sēdz] are "the useful or material results of an action or course; the return or yield." *Procedure* means (1) manner of proceeding or going forward; (2) a course of action. *Procedural* means "of or pertaining to procedure."

That was a strange proceeding on his part.
The secretary copied the proceedings of the last meeting.

43

The proceedings in the court went on and on.
Our financial proceeds from the transaction were good.
What procedure do you follow in getting a driver's license?
There were many small procedural details.

BEWARE: Do not confuse *precede* and *proceed*. *Precede* contains *pre-* meaning "before," and means "to go before or in front of." *Proceed* contains *pro-* meaning "forward," and means "to go forward; continue or begin."

process is formed from the Latin prefix *pro-* meaning "forward" and *cess-* meaning "to go." Thus, *process* means (1) a forward movement or ongoing operation; (2) a method of producing something; (3) a series of actions that bring about a result.

The baking process takes forty minutes.
What is the process used for mining coal?
Do you understand the process of growth?

Process may also mean "to subject to a routine procedure."

Please process this application without delay.

Two words based on *process* are *procession*, meaning "a parade or continued forward movement of people, vehicles, or events"; and *processional*, which means (1) of or pertaining to a procession; (2) the music played or sung during a procession.

The wedding procession entered the church.
What is the name of the processional hymn?

recede comes from the Latin prefix *re-* meaning "back" and *cede-* meaning "to go." Thus, *recede* means "to go back; withdraw."

The waters receded after the flood.

A word based on *recede* is *receding*, which means "going or sloping back."

He has a receding hairline.

recess is made up of the Latin prefix *re-* meaning "back" and *cess-* meaning "to go." *Recess* literally means "a going back." Hence, a *recess* is "an indentation or cavity" or "a time of withdrawal." To *recess* is "to withdraw for a time."

She put her umbrella in a recess near the door.

The court recess lasted for two hours.
The court recessed for two hours.

Two words based on *recess* are *recession* and *recessional*. *Recession* means (1) the act of receding; (2) a withdrawal from an economic peak; an economic setback; a slight depression. *Recessional* means (1) pertaining to a recession; (2) a hymn sung as the choir and clergy exit from the church.

The recession resulted in increased unemployment.
Kipling's "Recessional" is a splendid hymn.

There are many other words based on the root *ced-, cede-, ceed-,* or *cess-*. In all of them *ced-, cede-, ceed-,* or *cess-* means "to go; yield."

How good are you becoming at figuring out the meanings of words? For example, *inter-* means "between" and you know that *cede-* means "to go." Thus, if you did not know that *intercede* meant "to go between," especially "to mediate between two parties in a dispute," could you work out its meaning? Could you figure out that *intercession* means "a going between" or "an act of mediating between two parties"?

◊ Here is a list of *ced-, cede-, ceed-, cess-* words to practice on. Look them up in your dictionary and learn their meanings. Check the definitions of these words against their etymologies. Can you see how the words are built—how roots, prefixes, and suffixes affect their meanings?

abscess	intercede	succeed
accede	intercession	success
access	secede	successful
accessory	secession	succession

ROOT: CENT-

The Latin root *cent-* means "one hundred." Learn the following four core vocabulary words based on *cent-: centenary, centipede, century, percent.*

centenary comes from the root *cent-* meaning "one hundred" and the Latin suffix *-ary* meaning "pertaining to." Thus, *centenary* means "pertaining to a hundred; marking a period of a hundred years;

lasting for a hundred years; occurring every hundred years." It may also mean "a one-hundredth anniversary."

We planned a centenary celebration for our company.

centipede derives from *cent-* meaning "one hundred" and the Latin root *-pede* meaning "foot." Thus, *centipede* literally means "a creature with a hundred feet," although in fact this is an exaggeration.

BEWARE: Though *cent-* in *centipede* does mean "one hundred," the scientific root *centi-* means "one-hundredth." In any terms taken from the metric system, *centi-* means "a hundredth," not "a hundred." Look up *centimeter* (a hundredth of a meter) in your dictionary. Be sure not to confuse the meaning of *centi-* in the metric system with the root *cent-*.

century comes from a Latin word based on *cent-* meaning "one hundred." *Century* means "one hundred consecutive years," or "a period of a hundred years."

We live in the twentieth century.
Columbus lived more than four centuries ago.

percent comes directly from a Latin phrase meaning "by the hundred." *Percent* means "the number of parts in every hundred of something specified; hundredths."

More than 50 percent of the people are women.

Two words based on *percent* are *percentage* and *percentile*. *Percentage* means (1) the rate or proportion of anything per hundred; (2) a proportion in general. *Percentile* means "any in a series of one hundred points on a scale, each of which denotes the percentage of the total cases lying below it in the scale."

What percentage of the population is under thirty-five years of age?
Only a small percentage of the class attended the concert.
His College Board scores are in the second percentile.

◊ Here is a list of some less familiar *cent-* words to look up in your dictionary. Check the definitions against the etymologies. Can you see how the root *cent-* affects the meanings of the words?

centenarian	centurion
centuple	sesquicentennial

Fun With Words

MORE KEY ROOTS

The following thirteen words contain important roots. Choose the word or phrase you believe is closest in meaning to the key word. Answers follow.

1. **antithesis** [an·tith′ə·sis]—(a) an expository essay. (b) the direct opposite. (c) the subject. (d) a tentative theory.
2. **antidote** [an′ti·dōt]—(a) an amusing story. (b) opposition to a plan or idea. (c) a story about times gone by. (d) a remedy to counteract the effects of poison.
3. **adduce** [ə·dōōs′]—(a) to find a solution to. (b) to persuade. (c) to increase. (d) to cite or allege.
4. **amity** [am′ə·tē]—(a) a pardon granted to a political prisoner. (b) a truce. (c) soundness of mind. (d) good will.
5. **antecedent** [an′tə·sēd′nt]—(a) contemporary. (b) prior. (c) a future generation. (d) conflicting.
6. **antipathy** [an·tip′ə·thē]—(a) ancient times. (b) agreement. (c) deep dislike. (d) the opposite side of the earth.
7. **acoustics** [ə·kōōs′tiks]—(a) the furniture and color scheme of a room. (b) a type of word puzzle. (c) the sound-reflecting qualities of a place. (d) shrewdness.

8. **Anglophobe** [ang′glə·fōb]—(a) one who hates England. (b) one who loves England. (c) a member of the Anglo-Saxon race. (d) an instrument used in examining the eyes.
9. **annuity** [ə·nōō′ə·tē]—(a) a flower that blooms yearly. (b) a yearly celebration. (c) a life-insurance policy. (d) a yearly allowance or income.
10. **animate** [an′ə·māt]—(a) to enrage. (b) to cause to move or work faster. (c) to describe dramatically. (d) to make more alive.
11. **accredit** [ə·kred′it]—(a) to vouch for or authorize. (b) to sell. (c) to discount. (d) to find fault with.
12. **antagonism** [an·tag′ə·niz′əm]— (a) hatred toward women. (b) hostility. (c) boredom. (d) sympathy.
13. **aural** [ôr′əl]—(a) pertaining to speech. (b) a mountain range. (c) pertaining to the ear. (d) peaceful.

ANSWERS:

1. **antithesis**—(b) the direct opposite. 2. **antidote**—(d) a remedy to counteract the effects of poison. 3. **adduce**—(d) to cite or allege. 4. **amity**—(d) good will. 5. **antecedent**—(b) prior. 6. **antipathy**—(c) deep dislike. 7. **acoustics**—(c) the sound-reflecting qualities of a place. 8. **Anglophobe**—(a) one who hates England. (An *Anglophile* loves England.) 9. **annuity**—(d) a yearly allowance or income. 10. **animate**—(d) to make more alive. 11. **accredit**—(a) to vouch for or authorize. 12. **antagonism**—(b) hostility. 13. **aural**—(c) pertaining to the ear.

ROOT: CERN-, CRET-

The Latin root *cern-* or *cret-* means "to separate; see as being different; distinguish." Learn the three core vocabulary words based on this root —*concern, discern, secret*—and the additional words derived from them.

concern comes from the Latin prefix *con-* meaning "thoroughly" and *cern-* meaning "to see; distinguish." Thus, *concern* literally means "to see thoroughly in the mind." In practice, it may mean "to involve oneself" or "to relate to or affect." It may also mean "interest or worry" or "a business enterprise or firm."

> *He was concerned with improving himself.*
> *Don't concern yourself with small details.*
> *Emma expressed concern about Bob's health.*
> *What is the name of that new manufacturing concern?*

A word based on *concern* is *concerning*, which means "regarding; about."

> *The customer wrote to us concerning his bill.*

discern is made up of the Latin prefix *dis-* meaning "apart" and *cern-* meaning "to separate." Thus, *discern* means "to recognize as separate or apart from everything else; to perceive."

> *It was hard to discern the right road in the dark.*
> *Having seen through the lies, can you discern the truth?*

Three words based on *discern* are *discernible*, meaning "capable of being discerned; perceptible"; *discerning*, which means "quick to discern; discriminating; perceptive"; and *discernment*, meaning "insight."

> *There is no discernible difference between these two hats.*
> *Einstein had a discerning mind.*
> *Dr. Smith is a man of great discernment.*

NOTE: Two other words are based directly on *discern: discreet*, meaning "careful not to do or say the wrong thing; tactful"; and *discrete*, meaning "separated from others; distinct; totally different." You can tell they are related to *discern* by their roots. Learn the difference between these two words.

He maintained a discreet silence.
Sand is composed of tiny discrete grains of rocklike material.

secret is formed from the Latin prefix *se-* meaning "apart" and *cret-* meaning "to separate." Thus, a *secret* is "something separated or kept apart from others; something kept hidden; something not told or not to be revealed." *Secret* also means "concealed; hidden."

Don't tell your friend's secret.
This house is supposed to have a secret door.

Three words based on *secret* are *secretary*, meaning literally "a person who, dealing with the paperwork of an individual or business, can be trusted to keep business secrets"; *secretarial*, meaning "of or pertaining to a secretary or a secretary's work"; and *secretive*, which means "inclined to secrecy; close-mouthed."

The job involves some secretarial duties.
Mr. Thornton is unusually secretive about his business affairs.

ROOT: CLAM-, CLAIM-

The Latin root *clam-* or *claim-* means "to cry out; shout." Learn the three core vocabulary words based on this root—*declaim, exclaim, proclaim*—and the additional words derived from them.

declaim comes from the Latin prefix *de-* meaning "completely," and *claim-* meaning to "cry out; shout." Thus, *declaim* means "to cry out" or "to speak loudly and fully"; hence, "to give a formal speech, as opposed to speaking informally or softly."

The politician declaimed his speech to a large audience.

Two words based on *declaim* are *declamation*, meaning "a prepared, formal speech," and *declamatory*, meaning "characterized by declamation; bombastic."

The mayor delivered a long declamation on the Fourth of July.
What a boring, declamatory speech!

exclaim comes from the Latin prefix *ex-* meaning "out" and *claim-*

49

meaning "to cry out; shout." Thus, *exclaim* means "to cry out suddenly."

"Look! Look!" he exclaimed.

Two words based on *exclaim* are *exclamation* and *exclamatory*. *Exclamation* means (1) a sudden cry or shout; (2) a phrase or sentence that expresses surprise, shock, fear, or otherwise serves as a cry or shout. *Exclamatory* means "pertaining to or expressing surprise, shock, fear, etc."

He gave an exclamation of surprise.
The speech was full of angry, exclamatory sentences.

An exclamation mark (!) is used to end an *exclamatory* sentence or phrase in writing, showing that it is to be read as a cry or shout or is to carry emphasis.

proclaim is made up of the Latin prefix *pro-* meaning "before" and *claim-* meaning "to cry out." Thus, *proclaim* means "to cry something out before the people; make known before the public; announce; make clear."

The President proclaimed a national holiday.
His manner proclaimed his innocence.

A word based on *proclaim* is *proclamation,* meaning "a public announcement."

The White House has issued a Presidential proclamation.
The rooster's crowing is a proclamation of daybreak.

◊ Words that have the root *clam-* or *claim-* always have a meaning that relates to declaring something—to crying out, speaking out, or saying something in a certain way. For example, the prefix *re-* means "back." From this hint you could guess that *reclaim* means something like "to call back." Now look up the definition of *reclaim* in your dictionary. Is the meaning of *reclaim* related to calling back something? Look up the following list of words in your dictionary. Learn the meanings of these words and then read their etymologies. Can you see how the meanings of these words are built up from their prefixes and roots?

acclaim	clamorous	proclaimer
acclamation	disclaim	proclamatory
clamor	disclaimer	reclamation

ROOT: CLUD-, CLUS-, CLOS-

The Latin root *clud-, clus-,* or *clos-* means "to shut; close." Learn the six core vocabulary words based on this root: *conclude, disclose, enclose, exclude, include, preclude.*

conclude comes from the Latin prefix *con-* meaning "thoroughly" and *clud-* meaning "to shut." Thus, *conclude* literally means "to shut off thoroughly." Hence, it means (1) to bring to an end or finish; (2) to settle or decide.

> *The speaker concluded her speech in ten minutes.*
> *From the evidence, they concluded that the suspect was guilty.*

Two words based on *conclude* are *conclusion*, meaning "the end of something; a final outcome or decision"; and *conclusive*, which means "putting an end to doubt; decisive."

> *He left at the conclusion of the meeting.*
> *After seeing the evidence, what's your conclusion?*
> *The judge's ruling was conclusive.*

disclose comes from the Latin prefix *dis-* meaning "not" and *clos-* meaning "to shut." Thus, *disclose* literally means "not to shut." Hence, it means "to expose to view; reveal; make known to the public."

> *Please disclose everything you know about the incident.*
> *The President will disclose his new tax program tonight.*

A word based on *disclose* is *disclosure*, which means either "the act of disclosing or making known to the public," or "that which is disclosed or revealed."

> *The disclosure that he was a fraud forced him to leave town.*
> *The witness's disclosure helped to convict the defendant.*

enclose is formed from the Latin prefix *en-* meaning "in" and *clos-* meaning "to shut." Thus, *enclose* means (1) to shut in, fence in, or surround; (2) to put something inside an envelope, package, or other container; (3) to contain or hold.

> *The garden was enclosed by a wall.*
> *I am enclosing my check for $27.*
> *He herded the cattle into the enclosure.*

51

exclude comes from the Latin prefix *ex-* meaning "out" and *clud-* meaning "to shut." Thus, *exclude* means (1) to shut out; keep from entering; bar; (2) to leave out; (3) to put out; expel.

> *The apartment building excluded pets.*
> *The guest list included the Smiths but excluded the Browns.*
> *After the scandal, he was excluded from the club.*

Five words based on *exclude* are *excludable, exclusion, exclusive, exclusively,* and *exclusiveness. Excludable* means "able to be left out." *Exclusion* means (1) the act of excluding or leaving out; (2) that which is left out or excluded. *Exclusive* means (1) leaving out many; (2) admitting only a select group; restricted to one or a few; not shared; sole. *Exclusively* means (1) in an exclusive manner; (2) solely. *Exclusiveness* is "the condition or character of being exclusive."

> *You owe no tax on your excludable income.*
> *He liked movies to the exclusion of all other amusements.*
> *He is the exclusive owner of the house.*
> *That club is very exclusive.*
> *This story is exclusively yours.*
> *That club is noted for its exclusiveness.*

include is made up of the Latin prefix *in-* meaning "in" and *clud-* meaning "to shut." Thus, *include* means "to shut into a place"; hence, (1) to place in a general group or category; (2) to contain or take in.

> *Have you included bread on the grocery list?*
> *This price includes the delivery charge.*

Three words based on *include* are *includable, inclusion,* and *inclusive. Includable* means "able to be included." *Inclusion* means (1) that which is included; (2) the act of including. *Inclusive* means "comprehensive; including all."

> *Hotel bills are includable on your expense account.*
> *Their inclusion of the newcomer was kind.*
> *All the items are covered in an inclusive list.*

preclude comes from the Latin prefix *pre-* meaning "before" and *clud-* meaning "to shut." Thus, *preclude* means "to shut out in advance; make impossible by doing something in advance; prevent."

> *The heavy rain precluded our having the picnic.*
> *Your sloppy work precludes my giving you a raise.*

Fun With Words

REVIEW OF ROOTS

Here is a review test of roots and words you have already learned. Choose the answer which is closest in meaning to each of the key words. Answers follow.

1. **accept** [ak·sept′]—(a) a generalized idea, thought, or mental image. (b) a line connecting two other lines. (c) with the exclusion of; save for; but. (d) to receive with favor or consent.

2. **concept** [kon′sept]—(a) a specific idea. (b) a line connecting two other lines. (c) the circumference of a circle. (d) a generalized idea, thought, or mental image.

3. **conception** [kən·sep′shən]—(a) with the exclusion of; save for; but. (b) a beginning. (c) the circumference of a circle. (d) a specific idea.

4. **conceive** [kən·sēv′]—(a) to understand; grasp. (b) to bear a child. (c) self-love. (d) a large valley.

5. **abscess** [ab′ses]—(a) admittance; a way of approach or entrance. (b) a pain in or around a tooth. (c) a collection of pus in any part of the body. (d) a

boil or blister on the skin.

6. **access** [ak′ses]—(a) too much; more than enough. (b) friendship with important people. (c) admittance; a way of approach or entrance. (d) a large valley.

7. **accessory** [ak·ses′ər·ē]—(a) a necklace. (b) a witness for the defense. (c) an amount that is too large. (d) any item added for convenience or display.

8. **accede** [ak·sēd′]—(a) to agree; assent. (b) to be too much; be more than a limit. (c) to disagree; dissent. (d) to do more than one's share, as of work.

9. **secede** [si·sēd′]—(a) to accomplish what is attempted. (b) to prepare ground for planting. (c) to withdraw from a union or organization. (d) to grow old.

10. **succeed** [sək·sēd′]—(a) to accomplish what is attempted. (b) to prepare ground for planting. (c) to grow old. (d) to obtain wealth.

ANSWERS:

1. **accept**—(d) to receive with favor or consent. 2. **concept**—(d) a generalized idea, thought, or mental image. 3. **conception**—(b) a beginning. 4. **conceive**—(a) to understand; grasp. 5. **abscess**—(c) a collection of pus in any part of the body. 6. **access**—(c) admittance; a way of approach or entrance. 7. **accessory**—(d) any item added for convenience or display. 8. **accede**—(a) to agree, assent. 9. **secede**—(c) to withdraw from a union or organization. 10. **succeed**—(a) to accomplish what is attempted.

ROOT: CORD-

The Latin root *cord-* means "heart." Learn the following three important core vocabulary words that are based on *cord-: cordial, accord, record* and the additional words derived from them.

cordial comes from *cord-* meaning "heart" and the Latin suffix *-ial* meaning "pertaining to." Thus, *cordial* as an adjective means "pertaining to the heart"; hence, "warm and hearty; friendly and sincere." The noun *cordial* means "a stimulating drink, such as a liqueur," or "a medicine given as a stimulant for the heart or circulation."

> *We received a cordial welcome.*
> *I had a glass of blackberry cordial.*

A word based on *cordial* is *cordiality,* meaning "warmth of feeling."

> *He greeted the visitors with much cordiality.*

accord comes from the Latin prefix *ac-* (another spelling of *ad-*) meaning "to; at" and *cord-* meaning "heart." *Accord* literally means "at heart" or, as a verb, "to be of one heart or mind; to agree." It may also mean "to grant what is deserved." And as a noun it means "harmony; agreement."

> *My opinions accord with yours.*
> *The teacher accorded the student a prize.*
> *They all cheered with one accord.*
> *Our opinions are in accord.*

Three words based on *accord* are *accordance,* meaning "agreement; harmony; conformity"; *according,* which means "on the authority of; as stated by"; and *accordingly,* which can mean either (1) consequently, or (2) correspondingly.

> *I'll act in accordance with your wishes.*
> *According to the teacher, he was a good student.*
> *He was the best student and accordingly won the prize.*
> *The dinner is informal, so dress accordingly.*

record is formed from the Latin prefix *re-* meaning "back; again" and *cord-* meaning "heart." To *record* [ri·kôrd'] is "to put something in the heart or mind again, as by writing it down." Thus, *record* means "to write down, as for preserving an account of something; register in permanent form." As a noun, *record* [rek'ərd] means "a written or other permanent account, as a grooved disk that reproduces sound."

Will you record your impressions of your trip?
Do you keep a record of your expenditures?
What is that record on the phonograph?

◊ Learn the meaning of the following *cord-* words from your dictionary. Read the etymology of each word and see if you can figure out how each word's meaning is based on its word-building units.

concord	concordant	discord
concordance	concordantly	discordant

ROOT: CORPOR-, CORP-

The Latin root *corpor-* or *corp-* means "body; flesh." The most obvious modern word based on this root is *corpse*, which means "the body of a dead person." Thus, the root *corpor-* or *corp-* always refers to "body" or "flesh" in one way or another. In learning the following three core vocabulary words based on this root, note carefully their proper spellings: *corpulent, corpuscle, incorporate.*

corpulent comes from *corp-* meaning "body; flesh" and the Latin suffix *-ulent* meaning "abounding in; full of." Thus, *corpulent* means "fat; fleshy."

He grew increasingly corpulent as he grew older.

A word based on *corpulent* is **corpulence,** meaning "fatness; obesity."

The corpulence of the emperor impressed his people.

corpuscle comes from *corp-* meaning "body" and the Latin suffix *-cle* meaning "little." Therefore, a *corpuscle* is literally "a little body," and the word means "one of the small particles (or little bodies) that form part of the blood."

There are red and white corpuscles in the blood.

incorporate is made up of the Latin prefix *in-* meaning "into; in" and *corpor-* meaning "body" plus the Latin suffix *-ate*, which is merely a word-ending used to form verbs. Thus, *incorporate* means "to form into a body," and specifically "to form a legal association or company which can act as an individual."

He has just incorporated his business.

Two words related to or based on *incorporate* are *corporation,* meaning "a body of persons recognized by law as an individual person or entity," and *corporate* [kôr′pər·it], meaning "combined as a whole; collective."

He is president of a large business corporation.
Voting is our corporate responsibility.

QUICKIEQUIZQUICKIEQUIZQUICKIEQUIZQUICKIEQUIZQUICKIEQUIZQUICKIEQUIZQUICKIEQUIZQUICKIE

QUICKIE QUIZ
COLORS

How good is your color vocabulary? Can you match the color in the left-hand column with its description in the right-hand column? Answers follow.

1. **cerulean** [sə·rōō′lē·ən]	(a) pale yellowish green
2. **indigo** [in′də·gō]	(b) light yellowish brown
3. **ocher** [ō′kər]	(c) vivid blue
4. **azure** [azh′ər]	(d) purplish rose
5. **cerise** [sə·rēs′]	(e) dark yellow
6. **ecru** [ek′rōō]	(f) deep violet blue
7. **chartreuse** [shär·trōōz′]	(g) cherry red
8. **fuchsia** [fyōō′shə]	(h) reddish or yellowish brown
9. **sorrel** [sôr′əl]	(i) bright bluish red
10. **mauve** [mōv]	(j) clear sky blue

ANSWERS:

1. **cerulean**—(c) vivid blue. 2. **indigo**—(f) deep violet blue. 3. **ocher**—(e) dark yellow. 4. **azure**—(j) clear sky blue. 5. **cerise** —(g) cherry red. 6. **ecru** —(b) light yellowish brown. 7. **chartreuse**—(a) pale yellowish green. 8. **fuchsia**—(i) bright bluish red. 9. **sorrel**—(h) reddish or yellowish brown. 10. **mauve**—(d) purplish rose.

QUICKIEQUIZQUICKIEQUIZQUICKIEQUIZQUICKIEQUIZQUICKIEQUIZQUICKIEQUIZQUICKIEQUIZQUICKIE

ROOT: CRE-, CRESC-, CRET-

The Latin root *cre-*, *cresc-*, or *cret-* means "to grow." Here are three core vocabulary words to learn that are based on this root: *crescent, increase, concrete.*

crescent comes from *cresc-* meaning "to grow" and the Latin suffix *-ent*, which is the same as the English *-ing*. *Crescent* literally means "growing." That is why it has now come to mean "the visible part of the moon during its first or last quarter (which 'grows' larger or smaller)" or "anything shaped like a crescent moon."

Turkey has a crescent on its flag.

increase is derived from the Latin prefix *in-* meaning "in" and *cre-* meaning "to grow." Thus, *increase* means "to grow in size, amount, degree, or number; to become or cause to become greater or larger." It may also mean "growth" or "the amount of growth."

As his vocabulary grew, his confidence increased.
What was the rate of increase?

A word based on *increase* is *increment,* meaning "a quantity added to another to increase it; the amount of increase."

What increment did you receive on your investment?
My salary has gone up by a weekly increment of $10.

concrete comes from the Latin prefix *con-* meaning "together" and *cret-* meaning "to grow." Thus, *concrete* originally meant "grown or melded together; solidified." Today it means "relating to one solidified, definite idea, thing, or case; individual or particular, as opposed to general; real; specific." Of course, it also means "any mass of solidified particles, especially the material used in building."

Try to be less vague and more concrete in your statements.
The floor is made of concrete.

◊ Look up these *cre-*, *cresc-*, *cret-* "growth" words in your dictionary. Be sure to learn the meaning of each and try to relate the meaning to each word's etymology.

decrease	accretion
crescendo	excrescence

ROOT: CRED-

The Latin root *cred-* means "to believe; trust." Learn the following four core vocabulary words based on the root *cred-: credit, accredit, credentials, discredit.*

credit comes from a French word based on the Latin root *cred-* meaning "to believe; to trust." Thus, the noun *credit* basically means "trust or faith." This basic meaning has enlarged to include (1) a reputation for being trustworthy, especially in paying debts; (2) a source of honor; (3) acknowledgment for having done something; (4) confidence in a person's ability to be trusted; (5) money in one's favor or money entrusted to one as in a loan. To *credit* is (1) to give credit for; (2) to accept as true; (3) to attribute to, as honor or intelligence.

> *He has good credit at the bank.*
> *She is a credit to her school.*
> *He was given full credit for the work he did.*
> *The store sold her the goods on credit.*
> *The bank credited my account with $50.*
> *I cannot credit that story.*
> *Don't credit him with the idea, credit it to her.*

NOTE: In financial matters the opposite of *credit* is *debit.* If you write a check for $5 the bank will *debit* your account for that amount. You will have a $5 *debit.*

Two words based on *credit* are *creditable,* meaning "deserving credit; praiseworthy"; and *creditor,* meaning "a person or organization to whom money is owed."

> *The pianist gave a creditable performance.*
> *If you owe money to a store, the store is your creditor.*

accredit comes from the prefix *ac-* meaning "to" and the word *credit.* Thus, *accredit* means (1) to give credit to, as by acknowledging the work, effort, good qualities, etc., of; (2) to authorize officially; (3) to certify as meeting official requirements.

> *He was accredited with a quick intelligence.*
> *The ambassador was accredited by his government.*
> *The school board accredited the school.*

A word based on *accredit* is *accreditation,* meaning "the granting of recognition to a school, college, or the like, that fulfills official requirements of a state or country."

Our college has full accreditation.

credentials comes from *cred-* meaning "to believe" and the Latin suffix *-ent,* which is the same as the English *-ing,* plus the Latin suffix *-al* meaning "pertaining to." Thus, *credentials* can be "a certificate, letter, or other proof that gives evidence of a person's authority, identity, honesty, experience, etc."

The ambassador presented his credentials.
To enter this building, you must show your credentials.
His credentials as a doctor are excellent.

discredit comes from the Latin prefix *dis-* meaning "not" and the word *credit.* Thus, *discredit* means (1) not to credit; not to believe; (2) to harm the credit or reputation of someone; (3) to cause someone or something to be doubted. It also means "loss of reputation."

The lawyer discredited everything the witness said.
His acceptance of the bribe discredited him.
His rude behavior worked to his discredit.

◊ Here are six additional *cred-* words to learn. Look them up in your dictionary and learn their meanings. Can you relate the meaning of each word to the root *cred-* or the word *credit,* meaning "to believe; to trust"?

credible	incredible	credulous
credibility	incredibility	incredulous

ROOT: CUMB-, CUB-

The Latin root *cumb-* or *cub-* means "to lie down." Learn the following four core vocabulary words: *cubicle, incubate, incumbent, succumb.*

cubicle comes from *cub-* meaning "to lie down" and the Latin suffix *-cle* meaning "small." A *cubicle* was originally "a small room to lie down in; a bedroom." Today, *cubicle* means not only "a bedroom" but also "any small room or enclosed space."

> *Libraries often have cubicles in which students may study.*

incubate comes from the Latin prefix *in-* meaning "in; on" and *cub-* meaning "to lie down" plus the Latin suffix *-ate* which is used to form verbs. *Incubate* literally means "to lie on" and thus it now specifically means "to sit on eggs in order to hatch them." It also means "to give form to; develop."

> *A hen will try to incubate a wooden egg.*
> *The prisoners were incubating a plan for escape.*

A word based on *incubate* is *incubator,* meaning "a device used for hatching eggs." By extension, *incubator* has also come to mean "an apparatus for keeping a prematurely born baby warm."

> *There are five dozen eggs in the incubator.*
> *The quintuplets were kept in an incubator for several weeks.*

incumbent comes from the Latin prefix *in-* meaning "in; on" and *cumb-* meaning "to lie down" plus the Latin suffix *-ent,* which is the same as the English *-ing.* Thus, *incumbent* means "lying or resting on someone as an obligation." It also means "a person on whom an obligation rests—in other words, one who holds public office."

> *It is incumbent upon you to increase your vocabulary.*
> *It is hard for a newcomer to beat an incumbent in an election.*

A word based on *incumbent* is *incumbency,* meaning (1) the state of being incumbent; (2) the holding of an office; (3) the period in which an office is held.

> *The mayor's incumbency is for four years.*

succumb comes from the Latin prefix *suc-* (a variant of *sub-*) meaning "underneath" and *cumb-* meaning "to lie down." *Succumb* literally means "to give way underneath, or under the weight of, something." Thus, it means (1) to give way; yield; (2) to die.

> *The exhausted child finally succumbed to sleep.*
> *He succumbed to pneumonia at the age of eighty.*

◇ Look up the word *recumbent* in your dictionary. Be sure you understand all its parts—the prefix, the root, and the suffix.

60

EXPLORING WORDS
ELEVEN WORDS TAKEN FROM PLACE NAMES

Certain English words are based on the names of places. We all know that Panama hats originally came from Panama, Persian rugs from Persia, and French pastry from France. But do you know that the words *afghan, cantaloupe,* and *damask* are also based on place names? In some cases, the place name remains unchanged when it is used as a word, but at times it is hardly recognizable. How good are you at spotting words that come from places?

afghan a coverlet that is knitted or crocheted from soft woolen yarn. Such coverlets originally came from Afghanistan.

Argyle a plaid design of diamond-shaped blocks of solid color overlaid by a contrasting plaid. This design is the tartan of the clan Campbell of Argyll, a county of western Scotland.

bedlam a scene of wild uproar. The word is a corruption of Bethlehem, and comes from the name of a former insane asylum, the hospital of St. Mary of Bethlehem in London, England.

bologna [pronounced, and often spelled, baloney] a seasoned sausage of mixed meats. It was named after Bologna, Italy.

calico a cotton cloth printed in a figured pattern of bright colors. This word comes from Calicut cloth, named for the city where it was originally made, Calicut, India.

cantaloupe a variety of muskmelon. It was named after an Italian castle, Cantalupo, where this melon was first successfully grown in Europe.

champagne a sparkling white wine made in the region of Champagne, France, or wine made elsewhere in imitation of it.

cologne or **eau de cologne** a toilet water consisting of alcohol scented with aromatic oils. It was named for the city of Cologne in West Germany.

damask a silk or linen fabric with a woven pattern. Named after Damascus, Syria, where it was first made.

denim a heavy twilled cotton cloth used for work clothes. This word is shortened and changed from the French term for the cloth, *serge de Nîmes* (serge of Nîmes), after Nîmes, the French city where it was made.

frankfurter a smoked sausage made of beef or beef and pork, or one of these served on a long bun. This "American" dish comes from Frankfurt, Germany.

ROOT: CUR-, CURS-, COURS-

The Latin root *cur-*, *curs-*, or *cours-* means "to run; go." Learn the following four core vocabulary words based on this root: *concur, current, occur, recur.*

concur comes from the Latin prefix *con-* meaning "together" and *cur-* meaning "to run; go." Thus, *concur* literally means "to run together"; hence, (1) to agree or approve; (2) to happen at the same time.

> *The entire group concurred on what to do next.*

Two words based on *concur* are *concurrent*, meaning "happening together; simultaneous"; and *concourse*, which means "a coming together, as of streets, or a place where people, traffic, etc., come together."

> *The convict's two ten-year sentences were concurrent.*
> *The train station has a large concourse.*

current comes from *cur-* meaning "to run; go" and the Latin suffix *-ent*, which is the same as the English *-ing*. A *current* is literally "a going, running, or moving." Thus, *current* means "any continuous onward movement of something, as of water in a river or lake, or of electricity in an electric wire." *Current* as an adjective means "moving along with the times" or "belonging to the immediate present."

> *The current of the river is swift.*
> *This lamp works only on alternating current.*
> *Don't be a slave to current fashions.*

A word based on *current* is *currency*, meaning (1) money (that is, what is in *current* use as a medium of exchange); (2) general acceptance or circulation.

> *The dollar is the standard unit of currency of the United States.*
> *The rumor gained wide currency.*

occur comes from the Latin prefix *oc-* meaning "toward; against" and *cur-* meaning "to run; go." To *occur* is literally "to rush toward something or someone," as an event or an idea might do. Thus, *occur* means "to happen; come about; come to mind."

> *When did the auto accident occur?*
> *When did that idea occur to you?*

A word based on *occur* is *occurrence,* meaning (1) an event or instance; (2) the act or fact of occurring.

Let me tell you about a strange occurrence.
This is the third occurrence of robbery here this year.
The occurrence of a solar eclipse is rare.

recur comes from the Latin prefix *re-* meaning "back; again" and *cur-* meaning "to run; go." Thus, *recur* literally means "to run or go again," or "to happen again; to happen repeatedly."

John's asthma recurs every summer.

Two words based on *recur* are *recurrence,* meaning "a happening again," and *recurrent,* meaning "happening repeatedly."

After one bad attack, Harry has had no recurrence of malaria.
John has recurrent attacks of asthma.

◇ Look up the following words in your dictionary. Be sure to learn the meaning of each word. Can you relate the meaning of each word to the root *cur-, curs-,* or *cours-?*

discourse	excursive	precursor
discursive	incur	precursory
excursion	incursion	recourse

ROOT: DE-, DIV-

The Latin root *de-* or *div-* means "a god." Learn the following three core vocabulary words based on this root: *deify, deity, divine.*

deify comes from *de-* meaning "a god" and the Latin suffix *-ify* meaning "to make." Thus, *deify* means "to make a god of someone or something; to worship as a god."

In earlier times the Chinese deified their ancestors.
Some people almost deify neatness.

A word based on *deify* is *deification,* meaning "the act of making a god of" or "the state of being made a god."

Some pagans believed in the deification of the sun.

63

deity comes from *de-* meaning "a god" and the Latin suffix *-ity* meaning "the state or quality of being." Thus, *deity* means "the state of being a god" or, simply, "a god."

Jupiter was a Roman deity.

divine comes from the root *div-* meaning "a god" and the Latin suffix *-ine* meaning "pertaining to." Thus, *divine* means "pertaining to a god or to God; godlike; sacred."

Various churches have different forms of divine worship.

Two words based on *divine* are *divinely* and *divinity*. *Divinely* means (1) in a divine manner; (2) by or through God. *Divinity* means (1) the state or quality of being divine; (2) a god; (3) theology.

The prophet was divinely inspired.
Christians believe in the divinity of Christ.
Zeus and Athena were Greek divinities.
He is a divinity student.

ROOT: DICT-

The Latin root *dict-* means "to say or speak." Learn the following four core vocabulary words based on this root: *contradict, dictate, diction, predict.*

contradict comes from the Latin prefix *contra-* meaning "against" and *dict-* meaning "to say or speak." Thus, to *contradict* is "to speak against something; to hold that the opposite of what someone has said is true; to deny the truth of a statement."

Modern children aren't afraid to contradict their parents.
He contradicted his own previous testimony.

Two words based on *contradict* are *contradiction* and *contradictory*. *Contradiction* means (1) a denial; (2) a statement that denies another. *Contradictory* means "involving or given to contradiction."

His speech was confusing and full of contradictions.
The two witnesses made contradictory statements.

dictate comes from *dict-* meaning "to say or speak" and the Latin suffix *-ate,* which is used to form verbs. *Dictate* means "to say something aloud, so that it can be recorded; to say commands or lay down laws, etc., with authority."

> *She dictated three letters to her secretary.*
> *Hitler dictated German policy in World War II.*

Three words based on *dictate* are *dictation, dictator,* and *dictatorial. Dictation* means (1) the act of dictating letters, memos, etc.; (2) that which is dictated. A *dictator* is "one who dictates, especially a tyrant." *Dictatorial* means "of or like a dictator; over-authoritative."

> *The secretary took the dictation in shorthand.*
> *Mussolini was a dictator.*
> *Her parents were strict but not dictatorial.*

diction comes from *dict-* meaning "to say or speak" and the Latin suffix *-ion* meaning "the state or quality of." Thus, *diction* means "the quality of one's speech or of one's choice and use of words."

> *After her talk, the student was praised for her good diction.*

A word based on *diction* is *dictionary,* meaning "a reference book listing the words of a language with their definitions and usually with their pronunciations and etymologies."

> *Everyone should have a modern dictionary.*

predict comes from the Latin prefix *pre-* meaning "before" and *dict-* meaning "to say or speak." Thus, *predict* means "to say before the event; to foretell; to say what will happen in the future."

> *The weather report predicted rain for tomorrow.*

Two words based on *predict* are *predictable* and *prediction. Predictable* means "capable of being predicted; easily foretold." *Prediction* means "the act of predicting; a forecast."

> *Solar eclipses are always predictable.*
> *What's your prediction for tomorrow's weather?*

◊ Look up the following words in your dictionary. Learn their meanings and relate each meaning to the root *dict-*.

addict	dictum	edict	interdict

Fun With Words

WHICH ROOTS DO YOU KNOW?

The following words contain common roots. Check the word or phrase you believe is closest in meaning to the key word. Answers follow.

1. **anthropology** [an'thrə·pol'ə·jē] —(a) the science of animals. (b) the study of fossils. (c) the study of humanity. (d) the study of geological periods.

2. **bilingual** [bī·ling'gwəl]—(a) stuttering. (b) speaking two languages. (c) tongue-tied. (d) a translator.

3. **credence** [krēd'ns]—(a) a religion or personal belief. (b) reliance on the truth of something. (c) gullible. (d) simplicity.

4. **anachronism** [ə·nak'rə·niz'əm]— (a) government by a group of people. (b) old-fashioned. (c) a perpetual-motion clock. (d) something out of its proper time.

5. **biennial** [bī·en'ē·əl]—(a) occurring once every two years. (b) occurring twice a year. (c) a plant that blooms twice a year. (d) composed or created by two people.

6. **circumstantial** [sûr'kəm·stan'-shəl]—(a) furnishing conclusive proof. (b) dependent on circumstances. (c) not accepted in court. (d) vague or without details.

7. **credulous** [krej'oo·ləs]—(a) unbelievable. (b) firm in believing. (c) easily deceived. (d) suspicious.

8. **chronically** [kron'i·kəl·ē]—(a) irritably. (b) sickly. (c) habitually. (d) due to a generally run-down condition.

9. **misanthropic** [mis'ən·throp'ik] —(a) hating mankind. (b) charitable. (c) pertaining to non-human organisms. (d) pessimistic.

10. **circumlocution** [sûr'kəm·lō·kyoo'shən]—(a) a grammatical error. (b) a strolling around. (c) a roundabout expression. (d) sailing around the world.

11. **credo** [krē'dō]—(a) a disposition to believe on slight evidence. (b) doubt. (c) a set of professed beliefs. (d) a group to which a person owes allegiance.

12. **carnivora** [kär·niv'ə·rə]—(a) a very strong person. (b) the four pointed teeth on either side of the upper and lower incisors. (c) gypsies. (d) flesh-eating animals.

ANSWERS:

1. **anthropology**— (c) the study of humanity. 2. **bilingual**— (b) speaking two languages. 3. **credence**— (b) reliance on the truth of something. 4. **anachronism**— (d) something out of its proper time. 5. **biennial**— (a) occurring once every two years. 6. **circumstantial**— (b) dependent on circumstances. 7. **credulous**— (c) easily deceived. 8. **chronically**— (c) habitually. 9. **misanthropic**— (a) hating mankind. 10. **circumlocution**— (c) a roundabout expression. 11. **credo**— (c) a set of professed beliefs. 12. **carnivora**— (d) flesh-eating animals.

ROOT: DOC-, DOCT-

The Latin root *doc-* or *doct-* means "to teach." Here are four core vocabulary words based on the root *doc-* or *doct-*: *docile, doctor, doctrine, document.* Learn the meanings of these words and their derivatives.

docile comes from *doc-* meaning "to teach" and the Latin suffix *ile* meaning "able to be." Thus, docile means "easy to teach or train; or obedient and submissive."

   The horse was safe to ride because it was docile.

A word based on *docile* is *docility,* meaning "the state or condition of being submissive or easy to manage, teach, etc."

   This horse is noted for its docility.

doctor comes from the root *doct-* meaning "to teach" and the Latin suffix *-or* meaning "a person who." Thus, the word *doctor* originally meant "a teacher." Now, of course, *doctor* means "a person who has an advanced diploma, degree, or license in a certain field, especially a person trained and licensed to practice medicine or dentistry, or a person who holds an advanced degree from a graduate school."

   When Mimi fainted, we called the doctor.
   Andrew is a Doctor of Philosophy.

Two words based on *doctor* are *doctoral,* which means "pertaining or leading to the graduate-school degree of doctor," and *doctorate,* which means "the degree or title of doctor."

   Erik is writing his doctoral dissertation in history.
   He hasn't yet received his doctorate.

NOTE: We usually use the term *doctor* as a title for a person who is trained and licensed to practice medicine or dentistry—a physician or dentist. But people who have the degree of Ph.D. (Doctor of Philosophy) may also be called *doctors.* After finishing the usual four years of college and obtaining a bachelor's degree, they have attended a graduate school where, after completing many special requirements, including those for a master's degree, they have earned the highest graduate degree, the *doctorate. Doctoral* degrees are given in almost all fields of the arts and sciences. Remember, a *doctor* can be anyone—

a historian, a chemist, a lawyer, etc.— who has a *doctoral* degree. All *doctors* are not M.D.'s (Doctors of Medicine), although that is the type of *doctor* most of us know best.

doctrine comes from a Latin word based on *doct-* meaning "to teach." *Doctrine* means "a teaching or a body of teachings or beliefs, especially those of a political or religious group; a principle or set of principles."

> *What are the basic doctrines of Christianity?*
> *Buddhist and Hindu doctrines are different.*
> *The Monroe Doctrine (1823) warned European powers not to interfere in the affairs of the Western Hemisphere.*

A word based on *doctrine* is *doctrinal*, which means "pertaining to doctrine."

> *There are doctrinal differences between Roman Catholicism and Protestantism.*

document comes from *doc-* meaning "to teach" and the Latin suffix *-ment* meaning "the result of" or "the means of." A *document* is "a means of teaching something or of giving information." Thus, *document* is defined as "something written that gives conclusive information or evidence about something."

> *The Declaration of Independence is a famous historical document.*
> *What documents do you need to get a passport?*

Two words based on *document* are *documentary* and *documentation*. *Documentary* means (1) pertaining to or based upon descriptive facts or documents; (2) a motion picture or television program dealing with events in a factual way. *Documentation* is "the preparation or use of documents, factual references, records, etc., as in support of an idea or as evidence."

> *I have documentary evidence of my citizenship.*
> *This movie isn't fiction; it's a real documentary.*
> *This author provides thorough documentation in support of his argument.*

◊ Learn the meaning of the word *indoctrinate* from your dictionary. Can you see how it is based on the root *doc-* or *doct-* meaning "to teach"?

68

ROOT: DUC-, DUCT-

The Latin root *duc-* or *duct-* means "to lead." Learn the following four core vocabulary words: *conduct, introduce, produce, reduce.*

conduct comes from the Latin prefix *con-* meaning "with; together" and *duct-* meaning "to lead." Thus, *conduct* [kən·dukt′] means "to go with someone in order to lead him; to guide, escort, or direct." It also means "to direct, guide, or behave oneself." Pronounced another way, *conduct* [kon′dukt] means "behavior."

> *Can you conduct me to the personnel office?*
> *Do you know how to conduct a business?*
> *The composer conducted the orchestra.*
> *John always conducts himself well in public.*
> *His conduct in school is excellent.*

A word related to *conduct* is *conducive,* which means "helping, guiding, or leading toward a result."

> *Lack of sleep is not conducive to alertness.*

introduce comes from the Latin prefix *intro-* meaning "within" and the root *duc-* meaning "to lead." Thus, *introduce* literally means "to lead someone within something or into something"; hence, (1) to make a person acquainted with something or with another person; (2) to present; (3) to insert; (4) to start or bring into use.

> *This course will introduce you to higher mathematics.*
> *Peter, may I introduce you to Sally?*
> *John introduced the main speaker.*
> *The speaker introduced some humor into his talk.*
> *The Spaniards introduced the horse to America.*

Two words based on *introduce* are *introduction* and *introductory.* *Introduction* means (1) the act of introducing; (2) a person's first knowledge of something; (3) something that leads up to what follows. *Introductory* means "serving as an introduction."

> *That course was my introduction to higher mathematics.*
> *The introduction to this history book is twenty pages long.*
> *The book has a twenty-page introductory chapter.*

produce comes from the Latin prefix *pro-* meaning forward and *duc-* meaning "to lead." Thus, *produce* [prə·dōōs′] literally means "to lead forward"; hence, (1) to bring forth or bear; (2) to bring about, make, create; (3) to exhibit or show. The noun *produce* [prod′ōōs] means "something brought forth; a yield, as of fruits and vegetables."

> *The land produced grapes.*
> *From the grapes men produced wine.*
> *The speech produced much disagreement.*
> *Our school is going to produce a play.*
> *The farmers sold their produce at the market.*

Four of the many words based on *produce* are *product, production, productive,* and *productivity.* A *product* is (1) anything produced; (2) a result. *Production* means (1) the act of producing; (2) that which is produced. *Productive* means (1) tending to produce; (2) tending to produce profits; (3) causing or resulting in. *Productivity* means either (1) the state of being productive; or (2) the rate of producing.

> *Wine is a product of grapes.*
> *The story was a product of his imagination.*
> *The production of word processors is increasing.*
> *Last year's production was 2 million cars.*
> *The workers in the company are very productive.*
> *Their experiments have been productive of new techniques.*
> *Productivity in the factory has risen.*

reduce comes from the Latin prefix *re-* meaning "back" and *duc-* meaning "to lead." Thus, *reduce* literally means "to lead back"; hence, (1) to bring from a higher to a lower condition; (2) to make less in size, amount, number, value, etc.; (3) to become less in any way.

> *He was reduced in rank from sergeant to corporal.*
> *He has reduced his daily quota of cigarettes.*
> *The fire reduced the building to ashes.*
> *They hope to reduce by dieting.*

Two words based on *reduce* are *irreducible,* meaning "incapable of being reduced," and *reduction,* meaning (1) the act or process of reducing; (2) the result of reducing.

> *We have cut costs to an irreducible minimum.*
> *The management plans a reduction in staff.*
> *He objected to the reduction in pay.*

◊ Look up the following words in your dictionary. Notice how the meaning of each is based on the root *duc-* or *duct-* meaning "to lead."

abduct	deductive	seduce
abduction	induce	seduction
deduce	induction	seductive
deduction	inductive	traduce

QUICKIEQUIZQUICKIEQUIZQUICKIEQUIZQUICKIEQUIZQUICKIEQUIZQUICKIEQUIZQUICKIEQUIZQUICKIE

90-SECOND QUICKIE QUIZ
WORD BUILDING

Knowing the meanings of their parts can help you to understand many words. Can you match these roots and prefixes with their meanings in the right-hand column? Answers follow.

1. **dextro-** as in ambidextrous [am′bə·dek′strəs]   (a) human
2. **ambi-** as in ambiguous [am·big′yōō·əs]   (b) self
3. **anthropo-** as in anthropology [an′thrə·pol′ə·jē]   (c) both
4. **bi-** as in bigamy [big′ə·mē]   (d) two
5. **hemi-** as in hemisphere [hem′ə·sfir]   (e) half
6. **auto-** as in automobile [ô′tə·mə·bēl′]   (f) right
7. **derm-** as in dermatologist [dûr′mə·tol′ə·jist]   (g) equal
8. **cosmo-** as in cosmopolitan [koz′mə·pol′ə·tən]   (h) nation
9. **ethno-** as in ethnology [eth·nol′ə·jē]   (i) universe
10. **equi-** as in equilibrium [ē′kwə·lib′rē·əm]   (j) skin

ANSWERS:

1. **dextro-** — (f) right. Ambidextrous means being able to use both hands equally well. 2. **ambi-** — (c) both. Ambiguous means capable of being understood in two or more senses; hence, unclear. 3. **anthropo-** — (a) human. Anthropology is the study of the human race, its origin, evolution, customs, etc. 4. **bi-** — (d) two. Bigamy is the criminal offense of having two wives or husbands at the same time. 5. **hemi-** — (e) half. A hemisphere is half a sphere or half of the terrestrial or celestial globe, as either the Northern Hemisphere or the Southern Hemisphere. 6. **auto-** — (b) self. An automobile is a self-propelled vehicle. 7. **derm-** — (j) skin. A dermatologist is a doctor who specializes in treating diseases of the skin. 8. **cosmo-** — (i) universe. Cosmopolitan means at home in all parts of the world; not limited to local interests. 9. **ethno-** — (h) nation. Ethnology is the branch of anthropology dealing with racial and ethnic groups. 10. **equi-** — (g) equal. Equilibrium means a state of balance or the condition of being well-balanced.

QUICKIEQUIZQUICKIEQUIZQUICKIEQUIZQUICKIEQUIZQUICKIEQUIZQUICKIEQUIZQUICKIEQUIZQUICKIE

71

ROOT: EQU-

The Latin root *equ-* means "equal; even." Since this root appears even in its own definition, "equal," you can see how important it is to English. Keep *equal* in mind as your key word while you learn the three core vocabulary words: *adequate, equilibrium, equivocal.*

adequate comes from the Latin prefix *ad-* meaning "to" and *equ-* meaning "equal" plus the Latin suffix *-ate*, which is used to form adjectives. Thus, *adequate* means "equal to the job; equal to what is required."

> *She's not a perfect parachutist, but she's adequate.*
> *We had an adequate amount of money for a two-week trip.*

equilibrium comes from *equ-* meaning "equal; even" and the Latin word *libra* meaning "balance." Thus, *equilibrium* means "an even balance; a state of balance; physical, mental, or emotional balance."

> *How does a tight-rope walker keep his equilibrium?*
> *May was upset by the bad news but soon regained her equilibrium.*

equivocal comes from *equ-* meaning "equal" and the Latin root *voc-* meaning "voice" plus the Latin suffix *-al* meaning "pertaining to." Thus, *equivocal* literally means "pertaining to something of equal voice or significance"; hence, "having a double meaning; misleading; purposely vague."

> *I want all the facts, so stop giving me equivocal answers.*

Two words related to or based on *equivocal* are *unequivocal*, meaning "not doubtful or vague; straightforward"; and *equivocate*, meaning "to use vague language in an attempt to mislead."

> *He made an unequivocal denial of the charges against him.*
> *The politician equivocated about his campaign expenses.*

◊ Look up the following words in your dictionary. Notice how the meaning of each is based on *equ-* meaning "equal; even."

equable	equator	equipoise	equivalent
equate	equilibrist	equinox	inequitable
equation	equidistant	equitable	inequity

Fun With Words

COMMON ROOTS

The following twelve words contain common roots used in word building. Check the word or phrase you believe is closest in meaning to the key word. Answers follow.

1. **dexterity** [dek·ster′ə·tē]—(a) superabundant strength. (b) ability to use both hands equally well. (c) sweetness. (d) skill in using the hands or body.
2. **dermatology** [dûr′mə·tol′ə·jē]— (a) the study of insects. (b) heat treatment. (c) the study of infectious disease. (d) the study of the skin and its diseases.
3. **feline** [fē′līn]—(a) delicate. (b) catlike. (c) feminine. (d) to libel or slander.
4. **demagogic** [dem′ə·goj′ik]—(a) given to unprincipled political agitation. (b) the art of public speaking. (c) having only half knowledge. (d) the investigation of evil spirits.
5. **equilibrium** [ē′kwə·lib′rē·əm]— (a) seeing equally well with both eyes. (b) stability or balance. (c) one who rides horses. (d) skill or dexterity.
6. **edict** [ē′dikt]—(a) a correction. (b) an abbreviation. (c) an explanation. (d) any proclamation or command.

7. **ambidextrous** [am′bə·dek′strəs] —(a) able to use both hands equally well. (b) good handwriting skill. (c) cross-eyed. (d) very graceful.
8. **dictum** [dik′təm]—(a) enunciation. (b) a law. (c) an authoritative statement. (d) an autocratic ruler
9. **decimate** [des′ə·māt]—(a) to cut into small pieces. (b) to count in tens. (c) to extract the moisture from. (d) to destroy a large part of.
10. **endemic** [en·dem′ik]—(a) a contagious disease. (b) peculiar to a particular locale. (c) tending to produce vomiting. (d) a disease affecting children.
11. **enamored** [in·am′ərd]—(a) inflamed with love. (b) coated with a shellac. (c) faded. (d) endorsed.
12. **filial** [fil′ē·əl]—(a) faithful. (b) of a father or mother. (c) of a son or daughter. (d) frail.

ANSWERS:

1. **dexterity**—(d) skill in using the hands or body. 2. **dermatology**—(d) the study of the skin and its diseases. 3. **feline**—(b) catlike. 4. **demagogic**—(a) given to unprincipled political agitation. 5. **equilibrium**—(b) stability or balance. 6. **edict**—(d) any proclamation or command. 7. **ambidextrous**—(a) able to use both hands equally well. 8. **dictum**—(c) an authoritative statement. 9. **decimate**—(d) to destroy a large part of. 10. **endemic**—(b) peculiar to a particular locale. 11. **enamored**—(a) inflamed with love. 12. **filial** —(c) of a son or daughter.

ROOT: FAC-, FIC-, FACT-, FECT-

The Latin root *fac-*, *fic-*, *fact-*, or *fect-* means "to do; make." It is one of the most frequently used roots in English, probably because the ideas of doing and making are so important to us. Learn the five core vocabulary words based on this important root: *facile, fiction, efficient, infect, manufacture.*

facile comes from *fac-* meaning "to do; make" and the Latin suffix *-ile* meaning "able to be." Thus, *facile* means "able to be done"; hence, "easy; requiring little effort; so skilled or talented as to do something very easily." Note that *facile* can also mean "too smooth and superficial to be serious."

> *His writing is merely facile; it lacks depth.*
> *Being a facile speaker, she is an effective politician.*

A word based on *facile* is *facility*, which means (1) ready skill or ability; (2) a building, room, piece of equipment, etc., that is provided to make some action or operation easier.

> *Professor Smith speaks French with facility.*
> *The university has many research facilities.*

fiction comes from *fic-* meaning "to make" and the Latin suffix *-tion*, which is used to form nouns. Thus, *fiction* is literally "a making" or "a made-up piece of writing"; hence, "prose writing about imaginary characters and events."

> *Mr. Jones has written both history and fiction.*

Two words based on *fiction* are *fictional*, which means "pertaining or belonging to fiction; imaginary"; and *fictitious*, meaning "imaginary; not real; false."

> *The characters in the story are fictional.*
> *The criminal gave a fictitious address.*

efficient comes from the Latin prefix *ef-* (another spelling of *ex-*) meaning "out" and *fic-* meaning "to do; make" plus the Latin suffix *-ent*, which is the same as the English *-ing*. Thus, *efficient* means "making, or turning out results with little wasted effort."

> *Reading is an efficient way of building your vocabulary.*

A word based on *efficient* is *efficiency,* meaning "the quality of being efficient or of producing results; effectiveness."

A firm's success depends on its workers' efficiency.

infect comes from the Latin prefix *in-* meaning "in" and *fect-* meaning "to do; make." Thus, *infect* literally means "to do into or inside of"; hence, "to affect with a disease; contaminate."

Is the wound infected?

Two words based on *infect* are *infection,* meaning "an invasion of the body by disease germs; a disease"; and *infectious,* meaning (1) liable to produce infection; (2) contagious; spreading to others.

The infection was checked by penicillin.
He has an infectious disease.
Her laughter was infectious.

manufacture comes from the Latin root *manu-* meaning "hand" and *fact-* meaning "to do; make" plus the Latin suffix *-ure* meaning "the act of." Thus, *manufacture* originally meant "a making by hand; making handmade products." Of course the meaning of *manufacture* has now enlarged to mean (1) to make a product, especially on a large scale; (2) to make up or invent, as an excuse or alibi.

Many cars are manufactured in Detroit.
He was late and had to manufacture an excuse.

◊ Listed below are eighteen more common words based on the root *fac-, fic-, fact-,* or *fect-.* Learn their meanings from your dictionary and relate each to the common root *fac-, fic-, fact-,* or *fect-* meaning "to do; make."

affect	defective	factory
affective	effect	perfect
affection	effective	perfection
deficient	fact	proficient
defect	factual	proficiency
defection	factor	unification

NOTE: *Affect* and *effect* are confused by many people. Pay particular attention to the difference between these two words. The verb *affect* means "to influence or have an effect on." The verb *effect* means "to bring about or produce as a result." As a noun, *effect* means "a result or influence." The relationship between the noun and the two verbs may be seen in the sentence below:

The mountain air had a noticeable effect on the invalid; it affected his health for the better and helped to effect a cure.

ROOT: FER-

The Latin root *fer-* means "to carry; bring." Here are four core vocabulary words based on *fer-: confer, differ, offer, transfer.*

confer comes from the Latin prefix *con-* meaning "together; with" and *fer-* meaning "to carry; bring." Thus, *confer* literally means "to carry or bring together"; hence, "to give or bestow" or "to consult together."

The school conferred an award on the student.
The business executives conferred about costs.

A word based on *confer* is *conference*, meaning "a formal meeting for discussion of some important matter."

The executives held a business conference.
The annual conference of women's clubs was held in Chicago.

differ comes from the Latin prefix *dif-* (another spelling of *dis-*) meaning "apart" and *fer-* meaning "to carry; bring." Thus, *differ* means "to carry oneself apart from someone else; to be unlike; to disagree."

These colors differ.
My opinion differs from yours.

A word based on *differ* is *difference*, meaning (1) the state or an instance of being unlike; (2) a distinguishing characteristic.

We had a slight difference of opinion.
There is a difference between these two colors.

offer comes from the Latin prefix *of-* (another spelling of *ob-*) meaning

76

"before" and *fer-* meaning "to carry; bring." Thus, to *offer* means "to bring something before someone; to present something for acceptance or rejection; to propose." An *offer* is "that which is presented or proposed."

He offered to walk her home.
He offered us a ride.
We accepted his offer of a ride.
Shall we make an offer of $60,000 for the house?

Two words based on *offer* are *offering*, meaning "something offered, especially a gift or contribution made in church"; and *offertory*, meaning (1) the part of a religious service during which the offering is collected; (2) a hymn sung, a prayer said, or music played during this part of the service.

The ushers collected the congregation's offerings.
The choir sang the offertory anthem.

transfer comes from the Latin prefix *trans-* meaning "across" and *fer-* meaning "to carry; bring." Thus, to *transfer* means "to carry, move, or cause to go from one person, place, carrier, etc., to another."

The company transferred him from New York to Boston.
She transferred her property to her daughter.
Take the bus and transfer at Chestnut Street.

Three words based on *transfer* are *transferable*, meaning "capable of being transferred from one person to another"; *nontransferable*, meaning "incapable of or prohibited from being transferred"; and *transference*, meaning "the act of transferring or the state of being transferred."

Bonds may be either transferable or nontransferable.
The transference of the property was handled by a lawyer.

◊ Look up the following twelve frequently used *fer-* words in your dictionary. Be sure you know the true meaning and use of each. Can you relate the meaning of each to the root *fer-* meaning "to carry; bring"?

defer	preferential	referent
deferential	refer	suffer
prefer	reference	sufferance
preference	referendum	transferal

77

REVIEW OF ROOTS

Here is another review vocabulary test containing roots and words you have already learned. Choose the answer nearest in meaning to the key word. Answers follow.

1. **credible** [kred′ə·bəl]—(a) owing money. (b) easily convinced. (c) capable of being believed. (d) despicable.
2. **credulous** [krej′ŏŏ·ləs]—(a) owing money. (b) easily convinced. (c) despicable. (d) surprised.
3. **crescendo** [krəs·hen′dō *or* krə·sen′dō]—(a) a gradual increase in volume of sound. (b) a loud noise. (c) a waterfall. (d) an oily liquid.
4. **recumbent** [ri·kum′bənt]—(a) reclining; leaning. (b) twisted; bent. (c) sleeping. (d) elected for a second term of office.
5. **discursive** [dis·kûr′siv]—(a) loud or raucous. (b) rude. (c) passing quickly from one subject to another. (d) decisive, coming to the point or making a decision quickly.
6. **incur** [in·kûr′]—(a) to become angry. (b) to agree; give assent. (c) to get rid of. (d) to become subject to; bring on oneself.
7. **recourse** [rē′kôrs] *or* ri·kôrs′]—

(a) that which precedes and suggests the course of future events. (b) that which follows. (c) access to a person or thing for help or aid. (d) an alternative.

8. **precursor** [pri·kûr′sər]—(a) that which precedes and suggests the course of future events. (b) that which follows. (c) one who has given help or aid. (d) one who introduces a speaker.
9. **edict** [ē′dikt]—(a) to cast out. (b) a secret meeting. (c) to judge guilty. (d) an official decree publicly proclaimed.
10. **indoctrinate** [in·dok′trə·nāt]—(a) to inject medicine, drugs, etc., with a hypodermic needle. (b) to instruct in principles of belief. (c) to punish severely. (d) to dilute or add impurities to.
11. **deduce** [di·dōōs′ *or* di·dyōōs′]—(a) to entice to immoral acts. (b) to guess or suppose. (c) to gather facts. (d) to reach a conclusion by reasoning.

ANSWERS:

1. **credible**—(c) capable of being believed. 2. **credulous**—(b) easily convinced. 3. **crescendo**—(a) a gradual increase in volume of sound. 4. **recumbent**—(a) reclining, leaning. 5. **discursive**—(c) passing quickly from one subject to another. 6. **incur**—(d) to become subject to; bring on oneself. 7. **recourse**—(c) access to a person or thing for help or aid. 8. **precursor**—(a) that which precedes and suggests the course of future events. 9. **edict**—(d) an official decree publicly proclaimed. 10. **indoctrinate**—(b) to instruct in principles of belief. 11. **deduce**—(d) to reach a conclusion by reasoning.

ROOT: FIRM-

Can you guess what the Latin root *firm-* means? It's easy. It means what it says, "firm; strong." This root is used in three important core vocabulary words: *affirm, confirm, infirm.*

affirm comes from the Latin prefix *af-* (another spelling of *ad-*) meaning "to" and *firm-* meaning "firm; strong." Thus, *affirm* means "to make firm; declare positively; state something to be true."

> *He affirmed the truth of the statement while under oath.*
> *She affirmed her belief in God.*

Two words based on *affirm* are *affirmation,* which means "the act of affirming; assertion; confirmation"; and *affirmative,* which means "characterized by affirming; positive; accepting or agreeing."

> *The voters expressed affirmation of the platform by electing the party's candidate.*
> *His answer was affirmative.*
> *The majority of the votes were in the affirmative.*

confirm comes from the Latin prefix *con-* meaning "thoroughly" and *firm-* meaning "firm; strong." *Confirm* means "to make thoroughly strong; strengthen; verify; ratify." It also means "to admit to the privileges of a church after having been strengthened in religious faith by training in religious teachings."

> *Success confirmed him in his resolution to work hard.*
> *The results confirmed our suspicions.*
> *Congress confirmed the President's appointment of the new ambassador to Peru.*
> *Will you confirm your order in writing?*
> *She was confirmed in church last week.*

A word based on *confirm* is *confirmation,* meaning (1) the act of confirming; (2) proof; (3) a religious rite in which a person who has been strengthened in his faith is admitted to the privileges of a church.

> *The evidence gave confirmation of his theory.*
> *After her confirmation she began to teach Sunday school.*

infirm comes from the Latin prefix *in-* meaning "not" and *firm-* meaning "firm; strong." Thus, to be *infirm* is "not to be strong; to be feeble or weak; to be sick or weak with sickness."

Arthritis has made my grandmother infirm.

A word based on *infirm* is *infirmary*, meaning "a place for the treatment of sick people."

They rushed the sick student to the college infirmary.

ROOT: FLECT-, FLEX-

Can you *flex* your muscles? Here's a chance to *flex* your mind on another Latin root. The root *flect-* or *flex-* means "to bend." The three common *flect-*, *flex-* words for your core vocabulary are: *deflect, flexible, reflect.*

deflect comes from the Latin prefix *de-* meaning "down; away" and *flect-* meaning "to bend." Thus, *deflect* means "to bend away; turn aside; swerve or cause to swerve."

He deflected the blow with his left hand.
The warrior used his shield to deflect the enemy's spears.

flexible comes from the root *flex-* meaning "to bend" and the suffix *-ible* meaning "capable of being." Thus, *flexible* means "capable of being bent, twisted, etc., without breaking; pliant." It also means "giving in to persuasion" or "able to adjust easily to change."

Radio aerials on cars are made of flexible metal.
Our employer is open-minded and flexible.
Let's keep our traveling plans flexible.

Two words based on *flexible* are *flexibility*, meaning "the state or condition of being flexible," and *inflexible*, meaning "not flexible."

He's stubborn and shows no flexibility.
He maintains an inflexible political stand.

reflect comes from the Latin prefix *re-* meaning "back" and *flect-* meaning "to bend." *Reflect* means "to bend back; turn or throw back waves of light, sound, or heat." It also means "to think back; think again; review in the mind."

The water reflected the sunlight.
The mirror reflected his face.
Stop and reflect a minute before you act.
Phyllis sat and reflected on the events of the past year.

Two words based on *reflect* are *reflection* and *reflective*. *Reflection* means (1) the act of reflecting; (2) that which is reflected. *Reflective* means "given to mental reflection; thoughtful."

On reflection, I've decided not to go to Europe this year.
He saw his reflection in the mirror.
Charles has a calm, reflective nature.

◊ Look up these two words in your dictionary and learn their meanings: *inflection, reflex.*

QUICKIEQUIZQUICKIEQUIZQUICKIEQUIZQUICKIEQUIZQUICKIEQUIZQUICKIEQUIZQUICKIEQUIZQUICKIE

60-SECOND QUICKIE QUIZ

WORD BUILDING

Knowing the meanings of roots can help you understand many words. You have already learned the roots and words given below. Match each root in the left-hand column with its meaning in the right-hand column. Answers follow.

1. **fact-** as in manufacture [man'yə·fak'chər]   (a) hand
2. **manu-** as in manufacture [man'yə·fak'chər]   (b) equal; even
3. **equ-** as in equilibrium [ē'kwə·lib'rē·əm]   (c) to carry; bring
4. **fer-** as in transfer [trans'fər]   (d) to love
5. **am-** as in amateur [am'ə·choŏr]   (e) to do; make

ANSWERS:

1. **fact-** —(e) to do; make. To manufacture now means to make any product, especially on a large scale.
2. **manu-** —(a) hand. To manufacture originally meant "to make by hand."
3. **equ-** —(b) equal; even. Equilibrium means an even balance; physical, mental, or emotional balance.
4. **fer-** —(c) to carry; bring. Transfer combines the prefix *trans-* meaning across with the root *fer-*. Thus, *transfer* means to carry, bring, or move from one person, place or carrier to another.
5. **am-** —(d) to love. An amateur is someone who does something, such as paint or play golf, for the love of it rather than for money.

QUICKIEQUIZQUICKIEQUIZQUICKIEQUIZQUICKIEQUIZQUICKIEQUIZQUICKIEQUIZQUICKIEQUIZQUICKIE

ROOT: FLU-, FLUX-

Do you know what the word *flux* means? It means "a flow"—coming from the Latin root *flu-* or *flux-*: "to flow." Now how would you explain the meaning of the word *fluid?* If you explain it as "that which flows; a liquid," you are well on your way to understanding how words are formed and how to improve your vocabulary. The three core vocabulary words based on the root *flu-* or *flux-* are: *affluent, fluency, influence.*

affluent comes from the Latin prefix *af-* (another spelling of *ad-*) meaning "to" and *flu-* meaning "to flow" plus the Latin suffix *-ent,* which is the same as the English *-ing.* Thus, *affluent* literally means "flowing to a person"; hence, "abundant or wealthy."

> *We live in an affluent country.*
> *My uncle was the most affluent man in town.*

A word based on *affluent* is *affluence,* meaning "riches or wealth."

> *Some men are noted for their affluence, others for their good deeds.*

fluency comes from *flu-* meaning "to flow" and the Latin suffix *-ency* meaning "the state or condition of." Thus, *fluency* means "the state or condition of flowing," or, more precisely, "smoothness, especially smoothness or readiness of speech."

> *Professor Karl has great fluency in German.*

A word based on *fluency* is *fluent,* which means "showing smoothness or effortless ease, especially in speech."

> *Professor Karl is fluent in German.*

influence comes from the Latin prefix *in-* meaning "in" and *flu-* meaning "to flow" plus the Latin suffix *-ence* meaning "the state or condition of." Thus, *influence* means "a flowing in of one person's thought upon others"; hence, (1) the power to produce effects on others; (2) a person or thing possessing such power; (3) an effect produced by such power. As a verb, *influence* means "to produce or have an effect on; to affect or change."

> *I wish I had more influence on the boss's decisions.*
> *Gloria's father was a major influence on her life.*

Don't drive while under the influence of alcohol.
Someone has said that influence is the effluence of affluence.
People once believed that the planets influenced people's lives.

A word based on *influence* is *influential,* which means "having or using influence."

The mayor is the most influential man in our town.

◊ Here are three other *flu-, flux-* words you should learn. Look them up in your dictionary and learn their meanings. Be sure you can relate their meanings to the root *flu-* or *flux-* meaning "to flow."

fluctuation effluence influx

ROOT: FRANG-, FRING-, FRACT-, FRAG-

Can you see the relationship of these four core vocabulary words: *fraction, fragile, fragment, infringe?* They are all based on the Latin root *frang-, fring-, fract-,* or *frag-,* which means "to break."

fraction comes from *fract-* meaning "to break" and the Latin suffix *-ion,* which is used to form nouns. Thus, a *fraction* is "something broken off from the whole; a disconnected part; a small portion; a quantity less than a whole unit."

Five dollars was only a fraction of the money he owed.
One half is a fraction.

A word based on *fraction* is *fractional,* meaning "relating to or being a fraction; small in size; partial."

He made a fractional payment, not a full one.

fragile comes from *frag-* meaning "to break" and the Latin suffix *-ile* meaning "able to be." Thus, *fragile* means "breakable; easily broken or damaged; frail."

Be careful; that vase is fragile!
The box contained glass and was marked "Fragile."
The leaf looked thin and fragile.

83

A word based on *fragile* is *fragility*, meaning "the state or condition of being easily broken or damaged; frailness."

I decided not to buy the vase because of its fragility.
The child's fragility worries the family.

fragment comes from *frag-* meaning "to break" and the Latin suffix *-ment* meaning "the condition of being." Thus, a *fragment* is "something broken off; a part broken off; a small detached portion." *Fragment* can also mean "a small part of something that has been left unfinished."

He tried to glue together the fragments of the vase.
I heard only fragments of the conversation.
He had written a fragment of a symphony before his death.

Two words based on *fragment* are *fragmentary*, meaning "made up of unconnected bits and pieces; broken"; and *fragmentation,* meaning "a breaking up into fragments."

We overheard fragmentary bits of the conversation.
I dislike the fragmentation of society into self-seeking groups.
A fragmentation bomb explodes into many small pieces.

infringe comes from the Latin prefix *in-* meaning "in" and *fring-* meaning "to break." Thus, *infringe* means "to break in or into another person's time, rights, etc." Specifically, it means "to break the terms or requirements of something, such as a promise or a law; to violate; to trespass on."

Do not infringe on the rights of others.
He was fined for infringing the law.
You're infringing on my territory.
This invention does not infringe on any other patent.

A word based on *infringe* is *infringement,* meaning "the violation or breach of a law, right, etc."

Sparta was guilty of an infringement of its treaty with Athens.

◊ Knowing that *fract-* means "to break," can you explain what the word *fracture* means? Look up these *fract-, frang-* words in your dictionary and learn their meanings:

fracture	infraction	refraction
frangible	refract	refractory

84

EXPLORING WORDS

In the vast field of physical care almost every part and function of the body has its own specialist or therapist. If you were sent to the following specialists or practitioners (not all of whom, incidentally, are M.D.'s), would you know what they do?

anesthetist a person trained to administer anesthetics, as during an operation.

cardiologist a doctor who specializes in the study of the heart and its functions.

chiropodist a specialist in the minor ailments of the foot, including bunions, corns, etc. Also called a *podiatrist*.

dermatologist a physician who specializes in treating diseases of the skin.

gynecologist a doctor who specializes in the care of women, especially in matters concerning the reproductive organs.

internist a doctor who specializes in the large, general branch of medicine called *internal medicine. Internist* is a somewhat more modern and more restricted name for the "general practitioner" who treats all types of health problems.

WARNING: Do not confuse the words *internist* and *intern*. An *intern* is a medical graduate receiving clinical training in a hospital before being licensed to practice medicine.

neurologist a doctor who specializes in treating disorders of the nervous system.

obstetrician a doctor who specializes in delivering babies and in medical problems related to childbirth.

ophthalmologist a doctor who specializes in the anatomy, functions, and diseases of the eye.

orthodontist a dentist who specializes in preventing and correcting irregularities of the teeth, such as crooked or otherwise defective teeth.

orthopedist a doctor who specializes in correcting deformities of the skeletal system and treating diseases of the bones, spine, joints, muscles, etc.

pediatrician a doctor who specializes in the care and treatment of babies and young children.

podiatrist a therapist whose specialty is treating ailments of the feet.

ROOT: FUS-, FUND-, FOUND-

The Latin root *fus-*, *fund-*, or *found-* means "to melt; pour." Here are four core vocabulary words based on this root: *confuse, foundry, fusion, refund.*

confuse comes from the Latin prefix *con-* meaning "together" and *fus-* meaning "to melt; pour." *Confuse* literally means "to melt together." Thus, *confuse* means "to mix up mentally; to jumble."

> *He confused the names of his two new friends.*
> *He was confused about their names.*

Two words related to or based on *confuse* are *confound* and *confusion*. *Confound* means (1) to confuse, bewilder, or amaze; (2) to damn (used in mild oaths or curses). *Confusion* is "the state of being confused."

> *He was confounded by the noise and the crowds.*
> *Confound that young whippersnapper!*
> *Sudden screams threw the entire office into confusion.*

foundry comes from a word which is based on the root *found-* meaning "to melt; pour." Thus, *foundry* means "a place in which metal is cast" (melted and poured).

> *There are two steel foundries in town.*

fusion comes from *fus-* meaning "to melt; pour" and the Latin suffix *-ion* meaning "the state or process of." Thus, *fusion* means (1) a melting or blending together; (2) the result of a melting or combining.

> *He was elected by a fusion of the two political parties.*
> *Brass is formed by the fusion of copper and zinc.*

Two words related to or based on *fusion* are *infuse* and *fuse*. *Infuse* means (1) to pour in, instill, or inspire something; (2) to soak a substance in a liquid in order to extract its properties. *Fuse* means (1) to melt or to join by melting; (2) a device intended to melt or break an electric circuit before an overload causes a fire or other damage.

> *The captain infused courage into the troops.*
> *Tea leaves are infused, or steeped, in hot water.*

The two pieces of metal were fused by the heat.
He put a new fuse in the fuse box.

refund comes from the Latin prefix *re-* meaning "back" and *fund-* meaning "to pour." To *refund* is "to pour something back." Thus, *refund* means (1) to give or pay back; (2) a repayment.

If I'm not satisfied, will my money be refunded?
Did you get a refund for the damaged article?

◇ Can you now figure out why *transfusion* means what it does? What is a blood *transfusion?* Look up the following words in your dictionary and learn their meanings. Be sure that you can relate each meaning to the root *fus-* meaning "to melt; pour."

diffuse	profuse	suffuse
diffusion	profusion	suffusion
effusion	profusive	transfuse
effusive	refuse	transfusion

ROOT: GAM-

The Greek root *gam-* means "marriage." Three core vocabulary words relating to marriage are based on the root *gam-: bigamy, monogamy, polygamy.*

bigamy comes from *bi-* meaning "twice; doubly; two" and *gam-* meaning "marriage." Thus, *bigamy* means "marrying another person while one still has a legal, living husband or wife."

Bigamy is a crime in all states.

monogamy comes from the Greek prefix *mono-* meaning "one; single" and *gam-* meaning "marriage." Thus, *monogamy* means "the practice of having only one wife or husband at a time."

Monogamy is the type of marriage prevailing in most civilized countries.

polygamy comes from the Greek prefix *poly-* meaning "many" and *gam-* meaning "marriage." Thus, *polygamy* means "the practice of having more than one wife or husband at a time; plural marriage."

A sultan with three wives is practicing polygamy.

◊ Almost all the vocabulary words taught in this book are common words for your everyday vocabulary. However, it's fun to know a few uncommon words. Here are two uncommon words based on the root *gam-* that you may find in sociology books or even in crossword puzzles: *exogamy, endogamy.*

ROOT: GEN-, GENIT-

The Greek and Latin root *gen-* or *genit-* means "to produce; give birth to; beget." Learn the six core vocabulary words based on *gen-* or *genit-*: *genesis, genius, genial, genuine, genital, progenitor.*

genesis comes directly from a Greek word which is based on the root *gen-* meaning "to produce; give birth to." Hence, *genesis* means "creation; beginning; the birth or origin of anything."

> *The genesis of the universe may have been a big explosion.*
> *Genesis, the story of the Creation, is the first book of the Bible.*

genius comes directly from a Latin word based on *gen-* meaning "the inborn or guardian spirit of a person or place." Hence, *genius* came to mean "extraordinary inborn intelligence" or "an outstanding natural aptitude for doing something." It also means "a person who has a brilliant mind, especially one of great intellectual achievements."

> *Einstein had a genius for mathematics.*
> *Shakespeare was a genius.*

genial comes from the same Latin word as *genius* and literally means "of one's guardian spirit." Hence, *genial* means "showing inborn or natural kindliness or pleasantness; giving comfort, warmth, or life."

> *She has a friendly, genial personality.*

88

A word based on *genial* is *congenial,* meaning "sympathetic or agreeable" and used to describe people or situations that one is naturally happy with or suited to.

> *His colleagues are all congenial.*
> *She finds her job very congenial.*

genuine comes from a Latin word based on *gen-* meaning "natural; inborn; innate." Hence, *genuine* means "native; original; authentic; real."

> *He is a genuine New Englander.*
> *This is genuine leather, not an imitation.*

genital comes from *genit-* meaning "to give birth to; beget" and the Latin suffix *-al* meaning "pertaining to." Thus, *genital* means "pertaining to the birth-giving or reproductive organs or processes." The *genitals* are "the external sexual organs."

A word based on *genital* is *congenital,* meaning (1) existing at or before birth, but not inherited; (2) by nature; natural; born.

> *The baby had a congenital defect.*
> *That boy is a congenital liar.*

progenitor comes from the Latin prefix *pro-* meaning "before" and *genit-* meaning "to give birth to; beget," plus the suffix *-or* meaning "the person or thing performing the action." Thus, *progenitor* means "an ancestor, usually remote; forebear."

> *The woolly mammoth is a progenitor of the elephant.*

◊ Look up these *gen-* words in your dictionary. Notice how the meaning of each word is based on the root *gen-* or *genit-* meaning "to produce; give birth to."

genitive	ingenious	ingenuous
hydrogen	ingenuity	oxygen

NOTE: There is a difference in meaning between *ingenious* and *ingenuous.* If you have trouble distinguishing between these two words, study their different definitions and the following sample sentences:

> *That was an ingenious solution to the problem.*
> *The naive child asked many ingenuous questions.*

REVIEW OF ROOTS

This vocabulary test contains roots and words you have already learned. Choose the answer nearest in meaning to the key word. Answers follow.

1. **deferential** [def′ə·ren′shəl]—(a) lazy; uncaring. (b) the total difference between two things. (c) a number that is subtracted from another. (d) respectful; courteous.
2. **preference** [pref′ər·əns]—(a) that which precedes or comes first in time. (b) the largest portion. (c) an indirect statement; hint. (d) a choosing of one thing over another.
3. **reference** [ref′ər·əns *or* ref′rəns] —(a) second choice. (b) direction of the attention to a person or thing. (c) praise; a compliment. (d) printed material, as a book.
4. **referendum** [ref′ə·ren′dəm]—(a) a period of waiting. (b) the submission of a proposed law to a popular vote. (c) a ballot. (d) the submission of a dispute to a mediator or judge.
5. **transferal** [trans·fûr′əl]—(a) a method or means of transfer. (b) an official document. (c) trespassing. (d) the state or process of growth.
6. **reflex** [rē′fleks]—(a) the main muscle of the upper arm. (b) an involuntary movement, such as sneezing. (c) any quick movement. (d) an inverted image, such as seen in a mirror.
7. **inflection** [in·flek′shən]—(a) a modulation of the voice. (b) any quick movement. (c) a physical defect. (d) the thigh bone.
8. **influx** [in′fluks′]—(a) constant change. (b) magnetic force, as around the North Pole. (c) a continuous flowing in, as of people or things. (d) unyielding; stubborn.
9. **fluctuation** [fluk′chōō·ā′shən]— (a) a flood. (b) a confusing situation. (c) the monthly cycle of the tides. (d) continual change; vacillation.
10. **effluence** [ef′lōō·əns]—(a) power to effect by indirect means. (b) political power. (c) a flowing out; emanation. (d) an oily scum, as on water.
11. **infraction** [in·frak′shən]—(a) the breaking of a law or rule. (b) a minor fracture, as of a small bone. (c) reflected light, as from a mirror. (d) a number that is divided by another.

ANSWERS:

1. **deferential**—(d) respectful; courteous. 2. **preference**—(d) a choosing of one thing over another. 3. **reference**—(b) direction of the attention to a person or thing. 4. **referendum**—(b) the submission of a proposed law to a popular vote. 5. **transferal**—(a) a method or means of transfer. 6. **reflex** —(b) an involuntary movement, such as sneezing. 7. **inflection**—(a) modulation of the voice. 8. **influx**—(c) a continuous flowing in, as of people or things. 9. **fluctuation**—(d) continual change; vacillation. 10. **effluence**—(c) a flowing out; emanation. 11. **infraction**—(a) the breaking of a law or rule.

ROOT: GEO-

Can you think of what *geography* and *geology* have in common? They both apply to the earth. In fact, both words are based on the Greek root *geo-* meaning "earth." The root *geo-* appears chiefly in words for certain common and important sciences or branches of knowledge. Here are the three "earthy" core vocabulary words based on *geo-: geography, geology, geometry.*

geography comes from *geo-* meaning "earth" and the Greek root *-graphy* meaning "writing; description." Thus, *geography* is "the description of the earth"; that is, "the science that describes the surface of the earth, or of other planets, especially in terms of large areas and how they are related."

> *Everyone studies some geography in school.*
> *We have learned a great deal about the moon's geography.*

Three words based on *geography* are *geographic* and *geographical,* which mean "pertaining to geography," and *geographer,* meaning "a specialist in or student of geography."

> *He is a member of the local geographic society.*
> *What was the expedition's exact geographical location?*
> *The expedition included a geographer to map the region.*

geology comes from *geo-* meaning "earth" and the Greek root *-logy* meaning "the science or study of." Thus, *geology* means "the science that deals with the origin and structure of the earth, especially its rocks and rock formations."

> *Gold prospectors must have some knowledge of geology.*

Three words based on *geology* are *geologic* and *geological,* which mean "pertaining to geology," and *geologist,* meaning "a specialist in or student of geology."

> *This is a geologic textbook.*
> *This is a geological map, showing ore deposits and rock formations.*
> *A geologist could tell us what kind of rock this is.*

geometry comes from *geo-* meaning "earth" and the Greek root *-metry* meaning "measure; measurement." *Geometry* was originally thought of as a way to measure the earth. Today, of course, *geometry* means "the branch of mathematics dealing especially with the measurements of and the relationships between points, lines, angles, surfaces, and solids."

I found geometry harder than algebra.

Three words based on *geometry* are *geometric, geometrical,* and *geometrician. Geometric* and *geometrical* mean (1) pertaining to or according to the rules of geometry; (2) characterized by straight lines, crosses, zigzags, etc., as some designs or paintings. A *geometrician* is "a specialist in geometry."

What is the geometric relation between these two lines?
The wallpaper has a geometrical design.

◊ Here are three more words based on the root *geo-*. These words apply to important concepts; you will find them mentioned in your newspaper from time to time. Look up these words in your dictionary. If you know that *geo-* means "earth," you will learn and remember these words easily.

geochemistry   geophysics   geopolitics

ROOT: GER-, GEST-

Did you know that there is a relationship between the words *belligerent* and *digestion?* They are both based on the Latin root *ger-* or *gest-* meaning "to carry; carry on; produce." Learn the following three core vocabulary words based on this root—*belligerent, digest, gestate*—and the additional words derived from them.

belligerent comes from the Latin root *belli-* meaning "war" and *ger-* meaning "to carry on" plus the Latin suffix *-ent,* which is the same as the English ending *-ing.* Thus, *belligerent* means "carrying on in a warlike way; warlike; antagonistic; engaged in warfare." As a noun, *belligerent* means "a person or nation engaged in warfare or fighting."

He was belligerent toward strangers, always picking fights.

A mediator tried to reconcile the belligerent factions.
The belligerents are going to hold truce talks.

A word based on *belligerent* is *nonbelligerent,* meaning (1) not war-like or not at war; (2) a person or nation that is not at war.

Switzerland is a nonbelligerent country.
A nonbelligerent may aid one of the belligerents in a war.

digest comes from the Latin prefix *di-* meaning "away" and *gest-* meaning "to carry." *Digest* is "to carry away something inside; to take in." Thus, the verb *digest* [di·jest'] means (1) to take in and assimilate, especially food for the body; (2) to take in and understand mentally; (3) to take in and condense or summarize. As a noun, *digest* [dī'jest] means "a condensation or summary."

Are cucumbers hard to digest?
I need time to digest this new idea.
Please digest this long report into a two-page summary.
Have you read the digest of his latest book?

Four words based on *digest* are *digestion, indigestion, digestive,* and *indigestible. Digestion* is "the act or process of digesting." *Indigestion* is "faulty digestion; painful or imperfect digestion, as from overeating or from eating rich or unsuitable foods." *Digestive* means "pertaining to or aiding digestion." *Indigestible* means "incapable of being digested."

Father claims to have a good digestion.
Bart took bicarbonate of soda for his indigestion.
Where is the digestive tract?
He finds cucumbers indigestible.

gestate comes from *gest-* meaning "to carry" and the Latin suffix *-ate,* which is used to form verbs. *Gestate* is "to carry young inside the body." Thus, *gestate* means "to carry young in the uterus."

The human female gestates for nine months.

A word based on *gestate* is *gestation,* meaning "the period during which the unborn young are carried in the uterus; pregnancy."

Gestation in human beings is nine months.

◊ Look up the following words in your dictionary and learn their

93

meanings. Notice how each word is based on the root *ger-* or *gest-* meaning "to carry; carry on; produce."

congest	gesticulate	gesture
congestion	gesticulation	ingest

NOTE: In this chapter you learned that the Latin root *belli-* means "war," as in *belligerent.* Knowing what the root *belli-* means, can you figure out the meanings of *bellicose* and *antebellum?* If you don't know what *bellicose* and *antebellum* mean, look them up in your dictionary and note how both are based on the root *belli-* meaning "war."

ROOT: GRAD-, GRESS-

The Latin root *grad-* or *gress-* means either "a step" or "to step or go." Learn the following four core vocabulary words based on *grad-* or *gress-: aggression, gradual, graduate, progress.* Here are ten progressive words leading to graduation.

aggression comes from the Latin prefix *ag-* (another spelling of *ad-*) meaning "to; toward" and *gress-* meaning "to step or go" plus the Latin suffix *-ion* meaning "the act or state of." An *aggression* is literally "an act of going to, or an approach toward, someone." Thus, *aggression* means "an attack."

The warring nations accused each other of aggression.

Two words related to *aggression* are *aggressive,* meaning "characterized by vigorous activity; disposed toward a forceful approach or attack"; and *aggressor,* which means "commits aggression."

Tom is an aggressive salesman—a real go-getter.
The United Nations condemned the aggressors.

gradual comes from *grad-* meaning "a step" and the Latin suffix *-al* meaning "pertaining to." *Gradual* means "moving or changing slowly, as if by steps; little by little; step by step."

The change in the weather was gradual.
Gradually his broken bones began to mend.

A word based on *gradual* is *gradualism,* meaning "the principle of gradual change, especially in social or political matters."

The governor is not against change but practices gradualism.

graduate comes from the root *grad-* meaning "a step" and the suffix *-ate* meaning "to take or make." The verb *graduate* [graj′oo·āt] literally means "to take a step." Hence, it means "to grant or receive a diploma or degree for completing a course of study at a school or college." A *graduate* [graj′oo·it] is "a person who holds a diploma or degree, especially a bachelor's degree." In other senses, the verb *graduate* means "to mark off in measured units" or "to adjust or change by steps."

The school graduated him at the top of his class.
He graduated from college in June.
She is a graduate of the University of Michigan.
Thermometers are graduated for the measurement of temperature.
The income tax is graduated; the more you earn, the higher your tax bracket.

A word based on *graduate* is *graduation,* meaning (1) the act of graduating; (2) a ceremony at which degrees or diplomas are given out; (3) an equal division or mark of measurement, as on a scale.

We attended the graduation exercises.
The graduations on this thermometer are hard to see.

progress comes from the Latin prefix *pro-* meaning "forward" and *gress-* meaning "to step or go." Thus, the noun *progress* [prog′res] means "a going forward; advancement; improvement." The verb *progress* [prǝ·gres′] means "to go forward; advance; improve."

Have you noticed progress in your vocabulary building?
We must progress to our final goal.

Two words based on *progress* are *progression* and *progressive. Progression* means (1) the act of progressing; (2) an advancing sequence of things. *Progressive* means (1) moving forward, proceeding, or increasing; (2) aiming at progress.

The series 2, 4, 8, 16 is a mathematical progression.
There has been a progressive worsening of air pollution.
He is a progressive politician.

95

◊ Look up the following words in your dictionary. Learn the meaning of each and note how it is based on the root *grad-* or *gress-* meaning "to step or go."

digress	regress	transgress
digression	regression	transgression
digressive	regressive	transgressor

QUICKIEQUIZQUICKIEQUIZQUICKIEQUIZQUICKIEQUIZQUICKIEQUIZQUICKIEQUIZQUICKIEQUIZQUICKIE

90-SECOND QUICKIE QUIZ

WORD BUILDING

Reviewing the meanings of roots you have learned will help you remember them. You have already learned the roots and words given below. Match each root in the left-hand column with its meaning in the right-hand column. Answers follow.

1. **geo-** as in geology [jē·ol′ə·jē]   (a) ancient
2. **anthropo-** as in anthropology [an′thrə·pol′ə·jē]   (b) pleasing
3. **archeo-** as in archeology [är′kē·ol′ə·jē]   (c) a step
4. **flux-** as in influx [in′fluks′]   (d) a flow
5. **fract-** as in fraction [frak′shən]   (e) to melt; pour
6. **grad-** as in gradual [graj′ōō·əl]   (f) earth
7. **grat-** as in gratitude [grat′ə·tōōd]   (g) man; human
8. **fus-** as in fusion [fyōō′zhən]   (h) to break

ANSWERS:

1. **geo-** —(f) earth. Geology is the science that deals with the origin and structure of the earth, especially its rocks and rock formations.
2. **anthropo-** — (g) man; human. Anthropology is the science that deals with the physical, social, cultural, and material development of the human race; it is the study of mankind.
3. **archeo-** —(a) ancient. Archeology is the study of history from the remains of ancient human cultures.
4. **flux-** —(d) a flow. An influx is a flowing or coming in, as of a large number of people or things.
5. **fract-** —(h) to break. A fraction is something broken off from the whole; a small portion or part; a quantity less than a whole number or unit.
6. **grad-** —(c) a step. Gradual means moving or changing slowly; step-by-step, little-by-little.
7. **grat-** —(b) pleasing. Gratitude is the state of being pleased or thankful; thankfulness, appreciation.
8. **fus-** —(e) to melt; pour. A fusion is a melting or blending together; a combination.

QUICKIEQUIZQUICKIEQUIZQUICKIEQUIZQUICKIEQUIZQUICKIEQUIZQUICKIEQUIZQUICKIE

ROOT: GRAT-

The Latin root *grat-* means "pleasing." The five core vocabulary words based on this root are: *congratulate, grateful, gratify, gratitude, gratuity.*

congratulate comes from the prefix *con-* meaning "together" and a Latin word meaning "to rejoice," which is based on the root *grat-* meaning "pleasing." *Congratulate* means "to express one's pleasure at the success, joy, etc., of someone else."

We congratulated John when he won the prize.

A word based on *congratulate* is *congratulation,* meaning "the act of expressing one's pleasure at another's success or good fortune."

We sent our congratulations when our neighbors had a baby.

grateful comes from *grat-* meaning "pleasing" and the suffix *-ful* meaning "tending to; characterized by." Thus, *grateful* means "characterized by being well pleased"; hence, "thankful or appreciative."

She was grateful for our help.

gratify comes from *grat-* meaning "pleasing" and the Latin suffix *-ify* meaning "to make." Thus, to *gratify* is "to make pleased; to give pleasure or satisfaction to." *Gratify* also means "to satisfy or indulge."

She was gratified by the response to her suggestion.
He gratified his wife's every wish.

A word based on *gratify* is *gratification,* meaning "pleasure or satisfaction."

What gratification do you get from studying?

gratitude comes from *grat-* meaning "pleasing" and the suffix *-itude* meaning "the quality or state of." *Gratitude* means "the state of being pleased or thankful; thankfulness; appreciation."

We were full of gratitude for the help she gave us.

A word based on *gratitude* is *ingratitude,* meaning "lack of thankfulness or appreciation."

Parents sometimes accuse their children of ingratitude.

gratuity comes from *grat-* meaning "pleasing" and the Latin suffix *-ity* meaning "the quality or state of." Thus, *gratuity* means "something given for having pleased another; especially, a gift of money given in return for some service." In short, *gratuity* is a very formal word for a tip.

> *Do you think the doorman expects a gratuity at Christmastime?*

A word based on *gratuity* is *gratuitous,* meaning (1) free; (2) lacking cause; unwarranted.

> *Some people like to give gratuitous advice.*
> *That was a gratuitous insult.*

◊ Look up the following words in your dictionary. Learn their meanings and relate each to the root *grat-* meaning "pleasing": *gratis, ingrate.*

ROOT: GRAV-

The Latin root *grav-* means "heavy." A key word to remember in learning the root *grav-* is our modern adjective *grave,* meaning "of great importance; solemn; dignified; somber."

> *The town banker always had a grave look on his face.*
> *This is a grave political issue.*

Add *grave* to your core vocabulary, along with two additional words based on the root *grav-: aggravate* and *gravity.*

aggravate comes from the Latin prefix *ag-* (another spelling of *ad-*) meaning "to" and *grav-* meaning "heavy" plus the Latin suffix *-ate,* which can be used to form verbs. Thus, *aggravate* means "to make heavy"; hence, "to make worse, more unpleasant, or more burdensome."

> *His cold was aggravated by the rainy weather.*
> *He is aggravating his cold by going out in the rain.*

NOTE: Precise writers and speakers do not use *aggravate* to mean "annoy" or *aggravating* to mean "annoying, provoking, or exasperating." These usages are informal.

gravity comes from *grav-* meaning "heavy" and the Latin suffix *-ity* meaning "the state or quality of." Thus, *gravity* means "heaviness," or more specifically, "the force that causes material objects to fall toward the center of the earth." In another sense, *gravity* means "seriousness."

> *Who discovered the force of gravity?*
> *Are you aware of the gravity of the current political situation?*

Three words related to or based on *gravity* are *gravitate, gravitation,* and *gravitational. Gravitate* means "to move or be attracted as if by the force of gravity." *Gravitation* is (1) the act or state of gravitating; (2) in physics, the force whereby any two bodies attract each other; (3) gravity. *Gravitational* means "of or having to do with gravity or gravitation."

> *He gravitates toward people his own age.*
> *The gravitation of one suspended object toward another can be measured by delicate instruments.*
> *The earth's gravitational pull is greater than that of the moon.*

◊ Now that you know what *gravity* means and that it is based on the root *grav-* meaning "heavy," look up the scientific term *specific gravity* in your dictionary. Note the difference between mere *weight* and *specific gravity.*

ROOT: HER-, HES-

The Latin root *her-* or *hes-* means "to stick." Learn the two core vocabulary words based on *her-* or *hes-: adhere* and *cohere.*

adhere comes from the Latin prefix *ad-* meaning "to" and *her-* meaning "to stick." Thus, *adhere* means "to stick to; stick fast; be attached to."

> *This tape won't adhere to a slick surface.*
> *He always adheres to his principles.*
> *In spite of opposition he adhered to his plan.*

Four words based on *adhere* are *adherence, adherent, adhesion,* and *adhesive. Adherence* means "firm or faithful attachment." An *adherent* is "a follower or supporter of a cause, doctrine, or leader." *Adhesion* means (1) sticking fast; (2) firm attachment or fidelity. *Adhesive* means (1) sticky or designed to stick; (2) a substance that sticks things together, as glue.

> *Their strict adherence to their beliefs brought them persecution.*
> *He is an adherent of the philosophy of nonviolence.*
> *The tape holds the bandage in place by adhesion.*
> *Where is the adhesive tape?*
> *Animal glue is a strong adhesive.*

cohere comes from the Latin prefix *co-* meaning "together" and *her-* meaning "to stick." *Cohere* means "to stick together"; hence, "to be firmly or logically connected; to hold together or be consistent."

> *The snowball wouldn't cohere and flew apart when he threw it.*
> *The stories of the three witnesses don't cohere.*

Four words based on *cohere* are *coherence, coherent, cohesion,* and *cohesive. Coherence* means (1) a sticking together; (2) logical connection or consistency. *Coherent* means (1) sticking together; (2) logically connected and consistent; (3) understandable. *Cohesion* is "the act or state of sticking together." *Cohesive* means "sticking close together."

> *His speech lacked coherence; he rambled and digressed aimlessly.*
> *Did you think his speech was coherent?*
> *She was too terrified to speak coherently.*
> *The cohesion of their family group is remarkable.*
> *He belongs to a very cohesive group of friends.*

NOTE: Many people confuse the words *adhesive* and *cohesive* because both are based on the root *hes-* meaning "to stick." Remember that the prefix *ad-* means "to," so that *adhesive* means "sticking to something else." Remember that the prefix *co-* means "together," so that *cohesive* means "sticking together." Something that is *adhesive* sticks *to* something else. Something that is *cohesive* sticks *together* in a solid mass.

◊ Learn the meaning of the following *her-* or *hes-* words from your dictionary. All these words also have the prefix *in-*, which has two possible meanings: "in" or "into" and "not." In which of the following *her-, hes-* words does the prefix *in-* mean "in"? In which word does it mean "not"?

incoherent   inhere   inherent   inhesion

Fun With Words

TOUGHER ROOTS

Some of the roots you learned in the preceding pages are found in these twelve words. Choose the word or phrase you believe is closest in meaning to the key word. Answers follow.

1. **genocide** [jen′ə·sīd]—(a) the extermination of an entire race or people. (b) self-destruction. (c) the murder of one's father. (d) the assassination of a king.
2. **homogeneity** [hō′mə·jə·nē′ə·tē] —(a) longevity. (b) comfort. (c) uniformity or likeness in kind. (d) manliness.
3. **genealogy**[jē′nē·al′ə·jē]—(a) the study of genes and chromosomes. (b) the study of humanity. (c) the study of old age. (d) a record of family descent.
4. **misogyny** [mis·oj′·ə·nē]—(a) hatred of people. (b) hatred of women. (c) hatred of marriage. (d) rule by a woman or women.
5. **juxtaposition** [juks′tə·pə·zish′ən] —(a) wide separation. (b) fairmindedness. (c) stubborn opposition. (d) placement side by side.
6. **luminary** [lōō′mə·ner′ē]—(a) a famous person. (b) pertaining to the moon's atmosphere. (c) hopeful. (d) a person who is very vain.
7. **homonym** [hom′ə·nim]—(a) a word with the same sound as another word but with a different meaning. (b) in complete accord. (c) a false name. (d) internal secretion of the endocrine glands.
8. **heterogeneous** [het′ər·ə·jē′nē·əs] —(a) pertaining to men and women. (b) foreign. (c) consisting of different elements; unlike. (d) unorthodox opinions,
9. **misogamy** [mis·og′ə·mē]—(a) hatred of marriage. (b) hatred of human society. (c) rule by a woman or women. (d) hatred of women.
10. **linguistics** [ling·gwis′tiks]—(a) the study of diction and enunciation. (b) geometric patterns. (c) the science of light. (d) the science and study of language.
11. **iconoclast** [ī·kon′ə·klast]—(a) a type of spring flower. (b) a destroyer of images. (c) a revolutionist. (d) a pioneer.
12. **monogamous** [mə·nog′ə·məs]— (a) boring and tiresome. (b) all of the same kind. (c) womanhating. (d) having only one spouse.

ANSWERS:

1. **genocide**—(a) the extermination of an entire race or people. 2. **homogeneity**—(c) uniformity or likeness in kind. 3. **genealogy**—(d) a record of family descent. 4. **misogyny**—(b) hatred of women. 5. **juxtaposition**—(d) placement side by side. 6. **luminary**—(a) a famous person. 7. **homonym**—(a) a word with the same sound as another word but with a different meaning. 8. **heterogeneous**—(c) consisting of different elements; unlike. 9. **misogamy**—(a) hatred of marriage. 10. **linguistics**—(d) the science and study of language. 11. **iconoclast**—(b) a destroyer of images. 12. **monogamous**—(d) having only one spouse.

ROOT: JAC-, JECT-

The Latin root *jac-* or *ject-* means "to throw, lie, or be thrown down." Learn the three core vocabulary words based on *jac-* or *ject-: adjacent, inject, project.*

adjacent comes from the Latin prefix *ad-* meaning "near" and *jac-* meaning "to be thrown down" plus the Latin suffix *-ent* which is the same as our English ending *-ing. Adjacent* therefore means "thrown down, or lying, next to or near something else; situated or located next to or near one another; adjoining."

> *Mr. Green's farm is adjacent to ours.*
> *We took adjacent rooms at the hotel.*

inject comes from the Latin prefix *in-* meaning "into" and *ject-* meaning "to throw." To *inject* is "to throw or shoot something into something else." Thus, *inject* means "to force into, as when shooting a fluid, drug, etc., into the body with a syringe or hypodermic needle," or "to introduce into, as when throwing in a comment or bringing in a new element."

> *The doctor injected the vaccine into my arm.*
> *Simon injected a touch of humor into the conversation.*

A word based on *inject* is *injection,* meaning (1) the act of forcing or introducing something into something else; (2) that which is injected.

> *Have you had a typhoid injection?*

project comes from the Latin prefix *pro-* meaning "forward; before" and *ject-* meaning "to throw." Thus, the verb *project* [prə·jekt'] literally means "to throw forward or throw forth"; hence, "to put forth one's words, ideas, etc.; to make oneself heard or understood." Pronounced another way, the noun *project* [proj'ekt] means "something that is proposed; a plan."

> *The speaker projected his voice all the way to the back row.*
> *The business project was approved.*

Four words based on *project* are *projectile, projection, projector,* and *projectionist.* A *projectile* is "something that is thrown forward by force." *Projection* means (1) the act of throwing forward; putting forth or presenting something; (2) something that is projected, presented, or proposed. A *projector* is "a person or thing that projects; especially, a machine for throwing film images on a screen." A *projectionist* is "an operator of a motion-picture film projector."

> *Both spears and bullets are projectiles.*
> *The projection of the film was delayed because of a missing reel.*
> *This chart is a projection of next year's income and expenses.*
> *The film projector is broken, and the projectionist can't fix it.*

◊ Look up the following words in your dictionary. Learn the meaning of each word and be sure you understand how each is built on the root *jac-* or *ject-* meaning "to throw."

abject	ejaculate	object
adjective	eject	reject
dejection	interjection	subject

ROOT: JUNCT-, JOIN-, JOINT-

Can you guess what the Latin root *junct-, join-,* or *joint-* means? It is as easy as it looks. This root means "to join." Of course, *join* and *joint* are key words to remember with this root. We all know what *join* means, and it is obvious that a *joint* in the body is "a place where two bones are joined together." Learn the following four core vocabulary words based on the root *junct-, join-,* or *joint-: adjoin, conjunction, injunction, junction.*

adjoin comes from the Latin prefix *ad-* meaning "to" and *join-* meaning "to join." Thus, *adjoin* means "to join to"; hence, "to be next to and often connected with something."

> *Our farm adjoins the road.*

NOTE: *Adjacent* and *adjoining* both mean "lying next to," but *adjoining* sometimes carries the additional meaning of being connected. Thus, two *adjacent* hotel rooms are next to each other, while two *adjoining* hotel rooms are next to each other and are connected by a door.

103

A word related to *adjoin* is *adjunct,* meaning "something of less importance joined to something of greater importance."

> *The orchard is a valuable adjunct of the farm.*

conjunction comes from the Latin prefix *con-* meaning "together" and *junct-* meaning "to join" plus the Latin suffix *-ion* meaning "the act or result of." Thus, *conjunction* means "the act or result of joining together; association." It also means "an occurrence of events joined together in time; a simultaneous occurrence." In grammar a *conjunction* is a word that joins grammatical elements together.

> *Our club is giving a dance in conjunction with two other organizations.*
> *The conjunction of the two accidents at midnight was strange.*
> *The conjunction* and *may be used to join independent clauses together in a compound sentence.*

Two words based on or related to *conjunction* are *conjoin,* meaning "to join together; combine; unite"; and *conjunctive,* meaning "connective."

> *We believe in justice conjoined with mercy.*
> And *is a conjunctive word.*

injunction comes from the prefix *in-* meaning "in; into" and *junct-* meaning "to join" plus the suffix *-ion* meaning "the act or state of." Thus, *injunction* means "the act of legally joining in or butting in"; hence, (1) the act of ordering something authoritatively; (2) an authoritative order or direction, especially one issued by a court of law that forbids a party from taking a certain action.

> *The judge issued an injunction against the strike.*

junction comes from the root *junct-* meaning "to join" and the suffix *-ion* meaning "the act or state of." Thus, *junction* means "the act of joining or the state of being joined"; hence, "the place where lines or routes, such as roads, railways, streams, etc., come together or cross."

> *The railway junction is two miles from town.*

◊ Look up the following words in your dictionary. Learn their meanings and how they are based on the root *junct-, join-,* or *joint-.*

> disjunctive   enjoin   juncture   subjunctive

ROOT: LEG-, LIG-, LECT-

The Latin root *leg-*, *lig-*, or *lect-* means "to choose" or "to read." It is the basic root of such common words as *lecture, elect,* and *collect.* Learn the following six core vocabulary words based on *leg-*, *lig-*, or *lect-*: *collect, elect, eligible, lecture, legible, select.*

collect comes from the prefix *col-* meaning "together" and *lect-* meaning "to choose." *Collect* originally meant "to choose together." Now, of course, *collect* means (1) to gather together or assemble; (2) to bring together for study or as a hobby; (3) to gather payments of money, donations, etc.; (4) to accumulate, as dust or dirt.

> *People collected in the street to see the fire.*
> *He collects coins and stamps.*
> *The state collects taxes every year.*
> *Dust collects on this windowsill.*

Three words based on *collect* are *collection, collective,* and *collector.* *Collection* means (1) the act of gathering together; (2) that which is gathered together or assembled; (3) a collecting of money, as for a church, charity, etc. *Collective* means (1) of, related to, or proceeding from a number of persons or things together; common; (2) a group enterprise. A *collector* is "a person who collects anything."

> *Have you seen my stamp collection?*
> *We made a collective effort to win the game.*
> *He works on a collective farm in Russia.*
> *She is a coin collector.*
> *He is a tax collector.*

elect comes from the Latin prefix *e-* (another spelling of *ex-*) meaning "out" and *lect-* meaning "to choose." Thus, the verb *elect* means "to pick out, or choose; especially, to choose for an office by vote; select." The adjective *elect* means "chosen; chosen for office but not yet installed." The noun *elect* means "those chosen or favored."

> *Linda elected to take a course in dramatics.*
> *This year we vote to elect a president.*
> *He is the president-elect.*
> *Leonardo da Vinci is among the elect in the fine arts.*

QUICKIE QUIZ
SOME FAMILIAR ROOTS

Here are some roots you have already learned. Can you match them with their meanings? Answers follow.

1. **cumb-** as in recumbent [ri·kum′bənt]   (a) to teach
2. **doct-** as in indoctrinate [in·dok′trə·nāt]   (b) to step
3. **cresc-** as in excrescence [iks·kres′əns]   (c) to grow
4. **grad-** as in gradation [grā·dā′shən]   (d) to lie

ANSWERS:

1. **cumb-**—(d) to lie. Recumbent means lying down. 2. **doct-**—(a) to teach. Indoctrinate means to instruct in principles or doctrines. 3. **cresc-**—(c) to grow. An excrescence is an unnatural outgrowth, as a wart. 4. **grad-**—(b) to step. Gradation means a gradual change by steps.

Three words based on *elect* are *election, elector,* and *electorate.* *Election* means (1) the formal choice of a person or persons for any position, especially by ballot; (2) a popular vote on any question; (3) the act of choosing. An *elector* is "a person who elects; one who is qualified to vote in an election." The *electorate* is "the whole body of voters."

He is running in the congressional election.
Many electors vote a straight party ticket.
Twenty percent of the electorate voted for the losing candidate.

eligible comes from the Latin prefix *e-* (another spelling of *ex-*) meaning "out" and *lig-* meaning "to choose" plus the Latin suffix *-ible* meaning "able to be." Thus, *eligible* means "able to be chosen or picked out for something; worthy of being chosen; qualified for a position, office, or function; suitable; qualified and desirable, as for marriage."

Mr. Jones is an eligible candidate for mayor.
All adult citizens are eligible to vote.
Tony is an eligible bachelor.

A word based on *eligible* is *eligibility,* meaning "the quality of being eligible; suitableness."

Have you checked his eligibility to run for office?

106

lecture comes from *lect-* meaning "to read" and the Latin suffix *-ure* meaning "the act of." Originally, *lecture* meant "the act of reading." Now, of course, a *lecture* is "a discourse, read or spoken, on a specific subject, given before an audience for information or instruction." To *lecture* is "to deliver a lecture or lectures."

The professor gave lectures twice a week.
She lectured at the university.

legible comes from *leg-* meaning "to read" and the Latin suffix *-ible* meaning "able; able to be." Hence, *legible* means "able to be read; readable; clear, as handwriting."

This scrawled note is barely legible.
Please try to write legibly.

A word based on *legible* is *illegible,* meaning "not able to be read, as the result of poor handwriting, smears, bad printing, etc."

Your handwriting is illegible.

select comes from the Latin prefix *se-* meaning "apart" and *lect-* meaning "to choose." Thus, the verb *select* means "to choose something apart from the rest; pick out in preference to others." As an adjective, *select* means "set aside by having been chosen; choice or exclusive."

Have you selected the book you want to buy?
These are our best, select tomatoes.
That club has a select membership.

Two words based on *select* are *selection* and *selective. Selection* means (1) the act of choosing; (2) a choice; (3) a collection chosen with care. *Selective* means (1) pertaining to selecting or that which is selected; (2) careful in choosing.

Have you made a selection of books to buy?
The store had a good selection of shoes.
She had a highly selective taste in clothes.

◇ Look up the following words in your dictionary. Learn their meanings and relate each to the root *leg-, lig-,* or *lect-* meaning "to choose" or "to read."

elective	lectern	legend	selectivity
intelligent	lecturer	predilection	selectman

Fun With Words

STORIES BEHIND THE WORDS

Here is a vocabulary test of twenty words that have interesting etymologies. Check the word or phrase you believe is closest in meaning to the key word. Answers and etymologies follow.

1. **tantalize** [tan′tə·līz]—(a) to tease or torment by holding out false hopes. (b) to dance in a lively manner. (c) to make one's mouth water. (d) to inoculate.

2. **titan** [tīt′n]—(a) a large cloud formation. (b) a pale blue color. (c) a figure or person of gigantic size. (d) the presiding officer.

3. **mausoleum** [mô′sə·lē′əm]—(a) a museum. (b) a floor covering. (c) a stately tomb. (d) an enclosure for animals.

4. **hegira** [hi·jī′rə]—(a) departure. (b) deceit. (c) bargaining. (d) a burden.

5. **nemesis** [nem′ə·sis]—(a) a fearsome opponent or antagonist. (b) favoritism extended toward relatives. (c) a kidney disease. (d) a bad omen.

6. **hallmark** [hôl′märk′]—(a) a disfigurement. (b) a proof of excellence. (c) a piece of furniture. (d) a decoration.

7. **Thespian** [thes′pē·ən]—(a) a tramp. (b) one who lisps. (c) an actor. (d) a gypsy.

8. **solecism** [sol′ə·siz′əm]—(a) comfort. (b) a factor in astronomy. (c) loneliness. (d) a grammatical error.

9. **meander** [mē·an′dər]—(a) to flirt. (b) to waste time. (c) to wander aimlessly. (d) to mumble.

10. **chauvinism** [shō′vən·iz′əm]—(a) exaggerated, vainglorious patriotism. (b) a vulgar display. (c) capitalism. (d) complete and utter defeat.

11. **shambles** [sham′bəlz]—(a) a scene of disorder or ruin. (b) forest path. (c) aimless wandering. (d) an overcrowded area.

12. **pariah** [pə·rī′ə]—(a) a Hindu ruler. (b) an underling. (c) a diseased person. (d) a social outcast.

13. **shanghai** [shang′hī]—(a) to kidnap for service on a ship. (b) a fancy beverage. (c) to deceive. (d) to render incapable.

14. **maverick** [mav′ər·ik]—(a) an undomesticated animal. (b) a criminal. (c) an immigrant. (d) a nonconformist.

15. **churlish** [chûr′lish]—(a) childlike. (b) effeminate. (c) rude. (d) foolish.

16. **stentorian** [sten′tôr′ē·ən]—(a) infuriated. (b) dignified. (c) loud-voiced. (d) grim.

17. **behemoth** [bi·hē′məth]—(a) a colossal beast. (b) a tomb. (c) a human giant. (d) a heathen idol.

18. **Pyrrhic victory** [pir′ik]—(a) a victory gained by ruinous loss. (b) an overwhelming victory. (c) a quick victory. (d) a victory by a few over many.

19. **braggadocio** [brag′ə·dō′shē·ō] —(a) humor. (b) jargon. (c) empty boasting. (d) long-windedness.

20. **mecca** [mek′ə]—(a) any temple. (b) a small, high plateau. (c) a wasteland. (d) a place of pilgrimage.

STORIES BEHIND THE WORDS

1. **tantalize**—(a) to tease or torment by holding out false hopes. (Tantalus, according to Greek mythology, was punished for a misdeed by being made to stand in water that receded when he tried to drink it and under fruit-laden branches which he could not reach.)

2. **titan**—(c) a figure or person of gigantic size. (The Titans were a race of gigantic Greek gods.)

3. **mausoleum**—(c) a stately tomb. (The tomb of King Mausolus at Halicarnassus was one of the Seven Wonders of the World in ancient times.)

4. **hegira**—(a) departure. (Mohammed's flight from Mecca to Medina in 622 was called his Hegira, which means "departure" in Arabic.)

5. **nemesis**—(a) a fearsome opponent or antagonist. (Nemesis was the Greek goddess of vengeance.)

6. **hallmark**—(b) a proof of excellence. (In medieval times, a hallmark was an official mark stamped on genuine gold and silver articles at the Goldsmiths' Hall in London.)

7. **Thespian**—(c) an actor. (Thespis, an ancient Greek poet and actor, was considered the father of tragic drama.)

8. **solecism**—(d) a grammatical error. (Soloi was an ancient town in Asia Minor, whose inhabitants spoke a substandard dialect of Greek.)

9. **meander**—(c) to wander aimlessly. (The Meander—now called Menderes—is one of the most winding rivers in Asia.)

10. **chauvinism**—(a) exaggerated, vainglorious patriotism. (Nicholas Chauvin was a zealous patriot in Napoleonic France.)

11. **shambles**—(a) a scene of disorder or ruin. (From the Old English word *scamol*, a table on which butchers displayed meat for sale.)

12. **pariah**—(d) a social outcast. (In the caste system of India a pariah belonged to a very low caste, at the botton of the social scale.)

13. **shanghai**—(a) to kidnap for service on a ship. (Men used to be drugged, kidnapped, and forced into service on ships bound for Oriental ports such as Shanghai.)

14. **maverick**—(d) a nonconformist. (Samuel A. Maverick was a Texan who didn't brand his cattle, claiming that all unbranded cattle were his.)

15. **churlish**—(c) rude. (In Anglo-Saxon England a churl was a freeman of low birth.)

16. **stentorian**—(c) loud-voiced. (In Homer's *Iliad*, Stentor is a herald famous for his loud voice.)

17. **behemoth**—(a) a colossal beast. (The behemoth is a mighty Biblical beast described in Job 40: 15–24.)

18. **Pyrrhic victory**—(a) a victory gained by ruinous loss. (King Pyrrhus of Epirus defeated the Romans in battle in 279 B.C., but suffered such heavy losses that the better part of his army was wiped out.)

19. **braggadocio**—(c) empty boasting. (Braggadochio is a boastful character in Edmund Spenser's poem *The Faerie Queen*.)

20. **mecca**—(d) a place of pilgrimage. (Mecca, Mohammed's birthplace, is a holy city to which Moslems make pilgrimages.)

ROOT: LOQU-, LOCUT-

Since the ancient Romans loved to give speeches and orations, it is no surprise that they had an important root meaning "to speak." This Latin root is *loqu-* or *locut-*. Learn the four core vocabulary words based on this important root: *colloquial, eloquent, elocution, interlocutor.*

colloquial comes from the Latin prefix *col-* (another spelling of *com-*) meaning "together" and *loqu-* meaning "to speak" plus the Latin suffix *-ial* meaning "pertaining to." Thus, *colloquial* means "pertaining to speaking together or to conversation"; hence, "belonging to informal or conversational speech or writing; informal and conversational."

> *Some colloquial words should never be used in formal writing.*
> *This novel is written in a lively, colloquial style.*

A word based on *colloquial* is *colloquialism,* meaning "an expression or word that is used in or suitable for informal speech or conversation, as opposed to formal speech or writing."

> *"Hi" is a colloquialism for "hello."*

eloquent comes from the Latin prefix *e-* (another spelling of *ex-*) meaning "out" and *loqu-* meaning "to speak" plus the Latin suffix *-ent,* which is the same as the English ending *-ing.* Thus, *eloquent* literally means "speaking out fully"; hence, "making effective use of language, especially in public speaking; forceful or moving."

> *The Gettysburg Address is an eloquent speech.*
> *Patrick Henry was noted as an eloquent speaker.*

A word based on *eloquent* is *eloquence,* meaning "highly effective use of language, especially in public speaking."

> *Were you moved by the eloquence of his speech?*

elocution comes from the Latin prefix *e-* meaning "out" and *locut-* meaning "to speak" plus the Latin suffix *-ion* meaning "the act of." Thus, *elocution* literally means "the act of speaking out"; hence, (1) the act or art of public speaking; (2) one's manner of speaking.

> *Lawyers have to study elocution.*
> *The nervous speaker was criticized for his poor elocution.*

interlocutor comes from the Latin prefix *inter-* meaning "between; among" and *locut-* meaning "to speak" plus the Latin suffix *-or* meaning "a person who." Thus, an *interlocutor* is literally "a person who speaks between others"; hence, "a person who takes part in a conversation or who keeps a conversation going by asking questions."

Dr. Harris was my interlocutor at dinner.
The lawyer served as an interlocutor, trying to get the full story from the witnesses.

◊ Look up the following words in your dictionary. Learn the meaning of each word and relate the meanings to the root *loqu-* or *locut-* meaning "to speak."

colloquy	locution	loquacious
interlocutory	circumlocution	loquacity

ROOT: MIT-, MISS-

The Latin root *mit-* or *miss-* means "to send; let go." Learn the eight core vocabulary words based on this root: *admit, commit, dismiss, emit, missile, omit, permit, transmit.*

admit comes from the Latin prefix *ad-* meaning "to" and *mit-* meaning "to send; let go." *Admit* literally means "to let go." In practice, *admit* means (1) to let in; let enter; (2) to allow to join; (3) to have or leave room for; (4) to grant something as true.

This ticket admits one person to the theater.
The theater could admit only 500 people.
This key will admit you to the office.
Have you been admitted to the club?
His impatience admits no delay.
I admit you are right about that.

Four words based on *admit* are *admissible, inadmissible, admission,* and *admittance. Admissible* means "allowable." *Inadmissible* means "not allowable." *Admission* is (1) the act of admitting; (2) permission to go in or enter; (3) the price charged for letting a person enter a

111

theater, stadium, etc.; (4) a confession. *Admittance* is "the right or power to enter a place; entrance or admission."

> *The gun was shown to the jury as admissible evidence.*
> *Since the gun had not belonged to the suspect for the last five years, it was judged inadmissible evidence.*
> *Did you gain admission to the college of your choice?*
> *The theater charged a lower admission for children than for adults.*
> *He stole the money by his own admission.*
> *Did you gain admittance through the front door?*

commit comes from the Latin prefix *com-* meaning "together" and *mit-* meaning "to send." *Commit* literally means "to send together." Thus, it actually means (1) to do; (2) to entrust to the care of something or someone; (3) to devote oneself to something; (4) to place someone in custody, as in a prison or mental institution.

> *Did he commit the crime?*
> *Jack committed the speech to memory.*
> *She committed herself to her studies.*
> *He was committed to prison.*

Two words based on *commit* are *commission* and *committee*. *Commission* means (1) an entrusting; (2) an authorization to act as specified; (3) the act of doing or performing; (4) a body of persons acting under lawful authority to perform certain duties; (5) a fee given an agent or salesman for his services. A *committee* is "a group of people chosen to investigate, report, or act on a matter."

> *He has a commission from the president to take charge of this area.*
> *He was charged with the commission of the crime.*
> *A commission was appointed to investigate the assassination.*
> *The broker's commission on the sale was $100.*
> *Congress has a large number of committees.*

dismiss comes from the Latin prefix *dis-* meaning "away" and *miss-* meaning "to send." Thus, *dismiss* means "to send away"; hence, (1) to discharge from a job; (2) to tell or allow to go; (3) to reject; (4) to get rid of or have done with quickly.

> *The boss dismissed him because of his laziness.*
> *The teacher dismissed the students for the day.*
> *The politician dismissed the charges against him as lies.*

A word based on *dismiss* is *dismissal*, meaning (1) the act of dismissing or the state of being dismissed; (2) a notice of discharge.

His dismissal from the job came as a shock.

emit comes from the Latin prefix *e-* (another spelling of *ex-*) meaning "out" and *mit-* meaning "to send." Thus, *emit* means "to send out; send forth or give off sound, light, heat, etc.; give expression to something."

The electric typewriter was emitting a low buzz.
The firecracker emitted sparks in all directions.
The radioactive material emitted electromagnetic radiation.
The injured man emitted a moan.

A word based on *emit* is *emission*, meaning (1) the act of emitting something; (2) that which is emitted.

Can you hear the emission of a low buzz from the radio?
Radioactive emissions can be very dangerous.

missile comes from *miss-* meaning "to send" and the Latin suffix *-ile* meaning "able to be." Thus, *missile* literally means "something that can be sent or let go"; hence, "any object intended to be thrown or discharged, such as a rock, spear, arrow, or bullet." In modern times, *missile* has come to mean "a guided rocket."

The boy was collecting missiles for his slingshot.
"Apollo 12" was the first missile to take man to the moon.

omit comes from the Latin prefix *o-* (another spelling of *ob-*) meaning "toward" and *mit-* meaning "to send." *Omit* originally meant "to send something toward another person." Now *omit* means "to let something go away from oneself; let go; leave out; fail to include or do something."

I omitted sugar from the shopping list.
Don't omit any answers required on this test.

A word based on *omit* is *omission*, meaning (1) the act of leaving something out; (2) something that is left out.

The shopping list was complete except for the omission of sugar.
Sugar was not a serious omission.

permit comes from the Latin prefix *per-* meaning "through" and *mit-*

113

meaning "to send; let go." Thus, *permit* [pər·mit′] means "to send or let something go through"; hence, "to allow, consent to, authorize, or offer an opportunity for." A *permit* [pûr′mit] is "a written authorization to do something; any official document authorizing the performance of a specified activity."

> *The mother permitted the children to go to the movies.*
> *You are not permitted to park here.*
> *His explanation did not permit of any misunderstanding.*
> *Do you have a learner's permit to drive?*

Three words based on *permit* are *permissible, permission,* and *permissive. Permissible* means "allowable." *Permission* is (1) the act of allowing; (2) formal authorization or consent. *Permissive* means (1) granting permission; (2) not strict in discipline; lenient.

> *It is not permissible to park here.*
> *Do you have permission to park here?*
> *The teacher is permissive and allows some talking in the classroom.*

transmit comes from the Latin prefix *trans-* meaning "across" and *mit-* meaning "to send." Thus, *transmit* means "to send something across"; hence, "to send something from one place to another; pass on anything, such as news, a disease, a message, etc."

> *The message was transmitted from New York to London by cable.*
> *Influenza is easily transmitted from person to person.*

Two words based on *transmit* are *transmitter* and *transmission.* A *transmitter* is "a person or thing that transmits; especially, the part of an instrument, such as a telephone or telegraph or a radio or television system, that sends messages or that transmits electrical waves." *Transmission* means (1) the act of transmitting or the state of being transmitted; (2) that which is transmitted; (3) the device in an automobile that transmits the power from the engine to the driving wheels.

> *The transmitter of a telephone changes sound waves to electrical waves.*
> *The transmitter of this station is located on a hill near town.*
> *The transmission of the TV program was interrupted by a power failure.*
> *Does this car have an automatic transmission?*

◊ Look up the following words in your dictionary. Learn the meaning of each word and relate each meaning to the root *mit-* or *miss-* meaning "to send; let go."

intermittent	emissary	missive	remission
missionary	intermission	remiss	remit

ROOT: MON-, MONIT-

The Latin root *mon-* or *monit-* means "to warn; advise." Learn the four core vocabulary words based on this root: *admonish, monument, monitor, premonition.*

admonish comes from the Latin prefix *ad-* meaning "to" and *mon-* meaning "to warn; advise" plus the suffix *-ish,* which appears as a verb ending. Thus, *admonish* means "to warn or advise someone of a fault; caution someone about a danger; reprove someone about an error."

The teacher admonished the dozing student to pay attention.

A word based on *admonish* is *admonition,* meaning (1) the act of admonishing; (2) a mild warning or gentle reproof.

The student didn't hear the teacher's admonition.

monument comes from *mon-* meaning "to warn; advise" and the Latin suffix *-ment* meaning "the act or means of." A *monument* is literally "a means of advising or reminding people of something." Thus, *monument* means "something, such as a statue, arch, pillar, etc., built as a reminder of a person, event, or the like." In more specific senses, *monument* means "a tombstone," or "a work of art, literature, scholarship, etc., that is considered to be of lasting value."

Have you seen the Washington Monument?
There are thousands of monuments in this cemetery.
Michelangelo's great fresco on the Sistine Chapel ceiling is a monument to Renaissance art.

A word based on *monument* is *monumental,* meaning (1) pertaining to, like, or serving as a monument; (2) of great importance; memorable; (3) larger than life; huge or massive.

This is a monumental day in the history of our town.
The Statue of Liberty is of monumental size.

monitor comes from *monit-* meaning "to warn; advise" and the Latin suffix *-or* meaning "a person who or a thing that does something." Thus, a *monitor* is literally "one who advises or warns"; hence, (1) a student chosen to help maintain order in class, oversee tests, or perform other assigned duties; (2) an apparatus used to check radio and television broadcasts for quality, compliance with laws, etc. To *monitor* is "to listen to or check conversations, radio or television broadcasts, etc., for quality, compliance with the law, or for other specific information."

As monitor, Gene has to see that no one cheats on exams or leaves the room without permission.
We are going to monitor all news broadcasts to see which stations give sports results.

A word based on *monitor* is *monitory,* meaning "warning."

The teacher gave Jim a monitory look and he stopped whispering.

premonition comes from the Latin prefix *pre-* meaning "before" and *monit-* meaning "to warn; advise" plus the Latin suffix *-ion* meaning "the state or result of." Thus, a *premonition* is "the state of being warned beforehand"; hence, "an instinctive sense of what is going to happen in the future, based on intuition, not information."

Carl had a premonition that he would be in an accident.

A word based on *premonition* is *premonitory,* meaning "giving warning beforehand; giving or containing a premonition."

Headache and sore throat are the first premonitory symptoms of many infectious childhood diseases.

◇ Look up *admonishment* and *admonitory* in your dictionary. Learn their meanings and note how they are based on the root *mon-* or *monit-* meaning "to warn; advise."

EXPLORING WORDS

FROM THE ART WORLD

Painting, sculpture, and drawing have a special vocabulary of their own. If you like art, know someone who does, or would like to know more about it, here are some useful terms.

abstract a painting that does not portray natural objects or figures, but uses lines, masses of color, and geometrical forms such as oblongs, squares, circles, etc.

bas-relief [bä′ri·lēf′] a piece of sculpture in which the figures are raised out only slightly from a background panel or wall, such as a frieze on a building.

chiaroscuro [kē·är′ə·skyo͞or′ō] (1) the distribution and treatment of light and shade in a picture; (2) a kind of picture using only light and shade and no definite lines.

fresco a painting made by applying colors to a wet plaster surface, so that they sink in deeply and dry with it.

frieze a long strip or band of decoration, as on a building, ornamented with lettering, sculpture, scrolls, etc.

gouache [gwosh] a painting using opaque colors mixed with water and gum.

impasto [im·päs′tō] a method of painting in which colors are applied thickly so that they stand out from the canvas.

impressionism a late nineteenth-century theory and style of painting that tried to produce the visual impression of the subject with the color values of light and air—sometimes purposely resulting in paintings that seem misty or vaguely out of focus.

mobile a piece of sculpture made of wire, strips of metal, etc., in such a way that it moves when touched or blown by the wind.

mural a painting applied directly to a wall or ceiling.

palette a flat, thin piece of wood, plastic, etc., which holds the different paints used by an artist, and which is often held in the hand.

pastel [pas·tel′] a drawing made with colored crayons, especially soft crayons made of pipe clay, pigment, and gum water.

study a preliminary sketch or exercise, as a preliminary rough sketch of an object or landscape that will later be the subject of a painting.

tempera (1) a fast-drying paint made of colors that are mixed with water and egg yolk; (2) a painting made from such paint.

water color (1) a painting made with pigments mixed in water; (2) paint having water as the medium.

ROOT: MOV-, MOT-

The Latin root *mov-* or *mot-* means "to move." The common words *move, movement,* and *motion* are all directly based on the Latin root *mov-* or *mot-*. Keep them in mind as you master four more core vocabulary words based on this root: *emotion, promote, remote, remove.*

emotion comes from the Latin prefix *e-* (another spelling of *ex-*) meaning "out" and *mot-* meaning "to move" plus the Latin suffix *-ion* meaning "the act or state of." *Emotion* is literally "the act of moving out or outward." Hence, *emotion* means "a strong surge of feeling that is expressed outwardly; any intense feeling, such as love or hate."

> *Fear is a powerful emotion.*
> *His voice was full of emotion as he told us his story.*

A word based on *emotion* is *emotional,* meaning "full of emotion; pertaining to an emotion or to the feelings in general."

> *We had an emotional meeting with old friends.*
> *The actor gave an emotional performance.*

promote comes from the Latin prefix *pro-* meaning "forward" and *mot-* meaning "to move." Thus, *promote* literally means "to move someone or something forward"; hence, (1) to contribute to the progress or growth of something; (2) to advance someone; (3) to work on behalf of something; (4) to seek to make a product popular or successful.

> *He is famous for promoting public education.*
> *Did your teacher promote you to the next grade?*
> *The company launched an advertising campaign to promote its new product.*

A word based on *promote* is *promotion,* meaning (1) advancement in rank, position, etc.; (2) work on behalf of something.

> *She got a promotion to a more responsible job.*
> *Did the company's promotion campaign succeed in selling the new product?*

remote comes from the Latin prefix *re-* meaning "back" and *mot-* meaning "to move." Something *remote* is "something moved back or away from the place specified." Thus, *remote* means "located far away from a specified place; distant." It also means "not obvious; slight." A third meaning of remote is "distant in manner; aloof."

The beach is remote from the city.
He is a remote cousin of mine.
There is a remote possibility that it may rain tonight.
My grandfather was a remote, silent man.

remove comes from the Latin prefix *re-* meaning "back" plus the English word *move*, which is directly based on the Latin root *mov-* meaning "to move." To *remove* is literally "to move back." Thus, *remove* means (1) to take or move away; (2) to dismiss; (3) to take off; (4) to take out; extract.

They removed the extra chairs after the meeting.
He was removed from his position as head of the bus company.
He removed his coat when he entered the house.
How is the wheat removed from the chaff?
Charlie's tonsils were removed last week.

A word based on *remove* is *removal*, meaning (1) the act of removing or the state of being removed; (2) dismissal.

The operation was for the removal of gallstones.
Brown's removal as head of the bus company was the result of local politics.

NOTE: You have probably already noticed that *remote* and *remove* are based on the same prefix and root, despite the difference in their spellings and in their modern meanings. Their meanings really are very close: Something *remote* is something that has been moved far away; to *remove* is to move something away.

◊ Look up the following words in your dictionary. Learn the meaning of each and note how each meaning is based on the root *mov-* or *mot-* meaning "to move."

commotion	immovable	motivation
demobilize	mobile	motive
demote	mobilize	motor
demotion	mobilization	remoteness
immobilize	motility	unmoved

119

REVIEW OF ROOTS

Here are more roots and words you have already learned. Choose the answer that is nearest in meaning to the key word. Answers follow.

1. **digress** [di·gres′ *or* dī·gres′]—(a) to separate. (b) to ramble; wander away from the main topic. (c) to move sideways. (d) to stop suddenly.

2. **regress** [rē′gres *or* ri·gres′]—(a) to right a wrong. (b) to break a promise. (c) to go backward; revert to an earlier state. (d) to complain repeatedly.

3. **transgress** [trans·gres′ *or* tranz·gres′]—(a) to change sides in a debate or argument. (b) to sin; offend. (c) to forgive. (d) to transport over a specific route.

4. **gratis** [grat′is *or* grā′tis]—(a) served with melted cheese on top. (b) to cut up into small pieces. (c) worthless. (d) free of charge.

5. **inherent** [in·hir′ənt *or* in·her′ənt]—(a) pertaining to a male heir. (b) vital; necessary. (c) inborn. (d) the beneficiary of a will.

6. **incoherent** [in′kō·hir′ənt]—(a) lacking logical connection; disjointed; confused. (b) illegible; hard to read. (c) shared equally by two or more heirs. (d) slick; smooth; not sticky.

7. **eject** [i·jekt′]—(a) to refuse to accept. (b) to throw out with sudden force; expel. (c) to sadden or depress. (d) to pull apart; disassemble.

8. **dejection** [di·jek′shən]—(a) anger; a stormy mood. (b) a pensive, reflective mood. (c) stubbornness. (d) lowness of spirits; depression.

9. **interjection** [in′tər·jek′shən]—(a) a command. (b) an action verb. (c) a one-word exclamation. (d) a question mark.

10. **enjoin** [in·join′]—(a) to share good times. (b) to order, direct, or prohibit authoritatively. (c) to settle a labor dispute. (d) to meet with in order to negotiate.

11. **juncture** [jungk′chər]—(a) a point in time, especially at which a critical decision must be made. (b) the place where two roads cross. (c) a break or rupture. (d) a short vacation or quick trip.

ANSWERS:

1. **digress**—(b) to ramble; wander away from the main topic. 2. **regress**—(c) to go backward; revert to an earlier state. 3. **transgress**—(b) to sin; offend. 4. **gratis**—(d) free of charge. 5. **inherent**—(c) inborn. 6. **incoherent**—(a) lacking logical connection; disjointed; confused. 7. **eject**—(b) to throw out with sudden force; expel. 8. **dejection**—(d) lowness of spirits; depression. 9. **interjection**—(c) a one-word exclamation. 10. **enjoin**—(b) to order, direct, or prohibit authoritatively. 11. **juncture**—(a) a point in time, especially at which a critical decision must be made.

ROOT: NASC-, NAT-

The Latin root *nasc-* or *nat-* means "to be born." Learn the four core vocabulary words based on *nasc-* or *nat-*: *nascent, nation, native, prenatal.*

nascent [nā′sənt] comes from *nasc-* meaning "to be born" and the Latin suffix *-ent*, which is the same as the English ending *-ing*. Thus, *nascent* means "being born; beginning to exist or develop; newly conceived."

> *The survey uncovered nascent discontent among students.*

nation comes from *nat-* meaning "to be born" plus the suffix *-ion* meaning "the state of." *Nation* literally means "the place of one's birth." Today, of course, *nation* means "a body of persons in a place organized under one government" or "a body of persons having a common origin and language."

> *At what date did this country become a nation?*
> *He is a member of the Cherokee nation.*

Two words based on *nation* are *national*, meaning "of, belonging to, or representative of a nation," and *nationalism*, which means (1) devotion, often extreme devotion, to the interests of one's own nation; (2) a political belief that the welfare of human beings is best served by the nations acting independently rather than in collective or cooperative action.

> *How much is the national debt?*
> *Nazism was an extreme form of nationalism.*

native comes from *nat-* meaning "to be born" and the Latin suffix *-ive* meaning "tending to" or, in this case, "a person who is." Thus, the noun *native* means "a person or animal born in a particular place," or "something that was originated, developed, or grown in a particular place." The adjective *native* means "by birth or origin; not foreign; inborn or natural."

> *Clarence is a native of Colorado.*
> *These are native New Jersey tomatoes.*
> *Folk art has a lot of native charm.*

121

A word based on *native* is *nativity,* meaning "birth, especially in regard to its time, place, or circumstances." *The Nativity* refers to the birth of Christ, or to Christmas Day.

prenatal comes from the Latin prefix *pre-* meaning "before" and *nat-* meaning "to be born" plus the Latin suffix *-al* meaning "pertaining to." Thus, *prenatal* means "pertaining to the time before birth; prior to birth."

    Good prenatal care produces healthy babies.

◊ Look up the word *natal* in your dictionary. Learn its meaning and note how it is based on the root *nat-* meaning "to be born." If you have paid attention to the explanation of the word *prenatal,* you can probably figure out the exact meaning of *natal* without using your dictionary. What is someone's *"natal* day"?

ROOT: PEL-, PELL-, PULS-

The Latin root *pel-, pell-,* or *puls-* means "to drive; push." Learn the following three core vocabulary words: *compel, impel, repel.*

compel comes from the Latin prefix *com-* meaning "together" and the root *pel-* meaning "to drive; push." *Compel* originally meant "to drive together; herd." Now it means (1) to urge forcefully; (2) to force or require by law, threat, necessity, etc.

    My conscience compels me to tell the truth.
    All children are compelled to attend school.

Four words based on *compel* are *compelling, compulsion, compulsive,* and *compulsory. Compelling* means "forceful; overpowering." *Compulsion* is (1) the act of compelling or the state of being compelled; force; coercion; (2) an irresistible impulse or desire. *Compulsive* means (1) compelling; (2) moved by or involving compulsion. *Compulsory* means (1) required; (2) using compulsion.

    You have no compelling need to leave now.
    Did he do it voluntarily or under compulsion?
    The cook has a compulsion to change his mind several times a day.

She had a compulsive desire to buy too many books.
Many alcoholics are compulsive drinkers.
The United States has compulsory education.

impel comes from the Latin prefix *im-* meaning "on" and *pel-* meaning "to drive; push." Thus, *impel* means "to drive on; force or drive someone or something to an action; urge on."

His desire for more money impelled him to get more education.

Three words based on *impel* are *impulse, impulsion,* and *impulsive.* *Impulse* means "a sudden, unplanned inclination to some action." *Impulsion* means (1) the act of impelling or the state of being impelled; (2) an impulse. *Impulsive* means (1) brought about by impulse rather than by reason or planning; unpremeditated; (2) acting on impulse and without forethought.

He followed his impulse and gave the stranger a lift.
He acted under the impulsion of the moment.
His purchase of an expensive new car was impulsive.

NOTE: *Impel* means "to urge on." It differs from *compel* in that it does not contain the idea of force, law, or coercion. When a person is *compelled* to do something, he has no choice. When he is *impelled* to do something, he feels a strong urge to do it, but he can choose not to.

repel comes from the Latin prefix *re-* meaning "back" and *pel-* meaning "to drive; push." Thus, *repel* means (1) to drive or force someone or something back; (2) cause one to feel distaste or disgust; (3) push or keep away.

The soldiers repelled the enemy attack.
Snakes repel me.
Will this coat repel water?

Three words based on *repel* are *repellent, repulsion,* and *repulsive.* *Repellent* means (1) tending to repel; resistant; (2) offensive or disgusting. *Repulsion* is "aversion; a feeling of extreme dislike, horror, or disgust." *Repulsive* means "horrifying or disgusting; abhorrent."

Is this a water-repellent raincoat?
Their way of life was repellent to him.
I feel nothing but repulsion for snakes.
George doesn't think snakes are repulsive.

123

◊ Another important vocabulary word based on the root *pel-*, *pell-*, or *puls-* is *propel*, from which the words *propeller* and *propulsion* are derived. Look up these words in your dictionary, along with the words that follow. Learn their meanings and be sure you can relate each word to the root *pel-*, *pell-*, or *puls-* meaning "to drive; push."

dispel	expulsion	pulsation
expel	pulsate	pulse

QUICKIEQUIZQUICKIEQUIZQUICKIEQUIZQUICKIEQUIZQUICKIEQUIZQUICKIEQUIZQUICKIEQUIZQUICKIE

90-SECOND QUICKIE QUIZ

WORD BUILDING

Here is another quick review quiz of roots and words you have already learned. Match the roots with their meanings. Answers follow.

1. **grav-** as in aggravate [ag′rə·vāt]
2. **lect-** as in election [i·lek′shən]
3. **nat-** as in nation [nā′shən]
4. **anim-** as in unanimous [yōō·nan′ə·məs]
5. **cord-** as in accord [ə·kôrd′]
6. **gam-** as in monogamy [mə·nog′ə·mē]
7. **loque-** as in eloquent [el′ə·kwənt]
8. **audit-** or **aud-** as in audible [ô′də·bəl]
9. **bio-** as in biography [bī·og′rə·fē]

(a) to speak
(b) to hear
(c) marriage
(d) life
(e) to choose; to read
(f) heavy
(g) to be born
(h) life, mind, spirit
(i) heart

ANSWERS:
1. **grav-** —(f) heavy. To aggravate is to make worse or more burdensome or unpleasant.
2. **lect-** —(e) to choose; to read. An election is the choosing of a person or persons by ballot or by popular vote.
3. **nat-** —(g) to be born. Originally nation meant the place of one's birth. Now it means a country or a body of persons having a common origin and language or organized under one government.
4. **anim-** —(h) life, mind, spirit. Unanimous combines the root *un-* meaning one and the root *anim-*. It means being of one mind, sharing the same views.
5. **cord-** —(i) heart. Accord means to be of one heart; agreement.
6. **gam-** —(c) marriage. Monogamy is the practice of having only one wife or husband at a time.
7. **loque-** —(a) to speak. Eloquent means making effective use of language; forceful or moving in public speaking.
8. **audit-** or **aud-** —(b) to hear. Audible means capable of being heard; loud enough to be heard.
9. **bio-** —(d) life. A biography is a written account of a person's life.

QUICKIEQUIZQUICKIEQUIZQUICKIEQUIZQUICKIEQUIZQUICKIEQUIZQUICKIEQUIZQUICKIEQUIZQUICKIE

ROOT: PEND-, PENS-

The Latin root *pend-* or *pens-* means "to hang, weigh, or pay." The reason this root has three meanings is that in Roman times it referred to the weighing of gold on scales. Since weights were hung on one side of the scale and gold was weighed to determine the amount of money to pay, the root *pend-* or *pens-* developed all three meanings: "to hang," "to weigh," and "to pay." Learn the following four core vocabulary words based on the root *pend-* or *pens-: depend, dispense, expend, suspend.*

depend comes from the Latin prefix *de-* meaning "down" and *pend-* meaning "to hang." *Depend* originally meant "to hang down." The modern meanings of *depend* came from the idea of something hanging down from, or being supported by, something else. Hence, *depend* means (1) to trust or rely on; (2) to rely for support on someone or something; (3) to be determined.

> *The children depend on their parents in many ways.*
> *Whether we have the picnic or not will depend on the weather.*

Three words based on *depend* are *dependable, dependence,* and *dependent. Dependable* means "trustworthy or reliable." *Dependence* is (1) the state of relying on someone or something for support; (2) the state of being determined by something else; (3) subjection to the control of another. *Dependent* means (1) conditioned by something else; (2) subject to outside control; (3) relying on someone else for support; (4) a person who depends on another for support.

> *Walter owns a dependable car.*
> *The youth disliked his long dependence on his parents.*
> *Your success is dependent on your luck and intelligence.*
> *The income tax form allows you a deduction for each dependent.*

dispense comes from the Latin prefix *dis-* meaning "away" and *pens-* meaning "to weigh." Thus, *dispense* literally means "to weigh and give away"; hence, (1) to give or deal out something in portions; (2) to administer, as laws; (3) to get along without.

> *A pharmacist dispenses medicines.*
> *The judge dispenses justice.*
> *Let's dispense with these wild accusations and discuss the facts.*

Three words based on *dispense* are *dispensable,* meaning "capable of being dispensed with; unnecessary; not essential"; *indispensable,* meaning "incapable of being done without; necessary; essential"; and *dispensary,* which is "a place where medicines and medical advice are given out."

During the emergency they cut off all dispensable services.
A car is indispensable to a traveling sales representative.
She was a nurse at the school dispensary.

expend comes from the Latin prefix *ex-* meaning "out" and *pend-* meaning "to pay." Thus, *expend* means "to pay out; spend; use up."

What did the firm expend on new equipment last year?
Don't expend all your energy on one thing.

Five words based on *expend* are *expendable, expenditure, expense, expenses,* and *expensive. Expendable* means (1) available for spending; (2) able to be used up or sacrificed: applied especially to military equipment or supplies that can be sacrificed if necessary. *Expenditure* means (1) the act of expending; outlay; (2) what is spent; expense. *Expense* means (1) cost, outlay, or expenditure; (2) something requiring the continued spending of money; (3) loss or sacrifice necessarily involved in doing something. *Expenses* are "funds provided, spent, or required to cover costs." *Expensive* means "costly."

The company has $50,000 in expendable funds.
Rescue the crew and save the records; the ship is expendable.
What were the firm's expenditures for new equipment?
What was the total expense of your trip?
Owning a car is an expense.
Don't work fast at the expense of accuracy.
He receives a salary plus traveling expenses.
A mink coat is very expensive.

suspend comes from the prefix *sus-* (another spelling of *sub-*) meaning "under" and *pens-* meaning "to hang." *Suspend* literally means "to hang something under, or from, a support above." Hence, *suspend* means (1) to hang from a support, so as to allow free movement; (2) to bar for a time from a privilege or function; (3) to withhold temporarily; (4) to defer action on.

The chandelier was suspended from the ceiling.

The student was suspended from school for a term.
Todd suspended payments on the car until the company had corrected the mechanical defects.
The judge suspended the sentence.

Three words based on *suspend* are *suspenders, suspense,* and *suspension. Suspenders* are "a pair of straps worn over the shoulders for supporting the trousers." *Suspense* is (1) the state of being uncertain or undecided, usually accompanied by fear, worry, agitation, etc.; (2) an uncertain or doubtful situation. *Suspension* means (1) a debarring; (2) an interruption; (3) a putting off of an action; (4) a stopping of payments in business; (5) any device from which something is suspended; (6) any mechanical system, as the springs in an automobile, intended to support the body or chassis of the machine and insulate it from shocks.

He always wears suspenders instead of a belt.
The outcome of the election kept us in suspense.
Have you heard about Richard's suspension from school?
The road of a suspension bridge is hung from cables.

◊ Look up the following words in your dictionary. Learn their meanings and relate each to the root *pend-* or *pens-* meaning "to hang, weigh, or pay."

append	compensate	pendant
appendage	impending	pending
appendix	independent	pendulum

ROOT: PET-, PETIT-

The Latin root *pet-* or *petit-* means "to go; seek; strive." Learn the following five core vocabulary words based on this root: *appetite, compete, competent, petition, repetition.*

appetite comes from the Latin prefix *ap-* (another spelling of *ad-*) meaning "to" and *pet-* meaning "to seek; strive" plus the Latin suffix *-ite,* which is used to form nouns. Thus, *appetite* originally meant "a striving to satisfy a desire." In modern times *appetite* means (1)

127

a desire for food or drink; (2) a physical craving; (3) a strong liking for anything.

He lost his appetite from eating too much candy.
Americans today have an insatiable appetite for electronic gadgets.

Two words based on *appetite* are *appetizer*, meaning "something that arouses the appetite; especially, tidbits of food served before a meal"; and *appetizing*, which means "stimulating to the appetite; arousing hunger or desire."

Nuts and cheese were served as appetizers.
There was an appetizing aroma coming from the kitchen.

compete comes from the Latin prefix *com-* meaning "together" and *pet-* meaning "to strive." Thus, *compete* means "to strive with others, as for a prize"; hence, "to take part in a contest" or "to be a rival, as in business."

The two teams competed for the championship.
These two stores always compete with each other.

Three words based on *compete* are *competition, competitive,* and *competitor. Competition* means (1) a contest, as for a prize or business; (2) rivalry; (3) a rival or rivals. *Competitive* means "characterized by competition; inclined to compete; competing aggressively." A *competitor* is "a person or organization that competes, as in games or in business; a rival."

Did you enter last week's crossword competition?
The two oil companies are in competition.
I think our football team can beat the competition.
Business in this town is highly competitive.
Japan is our biggest competitor in the world's markets.

competent comes from the Latin prefix *com-* meaning "together" and *pet-* meaning "to go" plus the Latin suffix *-ent,* which is the same as our English ending *-ing. Competent* originally referred to "something that goes together with something else"; that is, "something that is proper or fitting." Hence, *competent* means "capable; qualified."

He is a competent worker.
She is competent to do the job.

Two words based on *competent* are *competence* and *incompetent*. *Competence* means (1) ability; skill; (2) sufficient means for a comfortable life. *Incompetent* means "not capable; inadequate."

> *His competence as a violinist is well known.*
> *The huge dairy farm provided the family with a competence.*
> *He is a totally incompetent bookkeeper.*

petition comes from *petit-* meaning "to seek" and the Latin suffix *-ion* meaning "the act or state of." A *petition* is "an act of seeking something." Hence, a *petition* is "a request, especially a formal request or application to a law court, authority, etc., asking that some entreaty or demand be granted." To *petition* is (1) to make or sign such a request; to ask for something; (2) to ask, plead, or appeal for something, especially from a higher authority.

> *Have you signed the petition against higher taxes?*
> *O, Lord, hear my petition.*
> *They petitioned the city for better transportation.*

A word based on *petition* is *petitioner,* meaning (1) a person who makes or signs a petition; (2) one who makes an appeal or a claim, especially a formal written request.

repetition comes from the Latin prefix *re-* meaning "again" and *petit-* meaning "to seek" plus the Latin suffix *-ion* meaning "the act of." Thus, *repetition* literally means "the act of seeking something again"; hence, (1) the act of repeating; a doing or saying of something over again; (2) that which is repeated; a repeated instance.

> *His writing is long-winded and full of repetition.*
> *This morning's traffic jam was a repetition of yesterday's.*

Two words based on *repetition* are *repetitious,* meaning "full of repetition, especially useless or tedious repetition," and *repetitive,* which means "involving, using, or like repetition; repetitious."

> *He gave a long, repetitious report at the meeting.*
> *Bad teaching can make the learning process dull and repetitive.*

◊ Look up *impetus* and *impetuous* in your dictionary. Learn their meanings and relate each to the root *pet-, petit-* meaning "to go; seek; strive."

VOCABULARY BUILDING

The following fourteen words contain common roots. Check the word or phrase you believe is closest in meaning to the key word. Answers follow.

1. **matriarch** [mā′trē·ärk]—(a) a woman who rules a family or group. (b) an elderly and wise woman. (c) a wise old man. (d) a mother-in-law.

2. **magnification** [mag′nə·fə·kā′shən]—(a) the process of beautifying. (b) extreme boldness. (c) generosity. (d) enlargement.

3. **matriculate** [mə·trik′yə·lāt]—(a) to come to maturity. (b) to join together. (c) to enroll. (d) to graduate, as from college.

4. **manipulate** [mə·nip′yə·lāt]—(a) to handle skillfully. (b) to construct. (c) to write illegibly. (d) many times over.

5. **manifest** [man′ə·fest]—(a) boasting. (b) evident. (c) destined. (d) generous.

6. **malefactor** [mal′ə·fak′tər]—(a) a criminal or evildoer. (b) a witch. (c) a violent windstorm. (d) a bad omen.

7. **nomenclature** [nō′mən·klā′chər] —(a) pen names. (b) law records. (c) the history of names. (d) names used in classifications.

8. **nominal** [nom′ə·nəl]—(a) understood; known. (b) unnamed. (c) too small to be considered. (d) believable.

9. **omniscience** [om·nish′əns]—(a) threatening or foretelling evil. (b) infinite knowledge. (c) conceit. (d) wide popularity.

10. **omnivorous** [om·niv′ər·əs]—(a) meat-eating. (b) heartless. (c) all-seeing. (d) devouring indiscriminately.

11. **phonetics** [fə·net′iks]—(a) the science of grammar. (b) diacritical marks. (c) speech sounds. (d) a study of rhetoric.

12. **orifice** [ôr′ə·fis]—(a) an oral report. (b) an opening or aperture. (c) an overlord. (d) a device used in examining the ears.

13. **cognomen** [kog·nō′mən]—(a) a family title. (b) an alias. (c) a political-party nominee. (d) surname or a nickname.

14. **permissive** [pər·mis′iv]—(a) ungrudging. (b) immoral. (c) lenient. (d) relaxed.

ANSWERS:

1. **matriarch**—(a) a woman who rules a family or group. 2. **magnification**—(d) enlargement. 3. **matriculate**—(c) to enroll. 4. **manipulate**—(a) to handle skillfully. 5. **manifest**—(b) evident. 6. **malefactor**—(a) a criminal or evildoer. 7. **nomenclature**—(d) names used in classifications. 8. **nominal**—(c) too small to be considered. 9. **omniscience**—(b) infinite knowledge. 10. **omnivorous**—(d) devouring indiscriminately. 11. **phonetics**—(c) speech sounds. 12. **orifice**—(b) an opening or aperture. 13. **cognomen**—(d) a surname or a nickname. 14. **permissive**—(c) lenient.

ROOT: PLE-, PLET-

The Latin root *ple-* or *plet-* means "to fill." Learn the following four core vocabulary words based on this common root: *complete, deplete, implement, replete.*

complete comes from the Latin prefix *com-* meaning "thoroughly" and *plet-* meaning "to fill." Thus, the adjective *complete* means "filled thoroughly; full; with all the needed parts or items included; wholly finished; perfect." As a verb, *complete* means "to finish; conclude."

> *Did you order the complete dinner?*
> *The clothing store carries a complete range of sizes.*
> *The author said his book was finally complete.*
> *He completed the book after years of work and study.*

Three words based on *complete* are *completely,* meaning "totally; entirely"; *completion,* meaning "the act of completing or the state of being complete"; and *incomplete,* meaning "not complete; unfinished."

> *I am completely satisfied.*
> *The completion of the work took two years.*
> *He left his task incomplete at the end of the day.*

deplete comes from the Latin prefix *de-* meaning "not" and *plet-* meaning "to fill." *Deplete* literally means "not to fill" or "to reverse the process of filling"; hence, "to lessen by use or waste; to use up or empty."

> *We have depleted many of our natural resources.*
> *The child's energy was depleted by malnutrition.*

A word based on *deplete* is *depletion,* meaning (1) the act of lessening or reducing something by use or waste; a using up; (2) the state of being used up or lessened.

> *The depletion of oil reserves is a major problem.*

implement comes from the Latin prefix *im-* (another spelling of *in-*) meaning "in" or "up" and *ple-* meaning "to fill" plus the Latin suffix *-ment* meaning "the act of." To *implement* originally meant "to fill something up with what is needed"; hence, "to give or do what is necessary to accomplish something; supply what is needed." An

131

implement is "something used to accomplish a purpose; especially, a tool or piece of equipment used in some form of work."

> *The President implemented the welfare program with federal funds.*
> *The farm implements are stored in the barn.*

A word based on *implement* is *implementation,* meaning "a putting of something into effect; a carrying through of something."

> *The implementation of the welfare program was successful.*

replete comes from the Latin prefix *re-* meaning "again" and *plet-* meaning "to fill." *Replete* originally meant "filled again" or "filled up again." Today, *replete* means "completely full; supplied in abundance; well-provided."

> *Cod-liver oil is replete with vitamins A and D.*

A word based on *replete* is *repletion,* meaning "the state of being completely or excessively full."

> *We have dined to repletion.*

ROOT: PLIC-, PLICIT-, PLEX-, PLY-

The Latin root *plic-, plicit-, plex-,* or *ply-* means "to fold; twist; bend; tangle; connect." Learn the seven core vocabulary words based on this important root: *complex, complexion, complicate, explicit, implicate, implicit, imply.*

complex comes from the Latin prefix *com-* meaning "together" and *plex-* meaning "to twist; connect." Thus, *complex* means (1) consisting of various parts connected together; composite; (2) complicated, as in structure; involved; intricate. A *complex* is "a whole made up of connected or interwoven parts."

> *A computer is a complex machine.*
> *This is a complex problem; there is no easy solution.*
> *Have you seen the new housing complex?*

A word based on *complex* is *complexity,* meaning "the state of being complex or involved."

The complexity of a computer is amazing.

complexion comes from the Latin prefix *com-* meaning "together" and *plex-* meaning "to twist; connect" plus the Latin suffix *-ion* meaning "the state of." *Complexion* originally meant "the state of things closely connected in a whole," referring to the constitution of the human body. Today, of course, *complexion* means "the color and appearance of the skin, especially of the face," or "the general appearance, quality, or character of a person or thing."

She has a light, clear complexion.
What is the political complexion of the new legislature?

complicate comes from the Latin prefix *com-* meaning "together" and *plic-* meaning "to twist; tangle" plus the Latin suffix *-ate* meaning "to make." To *complicate* is literally "to make twisted or tangled together"; hence, "to make or become complex or difficult."

Don't complicate your life by worrying too much.
The strike complicates our production problems.

Two words based on *complicate* are *complicated,* meaning "difficult to understand; involved," and *complication,* which means (1) the act of complicating; (2) a complicated situation, condition, element, or structure; (3) anything that causes difficulty, as a problem added to one already existing.

This book is too complicated for children.
The complications of the job are more than one person can handle.
He had a slight case of the flu, but then complications set in.

explicit comes from the Latin prefix *ex-* meaning "out" and *plicit-* meaning "to fold." *Explicit* originally meant "folded out" or "unfolded." Hence, *explicit* means "clearly expressed; straightforward; direct."

He gave us explicit instructions on how to reach the house.
You explicitly told me I would get a raise.

implicate comes from the Latin prefix *im-* (another spelling of *in-*) meaning "in" and *plic-* meaning "to fold; twist; tangle" plus the Latin suffix *-ate* meaning "to make." Thus, to *implicate* literally means "to entangle someone in something, as in an accusation of guilt"; hence, "to show that someone is involved in something, such as a crime or plot."

The informer's testimony implicated five people in the robbery.

A word based on *implicate* is *implication,* meaning (1) the act of involving or implying; (2) a hint or suggestion.

There is an implication of hostility in his remarks.
Your implication that I am wealthy makes me laugh.

implicit comes from the Latin prefix *im-* (another spelling of *in-*) meaning "in" and *plicit-* meaning "to fold." *Implicit* originally meant "folded in." Hence, *implicit* means "understood or suggested but not directly expressed." It also means "complete or total; unreserved; unqualified."

The partners have an implicit understanding rather than a contract.
I have implicit trust in my partner's judgment.
That theologian believes implicitly in original sin.

NOTE: *Explicit* and *implicit* have opposite meanings. *Explicit* means "unfolded." When you unfold your ideas explicitly, you clearly and directly express them. *Implicit* means "folded in." When you fold in your ideas implicitly, you express them only indirectly; you suggest or hint things instead of stating them straightforwardly.

imply comes from the Latin prefix *im-* (another spelling of *in-*) meaning "in" and *ply-* meaning "to fold; twist." Thus, *imply* is closely related to *implicit,* literally meaning "to fold in." Hence, *imply* means (1) to suggest without stating; suggest or convey indirectly; (2) to indicate or involve as an obvious cause or consequence.

Her blushing implied that she was embarrassed.
Smoke implies fire.

◊ Look up the following words in your dictionary. Learn their meanings and be sure you can relate each to the root *plic-, plicit-, plex-,* or *ply-* meaning "to fold; twist; bend; tangle; connect."

complicity	duplicity	replica
duplex	multiply	reply
duplicate	ply	supplication

EXPLORING WORDS
WHAT KIND OF PERSON IS THAT?

There are many words that describe types of people and the ways they react to the world about them. Here are fourteen words that deal with human behavior, both normal and abnormal. Do you recognize yourself or any of your friends and acquaintances in this list?

aesthete (1) a person who is devoted to beauty in nature, art, painting, music, etc.; (2) a person who displays an extravagant or affected admiration for beauty and the arts.

altruist a person who is selflessly concerned with the welfare of others; one who puts the comfort and happiness of others before his own.

ascetic a person who leads a simple, austere life, avoiding luxury and pleasure, seeking solitude, practicing self-discipline, and devoting himself to contemplation or meditation.

conservative a person who wants to preserve the existing order of things, feeling content or safe with things as they are.

hypochondriac a person who worries constantly—usually without any real reason—about the state of his health, believing that he has many ailments, taking extreme health precautions, etc.

kleptomaniac a person who has an irresistible desire to steal and shoplift—not because he is in need of what he steals, but because stealing gives him an emotional satisfaction.

megalomaniac a person who suffers from delusions of greatness.

optimist a person who tends to look on the bright side of things, or one who tends to think that the world is basically good and that what happens is for the best: the opposite of *pessimist*.

paranoid a person who believes that other people are always plotting against him, cheating and persecuting him, feeling hate for him, etc.

pessimist a person who tends to look on the darker side of things, or one who believes that the world is basically bad or evil.

pragmatist a person who believes that ideas have value only in terms of their practical consequence and that practical results are the sole test of the truth or validity of beliefs.

realist a person who believes in basing his life on facts and who dislikes anything that seems imaginary, impractical, theoretical, or utopian.

romantic a person who approaches everything in life emotionally and who enjoys adventures, falling in love, fighting for causes, etc.

ROOT: PON-, POSIT-, POUND-, POSE-

The Latin root *pon-*, *posit-*, *pound-*, or *pose-* means "to put; place." This is one of the most important roots you will ever learn; it is used in making a great many common English words. Learn carefully the core vocabulary words based on this root: *component, compose, composite, compound, depose, deposit, dispose, expose, exposition, expound, impose, oppose, positive, postpone, propose, suppose.*

component comes from the Latin prefix *com-* meaning "together" and *pon-* meaning "to put; place" plus the Latin suffix *-ent*, which is the same as our English ending *-ing*. Thus, the noun *component* means "a part used in putting together a whole." As an adjective, *component* means "helping to make up a whole."

> *Flour is a basic component of bread.*
> *Turntable, amplifier, and speakers are components of a stereo set.*
> *Sugar and water are component parts of syrup.*

compose comes from the Latin prefix *com-* meaning "together" and *pose-*,meaning "to put; place." Thus, *compose* literally means "to put something together"; hence, (1) to make up, or form as a whole, from different elements; (2) to create, as a literary or musical work; (3) to arrange, settle, or calm.

> *Water is composed of hydrogen and oxygen.*
> *Beethoven composed nine symphonies.*
> *Relax and compose yourself.*

A word based on *compose* is *composure,* meaning "calmness or serenity."

> *Though he was heckled, the speaker maintained his composure.*

composite comes from the Latin prefix *com-* meaning "together" and *posit-* meaning "to put; place." Thus, *composite* means "put together or made up of separate parts." A *composite* is "something made up of separate parts."

> *This composite photograph was made by combining halves of two different negatives.*
> *This jigsaw puzzle is a composite of 200 pieces.*

136

compound comes from the Latin prefix *com-* meaning "together" and *pound-* meaning "to put; place." Thus, a *compound* [kom′pound] is "a combination of two or more separate parts or ingredients." To *compound* [kom·pound′] means (1) to make by combining parts or ingredients; (2) to complicate something by bringing in a new element; (3) in finance, to compute interest on both the original principal and the accumulated interest.

Most drugs are compounds of several chemicals.
Blackberry *is a compound word made up of* black *and* berry.
The pharmacist compounded the prescribed medicine.
Tom's uncooperative attitude compounded the difficulty.
The bank compounds interest on savings accounts.

depose comes from the Latin prefix *de-* meaning "down" and *pose-* meaning "to put; place." *Depose* originally meant "to put someone down in position or rank; demote." Today, *depose* means "to take an office, position, etc., away from the person holding it; oust, as a monarch." In law, *depose* has a special meaning: "to give testimony under oath, especially in writing."

The revolutionary mobs deposed the king.

A word related to *depose* is *deposition*, meaning "the act of deposing." In law, a *deposition* is "the written testimony of a witness who is under oath."

deposit comes from the Latin prefix *de-* meaning "down" and *posit-* meaning "to put; place." To *deposit* is "to put or set something down." Thus, *deposit* also means (1) to put something down in the form of a layer, as of dirt; (2) to put down and entrust money to a bank; (3) to put down money as a partial payment on something.

The Nile River deposited silt over the ages to form a delta.
She deposited $25 in her savings account.
He made a $500 deposit on the car.

A word based on *deposit* is *depository*, meaning "a place where anything is deposited; a storehouse."

An arsenal is a depository for weapons.

dispose comes from *dis-* meaning "apart" and the root *pose-* meaning "to put." *Dispose* literally means "to put apart or set aside." Hence,

137

dispose means (1) to get rid of; (2) to put in order, arrange, or settle; (3) to put into a receptive frame of mind for; (4) to condition toward something.

> *Have you disposed of your old car?*
> *He disposed the business affairs of his ailing brother.*
> *The news disposed them to accept our offer of help.*
> *Lack of sleep disposes some people to headaches.*

Two words based on or related to *dispose* are *disposal* and *disposition*. *Disposal* means (1) a transfer of something to another, as by sale or gift; (2) a getting rid of something. *Disposition* means (1) one's usual frame of mind; (2) a tendency or habit; (3) management or settlement, as of business affairs; (4) a particular ordering or arrangement, as of troops.

> *His will provided for the disposal of his property.*
> *This sink takes care of waste disposal.*
> *Amy has a cheerful disposition.*
> *What did you think of the disposition of the lawsuit?*
> *The map showed the disposition of troops in the area.*

expose comes from the Latin prefix *ex-* meaning "out" and *pose-* meaning "to put; place." Thus, *expose* means "to put something out so that it is seen or known"; hence, (1) to reveal something, especially something that was deliberately hidden; (2) to lay something open to ridicule or criticism; (3) to uncover; (4) to lay open to the effect of sunlight, the elements, etc.

> *The newspaper reporter exposed the corruption in government.*
> *When Gary tries to discuss baseball, he exposes his ignorance.*
> *If you expose yourself to the sun too long, you get burned.*

Two words based on *expose* are *exposé* and *exposure*. An *exposé* is "a making known publicly of something hidden, especially something evil or scandalous." *Exposure* means (1) the act of exposing or the state of being exposed; (2) position in relation to the sun, elements, or compass points; (3) the act of exposing film in order to make a photograph; (4) the time that a film is exposed; (5) a segment of film from which a single picture is made.

> *The newspaper ran an exposé of corruption in local government.*
> *The exposure of government corruption brought about reforms.*

138

This room has a southern exposure.
The photograph needed an exposure of ten seconds.
There are twelve exposures on this roll of film.

exposition comes from the Latin prefix *ex-* meaning "out" and *posit-* meaning "to put; place" plus the Latin suffix *-ion* meaning "the state or act of." Hence, *exposition* means "the act of setting out, explaining, or displaying one's facts, ideas, products, works of art, etc." More specifically, it means (1) a detailed presentation of a subject; (2) a public display, show, or exhibition; (3) the part of a literary work, as a play, that gives the background of the plot and characters.

The teacher gave a clear exposition of the contents of the course.
The museum has an exposition of new paintings.

A word based on *exposition* is *expository,* meaning "of or pertaining to exposition; explanatory."

The novel Moby Dick *is full of expository chapters about whales.*

expound comes from the Latin prefix *ex-* meaning "out" and *pound-* meaning "to put; place." Thus, *expound* means "to put something out in the form of words; to state, reveal, explain, or interpret something."

The professor expounded Einstein's theory of relativity.

impose comes from the Latin prefix *im-* meaning "on" and *pose-* meaning "to put; place." Thus, *impose* means "to put or force something upon others"; hence, (1) to force oneself or one's views on others; (2) to establish or enforce something by authority.

He imposed on our hospitality by staying two weeks.
The governor imposed martial law during the riots.

Two words based on or related to *impose* are *imposing,* meaning "impressive, grand, or stately," and *imposition,* which means (1) the act of imposing; (2) that which is imposed, as a tax or an excessive requirement.

The governor's mansion is an imposing edifice.
His unexpected visit was an imposition.

oppose comes from the Latin prefix *op-* (another spelling of *ob-*) meaning "against" and *pose-* meaning "to put; place." Thus, *oppose*

139

90-SECOND QUICKIE QUIZ

WORD BUILDING

Here is another short review quiz of roots and words you have already learned. Match the roots with their meanings. Answers follow.

1. **pend-** as in depend [di·pend']
2. **plex-** as in complex [kom'pleks]
3. **corp-** as in corpulent [kôr'pyə·lənt]
4. **dict-** as in contradict [kon'trə·dikt']
5. **cred-** as in credentials [kri·den'shəls]
6. **ag-** as in agenda [ə·jen'də]
7. **posit-** as in deposit [di·poz'it]
8. **acu-** as in acute [ə·kyo͞ot']

(a) to say or speak
(b) to hang, weigh, or pay
(c) to put; place
(d) to fold; connect
(e) to believe; trust
(f) body; flesh
(g) to do
(h) sharp

ANSWERS:

1. **pend-** —(b) to hang, weigh, or pay. To depend means to trust or rely on; to rely for support on.
2. **plex-** —(d) to fold; connect. Complex means consisting of various connected parts, not simple; a whole made up of connected parts.
3. **corp-** —(f) body; flesh. Corpulent means abounding in flesh; fat.
4. **dict-** —(a) to say or speak. To contradict means to say the opposite, as of what someone else has said.
5. **cred-** —(e) to believe; trust. Credentials are proof or evidence that cause others to believe the identity, experience, or authority of someone.
6. **ag-** —(g) to do. An agenda is a list of things to be done, discussed, or decided.
7. **posit-** —(c) to put; place. Deposit means (1) to put something down in the form of a layer, as of dust or mud; (2) to put down or entrust money to a bank; (3) to put down money as a partial payment on something.
8. **acu-** —(h) sharp. Acute means coming to a sharp point; reaching a crisis, critical; keen, intense.

means "to put oneself against something or someone; to be or act against; resist or fight."

The senator opposed new taxes.
The United States opposed Germany in both world wars.

Three words related to *oppose* are *opponent, opposite,* and *opposition.* An *opponent* is "a person who opposes someone or something." *Opposite* means (1) being on the other side or on each side of something; (2) facing or moving the other way; (3) contrary or different

140

in character. *Opposition* means (1) the act of opposing or the state of being opposed; (2) that which opposes; especially, a political party in power.

> *The senator beat his opponent in the election.*
> *The two men shouted at each other from opposite ends of the room.*
> *My views are in opposition to those of Marx.*
> *The opposition voted against the President's bill.*

positive comes from *posit-* meaning "to put; place" and the Latin suffix *-ive* meaning "inclined to." Thus, *positive* means "definitely put forth and accepted; affirmative or affirmed; not open to doubt."

> *He gave positive proof of his innocence.*
> *I'm positive that I left my umbrella at your house.*

postpone comes from the Latin prefix *post-* meaning "after" and *pone-* meaning "to put; place." Thus, *postpone* means "to put off until later; delay."

> *We postponed our picnic because of rain.*

A word based on *postpone* is *postponement,* meaning "a putting off of something; a delay."

> *Bad weather caused a three-day postponement of our trip.*

propose comes from the Latin prefix *pro-* meaning "forward" and *pose-* meaning "to put; place." Thus, *propose* means (1) to put something forward for consideration; (2) to nominate; (3) to make an offer of marriage.

> *The President proposed an increase in taxes.*
> *I proposed Tom Smith for president of the club.*
> *Jonathan proposed to Kate Friday night.*

Two words based on or related to *propose* are *proposal* and *proposition.* A *proposal* is (1) an offer proposing something to be accepted or adopted; (2) an offer of marriage; (3) something proposed, such as a plan. *Proposition* means (1) a plan or proposal; (2) a subject or statement presented for discussion.

> *He made two proposals at the business meeting.*
> *She accepted his proposal of marriage.*
> *The chairman read his proposition to the committee.*

141

suppose comes from the Latin prefix *sup-* (another spelling of *sub-*) meaning "under; secretly" and *pose-* meaning "to put; place." Thus, *suppose* means "to put something secretly to oneself"; hence, (1) to think or imagine something to oneself as true; (2) to believe probable; (3) to require or expect; (4) to assume to be true for the sake of argument.

> *He actually supposed that people were spying on him.*
> *I suppose you are right.*
> *What are you supposed to be learning?*
> *Suppose he arrives late; what will we do?*

Two words based on or related to *suppose* are *supposed*, meaning "accepted as genuine or true, though perhaps not so," and *supposition*, which means (1) the act of supposing; (2) a guess.

> *Her supposed remorse proved to be a sham.*
> *It is my supposition that he will arrive late.*

◊ Look up the following words in your dictionary. Learn the meaning of each, and be sure you can relate each meaning to the root *pon-*, *posit-*, *pound-*, or *pose-* meaning "to put; place."

composition	juxtaposition	purpose
deponent	preposition	repository
exponent	proponent	superimpose
interpose	propound	transpose

ROOT: PORT-

The Latin root *port-* means "to carry." Learn the following core vocabulary words based on this root: *deport, export, import, portable.*

deport comes from the Latin prefix *de-* meaning "away" and *port-* meaning "to carry." To *deport* is literally "to carry someone away." Hence, *deport* means "to expel or banish someone from a country, often for political reasons."

> *Most governments have the right to deport undesirable aliens.*

Two words based on *deport* are *deportation,* meaning "banishment," and *deportment,* meaning "behavior or conduct; bearing."

The deportation of the spy is scheduled for today.
Grandfather was noted for his dignified deportment.
When I was in school we were graded on our deportment.

export comes from the Latin prefix *ex-* meaning "out" and *port-* meaning "to carry." Thus, to *export* is "to send merchandise or raw materials out of a country for sale or trade." An *export* is "an exported commodity."

The United States exports wheat.
Wheat is a major export.

import comes from the Latin prefix *im-* meaning "in" and *port-* meaning "to carry." Thus, to *import* [im·pôrt'] means "to bring merchandise or raw materials into a country for commercial use." An *import* [im'pôrt] is "an imported commodity."

The United States imports coffee.
Coffee is a major import.

Import also has the meaning of "implication, purport, or consequence."

John felt the import of the speaker's words.
The article discussed matters of great import.

portable comes from *port-* meaning "to carry" and the Latin suffix *-able* meaning "capable of being." Thus, *portable* means "capable of being carried; easily or readily movable." A *portable* is "something that can be moved easily, as a lightweight typewriter or a small radio."

Do you have a portable television set?
I have a desktop computer, not a portable.

◊ You already know the meanings of the nine words below. Can you relate the meaning of each word to the root *port-* meaning "to carry"? Check yourself by looking up the words in your dictionary.

disport	report	supporter
porter	reporter	transport
portfolio	support	transportation

143

REVIEW OF ROOTS

Here are more roots and words you have learned. Choose the answer nearest in meaning to the key word. Answers follow.

1. **mobile** [mō′bəl *or* mō′bēl]—(a) movable; capable of being moved easily. (b) agile; nimble. (c) a small truck. (d) a small mob.
2. **motive** [mō′tiv]—(a) slow, deliberate motion or action. (b) mechanical force. (c) a reason for a person's action or behavior. (d) actions leading up to a crime.
3. **motivation** [mō′tə·vā′shən]—(a) slow, deliberate motion or action. (b) the act of providing an incentive; drive. (c) actions leading up to a crime. (d) political power.
4. **natal** [nāt′l]—(a) pertaining to one's mother's family. (b) happening before one's birth. (c) happening after one's birth. (d) of or pertaining to one's birth.
5. **dispel** [dis·pel′]—(a) to doubt. (b) to be certain; have no doubts. (c) to disperse. (d) to swear to an oath.
6. **expel** [ik·spel′]—(a) to breathe out. (b) to spit. (c) to gather in. (d) to force out; eject.

7. **expulsion** [ik·spul′shən]—(a) forcible ejection. (b) rate of movement or progress. (c) an oath or curse. (d) death.
8. **compensate** [kom′pən·sāt]—(a) sad; pensive. (b) thoughtful. (c) to counterbalance; make up for. (d) to pay more than something is worth.
9. **dispensation** [dis′pən·sā′shən]— (a) to sell drugs or medicine. (b) distribution; an orderly dealing out or administering. (c) an excuse. (d) a gift to a charity or religious order.
10. **pending** [pen′ding]—(a) officially registered or recorded, as a patent. (b) urgent; most necessary. (c) remaining to be finished or decided. (d) supported from above.
11. **impending** [im·pen′ding]—(a) about to occur; imminent. (b) urgent; most necessary. (c) foreboding; forecasting bad luck or disaster. (d) restricting; confining.

ANSWERS:

1. **mobile**—(a) movable; capable of being moved easily. 2. **motive**—(c) a reason for a person's action or behavior. 3. **motivation**—(b) the act of providing an incentive; drive. 4. **natal**—(d) of or pertaining to one's birth. 5. **dispel**—(c) to disperse. 6. **expel**—(d) to force out; eject. 7. **expulsion**—(a) forcible ejection. 8. **compensate**—(c) to counterbalance; make up for. 9. **dispensation**—(b) distribution; an orderly dealing out or administering. 10. **pending**—(c) remaining to be finished or decided. 11. **impending**—(a) about to occur; imminent.

ROOT: QUIR-, QUISIT-, QUEST-

The Latin root *quir-*, *quisit-*, or *quest-* means "to seek or ask." This root is the basis of many common English words such as *question* and *quest*. Learn the three core vocabulary words based on the root *quir-*, *quisit-*, or *quest-*: *acquire*, *inquire*, and *require*.

acquire comes from the Latin prefix *ac-* (another spelling of *ad-*) meaning "to; for" and *quir-* meaning "to seek or ask." Thus, *acquire* means "to seek something for oneself and get it; obtain something by one's own efforts; get."

> *He has acquired a house in the country.*
> *Where did you acquire that Southern accent?*

Three words based on *acquire* are *acquirement, acquisition,* and *acquisitive.* Both *acquirement* and *acquisition* mean (1) the act of acquiring; (2) something acquired. An *acquirement,* however, is a skill gained by study or practice, while an *acquisition* is usually an object that has been acquired. *Acquisitive* means "inclined to acquire things; grasping."

> *She is a person of notable scholarly acquirements.*
> *The library has a display of its recent acquisitions.*
> *His acquisitive nature makes him a compulsive shopper.*

inquire comes from the Latin prefix *in-* meaning "in; into" plus *quir-* meaning "to seek or ask." Thus, *inquire* means "to ask or seek into something; seek information by asking questions; make an investigation or search into something."

> *"Why are you staring at me?" he inquired.*
> *He inquired about your health.*
> *The police are inquiring into the circumstances of the crime.*

Three words based on *inquire* are *inquiry, inquisition,* and *inquisitive. Inquiry* means (1) the act of inquiring; investigation; (2) a question. An *inquisition* is "an official inquiry or investigation into the beliefs of individuals or groups, for the purpose of enforcing dominant social, political, or religious beliefs." (The Spanish Inquisition was a judicial court of the Roman Catholic Church set up in Spain in the fifteenth century for the purpose of discovering and punishing heretics.) *Inquisitive* means (1) given to questioning, especially when too curious about the affairs of others; (2) eager for knowledge.

> *Discoveries are made through scientific inquiry.*
> *She handles customers' inquiries about merchandise.*
> *Jean has an inquisitive old cat.*
> *Bill has an inquisitive mind and will make a good scientist.*

require comes from the Latin prefix *re-* meaning "back; again" and *quir-* meaning "to seek or ask." *Require* literally means "to ask again"; that is, "to ask as if demanding something." Hence, *require* means "to demand, order, or insist upon" or "to have need of something."

> *The hotel requires guests to dress formally for dinner.*
> *English is a required course.*
> *The patient requires rest and quiet.*

Two words based on *require* are *requirement,* meaning "that which is required; an essential or demand"; and *requisite,* which means (1) required by the nature of things; necessary; (2) a necessity or requirement.

> *Good grades are a requirement for graduation.*
> *Have you done the requisite amount of work, fulfilling all the requisites for the degree?*

◊ Look up the following words in your dictionary. Learn the meaning of each, and be sure you can relate each to the root *quir-, quisit-,* or *quest-* meaning "to seek or ask."

conquest   exquisite   perquisite   request

ROOT: RUPT-

The Latin root *rupt-* means "to break; burst." Learn the five core vocabulary words based on this root—*corrupt, disrupt, erupt, interrupt, rupture.*

corrupt comes from the Latin prefix *cor-* (another spelling of *con-*) meaning "thoroughly" and *rupt-* meaning "to break." Thus, to *corrupt* is "to ruin or destroy morally; to debase or spoil." As an adjective, *corrupt* means "dishonest; immoral."

Joe's dishonest friends corrupted him.
There is nothing worse than a corrupt politician.

A word based on *corrupt* is *corruption,* meaning (1) the act of corrupting, or the state of being corrupt; (2) dishonesty or bribery.

Several local politicians have been accused of corruption.

disrupt comes from the Latin prefix *dis-* meaning "apart" and *rupt-* meaning "to break; burst." Thus, *disrupt* means "to break apart or break up; throw into disorder; upset."

Some of the students tried to disrupt classes.

Two words based on *disrupt* are *disruption,* meaning "the act of disrupting, or the state of being disrupted," and *disruptive,* which means "causing or tending to cause disruption."

Guards were posted to prevent the disruption of the meeting.
The dean expelled the disruptive students.

erupt comes from the Latin prefix *e-* (another spelling of *ex-*) meaning "out" and *rupt-* meaning "to break; burst." Thus, *erupt* means "to burst forth with lava, steam, etc., in the manner of a volcano or geyser; burst out or burst open suddenly or violently."

The volcano erupted at midnight.
Their anger erupted into a fight.
Riots erupted in several countries last year.

A word based on *erupt* is *eruption,* which means (1) a breaking forth or outbreak; (2) a bursting forth of lava, steam, etc.

He suffers from a skin eruption similar to acne.

interrupt comes from the Latin prefix *inter-* meaning "between; in between" and *rupt-* meaning "to break; burst." Thus, *interrupt* means "to break into the continuity of something, such as conversation or speech; stop temporarily."

The heckler interrupted the speaker several times.
The regular train schedule has been interrupted by snow.

A word based on *interrupt* is *interruption,* meaning (1) the act of

147

interrupting or state of being interrupted; (2) something that interrupts.

The speaker tried to ignore the heckler's interruption.

rupture comes from *rupt-* meaning "to break; burst" and the Latin suffix *-ure* meaning "the act or state of." Thus, to *rupture* is "to break open or break apart." A *rupture* is "the act of bursting or breaking; a bursting or break; a breaking off, as of friendship or good relations between persons or countries."

His appendix ruptured.
He suffered a rupture of the appendix.
The rupture between England and Ireland has never been healed.

ROOT: SCRIB-, SCRIPT-

The Latin root *scrib-* or *script-* means "to write." Can you describe or scribble down two words containing this root? *Script,* you will note, is a word in itself, meaning "writing or a piece of writing, such as a copy of a play prepared for actors' use." With the addition of the letter *e,* *scrib-* becomes the word *scribe,* meaning "one who copies manuscripts." Learn the five core vocabulary words based on the root *scrib-* or *script-:* *describe, inscribe, prescribe, proscribe, subscribe, transcribe.*

describe comes from the Latin prefix *de-* meaning "down" and *scrib-* meaning "to write." *Describe* originally meant "to write something down." Today, *describe* means "to present something in spoken or written words; to give an account of something."

He described what he had seen on his trip.
Can you describe the burglar's appearance?

Two words based on *describe* are *description* and *descriptive.* *Description* is (1) an account that describes; (2) the act or technique of describing. *Descriptive* means "containing description or serving to describe."

He wrote a vivid description of the trip.
This is colorful, descriptive writing.

148

inscribe comes from the Latin prefix *in-* meaning "in; on" and *scrib-* meaning "to write." Thus, *inscribe* means (1) to write words, names, etc., on something for a public or formal purpose; (2) to write in a book or on a photograph, etc., as when autographing or dedicating it; (3) to enter a name on a formal or official list.

> *The monument was inscribed with the names of the war dead.*
> *The author inscribed a copy of his book to his best friend.*
> *He inscribed his name on the petition.*

A word based on *inscribe* is *inscription,* meaning (1) the act of inscribing; (2) writing that has been inscribed on a tablet, statue, etc.; (3) an informal written dedication in a book.

> *The inscription on the old tombstone was hard to read.*

prescribe comes from the Latin prefix *pre-* meaning "before" and *scrib-* meaning "to write." *Prescribe* literally means "to write before someone else acts, as when giving an order." Hence, *prescribe* means (1) to set something down as a rule to be followed; (2) to order the use of a medicine or treatment for a patient.

> *The engraved invitation prescribed formal dress.*
> *The doctor prescribed an antibiotic.*

Two words based on *prescribe* are *prescription* and *prescriptive.* A *prescription* is (1) a doctor's written formula authorizing a druggist to prepare a medicine; (2) a remedy recommended by a doctor. *Prescriptive* means "making strict rules."

> *Did the druggist fill your prescription?*
> *Has the new prescription helped your allergy?*
> *This book deals with prescriptive grammar.*

proscribe comes from the Latin prefix *pro-* meaning "before" and *scrib-* meaning "to write." *Proscribe* originally meant "to write an outlaw's name in public." Today, *proscribe* means "to outlaw or banish; denounce or condemn someone or something; prohibit."

> *The nations agreed to proscribe germ warfare.*

A word based on *proscribe* is *proscription,* meaning "a prohibition" or "banishment."

> *Nations should try to agree on a proscription of nuclear weapons.*

149

NOTE: Be careful to learn the difference between *prescribe* and *proscribe*.

> *The doctor prescribed aspirin for my headache.*
> *Many states have proscribed the use of certain insecticides.*

subscribe comes from the Latin prefix *sub-* meaning "underneath" and *scrib-* meaning "to write." Thus, *subscribe* means (1) to write one's name underneath, or at the end of, a document, as to show agreement; sign; (2) to agree with, support, approve, or sanction; (3) to agree to pay money to a cause, or to a newspaper or periodical for its delivery.

> *I subscribe to everything the speaker said.*
> *Do you subscribe to the* Daily Record?

Two words based on *subscribe* are *subscriber*, meaning "a person who subscribes, as to a newspaper or magazine," and *subscription*, which means (1) the act of subscribing; (2) a signature; (3) the sale or purchase of prepaid orders for books, magazines, tickets, etc., as by mail or through a door-to-door salesman.

> *Are you a subscriber of your local newspaper?*
> *Tickets for some charity balls are sold only by subscription.*
> *When does your magazine subscription expire?*

transcribe comes from the Latin prefix *trans-* meaning "across; beyond; through" and *scrib-* meaning "to write." Thus, *transcribe* means (1) to copy or recopy from an original or from shorthand notes; (2) to adapt a musical composition for a change of instrument or voice.

> *It is difficult to transcribe another person's shorthand notes.*
> *The symphony was transcribed for two pianos.*

A word based on *transcribe* is *transcript*, meaning "a copy, especially of a student's academic courses and grades."

◊ Look up the following words in your dictionary. Learn the meaning of each, and be sure you can relate each to the root *scrib-* or *script-* meaning "to write."

ascribe	indescribable	scribble
circumscribe	manuscript	Scripture
conscript	postscript	scrip

Fun With Words

SPOT THE SPECIALISTS

Do you know what profession or field of study the following people are associated with? The roots you are learning in this section will help you. Check the word or phrase you believe is closest in meaning to the key word. Answers follow.

1. **agronomist** [ə·gron'ə·mist]—(a) an expert in finance. (b) an expert in botany. (c) an expert in field-crop production. (d) an expert in home economics.

2. **antiquary** [an'ti·kwer'ē]—(a) a student of antiques. (b) a doctor who specializes in the care and treatment of elderly persons. (c) the curator of a zoo. (d) a stamp collector.

3. **etymologist** [et'ə·mol'ə·jist]—(a) a student of the meaning of words. (b) an expert in the pronunciation of words. (c) an expert in the derivation of words. (d) a student of insects.

4. **ichthyologist** [ik'thē·ol'ə·jist]— (a) one who studies religious characteristics. (b) an expert in fishes. (c) a professional hunter and fisherman. (d) one who grows herbs.

5. **philologist** [fi·lol'ə·jist]—(a) a handwriting expert. (b) a philosopher. (c) a student of words and languages. (d) an expert in map making.

6. **archeologist** [är'kē·ol'ə·jist]—(a) a student of medieval architecture. (b) a student of cathedrals. (c) a student of government. (d) one who uncovers and studies the remains of early human cultures.

7. **lexicographer** [lek'sə·kog'rə·fər] —(a) a printer. (b) one who writes or compiles a dictionary. (c) one who studies the science of law. (d) a map maker.

8. **anthropologist** [an'thrə·pol'ə·jist]— (a one who studies the development of humanity. (b) a zoo attendant. (c) a geologist specializing in the study of coal and coal mines. (d) a professional boxer.

9. **zoologist** [zō·ol'ə·jist]—(a) a zoo keeper. (b) the curator of a museum. (c) a taxidermist. (d) one who studies the development and structure of animals.

10. **choreographer** [kôr'ē·og'rə·fər] —(a) one who devises dance movements and patterns. (b) a singer. (c) a priest. (d) a map maker.

ANSWERS:

1. **agronomist**—(c) an expert in field-crop production. 2. **antiquary**—(a) a student of antiques. 3. **etymologist**—(c) an expert in the derivation of words. 4. **ichthyologist**—(b) an expert in fishes. 5. **philologist**—(c) a student of words and languages. 6. **archeologist**—(d) one who uncovers and studies the remains of early human cultures. 7. **lexicographer**—(b) one who writes or compiles a dictionary. 8. **anthropologist**—(a) one who studies the development of humanity. 9. **zoologist**—(d) one who studies the development and structure of animals. 10. **choreographer**—(a) one who devises dance movements and patterns.

ROOT: SED-, SID-, SESS-

The Latin root *sed-*, *sid-*, or *sess-* means "to sit; settle." Learn the following four core vocabulary words based on this root: *preside, reside, sediment, session.*

preside comes from the Latin prefix *pre-* meaning "before" and *side-* meaning "to sit." Thus, *preside* means "to sit before others in the place of a leader; sit in authority; act as chairman."

> *Tom Smith presided at the meeting of the club.*

Three words based on *preside* are *president,* meaning "the person chosen to preside over any organization, group, nation, etc.; the chief executive"; *presidency,* meaning "the office of a president or the time that a president is in office"; and *presidential,* which means "of, for, or pertaining to a president, the presidency, or the election of a president."

> *World War II ended during Truman's presidency.*
> *Do you remember John Kennedy's presidential campaign?*

reside comes from the Latin prefix *re-* meaning "back" and *side-* meaning "to sit; settle." Thus, *reside* means "to settle back or stay at a place"; hence, (1) to make one's home at a particular place; (2) to exist as a quality in something; (3) to be vested in as a right.

> *Washington resided at Mount Vernon.*
> *The power to confirm presidential appointments resides in the Senate.*

Three words based on *reside* are *residence, resident,* and *residential.* *Residence* means (1) the place or house where a person lives; (2) the fact of being officially present at a place. *Resident* means (1) a person who lives in a place; (2) having a residence; (3) staying in or being affiliated with a place in connection with one's official work. *Residential* means "of, pertaining to, or suitable for residences or homes."

> *Is your residence in St. Louis?*
> *Randall Jarrell was once writer in residence at my college.*
> *She is a resident of Columbus, Ohio.*
> *Dr. Jones is the resident physician at this hospital.*
> *The town has several beautiful residential districts.*

sediment comes from *sed-* meaning "to sit; settle" and the Latin suffix
-ment meaning "the act or result of." Thus, *sediment* means "the result of something settling"; that is, "matter that settles or is settling
to the bottom of a body of liquid."

> *The drinking water was full of sediment.*

session comes from *sess-* meaning "to sit; settle" and the Latin suffix
-ion meaning "the act or state of." Thus, *session* means (1) the
sitting together of a legislative body, a court, etc., for the purpose
of doing business; (2) a single meeting of an organized group; (3)
a school term.

> *Congress is meeting for its winter session.*
> *The afternoon session of the conference lasted three hours.*
> *Did you attend the summer session at school?*

◊ Look up the following words in your dictionary. Learn the meaning
of each, and be sure you can relate each meaning to the root *sed-*, *sid-*,
or *sess-* meaning "to sit; settle."

dissident	residue	subside
obsession	sedate	subsidiary
residual	sedative	subsidy

ROOT: SPEC-, SPIC-, SPECT-

The Latin root *spec-*, *spic-*, or *spect-* means "to look; look at." Learn the
five core vocabulary words based on this root: *conspicuous, expect,
inspect, respect, spectacle.*

conspicuous comes from the Latin prefix *con-* meaning "together" and
spic- meaning "to look; look at" plus the Latin suffix *-uous* meaning
"tending to; inclined to." Something *conspicuous* tends to be looked
at altogether, at once, and isn't hard to see. Hence, *conspicuous*
means "easily visible; attracting attention."

> *The lighthouse was conspicuous for miles.*
> *She was carrying a loud, conspicuous parrot*

153

A word based on *conspicuous* is *inconspicuous,* meaning "not easily visible; not attracting attention; not noticeable."

The brown bird was inconspicuous among the branches.
Mr. Burns is a quiet, inconspicuous man.

expect comes from the Latin prefix *ex-* meaning "out" and *spect-* meaning "to look at." Thus, to *expect* is "to look out for something"; hence, "to look forward to something as certain or likely" or "to look for something as right or essential; require."

I expect that he will arrive tonight.
He expected to be paid for his trouble.
The teacher expected the students to write a paper every week.

Three words based on *expect* are *expectancy, expectant,* and *expectation. Expectancy* is (1) the act or state of expecting; (2) something expected. *Expectant* means (1) expecting; (2) awaiting the birth of a child. *Expectation* is (1) the act of expecting or state of mind of a person who expects something; anticipation; (2) a prospect of some good to come.

What is the life expectancy of a fifty-year-old American?
She is an expectant mother.
Do you have any expectation of success?
He has great expectations in life.

inspect comes from the Latin prefix *in-* meaning "in; into" and *spect-* meaning "to look." Thus, to *inspect* is "to look into something; examine something carefully; examine or review something officially."

Holmes inspected the butterfly under a magnifying glass.
The man was nervously inspecting his fingernails.
The general inspected his troops.

Two words based on *inspect* are *inspection,* meaning "a careful examination; an official examination or review"; and *inspector,* which means "a person who inspects, as an official examiner or a police officer ranking below a superintendent."

The fire department's inspection of the building was thorough.
The troops stood inspection for the general.
He is an inspector with Scotland Yard.

respect comes from the Latin prefix *re-* meaning "back; again" and *spect-* meaning "to look; look at." *Respect* literally means "to look again at someone"; that is, "to treat someone with consideration." Hence, the verb *respect* means "to have regard for a person or to treat a person with consideration." The noun *respect* means "honor and esteem" or "a specific detail or aspect."

Children should respect their parents.
Parents should also have respect for their children.
In what respect do you feel we have failed in our mission?

Two words based on *respect* are *respectable,* meaning (1) deserving respect; having a good reputation; (2) fairly good or average; and *respectful,* which means "showing respect."

Her family is highly respectable.
He received a respectable raise.
Children should be respectful to their parents.

spectacle comes from a Latin word based on *spect-* meaning "to look; look at." *Spectacle* means "something exhibited to public view"— either "an unusual sight or grand display" or "a painful or embarrassing sight." The plural form of the word, *spectacles,* means "a pair of eyeglasses."

The three-ring circus was quite a spectacle.
John drank too much at the party and made a spectacle of himself.
Eloise is constantly breaking her spectacles.

A word based on *spectacle* is *spectacular,* meaning "of or like a spectacle; characterized by a grand display that excites wonder or amazement." A *spectacular* is "an impressive exhibition or production, as a show having a large cast, elaborate sets, exciting acts, etc."

We saw a spectacular display of fireworks on the Fourth of July.
The race ended in a spectacular neck-and-neck finish.
Did you see the television spectacular last night?

◊ Look up the following words in your dictionary. Learn the meaning of each. Be sure you can relate each meaning to the root *spec-, spic-,* or *spect-* meaning "to look; look at."

auspicious	perspicuity	speculate
despicable	specimen	suspect
perspective	spectator	suspicion

155

ROOT: TANG-, TING-, TACT-

The Latin root *tang-*, *ting-*, or *tact-* means "to touch." Here are eleven "touching" words. First learn the six core vocabulary words based on this root: *contact, contingent, intact, tact, tangent, tangible.*

contact comes from the Latin prefix *con-* meaning "together" and *tact-* meaning "to touch." Thus, the verb *contact* means (1) to come or bring together; touch; (2) to get in touch with someone. As a noun, *contact* means (1) the coming together or touching of two things; (2) a being in touch with someone or something; (3) a person with whom one is in touch and who can perhaps help one.

> *If these electric wires contact, the fuse will be blown.*
> *I think you should contact a good lawyer.*
> *It wasn't a collision; the two cars barely came into contact.*
> *Are you in contact with your brother?*
> *He has a contact in Washington who could help us.*

contingent comes from the Latin prefix *con-* meaning "together" and *ting-* meaning "to touch" plus the Latin suffix *-ent*, which is the same as our English ending *-ing*. *Contingent* literally indicates that two unrelated things are touching or happening together. Hence, *contingent* means (1) occurring by chance; accidental; (2) probable or liable to occur but not certain or logical; (3) dependent upon an uncertain event. A *contingent* is (1) a representative group in an assemblage; (2) a quota of something to be furnished, as troops.

> *Their budget allowed for contingent expenses as well as fixed costs.*
> *Our trip is contingent upon good weather.*
> *At the convention there was a large contingent from Chicago.*
> *A contingent of Australian troops joined the peace-keeping force.*

A word based on *contingent* is *contingency*, meaning "an unforeseen but possible occurrence, as an accident or emergency."

> *Before setting out, we tried to prepare for all contingencies.*

intact comes from the Latin prefix *in-* meaning "not" and *tact-* meaning "to touch." Thus, *intact* literally means "not touched or spoiled; remaining whole or unchanged; undamaged."

> *The fire destroyed the garage but left the house intact.*

156

tact comes directly from the root *tact-*. *Tact* means "just the right social 'touch'; a quick sense of what is appropriate, proper, or right; skill in avoiding what would offend."

An ambassador must have tact.

Two words based on *tact* are *tactful,* meaning "having or showing tact; considerate"; and *tactless,* meaning "lacking tact; boorish."

An ambassador clearly has to be a tactful man.
Jenny often makes tactless remarks to her friends.

tangent comes from *tang-* meaning "to touch" and the Latin suffix *-ent,* which is the same as our English ending *-ing.* Thus, *tangent* means "touching." In geometry, the adjective *tangent* means "being in contact at a single point or along a line"; hence, a *tangent* is a "straight line that is in contact with a curved line at one point." The expression *to go off on a tangent* means "to make a sharp or sudden change in direction, especially when discussing a subject."

The line is tangent to the circle.
The line is a tangent of the circle.
He is an interesting speaker but tends to go off on tangents.

A word based on *tangent* is *tangential,* meaning (1) of or pertaining to a tangent; (2) touching only slightly on something; (3) only slightly relevant to the main topic.

He kept introducing tangential questions into the debate.

tangible comes from *tang-* meaning "to touch" and the Latin suffix *-ible* meaning "able to be; capable of being." *Tangible* literally means "capable of being touched; touchable." Hence, *tangible* means "perceptible by touch; having a definite shape; solid."

The oasis wasn't tangible; it was just a mirage.
The storm seems to have had no tangible effect on our roofing.

A word based on *tangible* is *intangible,* meaning "not tangible; real, but not material or concrete; hard to define or explain in words."

He cares more for material things than for intangible ideas.
She has that intangible quality of good taste.

◇ Sculptors may have more *tactile* sensitivity than most other people. Can you explain why?

Here are some fun words you might like to try on your friends. Check the word or phrase you believe is closest in meaning to the key word. Answers follow.

1. **amanuensis** [ə·man′yoō·en′sis]— (a) a magician. (b) stuttering. (c) a secretary. (d) one who hates men.

2. **bibelot** [bib′lō]—(a) a small object of art. (b) an old-fashioned neckpiece. (c) a marker for Holy Writ. (d) a love letter.

3. **bailiwick** [bā′lə·wik]—(a) a reed basket. (b) a prison. (c) one's own special place or province. (d) a whip.

4. **caravansary** [kar′ə·van′sə·rē]— (a) a traveling show. (b) an inn. (c) a camel train. (d) seeded bread from Arabia.

5. **cabalistic** [kab′ə·lis′tik]—(a) pertaining to black magic. (b) having a mystical meaning. (c) pertaining to those secretly united for intrigue. (d) pertaining to an acrostic.

6. **entrepreneur** [än′trə·prə·nûr′]— (a) a nightclub entertainer. (b) a person who is between jobs. (c) one who originates and conducts an enterprise. (d) an actor.

7. **furbelow** [fûr′bə·lō]—(a) a silly action. (b) a fussy or showy trimming. (c) a deep valley. (d) cheap jewelry.

8. **hoi polloi** [hoi′ pə·loi′]—(a) Japanese emperor. (b) a Hawaiian fruit salad. (c) the common people. (d) a flowering shrub of the Pacific.

9. **leprechaun** [lep′rə·kôn]—(a) an elf in Irish folklore. (b) a disease of the skin. (c) a small leopard of the African highlands. (d) a medieval spell or charm.

10. **legerdemain** [lej′ər·də·mān′]— (a) a record of accounts. (b) magic tricks or sleight of hand. (c) witchcraft. (d) a chronicle of events.

11. **mountebank** [moun′tə·bangk]— (a) an area reserved for skiing. (b) a doctor. (c) an antelope of the African highlands. (d) a charlatan.

12. **nimrod** [nim′rod]—(a) an acrobat. (b) a fisherman. (c) a humorous character in puppet shows. (d) a hunter.

ANSWERS:

1. **amanuensis**—(c) a secretary. 2. **bibelot**—(a) a small object of art. 3. **bailiwick**—(c) one's own special place or province. 4. **caravansary**—(b) an inn. 5. **cabalistic**—(b) having a mystical meaning. 6. **entrepreneur**—(c) one who originates and conducts an enterprise. 7. **furbelow**—(b) a fussy or showy trimming. 8. **hoi polloi**—(c) the common people. 9. **leprechaun**—(a) an elf in Irish folklore. 10. **legerdemain**—(b) magic tricks or sleight of hand. 11. **mountebank**—(d) a charlatan. 12. **nimrod**—(d) a hunter.

ROOT: TEN-, TIN-, TENT-, TAIN-

The Latin root *ten-*, *tin-*, *tent-*, or *tain-* means "to hold." Learn the eight core vocabulary words based on this root: *contain, continent, detain, lieutenant, pertain, pertinacious, retain, tenacious.*

contain comes from the Latin prefix *con-* meaning "together" and *tain-* meaning "to hold." *Contain* literally means "to hold something together in a holder"; hence, (1) to hold or be able to hold; (2) to include; (3) to keep within bounds or restrain.

> *That bottle contains a quart of milk.*
> *This book contains useful information.*
> *A foot contains twelve inches.*
> *He was so angry he couldn't contain himself.*
> *Try to contain the enemy attack until reinforcements arrive.*

Three words based on *contain* are *container,* meaning "a box, carton, can, jar, etc., that holds or encloses something"; *containment,* meaning "the act or fact of containing; especially, the prevention of a nation from expanding its territories or political control"; and *content* [kon′tent], which means (1) that which a thing contains; (2) the amount of something contained; (3) subject matter.

> *She opened the container and removed the contents.*
> *We still have a policy of containment with regard to China.*
> *What is the silver content of the ore?*
> *They studied the style and content of Shakespeare's plays.*

continent comes from the Latin prefix *con-* meaning "together" and *tin-* meaning "to hold" plus the Latin suffix *-ent,* which is the same as our English ending *-ing.* Thus, a *continent* is "a mass of land that is holding together; one of the large land masses of the earth."

> *Africa is a continent.*
> *Englishmen and Americans sometimes refer to Europe as "the Continent."*

A word based on *continent* is *continental,* meaning (1) of, on, or resembling a continent; (2) pertaining to Europe or Europeans.

> *Hawaii is not part of the continental United States.*
> *He has old-fashioned, Continental manners.*

detain comes from the Latin prefix *de-* meaning "away" and *tain-* meaning "to hold." *Detain* originally meant "to hold away from someone that which belonged to him; to withhold freedom from someone." Thus, *detain* means (1) to stop or delay; (2) to confine in jail.

I was detained by heavy traffic.
The police detained the suspect for further questioning.

A word based on *detain* is *detention,* meaning (1) the act of detaining or confining someone; (2) the state of being confined or delayed.

As a suspect, he was held in detention by the police.

lieutenant comes from the French word *lieu* meaning "place" and the Latin root *ten-* meaning "to hold" plus the Latin suffix *-ant,* which is the same as our English ending, *-ing. Lieutenant* literally means "holding the place of another or acting in lieu of another." Hence, a *lieutenant* is (1) a person having the power to act for or represent his superior; (2) a commissioned officer ranking below a captain in the army and below a lieutenant commander in the navy.

His most reliable lieutenant managed the business in his absence.
In the army, a second lieutenant ranks below a first lieutenant.

pertain comes from the Latin prefix *per-* meaning "through; throughout" and *tain-* meaning "to hold." *Pertain* literally means "to have a hold throughout something"; hence, "to have to do with or have reference to something."

I don't see how your statement pertains to my question.

Two words based on *pertain* are *pertinent,* meaning "related to the matter at hand; relevant" and *impertinent,* which means (1) disrespectful; unmannerly; impudent; (2) not pertinent; irrelevant.

His suggestion was pertinent; it was to the point.
That child is rude and impertinent.
Ed's wife has a way of breaking into serious conversations with impertinent small talk.

pertinacious comes from the Latin prefix *per-* meaning "thoroughly; completely" plus the word *tenacious. Pertinacious* means "sticking stubbornly or with determination to a purpose or opinion."

The pertinacious detective tracked down the suspect.

retain comes from the Latin prefix *re-* meaning "back" and *tain-* meaning "to hold." *Retain* literally means "to hold back something for oneself"; hence, (1) to keep or continue to keep something in one's possession; (2) to keep something in use, practice, etc.; (3) to keep in mind or remember; (4) to reserve the services of a lawyer or other representative by paying him a fee.

Mr. Smith retains complete control of the family business.
Though he became famous, he retained his modesty.
My mind doesn't retain facts as well as it used to.
The firm retained a lawyer for any lawsuits that might arise.

Three words based on *retain* are *retainer, retention,* and *retentive.* A *retainer* is (1) a servant; (2) a fee paid to engage or keep a representative, such as a lawyer. *Retention* means (1) the act of retaining or state of being retained or kept; (2) the ability to remember; memory. *Retentive* means "able to keep things, especially in memory."

The butler was an old family retainer.
The lawyer collected his yearly retainer from the firm.
The child has a retentive mind; his retention of new words is excellent.

tenacious comes from *ten-* meaning "to hold" and the Latin suffix *-acious* meaning "tending to; inclined to." Thus, *tenacious* means "tending to hold something strongly, such as an opinion, belief, etc.; stubborn."

He is tenacious in his support of free speech.
The wounded man clung to life tenaciously.

A word based on *tenacious* is *tenacity,* meaning "the state or quality of holding firm; stubbornness; determination."

Though badly wounded, he clung to life with tenacity.

◊ Look up the following words in your dictionary. Be sure you know the meaning of each. Relate each meaning to the root *ten-, tin-, tent-,* or *tain-* meaning "to hold."

abstain	entertain	sustenance
abstention	maintain	tenable
continuation	obtain	tenant
continue	sustain	tenancy

161

EXPLORING WORDS
MORE PEOPLE WHO BECAME WORDS

July the seventh month of the year. Literally, it means "the month of Julius" because it was inserted into the calendar by Julius Caesar.

macadamize to pave a road with layers of small or cracked stones, usually with a tar or asphalt binder. The word comes from J. L. McAdam, a Scottish engineer who invented the method.

mansard a roof that is flat on the top and has sharp, vertical slopes at the edges. Named after a French architect, François Mansard, who popularized this style in the seventeenth century.

martinet a person, such as a teacher, army officer, etc., who believes in and enforces strict discipline. The word comes from Gen. Jean Martinet, a French drillmaster in the seventeenth century who invented a new system of military drill.

maudlin excessively and tearfully emotional or sentimental. From Mary Magdalen, who is often depicted with her eyes swollen from weeping.

mausoleum a large, stately tomb. From King Mausolus of Caria, whose large tomb, erected by Queen Artemisia at Halicarnassus in Asia Minor about 350 B.C., was one of the Seven Wonders of the World.

maverick (1) an unbranded or orphaned animal, as a calf; (2) an unorthodox person. From Samuel A. Maverick, a nineteenth-century Texas lawyer who refused to brand his cattle.

nicotine a poisonous, oily alkaloid found in tobacco leaves. Named after Jean Nicot, the French courtier who introduced tobacco into France from Portugal in the sixteenth century.

pasteurize to destroy germs and check fermentation in milk, beer, wine, etc., by the use of high temperatures. The word comes from Louis Pasteur, the famous nineteenth-century French chemist and the father of modern bacteriology.

quisling a person who betrays his own country by helping an invader. Named after a Norwegian traitor, Vidkun Quisling, who collaborated with the Nazis and became a Nazi party leader during World War II.

shrapnel a kind of shell containing pieces of sharp metal that shoot out in all directions when the charge is exploded. Named after its inventor, Henry Shrapnel (1761–1842), an English artillery officer.

sideburns short side whiskers reaching from the hairline to below the ears. The word comes from *burnsides*—side whiskers and mustache, worn with the chin clean-shaven—named after the Civil War Union general, A. E. Burnside.

162

ROOT: TRACT-

The important Latin root *tract-* means "to drag; draw; pull." Learn the eleven core vocabulary words based on the root *tract-: attract, contract, detract, distract, extract, protract, retract, subtract, tract, traction, tractor.*

attract comes from the Latin prefix *at-* (another spelling of *ad-*) meaning "to; toward" and *tract-* meaning "to draw; pull." Thus, *attract* means (1) to draw something or someone to or toward oneself, as by magnetism; (2) to gain the admiration or attention of someone.

> *A magnet will attract iron.*
> *The candle flame attracted several moths.*
> *The baby cried to attract attention.*

Two words based on *attract* are *attraction* and *attractive. Attraction* means (1) the act or power of attracting; (2) a characteristic or feature that attracts. *Attractive* means "having the quality of drawing interest or affection; pleasing."

> *Things fall downward because of the attraction of the earth's gravity.*
> *The dolphin's intelligence was its chief attraction.*
> *What is the main attraction at the local theater?*
> *The store's bargain prices were attractive.*
> *The Siamese cat has an attractive face.*

contract comes from the Latin prefix *con-* meaning "together" and *tract-* meaning "to draw; pull." Thus, *contract* [kən·trakt′] means (1) to draw together; to shrink or become more compact; (2) to cause something to draw together; (3) to take on or become affected with, as a debt or a disease; (4) to make a legal agreement. A *contract* [kon′trakt] is "a legal agreement that draws together two people or parties."

> *The pupils of his eyes contracted in the bright light.*
> *Cold contracts metals.*
> *Mr. Vernon contracted large debts in his business.*
> *He contracted pneumonia.*
> *The construction company contracted to build the new school.*
> *The lawyer drew up a contract for his clients.*

Three words based on *contract* are *contraction, contractor,* and *contractual. Contraction* means (1) a drawing or pulling together; a shrinkage or reduction; (2) a shortened form of a word. *Contractor* means "a person who makes a contract, especially one who agrees to supply certain materials or to perform a job for an agreed price." *Contractual* means "of or concerning a contract."

Cold causes the contraction of liquids.
The word can't *is a contraction of* cannot.
Mr. Smith is a building contractor.
The business partners trusted each other so much that they did not have a contractual agreement.

detract comes from the Latin prefix *de-* meaning "away" and *tract-* meaning "to draw." Thus, *detract* means "to draw or take away a part of something, as part of one's good reputation, enjoyment, etc."

His laziness detracts from his efficiency.
The rainy weather detracted from our enjoyment of the scenery.

Two words based on *detract* are *detractor,* meaning "a person who defames or disparages another"; and *detraction,* meaning "a taking away of something, such as someone's good reputation; slander."

He has always been one of the mayor's greatest detractors.
He stood firm, despite the detractions of his critics.

distract comes from the Latin prefix *dis-* meaning "away" and *tract-* meaning "to draw." Thus, *distract* means (1) to draw away or divert the mind, attention, etc., in a different direction; (2) to bewilder.

He went to a movie to distract his mind from his worries.
The speed and roar of the traffic distracted the student driver.

Two words based on *distract* are *distracted* and *distraction. Distracted* means (1) bewildered; confused; preoccupied with worry; (2) insane. *Distraction* means (1) a drawing away of the mind from an object or from cares; (2) anything that distracts, as a diversion or interruption; (3) extreme mental distress.

He was in a distracted, anxious frame of mind.
He tries to avoid distractions such as telephone calls.
A trip to the beach offered a welcome distraction for the children.
The earsplitting noise of the drill is driving us to distraction.

NOTE: Another word having almost the same meaning as *distracted* is *distraught*. Though it is spelled differently, *distraught* comes from the same Latin word as *distracted*. *Distraught* means "deeply agitated in mind; worried, tense, and bewildered."

Millie was distraught until her missing child was found.

extract comes from the Latin prefix *ex-* meaning "out" and *tract-* meaning "to draw; pull." Thus, *extract* [ig·strakt′] means (1) to draw or pull out; (2) to obtain something from a substance by squeezing it, distilling it, etc.; (3) to obtain or draw out pleasure, knowledge, a promise, etc., from something or someone; (4) to copy out information from a book. An *extract* [eks′trakt] is "anything drawn out of a thing or substance, as a passage or quotation copied out of a book or a preparation containing the essence of a substance in concentrated form."

The dentist extracted the bad tooth.
He extracted a big gold watch from his pocket.
This machine extracts juice from oranges.
Did you extract a promise of payment from the customer?
Dr. Lindon extracted a verse from the Bible for his sermon.
He read an extract from the Old Testament.
Don't forget to buy some vanilla extract.

A word based on *extract* is *extraction*, meaning (1) a drawing or pulling out of something; (2) a person's national origin or line of descent; ancestry.

The dentist charged $100 for the extraction of the wisdom tooth.
Mr. McLean is of Scottish extraction.

protract comes from the Latin prefix *pro-* meaning "forward" and *tract-* meaning "to draw." Thus, *protract* means "to draw forward in time"; hence, "to extend for a longer time than was expected; prolong."

The meeting should not be protracted beyond 5:00 P.M.

Two words based on *protract* are *protraction*, meaning "the act of prolonging something; an extension"; and *protractor*, meaning "an instrument for measuring and laying out angles."

The heated argument caused a protraction of the meeting.
A protractor is used in geometry.

retract comes from the Latin prefix *re-* meaning "back" and *tract-* meaning "to draw; pull." Thus, *retract* means (1) to draw and take something back, such as a remark, statement, promise, etc.; (2) to draw back in, as a cat draws in its claws.

He retracted the insult and apologized.
The landing gear retracted into the fuselage of the airplane.

Two words based on *retract* are *retractable*, or *retractible*, meaning "able to be taken back or drawn back in"; and *retraction*, meaning "a taking back of something, especially something said or written."

Are the wheels of all airplanes retractable?
He published a retraction of his unsupported accusations.

subtract comes from the Latin prefix *sub-* meaning "beneath; away from; under" and *tract-* meaning "to draw." Thus, *subtract* means "to take away from something by deducting a quantity, number, etc."

He subtracted the expenses from the profits.

A word based on *subtract* is *subtraction*, meaning "the act or process of taking a quantity, number, etc., away from something."

Addition and subtraction are taught in elementary school.

tract comes directly from the root *tract-* meaning "to draw." The word *tract* means (1) an extended area, as of land or water; (2) an extensive region of the body, especially a system of parts or organs. It can also mean "a short written discussion on some subject, especially a pamphlet on politics or religion."

This tract of land is about ten acres.
Food is digested in the alimentary tract.
Alexander Hamilton wrote a number of political tracts.

traction comes from *tract-* meaning "to draw; pull" and the Latin suffix *-ion* meaning "the act or result of." Thus, *traction* means (1) the act or result of a pulling force; (2) a pulling force itself; (3) the state or condition of being subject to a pulling force; (4) the ability to grip and move on a surface without slipping.

The broken leg was placed in traction to keep the parts of the fractured bone in place.
Trains used to be powered by steam traction.
It is hard for tires to get good traction on an icy road.

tractor comes from *tract-* meaning "to draw; pull; drag" and the Latin suffix *-or* meaning "a thing that does." Thus, a *tractor* is "a thing that pulls or draws something"; hence, "a vehicle used for pulling a piece of farm equipment, a trailer, etc."

QUICKIEQUIZQUICKIEQUIZQUICKIEQUIZQUICKIEQUIZQUICKIEQUIZQUICKIEQUIZQUICKIE

90-SECOND QUICKIE QUIZ
TEN MORE WORD BUILDING BLOCKS

Knowing the meaning of the roots that make up words can help you to define them. Can you match these word elements with their meanings? Answers follow.

1. **mono-** as in monocle [mon′ə·kəl]	(a) sleep
2. **gam-** as in monogamy [mə·nog′ə·mē]	(b) writing
3. **matri-** as in matriarchy [mā′trē·är′kē]	(c) woman
4. **hydro-** as in hydroelectric [hī′drō·i·lek′trik]	(d) one
5. **-graphy** as in photography [fə·tog′rə·fē]	(e) image
6. **mega-** as in megaphone [meg′ə·fōn]	(f) water
7. **gyn-** as in gynecologist [gī′nə·kol′ə·jist]	(g) mother
8. **icon-** as in iconoclast [ī·kon′ə·klast]	(h) marriage
9. **omni-** as in omnipotent [om·nip′ə·tənt]	(i) great
10. **hypno-** as in hypnosis [hip·nō′sis]	(j) all

ANSWERS:

1. **mono-** —(d) one. A monocle is an eyeglass for one eye.
2. **gam-** —(d) marriage. Monogamy is the practice of having only one marriage, or one husband or wife, at a time.
3. **matri-** —(g) mother. A matriarchy is a tribe, race, or family of which a woman is the head.
4. **hydro-** —(f) water. Hydroelectric refers to electricity generated by the energy of water, as a hydroelectric plant located near a dam or on a river.
5. **-graphy**—(b) writing. Photography literally means "writing with light."
6. **mega-** —(i) great. A megaphone is a funnel-shaped device for amplifying sound.
7. **gyn-** —(c) woman. A gynecologist is a doctor who specializes in diseases peculiar to women.
8. **icon-** —(e) image. An iconoclast seeks to destroy conventions and cherished beliefs (literally, to destroy the use of images in religious worship).
9. **omni-** —(j) all. Omnipotent means all-powerful; almighty.
10. **hypno-** —(a) sleep. Hypnosis is a trancelike condition resembling sleep.

QUICKIEQUIZQUICKIEQUIZQUICKIEQUIZQUICKIEQUIZQUICKIEQUIZQUICKIEQUIZQUICKIE

ROOT: VEN-, VENT-

The Latin root *ven-* or *vent-* means "to move toward; come." Learn the seven core vocabulary words based on *ven-* or *vent-*: *adventure, circumvent, convene, convenient, event, invent, prevent.*

adventure comes from the Latin prefix *ad-* meaning "to" and *ven-* meaning "to come" plus the Latin suffix *-ure* meaning "the act or state of." *Adventure* literally means "that which is about to come upon, or happen to, someone." Thus, *adventure* means "a thrilling experience; a risky or daring undertaking."

> *Huckleberry Finn's great adventure was a trip down the Mississippi on a raft.*

Two words based on *adventure* are *adventurer*, meaning "a person who takes part in adventures or who seeks them"; and *adventurous*, meaning "liking to seek adventures or take risks."

> *Explorers are all adventurers.*
> *Astronauts are adventurous.*

circumvent comes from the Latin prefix *circum-* meaning "around" and *vent-* meaning "to come." Thus, *circumvent* means (1) to come around or get around something; (2) to avoid something, especially by using one's wits.

> *Many modern highways circumvent large towns.*
> *Don't try to circumvent the law!*

convene comes from the Latin prefix *con-* meaning "together" and *ven-* meaning "to come." Thus, *convene* means "to call or come together; assemble."

> *The President convened an emergency session of Congress.*
> *The committee convened every Monday.*

Four words based on *convene* are *convent, convention, conventional,* and *unconventional. Convent* means (1) an assembly or community of nuns; (2) the building in which nuns live. *Convention* means (1) an assembly of delegates or members, meeting for political, professional, or other purposes; (2) a custom or rule that is generally followed by a group or by society as a whole. *Conventional* means (1) growing out of or following custom, established by general agreement; (2) lacking originality. *Unconventional* means "not following custom, tradition, or established rules."

> *Having chosen the religious life, she entered the convent.*
> *Where did the Elks' convention meet?*
> *According to convention, men wear coats and ties in business offices.*
> *An S.O.S. is a conventional signal for help.*
> *It is a rather dull, conventional movie, in which boy meets girl.*
> *Her teaching methods were unconventional but effective.*

convenient comes from the Latin prefix *con-* meaning "together" and *ven-* meaning "to come" plus the Latin suffix *-ient,* which is the same as our English ending *-ing.* Thus, *convenient* means (1) coming or fitting together so as to be proper or easy for a person; suited to what one needs; (2) within easy reach; handy.

> *Let's discuss this matter at a more convenient time.*
> *The house is in a convenient location for shopping.*

Two words based on *convenient* are *inconvenient* and *convenience.* *Inconvenient* means (1) not suitable for one's needs; troublesome; (2) not within easy reach; not handy. *Convenience* means (1) the quality of being suited to one's needs; (2) comfort; ease; (3) something that increases comfort or saves work, effort, or trouble.

> *The kitchen is poorly planned and inconvenient.*
> *It would be inconvenient for me to meet you for lunch.*
> *I'd like to discuss the matter with you at your convenience.*
> *A swimming pool was provided for the convenience of the guests.*
> *We don't really need a car, but it would be a convenience.*

event comes from the Latin prefix *e-* (another spelling of *ex-*) meaning "out" and *vent-* meaning "to come." Thus, *event* means (1) something that takes place; a situation or happening; (2) one of the items or "happenings" on a sports program.

> *He is interested in reading about historical events.*
> *The main event was the fight for the heavyweight championship.*

Four words based on *event* are *eventful,* meaning "marked by important events"; *eventual,* meaning "happening in the due course of

INCREASE YOUR WORD POWER

time"; *eventuality,* meaning "a possible happening, situation, or out-come"; and *eventually,* meaning "finally; in due course."

> *The 1960s was an eventful decade.*
> *Their eventual victory made up for past defeats.*
> *If he keeps trying, he will eventually succeed.*
> *If you travel alone in the jungle, you must be prepared for any eventuality.*

invent comes from the Latin prefix *in-* meaning "on" and *vent-* meaning "to come." *Invent* literally means "to come on or come upon some-thing." Hence, *invent* means "to think up or make something new; originate or create; make something up."

> *Edison invented the incandescent bulb.*
> *The author has invented some interesting characters in this book.*
> *Did you invent an excuse for your absence?*

Three words based on *invent* are *invention, inventive,* and *inventor.* *Invention* means (1) that which is invented or made up; (2) the act of inventing something. *Inventive* means (1) good at inventing things; (2) showing the power of invention. *Inventor* means "a person who invents something."

> *How many of Edison's inventions can you name?*
> *That story Donna told was pure invention.*
> *The invention of the airplane revolutionized transportation.*
> *She has an inventive mind.*
> *This is a very inventive solution to the problem.*
> *Thomas Edison was a famous American inventor.*

prevent comes from the Latin prefix *pre-* meaning "before" and *vent-* meaning "to come." Thus, *prevent* literally means "to make something come before something else in order to keep it from happening." Hence, *prevent* means "to keep something from happen-ing or to keep someone from doing something, by taking measures beforehand."

> *You can help prevent forest fires by dousing your campfire.*
> *A snowstorm prevented them from driving home.*
> *A poor vocabulary prevented him from getting ahead.*

Two words based on *prevent* are *prevention* and *preventive. Preven-tion* means (1) the act of preventing; (2) a hindrance. *Preventive* means "intended or serving to prevent or ward off harm, disease, etc."

The prevention of forest fires is necessary for the protection of wildlife.
A proper diet helps in the prevention of disease.
Vaccines are a form of preventive medicine.

◇ Look up the following words in your dictionary. Learn the meaning of each. Be sure you can relate each meaning to the root *ven-* or *vent-* meaning "to move toward; come."

    advent   intervene   venture   venturesome

ROOT: VERT-, VERS-

The Latin root *vert-* or *vers-* means "to turn." Learn the five core vocabulary words based on this root: *avert, convert, divert, reverse, subversive.*

avert comes from the Latin prefix *a-* (another spelling of *ab-*) meaning "away" and *vert-* meaning "to turn." Thus, *avert* means "to turn one's eyes or head away from something; to ward off a danger."

When he opened the furnace door, he averted his face.
He tried to avert the accident by slamming on his brakes.

A word based on *avert* is *aversion,* meaning "extreme dislike," literally, "that which makes one turn away."

She has an aversion to large crowds.

convert comes from the Latin prefix *con-* meaning "thoroughly; completely" and *vert-* meaning "to turn." Thus, *convert* [kən·vûrt′] means "to turn completely from one thing to another; change to another form, character, religion, etc.; transform." A *convert* [kon′vûrt] is "a person who changes his belief, especially his religious beliefs."

They converted the old barn into a summer house.
When I reached France, I had to convert my dollars to francs.
John Henry Newman converted to Catholicism.
Cardinal Newman was a Catholic convert.

171

Eight words based on *convert* are *conversant, conversation, conversational, conversationalist, converse, conversion, converter,* and *convertible. Conversant* means "familiar with." *Conversation* means "friendly talk or an exchange of ideas." *Conversational* means "having to do with or resembling conversation, especially informal conversation." *Conversationalist* means "a person who likes to talk or who is good at conversation." *Converse* means (1) to talk informally together; exchange ideas; (2) the opposite or "turned around" side of something; the contrary or reverse. *Conversion* means (1) the act of changing something into another form; (2) the act of changing to a new religion or way of thinking. *Converter* means "a person or thing that converts." *Convertible* means (1) capable of being converted or changed in character; (2) a convertible thing, especially an automobile with a folding top that can be lowered or raised.

> *He is conversant with many fields of study.*
> *We were having a conversation on politics.*
> *His style of writing is easy and conversational.*
> *He is too shy to be a good conversationalist.*
> *The old friends conversed late into the night.*
> *I believe that the converse of what he said is true.*
> *Extreme cold brings about the conversion of water into ice.*
> *Last year he experienced a conversion to Buddhism.*
> *A Bessemer converter is used to turn pig iron into steel.*
> *Checks are convertible into cash.*
> *Her father drives a sedan, and she drives a convertible.*

divert comes from the Latin prefix *di-* (another spelling of *dis-*) meaning "apart; in different directions" and *vert-* meaning "to turn." Thus, *divert* means (1) to turn in a different direction; turn aside from a set course; (2) to distract; (3) to entertain.

> *Traffic was diverted to a side road because of an accident.*
> *A loud noise diverted his attention from his book.*
> *The children were diverted by the puppet show.*

Three words based on *divert* are *diverse, diversion,* and *diversity. Diverse* means (1) marked by differences; not alike; (2) varied in kind or form. *Diversion* means (1) a turning aside; (2) an entertainment, amusement, or pleasant pastime. *Diversity* means (1) complete difference; (2) variety; multiplicity.

172

America is made up of people of diverse backgrounds.
His diverse interests range from baseball to classical music.
The dam caused a diversion of the river from its natural bed.
A visit to the zoo was a diversion for the children.
There was a diversity of opinions at the political convention.
Big cities offer a diversity of amusements.

reverse comes from the Latin prefix *re-* meaning "back" and *vers-* meaning "to turn." *Reverse* literally means "turned backward; having an opposite direction, character, etc." Hence, *reverse* means "to turn upside down, inside out, or in an opposite direction; set aside, overturn, or turn backward or to the rear." The *reverse* is "that which is directly opposite." A *reverse* means "a setback."

You may reverse this coat so that the fur is on the outside.
The Supreme Court reversed several lower court decisions.
He disagreed and took the reverse side of the argument.
The names were listed in reverse alphabetical order.
That is the reverse of the truth.
The business suffered reverses during the strike.

Four words based on *reverse* are *reversal, reversible, reversion,* and *revert. Reversal* means (1) the act of reversing; (2) something that is reversed; a setback. *Reversible* means "capable of being reversed." *Reversion* means "a return to a former condition, state, belief, practice, etc." *Revert* means "to go back to a former place, state, condition, etc."

Not getting the promotion was a major reversal in his career.
This raincoat is reversible—tan on one side and blue on the other.
After the war, industry underwent a reversion to peacetime products.
If the college does not use the money according to the will, the fund will revert to the family.

subversive comes from the Latin prefix *sub-* meaning "from beneath; up from under" and *vers-* meaning "to turn" plus the Latin suffix *-ive* meaning "tending to." Thus, *subversive* means "tending to overturn or overthrow something, especially a government, from its very foundations."

The British considered the Boston Tea Party a subversive act.

Two words based on *subversive* are *subversion,* meaning "the act of overthrowing something or the state of being overthrown"; and *subvert,* meaning "to overthrow from the very foundation."

> *Dictatorship is a subversion of the rights of the people.*
> *Discontented people tried to subvert the new government.*

◊ Look up the following words in your dictionary. Learn the meaning of each. Try to relate each meaning to the root *vert-* or *vers-* meaning "to turn."

controversy   irreversible   traverse

ROOT: VID-, VIS-

You probably own something whose name contains this root. Can you think of what it is? Did you think of a television set? If you did, you are right. The Latin root *vid-* or *vis-* appears in the word *television* and means "to see." Learn the five core vocabulary words based on the root *vid-* or *vis-: evident, provide, television, video, vision.*

evident comes from the Latin prefix *e-* (another spelling of *ex-*) meaning "out" and *vid-* meaning "to see," plus the Latin suffix *-ent,* which is the same as our English ending *-ing.* Thus, *evident* means "seeing something out in the open"; hence, "easily seen or recognized; clear."

> *It is evident that you are learning many new words.*
> *He was evidently in great pain.*

Two words based on *evident* are *self-evident,* meaning "requiring no proof of its truth; obvious in itself," and *evidence,* meaning "that which proves or disproves something; proof."

> *The thief was caught in the act; his guilt was self-evident.*
> *The evidence was overwhelming that the accused man was guilty.*
> *A gun was produced as evidence of the crime.*

provide comes from the Latin prefix *pro-* meaning "before" and *vid-* meaning "to see." Thus, *provide* literally means "to foresee"; hence,

174

(1) to prepare or supply beforehand; (2) to furnish necessary food, clothing, and shelter; support.

Who will provide the food for the picnic?
In case of your death, this life insurance policy will provide for your family.

Seven words based on *provide* are *provided, provider, providence, provident, provision, provisions,* and *provisional. Provided* means "if; depending on preparations or on expectations being fulfilled." A *provider* is "one who provides; especially, a person whose income supports a family." *Providence* means (1) concern for the future; foresight; (2) *spelled with a capital first letter* the care exercised by God over the universe. *Provident* means "preparing for future needs." *Provision* means (1) to supply with basic items or supplies of food; (2) the act of providing, or the state of being provided; (3) part of an agreement referring to one specific thing. *Provisions* are "supplies, especially of basic items of food." *Provisional* means "provided for a temporary need; adopted on a tentative basis or for lack of something permanent."

We'll have the picnic, provided the weather is good.
To feed their young, eagles must be good providers.
The Puritans trusted in Providence.
He was provident and saved most of his earnings.
Napoleon provisioned his army well.
The treaty had no provision for settling the disputed boundary between the two nations.
Have you bought the provisions for the camping trip?
The general raised a provisional army to fight the invaders.

television comes from the Greek root *tele-* meaning "far; at a distance" and the word *vision. Television* means "the transmission of visual images over a distance as a series of electrical impulses." It can also mean "the television broadcasting industry" or "a television receiver."

Television has replaced radio in popularity.
Last night there was an old movie on television.

A word based on *television* is *televise,* meaning "to send or receive by television."

The political conventions are usually televised.

video comes directly from a Latin word based on the root *vid-* meaning

"I see." In modern English, the adjective *video* means "the picture portion of television."

> *Television shows are filmed on video tape.*
> *How does the video news compare with newspaper and weekly magazine coverage?*
> *In our television set, the sound is good, but the video needs adjusting.*

vision comes from *vis-* meaning "to see" and the Latin suffix *-ion* meaning "the act, state, or result of." Thus, *vision* means (1) the sense of sight; (2) insight or imagination; (3) something seen as in a plan, dream, trance, etc.

> *She wears glasses to improve her vision.*
> *We need a man of vision to head the planning commission.*
> *He had a vision of owning a large ranch and raising cattle.*

Five words based on or related to *vision* are *visible, invisible, visionary, visual,* and *visualize. Visible* means (1) capable of being seen; (2) evident, obvious, or apparent. *Invisible* means "not capable of being seen." *Visionary* means (1) impractical or unreal; (2) a person who has visions of any kind, such as highly imaginative plans, unusual insight, dreams, trances, etc. *Visual* means "pertaining to, resulting from, or serving the sense of sight." *Visualize* means "to see in the mind; to form a mental image of something."

> *The camouflaged trucks were not visible from the airplane.*
> *The tramp had no visible means of support.*
> *A colorless gas such as oxygen is invisible.*
> *He lost money on several of his visionary schemes.*
> *Many Christian saints were visionaries.*
> *The school uses slides and movies as visual aids to learning.*
> *I can't visualize you as a lion hunter.*

◇ Look up the following words in your dictionary. You should know the meaning of each, but check to see how they are related to the root *vid-* or *vis-* meaning "to see."

advise	ill-advised	visibility
advisement	improvident	visit
adviser	proviso	visitation
advisory	visage	visitor

ROOT: VOC-, VOK-

The Latin root *voc-* or *vok-* means "voice" or "to call." Two simple words that you already know, *voice* and *vocal,* are based on this root. Learn the seven core vocabulary words based on *voc-* or *vok-*: *advocate, evoke, invoke, provoke, revoke, vocabulary, vocation.*

advocate comes from the Latin prefix *ad-* meaning "to" and *voc-* meaning "to call" plus the suffix *-ate,* which is used to form verbs. *Advocate* originally referred to someone who is "called to" another person in order to give assistance. Hence, to *advocate* [ad′və·kāt] means "to speak or write in favor of someone or something." An *advocate* [ad′və·kit] is "a person who pleads the cause of another or who defends a cause."

> *He advocates free speech.*
> *Dr. Smith is an advocate of strenuous exercise.*

evoke comes from the Latin prefix *e-* (another spelling of *ex-*) meaning "out" and *vok-* meaning "to call." Thus, *evoke* means (1) to call out or summon forth something, such as memories; (2) to produce a reaction, response, etc.

> *The writer evoked the days of his youth.*
> *His sarcastic letter evoked an angry reply.*

Two words based on *evoke* are *evocation,* meaning "the act of calling something forth, as memories," and *evocative,* meaning "tending to call something forth, as memories."

> *The author was praised for his moving evocation of a bygone era.*
> *He wrote an evocative description of his childhood.*

invoke comes from the Latin prefix *in-* meaning "on" and *vok-* meaning "to call." Thus, *invoke* means "to call upon someone or something, especially a spirit or god, for aid, protection, etc.; appeal to a law, power, etc., for aid or support; ask or call for something, especially a blessing."

> *The poet invoked the muses to inspire him.*
> *The accused man invoked the Fifth Amendment.*
> *The priest invoked God's blessing on the congregation.*

A word based on *invoke* is *invocation,* meaning "an appeal to a god, power, or other agent, for aid, protection, etc., especially a prayer said before and for a group."

The chaplain gave the invocation at the opening of Congress.

provoke comes from the Latin prefix *pro-* meaning "forward; forth" and *vok-* meaning "to call." Thus, *provoke* means (1) to call forth or arouse anger in someone; irritate; stir up; (2) to arouse or cause some action or reaction.

He was provoked by the waiter's lack of attention.
Their disagreement over politics provoked a serious quarrel.
His slip of the tongue provoked shouts of laughter.

Two words based on *provoke* are *provocation,* meaning "an act that causes anger or irritation; an act calling forth an angry response"; and *provocative,* meaning "calling forth anger or any strong feeling; irritating or stimulating."

He started the fight without provocation.
The country responded to the hostile nation's provocations by declaring war.
Did his provocative remarks really justify your hitting him?
The perfume had a provocative aroma.

revoke comes from the Latin prefix *re-* meaning "back" and *vok-* meaning "to call." Thus, *revoke* means "to make something void by calling it back or recalling it; cancel."

The captain revoked the soldier's weekend pass.
His driver's license was revoked because he had had several accidents.

Two words based on *revoke* are *irrevocable,* meaning "incapable of being repealed, changed, or canceled," and *revocation,* meaning "a repeal, reversal, or cancellation."

Once in writing, his decision to resign was irrevocable.
The past is irrevocable.
Drunken driving will result in the revocation of one's driver's license.

vocabulary comes from the Latin root *vocabul-* based on *voc-,* which means "a word," and *-ary* meaning "connected with." Thus, *vocabu-*

lary means "a list of words or phrases, especially one arranged alphabetically and including definitions or translations." It may also mean "all the words of a language," or "all the words known or used by a particular person or in a particular field."

The French vocabulary was printed in the back of the textbook.
The English vocabulary includes hundreds of thousands of words.
A scientific vocabulary includes many words from Greek.

NOTE: Remember these different meanings of vocabulary. Your vocabulary is made up of the words you know or use. The English vocabulary is made up of all the words that have been used by English writers and speakers. A foreign language vocabulary is compiled for the use of persons learning that language.

vocation comes from *voc-* meaning "to call" and the Latin suffix *-ation* meaning "the act or state of." *Vocation* literally means "the state of being called"; hence, "a calling; a regular occupation; one's main job or interest." *Vocation* may also refer to "fitness for a certain career, especially religious work."

He chose medicine as his vocation.
The student felt he had a vocation for the priesthood.

A word based on *vocation* is *vocational,* meaning "of or pertaining to a job or career."

He learned welding in a vocational school.
Most schools offer vocational guidance.

NOTE: *Avocation* is built on the prefix *a-* (a form of the prefix *ab-* meaning "away") and the word *vocation.* Literally, an *avocation* is something that takes or calls a person "away" from his occupation or main job or interest. Thus, an *avocation* is "a hobby or diversion; a secondary job or interest."

The doctor's vocation is medicine; his avocation is golf.

◊ Look up the following words in your dictionary. Learn the meaning of each. Try to relate each meaning to the root *voc-* or *vok-* meaning "voice" or "to call."

vocal	vocalize	vociferous
vocalist	vociferate	vox populi

179

ROOT: VOLV-, VOLUT-

The Latin root *volv-* or *volut-* means "to roll." Learn the four core vocabulary words based on this root: *evolve, involve, revolve, revolt.*

evolve comes from the Latin prefix *e-* (another spelling of *ex-*) meaning "out" and *volv-* meaning "to roll." Thus, *evolve* means (1) to roll out or unroll, hence: to unfold or expand; (2) to work out or develop something gradually; (3) to develop from a lower to a higher stage of organization; (4) to undergo the process of evolution.

> *He evolved a plan for increasing sales.*
> *Over the years, the small business evolved into a large corporation.*
> *The jet airliner has evolved from the Wright brothers' small airplane.*
> *Birds evolved from prehistoric reptiles.*

A word based on *evolve* is *evolution,* meaning "the process of developing from one state to another, usually slowly and by stages" or "anything that develops by such a process."

> *The evolution of the airplane is an example of technological development.*
> *The evolution of living things took place over millions of years.*

involve comes from the Latin prefix *in-* meaning "in" and *volv-* meaning "to roll." *Involve* literally means "to roll in or roll up." Thus, *involve* means (1) to include as a necessary part of something; (2) to take in or have an effect on; (3) to bring someone or something into trouble, difficulty, danger, etc.; (4) to take up the attention; engross.

> *Building a good vocabulary involves study.*
> *The depression involved almost everyone in the country.*
> *I don't want to get involved in your argument with him.*
> *The girl was completely involved in her work.*

Two words based on *involve* are *involved,* meaning "complicated; intricate," and *involvement,* meaning "an involving or being involved."

> *The directions he gave us were so involved that we were lost.*
> *They were having an involved scientific discussion.*
> *The nightclub owner's involvement with gangsters was well known.*

revolve comes from the Latin prefix *re-* meaning "back" and *volv-* meaning "to roll." *Revolve* literally means "to roll back to the starting point; roll around." Thus, *revolve* means (1) to move in a circle around a center; rotate; (2) to occur regularly again and again, as in cycles.

> *The earth revolves around the sun.*
> *Many large buildings have revolving doors.*
> *The whole movie revolved around the star.*
> *The seasons revolve every year.*

Three words based on *revolve* are *revolution, revolutionary, revolver.* *Revolution* means (1) the act or state of revolving; (2) the overthrow and replacement of a government, group, or system by its members; (3) any drastic change in something, as in a condition, plan, etc. *Revolutionary* means (1) a person who leads or joins a revolution or who brings about a drastic change; (2) of, pertaining to, or causing a revolution or drastic change. A *revolver* is "a hand gun having a revolving chamber to hold several cartridges."

> *One complete revolution of the earth around the sun takes 365 days.*
> *The American Revolution led to independence.*
> *The invention of the automobile caused a revolution in our way of life.*
> *Patrick Henry and George Washington were leading American revolutionaries.*
> *Henry Ford introduced the revolutionary idea of mass production into car manufacturing.*
> *Was the bullet fired from a pistol or from a revolver?*

revolt comes from the Latin prefix *re-* meaning "back" and the root *volt-*, which is based on *volv-* meaning "to roll." *Revolt* literally means "to roll back on or turn against." Thus, *revolt* as a verb means (1) to rise in rebellion against the constituted authority; (2) to disgust or repel. As a noun, *revolt* means (1) an uprising; a rebellion against authority; (2) the state of a person or persons who revolt.

> *The colonists revolted against taxation without representation.*
> *She was revolted by the strong smell of garlic.*
> *Troops were dispatched to put down an armed revolt.*
> *The nation was in revolt.*

181

REVIEW OF ROOTS

Here is another review test of roots and words you have already
learned. Choose the answer nearest in meaning to each of the key
words. Answers follow.

1. **ascribe** [ə·skrīb′]—(a) to attribute to a specific cause or source.
(b) to write down officially. (c)
to mark out the limits of; confine
within bounds. (d) to slander or
libel.
2. **circumscribe** [sûr′kəm·skrīb′]—
(a) to write down officially. (b)
to mark out the limits of; confine
within bounds. (c) to sail around
the world. (d) an accent mark
placed over certain vowels to
indicate their correct pronunciation.
3. **transcribe** [tran·skrīb′]—(a) to
write down officially. (b) to keep
a diary. (c) a person who can
speak or write many languages.
(d) to make a written copy, as
of a speech, lecture, shorthand
notes, etc.
4. **indescribable** [in′di·skrī′bə·bəl]
—(a) too good to be true. (b)
too complex or unusual to be described. (c) extremely beautiful.
(d) extremely ugly.
5. **postscript** [pōst′skript′]—(a)

money or checks sent through
the mail. (b) the opening or initial greeting beginning a letter.
(c) the closing or final line of a
letter. (d) a sentence or paragraph added to a letter after the
the writer's signature.
6. **obsession** [əb·sesh′ən]—(a) a
shadow, semidarkness, as at
dusk. (b) high regard; esteem.
(c) a persistent idea or emotion.
(d) an irrational scheme.
7. **sedate** [si·dāt′]—(a) old or old-
fashioned. (b) sickly or feeble.
(c) calm; quiet; composed. (d)
dignified; poised.
8. **sedative** [sed′ə·tiv]—(a) any
means of soothing distress or allaying pain. (b) a deep sleep.
(c) old or old-fashioned. (d)
sick or feeble.
9. **sedentary** [sed′ən·ter′ē]—(a) incapable of moving; stationary.
(b) a sleeping pill. (c) a layer
of silt or mud, as in a river. (d)
sitting; inactive.

ANSWERS:

1. **ascribe**—(a) to attribute to a specific cause or source. 2. **circumscribe**
—(b) to mark out the limits of; confine within bounds. 3. **transcribe**—(d) to
make a written copy, as of a speech, lecture, shorthand notes, etc. 4. **indescribable**—(b) too complex or unusual to be described. 5. **postscript**—(d) a
sentence or paragraph added to a letter after the writer's signature. 6. **obsession**—(c) a persistent idea or emotion. 7. **sedate**—(c) calm; quiet; composed. 8. **sedative**—(a) any means of soothing distress or allaying pain.
9. **sedentary**—(d) sitting; inactive.

2 PREFIXES—YOUR SECOND KEY TO WORD POWER

A prefix consists of a letter or group of letters placed before a root or word to alter its meaning. The word *prefix* is derived from two Latin words meaning "to place or attach before." Prefixes rank next in importance to roots as building blocks for a greater vocabulary.

Sometimes the same building block may seem to fit two different categories. For example, the Latin *bene-* meaning "good" is typically a prefix in position, being attached to the beginning of a word, as in *benefactor.* But *bene-* actually is, and functions as, a root, since it furnishes half the basic meaning of any word it forms. A *benefactor* is not simply "one who does something" but "one who does good." The same thing occurs in the related words *benefit, benediction,* and *benefice.* Hence, the fact that *bene-* looks like a prefix does not mean that we may not refer to it as a root.

The prefixes discussed in the following pages generally fall into one of four groups. The first is made up of mostly Latin and Greek words that have the meaning of English prepositions. Here are a few of them:

ante- (*before*), as in *antechamber,* meaning "a room coming before or leading into another room."

circum- (*around*), as in *circumvent,* meaning "to go around or to avoid."

com- (*with; together*), as in *combine,* meaning "to bring together in close union; blend; merge; unite."

intra- (*within; inside of*), as in *intramural,* meaning "situated or occurring within the limits of a city, building, organization, etc."

sub- (*under*), as in *substandard,* meaning "below the standard; lower than the established rate or requirement."

super- (*above in position; over*), as in *superstructure,* meaning "the parts of a ship's structure above the main deck."

ultra- (*on the other side of; beyond*), as in *ultramodern,* meaning "extremely modern."

The second group of prefixes serve to give a negative meaning to a word or to reverse and undo an action: *dis-* (as in *disease,* literally "a state of being not at ease; illness"); *in-* (as in *incapable,* meaning "not capable; not able to"); *mal-* (as in *malfunction,* meaning "a failure to function properly"); *mis-* (as in *misinform,* which means to "inform incorrectly; to give wrong information to"); *non-* (as in *nonflammable,* meaning "not flammable; not apt to catch on fire easily"); *un-* (as in *unbend,* which means to "become straight again or to relax").

The third group of prefixes have to do with amount, number, or degree: *ambi-* (as in *ambidextrous,* which means "able to use both hands equally well"); *bi-* (as in *bicuspid,* which means "having two points or cusps"); *hypo-* (as in *hypothyroidism,* meaning "a condition in which the thyroid gland is underactive"); *hyper-* (as in *hypercritical,* meaning "overly critical; excessively faultfinding").

The last group consists of common English words such as *extra-* (as in *extraordinary*), *out-* (as in *outspoken*), *over-* (as in *overweight*), and *under-* (as in *underprivileged*). Since these prefixes are perfectly familiar, you will have no difficulty in working out their meanings.

As you will see later, a number of prefixes have "disguises"—that is, their spelling changes before roots or words beginning with certain letters. This occurs in order to make pronunciation easier and more musical. For example, *sub-* meaning "under" becomes *sug-* in *suggest; com-* meaning "with" becomes *col-* in *collect.*

Let us try "taking apart" a few terms containing prefixes so that you can see how prefixes change the meaning of words or roots.

antisocial is made up of the prefix *anti-* meaning "against" plus the word *social* meaning (1) disposed to having friendly relations with persons living in a society; (2) having to do with society and the general good. Therefore, *antisocial* means (1) not friendly or outgoing; unsociable; (2) disruptive of society and the general good.

> *Hermits are generally considered antisocial.*
> *Robbery and assault are antisocial acts.*

refund comes from the Latin prefix *re-* meaning "again or back," plus the Latin root *fund-* meaning "to pour." Thus *refund* means "to pay back money." It also means "the money to be paid back."

> *We received a refund for our unused theater tickets.*

submerge comes from the Latin prefix *sub-* meaning "under" and the Latin root *merg-* one of whose meanings is "to plunge." Thus, *submerge* means "to plunge or dive under the surface of water."

> *The flood submerged all of the farmland in the area.*
> *With a flick of his tail, the porpoise submerged.*

unsound comes from the prefix *un-* meaning "not; opposed to," and the word *sound*, which means "healthy or strong." Therefore, *unsound* means "not strong, healthy, or solid; weak."

> *The platform was rickety and unsound.*
> *He was adjudged unsound of mind.*

The prefix section of *How to Increase Your Word Power* gives you 38 of the most common prefixes in English. You will enjoy testing your knowledge of prefixes in the vocabulary tests, called "Fun With Words," and the "Quickie Quizzes" that are included in many of the chapters. All of the tests relate to prefixes discussed in the preceding pages; many of them will also go on testing your knowledge of roots and of the special vocabularies that have appeared earlier in this book.

PREFIX: AB-, ABS-

The Latin prefix *ab-* or *abs-* means "off; away; from." Learn these ten core vocabulary words in which *ab-* appears: *abduct, abhor, abjure, abnormal, abort, absent, absolve, absorb, abstain, abuse.*

abduct comes from *ab-* meaning "away" and the root *-duct* meaning "to lead." Thus, *abduct* means "to lead or carry away wrongfully; to kidnap."

> *The kidnaper abducted the baby.*

abhor is formed from *ab-* meaning "from" and the Latin word *horrere* meaning "to shudder." Thus, *abhor* means "to hate or loathe."

> *Jane abhors spiders.*

A word based on *abhor* is *abhorrent*, meaning "hateful; disgusting."

> *Snakes are abhorrent to Mary.*

abjure derives from *ab-* meaning "away" and the Latin word *jurare* meaning "to swear." Thus, *abjure* means "to swear away an opinion or belief; to renounce or repudiate something under oath."

> *The convert abjured his old beliefs.*

185

abnormal stems from *ab-* meaning "away" or "from" and the Latin root *norm-* meaning "rule." Thus, *abnormal* means "unusual; irregular."

> *A bodily temperature of 102° F is abnormal.*

A word based on *abnormal* is *abnormality,* meaning (1) the condition of being abnormal; (2) an abnormal or unusual thing.

> *A harelip is a correctable abnormality.*

abort is formed from *ab-* meaning "away" or "from" and the Latin root *ort-* meaning "to be born." *Abort* means "to be born away from the right time"; hence, "to miscarry" or "to end something prematurely or unsuccessfully."

> *The mother cat aborted after being frightened by a dog.*
> *The space flight was aborted after only one orbit.*

Two words based on *abort* are *abortion,* which means "a miscarriage, especially one that is artificially induced," and *abortive,* meaning "coming to nothing; fruitless."

> *After many abortive attempts, they finally launched the boat.*

absent comes from *abs-* meaning "away" and a form of the Latin verb *esse* meaning "to be." As an adjective, *absent* [ab′sənt] means "away; not present." Thus, the verb *absent* [ab·sent′] means "to take or keep oneself away."

> *Many workers were absent because of sickness.*
> *Try not to absent yourself more than necessary.*

Two words based on *absent* are *absenteeism,* meaning "habitual or frequent absence," and *absent-minded,* meaning "inattentive to what is going on; forgetful."

> *Absenteeism has been a problem at the factory.*
> *Brian absent-mindedly wore bedroom slippers to the party.*

absolve is derived from *ab-* meaning "from" and the Latin word *solvere* meaning "to loosen." Thus, *absolve* means "to free from something, as guilt or a mistake; forgive or acquit."

> *The youth confessed his sins and was absolved.*
> *One motorist involved in the accident was absolved from blame.*

QUICKIE QUIZ
PREFIX AB-, ABS-

Here are ten more words beginning with the prefix *ab-, abs-*. Check the word or phrase you believe is closest in meaning to the key word. Answers follow.

1. **absolute** [ab′sə·lo͞ot]—(a) positive; certain. (b) cleansing. (c) sympathetic. (d) careless.
2. **abstracted** [ab·strak′tid]—(a) emotionally upset. (b) lost in thought. (c) scholarly. (d) faithful.
3. **abstemious** [ab·stē′mē·əs]—(a) squeamish. (b) dreary. (c) dignified. (d) eating and drinking sparingly.
4. **abstruse** [ab·stro͞os′]—(a) abundant. (b) hard to understand. (c) negligent. (d) official.
5. **abscess** [ab′ses]—(a) a leavetaking. (b) the act of cutting. (c) a collection of pus in the body. (d) rudeness.

6. **abrade** [ə·brād′]—(a) to scrape away. (b) to frighten. (c) to annoy. (d) to scold.
7. **abrogate** [ab′rə·gāt]—(a) to question. (b) to repeal, as a law. (c) to deprive. (d) to condense or abridge.
8. **abscond** [ab·skond′]—(a) to depart suddenly and secretly. (b) to steal. (c) to perjure. (d) to say farewell.
9. **abject** [ab′jekt]—(a) thrown aside. (b) miserable or despicable. (c) skillful. (d) exceptional.
10. **abstract** [ab·strakt′]—(a) used wrongly; misapplied. (b) forgiven. (c) theoretical; ideal. (d) traditional.

ANSWERS:

1. **absolute**—(a) positive; certain. 2. **abstracted**—(b) lost in thought. 3. **abstemious**—(d) eating and drinking sparingly. 4. **abstruse**—(b) hard to understand. 5. **abscess**—(c) a collection of pus in the body. 6. **abrade**—(a) to scrape away. 7. **abrogate**—(b) to repeal, as a law. 8. **abscond**—(a) to depart suddenly and secretly. 9. **abject**—(b) miserable or despicable. 10. **abstract**—(c) theoretical; ideal.

Two words based on *absolve* are *absolution*, which means "forgiveness; especially, pardon from sin"; and *absolute*, meaning (1) unlimited; unrestricted; (2) perfect or positive.

He was given absolution by the priest.
Catherine the Great reigned as an absolute monarch.
We are in absolute agreement.

absorb is made up of *ab-* meaning "from" and the Latin word *sorbere*

187

meaning "to suck in." Thus, *absorb* means "to suck or drink in something; to take up or swallow; to take over or occupy completely."

Sponges absorb water.
The nearby towns were eventually absorbed by the expanding city.
The student was absorbed in his work.

Two words based on *absorb* are *absorbent* and *absorption*. *Absorbent* means (1) absorbing or tending to absorb; (2) a substance that absorbs. *Absorption* means (1) the act of absorbing; (2) assimilation, as by incorporation or the digestive process; (3) preoccupation of the mind.

Cotton is used as an absorbent in surgical dressings.
Technology is improved through the absorption of new techniques.

abstain is formed from *ab-*, or in this case *abs-*, meaning "from" and *-tain*, which comes from the Latin word *tenere* meaning "to hold." Thus, *abstain* means "to hold away from; to choose not to do something."

She decided to abstain from eating meat.
Since I can vote neither for nor against the issue, I will abstain.

Two words based on *abstain* are *abstention*, meaning "a refraining or abstaining from something," and *abstinence*, meaning "the act or practice of abstaining, as from food, drink, etc.; self-denial."

There were three votes for, two against, and one abstention.
Not having smoked in a week, Jack boasted of his abstinence.

abuse derives from *ab-* meaning "away" and the Latin root *us-* meaning "to use." Thus, to *abuse* [ə·byōōz′] means "to use away from what is proper or right; misuse; mistreat; injure by speech or action." The noun *abuse* [ə·byōōs′] means "improper use; wrongful treatment; physical injury or verbal insults."

Do not abuse a friendship by asking too many favors.
If you abuse your privileges, they will be withdrawn.
Unlawful search is an abuse of police power.
The child had suffered abuse at the hands of his stepfather.

A word based on *abuse* is *abusive*, meaning "injurious or insulting."

He said that the man had used shocking and abusive language.

188

◊ The prefix *ab-* or *abs-* appears in many other words besides those listed above. Whenever you see an unfamiliar word beginning with *ab-* or *abs-*, remember that this prefix always means "away, off, or from." Sometimes, though, it may appear simply as *a-*, especially when it occurs before the letters *m, p,* or *v.* Now look up *avocation* in your dictionary. Note that this word is really *ab-* meaning "away from" plus the word *vocation.*

Look up the word *abscond* in your dictionary. Note that it comes from *abs-* meaning "away" and the Latin root *cond-* meaning "to hide or conceal." Thus, *abscond* means "to hide away"; hence, "to depart suddenly and secretly, especially in order to escape the law."

> *The thief absconded with the jewels.*

Other words beginning with the prefix *ab-* include:

abdicate	abominate	abstemious
aberrant	abrogate	abstract
abject	abscess	abstruse

PREFIX: AD-

The Latin prefix *ad-* means "to; toward; near; at." Learn the three core vocabulary words beginning with *ad-: adapt, adjacent, admire.*

adapt comes from *ad-* meaning "to" and the Latin root *apt-* meaning "to fit." Thus, *adapt* means "to fit for a new use; adjust."

> *The author adapted his novel for the stage.*
> *He adapted himself easily to his new job.*

NOTE: Do not confuse the words *adapt* and *adopt. Adopt* comes from *ad-* meaning "to" and the Latin root *opt-* meaning "to choose." Thus, *adopt* means (1) to choose or take a new relationship or a new course of action; (2) to take up from someone else and use as one's own, as an idea; (3) to vote to accept, as a motion or committee report.

> *The Wilsons adopted two baby boys.*
> *I've decided to adopt my wife's political views.*
> *We willingly adopted the chairman's recommendations.*

189

adjacent derives from *ad-* meaning "near; at" and the Latin root *jac-* meaning "to lie" plus the Latin suffix *-ent,* which is the same as the English ending *-ing.* Thus, *adjacent* means "lying or located near or next to something."

> *Alaska is adjacent to Canada.*

admire is formed from *ad-* meaning "at" and the Latin root *mir-* meaning "to wonder." Thus, *admire* means "to have esteem for."

> *They admired the courage of the astronauts.*

The following six words also use the prefix *ad-*. Study them and learn how the prefix enters into the meaning of the word.

addict a person who is enslaved by some habit, especially the use of narcotic drugs.

> *Drug addicts can be cured.*

address (1) to speak to; (2) to direct. As a noun, *address* means (1) a speech; (2) a place of residence.

> *The chairman addressed the club.*
> *She addressed the letter carefully.*
> *The President was preparing his inaugural address.*
> *What is your address?*

adhere (1) to stick; (2) to follow closely.

> *The tape will not adhere to this slick surface.*
> *We try to adhere to the principles of democracy.*

administer (1) to manage; (2) to apply or supply.

> *The President administers the government.*
> *The doctor administered the medicine to his patient.*

adore literally, to pray to or worship; hence, (1) to honor as divine; (2) to love or honor with great devotion.

> *Gandhi's followers adored him.*
> *George adores his wife.*

advice a view or opinion on what should be done.

> *You should follow the doctor's advice.*

The prefix *ad-* also has many disguises which you will learn next.

FROM A TO AB

The following words all begin with the letter *a* or the prefix *a-* or *ab-*, meaning "away" or "from." Check the word or phrase you believe is closest in meaning to the key word. Answers follow.

1. **adipose** [ad'ə·pōs]—(a) fatty. (b) well-balanced. (c) avoiding excess. (d) emaciated.
2. **aversion** [ə·vûr'zhən]—(a) bitterness. (b) intense dislike. (c) interpretation. (d) unwillingness.
3. **addle** [ad'l]—(a) to unravel. (b) to spread out. (c) to confuse or muddle. (d) to accuse.
4. **avocation** [av'ə·kā'shən]—(a) a side interest. (b) the pleading of a legal cause. (c) a cancellation. (d) a main occupation or calling.
5. **abductor** [ab·duk'tər]—(a) a leader. (b) the usurper of a throne. (c) a kidnaper. (d) part of an electric circuit.
6. **abnegation** [ab'nə·gā'shən]—(a) self-denial. (b) humiliation. (c) contradiction. (d) escape.
7. **abortive** [ə·bôr'tiv]—(a) contorted. (b) explosive. (c) enraged. (d) resulting in nothing.
8. **agrarian** [ə·grâr'ē·ən]—(a) pertaining to birds. (b) favorably inclined. (c) pertaining to land and agriculture. (d) causing fear.
9. **aberration** [ab'ə·rā'shən]—(a) a deviation from the normal course. (b) an illusion. (c) trembling. (d) a falsehood.
10. **abjure** [ab·jŏŏr']—(a) to denounce. (b) to take away a judicial decision. (c) to surrender. (d) to repudiate or renounce.
11. **abdicate** [ab'də·kāt]—(a) to give up formally. (b) to wander away. (c) to condense, as a novel. (d) to accompany.
12. **abstinence** [ab'stə·nəns]—(a) self-denial. (b) excessive use. (c) an eroding away. (d) self-righteousness.
13. **abrasive** [ə·brā'siv]—(a) unpleasant. (b) evasive. (c) harsh-sounding. (d) tending to wear away.
14. **albatross** [al'bə·trôs]—(a) a large sea bird. (b) a type of coal. (c) the white of an egg. (d) a chemical compound.
15. **amalgamate** [ə·mal'gə·māt]—(a) to gather. (b) to fill, as a tooth. (c) to astonish greatly. (d) to unite or combine.

ANSWERS:

1. **adipose**—(a) fatty. 2. **aversion**—(b) intense dislike. 3. **addle**—(c) to confuse or muddle. 4. **avocation**—(a) a side interest. 5. **abductor**—(c) a kidnaper. 6. **abnegation**—(a) self-denial. 7. **abortive**—(d) resulting in nothing. 8. **agrarian**—(c) pertaining to land and agriculture. 9. **aberration**—(a) a deviation from the normal course. 10. **abjure**—(d) to repudiate or renounce. 11. **abdicate**—(a) to give up formally. 12. **abstinence**—(a) self-denial. 13. **abrasive**—(d) tending to wear away. 14. **albatross**—(a) a large sea bird. 15. **amalgamate**—(d) to unite or combine.

PREFIX: AD- AND ITS DISGUISES

In the last section you learned that the Latin prefix *ad-* means "to; toward; near; at." This prefix appears in many disguises, with its last letter—*d*—changed in spelling to agree with the letter that follows it. This spelling change is natural; it happens simply because we pronounce the words in a certain way. For example, you would probably have trouble saying *adbreviate* instead of *abbreviate*. The *ad-* has been changed to *ab-* because it's easier and more natural to *say* the word that way.

Learn the ten core vocabulary words in which the last letter of the prefix *ad-* is changed to match the letter following it: *abbreviate, accord, affair, aggravate, alleviate, annex, appear, arrive, associate, attend.*

abbreviate is formed from the prefix *ad-* meaning "to" and the Latin root *breviat-* from *breviare* meaning "to shorten." Thus, *abbreviate* means "to shorten."

> *Mister is usually abbreviated "Mr."*

accord stems from *ad-* meaning "to; near" and the Latin root *cord-* meaning "heart." To *accord* originally meant "to be of one heart or mind." It now means (1) to agree or bring into agreement; (2) to grant in agreement with what is deserved. As a noun, *accord* means "agreement or harmony."

> *His views on the subject accord with mine.*
> *The general accorded the soldier the highest honors.*
> *Are our opinions in accord?*

Two words based on *accord* are *according* and *accordingly*. *According* means (1) as stated by; (2) in conformity with. *Accordingly* means (1) correspondingly; (2) consequently; so.

> *According to all reports, the world's population is still growing.*
> *They lined up according to height.*
> *He advised caution, and we acted accordingly.*
> *The fighters were eager; accordingly, they sprang forward at the sound of the bell.*

affair is formed from *ad-* meaning "to" and a French word that comes from the Latin root *fac-* meaning "to do; make." Thus, *affair* means

(1) anything done or made; (2) concern or business; (3) an event.

The raft was a crude affair.
My private life is not your affair.
The ambassador is busy with affairs of state.
The masked ball was quite an affair.

aggravate comes from *ad-* meaning "to" and the Latin root *grav-* meaning "heavy." *Aggravate* has come to mean "to make worse," and some people use it informally to mean "antagonize or irritate."

His business troubles were aggravated by his partner's death.

alleviate is formed from *ad-* meaning "to" and the Latin root *lev-* meaning "light." *Alleviate* literally means "to make lighter"; hence, "to make easier to bear; to relieve." Note that *aggravate* and *alleviate* are exactly opposite in meaning.

The medicine alleviated his pain, which exercise had aggravated.

annex stems from *ad-* meaning "to; at" and the Latin root *nex-* meaning "tied together." Thus, to *annex* [ə·neks'] means "to bind one thing to something else; to add or attach an additional part or area to another." An *annex* [an'eks] is "an addition to a building."

The large nation annexed its small neighbor.
The choir director's office is in the church annex.

appear comes from *ad-* meaning "to" and the Latin root *par-* meaning "to come forth." Thus, *appear* means "to come forth to the eye or mind; to come into view; to seem."

The sun appeared after the rain.
You appear to be busy.

Three words based on *appear* are *appearance, apparent,* and *apparition. Appearance* means (1) the act of appearing; a coming into view; (2) outward show or physical aspect. *Apparent* means (1) readily perceived or obvious; (2) seeming. *Apparition* means "something that seems to appear out of nowhere, as a phantom or ghost."

Though he is poor, he keeps up an appearance of wealth.
Cats generally take good care of their appearance.
His apparent boredom masked a keenly observant eye.
She looked so pale that I thought I was seeing an apparition.

arrive is made up of *ad-* meaning "to" and *-rive*, which comes from the Latin word *ripa* meaning "the shore." To *arrive* originally meant "to come to shore; to land." It long ago broadened in usage to mean "to reach a destination or goal."

> *The train arrived at the station on time.*
> *Helen's baby arrived at 3 A.M.*

associate stems from *ad-* meaning "to" and the Latin root *sociat-*, meaning "to join." Thus, to *associate* means "to join an idea or person to another or to bring or come into the company of others; to connect things mentally." An *associate* is "a companion or partner."

> *Don't associate with liars.*
> *We associate silk with China.*
> *The two men are business associates.*

A word based on *associate* is *association,* meaning (1) the act of associating or the state of being associates; (2) a group of people joined together; (3) the mental connection of two things or ideas.

> *The Robinsons belong to an association of homeowners.*
> *Do you make any association of silk with China?*

attend derives from *ad-* meaning "toward" and the Latin root *tend-* meaning "to stretch." Thus *attend* means (1) to stretch the mind toward or give attention to; (2) to be present at; (3) to go with, escort, accompany, or serve.

> *Did you attend to your duties?*
> *Are you going to attend the party?*
> *Two servants will attend the king.*

Two words based on *attend* are *attention* and *attentive. Attention* means (1) the concentrated direction of the mental powers; (2) care; (3) a soldier's position of readiness. *Attentive* means "thoughtful or considerate."

> *Pay attention!*
> *That cut on your hand needs attention.*
> *The soldiers stood at attention*
> *He is a very attentive husband.*

NOTE: The prefix *ad-* changes to *a-* before *sc, sp,* and *st,* as in *ascribe, aspect,* and *astringent.* It also changes to *ac-* before *q,* as in *acquire.*

194

Fun With Words

PREFIX AD- AND ITS DISGUISES

The words in the following list begin with *ad-* or one of several other prefixes that mean "to, toward, near, or at." Check the word or phrase you believe is closest in meaning to the key word. Answers follow.

1. **abeyance** [ə·bā′əns]—(a) suspension or temporary suppression. (b) discipline. (c) reduction in number. (d) low tide.
2. **abate** [ə·bāt′]—(a) to increase. (b) to suppress. (c) to tease. (d) to reduce or diminish.
3. **adroit** [ə·droit′]—(a) skillful. (b) a game resembling checkers. (c) temporary. (d) destructive.
4. **advent** [ad′vent]—(a) an increase in numbers. (b) an approach or arrival. (c) a salesman or merchant of small wares. (d) a departure.
5. **abut** [ə·but′]—(a) to carve. (b) to hammer out. (c) to border on. (d) to protrude.
6. **aspirant** [ə·spīr′ənt]—(a) one eager for advancement. (b) one who holds a high rank or position. (c) a low, crackly voice. (d) a deep, resonant voice.
7. **affirmation** [af′ər·mā′shən]—(a) a code of laws. (b) denial. (c) a solemn assertion. (d) graduation from a religious school.
8. **assignment** [ə·sīn′mənt]—(a) a conflict of interests. (b) a pro-cessional. (c) a secret meeting. (d) a fixed task.
9. **annulment** [ə·nul′mənt]—(a) an annual growth. (b) a careful measurement. (c) a destruction of the force or validity of something. (d) a faking of documents.
10. **affability** [af′ə·bil′ə·tē]—(a) sense of humor. (b) pretense. (c) sociability. (d) talkativeness.
11. **adage** [ad′ij]—(a) the total amount. (b) a wise elder. (c) a proverb handed down from the past. (d) a weight or mass.
12. **acquisition** [ak′wə·zish′ən]—(a) curiosity. (b) the act of obtaining. (c) a passive consent. (d) miserliness.
13. **aspersion** [ə·spûr′zhən]—(a) a distribution. (b) a compliment. (c) the act of diverting. (d) a slanderous remark.
14. **affront** [ə·frunt′]—(a) to advance abreast. (b) to offend purposely. (c) to bluff. (d) to display anger.

ANSWERS:

1. **abeyance**—(a) suspension or temporary suppression. 2. **abate**—(d) to reduce or diminish. 3. **adroit**—(a) skillful. 4. **advent**—(b) an approach or arrival. 5. **abut**—(c) to border on. 6. **aspirant**—(a) one eager for advancement. 7. **affirmation**—(c) a solemn assertion. 8. **assignment**—(d) a fixed task. 9. **annulment**—(c) a destruction of the force or validity of something. 10. **affability**—(c) sociability. 11. **adage**—(c) a proverb handed down from the past. 12. **acquisition**—(b) the act of obtaining. 13. **aspersion**—(d) a slanderous remark. 14. **affront**—(b) to offend purposely.

PREFIX: AMBI-

The prefix *ambi-* means "both; on both sides; around." Here are three words that are typical of the use of this prefix: *ambidextrous, ambiguous, ambitious.*

ambidextrous is formed from *ambi-* meaning "on both sides; both" and the word *dextrous,* a variant of *dexterous* meaning "skillful." Thus, *ambidextrous* means "able to use both hands with equal skill."

> *A switch hitter in baseball is an ambidextrous batter.*

ambiguous is derived from the Latin word *ambigere,* meaning to wander around, which comes in turn from *ambi-* meaning "around" and *agere* meaning "to go." *Ambiguous* means (1) having a double meaning; (2) doubtful or uncertain; (3) unclear, indistinct.

> *The ambiguous testimony of the witness did not help to clarify the case.*
> *Chemists will test this ambiguous substance to determine its composition.*
> *An ambiguous form loomed in the shadows.*

ambitious comes from *ambi-* meaning "around" and the Latin root *it-* meaning "to go" plus the Latin suffix *-ous* meaning "given to." *Ambitious* originally meant "given to going around and getting votes, as a politician does." Thus, *ambitious* means "eager to succeed or to achieve fame, power, wealth, etc.; having a high goal."

> *Ambitious people work hard.*
> *The state had an ambitious highway-development program.*

◇ Two words that you should look up in your dictionary and relate to the prefix *ambi-* are *ambience* and *ambivalence. Ambience* means "the overall atmosphere or mood of a situation, place, etc." *Ambivalence* means "the state of feeling or thinking two different things toward the same person or situation at the same time; the condition of feeling both love and hate, like and dislike, or other contradictory emotions."

> *The ambience of the little French restaurant delighted Ellen.*
> *His attitude toward his family was marked by ambivalence—love and loyalty warring with deep resentment.*

196

EXPLORING WORDS

As our most widely read book, and the basis of the Jewish and Christian religions, the Bible has given many words to the English language. Which of these words do you know?

Armageddon any great and decisive battle: from the name of the place where the Bible prophesies that the final battle between good and evil will be fought at the end of the world. *Revelation* 16:16.

calvary any great suffering: from the name sometimes associated with the hill where Christ was crucified; Golgotha. *Mark* 15:22.

Eden any delightful region or abode: from the Garden of Eden; Paradise. *Genesis* 2:8.

exodus a going forth or departure from a place or country by many people: from *The Exodus*, the departure of the Israelites from Egypt under the guidance of Moses, described in *Exodus*, the second book of the Old Testament. *Exodus* 13:18.

Gehenna any place of extreme torment or suffering; hell. Gehenna was the valley near Jerusalem where refuse was thrown and fires were kept burning to purify the air; in ancient times, it was likened to hell.

golden calf money or material goods as opposed to spiritual values: from the name of a molten image made by Aaron and worshiped by the Israelites. *Exodus* 32.

jeremiad a lament or tale of woe: from *Jeremiah,* a Judean prophet who lamented the ruin of Jerusalem.

Jezebel a bold, vicious woman: from the name of Ahab's wife, who was notorious for her evil actions. *I Kings* 16:31.

Judas a betrayer or traitor: from the name of the disciple of Christ who betrayed him with a kiss. *Matthew* 26:49.

magdalen a reformed prostitute: from Mary Magdalene, a penitent sinner whom Christ forgave. *Luke* 7:36–50.

pharisee a formal, sanctimonious, hypocritical person: from the name of an ancient Jewish sect that practiced strict observance of Mosaic law and religious ritual.

shibboleth password, watchword, pet phrase, or distinguishing custom. The word was used by Jephthah as a test word to distinguish his own men from the Ephraimites, who could not pronounce the *sh* sound. *Judges* 12:4–6.

widow's mite a small contribution given with good will by someone who is poor. This phrase refers to a poor woman whom Christ praised for her selfless spirit of giving. *Mark* 12:42.

PREFIXES: ANTE-, ANTI-

The prefixes *ante-* and *anti-* look somewhat alike and are usually pronounced alike. But their meanings are very different. Be sure that you learn the difference between *ante-* and *anti-*, since these prefixes appear in many words.

The Latin prefix *ante-* means "before" or "in front of." Here are five core vocabulary words beginning with *ante-: antebellum, antecede, antechamber, antedate, anteroom.*

antebellum comes directly from Latin and is made up of *ante-* meaning "before" and the Latin word *bellum* meaning "war." Thus, *antebellum* means "before the war." In the United States it often means "before the Civil War" or "made or done before the Civil War."

Many beautiful antebellum mansions still stand in the South.

antecede is formed from *ante-* meaning "before" and the Latin root *cede-* meaning "to go." Thus, *antecede* means "to go before, in time, rank, order, etc." This verb is seldom used, however. Much commoner is the form *antecedent,* which means (1) going before; (2) a person or thing that goes before in time.

World War II was antecedent to the Korean War.
They knew nothing of the stranger's antecedents (his ancestors or his early life).

antechamber derives from *ante-* meaning "before" and the word *chamber.* Thus, *antechamber* means "a chamber or room coming before or leading to another room."

The duke waited in the king's antechamber.

antedate comes from *ante-* meaning "before" and the word *date.* Thus, *antedate* means "to come or happen before something else."

Radio antedates television.

anteroom is formed from *ante-* meaning "before" and the word *room.* Thus, *anteroom* means "a room that leads to another room; a waiting room." *Anteroom* is a modern form of *antechamber.*

The patient waited in the doctor's anteroom.

The Greek prefix *anti-* means "against; opposed to." Learn these three core vocabulary words beginning with *anti-: antiaircraft, antidote, antipathy.*

antiaircraft is a common and obvious *anti-* word. It comes, of course, from *anti-* meaning "against" plus *aircraft.* This use of *anti-* meaning "for use as a weapon or defense against" is common, and we have *antisubmarine* warfare, *antitank* guns, *antiballistic* missiles, *antiwar* protests, etc.

antidote is formed from *anti-* meaning "against" and the Greek root *dot-* meaning "given." An *antidote* is literally "something given against something else." Thus, *antidote* means "anything that will counteract the effects of a poison or other evil."

What is the antidote for arsenic?
Work is a good antidote for self-pity.

antipathy derives from *anti-* meaning "against" and the Greek root *path-* meaning "to feel." An *antipathy* is "a feeling against someone or something; an instinctive dislike, or the object of such a dislike."

She had a strong antipathy for cats.

A word based on *antipathy* is *antipathetic,* meaning "naturally opposed" or "arousing instinctive dislike."

The climate of Ireland is antipathetic to the growth of roses.
Even harmless snakes are antipathetic to her.

◊ There are hundreds of other *anti-* words in English. For example:

antibiotic a substance "used against" or to arrest or destroy microorganisms that infect the body.

Penicillin is an antibiotic.

anticlimax a disappointing shift from something important, impressive, or moving to something petty or trivial.

The last chapter of detective novels is often an anticlimax.

antiseptic a substance used in order to prevent the growth of certain harmful bacteria.

You'd better put some antiseptic on that scratch.
Some people believe that antiseptic mouth washes prevent colds.

199

antitrust opposing or attacking trusts, cartels, or monopolies in business.

The government filed an antitrust suit in court.

Open your dictionary and see how many *anti-* words are listed. You should learn many of these words and be able to use them when necessary. Notice that many of the *anti-* words are simple and obvious: *anticommunist, antifreeze, antiknock, antiperspirant, antisocial, antislavery,* and *antitoxic.* Other *anti-* words are based on less obvious Greek and Latin roots, but *anti-* almost always means "against; opposed to." Your dictionary will give you all meanings and etymologies.

REMEMBER: The prefix *ante-* means "before; in front of," whereas *anti-* means "against; opposed to."

PREFIX: BI-

The Latin prefix *bi-* means "twice; doubly; occurring twice or having two." Here are seven core vocabulary words formed with the prefix *bi-*: *biannual, bicameral, bicycle, bigamy, bilateral, bilingual, binoculars.*

biannual comes from *bi-* meaning "occurring twice" and the word *annual* meaning "yearly." Thus, *biannual* means "occurring twice a year; semiannual."

Our club has a biannual meeting.

BEWARE: Look up the word *biennial* in your dictionary. This word is made up of exactly the same word-building parts as *biannual.* But notice the difference in meaning. Whereas *biannual* means "two times every year," *biennial* means "once every two years." Learn this difference.

bicameral comes from *bi-* meaning "having two" and the Latin word *camera* meaning "chamber" plus the Latin suffix *-al* meaning "of or pertaining to." Thus, *bicameral* means "consisting of two legislative chambers, houses, or branches."

The United States Congress is bicameral.

bicycle is the most obvious *bi-* word. It is made up of *bi-* meaning "having two" and the Greek root *cycl-* meaning "wheel." A *bicycle* is, literally, "a two-wheeled vehicle."

bigamy comes from *bi-* meaning "twice; doubly" and the Greek root *gam-* meaning "marriage." Thus, *bigamy* means "the act of being doubly married; the offense of being married to two wives or two husbands at the same time."

> *Bigamy is a crime in the United States.*

bilateral is formed from the prefix *bi-* meaning "having two" and the Latin *latus* meaning "side." Thus, *bilateral* means "having two sides; arranged symmetrically on two sides; binding on two parties (as an agreement)."

> *The Senator proposed a bilateral system of wage and price controls.*
> *Our biology teacher explained that starfish show radial symmetry, but animals and insects show bilateral symmetry.*
> *The two countries signed a bilateral disarmament pact.*

bilingual derives from the prefix *bi-* meaning "having two" and the Latin root *ling-*, which means "tongue." Thus, *bilingual* means "having two tongues; able to speak two languages with ease; in two languages."

> *Many people in Quebec, Canada, are bilingual; they speak both English and French.*
> *The bilingual edition of the magazine was in English and Spanish.*

binoculars comes from *bin-* (the form of the prefix *bi-* that is used before a vowel) meaning "having two" and the Latin root *ocular-* meaning "of the eyes." *Binoculars* are "telescopes or opera glasses that are made to be used with both eyes at once."

◊ There are numerous other important words based on *bi-* meaning "twice" or "having two." Look up the following words in your dictionary and learn their meanings:

bifocal	bimonthly	bipartisan
bifurcate	binomial	bipartite

BEWARE: Do not confuse the prefix *bi-* with the root *bio-*. *Bi-* means "twice" and *bio-* means "life." The two usually have nothing to do with each other in meaning.

PREFIX: CIRCUM-

The prefix *circum-* means "around; on all sides." Here are two typical words in which *circum-* appears: *circumambulate, circumlocution*.

circumambulate is formed from *circum-* meaning "around" and the word *ambulate* meaning "to walk." Thus, *circumambulate* means "to walk around; especially, to walk around an object as part of a religious ritual or as a form of worship."

> *The pilgrims circumambulated the holy shrine.*

circumlocution is formed from *circum-* meaning "around" and the word *locution* meaning "a phrase or saying; an expression." Thus, *circumlocution* means "an indirect, roundabout way of saying something."

> *The speech was full of ponderous circumlocutions.*

Learn the following seven words, all of which have the prefix *circum-*. You will already know several of them.

circumference (1) the boundary line of a circle or any closed curve; (2) the length of such a line or the distance around it.

> *The equator is the largest circumference that can be drawn around the earth.*

circumflex a mark written over a letter, to indicate pronunciation.

> *The letter "e" often has a circumflex over it in French, as in the word "fête."*

circumnavigate to sail around something, such as an island, the world, etc.

> *Magellan died before he could finish circumnavigating the globe.*

circumscribe (1) to draw a line around something; (2) to mark the limits of or restrict something.

> *The triangle was circumscribed by a circle.*
> *For months after John's illness, his activities were severely circumscribed.*

circumspect watchful in all directions, as for danger or error; being careful about one's reputation.

Politicians should be quite circumspect in their behavior.

circumstance a detail or factor that is part of a surrounding condition; a factor connected with an act, event, or condition.

Under what circumstances did you leave your last job?

circumvent (1) to "get around" or outwit; (2) to surround or trap, as an enemy.

It's foolhardy to try to circumvent the law.

PREFIX: COM- AND ITS DISGUISES

The prefix *com-* means "with; together; thoroughly." Like the prefix *ad-*, *com-* sometimes changes its spelling depending on the letters that follow it. Thus, *com-* may appear as *co-*, *col-*, *con-*, or *cor-*. Of these different spellings, *co-* is the most frequent and important.

Here are three typical words using *com-* or a variant of it: *combat, compatriot, concede.* Learn all the words in this section, and remember that all are based on the prefix *com-* meaning "with; together; thoroughly."

combat is derived from *com-* meaning "with" and the Latin root *bat-* meaning "to fight." Thus, to *combat* [kəm·bat′] means "to fight with; fight against; oppose in battle; resist." As a noun, *combat* [kom′bat] means "battle; fighting" or "a battle or fight."

We must combat disease with better health programs.
Did you see much combat during the war?

compatriot is formed from *com-* meaning "together" and the Latin word *patriota*, meaning "countryman." Thus, *compatriot* means "a fellow countryman."

I saw many of my compatriots in Europe last summer.

concede comes from *con-* meaning "thoroughly" and the Latin root

203

ced- meaning "to yield; withdraw." Thus, *concede* means "to yield thoroughly on some point; to admit; to give up or grant as a right or privilege."

> *After a long argument, Bob conceded that Jim was right.*
> *Even before the votes were counted, the Senator conceded the election to his opponent.*

The following words use the prefix *com-* or one of its variants. Study these words carefully and learn how the meaning of the prefix enters into the meaning of the word.

coequal (1) an equal of another person or thing; (2) equal with one another; of the same value, size, rank, etc.

> *All the lawyers were coequals in the firm.*
> *In the United States Senate, Rhode Island and Texas are coequal.*

coerce to force by means of intimidation, threats, authority, etc.

> *The racketeer coerced the businessman into paying a bribe.*

coeval belonging to the same age, time, or era.

> *The Aztec empire was coeval with the reign of Henry VIII.*

coexist to exist together at the same place or time.

> *Can democracy and communism coexist?*

cohere to stick or hold firmly together; be consistent.

> *This pie crust keeps crumbling; it doesn't cohere.*

cohort a companion or follower.

> *He and his cohorts started the brawl.*

collaborate to work with another person or group of persons.

> *The musician and the lyricist collaborate on writing songs.*
> *Quisling was accused of collaborating with the enemy.*

colleague a fellow member of a profession, organization, etc.

> *Dr. Martin and his colleagues worked hard during the epidemic.*

collide to come together with violent impact.

> *The two cars collided at the intersection.*

QUICKIE QUIZ
PREFIX COM-

Here are six more words beginning with the prefix *com-*. Check the word or phrase you believe is closest in meaning to the key word. Answers follow.

1. **complaisant** [kəm·plā′zənt]—(a) careless. (b) showing a desire to please, as by yielding. (c) not energetic or active. (d) immoral.
2. **compile** [kəm·pīl′]—(a) to compromise. (b) to store. (c) to bring together. (d) to force.
3. **compliance** [kəm·plī′əns]—(a) conformance or obedience. (b) solicitation. (c) faithfulness. (d) limitation.
4. **commendable** [kə·men′də·bəl]—(a) advisable. (b) tentative. (c) satisfactory. (d) praiseworthy.
5. **commotion** [kə·mō′shən]—(a) violent anger. (b) despair. (c) monotony. (d) excitement.
6. **complacent** [kəm·plā′sənt]—(a) sympathetic. (b) constantly complaining. (c) self-satisfied. (d) all-knowing.

ANSWERS:

1. **complaisant**—(b) showing a desire to please, as by yielding. 2. **compile**—(c) to bring together. 3. **compliance**—(a) conformance or obedience. 4. **commendable**—(d) praiseworthy. 5. **commotion**—(d) excitement. 6. **complacent**—(c) self-satisfied.

combine to bring or come together into a close union; blend; unite.

Combine the flour and milk before adding the eggs.
Oil and water won't combine.
Let's combine our efforts and get the work done.

commerce the exchange of materials, products, etc., especially on a large scale; trade.

Is there much commerce between Japan and Italy?

commit (1) to do; (2) to place someone or something in the trust of another; (3) to devote oneself to something.

The gangster committed many crimes.
The murderer was committed to a hospital for the mentally ill.
I am committed to my ideals.

community (1) a group of people living together in one location, sub-

205

ject to the same laws, having similar interests, etc.; (2) any group united by a common characteristic or common interests.

Our small town is a pleasant community.
A university is a community of scholars.
The business community favors this law.

compact (1) pressed together; firmly united; made small or packed into a small space; (2) an agreement or contract.

A snowball must be compact if it's to be any good.
He bought a compact car.
France has a commercial compact with its former colonies.

compassion pity for the suffering of another; fellow feeling.

She feels genuine compassion for the old and infirm.

compatible capable of existing together; able to get along peacefully.

Your ideas are not compatible with mine.
To have a happy marriage, a couple must be compatible.

compel (1) to force or urge irresistibly; (2) to obtain by force.

The general was compelled to surrender.
Duty compels me to go.
They compelled a confession at gunpoint.

compete to take part in a contest.

He will compete in the broad jump.

complete (1) having all needed parts; lacking nothing; (2) to add a needed part or parts to; to finish.

I'm going to order the complete dinner.
John completed the painting job the landlord had started.

complex [kəm·pleks′] having many related parts; complicated or intricate. As a noun, *complex* [kom′pleks] means "an intricate whole made up of many different but related parts."

Computers are complex machines.
This is a complex problem.
The manufacturing complex covered fifty acres.

composition (1) a putting together of different parts, ingredients, etc.,

206

to form a whole; (2) a whole formed in this way; (3) a written theme, essay, or piece of music.

This flooring is a composition of cork and wood fibers.
The student's composition was entitled "How I Spent the Summer."

compress (1) to condense; (2) to press together or into a smaller space. As a noun *compress* means "a cloth used to apply cold, heat, or pressure to a part of the body."

Compress this report into two pages.
The machine compresses cotton into bales.
Louise placed a compress on the cut.

concave hollow and curving inward. The opposite of *concave* is *convex*, meaning "curving outward."

The old man had a concave chest.
A baseball has a convex surface.

confide (1) to trust with one's secrets; (2) to reveal something in trust.

I asked Cathy to confide in me, and she confided that she was going to elope.

congregate to come together in a crowd; assemble.

The passers-by congregated around the shouting man.

correspond (1) to be in agreement; (2) to be similar in character; (3) to exchange letters with another person.

Your version of the accident corresponds with mine.
The claws of a cat correspond to the nails of a person.
We've been corresponding for fifteen years.

◊ How many additional words can you build from the words listed above? If you now know what *coerce* means, can you use *coercion* in a sentence? You have learned *coexist;* what does *coexistence* mean? Does the word *collaborate* remind you of *collaborator?* How many words can you build from *cohere, collide, combine, commit?* What does *compassionate* mean? *Incompatible? Competitor? Congregation? Correspondence?*

Many, many more words begin with the prefix *com-* or one of its variants. You will find scores of them in your dictionary. How many are familiar to you?

TOGETHERNESS WORDS

Here are twelve words beginning with the prefix *con-*, meaning "with; together; thoroughly." Check the word or phrase you believe is closest in meaning to the key word. Answers follow.

1. **conclave** [kon′klāv]—(a) a secret council. (b) a church law. (c) any body of people meeting in council. (d) one of the sustaining arches of a cathedral.

2. **concomitant** [kon·kom′ə·tənt]— (a) an agreeable friend. (b) something that accompanies or attends. (c) a contestant. (d) a collaborator.

3. **concurrent** [kən·kûr′ənt]—(a) happening in sequence. (b) meeting by accident. (c) unexpected. (d) occurring or acting together.

4. **congenital** [kən·jen′ə·təl]—(a) idiotic. (b) natural, as though from birth. (c) diseased. (d) prolific.

5. **contrite** [kən·trīt′]—(a) penitent. (b) accompanying. (c) hackneyed. (d) irritable.

6. **conjoin** [kən·join′]—(a) to be awkward. (b) to follow. (c) to unite. (d) to distort.

7. **concordant** [kon·kôr′dənt]—(a) harmonious. (b) following one after another. (c) occurring together. (d) combative.

8. **connotation** [kon′ə·tā′shən]— (a) earnest thought. (b) notes added by way of explanation. (c) an implied, additional meaning of a word. (d) the direct, basic meaning of a word.

9. **conviviality** [kən·viv′ē·al′ə·tē]— (a) foolishness. (b) sociability or good fellowship. (c) superficiality. (d) wit and lightheartedness.

10. **consanguinity** [kon′sang·gwin′ə· tē]—(a) a succession of mutually dependent events. (b) friendship. (c) a simultaneous occurrence. (d) blood relationship.

11. **conglomerate** [kən·glom′ər·it]— (a) pertaining to the total. (b) inherent. (c) a cluster or collection of various parts or materials. (d) gluey.

12. **convocation** [kon′vō·kā′shən]— (a) a speech. (b) an opening prayer. (c) an agreement. (d) a meeting.

ANSWERS:

1. **conclave**—(a) a secret council. 2. **concomitant**—(b) something that accompanies or attends. 3. **concurrent**—(d) occurring or acting together. 4. **congenital**—(b) natural, as though from birth. 5. **contrite**—(a) penitent. 6. **conjoin**—(c) to unite. 7. **concordant**—(a) harmonious. 8. **connotation**—(c) an implied, additional meaning of a word. 9. **conviviality**—(b) sociability or good fellowship. 10. **consanguinity**—(d) blood relationship. 11. **conglomerate**—(c) a cluster or collection of various parts or materials. 12. **convocation**—(d) a meeting.

PREFIX: CONTRA-, COUNTER-

The prefix *contra-* or *counter-* means "against; opposite; contrary; opposing." Here are two typical *contra-, counter-* words: *contraband, counterclockwise.*

contraband comes from *contra-* meaning "against" and the root *band-*, which goes back to a Latin word meaning "law." Thus, *contraband* means "articles brought into a country against the law; smuggled articles." It also means "the act of smuggling."

> *The customs agents seized $500,000 worth of contraband goods.*
> *To engage in contraband is to defy international law.*

counterclockwise comes from *counter-* meaning "opposite" and the word *clockwise* meaning "in the direction taken by the hands of a clock; in a circle, from left to right." Thus, *counterclockwise* means "opposite to the direction taken by the hands of a clock; in a circle from right to left."

> *Most horse races are run counterclockwise around the track.*

Other words using *contra-* or *counter-* include:

contraceptive (1) used against conception, to prevent pregnancy; (2) a device or medicine for preventing conception.

contradict (1) to say the opposite, or to maintain the opposite of a statement; (2) to be inconsistent with.

counterattack an attack made against and in answer to an enemy's attack.

counterbalance to oppose something with an equal weight or force.

counterespionage measures taken against enemy spying; operations and measures carried out by intelligence agents or spies against enemy spying.

counterfeit (1) to make an imitation of money, stamps, a feeling, etc., with the intent to defraud or mislead; (2) false; fraudulent; feigned; pretended; (3) a false imitation or copy.

counterpart someone or something closely resembling another person or thing in a different or "opposite" country, firm, region, etc.

counterpoise (1) to bring to a balance by opposing with an equal weight or force. (2) a counterbalancing weight.

countersign to sign a document already signed by another person in order to establish the authenticity of the first signature; to sign "against" another's signature as proof of its authenticity.

counterstatement a statement opposing or denying another statement.

There are many more words using the prefix *contra-* or *counter-*. Look them up in your dictionary. How many of them can you define?

PREFIX: DE-

The prefix *de-* means (1) away; off; (2) down; a lessening; (3) completely; (4) undoing or reversal of an action. Here are four typical words that make use of *de-: debar, debark, declare, dehumidify.*

debar comes from *de-* meaning "away; off" and the word *bar* meaning "to shut." Thus, *debar* means "to shut out; to exclude."

He was debarred from club membership because of the scandal.

debark is derived from *de-* meaning "away; off" and the old word *bark* meaning "a ship." Thus, *debark* means "to go away from, or off, a ship; to put something off a ship; to go ashore; to unload."

The ship docked at noon and we debarked immediately.

declare is formed from *de-* meaning "completely" and the Latin root *clar-* meaning "to make clear." Thus, *declare* means "to make completely clear"; hence, "to say something emphatically; to reveal or prove."

He declared that he was completely innocent.
The judges declared Sam the winner of the race.

dehumidify is made up of *de-* meaning "the reversal of an action" and the word *humidify* meaning "to make humid." Thus, *dehumidify* means "to make less humid."

An air conditioner both cools and dehumidifies the air.

Learn the following words that begin with the prefix *de-:*

decentralize to reorganize into smaller parts away from the center of something.

decipher (1) to break down a code or coded message; (2) to determine the meaning of something that is hard to read, such as a code or cipher, bad handwriting, etc.

declaim to speak loudly and in a set, formal way.

decline (1) to bend downward; (2) to sink downward or fail, as in health; (3) to turn down or refuse.

decrease (1) to grow less or smaller; (2) to take away a part, quantity, rank, etc.

defend to turn away injury, danger, etc.; to shield from danger; to protect.

defer (1) to put off or delay; (2) to yield to someone else's opinion.

deflect to turn something away; to swerve.

deform (1) to distort the form of something; (2) to mar the beauty of something or someone.

deliver (1) to set free from something; (2) to hand over; to carry and distribute; (3) to give or send forth.

demote to bring down or lower in rank.

deplete (1) to reduce a supply of something, as by use, waste, etc.; (2) to empty completely.

depopulate to take away the inhabitants of a place, as by death, war, disaster, etc.

depreciate (1) to lessen the value of; take away value from; (2) to become less valuable; lose value.

descend (1) to go or come down; (2) to lower oneself; (3) to be derived by heredity.

detract to take away a part of something; to lessen.

Many, many other words begin with the prefix *de-*. Look in your dictionary for words beginning with the prefix *de-*. How many of them do you know?

PREFIX DE-

The fifteen words below begin with the prefix *de-*, which can mean "away, off, down, a lessening, or completely." Check the word or phrase you believe is closest in meaning to the key word. Answers follow.

1. **decant** [di·kant']—(a) to talk insincerely. (b) to narrate at great length. (c) to pour off gently. (d) to complain.
2. **depredate** [dep'rə·dāt]—(a) to express disapproval of. (b) to disparage. (c) to despoil or plunder. (d) to make humble statements.
3. **deduce** [di·do͞os']—(a) to influence. (b) to infer or conclude. (c) to persuade. (d) to lead on.
4. **demise** [di·mīz']—(a) modesty. (b) a plan. (c) death. (d) a legal oath.
5. **decadent** [dek'ə·dənt]—(a) evil. (b) a successor in office. (c) characterized by deterioration. (d) recently deceased.
6. **deterrent** [di·tûr'ənt]—(a) something that prevents or discourages. (b) a soap or cleansing agent. (c) a separation. (d) a heavy rainfall.
7. **delegate** [del'ə·gāt]—(a) to demote. (b) to give over authority to another. (c) to dismiss. (d) to point out.
8. **defile** [di·fīl']—(a) filth. (b) a

long, narrow pass. (c) a dry river bed. (d) the pattern of troops marching side by side.
9. **defunct** [di·fungkt']—(a) not working properly. (b) putrid. (c) cowardly. (d) dead.
10. **deprecate** [dep'rə·kāt]—(a) to argue. (b) to lose value. (c) to implore. (d) to express disapproval of or regret for.
11. **detraction** [di·trak'shən]—(a) mental distress. (b) something that diverts the attention. (c) defamation. (d) a mountain path.
12. **derision** [di·rizh'ən]—(a) origin. (b) failure in duty. (c) act of throwing into disorder. (d) ridicule or scorn.
13. **defray** [di·frā']—(a) to tear to tatters. (b) to postpone. (c) to pay. (d) to avoid.
14. **debase** [di·bās']—(a) to lower in character or quality. (b) to lighten in color. (c) to remove troops from. (d) to benefit from.
15. **declivity** [di·kliv'ə·tē]—(a) a crack in a glacier. (b) an unwillingness to continue. (c) loyalty. (d) a downward slope.

ANSWERS:

1. **decant**—(c) to pour off gently. 2. **depredate**—(c) to despoil or plunder. 3. **deduce**—(b) to infer or conclude. 4. **demise**—(c) death. 5. **decadent**—(c) characterized by deterioration. 6. **deterrent**—(a) something that prevents or discourages. 7. **delegate**—(b) to give over authority to another. 8. **defile**—(b) a long, narrow pass. 9. **defunct**—(d) dead. 10. **deprecate**—(d) to express disapproval of or regret for. 11. **detraction**—(c) defamation. 12. **derision**—(d) ridicule or scorn. 13. **defray**—(c) to pay. 14. **debase**—(a) to lower in character or quality. 15. **declivity**—(d) a downward slope.

PREFIX: DIS-, DI-, DIF-

The prefix *dis-*, *di-*, or *dif-* means (1) away from; apart; in different directions; (2) the reversal or undoing of an action; (3) not. The meaning of the prefix *dis-* is close to that of the prefix *de-*. The important difference is: The prefix *de-* most often has the meaning "down" (and the associated meanings of "less; making smaller or less important"), whereas *dis-* has the stronger negative meaning of "not."

Here are seven words formed with the prefix *dis-* or its variants, *dif-* or *di-*:

diffuse [di·fyo͞oz'] comes from *dif-* meaning "in different directions" and the Latin root *fus-* meaning "to pour." Thus, *diffuse* means "to pour or send out something so that it spreads in all directions." The adjective *diffuse* [di·fyo͞os'] means "widely spread out" or "wordy."

> *The cloud cover diffused the light of the sun.*
> *His argument lacked force because it was diffuse.*

disable derives from *dis-* meaning "not" and the word *able*. Thus, *disable* means "to make unable; to cripple."

> *He was disabled by the car accident.*

disconnect is made up of *dis-* meaning "the reversal or undoing of an action" and the word *connect*. Thus, *disconnect* means "to break the connection of, or between, things or persons."

> *Operator, we've been disconnected!*
> *He spoke in disconnected sentences.*

discontinue is formed from *dis-* meaning "not" and the word *continue*. Thus, *discontinue* means "to break off or cease from doing, using, producing, etc.; to stop."

> *They have discontinued publication of the paper.*
> *With regret the two men discontinued their friendship.*

dislocate is a combination of *dis-* meaning "away from; apart" and the word *locate*. Thus, *dislocate* means "to put something out of its proper place."

> *Thousands of flood victims were dislocated last spring.*
> *The quarterback dislocated his shoulder during the game.*

disloyal is derived from *dis-* meaning "not" and the word *loyal*. Thus, *disloyal* means "not loyal."

A disloyal general caused the downfall of the government.

divert is made up of *di-* meaning "away from; apart" and the Latin root *vert-* meaning "to turn." Thus, *divert* means (1) to turn aside, as from a set course; (2) to distract the attention of; (3) to amuse.

The dam diverted the river.
The clowns diverted the children.

Now that you know the seven preceding words, learn the following words beginning with *dis-:*

disarm (1) to take away the weapons of a person or nation; (2) to allay or reduce suspicion, antagonism, etc.

The Allies forced Germany to disarm.
She was frowning angrily, but her friend's smile disarmed her.

discomfit (1) to defeat someone's plans or purposes; (2) to throw into confusion.

A sudden hailstorm discomfited the picknickers.
The teacher's unexpected arrival discomfited the mischievous students.

discriminate (1) to act toward someone with partiality or prejudice; (2) to draw a clear distinction between things.

Many colleges used to discriminate against minorities.
A true critic can discriminate between good and bad art.

disfigure to mar or destroy the appearance of something.

Deep scratches disfigured the surface of the table.

dishearten to weaken someone's spirit or courage.

Two quick touchdowns by Yale disheartened the Princeton team.
News of the general's death disheartened the troops.

disintegrate (1) to destroy the wholeness of something; (2) to become reduced to fragments.

Heat disintegrates many substances.
The sand castle was disintegrated by the waves.

dismantle (1) to strip something of its furniture or equipment; (2) to take apart.

Movers dismantled the apartment efficiently.

The maintenance crew dismantled the plane's engines for inspection.

disorient to confuse someone's sense of direction or perspective.

Heavy fog disoriented the ship's navigator.

disown to refuse to acknowledge or admit responsibility for something or someone.

The firm disowned any role in causing the disastrous warehouse fire.

dissect (1) to cut apart, as a plant or a dead animal in a laboratory, in order to examine the structure; (2) to analyze in detail.

Our biology class dissected frogs last week.
A good debater can dissect his opponent's argument.

disseminate to scatter something far and wide, as if sowing, especially ideas, knowledge, etc.

dissipate (1) to drive away or dispel; (2) to spend wastefully or squander.

Gusts of wind quickly dissipated the smoke.
The young playboy dissipated his father's fortune in gambling and entertaining lavishly.

dissuade to persuade someone not to do something.

Can't I dissuade you from eating so much candy?

◊ How many words can you build from the above list? Knowing the meanings of these words, can you define the words below, which are built on them?

disarmament	disintegration	dissemination
discrimination	dissection	dissuasion

If you are in doubt about the meanings or uses of these additional words, look them up in your dictionary.

Many other words are built on the prefix *dis-*. Look them up in your dictionary. How many do you know?

NOTE: A knowledge of word building will also help you perfect your spelling. Knowing that the prefix *dis-* is added to *own* to form the word *disown*, you know why *disown* has only one *s*. Now, can you figure out why *dissect* and *dissuade* have two *s*'s?

PREFIX DIS-

These fifteen words begin with the prefix *dis-*, which has a variety of meanings: "apart; away from; not," etc. Check the word or phrase you believe is closest in meaning to the key word. Answers follow.

1. **dissonance**   [dis′ə·nəns]—(a) keen dislike. (b) harshness of sound. (c) immorality. (d) discouragement.
2. **dissemble** [di·sem′bəl]—(a) to scatter. (b) to conceal or disguise. (c) to unravel. (d) to be embarrassed.
3. **dispense** [dis·pens′]—(a) to end. (b) to disagree. (c) to distribute. (d) to solve quickly.
4. **disparate** [dis·par′ət *or* dis′par·it] —(a) dissimilar. (b) discouraged. (c) reckless. (d) insufficient.
5. **dispensation** [dis′pən·sā′shən]— (a) a delaying. (b) a special exemption from an obligation. (c) a surrender of power. (d) a scattering.
6. **disingenuous** [dis′in·jen′yo͞o·əs] —(a) clever. (b) innocent. (c) dumb. (d) not sincere.
7. **disconsolate** [dis·kon′sə·lit]—(a) disorganized. (b) shabby. (c) forlorn. (d) untrustworthy.
8. **disclaim** [dis·klām′]—(a) to deliver an oration. (b) to avoid a direct statement. (c) to shout out. (d) to deny connection with.
9. **disavow** [dis′ə·vou′]—(a) to swear to. (b) to denounce. (c) to disclaim. (d) to apologize.
10. **distend** [dis·tend′]—(a) to expand. (b) to care for. (c) to wander aimlessly. (d) to keep away from.
11. **disdain** [dis·dān′]—(a) to be proud. (b) to flatter. (c) to dislike. (d) to scorn.
12. **distraught** [dis·trôt′]—(a) greatly agitated. (b) instinctive. (c) gullible or easily influenced. (d) morally binding.
13. **dismantle** [dis·man′təl]—(a) to upset. (b) to disillusion. (c) to shatter. (d) to strip or take apart.
14. **disinter** [dis′in·tûr′]—(a) to exhume. (b) to spread apart. (c) to become less active. (d) to question thoroughly.
15. **disparity** [dis·par′ə·tē]—(a) unjust criticism. (b) dissimilarity. (c) discouragement. (d) distaste.

ANSWERS:

1. **dissonance**—(b) harshness of sound. 2. **dissemble**—(b) to conceal or disguise. 3. **dispense**—(c) to distribute. 4. **disparate**—(a) dissimilar. 5. **dispensation**—(b) a special exemption from an obligation. 6. **disingenuous**— (d) not sincere. 7. **disconsolate**—(c) forlorn. 8. **disclaim**—(d) to deny connection with. 9. **disavow**—(c) to disclaim. 10. **distend**—(a) to expand. 11. **disdain**—(d) to scorn. 12. **distraught**—(a) greatly agitated. 13. **dismantle** —(d) to strip or take apart. 14. **disinter**—(a) to exhume. 15. **disparity**— (b) dissimilarity.

PREFIX: EX- AND ITS DISGUISES

The prefix *ex-* and its disguises *e-* or *ef-* means (1) out, out of, or from; (2) former; (3) thoroughly or completely. Learn the following core words in which *ex-*, *e-*, or *ef-* appears:

effervesce is formed from *ef-* meaning "out" and the Latin root *fervesc-* meaning "to boil." Thus, *effervesce* means (1) to give off bubbles of gas, as carbonated drinks; (2) to be exhilarated or vivacious.

> *The soda water is stale and doesn't effervesce.*
> *Mary has an effervescent way of speaking.*

evade derives from *e-* meaning "out" and the Latin root *vad-* meaning "to go." Thus, *evade* means "to go or get out of something; hence, to avoid or escape."

> *The witness tried to evade the lawyer's question.*
> *You can circumvent the law, but you can't evade it forever.*

exclude is made up of *ex-* meaning "out" and the Latin root *clud-* meaning "to shut." Thus, *exclude* means "to shut someone or something out, as from a group or place."

> *His poor grade in math excluded him from the honor roll.*

excruciate comes from *ex-* meaning "completely; thoroughly" and the Latin root *cruciat-* meaning "to torture." Thus, *excruciate* means "to inflict extreme pain on someone; to rack with pain."

> *Walking was excruciatingly painful for the wounded man.*

exhume stems from *ex-* meaning "out of; from" and the Latin root *hum-* meaning "the ground." Thus, *exhume* means "to dig up a corpse or other buried thing."

> *The soldier's body was exhumed and shipped home after the war.*

Learn these additional words that use the prefix *ex-*, *e-*, or *ef-*:

excavate (1) to hollow or dig out; (2) to make a tunnel or hole by digging out the earth.

> *Indians excavated the cores of fallen trees to make dugout canoes.*
> *Blasting crews will excavate a tunnel under the Alps.*

217

excerpt a passage picked out from a book, speech, etc., and used or quoted separately.

Several newspapers printed excerpts from the president's memoirs.

excommunicate to cut someone off from membership in a church.

exhale (1) to breathe out; (2) to breathe something out, such as tobacco smoke.

exonerate to free someone from blame; to acquit.

The court completely exonerated the defendant from charges of negligence.

expedite to speed up the progress of something.

Our new computer has expedited the company's billing operation.

expire (1) to breathe out one's last breath; to die; (2) to come to an end, as a contract or license.

The old woman expired peacefully in her sleep.
I hope you'll renew my lease when it expires next year.

exterminate to destroy; to wipe out a living thing or things.

extinguish (1) to put out or quench, as a fire; (2) to wipe out.

extort to wrest money, etc., from a person by threats or violence.

extricate to free from entanglements or other difficulties.

◊ Make up a sentence using each of the words in the preceding list. Now let's see how many of the following words you can figure out.

evasive	exhortation	ex-president
excrescent	expel	exterminator
exhaust	expiration	extortion

Many, many other words begin with the prefix *ex-*. Check under *ex-* in your dictionary; see how many of these words you know. What additional *ex-* words are you going to learn by reading the definitions and etymologies?

Fun With Words

PREFIX EX- AND ITS DISGUISES

Here are fifteen words beginning with the prefix *ex-, e-,* or *ef-* meaning "out, out of, former, or thoroughly." Check the word or phrase you believe is closest in meaning to the key word. Answers follow.

1. **emanate** [em′ə·nāt]—(a) to conspire. (b) to experience. (c) to flow forth. (d) to embrace.
2. **excoriate** [ik·skôr′ē·āt]—(a) to wipe out. (b) to strip off the skin or cover of. (c) to make clean and bright by friction. (d) to expel from a church.
3. **extenuate** [ik·sten′yōō·āt]—(a) to stretch out. (b) to become inactive. (c) to obtain by force. (d) to excuse the faults of.
4. **exonerate** [ig·zon′ə·rāt]—(a) to praise. (b) to free from blame. (c) to elevate. (d) to accuse.
5. **evolve** [i·volv′]—(a) to work out or develop gradually. (b) to entangle. (c) to explain and make clear. (d) to transmit or hand down.
6. **exacerbate** [ig·zas′ər·bāt]—(a) to encourage. (b) to overstate. (c) to bring to a high polish. (d) to aggravate.
7. **emit** [i·mit′]—(a) to leave out. (b) to forget. (c) to give out. (d) to let in.
8. **evasive** [i·vā′siv]—(a) gentle.

ANSWERS:

(b) abrasive. (c) elusive. (d) fleeting.
9. **exaction** [ig·zak′shən]—(a) a demand or requirement. (b) an inspection. (c) exhilaration. (d) the process of development.
10. **elide** [i·līd′]—(a) to omit a vowel or syllable in pronunciation. (b) to slip or fall. (c) to escape detection. (d) to wear away or be used up.
11. **evince** [i·vins′]—(a) to conquer. (b) to carry away. (c) to delay. (d) to make evident.
12. **extirpate** [ek′stər·pāt]—(a) to root out or eradicate. (b) to disturb. (c) to make extra work for someone. (d) to raise in rank.
13. **efface** [i·fās′]—(a) to be smug about something. (b) to mask. (c) to be friendly toward. (d) to obliterate.
14. **effeminate** [i·fem′ə·nit]—(a) opposed to women. (b) exaggeratedly womanish. (c) harsh and disagreeable. (d) happy-go-lucky.
15. **egregious** [i·grē′jəs]—(a) conspicuously bad. (b) egg-shaped. (c) like a chant. (d) very poor.

1. **emanate**—(c) to flow forth. 2. **excoriate**—(b) to strip off the skin or cover of. 3. **extenuate**—(d) to excuse the faults of. 4. **exonerate**—(b) to free from blame. 5. **evolve**—(a) to work out or develop gradually. 6. **exacerbate**—(d) to aggravate. 7. **emit**—(c) to give out. 8. **evasive**—(c) elusive. 9. **exaction**—(a) a demand or requirement. 10. **elide**—(a) to omit a vowel or syllable in pronunciation. 11. **evince**—(d) to make evident. 12. **extirpate**—(a) to root out or eradicate. 13. **efface**—(d) to obliterate. 14. **effeminate**—(b) exaggeratedly womanish. 15. **egregious**—(a) conspicuously bad.

PREFIX: EXTRA-

The prefix *extra-* means "outside of; beyond or outside the range, scope, or limits of something." As a word *extra* is used to mean "being over and above what is required; additional."

Here are two core vocabulary words beginning with the prefix *extra-*: *extraordinary, extrasensory.*

extraordinary is made up of *extra-* meaning "outside of; beyond" and the word *ordinary*. Thus, *extraordinary* means "being beyond or out of the ordinary; exceptional or remarkable."

She showed extraordinary presence of mind during the emergency.

extrasensory derives from *extra-* meaning "beyond the scope or range of" and the word *sensory* meaning "having to do with sensation or the sense impulses." Thus, *extrasensory* means "beyond the range of normal sense perception; perceived by unknown or unexplained senses beyond the ordinary ones of touch, sight, hearing, etc."

Do you believe in extrasensory perception?

◊ What is meant by *extracurricular* activities? You will find many words beginning with *extra-* listed in your dictionary. Study them and learn the ones that seem most useful. Their meanings should be obvious if you know the meaning of the words to which *extra-* is prefixed.

PREFIX: HYPER-

The prefix *hyper-* means "over; excessive or excessively." Learn the following three core vocabulary words that begin with *hyper-*: *hyperacidity, hypercorrect, hypersensitive.*

hyperacidity is formed from *hyper-* meaning "excessive" and the word *acidity*. Thus, *hyperacidity* means "an excess of stomach acid."

hypercorrect comes from *hyper-* meaning "excessively" or "over" and the word *correct*. Thus, *hypercorrect* means "excessively correct or finicky, especially in regard to such things as manners, appearance, writing, speaking, etc."

A hypercorrect person can be hard to live with.

hypersensitive derives from *hyper-* meaning "over" or "excessively" and the word *sensitive.* Thus, *hypersensitive* means "excessively sensitive or touchy; too easily insulted, angered, disappointed, etc."

Nancy's skin is hypersensitive to chlorine.

◊ Look up the words listed under *hyper-* in your dictionary. How many of them can you define?

PREFIX: HYPO-

B̄elieve it or not, a hypodermic needle and the hypotenuse of a triangle are related. The prefix *hypo-* means "under or beneath; less than." Do not confuse *hypo-* and *hyper-;* they are almost opposite in meaning. *Hyper-* means "over"; *hypo-* means "under." So remember the two core vocabulary words beginning with the prefix *hypo-: hypodermic, hypotenuse.*

hypodermic is formed from *hypo-* meaning "beneath" and the Greek root *derm-* meaning "skin" plus the Latin suffix *-ic* meaning "pertaining to." Thus, *hypodermic* means "of or pertaining to the area under the skin." As a noun, *hypodermic* means "a syringe for giving under-the-skin injections."

> *The doctor used a disposable hypodermic needle to give me the flu shot.*

hypotenuse comes from *hypo-* meaning "under" and the Greek root *tenus-* meaning "stretching." Thus, *hypotenuse* means "the side of a right triangle that stretches under (or lies opposite) the right angle."

Now learn three more words that begin with the prefix *hypo-:*

hypochondria persistent anxiety about one's health. *Hypochondria* literally means "under the cartilage of the breastbone"; this spot was once thought to be the physical seat of morbidity.

hypothesis an assumption that lies beneath or supports a line of reasoning, and that is therefore accepted as a basis for investigation, argument, or further reasoning.

> *On the hypothesis that the world was round, Columbus hoped to reach the East Indies by sailing westward.*

hypothetical pertaining to or of the nature of a hypothesis; based on an assumption.

> *There is no longer anything hypothetical about our ability to reach the moon.*

PREFIX: IN- AND ITS DISGUISES

Like the prefix *ad-*, the prefix *in-* changes spelling depending on the letter that follows it. Thus, *in-* may also be spelled *em-*, *en-*, *il-*, *im-*, and *ir-*.

The prefix *in-* has two basic meanings: (1) not; without; un-; non-; (2) in; into; within. *In-* is one of the most important prefixes of the English language. It appears in hundreds of English words, many of which you know, but you may not know how the prefix *in-* always adds its own particular meaning. Study the following *in-* words carefully. Learn the six core vocabulary words beginning with *in-* (or one of its variants): *embrace, enclose, illiterate, imbalance, incarnate, irresistible.*

embrace is derived from *em-* meaning "in" and the root *brac-*, which comes from a Latin word meaning "arm." Thus, *embrace* means (1) to clasp in one's arms; (2) to accept a concept or belief willingly, as if by hugging it; (3) to include or contain. An *embrace* is, of course, "a hug."

> *Bob embraced Arlene at the airport.*
> *Why do you embrace all the new fads?*
> *This plan embraces the major ideas you suggested.*

NOTE: Now that you know that the root *brac-* comes from a Latin word meaning "arm," can you figure out the etymology of the word *bracelet?*

enclose is formed from *en-* meaning "in" and the root *clos-*, which

QUICKIE QUIZ
"NOT" WORDS

These ten words begin with the prefix *in-*, meaning "without" or "not." Check the word or phrase you believe is closest in meaning to the key word. Answers follow.

1. **intestate** [in·tes′tāt]—(a) sick. (b) between states. (c) having gone bankrupt. (d) not having made a valid will.
2. **inviolate** [in·vī′ə·lit]—(a) calm. (b) excited. (c) brutal. (d) pure.
3. **insatiable** [in·sā′shə·bəl]—(a) greedy. (b) insecure. (c) unsatisfactory. (d) hungry.
4. **invalidate** [in·val′ə·dāt]—(a) to marry secretly. (b) to annoy. (c) unheroic. (d) to make void.
5. **inexorable** [in·ek′sər·ə·bəl]—(a) formidable. (b) inexcusable. (c) cruel. (d) relentless.
6. **incongruous** [in·kong′grōō·əs]—(a) not logical. (b) out of place. (c) foolish. (d) debatable.
7. **incessant** [in·ses′ənt]—(a) continuing without interruption. (b) unbelievable. (c) not cautious. (d) incomplete.
8. **insufferable** [in·suf′ər·ə·bəl]—(a) unqualified. (b) shameful or horrifying. (c) not enough. (d) not to be endured.
9. **indemnity** [in·dem′nə·tē]—(a) a compensation for loss or damage. (b) to owe money to. (c) damaging evidence. (d) a trivial amount.
10. **indomitable** [in·dom′i·tə·bəl]—(a) not intelligent. (b) domineering. (c) arch-shaped. (d) not easily defeated.

ANSWERS:

1. **intestate**—(d) not having made a valid will. 2. **inviolate**—(d) pure. 3. **insatiable**—(a) greedy. 4. **invalidate**—(d) to make void. 5. **inexorable**—(d) relentless. 6. **incongruous**—(b) out of place. 7. **incessant**—(a) continuing without interruption. 8. **insufferable**—(d) not to be endured. 9. **indemnity**—(a) a compensation for loss or damage. 10. **indomitable**—(d) not easily defeated.

derives from a Latin word meaning "to shut." Thus, *enclose* means (1) to shut in on all sides; (2) to send something inside an envelope; (3) to contain.

He enclosed the yard with shrubs.
I enclose a check for $10.
Her clenched fist enclosed the coins.

illiterate comes from *il-* meaning "not" and the word *literate* meaning "able to read and write; educated." Thus, *illiterate* means "unable to read and write; uneducated." An *illiterate* is "a person who is unable to read and write." *Illiterate* is also used to describe incorrect language that shows a lack of education.

> *Twenty percent of the population are virtually illiterate.*
> *Can you imagine what it's like to be an illiterate?*
> *"Drownded" is an illiterate word.*

imbalance is formed from *im-* meaning "not; without" and the word *balance*. Thus, *imbalance* means "the state or condition of being out of balance; inequality."

> *There is an imbalance between our exports and imports.*

incarnate derives from *in-* meaning "in" and the root *carnat-*, which comes from a Latin verb meaning "to make flesh; to give a body to." Thus, to *incarnate* [in·kär′nāt] means "to give a bodily form to." As an adjective, *incarnate* [in·kär′nit] means "embodied in a human form."

> *He was the Devil incarnate!*

irresistible is made up of *ir-* meaning "not" and the word *resistible*. Thus, *irresistible* means "not capable of being resisted." Specifically, it may mean "fascinating or enchanting."

> *The criminal said he'd had an irresistible impulse to steal.*
> *The child's irresistible smile won me over.*

Learn these additional words that make use of the prefix *in-:*

inarticulate (1) said or expressed without distinct words, as a cry or yell; said incoherently; (2) unable to express oneself fully or understandably; (3) incapable of speech; dumb.

inconsequential having little or no importance.

inequitable not just; unfair.

infamous having a bad reputation; notoriously bad.

insatiable not capable of being satisfied; extremely greedy.

insuperable not to be overcome or surmounted.

◊ Make up a sentence using each of the above words. Look up the many other *in-* words in your dictionary and learn the definitions of those you have heard most often. While studying them, remember the two basic meanings of *in-:* (1) not; without; (2) in; into; within.

EXPLORING WORDS

English has constantly borrowed words and expressions from other languages. Learn the following foreign expressions, which are often used in American speech and writing.

ad hoc [ad hok′]—*Latin* pertaining to this (particular thing); designating a committee formed for a specific purpose in a specific situation.

aficionado [ə·fē′syō·nä′dō]—*Spanish* an enthusiast; a devotee, as a fan of bullfights.

à la carte [ä′ lə kärt′]—*French* by the menu: applied to a meal in which each item on the menu has a separate price, as opposed to a complete meal for an all-in-one price.

à la mode [ä′ lə mōd′]—*French* in the latest fashion; specifically, with ice cream on top (which was once a new way to serve pie and cake).

alter ego [ôl′tər ē′gō]—*Latin* a second self; a close friend; a confidant.

auf Wiedersehen [ouf vē′dər·zā′ən]—*German* till we meet again; good-by.

bona fide [bō′nə fīd′]—*Latin* in good faith; genuine.

canapé [kan′ə·pā]—*French* a small piece of bread or a cracker, spread with cheese, caviar, etc., usually eaten as an appetizer.

carte blanche [kärt′ blänsh′]—*French* unrestricted authority; permission to do whatever one wishes.

coup d'état [kōō′ dä·tä′]—*French* an unexpected stroke of policy; especially, a sudden seizure of government.

cul-de-sac [kul′də·sak′]—*French* a blind alley; a dead end.

de facto [dē fak′tō]—*Latin* existing in fact, with or without legal sanction.

en rapport [än rä·pôr′]—*French* in sympathetic relation or harmonious agreement.

e pluribus unum [ē plŏŏr′ə·bəs yōō′nəm]—*Latin* out of many, one: the motto of the United States (because it is one country made up of many states).

esprit de corps [es·prē′ də kôr′]—*French* a spirit of devotion to one's group and its goals.

PREFIX: INTER-

The prefix *inter-* means "among; between; with each other." Here are four core vocabulary words beginning with *inter-: interbreed, interfere, interject, interlude.*

interbreed is formed from *inter-* meaning "between; with each other" and the word *breed.* Thus, *interbreed* means "to breed different stocks of animals with each other; crossbreed; hybridize."

> *He stocked his farm by interbreeding Jersey and Guernsey cattle.*

interfere derives from *inter-* meaning "between" and the Latin root *fer-* meaning "to strike." Thus, *interfere* literally means "to strike (or come forcefully) between"; hence, "to get in the way; to take part in the affairs of others, especially when uninvited to do so; to meddle."

> *If you'll stop interfering, I'll finish the job faster.*

interject is made up of *inter-* meaning "between" and the Latin root *ject-,* which comes from a Latin verb meaning "to throw." Thus, *interject* means "to throw in a comment or a remark between other things; to introduce something abruptly."

> *I'd like to interject a few words before you go on.*

interlude comes from *inter-* meaning "between" and the Latin root *lud-* meaning "a play or game." *Interlude* originally meant "a short dramatic or comic act or a transitional piece of music performed between the acts of a play." Today, *interlude* also means "something that occurs in and divides up a longer, more important process; a feature that is put into a larger whole to break up the monotony; a short episode in one's life, history, etc."

> *Their love turned out to be only a brief interlude.*
> *The essay chapters of* Tom Jones *serve as interludes between the narrative portions.*

Here are some other important *inter-* words that you should learn:

intercept to seize or stop something or someone and prevent it or him from reaching a destination.

> *He intercepted the pass and ran for a touchdown.*

QUICKIE QUIZ
"IN" WORDS

The prefix *in-* sometimes means "in; into; within," as in the following ten words. Check the word or phrase you believe is closest in meaning to the key word. Answers follow.

1. **incarnate** [in·kär′nit]—(a) vulgar. (b) personified. (c) appearing again. (d) crimson.
2. **innate** [i·nāt′]—(a) inside. (b) inborn. (c) inhibited. (d) intimate.
3. **incarcerate** [in·kär′sə·rāt]—(a) to flay. (b) to visit scorn upon. (c) to imprison. (d) to forgive.
4. **incumbency** [in·kum′bən·sē]—(a) clumsiness. (b) ownership of possessions. (c) involvement in crime. (d) the holding of an office.
5. **inhibit** [in·hib′it]—(a) to set free. (b) to weaken. (c) to hinder or restrain. (d) to insist upon.
6. **ingratiate** [in·grā′shē·āt]—(a) to place oneself in a favorable position. (b) to cut into small pieces. (c) to be in debt to. (d) to act unkindly toward.
7. **infringe** [in·frinj′]—(a) to surround. (b) to decorate. (c) to limit. (d) to encroach.
8. **inherent** [in·hir′ənt]—(a) restrained. (b) possessive. (c) calm. (d) inborn or innate.
9. **incipient** [in·sip′ē·ənt]—(a) just beginning to appear. (b) maladjusted. (c) humble. (d) unthinking.
10. **incursion** [in·kûr′zhən]—(a) to swear at. (b) an invasion. (c) an agreement. (d) an exploration.

ANSWERS:

1. **incarnate**—(b) personified. 2. **innate**—(b) inborn. 3. **incarcerate**—(c) to imprison. 4. **incumbency**—(d) the holding of an office. 5. **inhibit**—(c) to hinder or restrain. 6. **ingratiate**—(a) to place oneself in a favorable position. 7. **infringe**—(d) to encroach. 8. **inherent**—(d) inborn or innate. 9. **incipient**—(a) just beginning to appear. 10. **incursion**—(b) an invasion.

intercollegiate involving two or more colleges, as in sports.

Intercollegiate baseball is less glamorous than football.

interdenominational of, for, or pertaining to two or more religious denominations.

There will be an interdenominational prayer meeting tonight.

interdependent dependent on each other.

intermezzo [in′tər·met′sō] (1) a short musical or dramatic offering given between the acts of a play or opera; (2) a short movement connecting the main parts of a long musical composition.

A melodious intermezzo precedes Act III of the opera Manon Lescaut.

internecine [in'tər·nē'sin] (1) destructive to both sides, as in a war; (2) of or pertaining to a divisive conflict within a group.

Both armies withdrew after the internecine battle.
A bitter internecine feud split the party into factions.

Many other words begin with the prefix *inter-*. Look under *inter-* in your dictionary to see how many words you know. Be sure to study the definitions and learn the words that you don't yet know.

PREFIX: INTRA-

What do an intramural football game and an intravenous injection have in common? What is the difference between intramural sports and intercollegiate sports? The Latin prefix *intra-* means "inside; within." Thus, *intra-* is opposed in meaning to both the prefix *extra-* meaning "outside; beyond" and the prefix *inter-* meaning "among; between."

Here are two core vocabulary words that begin with *intra-*: *intramural, intravenous.*

intramural is formed from *intra-* meaning "inside; within" and the word *mural* meaning "having to do with a wall or walls." Thus, *intramural* means "occurring within the walls or confines of one place, such as a city, organization, school, etc."

The coach scheduled an intramural football game between the freshmen and sophomores.

intravenous derives from *intra-* meaning "inside of" and the word *venous* meaning "of or having to do with a vein or veins." Thus, *intravenous* means "inside of or affecting the inside of a vein."

Have you ever had an intravenous injection?
The patient had to be fed intravenously.

◊ Several words beginning with the prefix *intra-* appear in your dictionary. Note that many of these are medical terms and have to do with internal medicine and parts of the body. Read the definitions for these words in your dictionary; learn any that you have heard frequently.

PREFIXES: MAL- or MALE- and MIS-

The prefix *mal-* or *male-* means "bad; ill; evil; wrong." Here are four typical words beginning with *mal-* or *male-*: *maladroit, malcontent, malediction, malignant.*

maladroit comes from the prefix *mal-* meaning "bad or badly" and the word *adroit* meaning "skillful or expert." Thus, a *maladroit* person is clumsy or lacking in skill. Something awkward can also be termed *maladroit*.

> *That waiter is so maladroit that he dropped the ashtray into my soup.*
> *The young man's maladroit remarks about the hostess embarrassed everyone at the party.*

malcontent is formed from *mal-* meaning "bad or badly" and the word *content*. Thus, *malcontent* means "barely content or not at all content with the existing state of things." A *malcontent* is "a discontented or dissatisfied person, especially a habitually discontented person."

> *Booth allied himself with a malcontent political faction.*
> *A group of malcontents tried to disrupt the meeting.*

malediction is made up of *male-* meaning "ill or evil" and the Latin root *dict-* meaning "to say or speak" plus the suffix *-ion* meaning "the act of." Thus, *malediction* means "the act of speaking ill"; hence, "a curse or slander."

> *Shylock heaped maledictions on the head of his daughter's lover.*

NOTE: *Malediction* is the opposite of *benediction,* meaning "the act of speaking well; a blessing." *Malediction* is pronounced [mal′ə·dik′shən]. Do not confuse the prefix *male-* [mal′ə] with the word *male.*

malignant comes from a Latin word based on *mal-* and meaning "to act maliciously or spitefully." Hence, *malignant* means "tending to produce or inflict evil; tending to do great harm; deadly."

A cancer is a malignant growth.

NOTE: *Malignant* is the opposite of *benign,* meaning "kindly" or "harmless." Two other words based on *mal-* or *male-* are *malnutrition* and *malefactor.* Can you figure out what they mean? Look them up in your dictionary.

The prefix *mis-* means (1) bad; badly; wrongly; (2) hating; hatred. Here are four words beginning with *mis-*: *misanthrope, misrepresent, misspell, mistake.*

misanthrope comes from *mis-* meaning "hating" and the Greek root *anthrop-* meaning "humanity." Thus, a *misanthrope* is "a person who hates humanity; one who hates or does not trust people."

misrepresent is formed from the prefix *mis-* meaning "wrongly" and the word *represent,* meaning "to symbolize, describe, or express." *Misrepresent* thus means "to represent something falsely or poorly."

> *Your salespeople misrepresented the terms of the warranty on my new car.*
> *Senator Smith's stand on the tax bill misrepresents the wishes of the voters in his state.*
> *Some misers misrepresent their wealth.*

misspell comes from *mis-* meaning "wrongly" and the word *spell.* Thus, *misspell* means "to spell a word or words incorrectly."

> *If you look up unfamiliar words, you won't misspell them.*

mistake comes from *mis-* meaning "wrongly" and the word *take.* *Mistake* literally means "to take (or understand) something wrongly." Hence, *mistake* means "to identify someone or something wrongly or to misinterpret." A *mistake* is "an error in action, judgment, knowledge, perception, understanding, etc."

> *I mistook you for someone else.*
> *Do not mistake silence for consent.*
> *Did you make any mistakes on the test?*

Other words you should learn that begin with *mis-* include *misapprehension, misnomer,* and *misunderstand.* Look up these words in your dictionary and relate the meaning of each to the prefix *mis-*.

PREFIXES MAL-, MALE-, MIS

Here are fourteen words beginning with the prefix *mal-, male-,* or *mis-,* which can mean "bad, ill, or wrong." Check the word or phrase you believe is closest in meaning to the key word. Answers follow.

1. **malodorous** [mal·ō′dər·əs]—(a) wicked. (b) musically pleasing. (c) ugly. (d) ill-smelling.
2. **malfeasance** [mal·fē′zəns]—(a) an illegal deed. (b) a failure. (c) a disappointment. (d) an unpleasant manner.
3. **misconstrue** [mis′kən·strōō′]— (a) to scatter about. (b) to be defeated. (c) to demolish. (d) to misunderstand.
4. **miscreant** [mis′krē·ənt]—(a) a slanderer. (b) an evildoer. (c) a misunderstood command. (d) an error.
5. **malcontent** [mal′kən·tent]—(a) unmixed. (b) playful. (c) dissatisfied. (d) incorrect.
6. **misdemeanor** [mis′di·mē′nər]— (a) a minor offense. (b) a doubting look. (c) bad luck. (d) a medley.
7. **misnomer** [mis·nō′mər]—(a) a wicked person. (b) a misrepresentation. (c) a wrong turn. (d) a name wrongly applied to someone or something.
8. **misconception** [mis′kən·sep′-shən]—(a) poor management.

(b) a false notion or idea. (c) failure to fertilize. (d) wicked thoughts.
9. **malediction** [mal′ə·dik′shən]— (a) a curse against someone. (b) an opening prayer. (c) a closing prayer. (d) an unintelligible speech.
10. **malefactor** [mal′ə·fak′tər]—(a) poor addition. (b) a miser. (c) a criminal. (d) to misunderstand.
11. **misapprehension** [mis′ap·ri·hen′-shən]—(a) fear or dread. (b) an illegal act. (c) misunderstanding. (d) an escape.
12. **malaise** [mal·āz′]—(a) uneasiness. (b) hatred. (c) discouragement. (d) acute pain.
13. **malevolent** [mə·lev′ə·lənt]—(a) extremely violent. (b) wishing evil toward others. (c) in poor voice. (d) insane.
14. **mishap** [mis′hap]—(a) poor behavior. (b) to do something incorrectly. (c) to tear down or destroy. (d) an unfortunate accident.

ANSWERS:

1. **malodorous**—(d) ill-smelling. 2. **malfeasance**—(a) an illegal deed. 3. **misconstrue**—(d) to misunderstand. 4. **miscreant**—(b) an evildoer. 5. **malcontent**—(c) dissatisfied. 6. **misdemeanor**—(a) a minor offense. 7. **misnomer**—(d) a name wrongly applied to someone or something. 8. **misconception**—(b) a false notion or idea. 9. **malediction**—(a) a curse against someone. 10. **malefactor**—(c) a criminal. 11. **misapprehension**—(c) misunderstanding. 12. **malaise**—(a) uneasiness. 13. **malevolent**—(b) wishing evil toward others. 14. **mishap**—(d) an unfortunate accident.

PREFIX: NON-

The Latin prefix *non-* means "not." *Non-* is one of the easiest of prefixes to learn, since it is a simple negative that behaves exactly like a minus sign; it negates the word that follows. Many other prefixes have a similar negative function— for example, *dis-*, *de-*, *in-*, and *un-*. However, these other negative prefixes have various other meanings as well, whereas *non-* means "not" and only "not."

Here are four core vocabulary words that show how *non-* is used: *nonchalant, nonconformist, nonentity, nonsense.*

nonchalant is a French word made up of *non-* meaning "not" and *chalant* meaning "to be warm; to be desirous." Thus, *nonchalant* means "showing a lack of interest or excitement; casually indifferent; self-confidently cool."

> *You take a very nonchalant attitude toward your work.*
> *Nonchalantly, unemotionally, he waited for the first question.*

nonconformist is formed from *non-* meaning "not" and the word *conformist* meaning "a person who follows conventional behavior." Thus, *nonconformist* means "a person who does not think or behave like most other people."

> *Many writers and artists are nonconformists.*
> *A Nonconformist is an English Protestant who refuses to conform to the Church of England.*

nonentity comes from *non-* meaning "not" and the word *entity* meaning "something that really exists; a real being." Thus, *nonentity* means "a mere nothing; a person or thing of very little account."

> *Tom brags about his work, but his boss considers him a nonentity.*

nonsense derives from *non-* meaning "not" and the word *sense*. Thus, *nonsense* means "anything that does not make sense; anything meaningless or absurd."

> *Tom's bragging is a lot of nonsense.*
> *Most children love nonsense rhymes.*

◊ How many words beginning with *non-* can you think of? There are literally hundreds of *non-* words listed in your dictionary. Look them up.

PREFIX: OB- AND ITS DISGUISES

The prefix *ob-* means "toward; to; against; completely; over." As in the case of *ad-* and *in-*, the spelling of this prefix may change depending on the letter that follows it. Thus, *ob-* may be spelled *oc-*, *of-*, or *op-*.

Here are six common words beginning with *ob-* or one of its variant spellings: *obese, object, obtrude, occupy, offend, oppress.* Start with these and then learn all the other words in this chapter.

obese comes from a Latin word meaning "fat," made up of *ob-* meaning "completely" or "over" and a verb meaning "to eat." Thus, *obese* means "fat from overeating; very fat."

> *That dog used to be only a bit overweight, but now it's obese.*

object is formed from *ob-* meaning "against" and the Latin root *ject-* meaning "to throw." Thus, to *object* [əb·jekt′] is "to throw criticism against something; to oppose something, especially with words." An *object* [ob′jikt] is literally "something thrown in the way." Hence, the noun *object* means (1) something that can be seen or touched; (2) something that is sought for; a purpose or goal.

> *Mr. Harris objected to the noise.*
> *They spotted an unidentified flying object.*
> *The object of the meeting was to elect a new president.*

obtrude comes from *ob-* meaning "against" or "toward" and the Latin root *trud-* meaning "to thrust." Thus, *obtrude* means "to force or thrust oneself, an opinion, etc., upon another person without being asked."

> *You shouldn't obtrude your beliefs into every conversation.*

occupy is derived from *oc-* (another spelling of *ob-*) meaning "against" and the root *-cupy*, which is related to the Latin root *cap-* meaning "to take." Thus, *occupy* means (1) to take and hold possession of something, as by force or conquest; (2) to hold or fill, as an office or post; (3) to keep oneself busy at doing something.

> *Germany occupied France during World War II.*
> *He occupied the mayor's office for four terms.*
> *Can't you find something worthwhile to occupy your mind?*

offend stems from *of-* (another spelling of *ob-*) meaning "against" and the Latin root *fend-* meaning "to hit." Thus, *offend* literally means "to hit against or collide with"; hence, (1) to displease or anger someone; (2) to be disagreeable to the sense of smell, sight, etc.; (3) to commit a crime or sin, or to err in some other way.

> *I'm sorry if I've offended you.*
> *The blaring music offended Sue's ears.*
> *Nonconformists often offend against the customs of society.*

oppress is derived from *op-* (another spelling of *ob-*) meaning "against" and the word *press*. Thus, *oppress* means (1) to press or lie heavily upon someone, as a burden; (2) to keep in subjugation by harsh use of force or authority.

> *The atmosphere of uncertainty oppressed our spirits.*
> *They were an oppressed people, enslaved by conquerors.*

Learn the following thirteen additional words beginning with the prefix *ob-* or its disguises.

obfuscate (1) to confuse or perplex; (2) to darken or obscure something.

obligate to bind or force someone, as with a contract, promise, etc., that necessitates some action, such as the return of a favor or the performance of a duty.

oblique not following the perpendicular or horizontal; slanting.

oblong longer in one direction than in another.

obnoxious highly disagreeable; objectionable.

obsolete out of fashion; no longer used or done.

obstacle that which stands in the way; a hindrance.

obstetrics the branch of medicine dealing with pregnancy and childbirth; literally, the branch of medicine that "stands by" during the process.

obstreperous noisy and unruly; literally, making noise "against" a speaker, someone in authority, etc.

obtuse not quick in mind or feeling; stupid.

occult pertaining to various magical arts or practices, such as astrology, alchemy, and witchcraft, which are "hidden against" the light of reason.

opportune timely or favorable; literally, blowing "toward port," as a ship or a favorable wind.

opprobrium (1) the state of being reproached or scorned; (2) reproach mingled with disdain.

◊ You should be able to build many words from the ones presented in this chapter. Remembering the definitions given above, how would you define the words below?

obesity	offensive	obligatory
occupant	oppressive	opportunity

FOUR NATIVE ENGLISH PREFIXES: ON-, OUT-, OVER-, UNDER-

Latin and Greek are not only the only languages that give us prefixes. English has its own set of native prefixes. These are often simple words we all know—such as the words *on, out, over,* and *under*—which we prefix to other words (roots) in order to form new words. This simple manufacturing process is exactly how words are made from Greek and Latin prefixes and roots. The difference is that you need to learn the meaning of Greek and Latin prefixes and roots, whereas you already know the English words used in word building.

Here are eleven words that illustrate the way we use our own English words *on, out, over,* and *under* as prefixes to form new words:

onset a start or attack; literally, "the starting on" of something.

I've been suffering from the onset of a cold.

onslaught a strong attack on someone or something.

The troops fought back an onslaught of enemy soldiers.

outermost farthest out; farthest away from the center.

The outermost of our states is Hawaii.

235

outset the beginning or start.

> *We were seasick from the very outset of the voyage.*

outside (1) the outer side, part, surface, etc.; (2) the space beyónd an enclosure; (3) being, acting, etc., beyond an enclosure, limit, etc.

> *The outside of the car was muddy.*
> *Sounds of music came from outside.*
> *Robin Hood's activities were outside the law.*

oversight failure to notice; an error caused by carelessness.

> *Because of an oversight, our baggage was left in the plane.*

overweight weighing more than normal.

> *No one should be more than ten pounds overweight.*

overwrought excessively worked up; overstrained.

> *Overwrought young mothers need time away from their children.*

underhanded not open and honorable; secret and sly.

> *He made a fortune in underhanded business deals.*

underwear clothing worn under the outer clothes.

underweight weighing less than normal.

PREFIX: PER-

What do a percolator, a perambulator, and a perjurer have in common? The prefix *per-* means (1) through; throughout; by means of; by; (2) thoroughly; completely; (3) wrongly. Here are four core vocabulary words that begin with *per-*: *perambulate, percent, perfect, perjure.*

perambulate derives from *per-* meaning "through" and the word *ambulate* meaning "to walk." Thus, to *perambulate* means "to walk through or around; to stroll."

> *Their vast garden is marvelous for perambulating.*

percent is a combination of the prefix *per* meaning "by" and the Latin root *cent-* meaning "hundred." Thus, *percent* means "the number of parts in every hundred of something."

He lost nearly ten percent of his accounts.

perfect comes from *per-* meaning "thoroughly" and the Latin root *fect-*, meaning "to make or do." Thus, *perfect* [pûr′fikt] means "done thoroughly; without fault or blemish; completely suitable." To *perfect* [pər·fekt′] is "to make flawless; to improve, refine, or complete."

It's a perfect day for a picnic.
Our architect has been perfecting plans for the new house.

perjure is formed from *per-* meaning "wrongly" and the Latin root *jur-* meaning "to swear." Thus, to *perjure* means "to be guilty of swearing falsely or of giving false testimony while under oath."

If you falsify your tax return, you're guilty of perjury.

Learn these fourteen additional *per-* words:

percolate to pass a liquid or cause a liquid to pass through a filter or strainer; especially, to cause boiling water to filter down through ground coffee.

percussion (1) the sound produced by means of striking one thing against another; (2) musical instruments, such as drums, cymbals, etc., whose sound is caused in this manner.

perdition eternal damnation.

perfidious breaking faith, trust, or allegiance, especially through treachery.

permeate (1) to spread thoroughly through; (2) to pass through the pores of something, as of a filter or membrane.

pernicious having the power to destroy thoroughly; highly injurious; wicked.

perpendicular at right angles to or through the horizontal plane; vertical.

perpetual lasting forever.

perplexity doubt, confusion, or bewilderment.

persevere to continue striving for a purpose in spite of difficulties.

persist (1) to continue firmly in some course of action; (2) to be insistent, as in repeating an action.

perspective (1) the effect that distance has upon the appearance of objects, by means of which the eye judges spatial relationships; (2) the art or theory of portraying objects on a flat surface so that there is an effect of depth and distance, as in a painting; (3) judgment of facts, circumstances, etc., in regard to their proportional importance.

pertain (1) to have reference to; relate; (2) to belong to something, as a quality, function, adjunct, etc.

pervade to spread through every part of something.

An odor pervades a room by permeating the air in the room.

◊ Make up a sample sentence using each of the preceding words. Look up all the *per-* words listed in your dictionary. How many do you know? Learn any new *per-* words that seem especially *pertinent* to your own interests.

PREFIX: POST-

The word *postmeridian* may sound strange to you, but you use it—in a shortened form, to be sure—all the time!

The Latin prefix *post-* means "after; behind." Here are three core vocabulary words using the prefix *post-*: *postgraduate, postmeridian, postpone.*

postgraduate comes from *post-* meaning "after" and the word *graduate.* Thus, *postgraduate* means "pertaining to academic studies that are taken up after a degree has been received."

I took my B.S. at U.C.L.A. and did postgraduate work at Yale.

postmeridian comes from *post-* meaning "after" and the word *meridian*

238

meaning "a great circle or dividing line drawn from any point on the earth's surface and passing through both poles." Thus, *postmeridian* means "after the sun has passed the dividing line at noon." Our abbreviation P.M. is taken from the Latin form of this word (*post meridiem*) and, of course, means "in the afternoon" or "in the second half of the day, from noon to midnight."

He works from 3 P.M. to 11 P.M.

postpone comes from *post-* meaning "after" and the Latin root *pon-* meaning "to put; place." Thus, to *postpone* means "to put off until afterward; delay."

The game was postponed because of rain.

Learn these additional *post-* words:

posterior (1) situated behind something else; (2) coming after another in time or order; (3) the rump.

posterity generations that come after; future generations taken as a whole.

posthumous [pos'choo-məs] (1) arising or continuing after one's death; (2) born after the father's death, as a child; (3) published after the author's death, as a book.

Most of Dickinson's poems were published posthumously.

post-mortem (1) happening or performed after death; (2) a medical examination of a body performed after death.

postprandial after-dinner.

postscript a sentence or more added to a letter after the writer's signature. The familiar abbreviation of *postscript* is P.S.

◊ Other words formed with the prefix *post-* range from simple terms like *postwar* and *postdate* to specialized terms like *postdiluvian*. Look up *post* referring to *mail*. This is not the same as the prefix *post-* meaning "after." Obviously, *postcard* and *poster* are based on the root *post*, not the prefix. From the *post* words in your dictionary, see if you can figure out which are based on the prefix *post-* meaning "after; behind" and which on the root *post*, referring to mail.

Fun With Words

ALL, AROUND, AND BESIDE

The following ten words begin with three little-used but interesting Greek prefixes: *pan-* meaning "all," *peri-* meaning "around," and *para-* meaning "beside." Check the word or phrase you believe is closest in meaning to the key word. Answers follow.

1. **pandemonium** [pan'də·mō'nē·əm]—(a) a large area. (b) wild uproar. (c) plague. (d) a disease of the respiratory tract.
2. **peripatetic** [per'i·pə·tet'ik]—(a) talkative. (b) permissive. (c) amusing. (d) walking about from one place to another.
3. **panacea** [pan'ə·sē'ə]—(a) everywhere. (b) a cure-all. (c) equality. (d) a bodily organ of digestion.
4. **panoply** [pan'ə·plē]—(a) a magnificent array, especially of armor. (b) a covering for a four-poster bed. (c) a harplike musical instrument. (d) a fruit.
5. **periphery** [pə·rif'ər·ē]—(a) a straight line. (b) the diameter. (c) the outer bounds. (d) a diagonal line.
6. **paragon** [par'ə·gón]—(a) away. (b) an advocate. (c) a large building. (d) a model of excellence.

7. **perimeter** [pə·rim'ə·tər]—(a) an area bounded by certain limits. (b) the outer boundary. (c) a straight line through the center of an object. (d) a measurement of distance.
8. **paranoia** [par'ə·noi'ə]—(a) a mental disorder characterized by delusions of persecution. (b) double talk. (c) a disease of the nervous system. (d) a mental disorder characterized by lapses of memory.
9. **paraphernalia** [par'ə·fər·nā'lē·ə]—(a) a mental disorder characterized by alternating periods of anger and withdrawal. (b) a large suitcase. (c) abnormal sleep. (d) personal effects.
10. **panorama** [pan'ə·ram'ə]—(a) a comprehensive view of a subject. (b) a metropolis. (c) a confused state of mind. (d) a large screen to project pictures on.

ANSWERS:

1. **pandemonium**—(b) wild uproar. 2. **peripatetic**—(d) walking about from one place to another. 3. **panacea**—(b) a cure-all. 4. **panoply**—(a) a magnificent array, especially of armor. 5. **periphery**—(c) the outer bounds. 6. **paragon**—(d) a model of excellence. 7. **perimeter**—(b) the outer boundary. 8. **paranoia**—(a) a mental disorder characterized by delusions of persecution. 9. **paraphernalia**—(d) personal effects. 10. **panorama**—(a) a comprehensive view of a subject.

PREFIX: PRE-

W hat does the preface of a book have in common with a prefabricated house? The prefix *pre-* means "before in time or order; preceding; prior to; in front of." Here are four core vocabulary words beginning with *pre-: precaution, precursor, prefabricate, premolar.*

precaution is formed from *pre-* meaning "before" and the word *caution*. Thus, *precaution* means "caution taken as a preparation for a possible emergency."

> *Take the precaution of fastening your seat belt before starting.*

precursor comes from *pre-* meaning "before" and the Latin root *curs-* meaning "to run" plus the suffix *-or* meaning "a person who." Thus, a *precursor* is literally "a person who runs before; a forerunner"; hence, "a person or thing that precedes and suggests the course of events to come."

> *The first robin you see is a precursor of spring.*

prefabricate derives from *pre-* meaning "before" and the word *fabricate* meaning "to make; manufacture; build." Thus, to *prefabricate* is "to manufacture something beforehand; especially, to manufacture the parts of a house in standard sections that can be put together rapidly."

> *The workers erected the prefabricated house in three days.*

premolar derives from *pre-* meaning "in front of" and the word *molar*. Thus, *premolar* means "one of the teeth situated in front of the molars; a bicuspid."

> *The dentist filled one of my premolars.*

Learn these seventeen additional words that include the prefix *pre-:*

precept (1) a rule prescribing a particular kind of conduct; (2) a proverb.

precinct (1) an election district or a police district; (2) a place or enclosure marked off by fixed limits.

precipice the brink of a cliff; a high vertical or overhanging face of rock.

241

precipitate to bring something about suddenly and unexpectedly.

precipitation rain, snow, sleet, etc.

precise strictly accurate (originally, *precise* meant "to be sure before cutting or acting").

precocious (1) unusually developed or advanced for one's age; (2) developed before the usual time or age.

preface a brief, introductory statement or essay in the front of a book.

prelate [prel'it] a clergyman of high rank, as a bishop, archbishop, etc.

preliminary befoɪe or introductory to the main event, business, etc.

premeditate to plan or consider beforehand.

preposterous absurd; contrary to nature, reason, or common sense.

(Note that this word contains both the prefix *pre-* meaning "before" and the prefix *post-* meaning "after." Combining "before" and "after" is absurd, and that is how *preposterous* got its meaning.)

prerequisite something required before or necessary to something that follows, such as an academic course that must be taken before another, more advanced course.

prerogative an exclusive right or privilege belonging to a person or group; a right so obvious that it is given before it is asked for.

It is a prelate's prerogative to officiate at some functions.

presage (1) as a noun [pres'ij], an indication of something to come; an omen; (2) as a verb [pri·sāj'], to give an indication of something to come; to foreshadow.

presume (1) to take for granted beforehand; (2) to take an unwarranted liberty; dare; (3) to seem to prove; (4) to make excessive demands on or rely too heavily on.

prevaricator a person who acts or speaks in a deceptive manner (literally, "a person who walks crookedly before another").

◊ Make a sample sentence using each of the preceding words. You will find a long list of words beginning with *pre-* in your dictionary. How many of these words do you know? Learn any additional *pre-* words that you have heard frequently.

EXPLORING WORDS
CHEERS, OLD CHAP

People from America and England speak the same language—almost. Some of the thirty-one British words listed below are rarely used in American speech. Others are used by Americans, but with different meanings. If you read British books, see British movies, or talk to British people, you might like to know the American meanings of the British words listed below.

biscuit a cracker.
bonnet the hood of an automobile.
boot the trunk of an automobile.
braces a pair of suspenders.
cab rank taxi stand.
chemist a pharmacist or druggist.
chips French-fried potatoes.
circus a traffic circle.
cotton wool absorbent cotton.
crumpet a muffin or light biscuit.
draper's haberdashery.
dustbin a garbage can.
egg whisk eggbeater
flat apartment.
greengrocer a fruit-and-vegetable store, or the proprietor of one.
lift an elevator.
lorry a truck.
mute pallbearer.
nappy a baby's diaper.
petrol gasoline.
pram a baby carriage (short for *perambulator*).
pub a bar or tavern (short for *public house*).
spanner a wrench.
subway an underpass, especially one for pedestrians.
tin a can, as of food.
treacle molasses.
underground a subway or subway system.
vest an undershirt.
waistcoat [wes'kit] a vest.
windscreen the windshield of an automobile.
works factory.

PREFIX: PRO-

Such very different words as *promiscuous, propaganda, prodigal,* and *pronoun* have in common the Latin prefix *pro-* which means (1) forward; forth; (2) before; (3) in place of or on behalf of; for. Here are five core vocabulary words formed with the prefix *pro-: proceed, produce, profane, profess, pronoun.*

proceed derives from the prefix *pro-* meaning "forward" and the Latin root *ceed-* meaning "to go." Thus, to *proceed* means "to go on or go forward, especially after a stop or interruption."

If there are no more questions, I'll proceed with the lecture.

produce is formed from *pro-* meaning "forward" and the Latin root *duc-* meaning "to lead." Thus, to *produce* means "to lead or bring forth; to yield, make, or bring about; to lead forward into view; to show or display."

An accusation of treachery always produces a violent reaction.
It was hard to produce evidence of the man's innocence.

profane comes from *pro-* meaning "before" and the Latin root *fan-* meaning "temple." Thus, *profane* literally means "outside the temple"; hence, (1) not religious or concerned with religious things; (2) irreverent; (3) coarse, as language. To *profane* something sacred is to treat it with irreverence.

Cursing is sometimes called profane language.
The church was profaned by vandals who turned over the altar.

A word based on *profane* is *profanity,* meaning "profane speech or action; disrespect for religious things."

His speech was coarse and full of profanity.

profess is formed from *pro-* meaning "before" and the Latin root *fess-,* meaning "to confess; declare." Thus, to *profess* means (1) to declare before others; (2) to declare faith in; (3) to pretend.

The accused man professed his innocence.
The young singer professed Islam and became a Muslim.
People often profess to despise what they actually envy.

Two words based on *profess* are *profession* and *professor*. *Profession* means (1) an occupation calling for education and involving mental rather than manual labor, as law, medicine, or theology; (2) the act of declaring openly. *Professor* means (1) a college or university teacher of the highest rank; (2) one who professes opinions or beliefs.

Dr. Smith, who is a professor of English, is proud of his profession.

pronoun is made up of *pro-* meaning "for; in place of" and the word *noun* meaning "the part of speech that names a person, place, or thing." Thus, *pronoun* means "a word used in place of a noun."

He, she, *and* it *are pronouns.*

Learn these six additional words beginning with the prefix *pro-:*

proclivity a natural disposition or tendency.

procure (1) to obtain by some means or effort; (2) to bring about.

prodigal (1) wasteful, of money or time; (2) a spendthrift.

promiscuous (1) composed of individuals or things mingled together in confusion; (2) indiscriminate, especially in sexual relations.

promulgate to announce officially and formally before the people.

propaganda (1) an effort to persuade people to adopt a particular belief, attitude, course of action, etc.; (2) any selection of facts, claims, ideas, or allegations used in such an effort.

◊ Other words can be built on the *pro-* words given above, and there are many other words that begin with *pro-*. Remembering the definitions of the words you have just learned, can you figure out meanings for the six words that follow?

proceeds [prō′sēdz]	professoriate
procurement	promiscuity
production	propagandist

NOTE: The prefix *pro-* can also mean "in favor of," as opposed to *anti-* meaning "against." The word *pro* means "for" or "an argument in favor of something," as opposed to *con*, which means "against" or "an argument against something."

Some colonists were pro-British during the Revolutionary War. Before deciding, let's consider all the pros and cons.

PREFIXES PRO- AND PRE-

The following thirteen words begin with the prefix *pro-* meaning "forward; before; for" or the prefix *pre-* meaning "before; prior to." Check the word or phrase you believe is closest in meaning to the key word. Answers follow.

1. **prescient** ⌊prē′shē·ənt]—(a) prophetic. (b) patient. (c) pure. (d) peaceful.
2. **premonitory** [pri·mon′ə·tôr′ē]—(a) a headland. (b) sad. (c) giving warning of something to come. (d) resounding.
3. **promulgate** [prom′əl·gāt]—(a) to proclaim. (b) to thrash. (c) to intend. (d) to force upon others.
4. **propitiate** [prō·pish′ē·āt]—(a) to weaken. (b) to encourage. (c) to rain or snow. (d) to appease or win the favor of.
5. **propensity** [prə·pen′sə·tē]—(a) feebleness. (b) ability. (c) a tendency. (d) miserliness or penny-pinching.
6. **predilection** [prē′də·lek′shən]—(a) in the neighborhood of. (b) a preference for something. (c) an introduction. (d) an implication.
7. **precocity** [pri·kos′ə·tē]—(a) impetuousness. (b) perverseness. (c) a state of being mentally de-veloped earlier than usual. (d) a state of being mentally developed later than usual.
8. **prestige** [pres·tēzh′]—(a) pride. (b) performance. (c) distinction. (d) wealth.
9. **proviso** [prə·vī′zō]—(a) a condition or stipulation. (b) a supply. (c) a definite command. (d) a prophecy.
10. **provocation** [prov′ə·kā′shən]—(a) a narrow-minded viewpoint. (b) a cause of anger or resentment. (c) willingness to work. (d) an alliance.
11. **prognostication** [prog·nos′tə·kā′shən]—(a) mental absorption. (b) the act of prolonging. (c) diagnosis. (d) a prediction or forecast.
12. **pretext** [prē′tekst]—(a) a rule. (b) a promise. (c) an excuse. (d) a preface.
13. **profess** [prə·fes′]—(a) to become expert at. (b) to proclaim or declare. (c) to plan or teach. (d) to foretell.

ANSWERS:

1. **prescient**—(a) prophetic. 2. **premonitory**—(c) giving warning of something to come. 3. **promulgate**—(a) to proclaim. 4. **propitiate**—(d) to appease or win the favor of. 5. **propensity**—(c) a tendency. 6. **predilection**—(b) a preference for something. 7. **precocity**—(c) a state of being mentally developed earlier than usual. 8. **prestige**—(c) distinction. 9. **proviso**—(a) a condition or stipulation. 10. **provocation**—(b) a cause of anger or resentment. 11. **prognostication**—(d) a prediction or forecast. 12. **pretext**—(c) an excuse. 13. **profess**—(b) to proclaim or declare.

PREFIX: RE-

What do a rebel, a refrigerator, and a reconnaissance plane have in common?

The Latin prefix *re-* means "back; again, thoroughly." Here are four core vocabulary words using *re-*: *rebel, recall, refresh, refrigerate.*

rebel is formed from the prefix *re-* meaning "again" and the Latin root *bel-* meaning "to make war." The verb *rebel* [ri·bel′] literally means "to make war again; resume fighting." Hence, to *rebel* is (1) to rise in resistance against the established government of one's country; (2) to resist or disobey any authority; (3) to react with strong opposition or disapproval. A *rebel* [reb′əl] is "a person who refuses to submit to the established authority or conventions."

> *The army rebelled against the dictator.*
> *Billy rebelled against his parents' way of life.*
> *The student rebels demanded an end to the grading system.*

recall derives from *re-* meaning "back" and the word *call.* Thus, *recall* means (1) to call back; order to return or be returned; (2) to take back; revoke; (3) to call back to mind; remember.

> *The retired general was recalled to duty.*
> *The manufacturer recalled the defective cars.*
> *Can you recall the date of Washington's birth?*

refresh is formed from *re-* meaning "again" and the word *fresh.* Thus, *refresh* means (1) to make fresh or vigorous again; revive; (2) to stimulate, as the memory.

> *He refreshed himself with a short nap.*
> *The old snapshots refreshed Sally's memory of her first teacher.*

refrigerate is made up of *re-* meaning "thoroughly" and the Latin root *frigerat-*, meaning "to cool." Thus, *refrigerate* means "to make or keep thoroughly cool."

> *Refrigerate the milk so that it won't spoil.*

Learn these eighteen additional *re-* words:

rebuff (1) to reject or refuse abruptly or rudely; snub; (2) an abrupt or rude rejection, denial, or defeat.

recalcitrant defying or resisting a request or command; obstinate, stubborn; rebellious (literally, "kicking back" at a request).

reciprocal done or given by each of two persons, things, parties, etc., to the other; mutual.

reconnaissance [ri·kon′ə·səns] (1) a preliminary survey or examination, as of an area of a country, for information; (2) the act of obtaining information of military value, especially regarding the position, strength, and movement of the enemy.

reconnoiter to survey or examine, as for military, engineering, or geological purposes.

recoup to get something back; recover or make up, as a loss.

recriminate to accuse in return; meet one accusation by making another.

recuperate to get back one's health or strength.

reiterate to say or do again and again, as for emphasis; repeat.

relapse (1) to lapse back, as into a disease, after a partial recovery; (2) a lapsing back.

relegate (1) to send back or off, as to a less important person, position, or place; (2) to assign to a certain category.

relinquish to give up or leave behind; abandon.

reminiscence (1) the calling to mind of past events; (2) the telling of past experiences.

remunerate to make a just or adequate return to or for; pay back or pay for; compensate.

reprieve (1) to delay temporarily the execution of a sentence upon a condemned person (literally, "taken back"); (2) to relieve for a time from trouble, danger, or pain; (3) the temporary suspension of a sentence; especially, the commutation of a death sentence; (4) temporary relief or a respite.

rescind to take back; make void; repeal.

revile to attack with contemptuous language; to abuse.

revise (1) to read again or read over in order to correct errors, make changes, etc.; (2) to change.

QUICKIE QUIZ

BACK AGAIN

The following seven words begin with the prefix *re-* meaning "back; again; thoroughly." Check the word you believe is closest in meaning to the key word. Answers follow.

1. **reverberate** [ri·vûr′bə·rāt]—(a) to separate into the original parts. (b) to echo or resound. (c) to regain one's energy. (d) to resume a former habit.
2. **recessive** [ri·ses′iv]—(a) indented. (b) growing gradually greater. (c) tending to go back. (d) growing gradually smaller.
3. **retrenchment** [ri·trench′mənt] —(a) a strengthening of the foundations. (b) a forced withdrawal. (c) a cutting down of expenses. (d) a retraction of a promise.
4. **remiss** [ri·mis′]—(a) absentminded. (b) careless. (c) sinful. (d) sorrowful.
5. **redress** [ri·dres′]—(a) to make amends for. (b) to make neat. (c) to withdraw. (d) to make a reply.
6. **repletion** [ri·plē′shən]—(a) a state of weakness. (b) the act of doing something more than once. (c) a state of complete or excessive fullness. (d) an invitation.
7. **recompense** [rek′əm·pens]—(a) to remember. (b) to reconcile. (c) to resume. (d) to pay back.

ANSWERS:

1. **reverberate**—(b) to echo or resound. 2. **recessive**—(c) tending to go back. 3. **retrenchment**—(c) a cutting down of expenses. 4. **remiss**—(b) careless. 5. **redress**—(a) to make amends for. 6. **repletion**—(c) a state of complete or excessive fullness. 7. **recompense**—(d) to pay back.

◊ You can build many more words on the words listed above. Remembering the meanings of the words just discussed, can you figure out the meanings of the words that follow?

rebellious	recuperation
refreshment	reminiscent
refrigerator	remuneration
recrimination	revision

Hundreds of other words begin with the prefix *re-*. Look at the words beginning with this prefix in your dictionary (there will be several pages of them). How many do you know? Learn the meanings of the *re-* words that you hear or see most often. Study their etymologies to be sure that you know how the prefix *re-* is used in word building.

PREFIX: SE-

The Latin prefix *se-* means "aside; apart; away; without." This prefix occurs in only a few words, but they are important. A basic word containing the prefix *se-* is *separate,* which literally means "to prepare apart." Here are six core vocabulary words using the prefix *se-: secede, secure, sedition, seduce, segregate, select.*

secede stems from *se-* meaning "apart" and the Latin root *ced-* meaning "to go." Thus, *secede* means "to go apart"; hence, "to withdraw from an association, especially for political or religious reasons."

> *The Confederacy was composed of Southern states that seceded from the Union.*

secure derives from the prefix *se-* meaning "without" and the Latin root *cur-* meaning "care." Thus, *secure* means "free from care, fear, etc."; hence, (1) safe; (2) certain; (3) fixed firmly' or strongly in place; (4) so strong or well made as to make loss, breakage, escape, or defeat impossible; (5) to protect, fasten, or guarantee; (6) to obtain.

> *Little Joey feels secure only when he is with his parents.*
> *He was secure in his knowledge of the facts.*
> *Our nation rests on a secure foundation.*
> *They secured all the doors and windows before the full force of the hurricane hit.*
> *Have you secured the necessary supplies?*

sedition is made up of *sed-* (another spelling of *se-*) meaning "aside" and the Latin root *it-* meaning "a going" plus the suffix *-ion* meaning "the act or state of." Thus, *sedition* literally means "the act of going aside from law and order"; hence, "language or action directed against public order; the encouragement of disorder or revolt against the state."

> *In Stalin's Russia, sedition meant certain death.*

seduce is formed of *se-* meaning "apart; away" and the Latin root *duc-* meaning "to lead." Thus, *seduce* means "to lead astray; to lure into wrong, disloyalty, etc.; especially, to persuade a person to engage in illicit sexual intercourse."

Their offer of big money seduced him into joining the conspiracy.
The heroine of many an old melodrama was seduced and abandoned
by the villain.

segregate is derived from *se-* meaning "apart" and the Latin root *greg-*
meaning "the flock or herd" plus the suffix *-ate* meaning "to make."
Thus, to *segregate* is "to place a person, thing, or group apart from
the rest; to isolate; especially, to subject a racial group to the practice of using separate facilities."

A child with measles should be segregated from the rest of the
pupils.
Segregated schools are illegal in this country.

select is formed from *se-* meaning "apart" and the Latin root *lect-*
meaning "to choose." Thus, to *select* literally means "to choose something apart from others"; hence, "to make a choice." As an adjective,
select means (1) set aside as being the best; chosen for high quality;
(2) making careful, discriminating choices.

You may select any dress you wish.
These tomatoes are select.

◇ From the words discussed in this chapter you can build such additional words as *secession, security, seditious,* etc. See how many you
can think of, and consult your dictionary to find out whether you've
figured out the correct meanings for them.

PREFIX: SUB- AND ITS DISGUISES

The Latin prefix *sub-* means (1) under; beneath; below; (2) secondary; subordinate; (3) less than, almost, or imperfectly; (4) secretly.

NOTE: Like *ad-*, the prefix *sub-* changes spelling so that its last letter
will harmonize with the letter following it. Thus, *sub-* may be spelled
suc-, suf-, sug-, sum-, sup-, sur-, or *sus-,* as in *succumb, suffer, suggest,*
summon, support, surrogate, susceptible, suspect, sustain.

Here are six core vocabulary words beginning with *sub-: subcon-*
scious, submarine, submit, suborbital, subordinate, suborn.

251

subconscious is formed from *sub-* meaning "imperfectly" or "below" and the word *conscious*. Thus, *subconscious* means "not clearly or wholly conscious." The *subconscious* is "the part of the mind or the mind's activity of which a person is usually not aware; the workings of the mind just below the threshold of consciousness."

> *Some people have a subconscious desire for self-destruction.*
> *The psychoanalyst knew that Laura's problem was buried in her subconscious.*

submarine derives from *sub-* meaning "under" and the word *marine* meaning "of or having to do with the sea or ships; nautical." Thus, *submarine* means "existing or operating beneath the surface of the sea." A *submarine* is designed to operate below the surface of the sea.

> *Skin divers can study submarine life.*
> *An atomic submarine can sail around the world without surfacing.*

submit comes from *sub-* meaning "under; beneath" and the Latin root *mit-* meaning "to send or place." Thus, *submit* means (1) to place under or yield to the authority, will, or power of another; to surrender; (2) to present for consideration; (3) to present as one's opinion; suggest.

> *The English tribes submitted to Caesar's legions.*
> *Please submit your report to the board on Friday.*
> *I submit that we are in error and should change our ways.*

suborbital stems from *sub-* meaning "less than, almost, or imperfectly," and the word *orbital* meaning "having to do with an orbit." Thus, *suborbital* means "not going into orbit; falling short of a complete revolution around the earth or another heavenly body: said of rockets, artificial satellites, and spacecraft."

> *The missile had a suborbital flight, landing a thousand miles down-range from the launching pad.*

subordinate is derived from *sub-* meaning "under" and the Latin root *ordin-* meaning "to order" plus the suffix *-ate* meaning "characterized by." Thus, *subordinate* means "belonging to a lower position, class, or rank." A *subordinate* is a person or thing lower in rank or authority than another.

> *A captain is subordinate to a major.*

An officer is authorized to give orders to his subordinates.
A complex sentence has an independent clause and one or more subordinate clauses.

suborn is formed from *sub-* meaning "secretly" and the Latin root *orn-* meaning "to equip." Thus, to *suborn* means "to incite someone to an evil or criminal act; especially, to bribe someone to commit perjury or some other criminal act."

The lawyer was charged with suborning a witness.

Learn these eight additional words beginning with the prefix *sub-:*

subcutaneous situated, found, or applied beneath the skin.

The doctor gave Paul a subcutaneous injection.

subliminal perceived below the threshold of consciousness, as certain stimuli, images, etc., of too low an intensity to produce a clear awareness.

Subliminal advertising is sometimes used in television.

subservient adapted to promote some higher or more important purpose; useful as a subordinate; servile.

subsidiary (1) a company owned and controlled by another company; (2) functioning in a lesser or secondary capacity; auxiliary.

subsidy financial assistance, especially through government grants, for an individual or enterprise that is thought to be beneficial to the public; literally, money that "sits under" something in order to support it.

substantiate to establish as truth by evidence; to verify; literally, to "stand under" something with supporting evidence.

substitute (1) to put in the place of another; (2) a person or thing that takes the place of another.

subterranean situated or occurring underground.

◇ Look up the words beginning with *sub-* in your dictionary. How many do you know? Then look up the nine words listed at the beginning of this discussion that contain a disguised form of the prefix *sub-*. How does the meaning of the prefix contribute to the meanings of these nine words?

Fun With Words

PREFIX SUB-

The following fourteen words begin with the prefix *sub-* meaning "under" or "secretly." Check the word or phrase you believe is closest in meaning to the key word. Answers follow.

1. **suborn** [sə·bôrn′]—(a) to swear in. (b) to bribe or induce to commit perjury. (c) to summon. (d) to arrest for false testimony.
2. **sublimate** [sub′lə·māt]—(a) to refine or purify. (b) to reduce to slavery. (c) to dignify with great honors. (d) to sum up.
3. **substantiate** [səb·stan′shē·āt]— (a) to weaken. (b) to substitute one thing for another. (c) to verify. (d) to make wealthy.
4. **subservient** [səb·sûr′vē·ənt]— (a) fawning and servile. (b) second in command. (c) insincere. (d) unfaithful.
5. **subversive** [səb·vûr′siv]—(a) secret. (b) deceptive. (c) overly humble. (d) tending to overthrow.
6. **subjugate** [sub′jŏŏ·gāt]—(a) to conquer or subdue. (b) to define. (c) to confuse. (d) to cause to wither and decay.
7. **submerge** [səb·mûrj′]—(a) to walk on. (b) to sink. (c) to appear. (d) to join together.
8. **subordinate** [sə·bôr′də·nit]—(a)

extraordinary. (b) secondary or minor. (c) rebellious. (d) tamely submissive.
9. **subliminal** [sub·lim′ə·nəl]—(a) equal. (b) attached at the end of a line. (c) below the threshold of consciousness. (d) close to the seashore.
10. **subconscious** [sub·kon′shəs]— (a) mental activity of which a person is usually not aware. (b) below the level of human. (c) under hypnosis. (d) unaware.
11. **subscribe** [səb·skrīb′]—(a) to scorn. (b) to continue to exist. (c) to classify. (d) to give sanction, support, or approval.
12. **subsidiary** [səb·sid′ē·er′ē]—(a) an associate. (b) secondary. (c) government aid. (d) rock strata below the earth's surface.
13. **subtle** [sut′l]—(a) unwilling. (b) unsympathetic. (c) sociable or amiable. (d) keen or discriminating.
14. **subside** [səb·sīd′]—(a) to resist. (b) to become strong. (c) to become less agitated. (d) aligned in rows.

ANSWERS:

1. **suborn**—(b) to bribe or induce to commit perjury. 2. **sublimate**—(a) to refine or purify. 3. **substantiate**—(c) to verify. 4. **subservient**—(a) fawning and servile. 5. **subversive**—(d) tending to overthrow. 6. **subjugate**—(a) to conquer or subdue. 7. **submerge**—(b) to sink. 8. **subordinate**—(b) secondary or minor. 9. **subliminal**—(c) below the threshold of consciousness. 10. **subconscious**—(a) mental activity of which a person is usually not aware. 11. **subscribe**—(d) to give sanction, support, or approval. 12. **subsidiary**— (b) secondary. 13. **subtle**—(d) keen or discriminating. 14. **subside**—(c) to become less agitated.

PREFIX: SUPER-

You don't have to be a superman to have a "super" vocabulary. Of course, the slang word *super,* meaning "first-rate," comes from the prefix *super-,* which is also used in *superman,* "a man possessed of superhuman powers; a superior being." The Latin prefix *super-* means (1) above; over; beyond; (2) more than; greater than; superior; (3) excessively. Here are three core vocabulary words that include the prefix *super-: superficial, superhighway, supernatural.*

superficial derives from *super-* meaning "over" and the root *fic-,* which comes from a Latin word meaning "the face; surface" plus the suffix *-ial* meaning "of or having to do with." Thus, *superficial* literally means "on or over the surface"; hence, "affecting only the surface; going no deeper than the ordinary or obvious."

> *It was a superficial wound, not a serious one.*
> *This student has only a superficial knowledge of his subject.*

superhighway is formed from *super-* meaning "greater than; superior" and the word *highway.* Thus, a *superhighway* is "a highway designed to handle more or faster traffic than a regular highway."

> *The new superhighway cuts our driving time to Cleveland by two hours.*

supernatural comes from *super-* meaning "above or beyond" and the word *natural.* Thus, *supernatural* means "existing or occurring through some agency beyond the known forces of nature; lying outside the natural order." *The supernatural* comprises "those forces, powers, or events that exist, operate, or occur outside the known or natural order."

> *Ghosts are supernatural beings.*
> *Poe wrote strange tales of the supernatural.*

Here are ten additional words that begin with the prefix *super-:*

superannuated (1) retired on a pension because one is over a certain age; (2) too old to be useful; obsolete; out-of-date.

supercilious showing contempt or indifference; arrogant; literally, "with raised eyebrows," which is a way of showing contempt.

TWO-MINUTE QUICKIE QUIZ
SUPER-WORDS

These five words begin with the prefix *super-*, meaning "above, over, or greater than." Check the word or phrase you believe is closest in meaning to the key word. Answers follow.

1. **superlative** [sə·pûr′lə·tiv]—(a) lavish. (b) everlasting. (c) surplus. (d) supreme.
2. **supercilious** [sō͞o′pər·sil′ē·əs]—(a) highly intelligent. (b) above reproach. (c) scornfully superior. (d) tending to be a social climber.
3. **supervene** [sō͞o′pər·vēn′]—(a) to follow closely upon something. (b) to overcome. (c) to force out. (d) to come in between.
4. **supersonic** [sō͞o′pər·son′ik]—(a) characterized by a speed greater than that of sound. (b) high-velocity sound waves. (c) extremely loud and noisy. (d) of unusual size.
5. **superimpose** [sō͞o′pər·im·pōz′]—(a) to force one's demand on others. (b) to lay or place on something else. (c) to find to be above suspicion. (d) to make superfluous.

ANSWERS:

1. **superlative**—(d) supreme. 2. **supercilious**—(c) scornfully superior. 3. **supervene**—(a) to follow closely upon something. 4. **supersonic**—(a) characterized by a speed greater than that of sound. 5. **superimpose**—(b) to lay or place on something else.

superfluous exceeding what is needed; unnecessary; surplus.

superintendent (1) a person who is placed over others to supervise them, as a person in charge of an office, department, etc.; (2) a person who supervises the upkeep and repair of an apartment building.

superlative (1) of supreme excellence or eminence; (2) in grammar, the form of an adjective or adverb expressing the highest degree of comparison.

supernumerary (1) an extra or unnecessary person or thing; (2) being beyond a fixed, standard, or necessary number.

supersede (1) to take the place of, by reason of superior worth, right, newness, etc.; (2) to supplant, replace, annul.

supersensitive excessively sensitive; too easily offended.

superstition (1) a belief based on irrational feelings, marked by a trust in or respect for charms, omens, signs, the supernatural, etc.; literally, "excessive fear of the gods"; (2) any irrational belief.

supervise to have charge of directing workers, a project, etc.; literally, "to oversee."

◊ Look up the many other words in your dictionary that begin with the prefix *super-*. If you remember what *super-* means, you should be able to figure out the meaning of many of these words. Check your own definitions against the dictionary definitions.

PREFIX: SYN- AND ITS DISGUISES

What do synchronized watches have in common with syllables and symphonies? The Greek prefix *syn-* means "together; with." This prefix may also be spelled *syl-, sym-,* or *sys-,* as in *syllable, sympathy,* and *system.* Here are eight core vocabulary words making use of the prefix *syn-* or one of its variants: *syllable, sympathy, symphony, synchronize, syncopate, syndrome, synonym, syntax.*

syllable is formed from *syl-* meaning "together" and the root *lab-* meaning "to take." Originally, *syllable* referred to letters or sounds that were "taken together." Hence, a syllable is "the part of a word that is spoken as a single unit, consisting of a vowel alone or with one or more consonants."

   The word vocabulary *has five syllables:* vo·cab·u·lar·y.

sympathy derives from the prefix *sym-* meaning "with" or "together" and the Greek root *path-* meaning "to feel" plus the suffix *-y* meaning "the quality or state of being." Thus, *sympathy* means "the quality of feeling with or feeling for someone else; a feeling of compassion for another's suffering; fellow feeling."

   The neighbors expressed their sympathy to the widow.

symphony comes from *sym-* meaning "together" and the Greek root *phon-* meaning "sound" plus the suffix *-y* meaning "the act or state of." *Symphony* literally means "the act of sounding together." Hence,

257

a symphony is (1) a musical composition written for all the instruments of the orchestra playing together; (2) a large orchestra; (3) a harmonious blending, as of sounds.

A symphony usually has four movements.
Did you hear the Cleveland Symphony play last night?
Morning brings us a symphony of bird songs.

synchronize is made up of the prefix *syn-* meaning "together" and the Greek root *chron-* meaning "time" plus the suffix *-ize* meaning "to make." Thus, *synchronize* means "to time things together; to adjust two or more things so that they agree with respect to time or speed; to work or cause to work in unison."

Synchronize your watches before you go to your posts.
When a movie is dubbed, the words and lip movements of the actors must be synchronized.

syncopate derives from *syn-* meaning "together" and the Greek root *cop-* meaning "to strike; cut" plus the suffix *-ate,* which is a suffix used to form verbs. *Syncopate* originally meant "to shorten something by cutting part of it out and piecing the rest together." Now *syncopate* means "to place a tone in music so that its accent or beat does not coincide with the regular beat or accent of the music."

Modern jazz usually has syncopated rhythms.

syndrome comes from *syn-* meaning "together" and the Greek root *drom-* meaning "to run." Thus, *syndrome* literally means "something that runs along together with something else," hence "a set of symptoms that occur together and are characteristic of a certain disease or a social or psychological condition."

The delusion of being persecuted is one aspect of the paranoid's syndrome.
The dropout syndrome among students is characterized by increasing absenteeism and indifference to grades.

synonym derives from *syn-* meaning "together" and the Greek root *onym-* meaning "name." Thus, a *synonym* is "a word having the same or almost the same meaning as another word."

The words reply *and* answer *are synonyms.*

syntax is formed from *syn-* meaning "together" and the Greek root *tax-*

258

meaning "to arrange." Thus, *syntax* means "the arrangement and relationship of words in phrases and sentences; sentence structure."

When learning a foreign language, you must study syntax as well as vocabulary and grammar.

Here are five additional words beginning with the prefix *syn-* that you should know.

synagogue a meeting place where Jewish people gather for worship and religious instruction.

syndicate (1) an association of individuals united to transact a business or pursue a venture requiring a large amount of capital; (2) an agency that sells articles, columns, etc., to a number of newspapers or magazines.

synod (1) a church council; (2) any assembly where people come together to deliberate.

synopsis a summary or outline, as of a piece of fiction, setting down the major points in order; literally, "a general view."

Before seeing Hamlet *they read a synopsis of it.*

synthesis (1) the assembling of separate parts into a whole; (2) a complex whole composed of separate parts.

◊ Various other words begin with the prefix *syn-* or its variants *syl-*, *sym-*, and *sys-* meaning "with" or "together"—for example: *syllogism*, *symmetrical*, *symposium*, *symptom*, *synthetic*, and *system*. Look up these words in your dictionary to be sure you know their meanings and how they are built with the prefix *syn-* or one of its variants.

PREFIX: TRANS-

The Latin prefix *trans-* means (1) across; over; beyond; through; on the other side of; (2) completely; (3) surpassing. Here are six core vocabulary words that make typical use of the prefix *trans-: transact, transatlantic, transcribe, transfer, transform, transmit.*

transact is formed from *trans-* meaning "through" and the Latin root *act-* meaning "to do; drive." Thus, to *transact* means "to carry through; accomplish."

It took Philip ten minutes to transact his business at the bank.

transatlantic derives from *trans-* meaning "across, on the other side of" and the word *Atlantic*. Thus, *transatlantic* means (1) on the other side of the Atlantic Ocean; (2) across or crossing the Atlantic Ocean.

We've just heard from our transatlantic representative.
The dispatch was sent by transatlantic cable.

transcribe is made up of *trans-* meaning "over" and the Latin root *scrib-* meaning "to write." Thus, *transcribe* means "to write over; copy from an original or from notes." *Transcribe* may also mean "to record a radio or television program for later broadcasting."

The typist quickly transcribed the letter from the shorthand notes.
This program isn't live; it was transcribed earlier for broadcast.

transfer comes from *trans-* meaning "across" and the Latin root *fer-* meaning "to carry." Thus, to *transfer* is "to carry across; to move or convey from one person, place, possessor, vehicle, etc., to another." A *transfer* is (1) the act of transferring or state of being transferred; (2) a thing or person transferred; (3) a means of transfer, as a ticket permitting a passenger to change from one bus to another.

He transferred his keys from his right hand to his left.
The stock transfer between the two corporations will take place on Friday.
Some of the new students were transfers from other colleges.
Be sure to ask for a transfer to a cross-town bus at Fifth Street.

transform comes from *trans-* meaning "over, completely" and the word *form*. Thus, *transform* means (1) to give a different form or appearance to; (2) to change the character, nature, condition, etc., of.

The Greggs have transformed their garage into a guest house.

transmit is made up of *trans-* meaning "across" and the root *mit-* meaning "to send." Thus, *transmit* means "to send from one place or person to another; to pass on news, information, etc.; to broadcast."

He transmitted your message to me.
On what frequency does this radio station transmit?

30-SECOND QUICKIE QUIZ
DOCTORS AND THEIR SPECIALTIES

Here's a short quickie quiz. Can you match the doctor with his specialty? Answers follow.

1. **dermatologist** [dûr′mə·tol′·ə·jist]
2. **gynecologist** [gī′nə·kol′ə·jist]
3. **pediatrician** [pē′dē·ə·trish′ən]
4. **podiatrist** [pə·dī′ə·trist]
5. **ophthalmologist** [of′thal·mol′ə·jist]

(a) children and infants
(b) eye diseases
(c) women's disorders
(d) skin
(e) feet

ANSWERS:

1. **dermatologist**—(d) skin. 2. **gynecologist**—(c) women's disorders. 3. **pediatrician**—(a) children and infants. 4. **podiatrist**—(e) feet. 5. **ophthalmologist**—(b) eye diseases.

Here are five additional words prefixed by *trans-:*

transcend (1) to rise above in excellence or degree; (2) to overstep or exceed a limit.

transfusion the transfer of blood from one person or animal to another.

transgress to break a law, oath, etc.; to pass beyond a limit; literally, "to step across a forbidden line."

transparent (1) easy to see through; (2) obvious; open.

transpose (1) to reverse the order or change the place of something; (2) to change music to a different key.

By transposing the letters of rat, *you get* tar *and* art.

◊ From the words defined, you can build many additional words. Remembering the definitions that have just been given, can you figure out the meanings of the words below?

transaction
transcription
transformation

transformer
transgression
transmission

Many other words also begin with the prefix *trans-*. How many can you list? Some suggestions: *transient, transistor* (which has a very interesting etymology), *transit, transition, transom, transpire, transplant.*

261

PREFIX: ULTRA-

The Latin prefix *ultra-* means "beyond; surpassing; excessively." It is similar in meaning to the prefixes *super-* and *trans-*. However, *ultra-* is less often used than the other two prefixes. When used in non-technical contexts, it usually means "excessively." Here are two core vocabulary words using the prefix *ultra-* that you should learn: *ultraconservative, ultraviolet.*

ultraconservative is formed from *ultra-* meaning "excessively" and the word *conservative*. Thus, *ultraconservative* means "excessively conservative, especially in politics; reactionary." An *ultraconservative* is "an excessively conservative person."

Ultraconservatives often believe that many changes are dangerous.

ultraviolet comes from *ultra-* meaning "beyond" and the word *violet*. Thus, *ultraviolet* means "lying beyond the violet end of the visible spectrum: said of high-frequency wavelengths."

Sunburn is caused by exposure to the sun's ultraviolet rays.

◊ Look up the words beginning with the prefix *ultra-* in your dictionary. One you will recognize is *ultramodern,* meaning "extremely modern." Are there any others that you should learn because you hear or see them frequently?

PREFIX: UN-

The prefix *un-* means "not; opposed to; lacking; back" and is often used to indicate the reversal of an action.

The prefix *un-* is the last and most important of several negative prefixes that you have learned. What is the difference between *un-* and *in-*, the two most important of these negative prefixes? Notice that *un-* may often indicate a simple lack of something, whereas *in-* is more likely to indicate a definite negative, or "not." For example, *unapproachable* means "hard to approach, as a person who is aloof." In other

QUICKIEQUIZQUICKIEQUIZQUICKIEQUIZQUICKIEQUIZQUICKIEQUIZQUICKIEQUIZQUICKIE

QUICKIE QUIZ
MORE "NOT" WORDS

Here are ten more words begining with the prefix *un-* meaning "not; opposed to; lacking." Check the word or phrase you believe is closest in meaning to the key word. Answers follow.

1. **unscathed** [un·skā<del>th</del>d']—(a) innocent. (b) unharmed. (c) burned. (d) angered.
2. **uncompromising** [un·kom'prə·mī'zing]—(a) indifferent. (b) reserved. (c) strict or inflexible. (d) uneasy.
3. **unwonted** [un·wun'tid]—(a) unaccustomed. (b) not desirable. (c) unable to do wrong. (d) inconsistent.
4. **unkempt** [un·kempt']—(a) unknown. (b) unfurled. (c) untidy. (d) freed from a cage.
5. **untoward** [un·tôrd']—(a) unfortunate. (b) moving away or retreating. (c) uncovered. (d) absent-minded.
6. **uncivilized** [un·siv'ə·līzd]—(a) illegal. (b) barbarous. (c) unaffected. (d) barely within the law.
7. **unintelligible** [un'in·tel'ə·jə·bəl]—(a) incapable of being understood. (b) unable to be translated. (c) mutterings. (d) stupid.
8. **unparalleled** [un·par'ə·leld]—(a) out of line. (b) unmatched. (c) following a crooked course of action. (d) premeditated.
9. **unmitigated** [un·mit'ə·gā'tid]—(a) not wise. (b) incorrect. (c) unscrupulous. (d) as bad as can be.
10. **unwieldy** [un·wēl'dē]—(a) unaccustomed. (b) immoral. (c) bulky or clumsy. (d) slowly or carefully.

ANSWERS:

1. **unscathed**—(b) unharmed. 2. **uncompromising**—(c) strict or inflexible. 3. **unwonted**—(a) unaccustomed. 4. **unkempt**—(c) untidy. 5. **untoward**—(a) unfortunate. 6. **uncivilized**—(b) barbarous. 7. **unintelligible**—(a) incapable of being understood. 8. **unparalleled**—(b) unmatched. 9. **unmitigated**—(d) as bad as can be. 10. **unwieldy**—(c) bulky or clumsy.

QUICKIEQUIZQUICKIEQUIZQUICKIEQUIZQUICKIEQUIZQUICKIEQUIZQUICKIEQUIZQUICKIEQUIZQUICKIE

words, an *unapproachable* person lacks friendliness. *Inapproachable,* if used with precision, means "not approachable; incapable of being reached." An isolated place without a road is *inapproachable* by car.

Here are three core vocabulary words using the prefix *un-: unbroken, unbend, uncouth.*

unbroken comes from *un-* meaning "not; opposed to" and the word *broken.* Thus, *unbroken* means (1) whole or complete; (2) untamed; not trained for use; (3) without interruption; (4) unplowed.

The teacher maintained unbroken control of the students during the emergency.
Julia longed to tame the unbroken horse.
At rush hour, the highway fills with an unbroken stream of cars.
When they bought the farm, it had 160 acres of unbroken ground.

unbend stems from *un-* meaning "back," indicating the reversal of an action, plus the word *bend*. Thus, *unbend* means (1) to bend back into place again; straighten; (2) to relax, as after tension, exertion, restraint, or formality.

> *Can you unbend this crooked nail?*
> *I unbend after work by watching television.*

uncouth is formed from *un-* meaning "not" and an older English word that is no longer used: *couth*, meaning "known." *Uncouth* originally meant "unknown." Now, of course, *uncouth* means "unknowing"; hence, "lacking refinement; crude; awkward; boorish."

> *It is uncouth to eat peas with a knife.*
> *The peasant, though uncouth in manner and appearance, was nevertheless honest and hard-working.*

◊ There are literally hundreds of words in your dictionary that begin with the prefix *un-*. How many of them can you list in ten minutes? Here are a few to start with: *unable, unarmed, unavoidable, unbearable, unbelievable, uncertain, uncomfortable, undecided, undressed, uneven, unfaithful, ungrateful, unhappy, unjust, unknown, unnatural, unorganized, unprepared, unqualified, unsuccessful, untie, unusual, unwrap.*

Notice that *un-* can be prefixed to an almost endless variety of words. As is true with some other prefixes, you can easily make up a list of *un-* words yourself. Would you like to *uninvite* a guest who has made himself unwelcome, or *unpot* an unhealthy plant, or *uninvent* an unsuccessful excuse? How many valid *un-* words can you make up that are not in your dictionary? Few people know prefixes, roots, and suffixes well enough to make up intelligible words, but *un-* is a good place to start. English is a wonderful language when you know the building blocks! Make up an *un-* word and try it on your family or friends. The chances are good that they will understand exactly what you are trying to say.

EXPLORING WORDS

NUMBERING, COUNTING, AND MEASURING

English has borrowed many words, roots, and prefixes from Greek and Latin that are used in numbering, counting, and measuring. Here is a sample chart of such terms, showing the Greek and Latin forms and how we use them. Be sure you know the meaning of the words used as examples. Remember that September, October, November, and December were the seventh, eighth, ninth, and tenth months in the old Roman calendar.

MEANING	FROM THE GREEK	FROM THE LATIN
half	*hemi-* as in *hemisphere*	*semi-* as in *semicircle* *demi-* as in *demitasse*
one	*mono-* as in *monogamous, monologue*	*uni-* as in *union, unilateral*
first	*proto-* as in *prototype, protoplasm*	*prim-* as in *prime, primary, primitive*
two; twice; double; in two	*di-* as in *dichloride* *dicho-* as in *dichotomy*	*bi-* as in *bicycle, bigamy* *du-* or *duo-* as in *dual, duet, duplex, duodecimal*
three	*tri-* as in *tricycle, trigonometry, trimeter*	*tri-* as in *tricolor, trio* *ter-* as in *tercentenary*
four	*tetra-* as in *tetrameter*	*quadr-* as in *quadrangle, quadrilateral, quadruped* *quart-* as in *quarter, quartet*
five	*penta-* as in *pentagon, pentameter*	*quint-* as in *quintet, quintuplets*
six	*hexa-* as in *hexagonal, hexagram, hexameter*	*sex-* as in *sextet, sextuple*
seven	*hepta-* as in *heptameter*	*sept-* as in *September, septet*
eight	*oct-* as in *octopus, octagonal*	*oct-* as in *October, octave, octet*
nine	*ennea-* as in *ennead*	*Nov-* or *non-* as in *November, nonagon*
ten	*deca-* as in *decade*	*dec-* or *deci-* as in *December, decimal*

3 SUFFIXES—YOUR THIRD KEY TO WORD POWER

Suffixes are less important than roots and prefixes in vocabulary building because they are usually (though not always) added on to a root or word after the primary meaning of the word has been established by the basic root and prefix. In such cases, the suffix serves to indicate the function of the word (that is, its use or part of speech). You should be familiar with suffixes and know how they are used, but you need not learn them as fully as you learned roots and prefixes. The following chapters will tell you what you need to know about suffixes.

Remember what suffixes are and what they do. They are attached to the ends of words just as prefixes are attached to the beginnings. Suffixes can sometimes change the meaning of a word, but they are primarily used to reveal its function. Suffixes, for example, can indicate the number of a noun by changing the singular form to a plural form. Thus, the suffix -s added to the word *boy* forms *boys*—the suffix -s showing that *boy* is plural. For another example, suffixes can indicate the time of a verb by showing whether the action is in the past or the present. Thus, the suffix -ed added to the verb *walk* forms the past tense *walked*.

To state it another way, the meaning of many suffixes is general: they serve primarily to tell you whether a word is used as an action word (verb), a modifier (adjective or adverb), or the name of a person, place, or thing (noun); and they serve to distinguish between such things as number and tense.

NOUN SUFFIXES: ACTS, CONDITIONS, OR STATES

The following fifteen suffixes generally mean (1) the act, state, quality, means, process, result, or condition of (doing or being); (2) the beliefs, teachings, or system of; (3) devotion to.

-acity
> **audacity** the quality of being audacious; boldness.
> **capacity** (1) the ability to receive, hold, or contain; (2) mental ability; (3) specific character or office.

tenacity the quality of being tenacious; stubbornness; toughness.

-acy

celibacy the state of being unmarried.

confederacy the condition of being allied; hence, a union of persons or states for mutual support or action.

fallacy (1) the condition of being in error; hence, an erroneous or misleading notion; (2) any reasoning, argument, etc., that violates logical rules.

-al (or **-ial, -eal**)

betrayal the act of betraying or the state of being betrayed.

denial the act of denying.

refusal the act of refusing.

-ence (or **-ance, -ency, -ancy**)

influence the quality or condition of being able to produce effects on others.

acceptance the act of accepting or the state of being accepted.

-ion

audition (1) the act or sense of hearing; (2) a hearing, especially a trial hearing of a performer.

creation (1) the act of creating, or the fact of being created; (2) anything created, especially by human intelligence or imagination, as an artistic work; (3) everything created; the universe.

union (1) the act of uniting or the state of being united; (2) the joining of persons, parties, nations, etc., for a mutual purpose.

-ism

alcoholism an abnormal or diseased condition caused by excessive use of alcohol.

heroism the state or condition of being heroic; bravery.

skepticism the state or condition of being a skeptic.

-ment (or **-men**)

excitement the state of being excited.

monument literally, a means of remembering someone or something; hence (1) a memorial erected in memory of a person, event, etc.; (2) a tombstone.

specimen a person, animal, plant, or thing regarded as representative of its class or type; a sample.

-mony

matrimony (1) the state or condition of being married; (2) the act or ceremony of marriage.

267

parsimony the condition of being overly thrifty; stinginess.

-ness

coldness (1) the state or condition of being cold; chill. (2) the state of being unenthusiastic or unfriendly.

sleeplessness the condition of not being able to sleep.

goodness the state or condition of being good.

-or

ardor the condition or quality of being eager or enthusiastic; warmth of feeling.

error (1) the condition of being wrong; (2) a mistake.

-sis (or **-sy, -sia**)

analysis (1) an examination of the parts of any complex whole; (2) the act of separating a whole into its parts.

autopsy a medical examination of a corpse.

amnesia partial or total loss of memory; the state of having no memory.

-tude

longitude literally, the quality of being long (like the lines of longitude on a globe); hence, the distance east or west on the earth's surface, measured from the prime meridian that runs through Greenwich, England.

multitude literally, the condition of being many in numbers; hence, a great number or crowd.

-ty (or **-ety, -ity**)

notoriety the state of being widely known and generally disapproved of.

novelty (1) the quality of being new; (2) something new or unusual.

superiority the quality of being superior; excellence.

-ure

aperture an opening.

curvature the state of being curved; a curving.

pressure the act or result of pressing or weighing down on something.

-y

inquiry the act of inquiring or seeking for facts or truth; investigation.

perjury the act of giving false testimony.

victory the state or condition of being a victor; the act or result of winning a contest, a war, etc.; success; triumph.

268

COLORFUL ADJECTIVES

Below are sixteen colorful adjectives whose meanings you should know. Check the word or phrase that is closest in meaning to the key word. Answers follow.

1. **pristine** [pris′tēn]—(a) shining. (b) unspoiled or primitive. (c) priggish. (d) honest.
2. **raucous** [rô′kəs]—(a) boisterous. (b) flavorful. (c) strong and aggressive. (d) evil.
3. **mundane** [mun′dān]—(a) lazy. (b) pertaining to the moon. (c) sad or depressing. (d) routine or ordinary.
4. **nostalgic** [nos·tal′jik]—(a) wistfully sentimental. (b) harmless. (c) debonair. (d) nightmarish.
5. **aquiline** [ak′wə·līn]—(a) a blue-green color. (b) noble. (c) hooked or curved like an eagle's beak. (d) bulbous.
6. **dolorous** [dō′lər·əs]—(a) impoverished. (b) lazy. (c) foolish. (d) sad.
7. **lurid** [loor′id]—(a) black and blue. (b) sensational. (c) passionate. (d) enticing.
8. **innocuous** [i·nok′yoo·əs]—(a) empty. (b) immune. (c) simple-minded. (d) harmless.
9. **niggardly** [nig′ərd·lē]—(a) hot and humid. (b) cruel. (c) stingy. (d) gloomy.
10. **obstreperous** [əb·strep′ər·əs]—(a) disagreeable. (b) stubborn. (c) unruly. (d) conceited.
11. **precocious** [pri·kō′shəs]—(a) overconfident. (b) scholarly. (c) showing premature development. (d) conservative.
12. **sallow** [sal′ō]—(a) yellowish in color. (b) salty. (c) unused. (d) fertile.
13. **pallid** [pal′id]—(a) wise. (b) pale. (c) dull. (d) unused.
14. **callous** [kal′əs]—(a) sickly looking. (b) inexperienced. (c) nonchalant. (d) unfeeling.
15. **picaresque** [pik′ə·resk′]—(a) pertaining to a type of fiction with a rogue as a central character. (b) pertaining to a folk dance. (c) quaint. (d) pertaining to a bullfight.
16. **ribald** [rib′əld]—(a) funny. (b) coarse and indecent. (c) jeering. (d) disrespectful.

ANSWERS:

1. **pristine**—(b) unspoiled or primitive. 2. **raucous**—(a) boisterous. 3. **mundane**—(d) routine or ordinary. 4. **nostalgic**—(a) wistfully sentimental. 5. **aquiline** —(c) hooked or curved like an eagle's beak. 6. **dolorous**—(d) sad. 7. **lurid**—(b) sensational. 8. **innocuous**—(d) harmless. 9. **niggardly**—(c) stingy. 10. **obstreperous**—(c) unruly. 11. **precocious**—(c) showing premature development. 12. **sallow**—(a) yellowish in color. 13. **pallid**—(b) pale. 14. **callous**—(d) unfeeling. 15. **picaresque**—(a) pertaining to a type of fiction with a rogue as a central character. 16. **ribald**—(b) coarse and indecent.

NOUN SUFFIXES: PEOPLE, PLACES, AND THINGS

The following ten suffixes of nouns all mean (1) a person or thing that does, practices, or is characterized by or connected with something; (2) a native, citizen, or inhabitant of; (3) a follower of; (4) a place or instrument for.

·an (or **-ian, -ean, -ane**)

> **American** a native or inhabitant of America; specifically, an inhabitant or citizen of the United States.
>
> **crustacean** a type of animal characterized by crustlike shell, as a lobster or crab.

-ant (or **-ent**)

> **inhabitant** a person who lives in or inhabits a specific place.
>
> **resident** a person who resides in a specific house, city, state, etc.

-ar

> **beggar** a person who begs for his living.
>
> **scholar** a person connected with or characterized by knowledge or studying.

-ary

> **dictionary** literally, a book connected with speaking; hence, a reference book containing the words of a language, arranged alphabetically with meanings, pronunciations, etc.
>
> **library** a place for the collection and storage of books.
>
> **secretary** literally, a person who keeps secrets; hence, a person employed to handle the records, letters, etc.; of a business office or of an individual.

-er

> **baker** a person who bakes bread, cake, etc., for his living.
>
> **golfer** a person who plays golf.
>
> **traveler** a person who travels.

-ician

> **electrician** a person who designs, installs, operates, or repairs electrical wiring, equipment, etc.
>
> **logician** an expert in the use of logic.

-ist

> **communist** a person who believes in the doctrines of communism.
>
> **druggist** a person who prepares and deals in medical drugs.
>
> **genealogist** a specialist in the study of genealogy or family trees.

270

-ite
socialite a person connected with fashionable social life.
suburbanite a person who lives in the suburbs.

-or
agitator a person or thing that agitates; especially, a person who persists in political or social agitation for change.
competitor a person who competes against another.
donor a person who gives or donates something.

-ory
dormitory a large room with sleeping accommodations for many persons.
lavatory a place for washing, as a bathroom or sink.

The following three suffixes of nouns all mean (1) the art, science, or study of; (2) speech or discourse.

-ics (or **-tics**)
dramatics the art or study of drama, the theater, acting, etc.
linguistics the science of language.

-logy (or **-logue, -ology**)
biology the science of life in all its manifestations.
geology the science that deals with the origin and structure of the earth.

QUICKIEQUIZQUICKIEQUIZQUICKIEQUIZQUICKIEQUIZQUICKIEQUIZQUICKIEQUIZQUICKIEQUIZQUICKIE

30-SECOND QUICKIE QUIZ
-OLOGIES

Can you match the *-ology* with the field of study it pertains to? Answers follow.

1. theology [thē·ol′ə·jē]   (a) the development of humanity
2. anthropology [an′thrə·pol′ə·jē] (b) insects
3. geology [jē·ol′ə·jē]   (c) the earth
4. entomology [en′tə·mol′ə·jē]   (d) the weather
5. meteorology [mē′tē·ə·rol′ə·jē]   (e) religion

ANSWERS:

1. theology—(e) religion. 2. anthropology—(a) the development of humanity. 3. geology—(c) the earth. 4. entomology—(b) insects. 5. meteorology—(d) the weather.

QUICKIEQUIZQUICKIEQUIZQUICKIEQUIZQUICKIEQUIZQUICKIEQUIZQUICKIEQUIZQUICKIEQUIZQUICKIE

catalogue a list of names, objects, etc., usually in alphabetical order and often with accompanying descriptions.

dialogue a conversation between two or more people, actors, groups, etc.

monologue a long speech by one person.

-nomy

astronomy the science that deals with heavenly bodies, their motions, distances, etc.

economy (1) a system for developing and managing material resources; (2) careful management of money; thrift.

FIVE FAMILIAR SUFFIXES

The following five noun and verb suffixes are widely used, but are not related in meaning as are those already discussed.

-cracy means "rule by; government."

democracy literally, rule by the people; hence, a form of government in which political power is exercised by the people, either directly or through elected representatives.

plutocracy (1) government by the wealthy; (2) a class that controls a government by means of its wealth.

NOTE: The suffix *-cracy* has a related suffix *-crat* meaning "a person who supports a type of government or who belongs to a social class," such as *democrat, plutocrat, aristocrat.*

-graph means (1) a writing or drawing; (2) an instrument for writing, describing, or making sounds.

autograph (1) literally, a self-writing; hence, one's own signature; (2) to sign something with one's own signature.

telegraph (1) literally, distance-writing; hence, a device using coded impulses that are sent by wire or radio waves as messages; (2) to communicate by telegraph.

phonograph a motor-driven turntable with a pickup attachment for the playing of phonograph records.

NOTE: The suffix *-graph* has a related suffix *-graphy* meaning "the art of writing or drawing," as in *geography, photography, biography.*

-meter means (1) a measure; (2) an instrument for measuring.

    diameter (1) literally, the measure through; hence a straight line passing through the center of a circle and ending at the circumference; (2) the length of such a line.

    thermometer an instrument for measuring heat or temperature.

NOTE: The suffix -*meter* has a related suffix -*metry* meaning "the art or science of measuring," as in *geometry, trigonometry.*

-scope means "an instrument for viewing or observing."

    microscope literally, an instrument for viewing that which is smallest; hence, an instrument used for magnifying objects too small to be seen, or to be seen in detail, by the naked eye.

    stethoscope literally, an instrument for observing the chest; hence, a device for conveying the sounds of the chest to the doctor's ears.

    telescope literally, an instrument for viewing a distance; hence, an instrument for enlarging the image of a distant object.

-s (-es) indicates that the noun is in the plural form. It means that there are two or more persons, places, or things being spoken of.

> *The chairs are on the porch.*
> *Mr. Smith owns several houses.*
> *Foxes have been stealing our chickens.*

SUFFIXES THAT FORM VERBS

The seven suffixes discussed here are added to roots or words in order to form verbs (words indicating action) or to indicate the tense of a verb.

-ate, -fy, -ish, and **-ize** are verb suffixes that mean (1) to cause to be, become, have, or do; (2) to make; (3) to act or act upon; (4) to subject to; (5) to act in the manner of; practice. Here are some examples:

decimate literally, to act upon a whole so as to take away a tenth; to select a group by lot and kill one out of every ten; hence, to kill or destroy a large proportion.

nominate literally, to cause to be named; hence, to name or propose as a candidate.

terminate to cause to end or stop.

electrify literally, to make electric; hence, to install electricity.

gratify literally, to make pleasing; hence, (1) to please; (2) to satisfy or indulge.

pacify (1) to make peaceful; (2) to calm or soothe.

admonish literally, to cause to be warned; hence, (1) to advise someone of a fault; to reprove; (2) to caution against error or danger; to warn.

demolish (1) to tear down; (2) to destroy.

extinguish (1) to put out, as a fire; (2) to wipe out or destroy, as life.

Christianize to cause to become Christian.

terrorize to subject to terror.

criticize to act in the manner of a critic or to practice criticism.

-s indicates that the verb, or action word, is in the present tense. It means that the action is taking place in the present, or that it is habitual or takes place at a regular time. This suffix also indicates that the subject of the verb is the third person singular, that one person or thing—one *he, she,* or *it*—is responsible for the action.

> *Nanette comes to see us every Sunday.*
> *Mr. Smith goes to his office every day at nine.*
> *The young girl dances well.*
> *The late-morning train always arrives on time.*
> *It occurs to me that I made a mistake.*

-ed indicates that the verb is in some form of the past tense. It means that the action has taken place and is now either partly or completely finished.

> *He whisked out of sight as I approached.*
> *Jerry has already played in five professional football games.*
> *When he was in college, he played football.*
> *Before he entered Harvard, he had played football in high school.*

-ing indicates that the action word will appear with some form of the verb *to be* and will signify a continuing action. It means that *am,* *are, is, were, was, has been, have been,* or *had been* is part of the verb form.

> *I am depending on you.*
> *He was driving too fast.*
> *We have been trying to improve our vocabulary—and still are.*

TWENTY-NINE SUFFIXES THAT FORM MODIFIERS

All the suffixes listed here are added to roots or words in order to form modifiers; they indicate that the new word functions as an adjective or adverb.

Suffix: *-al* and Related Suffixes

-al (or its variant spelling **-ial**), **-ar, -ary, -ic, -id, -ile, -ine, -ish, -oid,** and **-ory** are adjective suffixes meaning (1) of, pertaining to, of the nature of, like; (2) having, related to, or serving for.

equal of the same size, quality, rank, character, etc.
filial of or pertaining to a son or daughter.
manual of or pertaining to the hand or hands; done by the hands.
postal pertaining to the mails.

popular (1) of or pertaining to the people at large; (2) liked by most people; (3) suited to the means of the people.
similar like something else or one another, but not identical.

honorary pertaining to an office, title, etc., bestowed as an honor, usually without powers, duties, or salary.
pecuniary consisting of or pertaining to money.
secondary of second rank, grade, influence, etc.; subordinate; subsequent.

academic pertaining to an academy, college, or university; scholarly.
chromatic pertaining to color or colors.
despotic of or like a despot; tyrannical.

gravid heavy with child; pregnant.
humid having much water vapor, as air.

lucid (1) having light; shining; bright; (2) clear; easily understood; (3) rational; mentally sound.

juvenile pertaining to the young; young; youthful.

volatile literally, flying; hence, (1) evaporating rapidly at ordinary temperature on exposure to the air; (2) easily influenced; fickle; changeable.

bovine belonging or pertaining to the family of animals that includes oxen, cows, etc.

canine (1) of or like a dog; (2) of the dog family.

feline (1) of or like a cat; (2) of the cat family.

boyish of or like a boy or boys.

greenish of or like green; somewhat green.

ovoid like an egg; egg-shaped.

spheroid similar to a sphere; nearly sphere-shaped.

compulsory (1) involving or using compulsion, or being coercive; (2) required.

introductory serving as an introduction.

laudatory of the nature of praise; complimentary.

Suffix: -*ate* and Related Forms

-ate, -fic, -ose, -ous, -ulent (and its variant spelling **-olent**), **-ulous,** and **-y** are adjective suffixes meaning "full of, like, having, making or causing, given to, or characterized by."

adequate equal to or having what is required.

caudate having a tail.

pinnate (1) like a feather; (2) having the shape or arrangement of a feather.

soporific causing or tending to cause sleep.

terrific literally, full of or causing terror; hence, (1) extreme, intense, or tremendous; (2) wonderful, great, or splendid.

grandiose (1) characterized by grandeur or producing an effect of grandeur; (2) pretentiously grand.

verbose wordy.

glorious (1) full of or deserving glory; (2) bringing glory or honor; (3) splendid; magnificent.

276

joyous full of joy; causing joy; joyful.

opulent having or showing great wealth; rich.
redolent full of a pleasant fragrance; giving off a scent.
violent (1) coming from or characterized by physical force; (2) harsh or severe; (3) extreme or intense.

credulous given to believing on slight evidence; gullible.
populous full of people; crowded.

feathery (1) covered with feathers; (2) light or airy.
risky characterized by risk; full of risk.

Suffix: -*able* and Related Forms

-able (and its variant spelling **-ible**), **-acious, -ile,** and **-ive** are adjective suffixes meaning (1) able, able to be, or capable of being; (2) given to, likely to, or tending to; (3) characterized by or having the character or quality of.

peaceable (1) given to keeping the peace; (2) peaceful or tranquil.
audible capable of being heard.
terrible (1) likely to arouse terror; appalling; (2) extreme; severe; (3) awe-inspiring; (4) inferior; very bad.

tenacious tending to hold on strongly; hence, (1) holding strongly to opinions, beliefs, etc.; (2) stubborn.
voracious (1) eating with greediness or given to devouring things; (2) greedy; (3) never satisfied.

agile able to move quickly and easily.
docile able to be taught; obedient.

attractive (1) tending to attract interest, admiration, or affection; (2) exerting physical attraction, as a magnet.
massive having the quality of mass; having great bulk and weight.
secretive given to secrecy; reticent.

Suffix: -*an*

-an (or its variant spellings **-ian, -ean, -ane**) is an adjective suffix meaning (1) of, pertaining to, belonging to, or living in; (2) following.
human of, belonging to, or characteristic of man.

277

Confucian of or pertaining to Confucius; following the teachings of Confucius.

Grecian of, from, or pertaining to Greece or its people; Greek.

European of, from, or pertaining to Europe or its peoples.

urbane literally, belonging to the city; hence, having the refinement or elegance of manner associated with city life; suave.

Suffix: -*less*

-less is an adjective suffix meaning (1) lacking or without; (2) not able to; (3) not susceptible to or capable of being.

lifeless without life; inanimate or dead.

countless not capable of being counted; too many to count.

priceless without a price; too valuable to have a price.

sleepless not able to sleep; wakeful.

stainless (1) without a stain or spot; (2) not susceptible to staining; easy to keep clean.

toothless (1) not characterized by teeth, as a bird; (2) having lost all of one's teeth.

Suffix: -*ent*

-ent (or its variant spelling **-ant**) is an adjective suffix meaning "having the quality of or performing the action of." In many cases -*ent* is equivalent to -*ing*.

incumbent (1) resting upon one as a moral obligation; obligatory; (2) resting, leaning, or weighing upon something.

stringent literally, drawing tight; hence, compelling adherence to strict requirements; severe.

dormant (1) sleeping or motionless through sleep; (2) inactive.

Suffix: -*ing*

-ing is used to form the present participle of verbs and to form adjectives based on these participles. Among other things, it can mean (1) now doing the action indicated; (2) for or used for; (3) that results in. It is used with these meanings in the following phrases:

a running man   a cooking apple   a winning number

Suffix: -ed

-ed is used to form adjectives based on the past participles of verbs. It means "one who or that which has been or was."

an educated person	an overrated book
an interrupted journey	a scratched table

The suffix **-ed** is also used to form adjectives based on nouns. When so used, it means "one who or that which has, is, or resembles."

a four-footed animal	a winged cupid
a blue-eyed cat	dogged determination
a stoop-shouldered man	an eared seal

Suffix: -er

-er may be used to form the comparative of both adjectives and adverbs. It means "more than another or others."

colder	higher	smaller	sooner
greater	longer	shorter	later
brighter	greener	duller	sleepier

Suffix: -est

-est may be used to form the superlative of both adjectives and adverbs. It means "the most; the most of any or of all."

coldest	highest	smallest	soonest
greatest	longest	shortest	latest

Suffix: -ly

-ly is a suffix added to words to form modifiers—sometimes forming adjectives from nouns, and sometimes forming adverbs from either nouns or adjectives. It can mean (1) being or acting as; (2) in a certain manner or time; (3) characterized by; (4) with respect to.

a friendly man	recently ill
speaking quickly	a perfectly lovely day
a daily delivery	physically sound
suddenly afraid	mentally unbalanced

279

EXPLORING WORDS

English has a number of suffixes that are called diminutives; they show that the word to which they are attached refers to a miniature-sized version of the object. The diminutive suffixes are: *-cle, -cule, -el, -et* (or *-ette*), *-il, -let, -ling,* and *-ule.* All these suffixes mean "small." Here are fourteen words using these diminutive suffixes:

booklet a small book.

capsule literally, a small box; hence, (1) a small soluble container for enclosing a dose of medicine; (2) a small, detachable compartment of an airplane or spacecraft.

cigarette literally, a small cigar; hence, a small roll of finely cut tobacco for smoking, wrapped in a cylinder of paper.

codicil [kod′ə·səl] literally, a small writing tablet; hence, a supplement to a will, changing or explaining something; an addition. A codicil is so called because it is brief.

darling literally, little dear (*dar-* is an ancient variant spelling of *dear*); hence, a person tenderly loved.

duckling a young duck.

globule [glob′yo͞ol] literally, a small globe; hence, a tiny sphere of matter or drop of liquid.

gosling a young goose.

islet a small island.

leaflet literally, a small leaf, as a leaf of folded paper; hence, a small printed sheet of paper or a brochure.

molecule literally, a small mass; hence, the smallest particle of an element or compound that can exist separately without losing its physical or chemical properties.

morsel literally, a small bite; hence, a small piece of anything.

particle (1) a small part or piece of matter; a speck; (2) a very small amount.

suckling literally, an unweaned young animal or child; hence, (1) an unweaned mammal; (2) an infant or very young child.

PART TWO

Spell It Right

SPELLING—A SKILL THAT CAN BE LEARNED

Do some people have an inborn talent for spelling that many of us lack? The answer is no. An ability to spell is not inherited, and neither is an inability to spell. Spelling is a skill that can be learned. If it seems to come easy for some people, it is because they have learned it. You can become an excellent speller if you want to.

There are four main reasons why many normal, intelligent adults have trouble with spelling: (1) They never acquire the habit of looking closely at words, of questioning the spelling as they read a word or write it down; (2) they learned to hate spelling at school because, instead of being taught helpful rules, they were forced to learn seemingly disorganized lists of words; (3) they lack the energy, will power, or ambition to succeed at spelling; (4) although they know they have bad spelling habits, they have not yet realized that they can change those habits by studying meaningful word lists and practical guides to spelling power. This section provides you with just such lists and guides. Study them carefully and you will soon discover that you have broken bad old habits and have acquired good new ones.

Let us begin by admitting that English is not an easy language to spell. There are twenty-six letters in our alphabet as against about forty-five basic sounds—and the letters seldom match the sounds! Thus, one specific sound can be (and often is) spelled in a number of different ways; and, to complicate the problem even further, a single letter may represent any one of a variety of sounds (for instance, *a* stands for one sound in *day*, another in *hat*, and still another in *call*). Similarly, two vowels used together can represent totally dissimilar sounds, as the *ou* in *bough* [bou], the *ou* in *tough* [tuf], and that in *slough* [slōō], when it means a swampy place.

Matching a letter of the alphabet with a familiar sound can sometimes stump even the best of spellers. Take, for example, the simple words *pArade, sickEn, clarIty, melOn,* and *focUs*. In those five words the letters *a, e, i, o,* and *u* are all pronounced precisely the same way, as "uh"[ə]. Is it any wonder that some people have a hard time getting the fourth letter right in *sepArate?* Or, for an even more striking example, say the following words out loud: *stAge, rAIn, gAUge, dAY, matinEE, brEAk, vEIl, rEIGn, wEIGH, thEY*. The very same sound in those ten words [ā] is spelled in ten entirely different ways—and there are others as well.

There is only one rule, therefore, that will solve all spelling problems for you: When in doubt, look up the word in your dictionary. You should always have a dictionary within easy reach—in school, in the office, and at home.

Remember, though, that a dictionary is a reference book, not a teaching book. It will tell you how to spell a hard word, but if you do not learn the word now, you'll probably have to look it up all over again next week. So, although you can rely on your dictionary in a pinch, you should not rely on it exclusively. There are dozens of useful and easy-to-learn rules and guides that can make you a competent speller without constant reference to the dictionary. In the following chapters you will find such spelling aids explained, along with lists of related words and tips on how to master individual words that are your own personal spelling demons. Even the best of spellers encounter a few stumbling blocks. The spellings of look-alike words with different meanings, such as *principal* and *principle,* have often been confused by writers who should know better.

The words in these pages have been chosen with care. They are the useful words most commonly misspelled, as revealed in hundreds of thousands of tests given to elementary-school, high-school, secretarial-school, and college students, to Civil Service and other government workers, to job applicants, and to employees and executives of large companies. The words also include spelling demons from the Fitzgerald Master List, the Remington Rand List, state-board and college-entrance examinations, Gregg Secretarial lists, *The American School Board Journal,* style books of newspapers, magazines, and book publishers, and even from the National Spelling Bee.

You will almost certainly find your personal spelling demons discussed here. Don't waste time on the many words whose spellings you have already mastered. Concentrate on the ones you aren't sure of. As with learning to drive a car, play a game, or bake a cake, learning to spell will take time and concentration. But if your heart is in it, you will succeed in teaching yourself to be a better speller by making the most of these rules, tips, and tests. You will find that it is fun to test yourself, the members of your family, and your friends.

Faulty spelling can hinder a person's progress in both business and social life. On the other hand, the man or woman who writes business reports, letters, club notes, and so on without mistakes in spelling is very often the person who gets ahead. Now is your chance. Be sure to take it. Perfecting your spelling will require some effort and practice on your part, but you will find it worthwhile.

1 THE MOST FREQUENTLY MISSPELLED WORDS

What is the most commonly misspelled word in the English language? No one knows for sure. But it may well be any of these four:

all right   receive

coming   separate

For school children, the most frequently misspelled word might be any of the above four or *bicycle, description, really, similar,* or *writing.*

For office workers, secretaries, and businessmen, the culprit might be any of these:

advertisement   envelope

correspondence   recommend

definite   schedule

Housewives might most frequently misspell any of these words:

acquaintance   pleasant

development   spinach

This chapter will concentrate on everyday words that cause more than eighty percent of all spelling mistakes. Learn these words, drill yourself on them, review them at every opportunity. After you master them, spelling should never again be a major problem for you.

Sixth-Grade Spelling Demons

Here is a list of some of the most common spelling demons of sixth-graders. Many well-educated adults still misspell some of them. Check yourself to see whether you need to relearn any of them.

accommodate	Christmas	minute
across	coming	missile
already (one word)	deceive	niece
arithmetic	description, describe	really
athletics, athlete	February	separate
balloon	forty	similar
bicycle	fourth	sincerely
business	good night (two words)	studying
ceiling	grammar	surprise
challenge	Halloween	writing, written

High-School Spelling Demons

The following list contains eighty-seven of the words that are most frequently misspelled by high-school seniors and graduates. It is based on classroom lists, studies in *The American School Board Journal,* state-board and regents' tests, college-entrance and placement exams, and job-application tests given by large firms. Thus, this list is based on tests given to more than 87,000 high-school seniors and graduates from 750 different American high schools. Note that the words in italics also appeared on the sixth-grade spelling list, and that high-school students have been misspelling them since the sixth grade!

absence	embarrass	occasion
absurd	environment	occurred
accidentally	equipped	occurrence
accommodate	escape	omitted
across	exaggerate	opportunity
advertisement	excellent	parallel
all right	existence	parliament
amateur	experience	performance
athletics	familiar	permanent
attendance	fascinate	pleasant
beginning	*February*	possess
believe	foreign	prejudice
business	*forty*	privilege
coming	government	professor
committee	*grammar*	receive
condemn	guidance	recommend
conscious	humorous	repetition
convenient	imaginary	restaurant
correspondence	immediately	rhythm
criticize	independent	schedule
definite	irresistible	*separate*
dependent	laboratory	*similar*
descend	lightning	success
description	losing	*surprise*
desperate	lovely	tragedy
develop	misspelled	truly
difference	necessary	villain
disappoint	neighbor	weird
dispensable	*niece*	*writing*

TWO-MINUTE QUICKIE QUIZ
EASY

Choose the correctly spelled word from each pair below. This quiz contains problems from the sixth-grade and high-school-graduate lists. Take the test repeatedly until you do not hesitate at any pair, and can give all the correct answers in two minutes. Answers follow.

1. (a) separate	(b) seperate
2. (a) cieling	(b) ceiling
3. (a) schedual	(b) schedule
4. (a) parliament	(b) parlament
5. (a) comming	(b) coming
6. (a) wierd	(b) weird
7. (a) posess	(b) possess
8. (a) condem	(b) condemn
9. (a) missile	(b) missle
10. (a) speech	(b) speach
11. (a) truely	(b) truly
12. (a) fourty	(b) forty
13. (a) ninty	(b) ninety
14. (a) writing	(b) writting
15. (a) written	(b) writen
16. (a) lovely	(b) lovly
17. (a) Halloween	(b) Haloween
18. (a) until	(b) untill
19. (a) decieve	(b) deceive
20. (a) restaurant	(b) resteraunt
21. (a) accommodate	(b) acommodate
22. (a) February	(b) Febuary
23. (a) beseige	(b) besiege
24. (a) balloon	(b) baloon
25. (a) excellent	(b) excelent

ANSWERS:

1. (a) separate. 2. (b) ceiling. 3. (b) schedule. 4. (a) parliament. 5. (b) coming. 6. (b) weird. 7. (b) possess. 8. (b) condemn. 9. (a) missile. 10. (a) speech. 11. (b) truly. 12. (b) forty. 13. (b) ninety. 14. (a) writing. 15. (a) written. 16. (a) lovely. 17. (a) Halloween. 18. (a) until. 19. (b) deceive. 20. (a) restaurant. 21. (a) accommodate. 22. (a) February. 23. (b) besiege. 24. (a) balloon. 25. (a) excellent.

Could You Pass a Civil Service Exam?

Since many people who take written Civil Service exams are likely to be high-school graduates, the words most frequently misspelled on these exams are almost the same as those on the high-school spelling list. In addition, Civil Service exams show twenty-five more spelling demons related to government, finance, and office work. Here are those additional words:

accident	federal	salary
auxiliary	filing (*vs.* filling)	simplified
career	legality	society
catalog	mechanism	supervisor
clerical	monetary	technical
county (*vs.* country)	municipal	tendency
comptroller [kən·trō′lər]	personnel (*vs.* personal)	yield
enforcement	president	
expedient	responsibility	

Two Years of College

This list contains seventy-six words most frequently misspelled by students after two years of college work. Note that forty-two of these, printed in italics, are carried over from the high-school list. Obviously these are words that many students cannot spell when they graduate from high school and still can't manage after two years of college. The list is based on spelling tests that were given to more than 27,000 students and adults who had completed two years of college at 135 institutions throughout the United States.

absence	cemetery	*dependent*	*environment*
accidentally	*coming*	descendant	*exaggerate*
achieve	*committee*	desirable	exceed
aggravate	competition	despair	exercise
all right	conscientious	*develop*	*existence*
amateur	*conscious*	dining	*foreign*
appearance	convenience	disappear	*forty*
argument	*correspondence*	*disappoint*	*government*
athlete	council	*dispensable*	grievance
believe	*criticize*	*embarrass*	*irresistible*
benefited	definitely	enforcement	knowledge

287

laboratory	*occurrence*	procedure	*rhythm*
losing	*omitted*	proceed	*schedule*
maintenance	*parallel*	pronunciation	*separate*
marriage	*permanent*	*receive*	superintendent
mischievous	permissible	*recommend*	supersede
noticeable	precede	*repetition*	*tragedy*
occasion	*prejudice*	responsibility	*villain*
occurred	*privilege*	restaurant	*weird*

Business and Professional People Often Have Spelling Problems

Many college graduates, business executives, and professional people still have spelling problems. Here are fifty-one words they misspell most often. In this list, the words printed in italics are carried over from the two-years-of-college list. The other words not printed in italics are "new."

accessible	*embarrass*	*permissible*
acquainted	envelope	perseverance
all right	*exceed*	*precede*
analyze	*existence*	*prejudice*
appearance	incidentally	*privilege*
assistant	insistent	*proceed*
burglar	intercede	recognize
campaign	*irresistible*	*recommend*
canceled	irritable	*repetition*
coming	*laboratory*	*restaurant*
conscientious	license	*schedule*
coolly	loneliness	seize
correspondence	mortgage	*superintendent*
desirable	*occasion*	*supersede*
develop	*occurred*	*villain*
dispensable	*occurrence*	*weird*
drunkenness	*omitted*	withhold

The typical high-school graduate can spell about half of the words in this list correctly. The typical college graduate can spell thirty-seven (73 percent) of them correctly. What is your score?

It is interesting that *coming* has been on all spelling-demon lists since the sixth-grade list. It is certainly not hard to learn, but it must be hard to remember. Twenty other words on the business and professional list were not only on the college-sophomore list but also on the high-school list. This indicates how difficult bad spelling habits are to break. Here's your chance. Learn every word on each of the above lists thoroughly; then wait two days and look at the list again. If you still can't spell every word without hesitation, restudy the words that stump you.

QUICKIEQUIZQUICKIEQUIZQUICKIEQUIZQUICKIEQUIZQUICKIEQUIZQUICKIEQUIZQUICKIEQUIZQUICKIE

TWO-MINUTE QUICKIE QUIZ
MEDIUM

Choose the correctly spelled word from each pair below. This quiz comes from the high-school, Civil Service, and college lists. Repeat the test until you can give all the correct answers in two minutes. Answers follow.

1. (a) rhythm   (b) rhithm
2. (a) foreign   (b) foriegn
3. (a) equiped   (b) equipped
4. (a) absence   (b) abcense
5. (a) criticise   (b) criticize
6. (a) priviledge   (b) privilege
7. (a) prejudise   (b) prejudice
8. (a) omitted   (b) omited
9. (a) dependant   (b) dependent
10. (a) irresistible   (b) irresistable
11. (a) recommend   (b) reccommend
12. (a) occurred   (b) occured
13. (a) occassion   (b) occasion
14. (a) professor   (b) proffesor
15. (a) committee   (b) commitee
16. (a) permanant   (b) permanent
17. (a) independent   (b) independant
18. (a) embarass   (b) embarrass
19. (a) escape   (b) excape
20. (a) humourus   (b) humorous
21. (a) argument   (b) arguement
22. (a) performence   (b) performance
23. (a) indifferance   (b) indifference
24. (a) attendence   (b) attendance

ANSWERS:

1. (a) rhythm. 2. (a) foreign. 3. (b) equipped. 4. (a) absence. 5. (b) criticize. 6. (b) privilege. 7. (b) prejudice. 8. (a) omitted. 9. (b) dependent. 10. (a) irresistible. 11. (a) recommend. 12. (a) occurred. 13. (b) occasion. 14. (a) professor. 15. (a) committee. 16. (b) permanent. 17. (a) independent. 18. (b) embarrass. 19. (a) escape. 20. (b) humorous. 21. (a) argument. 22. (b) performance. 23. (b) indifference. 24. (b) attendance.

QUICKIEQUIZQUICKIEQUIZQUICKIEQUIZQUICKIEQUIZQUICKIEQUIZQUICKIEQUIZQUICKIEQUIZQUICKIE

How Do the Spelling Experts Do?

Some people are particularly good spellers—among them English teachers, editors, and writers. The following list consists of sixty-two reasonably plain, everyday words that are most commonly misspelled by even such experts. Those words in the list that are followed by an asterisk (*) have determined high-school-student winners—and losers —of the annual United States National Spelling Bee. How many of these words can you spell correctly? (Where a second spelling is termed "also acceptable," the first is nonetheless preferred.)

abscess*	exhilarate*	phlegm
accelerator	fission*	picnicking
aggressor*	fricassee*	prairie
allotted	fuselage	prescription
annihilate*	gaiety	propeller
assassin	gynecologist	questionnaire*
battalion*	harebrained*	raspberry
besiege	hippopotamus*	requiem*
broccoli*	hypocrisy*	rhinoceros
catalyst*	immaculate	sacrilegious*
category	innocuous	sheriff
chrysanthemum*	inoculate	sieve
connoisseur*	liquefy*	solder [sod'ər]
demagogue	millionaire	subpoena*
desiccate*	miscellaneous	tariff
dilapidated	moccasin*	tonsillitis
discriminate	paraffin	tyranny
disheveled	paralyze	vacillate
dissipate	pedagogue	vanilla
ecstasy*	penitentiary	victuals* [vit'lz]
effervescent	perspiration	

Note that such "simple" words as *category, gaiety, raspberry,* and *vanilla* are on this experts' list. Are you surprised? Don't be. So-called "simple" words can be among the worst spelling demons.

No question about it: This last list is a tough one. Most college graduates can spell only about thirty-five (56 percent) of these words. Most experts get about fifty-three (85 percent) right. Use the experts' list for fun—to stump your family and friends and to hold your own spelling bees at home.

THREE-MINUTE QUICKIE QUIZ
HARD

Choose the correctly spelled word from each pair below. This quiz is from the college-graduate and experts' lists. Take the test repeatedly until you can give all the correct answers in three minutes. Answers follow.

1.	(a) campagne	(b) campaign
2.	(a) recognize	(b) reconize
3.	(a) sherrif	(b) sheriff
4.	(a) dissipate	(b) disippate
5.	(a) genealogy	(b) geneology
6.	(a) develope	(b) develop
7.	(a) an envelop	(b) an envelope
8.	(a) sieve	(b) seive
9.	(a) ecstasy	(b) exstacy
10.	(a) hypocracy	(b) hypocrisy
11.	(a) proceed	(b) procede
12.	(a) exceed	(b) excede
13.	(a) preceed	(b) precede
14.	(a) supercede	(b) supersede
15.	(a) responsability	(b) responsibility
16.	(a) desireable	(b) desirable
17.	(a) assistant	(b) assistent
18.	(a) seize	(b) sieze
19.	(a) cemetary	(b) cemetery
20.	(a) mischievious	(b) mischievous
21.	(a) questionnaire	(b) questionaire
22.	(a) millionnaire	(b) millionaire
23.	(a) auxilliary	(b) auxiliary
24.	(a) perscription	(b) prescription
25.	(a) millennium	(b) millenium

ANSWERS:

1. (b) campaign. 2. (a) recognize. 3. (b) sheriff. 4. (a) dissipate. 5. (a) genealogy. 6. (b) develop. 7. (b) an envelope. 8. (a) sieve. 9. (a) ecstasy. 10. (b) hypocrisy. 11. (a) proceed. 12. (a) exceed. 13. (b) precede. 14. (b) supersede. 15. (b) responsibility. 16. (b) desirable. 17. (a) assistant. 18. (a) seize. 19. (b) cemetery. 20. (b) mischievous. 21. (a) questionnaire. 22. (b) millionaire. 23. (b) auxiliary. 24. (b) prescription. 25. (a) millennium.

2 SAYING IT AND SPELLING IT

Many simple words are misspelled because they are mispronounced. Thus, if you mispronounce *Feb·ru·ar·y* as *Feb·yoo·ar·y* or *ath·lete* as *ath·a·lete,* you are likely to misspell them, too. Here is a list of fourteen simple words that are often mispronounced. You will have no trouble with the spellings if you say the words correctly.

accidentaALly
arCtic
asparAgus
atHlete
envirONment
eScape
FebRuary

goverNment
libRary
PERspiration
PREscription
sophOmore
temperAment
temperAture

When Pronunciation Isn't Much Help

Sometimes, of course, proper pronunciation won't help you to spell a word properly. For example, the "uh" sound (the schwa or ə sound) can be spelled in many different ways: as the letter *a, e, i, o,* or *u.* You must learn which of these letters is used in spelling certain words. Pronunciation won't help.

Silent letters are also a problem. A silent letter is one that is necessary for the correct spelling of a word but that is not pronounced. Thus, the *g* in *gnat* and the *b* in *climb* are silent letters. *Gnat* and *climb* are not spelling demons, of course, but some words having silent letters are. Here is a list of words in which pronunciation doesn't help in spelling. The silent letters appear in parentheses.

han(d)kerchief	r(h)yme	recei(p)t
We(d)nesday	r(h)ythm	ai(s)le
poi(g)nant	parl(i)ament	vi(s)count
rei(g)n	a(l)mond	apos(t)le
ex(h)ibition	colum(n)	ches(t)nut
r(h)apsody	condem(n)	gris(t)le
r(h)eumatism	cor(ps) (silent *p*	mor(t)gage
r(h)inoceros	and silent *s*)	gun(w)ale
r(h)ubarb	(p)tomaine	(w)retch

Many other words have silent letters, such as *han(d)some, g(h)ost, (h)our, i(s)land, lis(t)en, (w)rong,* etc., but most of them are not spelling demons for most adults.

Thus, pronunciation can sometimes help your spelling (as with *Feb(R)uary* and *at(H)lete*) and can sometimes be of no help at all (as with *parl(i)ament* and *mor(t)gage*). When pronunciation can help you, use it. When it can't help, use the spelling tips, rules, and lists that you will learn in the following chapters.

QUICKIEQUIZQUICKIEQUIZQUICKIEQUIZQUICKIEQUIZQUICKIEQUIZQUICKIEQUIZQUICKIEQUIZQUICKIE

ONE-MINUTE QUICKIE QUIZ
SPELLING AND PRONUNCIATION

Choose the correctly spelled word from each pair below. Repeat the test until you can give all correct answers in one minute. Answers follow.

1. (a) apostle (b) aposle
2. (a) environment (b) enviroment
3. (a) prespiration (b) perspiration
4. (a) perscription (b) prescription
5. (a) morgage (b) mortgage
6. (a) lisle (b) laile
7. (a) condem (b) condemn
8. (a) accidentally (b) accidently
9. (a) parlament (b) parliament
10. (a) athalete (b) athlete
11. (a) rhubarb (b) rubarb
12. (a) rhinestone (b) rinestone
13. (a) temperament (b) temperment
14. (a) aile (b) aisle
15. (a) poignant (b) poinant
16. (a) hankerchief (b) handkerchief
17. (a) receipt (b) receit
18. (a) artic (b) arctic
19. (a) chessnut (b) chestnut
20. (a) almond (b) amond
21. (a) exhibition (b) exibition
22. (a) asparagus (b) aspargus
23. (a) escape (b) excape
24. (a) tomaine (b) ptomaine
25. (a) rinoceros (b) rhinoceros

ANSWERS:

1. (a) aposTle. 2. (a) enviroNment. 3. (b) PERspiration. 4. (b) PREscription. 5. (b) morTgage. 6. (a) liSle. 7. (b) condemN. 8. (a) accidentALly. 9. (b) parlIament. 10. (b) atHlete. 11. (a) rHubarb. 12. (a) rHinestone. 13. (a) temperAment. 14. (b) aiSle. 15. (a) poiGnant. 16. (b) hanDkerchief. 17. (a) receiPt. 18. (b) arCtic. 19. (b) chesTnut. 20. (a) aLmond. 21. (a) exHibition. 22. (a) asparAgus. 23. (a) eScape. 24. (b) Ptomaine. 25. (b) rHinoceros.

QUICKIEQUIZQUICKIEQUIZQUICKIEQUIZQUICKIEQUIZQUICKIEQUIZQUICKIEQUIZQUICKIEQUIZQUICKIE

3 WHICH IS IT: -ABLE or -IBLE?

W ords ending in -able and -ible are spelling nightmares because their endings sound alike. Words such as *agreeable, comfortable, horrible, visible,* for example, usually cause problems. The -able words (adjectives) have related -ably forms (adverbs) and the -ible words (adjectives) have related -ibly forms, as in *agreeably, comfortably, horribly, visibly,* etc. Thus, whatever is said about -able and -ible in this chapter also applies to -ably and -ibly. Fortunately, two points about -able and -ible simplify the decision as to which spelling is correct. Here are the points:

Point 1: -able is the basic form. Many more words end in -able than in -ible. When in doubt, and if your dictionary is temporarily unavailable, use -able (or -ably).

Point 2: An *a* for an *a* and an *i* for an *i:* If the adjective is closely related to a noun that ends in -ation, the adjective is almost certain to end in -able; if a related noun ends in -ion instead of -ation, the adjective is pretty sure to end in -ible. To figure out that *demonstrable* should end in -able, think of the well-known noun *demonstration.* In like manner, you can figure out *considerable* from *consideration, impenetrable* from *penetration,* and so on for hundreds of -able (or -ably) words. Similarly, you can figure out *admissible* from *admission, destructible* from *destruction,* etc.

Here is a list of -able and -ible words that you will spell correctly every time if you remember Point 2 about *a* for an *a* and *i* for an *i:*

-ATION becomes -ABLE		-ION becomes -IBLE	
adaptation	adaptable	accession	accessible
adoration	adorable	admission	admissible
application	applicable	apprehension	apprehensible
commendation	commendable	audition	audible
consideration	considerable	coercion	coercible
demonstration	demonstrable	combustion	combustible
dispensation	dispensable	comprehension	comprehensible
duration	durable	compression	compressible
estimation	estimable	conversion	convertible
explication	explicable	corruption	corruptible

-ATION becomes -ABLE		-ION becomes -IBLE	
imitation	imitable	deduction	deductible
impregnation	impregnable	destruction	destructible
inflammation	inflammable	digestion	digestible
irritation	irritable	division	divisible
justification	justifiable	exhaustion	exhaustible
lamentation	lamentable	expansion	expansible
navigation	navigable	extension	extensible
penetration	penetrable	perception	perceptible
reparation	reparable	perfection	perfectible
separation	separable	permission	permissible
toleration	tolerable	reduction	reducible
transportation	transportable	reprehension	reprehensible
valuation	valuable	repression	repressible
		reversion	reversible
		suppression	suppressible
		transmission	transmissible
		vision	visible

NOTE: (1) As this list shows, when a negative prefix, such as *un-*, *non-*, *dis-*, *im-*, *in-*, or *ir-*, is added to the adjective or adverb, the basic fact about *-able* or *-ible* and *-ably* or *-ibly* remains unaffected.

(2) Some of the words in the list have minor internal changes. For instance, *conversion* is related to *convertible*, *inflection* to *flexible*, *reduction* to *reducible*, etc. Such internal changes are not important; the basic *-able, -ible* fact remains the same: *a* for an *a* and *i* for an *i*.

(3) Remember that Point 2 is not a rule. It is a helpful guide to the spelling of a great many *-able* and *-ible* words, but there are others to which this interesting relationship does not apply. And, too, there are certain exceptions to the *a*-for-an-*a* and *i*-for-an-*i* guideline. *Correctable* and *detectable* are the preferred spellings of the adjectives, for example, despite the noun forms *correction* and *detection*. *Sensible* is correct, in spite of *sensation;* and *predictable* is correct, in spite of *prediction*. These are only four major exceptions; there are several others.

-able Is Added to Whole Words, *-ible* to Stems

Here is another helpful guide to spelling these troublesome adjectives and adverbs: With some exceptions, provided later, the suffix *-able*

295

is often added to whole words such as *agree* (*agreeable*); to whole words minus their final *-e*, such as *cure* (*curable*); and to whole words whose final *-y* is changed to *-i*, such as *rely* (*reliable*). The suffix *-ible*, on the other hand, is often added to apparently meaningless groups of letters and to stems or roots that are not whole words, as in *horrible*, *terrible*. For example:

-ABLE		-IBLE	
(added to whole words; to whole words minus a final *-e;* and to whole words whose final *-y* is changed to *-i*)		(added to meaningless groups of letters and to non-word roots or stems)	
agree	agreeable	compat-	compatible
change	changeable	controvert-	controvertible
compar(e)	comparable	cred-	credible
deplor(e)	deplorable	cruc-	crucible
desir(e)	desirable	del-	indelible
enforce	enforceable	ed-	edible
env(y)	enviable	elig-	eligible
excus(e)	excusable	fall-	fallible
liv(e)	livable	feas-	feasible
marriage	marriageable	horr-	horrible
notice	noticeable	intellig-	intelligible
peace	peaceable	leg-	legible
pleasur(e)	pleasurable	neglig-	negligible
receiv(e)	receivable	ostens-	ostensible
rel(y)	reliable	plaus-	plausible
replace	replaceable	suscept-	susceptible
revok(e)	revocable	tang-	tangible
service	serviceable	terr-	terrible
trace	traceable	vinc-	invincible

-ABLE		-IBLE	
(added to roots and stems)		(added to whole words)	
ami-	amiable	collaps(e)	collapsible
cap-	capable	contempt	contemptible
despic-	despicable	defens(e)	indefensible
formid-	formidable	resist	irresistible
memor-	memorable	respons(e)	responsible

Spelling Test—Fourteen -able, -ible Spelling Mistakes

Add -able or -ible to complete the following words. These words are the fourteen most common -able, -ible spelling demons. Repeat this quiz as many times as you need until you can give all the correct answers.

1. convert_____
2. respons_____
3. suscept_____
4. depend_____
5. notice_____
6. change_____
7. contempt_____

8. desir_____
9. irresist_____
10. liv_____
11. compat_____
12. divis_____
13. irrit_____
14. indispens_____

ANSWERS:

1. convertIBLE. 2. responsIBLE. 3. susceptIBLE. 4. dependABLE. 5. noticeABLE. 6. changeABLE. 7. contemptIBLE. 8. desirABLE. 9. irresistIBLE. 10. livABLE. 11. compatIBLE. 12. divisIBLE. 13. irritABLE. 14. indispens-ABLE.

QUICKIEQUIZQUICKIEQUIZQUICKIEQUIZQUICKIEQUIZQUICKIEQUIZQUICKIEQUIZQUICKIEQUIZQUICKIEQUIZ

QUICKIE QUIZ
STUMP YOUR FRIENDS

Stump your family and friends with this -able, -ible paragraph, or test yourself by having someone dictate it to you.

The Internal Revenue Service said the tax form I filled out was *terribly illegible, incomprehensible,* and *noticeably implausible.* My financial records of *taxable* income were *accessible* to the tax bureau, but these records were said to be *undependable, unreliable, unsuitable, irresponsible,* and *inadmissible.* Though the tax bureau did not hold me *blamable,* its attitude made me *uncomfortable.* Thus, I hoped its attitude would be *changeable, revocable,* or *reversible.* My tax accountant was *irritable* and believed that such *horribly undesirable* and *unfavorable* objections were *insupportable, contemptible, intolerable, deplorable, reprehensible,* and *inexcusable.* The Internal Revenue Service was not *adaptable,* however. In fact, it was *predictably inflexible.*

QUICKIEQUIZQUICKIEQUIZQUICKIEQUIZQUICKIEQUIZQUICKIEQUIZQUICKIEQUIZQUICKIE

-ABLE AND -IBLE

As you take this vocabulary test, use it to increase your knowledge of *-able* and *-ible* spellings. Choose the word or phrase you believe is closest in meaning to the key word. Answers follow.

1. **untenable** [un·ten′ə·bəl]—(a) not divisible by ten. (b) stubborn. (c) that cannot be maintained or defended. (d) not relaxed.

2. **irrevocable** [i·rev′ə·kə·bəl]—(a) stubborn. (b) temporary. (c) that cannot be recalled or changed. (d) unwritten.

3. **inestimable** [in·es′tə·mə·bəl]—(a) famous. (b) of little worth. (c) without esteem. (d) invaluable.

4. **inscrutable** [in·skrōō′tə·bəl]—(a) incomprehensible. (b) unwholesome. (c) greedy. (d) Oriental.

5. **irrefutable** [i·ref′yə·tə·bəl]—(a) that can be conquered. (b) absurd. (c) that can be used as evidence. (d) that cannot be proved to be false.

6. **inalienable** [in·āl′yən·ə·bəl]—(a) that cannot be rightfully taken away. (b) not foreign. (c) inadmissible. (d) not transferable.

7. **implacable** [im·plā′kə·bəl]—(a) stubborn. (b) not to be appeased. (c) out of place. (d) given to violence.

8. **malleable** [mal′ē·ə·bəl]—(a) cheerful. (b) capable of being shaped by hammering. (c) prone to seasickness. (d) easily broken.

9. **negligible** [neg′lə·jə·bəl]—(a) trifling. (b) widespread. (c) sleepy. (d) unworthy.

10. **ostensible** [os·ten′sə·bəl]—(a) practical. (b) apparent. (c) obvious. (d) capable of being drawn into a wire between rollers.

11. **perceptible** [pər·sep′tə·bəl]—(a) agreeable. (b) helpful. (c) gradual. (d) visible.

12. **potable** [pō′tə·bəl]—(a) believable. (b) that can be carried. (c) drinkable. (d) edible.

13. **plausible** [plô′zə·bəl]—(a) worthy of applause. (b) deceitful. (c) contrived. (d) believable.

14. **personable** [pûr′sən·ə·bəl]—(a) human. (b) attractive. (c) gossipy. (d) insulting.

ANSWERS:

1. **untenable**—(c) that cannot be maintained or defended. 2. **irrevocable**—(c) that cannot be recalled or changed. 3. **inestimable**—(d) invaluable. 4. **inscrutable**—(a) incomprehensible. 5. **irrefutable**—(d) that cannot be proved to be false. 6. **inalienable**—(a) that cannot be rightfully taken away. 7. **implacable**—(b) not to be appeased. 8. **malleable**—(b) capable of being shaped by hammering. 9. **negligible**—(a) trifling. 10. **ostensible**—(b) apparent. 11. **perceptible**—(d) visible. 12. **potable**—(c) drinkable. 13. **plausible**—(d) believable. 14. **personable**—(b) attractive.

4 WHICH IS IT: -AL, -EL, or -LE?

No good rule has ever been devised that will help you to decide whether a word ends in *-al*, *-el*, or *-le*. Pronunciation will not help either, because all three endings sound alike. Although *-al*, *-el*, and *-le* words are troublesome, you undoubtedly mastered most of them in elementary school. You probably will find only two or three words in the following list that cause you trouble.

Here are the thirty-five words ending in *-al*, *-el*, and *-le* that are most frequently misspelled, especially by elementary-school students.

-AL		-EL	
accidental	essential	angel	label
acquittal	funeral	barrel	nickel
aerial	natural	colonel	squirrel
arrival	official		
chemical	principal (of a school;		
	capital for investment;		
	major)		
colonial	refusal		

-LE

angle	fiddle
assemble	marble
bangle	principle (a general
bauble	rule or truth)
candle	resemble
cradle	sample
dabble	trouble
double	whistle
example	wrestle

Don't Wrestle With Squirrels

One *-le* word, *wrestle*, is both a spelling and a pronunciation nuisance. It is spelled *wrestle* and pronounced [res′əl]. Do *not* spell or pronounce it as "rassle."

Another word in the above list, *squirrel*, bothers some spellers because they forget that it has two *r*'s.

Spelling Test— -al, -el, or -le?

Add *-al, -el,* or *-le* to complete the following sentences. Answers follow.

1. Can you assemb_____ the baby's crad_____?
2. Please lab_____ this offici_____ samp_____.
3. The princip_____ of the school said the boy behaved like an ang_____.
4. She wears too many bang_____s and baub_____s.
5. Does the colon_____ live in a coloni_____ house?
6. The boy borrowed a nick_____ to buy a marb_____.
7. It's not the troub_____ he caused, it's the princip_____ of the thing.
8. Put the cand_____ on the barr_____.
9. Nero fidd_____d while Rome burned, but who kind_____d the fire?
10. Whist_____ while you wrest_____ with the squirr_____.

ANSWERS:

1. assembLE, cradLE. 2. labEL, officiAL, sampLE. 3. principAL, angEL.
4. bangLEs, baubLEs. 5. colonEL, coloniAL. 6. nickEL, marbLE. 7.
troubLE, principLE. 8. candLE, barrEL. 9. fiddLEd. kindLEd. 10. whistLE,
wrestLE, squirrEL.

5 WHICH IS IT: -ANT or -ENT? -ANCE or -ENCE? -ANCY or -ENCY?

There has never been a rule to guide spellers when they hear words in which they must choose either *-ant, -ance,* or *-ancy* versus *-ent, -ence,* or *-ency.* If you know that a word ends in *-ant,* related words will always end in *-ance* and *-ancy.* If a word ends in *-ent,* related words will end in *-ence* and *-ency.* Thus, *abundant, abundance, abundancy; consistent, consistence, consistency.* The best thing you can do is to memorize the common words of this group.

The 20 Most Common *-ant, -ent* Puzzlers

Here are the twenty most troublesome *-ant* and *-ent* words, including

WORDS ENDING IN -AL, -EL, AND -LE

Choose the word or phrase you believe is closest in meaning to each of the key words below. Also learn their proper spellings. Answers follow.

1. **trivial** [triv′e·əl]—(a) amusing. (b) of little importance. (c) amateurish. (d) changeable.
2. **rankle** [rang′kəl]—(a) to be noisy. (b) to argue. (c) to cause continued resentment. (d) to confuse.
3. **arable** [ar′ə·bəl]—(a) capable of being plowed or cultivated. (b) healthy. (c) public. (d) praiseworthy.
4. **mettle** [met′l]—(a) stubbornness. (b) irritation. (c) foolhardiness. (d) courage and ardor.
5. **farcical** [fär′si·kəl]—(a) forlorn. (b) quaint. (c) very old. (d) ludicrous.
6. **tangible** [tan′jə·bəl]—(a) definite and real. (b) justifiable. (c) adjacent to. (d) capable of being hammered into shape.
7. **temporal** [tem′pər·əl]—(a) saintly. (b) warm. (c) worldly. (d) lasting a short time.
8. **lethal** [lē′thəl]—(a) painful. (b) sharp. (c) deadly. (d) a large quantity.
9. **fettle** [fet′l]—(a) a shackle. (b) state or condition. (c) good health. (d) courage.
10. **hurtle** [hûr′təl]—(a) to fling. (b) to jump over. (c) to overcome. (d) to rush headlong.
11. **staple** [stā′pəl]—(a) dependable. (b) a principal commodity (c) any starchy food. (d) strength.
12. **mercurial** [mər·kyoor′e·əl]—(a) humorous. (b) changeable. (c) mercenary. (d) hot.
13. **vernal** [vûr′nəl]—(a) truthful. (b) aged. (c) of the spring. (d) of the fall.
14. **rational** [rash′ən·əl]—(a) perceptive. (b) sensible. (c) scarce. (d) boring.
15. **sequel** [sē′kwəl]—(a) an agreement. (b) calm. (c) equality. (d) that which follows.
16. **sidle** [sīd′l]—(a) to move sideways. (b) to smile foolishly. (c) an oath. (d) a beer mug.
17. **insoluble** [in·sol′yə·bəl]—(a) too salty. (b) not able to be dissolved. (c) lubricated. (d) not able to be defeated.

ANSWERS:

1. **trivial**—(b) of little importance. 2. **rankle**—(c) to cause continued resentment. 3. **arable**—(a) capable of being plowed or cultivated. 4. **mettle**—(d) courage and ardor. 5. **farcical**—(d) ludicrous. 6. **tangible** —(a) definite and real. 7. **temporal**—(c) worldly. 8. **lethal**—(c) deadly. 9. **fettle**—(b) state or condition. 10. **hurtle**—(d) to rush headlong. 11. **staple**—(b) a principal commodity. 12. **mercurial**—(b) changeable. 13. **vernal**—(c) of the spring. 14. **rational**—(b) sensible. 15. **sequel**—(d) that which follows. 16. **sidle**—(a) to move sideways. 17. **insoluble**—(b) not able to be dissolved.

some representative *-ance, -ancy* and *-ence, -ency* examples. Learn these spellings by heart.

-ANT, -ANCE, -ANCY	-ENT, -ENCE, -ENCY
acceptance	apparent
assistant, assistance	coincident, coincidence
attendant, attendance	conference
insurance	confident, confidence
maintenance	consistent, consistence, consistency
relevant, relevance, relevancy	correspondent, correspondence
resistant, resistance	dependent, dependence, dependency
tolerant, tolerance	existence
	occurrence
	persistent, persistence
	reference
	superintendent

NOTE: The word *descendant* is spelled correctly with an *a* when used as a noun meaning "offspring." As an adjective meaning "descending," the preferred spelling is *descendent*.

More *-ant, -ent* Words

Here are additional lists of *-ant, -ent* words with some representative *-ance, ancy,* and *-ence, -ency* examples. They are not major stumbling blocks for most people. Are any of them problems for you?

-ANT, -ANCE, -ANCY

abundant, abundance	ignorant
acquaintance	inheritance
appearance	observant, observance
clearance	perseverant, perseverance
defendant	radiant, radiance, radiancy
dominant, dominance	repentant, repentance
endurance	resemblance
entrant, entrance	restaurant
extravagant, extravagance	significant, significance
grievance	substance
guidance	sustenance
hindrance	tenant, tenancy

-ENT, -ENCE, -ENCY

abhorrent, abhorrence
absent, absence
abstinent
adherent
antecedent
audience
coherent, coherence
competent, competence,
   competency
convalescent, convalescence
convenient
different
diffident
diligent, diligence
dissident, dissidence
divergent
efficient, efficiency
eminent, eminence
equivalent
excellent, excellence, excellency
impertinent, impertinence
indulgent, indulgence
inference

insistent, insistence
insolent, insolence
intelligent
magnificent
obedient, obedience
opponent
opulent, opulence
penitent, penitence
permanent, permanence
pertinent
precedent, precedence
preference
proficient, proficience, proficiency
prominent, prominence
recurrent
repellent
resident, residence, residency
reverent, reverence
subsistent, subsistence
sufficient
tendency
violent

Two Super Spelling Demons

Two words ending in -*ant* are difficult not only because of their endings but because they contain certain other letters. They are *lieutenant* and *sergeant*.

Lieutenant is an interesting word, the derivation of which will help you remember its proper spelling. *Lieutenant* is a combination of *lieu,* meaning "place," and *tenant,* which comes from the Latin verb "to hold." Thus, a *lieutenant* is someone who holds the place of another, especially someone who acts as a deputy in *lieu* of a higher officer, the king, or other superior.

The second letter in *sergeant* is *e* because the word is related to *serve,* which used to be pronounced [särv]. *Serve* is no longer pronounced that way, but the *är* sound remains in *sergeant.*

Spelling Test— -ant, -ance, -ancy or -ent, -ence, -ency

Complete the following sentences by adding -ant, -ance, -ancy, -ent, -ence, or ency in the blanks. Answers follow.

1. The descend_____ of the lieuten_____ was very effici_____.
2. The abs_____ of sunshine was a hindr_____ to her convales-c_____.
3. His mainten_____ of an opul_____ mansion is a personal indul-g_____.
4. An acquaint_____ left him an inherit_____ suffici_____ for all his needs.
5. At a clear_____ sale, a shopper needs endur_____, insist_____, and dilig_____.
6. The dog's tend_____ toward viol_____ was tempered by obedi-_____.
7. There is a signific_____ differ_____ in the guid_____ systems of the two missiles.
8. An observ_____ audi_____ saw the resembl_____ between the two actors.
9. A good employer should be consist_____ and compet_____ but toler_____ of the mistakes of others.
10. A good lawyer never makes irrelev_____, ignor_____, or imperti-n_____ statements in court.
11. The insur_____ office assist_____ is an extravag_____, ele-g_____ woman.

ANSWERS:

1. descendANT, lieutenANT, efficiENT.
2. absENCE, hindrANCE, convalescENCE.
3. maintenANCE, opulENT, indulgENCE.
4. acquaintANCE, inheritANCE, sufficiENT.
5. clearANCE, endurANCE, insistENCE, diligENCE.
6. tendENCY, violENCE, obediENCE.
7. significANT, differENCE, guidANCE.
8. observANT, audiENCE, resemblANCE.
9. consistENT, competENT, tolerANT.
10. irrelevANT, ignorANT, impertinENT.
11. insurANCE, assistANT, extravagANT, elegANT.

Fun With Words
-ANT AND -ENT

Choose the definition you believe is closest in meaning to each of the key words below. As you do this vocabulary test, notice the *-ant* and *-ent* spellings. Answers follow.

1. **rampant** [ram′pənt]—(a) noisy. (b) rising. (c) unrestrained. (d) gigantic.
2. **blatant** [blā′tənt]—(a) offensively loud. (b) cheap. (c) boastful. (d) notorious.
3. **aberrant** [ab·er′ənt]—(a) reformed. (b) confused. (c) wandering. (d) suffering.
4. **resplendent** [ri·splen′dənt]—(a) many-colored. (b) lustrous and shining. (c) famous. (d) luxurious.
5. **benignant** [bi·nig′nənt]—(a) wise. (b) religious. (c) old. (d) kindly.
6. **cognizant** [kog′nə·zənt]—(a) puzzled. (b) aware. (c) shrewd (d) modern.
7. **covenant** [kuv′ə·nənt]—(a) a solemn agreement. (b) a small bay. (c) a carefully guarded secret. (d) one of the Ten Commandments.
8. **coherent** [kō·hir′ənt]—(a) logically consistent. (b) very strong. (c) friendly. (d) slanderous.
9. **contingent** [kən·tin′jənt]—(a) continuous. (b) dependent upon an uncertain event. (c) side-by-side. (d) obligatory.
10. **consonant** [kon′sə·nənt]—(a) discordant. (b) consistent. (c) virtuous. (d) faithful.
11. **conversant** [kən·vûr′sənt]—(a) suave. (b) talkative. (c) intimately acquainted. (d) sophisticated.
12. **decadent** [di·kād′nt *or* dek′ə·dənt]—(a) evil. (b) a period of ten years. (c) deceased. (d) deteriorating.
13. **dormant** [dôr′mənt]—(a) extravagant. (b) modest. (c) inactive. (d) cruel.
14. **flamboyant** [flam·boi′ənt]—(a) charming. (b) blushing. (c) friendly. (d) showy or bombastic.
15. **extant** [ek′stənt]—(a) long and drawn out. (b) still existing. (c) far-reaching. (d) prominent.
16. **errant** [er′rənt]—(a) noble. (b) wandering. (c) eccentric. (d) serving a king.

ANSWERS:

1. **rampant**—(c) unrestrained. 2. **blatant**—(a) offensively loud. 3. **aberrant**—(c) wandering. 4. **resplendent**—(b) lustrous and shining. 5. **benignant**—(d) kindly. 6. **cognizant**—(b) aware. 7. **covenant**—(a) a solemn agreement. 8. **coherent**—(a) logically consistent. 9. **contingent**—(b) dependent upon an uncertain event. 10. **consonant**—(b) consistent. 11. **conversant** (c) intimately acquainted. 12. **decadent**—(d) deteriorating. 13. **dormant** (c) inactive. 14. **flamboyant**—(d) showy or bombastic. 15. **extant**—(b) still existing. 16. **errant**—(b) wandering.

WORDS ENDING IN -ANCE AND -ENCE

Choose the word or phrase you believe is closest in meaning to each of the key words below. As you do this vocabulary test, learn the spelling of these words that end in -*ance* or -*ence*. Answers follow.

1. **appurtenance** [ə·pûr′tə·nəns]— (a) an accessory. (b) an apt retort. (c) diligence. (d) disrespectfulness.

2. **irrelevance** [i·rel′ə·vəns]—(a) a divine disclosure. (b) the state of not being pertinent. (c) disrespect. (d) blasphemy.

3. **abeyance** [ə·bā′əns]—(a) obedience. (b) temporary inaction. (c) servile humility. (d) under consideration.

4. **diffidence** [dif′ə·dəns]—(a) disagreement. (b) respect. (c) self-confidence. (d) shyness.

5. **preponderance** [pri·pon′dər·əns] —(a) indebtedness. (b) superiority or excess of weight, influence, etc. (c) forethought. (d) an insufficient amount.

6. **turbulence** [tûr′byə·ləns]—(a) rage. (b) a violent disturbance. (c) muddiness. (d) quick-flowing water.

7. **resilience** [ri·zil′yəns]—(a) determination. (b) stupidity. (c) elasticity or buoyancy. (d) cleverness.

8. **dissonance** [dis′ə·nəns]—(a) shrillness. (b) anger. (c) discord. (d) disagreement.

9. **ordinance** [ôr′də·nəns]—(a) commonplace materials. (b) military supplies. (c) weapons and ammunition. (d) that which is decreed.

10. **sustenance** [sus′tə·nəns]—(a) believability. (b) moral support. (c) opportunity. (d) nourishment.

11. **clairvoyance** [klâr·voi′əns]—(a) the state of being lighter than water. (b) purity. (c) extraordinary insight. (d) transparency.

12. **incidence** [in′sə·dəns]—(a) anecdotes. (b) the range of occurrence. (c) stubbornness. (d) glowing with heat.

13. **inference** [in′fər·əns]—(a) a reasoned deduction. (b) inferiority. (c) an oversight. (d) inattention.

14. **pittance** [pit′əns]—(a) a small British coin. (b) a small amount. (c) alms. (d) punishment for sins.

ANSWERS:

1. **appurtenance**—(a) an accessory. 2. **irrelevance**—(b) the state of not being pertinent. 3. **abeyance**—(b) temporary inaction. 4. **diffidence**—(d) shyness. 5. **preponderance**—(b) superiority or excess of weight, influence, etc. 6. **turbulence**—(b) a violent disturbance. 7. **resilience**—(c) elasticity or buoyancy. 8. **dissonance**—(c) discord. 9. **ordinance**—(d) that which is decreed. 10. **sustenance**—(d) nourishment. 11. **clairvoyance**—(c) extraordinary insight. 12. **incidence**—(b) the range of occurrence. 13. **inference**—(a) a reasoned deduction. 14. **pittance**—(b) a small amount.

6 WHICH IS IT: -AR, -ER, or -OR? OR EVEN -RE or -OUR?

The word *beggar* (one who begs) ends in -*ar; purchaser* (one who purchases) ends in -*er;* and *collector* (one who collects) ends in -*or.* Obviously, the endings -*ar,* -*er,* and -*or* mean the same thing. Each is added to verbs (in these examples, to *beg, purchase,* and *collect*) to form nouns that mean "a person who or thing that" does what the verb says. Why do we have three different endings— -*ar,* -*er,* and -*or* —that mean the same thing?

The answer is that the English language was not created at one time or from one source. The standard ending -*er* is added to a verb to make it into a noun meaning "a person who or thing that," as in *farmer* (one who farms), *propeller* (that which propels), and *runner* (one who runs). The equivalent Latin ending is -*or.* Thus, in many Latin words taken into English, we keep the Latin -*or* spelling, as in *editor.*

The -*ar* ending originally meant "a person or thing like or connected with." A *scholar* is not "one who schools," but "one who is connected with learning." This original meaning has become blurred so that -*ar* is also a variant of -*er,* giving us a few words such as *beggar.*

Thus, -*ar,* -*er,* and -*or* can mean the same thing—and they sound alike! How, then, can we know which ending to use when spelling a word? Here are two tips on *ar,* -*er,* and -*or* words.

The first tip is this: The ending -*ar* is rare. All you need do is learn a few such common -*ar* words as *beggar, liar,* and *scholar.*

The more confusing endings are -*er* and -*or.* So, here's the second tip: For simple, common English words, the kind you learned to spell in elementary school, -*er* is usually the right ending. The Latin -*or* goes with more advanced words. Thus, very simple words like *doer, talker,* and *seller* tend to end in -*er.* More difficult words such as *administrator, orator,* and *vendor* tend to end in -*or.*

-*ar,* -*er,* and -*or* for Nouns Meaning "Doers" of Something

If the following lists of -*ar,* -*er,* and -*or* words seem easy to you, good! Some persons, though, have trouble with a few of these words.

-AR

beggar	registrar
liar	scholar

-ER

adjuster	eraser
advertiser	examiner
adviser (also acceptable: advisor)	executioner
amplifier	invader
announcer	laborer
appraiser	lecturer
baker	manager
batter	manufacturer
bearer	mourner
beginner	observer
believer	passenger
brewer	peddler
comptroller [kən·trō′lər]	producer
consumer	purchaser
defender	subscriber
designer	teller
digger	traveler
distiller	treasurer
employer	writer

-OR

accelerator	depositor
actor	dictator
administrator	director
advisor	distributor
auditor	editor
bettor	educator
calculator	elector
collector	escalator
commentator	executor
competitor	fumigator
conductor	governor
confessor	incinerator
conqueror	incubator
conspirator	indicator
contractor	inspector
contributor	inventor
counselor	investigator

investor	sculptor
legislator	speculator
mortgagor	sponsor
operator	successor
orator	supervisor
professor	surveyor
protector	survivor
radiator	translator
refrigerator	vendor
sailor	visitor

The endings *-ar, -er,* and *-or* also have other uses. Sometimes *-er* is used to form a noun that names a person according to the product he makes or sells: *hatter,* for instance, or *jeweler.* Or *-er* may indicate a person's place of birth or residence, as *villager, Westerner,* or *New Yorker.* Also, of course, any one of these endings may simply happen to be the last two letters of a word and have no special meaning at all. The following *-ar, -er,* and *-or* words are a mixed bag where meanings are concerned, but they have one thing in common: They are spelling problems for many people.

More *-ar, -er,* and *-or* Words

-AR

angular	insular
calendar (for dAtes)	jugular
cedar	molar
cellar	peculiar
circular	regular
collar	similar
dollar	singular
familiar	sugar
grammar	vicar
hangar (for plAnes)	vulgar

-ER

butler	character
calender (for papEr making)	confectioner
center	foreigner

309

grocer	milliner
haberdasher	miner (works in a minE)
hanger (in the closEt)	minister
jeweler	officer
lawyer	partner
ledger	stationer
meager	stenographer
messenger	theater

-OR-

ancestor	inferior
anchor	janitor
ardor	major
author	minor (a yOung person)
aviator	motor
bachelor	neighbor
behavior	predecessor
captor	proprietor
creditor	realtor
debtor	rumor
doctor	senator
emperor	spectator
favor	superior
harbor	tailor
honor	tractor
humor	traitor
impostor	tremor
	vigor

When Is the Ending -*re* Used?

In American English, -*re* is not a common ending, but it does appear occasionally. You'll do well to learn the correct spelling of these six -*re* words:

acre	massacre
lucre	mediocre
macabre	ogre

Don't let British custom confuse you. The English use the ending -*re* for many words that Americans spell with an -*er*. Thus, you will find such spellings as *centre, meagre, sabre, theatre,* etc., in English books and periodicals.

The only *-re* British spelling appearing frequently in the United States is *theatre.* Some Americans associate this British spelling with "elegance"; certain American theaters, especially those specializing in foreign films, classical drama, ballet, etc., are likely to call themselves *theatres.* But the preferred spelling for the word in this country is *theater.*

When Is the Ending *-our* Used?

In American spelling, the *-our* ending is generally preferred in only one common word (which prides itself on not being "common"): *glamour.* And even *glamour* reverts to the more common *-or* spelling in its derived forms, *glamorous* and *glamorize.*

The *-our* ending is a distinctive British ending, often used where *-or* is employed in the United States. The British spell *color, honor, humor,* and *neighbor* as *colour, honour, humour,* and *neighbour.* Remember that this *-our* spelling is not used in the United States. Even *glamour* may be acceptably spelled *glamor* if you prefer it that way.

Spelling Test— -ar, -er, -or, or -re

Complete the following sentences by adding *-ar, -er, -or,* or *-re* where necessary. Answers follow.

1. The begg____ told the passeng____ that the peddl____ was a li____.
2. Schol____s and educat____s acted as advis____s to the govern____.
3. The sail____'s superi____ offic____ had trouble with gramm____.
4. The spectat____s enjoyed the hum____ous charact____ that the act____ portrayed.
5. Since the coal min____ was a min____, he could not vote for senat____.
6. The jewel____'s apprais____ said the diamond was inferi____.
7. The rum____ was that the bachel____'s butl____ was an impost____.
8. He was a debt____ because he did not pursue the doll____.

9. Beginn_____s in gramm_____ use many eras_____s.
10. Refrigerat_____ manufactur_____s have many competit_____s.
11. Burs_____s, comptroll_____s, and treasur_____s use calculat_____s and write figures in ledg_____s.
12. The teetotal_____s criticized distill_____s with singul_____ ard_____.
13. The conquer_____s were invad_____s for their emper_____.
14. Minist_____s and vic_____s have somewhat simil_____ lives.
15. Do produc_____s and direct_____ hire min_____ act_____ for maj_____ roles in the theat_____?
16. Glam_____ous foreign_____s fav_____ famili_____ spons_____s.
17. The og_____'s farm consisted of a meag_____ half ac_____.
18. The trait_____ helped to massac_____ the troops.
19. The aviat_____ landed the seaplane in the harb_____.
20. The design_____ designed an instant pancake batt_____ for the consum_____.
21. The elevat_____ operat_____ became a stenograph_____ when the firm installed an escalat_____.

ANSWERS:

1. beggAR, passengER, peddlER, liAR.
2. scholARs, educatORs. advisERs (or -ORs), governOR.
3. sailOR's, superiOR, officER, grammAR.
4. spectatORs, humORous, charactER, actOR.
5. minER, minOR, senatOR.
6. jewelER's, appraisER, inferiOR.
7. rumOR, bachelOR's, butlER, impostOR.
8. debtOR, dollAR, vigOR.
9. beginnERs, grammAR, erasERs.
10. refrigeratOR, manufacturERs, competitORs.
11. bursARs, comptrollERs, treasurERs, calculatOR, ledgERs.
12. teetotalERs, distillERs, singulAR, ardOR.
13. conquerORs, invadERs, emperOR.
14. ministERs, vicARs, similAR.
15. producERs, directORs, minOR, actORs, majOR, theatER.
16. glamORous, foreignERs, favOR, familiAR, sponsORs.
17. ogRE's, meagER, acRE.
18. traitOR, massacRE.
19. aviatOR, harbOR.
20. designER, battER, consumER.
21. elevatOR, operatOR, stenographER, escalatOR.

WORDS ENDING IN -AR, -ER, AND -OR

Choose the word or phrase you believe is closest in meaning to each of the key words below. These key words all end in *-ar*, *-er*, or *-or*, and you should also learn their proper spelling. Answers follow.

1. **welter** [wel′tər]—(a) heat. (b) a crowd. (c) turmoil or commotion. (d) suffering.
2. **caper** [kā′pər]—(a) to gamble. (b) to joke. (c) to trifle with. (d) to prance.
3. **garner** [gär′nər]—(a) to decorate. (b) to cut down. (c) to gather. (d) to scatter.
4. **render** [ren′dər]—(a) suffer. (b) rip apart. (c) contribute. (d) take back.
5. **banter** [ban′tər]—(a) playful teasing. (b) gossip. (c) very small. (d) memorable.
6. **provender** [prov′ən·dər]—(a) forethought. (b) supplies in general. (c) wealth. (d) feed for cattle.
7. **secular** [sek′yə·lər]—(a) following after. (b) wicked. (c) carefully chosen. (d) worldly.
8. **ulterior** [ul·tir′ē·ər]—(a) undisclosed. (b) evil. (c) false. (d) outside.
9. **titular** [tich′oŏ·lər]—(a) famous. (b) in name only. (c) high in authority. (d) temporary.

10. **perpetrator** [pûr′pə·trāt·ər]—(a) a criminal. (b) one who performs an act. (c) an accomplice. (d) an interior decorator.
11. **engender** [in·jen′dər]—(a) to make angry. (b) to conspire. (c) to cause to develop. (d) to deceive.
12. **proffer** [prof′ər]—(a) to accumulate wealth. (b) to act skillfully. (c) to teach. (d) to offer for acceptance.
13. **roister** [rois′tər]—(a) to carouse. (b) to list. (c) a calendar of events. (d) a noisy gathering.
14. **squalor** [skwol′ər]—(a) noise. (b) poverty. (c) dirt and misery. (d) extravagance.
15. **insular** [in′sə·lər]—(a) proud. (b) narrow-minded. (c) insulting. (d) powerful.
16. **demeanor** [di·mē′nər]—(a) manner or deportment. (b) disgrace. (c) humility. (d) shrewdness.
17. **sinister** [sin′is·tər]—(a) unmarried female. (b) causing sadness. (c) murderous. (d) menacing.

ANSWERS:

1. **welter**—(c) turmoil or commotion. 2. **caper**—(d) to prance. 3. **garner**—(c) to gather. 4. **render**—(c) contribute. 5. **banter**—(a) playful teasing. 6. **provender**—(d) feed for cattle. 7. **secular**—(d) worldly. 8. **ulterior**—(a) undisclosed. 9. **titular**—(b) in name only. 10. **perpetrator**—(b) one who performs an act. 11. **engender**—(c) to cause to develop. 12. **proffer**—(d) to offer for acceptance. 13. **roister**—(a) to carouse. 14. **squalor**—(c) dirt and misery. 15. **insular**—(b) narrow-minded. 16. **demeanor**—(a) manner or deportment. 17. **sinister**—(d) menacing.

7 WHICH IS IT: -ARY or -ERY?

Because the word endings *-ary* and *-ery* sound alike, they can cause spelling problems. However, one fact will solve most of the problems: More than 300 words end in *-ary;* only a few words end in *-ery*. If you learn these few *-ery* words, you have the difficulty licked.

Here are seven *-ery* words that are easy to learn. First, let's look at the roots of these words:

baker	milliner
brewer	refiner
confectioner	stationer
distiller	

Note that these seven root words end in *-er*, a suffix meaning "a person who makes, sells, or does something." Thus, a baker bakes bread, a stationer sells stationery, and so forth. By adding a *-y* to this *-er* suffix, we get *-ery*. This new ending means "the product made or sold, or the place that makes or sells it." Thus, a *bakery* is the place where the baker's goods are made or sold, and *stationery* is the product sold by a stationer. In the seven *-ery* words that follow, the *-y* is merely added to an already existing *-er* ending:

bakery	millinery
brewery	refinery
confectionery	stationery
distillery	

Of these seven words, *confectionery, millinery,* and *stationery* are on many spelling-demon lists. Learn them well. In particular, remember that a stationER sells stationERY; his shop is stationARY because it stays in the same plAce.

A few other words also end in *-ery*. Some are no problem: *bribery, cutlery, finery, flattery, machinery, nunnery,* and *thievery*. However, five other *-ery* words do perplex some people:

artillery	dysentery
celery	monastery
cemetery	

Celery is on many high-school lists, and *cemetery* and *monastery* are on many college lists. Be sure you know how to spell them.

Are There Any -ary Puzzlers?

Although more than 300 words end in -ary, few of them are confusing. Some persons, however, find the following -ary words difficult to spell. If any of these words bother you, learn them now:

adversary	infirmary
auxiliary	library
boundary	necessary
commentary	revolutionary
contemporary	secondary
dictionary	secretary
elementary	stationary (in one plAce)
February	tributary
honorary	vocabulary
imaginary	voluntary

Spelling Test— -ary or -ery?

Complete the following sentences by adding -ary or -ery where needed. Answers will be found on the next page.

1. He fell from the distill_____ window, was sent to the infirm_____, and ended up in the cemet_____.
2. The volunt_____ artill_____ group received an honor_____ medal.
3. The bak_____ prepared a special confection_____.
4. The secret_____ bought millin_____ and other fin_____.
5. If the size of your vocabul_____ remains station_____, a diction-_____ may be necess_____ to improve it.
6. The brew_____ patented revolution_____ new machin_____.
7. In Febru_____, my advers_____ fled to a monast_____.
8. The auxili_____ libr_____ contains element_____ books.
9. The brib_____ attempt was written on pink station_____.
10. Cel_____ will not cure dysent_____, but remaining station_____ may help.

315

11. The monast_____ is on the St. Lawrence tribut_____.

12. In the Sahara it is necess_____ to ride a dromed_____.

13. People in sedent_____ jobs require salut_____ exercise.

14. Sir, my advers_____'s effront_____ is unbearable.

15. The rebels made incendi_____ and revolution_____ speeches.

16. Is the equator an imagin_____ bound_____?

17. Much thiev_____ goes on at the brew_____.

18. The comment_____ in the back of the book is element_____.

19. Every day the lapid_____ went to the bak_____ for rolls.

20. Flatt_____ is only second_____ to good will.

21. In Janu_____ she bought a propriet_____ medicine for colds.

22. Most people work for monet_____ gain.

ANSWERS:

1. distillERY, infirmARY, cemetERY.
2. voluntARY, artillERY, honorARY.
3. bakERY, confectionERY.
4. secretARY, millinERY, finERY.
5. vocabulARY, stationARY, dictionARY, necessARY.
6. brewERY, revolutionARY, machinERY.
7. FebruARY, adversARY, monastERY.
8. auxiliARY, librARY, elementARY.
9. bribERY, stationERY.
10. celERY, dysentERY, stationARY.
11. monastERY, tributARY
12. necessARY, dromedARY.
13. SedentARY, salutARY.
14. adversARY, effrontERY.
15. incendiARY, revolutionARY.
16. imaginARY, boundARY.
17. thievERY, brewERY.
18. commentARY, elementARY.
19. lapidARY, bakERY.
20. FlattERY, secondARY.
21. JanuARY, proprietARY.
22. monetARY.

WORDS ENDING IN -ARY AND -ERY

Choose the word or phrase you believe is closest in meaning to each of the key words below. These key words all end in *-ary* or *-ery,* and you should also learn their proper spelling. Answers follow.

1. **lapidary** [lap′ə·der′ē]—(a) a cutter of precious stones. (b) a roofer. (c) a mason. (d) an eskimo dog.

2. **supernumerary** [soo′pər·noo′mə·rer′ē]—(a) a servant. (b) an unknown person. (c) an unneeded extra person. (d) a very strong person.

3. **exemplary** [ig·zem′plər·ē]—(a) authoritative. (b) well-dressed. (c) fit to be imitated. (d) not subject to a rule or law.

4. **raillery** [rā′lər·ē]—(a) cruel ridicule. (b) complaints. (c) good-humored jesting. (d) absurdities.

5. **arbitrary** [är′bə·trer′ē]—(a) decisive but unreasonable. (b) sudden. (c) just and fair. (d) difficult.

6. **incendiary** [in·sen′dē·er′ē]—(a) angry. (b) ambitious. (c) inflammatory. (d) sweet-smelling.

7. **effrontery** [i·frun′tər·ē]—(a) lavish display. (b) humility. (c) false pride. (d) insolent boldness.

8. **commentary** [kom′ən·ter′ē]—(a) a long speech. (b) suggestions. (c) a list of questions. (d) anything serving to explain or illustrate.

9. **estuary** [es′choo·er′ē]—(a) an inlet or arm of the sea. (b) a religious home. (c) a cluster of islands. (d) a large estate.

10. **sedentary** [sed′ən·ter′ē]—(a) unhurried. (b) inactive. (c) aged. (d) full of mud and silt.

11. **cutlery** [kut′lə·rē]—(a) implements for cutting and serving food. (b) a thin piece of meat. (c) small sleigh. (d) a peddler.

12. **lamasery** [lä′mə·ser′ē]—(a) a South American beast of burden. (b) a Tibetan monastery. (c) a sheepfold. (d) a poisonous shrub.

13. **dromedary** [drom′ə·der′ē]—(a) a date palm. (b) a racecourse. (c) a medieval ship. (d) a camel with a single hump.

14. **proprietary** [prə·prī′ə·ter′ē]—(a) proper behavior. (b) made and sold by exclusive legal right, as a medicine. (c) a scheme. (d) real estate.

ANSWERS:

1. **lapidary**—(a) a cutter of precious stones. 2. **supernumerary**—(c) an unneeded extra person. 3. **exemplary**—(c) fit to be imitated. 4. **raillery**—(c) good-humored jesting. 5. **arbitrary**—(a) decisive but unreasonable. 6. **incendiary**—(c) inflammatory. 7. **effrontery**—(d) insolent boldness. 8. **commentary**—(d) anything serving to explain or illustrate. 9. **estuary**—(a) an inlet or arm of the sea. 10. **sedentary**—(b) inactive. 11. **cutlery**—(a) implements for cutting and serving food. 12. **lamasery**—(b) a Tibetan monastery. 13. **dromedary**—(d) a camel with a single hump. 14. **proprietary**—(b) made and sold by exclusive legal right, as a medicine.

8 WHICH IS IT: C or CK?

C is one of the strangest letters in the language. It doesn't have its own sound but is sounded either like an *s* (as in *city*) or like a *k* (as in *cat*). In fact, every *c* could be completely replaced by an *s* or a *k*, as is done in dictionary pronunciations.

C is pronounced like an *s* before the vowels *e, i,* and *y* (as in *CEdar, CIty,* and *biCYcle*). When *c* is pronounced with this *s* sound, it is called a "soft c."

C is pronounced like a *k* either before the vowels *a, o,* and *u* (as in *CAt, COol,* and *CUt*), or at the end of a word (as in *froliC, paniC,* and *picniC*). When *c* is pronounced with a *k* sound, it is called a "hard c."

The fact that a *c* at the end of a word is normally hard and a *c* before an *e, i,* or *y* is normally soft can cause a minor spelling problem. With a word like *frolic* or *picnic,* the *c* must remain hard even when you add a suffix beginning with an *e, i,* or *y*. For example, if you add the suffix *-ing* to picnic, you form the word *picnicing.* But this spelling simply won't do, because the *i* after the *c* forces it into an *s* sound. And so, to keep the original hard *c* sound, we add a *k* to it. Thus, the proper spelling becomes *picniCKing.* This is a good example of how the requirements of pronunciation can result in unexpected spellings.

REMEMBER: If a word ends in a *c,* you must add a *k* to it before a suffix beginning with *e, i,* or *y*. The dash (—) used in the following list is a substitute for the word "becomes."

Root ends in a hard C (K) sound		Add a K to keep the C hard
bivouac	—	bivouacked, bivouacking
colic	—	colicky
frolic	—	frolicked, frolicking
mimic	—	mimicked, mimicking
mosaic	—	mosaicked, mosaicking
panic	—	panicked, panicking, panicky
picnic	—	picnicked, picnicking
politic	—	politicking
shellac	—	shellacked, shellacking
traffic	—	trafficked, trafficking

9 WHICH IS IT: C, S, or SC?

The letters *c, s,* and *sc* may all be pronounced alike, as in *competenCe, licenSe,* and *adoleSCence.* When you hear this sound, you have no way of knowing whether it is spelled *c, s,* or *sc.* Here are the most common words in which *c, s,* and *sc* may be confused:

C	S	SC
competenCe	apprehenSive	abSCess
evidenCe	comprehenSive	adoleSCent
negligenCe	incenSe	convaleSCent
violenCe	licenSe	irideSCent
	pretenSe	laSCivious
	reprehenSible	resuSCitate
	suspenSe	viSCera

In addition, *c* and *sc* may both be pronounced *sh,* as in *capricious* and *luscious.* Learn the following words, which can be troublesome because of the possible confusion of *c* and *sc:*

C	SC
capriCious	conSCience
defiCient	conSCious
maliCious	luSCious
suspiCion	omniSCient

QUICKIE QUIZ

STUMP YOUR FRIENDS

Stump your friends and family with this paragraph, or have someone dictate it to you as a spelling test:

The *convalescent* manager was *apprehensive* about his new *adolescent* employee. There was *evidence* that the lad lacked *competence, diligence, obedience,* and *intelligence,* although he never did anything *reprehensible, capricious,* or *malicious.* Nor was he *lascivious* or given to *violence.* But the manager was *suspicious* that the boy's *license* was under *suspension* for *negligence* in driving.

QUICKIE QUIZ

C, S, OR SC?

Choose the preferred spelling for each of the words below. Answers follow.

1. (a) reprehensable	(b) reprehenscible	(c) reprehensible
2. (a) concious	(b) consious	(c) conscious
3. (a) violense	(b) violance	(c) violence
4. (a) comprehension	(b) comprehencion	(c) comprehenscion
5. (a) negligensce	(b) negligence	(c) negligense
6. (a) competence	(b) competense	(c) compitence
7. (a) lisence	(b) license	(c) licence
8. (a) suspicion	(b) suspision	(c) suspiscion
9. (a) unconsious	(b) unconcious	(c) unconscious
10. (a) adolesent	(b) adolescent	(c) adolecent
11. (a) insense	(b) incence	(c) incense
12. (a) evidense	(b) evidance	(c) evidence
13. (a) convalescence	(b) convalesence	(c) convelesence
14. (a) caprecious	(b) capricious	(c) capriscious
15. (a) apprehencive	(b) apprehensive	(c) apprehenscive
16. (a) adolesence	(b) adolescence	(c) adolecense
17. (a) abscess	(b) abcess	(c) absess
18. (a) iridesent	(b) iridescent	(c) iridecent
19. (a) delicious	(b) deliscious	(c) delishius
20. (a) pretense	(b) pretence	(c) pretensce
21. (a) lucious	(b) luscious	(c) lusious
22. (a) malisous	(b) malicous	(c) malicious
23. (a) vicera	(b) viscera	(c) visera
24. (a) senesent	(b) senecent	(c) senescent
25. (a) offinse	(b) offense	(c) offensce

ANSWERS:

1. (c) reprehensible. 2. (c) conscious. 3. (c) violence. 4. (a) comprehension. 5. (b) negligence. 6. (a) competence. 7. (b) license. 8. (a) suspicion. 9. (c) unconscious. 10. (b) adolescent. 11. (c) incense. 12. (c) evidence. 13. (a) convalescence. 14. (b) capricious. 15. (b) apprehensive. 16. (b) adolescence. 17. (a) abscess. 18. (b) iridiscent. 19. (a) delicious. 20. (a) pretense. 21. (b) luscious. 22. (c) malicious. 23. (b) viscera. 24. (c) senescent. 25. (b) offense.

10 WHICH IS IT: -CEDE, -CEED, or -SEDE?

Since the endings *-cede, -ceed,* and *-sede* sound alike, poor spellers can be confused. However, only about a dozen basic words (all of them verbs) end in *-cede, -ceed,* or *-sede,* and these words are easy to learn. Here is all you need to know:

1. Only one common word in the English language ends in *-sede: supersede,* along with its forms *supersedes, superseded,* and *superseding.*

2. Only three common words end in *-ceed: exceed, proceed,* and *succeed,* along with their many forms, such as *exceeds, exceeding, proceeded, succeeding,* and so forth.

NOTE: The noun formed from the verb *proceed* is not spelled with a double *e.* It is spelled *procEdure.*

Here is a sentence worth memorizing: *When you sucCEED in remembering this exCEEDingly easy list of three words, proCEED to the next.*

3. All the other common words ending in this sound end in *-cede,* and there are only half a dozen or so of them: *accede, antecede, concede, intercede, precede, recede,* and *secede.* And, of course, the word *cede* itself "ends" in *cede.*

Spelling Test— *-cede, -ceed,* or *-sede*

Add *-cede, -ceed,* or *-sede* to the following to form complete words. Answers follow.

1. se_____   7. pro_____
2. ac_____   8. con_____
3. ex_____   9. suc_____
4. re_____   10. inter_____
5. super_____   11. ante_____
6. pre_____   12. retro_____

ANSWERS:

1. seCEDE. 2. acCEDE. 3. exCEED. 4. reCEDE. 5. superSEDE. 6. preCEDE. 7. proCEED. 8. conCEDE. 9. sucCEED. 10. interCEDE. 11. anteCEDE. 12. retroCEDE.

Choose the word or phrase that you believe is closest in meaning to each of the key words below. Answers follow.

1. **accede** [ak·sēd′]—(a) to be successful. (b) to give consent to. (c) to be more than. (d) to replace.
2. **replete** [ri·plēt′]—(a) generous. (b) dangerous. (c) filled to the utmost. (d) reiterated.
3. **commentary** [kom′ən·ter′ē]—(a) haughty. (b) qualification. (c) explanatory remarks. (d) basic facts.
4. **exemplary** [ig·zem′plər·ē]—(a) worthy of imitation. (b) plainly expressed. (c) true to type. (d) unusual.
5. **concede** [kən·sēd′]—(a) to admit as true. (b) to suggest. (c) to consider. (d) self-approval.
6. **rudimentary** [rōō′də·men′tər·ē]—(a) blunt. (b) nasty. (c) cud-chewing. (d) elementary.
7. **unsavory** [un·sā′vər·ē]—(a) dangerous. (b) disagreeable. (c) not sociable. (d) not suitable.
8. **supersede** [sōō′pər·sēd′]—(a) to supplant. (b) exceptional. (c) to overcome. (d) to admit as true.
9. **monetary** [mon′ə·ter′ē]—(a) fault-finding. (b) pertaining to money. (c) tedious. (d) a warning.
10. **vagary** [və·gâr′ē *or* vā′gər·ē]—(a) a wanderer. (b) an excuse. (c) vanity. (d) a wild fancy.
11. **corollary** [kôr′ə·ler′ē]—(a) a paradox. (b) something that naturally follows. (c) a maxim. (d) a heart ailment.
12. **recede** [ri·sēd′]—(a) to withdraw. (b) to sow again. (c) to rely on. (d) to take out an application.
13. **perfunctory** [pər·fungk′tər·ē]—(a) surrounding. (b) not functioning. (c) superficial. (d) at intervals.
14. **mercenary** [mûr′sə·ner′ē]—(a) sympathetic. (b) cruel. (c) warlike. (d) moved by love of money.
15. **votary** [vō′tər·ē]—(a) a petty official. (b) a sacrifice. (c) a devoted adherent. (d) an expert.
16. **trumpery** [trum′pər·ē]—(a) tasteful decorations. (b) worthless finery. (c) cheap boasting. (d) brazenness.

ANSWERS:

1. **accede**—(b) to give consent to. 2. **replete**—(c) filled to the utmost. 3. **commentary**—(c) explanatory remarks. 4. **exemplary**—(a) worthy of imitation. 5. **concede**—(a) to admit as true. 6. **rudimentary**—(d) elementary. 7. **unsavory**—(b) disagreeable. 8. **supersede**—(a) to supplant. 9. **monetary**—(b) pertaining to money. 10. **vagary**—(d) a wild fancy. 11. **corollary**—(b) something that naturally follows. 12. **recede**—(a) to withdraw. 13. **perfunctory**—(c) superficial. 14. **mercenary**—(d) moved by love of money. 15. **votary**—(c) a devoted adherent. 16. **trumpery**—(b) worthless finery.

11 WHICH IS IT: -CY or -SY?

As a final syllable, -cy is much more common than -sy. In fact, words ending in -sy may be considered exceptions. Here is a list of the most common words ending in -cy and -sy:

-CY Endings (frequent)	-SY Endings (rare)
accuracy	apostasy
bankruptcy	ecstasy
bureaucracy	heresy
democracy	hypocrisy
diplomacy	idiosyncrasy
expediency	
fallacy	
legacy	
literacy	
obstinacy	
secrecy	

Spelling Test— -cy or -sy?

Choose the correctly spelled words within the parentheses below. Answers follow.

1. All the motels had their "no (vacancy, vacansy)" signs on.
2. The firm went into (bankruptcy, bankruptsy) in 1987.
3. He was excommunicated for (heresy, herecy).
4. Some countries have only a 20 percent (literasy, literacy) rate.
5. Sleeping late on Sundays is sheer (ecstacy, ecstasy).
6. Do you have any memories of your (infansy, infancy)?
7. Eating banana sandwiches is one of Sam's (idiosyncrasies, idiosyncracies).
8. Eating banana sandwiches isn't an (idiosyncracy, idiosyncrasy); it's (lunacy, lunasy)!
9. We began our (occupansy, occupancy) of the house last May.
10. Can a (democracy, democrasy) also be a (bureaucrasy, bureaucracy)?

ANSWERS:

1. vacanCY. 2. bankruptCY. 3. hereSY. 4. literaCY. 5 ecstaSY. 6. infanCY. 7. idiosyncraSIES. 8. idiosyncraSY, lunaCY. 9. occupanCY. 10. democraCY, bureaucraCY.

WORDS ENDING IN -CY OR -SY

Choose the word or phrase you believe is closest in meaning to each of the key words below. These key words all end in -cy or -sy and you should also learn their proper spellings. Answers follow.

1. **intricacy** [in′tri·kə·sē]—(a) secret. (b) familiarity. (c) that which is deceitful. (d) that which is complicated.
2. **potency** [pōt′n·sē]—(a) suitability for drinking. (b) fertility. (c) good health. (d) power.
3. **ascendancy** [ə·sen′dən·sē]—(a) domination. (b) an inheritance. (c) ashes. (d) a staircase.
4. **constancy** [kon′stən·sē]—(a) hardheartedness. (b) temperateness. (c) faithfulness. (d) unending.
5. **idiosyncrasy** [id′ē·ō·sing′krə·sē] —(a) a personal oddity. (b) a country ruled by a committee. (c) a hobby. (d) a folk song.
6. **exigency** [ek′sə·jən·sē]—(a) effort. (b) urgency. (c) an extreme emergency. (d) an unneeded item.
7. **contingency** [kən·tin′jən·sē]— (a) a body of troops. (b) a defeat. (c) a dangerous situation. (d) a possible occurrence.
8. **expediency** [ik·spē′dē·ən·sē]— (a) that which is moral. (b) that which is advantageous or

useful. (c) that which is evil. (d) that which is pleasing.
9. **fallacy** [fal′ə·sē]—(a) companionship. (b) a basic truth. (c) a mistaken notion. (d) deceit.
10. **magistracy** [maj′is·trə·sē]—(a) a king or queen. (b) the office or function of a magistrate. (c) a body of laws. (d) large and imposing.
11. **hypocrisy** [hi·pok′rə·sē]—(a) a theory. (b) a trancelike condition. (c) insincerity. (d) high blood pressure.
12. **apostasy** [ə·pos′tə·sē]—(a) desertion of one's faith or principles. (b) a chemical compound. (c) a digression. (d) a warding off of evil.
13. **heresy** [her′ə·sē]—(a) a person who lives in seclusion. (b) a belief contrary to established doctrine. (c) a future existence. (d) armorial bearings.
14. **literacy** [lit′ə·rə·sē]—(a) having to do with literature. (b) the ability to read and write. (c) a liquid measure. (d) actually; really.

ANSWERS:

1. **intricacy**—(d) that which is complicated. 2. **potency**—(d) power. 3. **ascendancy**—(a) domination. 4. **constancy**—(c) faithfulness. 5. **idiosyncrasy**—(a) a personal oddity. 6. **exigency**—(b) urgency. 7. **contingency**— (d) a possible occurrence. 8. **expediency**—(b) that which is advantageous or useful. 9. **fallacy**—(c) a mistaken notion. 10. **magistracy**—(b) the office or function of a magistrate. 11. **hypocrisy**—(c) insincerity. 12. **apostasy**— (a) a desertion of one's faith or principles. 13. **heresy**—(b) a belief contrary to established doctrine. 14. **literacy**—(b) the ability to read and write.

12 THE FINAL-E RULE

The final-*e* rule is one of the most important in spelling. Learn it now. A word ending in a consonant and a silent *e* (like *blame, confuse, hope*) usually drops the *e* before a suffix that starts with a vowel (like *-able, -ion, -ing*). Just using these examples, we get *blam*(e)*able*, *confus*(e)*ion*, and *hop*(e)*ing*.

This is just as easy every time. As you know, vowels are the letters *a, e, i, o, u,* and sometimes *y* (when it sounds like an *i*); all other letters are consonants. The rule says that the final *e* is normally dropped from a root word before a suffix when all three of the following facts apply:

1. The final *e* is silent, as in *ache, become, hope,* etc.
2. The final *e* is preceded by a consonant, as in the above examples.
3. The added suffix begins with a vowel, as *-able, -al, -er,* etc.

The Final-E Rule—Dropping the E

Here are some common words in which an understanding of the final-*e* rule will solve your spelling problems. The dash (—) used in the following list is a substitute for the word "becomes."

ache	—	aching	excite	—	exciting
achieve	—	achieving	grieve	—	grievance
admire	—	admirable	hope	—	hoping
adore	—	adorable	judge	—	judging
advertise	—	advertising	like	—	likable
advise	—	advisable	live	—	livable
arrive	—	arrival	love	—	lovable
believe	—	believable	move	—	movable
blame	—	blamable	noise	—	noisy
bone	—	bony	notice	—	noticing
care	—	caring	service	—	servicing
change	—	changing	size	—	sizable (also
come	—	coming			acceptable:
complete	—	completing			sizEable)
conceive	—	conceivable	sponge	—	spongy
confuse	—	confusion	stone	—	stony
debate	—	debatable	trace	—	tracing
deplore	—	deplorable	trouble	—	troubling
deserve	—	deserving	use	—	using

Hundreds of other words follow the final-*e* rule by dropping the silent *e* before a suffix beginning with a vowel. But there is another way in which the rule works. It also tells you when not to drop the *e*.

The Final-E Rule—Keeping the E

The final *e* normally is retained under any one of the following three circumstances:

1. The *e* is not silent but is pronounced, as in *be,* which becomes *being.*

2. It is preceded not by a consonant, but by a vowel, as in *shoe,* which becomes *shoeing.*

3. The added suffix begins with a consonant, as in the suffixes *-ful, -less, -ly, -ness, -ty,* etc.

The dash (—) used in the following list is a substitute for the word "becomes."

absolute	—	absolutEly	like	—	likEly
achieve	—	achievEment	live	—	livEly
advertise	—	advertisEment	lone	—	lonEly
bare	—	barEly	love	—	lovEly
care	—	carEful	mere	—	merEly
complete	—	completEly	move	—	movEment
decisive	—	decisivEness	nine	—	ninEty
definite	—	definitEly	rare	—	rarEly
dye	—	dyEing	replace	—	replacEment
encourage	—	encouragEment	severe	—	severEly
eye	—	eyEing	shoe	—	shoEing
hie	—	hiEing	sincere	—	sincerEly
hoe	—	hoEing	toe	—	toEing
immediate	—	immediatEly	use	—	usEful
immense	—	immensEly	whole	—	wholEsome

NOTE: In many pairs of words based on the same root word, the presence or absence of an *e* depends solely on whether the suffix starts with a vowel or a consonant. The final-*e* rule explains why English has such pairs as *advertising–advertisement, bony–boneless, hating–hateful, hoping–hopeful, lovable–lovely,* etc. In such pairs, the silent *e* of the root word is dropped before a suffix beginning with a vowel and kept before a suffix beginning with a consonant.

Exceptions to the Final-E Rule

Some words keep the silent *e* in spite of the rule. The usual reason is that the word might be mispronounced or misunderstood if the *e* were dropped. For instance, any word ending in *-ce* or *-ge* presents a special problem. The *c* and *g* are "soft" (that is, they are pronounced *s* and *j,* respectively) before the vowels *e* and *i,* but they are "hard" (pronounced *k* and *g*) before *a, o,* and *u.* For this reason, the final silent *e* often is retained before a suffix beginning with an *a, o,* or *u.* We drop the final *e* in *embracing,* but we keep it in *embraceable;* we drop the *e* in *charging,* but we keep it in *chargeable.* In that way the correct pronunciation is maintained.

For a different reason, we keep the *e* in *singeing* (meaning "burning slightly"). If we followed the final-*e* rule here, the resultant word could be confused with *singing* (meaning "making vocal music").

Here is a list of words you should have no trouble with if you remember why they are exceptions to the final-*e* rule. The *e* is kept for the sake of pronunciation or to avoid confusion. The dash (—) used in the following list is a substitute for the word "becomes."

acre	—	acrEage
advantage	—	advantagEous
change	—	changEable
charge	—	chargEable
courage	—	couragEous
embrace	—	embracEable
enforce	—	enforcEable
Europe	—	EuropEan
knowledge	—	knowledgEable
manage	—	managEable
marriage	—	marriagEable
notice	—	noticEable
outrage	—	outragEous
peace	—	peacEable
pronounce	—	pronouncEable
replace	—	replacEable
salvage	—	salvagEable
service	—	servicEable
singe	—	singEing
trace	—	tracEable

A number of words drop the silent *e* when, according to the rule, you would expect them to retain it. Learn the words in the following list now. Many of them can stump even the experts. The dash (—) used in the following list is a substitute for the word "becomes."

abridge	—	abridgment
acknowledge	—	acknowledgment
argue	—	arguing (argument)
blue	—	bluish
die	—	dying
judge	—	judgment
lie	—	lying
nine	—	ninth
tie	—	tying
true	—	truly
value	—	valuable
vie	—	vying
whole	—	wholly

In the above list, note that the *ie* of *die, lie, tie,* and *vie* changes to *y* before adding the *-ing.* And make a special point of learning how to spell *ninth* and *wholly.*

REMEMBER: *Ninth* has no *e,* but *ninety* does. *Wholly* has no *e,* but *wholesome* does!

NOTE: The preferred spelling for the word *mileage* retains the *e,* though *milage* is acceptable. And there are two correct ways to spell *line* plus the suffix *-age. Linage* without the *e* refers to the lines in a piece of written or printed matter, and it is pronounced [lī′nij]. *Lineage,* which is pronounced [lin′ē·ij], means "ancestry or pedigree."

Spelling Test—The Final-E Rule

Combine the following root words and suffixes to form properly spelled words. Be sure you know when to keep or drop a final *e* from the root before adding the suffix. Answers follow.

1. safe + -ty
2. amuse + -ing
3. amuse + -ment
4. nine + -ty
5. judge + -ment
6. believe + -ing
7. come + -ing
8. become + -ing
9. mile + -age
10. change + -able

11. true + -ly	21. sale + -able
12. ache + -ing	22. sue + -ing
13. rare + -ly	23. bone + -y
14. rare + -ity	24. knowledge + -able
15. courage + -ous	25. acknowledge + -ment
16. hope + -ing	26. advantage + -ous
17. bare + -ly	27. nose + -y
18. mere + -ly	28. adore + -able
19. argue + -able	29. die + -ing
20. argue + -ment	30. dye + -ing

ANSWERS:

1. safEty. 2. amusing. 3. amusEment. 4. ninEty. 5. judgment. 6. believing.
7. coming. 8. becoming. 9. milEage *or* milage. 10. changEable. 11. truly.
12. aching. 13. rarEly. 14. rarity. 15. couragEous. 16. hoping. 17. barEly.
18. merEly. 19. arguable. 20. argument. 21. salable *or* salEable. 22. suing.
23. bony. 24. knowledgEable. 25. acknowledgment. 26. advantagEous.
27. nosy. 28. adorable. 29. dying. 30. dyEing.

13 WHICH IS IT: -EFY or -IFY?—TestEFY or TestIFY? StupEFY or StupIFY?

The ending *-ify* is much more common than *-efy*. In fact, words ending in *-efy* may be considered exceptions. Here is a list of the most common words ending in *-efy* and *-ify*.

-IFY (the usual ending)	-EFY (the exceptions)
clarify	liquefy
codify	putrefy
deify	rarefy
fortify	stupefy
glorify	
intensify	
modify	
mortify	
purify	
ratify	
testify	
verify	

329

Spelling Test— -efy or -ify?

Choose the correctly spelled words within the parentheses below. Answers follow.

1. Should the Congress (ratefy, ratify) the new treaty?
2. The news (stupefied, stupified) me!
3. The witness for the prosecution will now (testefy, testify).
4. Please (clarify, clarefy) your last statement.
5. If Joe can't (verify, verefy) his facts, he will be (mortefied, mortified).
6. We must (intensify, intensefy) our sales efforts.
7. Meat soon (putrifies, putrefies) if it is not refrigerated.
8. This milk is (fortefied, fortified) with vitamin D.
9. Would you care to (modify, modefy) your report?
10. (Liquefied, liquified) oxygen is used as a rocket fuel.

ANSWERS:

1. ratify. 2. stupefied. 3. testify. 4. clarify. 5. verify, mortified. 6. intensify. 7. putrefies. 8. fortified. 9. modify. 10. liquefied *or* liquified.

14 THERE IS NO DG IN PRIVILEGE

Some words are spelling problems because the g sound in them is pronounced as *j* or *dg*. The letters *g*, *j*, and *dg* sometimes sound alike in English. Thus: *jam, gem, knowledge.* Very few people make the mistake of spelling simple g words with a *j* instead of a *g*. But a common error is to spell these words with a *dg*. Don't!

Three Simple G Words
privilege
allege
pigeon

Three Difficult G Words
cortege
sacrilege
sortilege

330

Spelling Test— –ege or –edge?

Choose the preferred spelling for the words between the parentheses below. Answers follow.

1. Criminals hate stool (pidgeons, pigeons).
2. The store's (legers, ledgers) are checked by an accountant.
3. In my (judgment, judgement), this house isn't (liveable, livable).
4. Have you read the (abridgement, abridgment) of the best-selling novel?
5. What are the (privileges, priviledges) that go with being an adult?
6. There are millions of (college, colledge) students in America.
7. The (alledged, alleged) thief has been arrested.
8. She carried a (lace-eged, lace-edged) handkerchief.
9. The funeral (cortedge, cortege) passed slowly by.
10. The boy (mimiced, mimicked) the (fledgling's, flegling's) walk.

ANSWERS:

1. pigeons. 2. ledgers. 3. judgment, livable. 4. abridgment. 5. privileges.
6. college. 7. alleged. 8. lace-edged. 9. cortege. 10. mimicked, fledgling's.

---

15 I BEFORE E EXCEPT AFTER C

Spelling rules can be helpful if you bear in mind that there are exceptions to almost every rule. One of the best-known rules in English spelling is this:

> Write *I* before *E*
> Except after *C*,
> Or when sounded like *A*
> As in *neighbor* and *weigh.*

This jingle is catchy, easy to remember, and, as far as it goes, correct. It just isn't complete. In fact, there are almost more exceptions to the rule than words that fit it. Contrary to the rule, *I* can come before *E* after *C* if it is a sh-sounding *C*, as in *conscience.* And after establishing that the *I*-before-*E* rule refers to words having an *e* sound, as either of the *e*'s in *even,* what about *codeine* and *heifer?*

Your best bet with *IE* and *EI* words is to learn the rule, learn to apply it, and then learn the exceptions.

I before E (when the word has a long or short *e* sound)

achieve	frieze	piece	wield
apiece	frontier	priest	yield
believe	grieve	relieve	
brief	hygiene	reprieve	
chief	liege	retrieve	
fiend	lien	shriek	
fierce	mien	siege	
friend	niece	thief	

Exceptions:

caffeine	heifer	nonpareil	sheik
codeine	leisure	protein	weir
either	neither	seize	weird

E before I after (an ess-sounding) C

ceiling	deceive
conceit	perceive
conceive	receipt
deceit	receive

Exceptions (after a sh-sounding C):

ancient	omniscient
conscience	proficient
deficient	species
efficient	sufficient
glacier	

E before I (when sounded like *a*)

beige	freight	neighbor	skein
chow mein	heinous	obeisance	sleigh
deign	heir	reign	surveillance
eight	heirloom	rein	veil
feign	inveigh	reindeer	vein
feint	neigh	seine	weigh

There are no exceptions to this part of the rule!

E before I (when the word has a long or short *i* sound)

counterfeit	leitmotif
eiderdown	seismograph
fahrenheit	sleight
foreign	stein
forfeit	surfeit
height	

Exceptions:

handkerchief	mischievous
mischief	sieve

There is one word, *financier,* that follows no rules at all. It must be memorized.

QUICKIEQUIZQUICKIEQUIZQUICKIEQUIZQUICKIEQUIZQUICKIEQUIZQUICKIEQUIZQUICKIEQUIZQUICKIE

TWO-MINUTE QUICKIE QUIZ

IE OR EI?

Add *ie* or *ei* to each of the words in this list. Answers follow.

1. anc____nt	13. glac____r
2. hyg____ne	14. f____nd
3. caff____ne	15. effic____ncy
4. bes____ge	16. s____zure
5. w____rd	17. s____ve
6. dec____tful	18. v____n
7. financ____r	19. ach____vement
8. repr____ved	20. l____utenant
9. chow m____n	21. rec____ving
10. forf____t	22. h____rloom
11. cloth____r	23. d____ty
12. r____ndeer	24. gr____vous

ANSWERS:

1. ancIEnt. 2. hygIEne. 3. caffEIne. 4. besIEge. 5. wEIrd. 6. decEItful. 7. financIEr. 8. reprIEved. 9. chow mEIn. 10. forfEIt. 11. clothIEr. 12. rEIndeer. 13. glacIEr. 14. fiEnd. 15. efficIEncy. 16. sEIzure. 17. sIEve. 18. vEIn. 19. achIEvement. 20. lIEutenant. 21. recEIving. 22. hEIrloom. 23. dEIty. 24. grIEvous.

QUICKIEQUIZQUICKIEQUIZQUICKIEQUIZQUICKIEQUIZQUICKIEQUIZQUICKIEQUIZQUICKIEQUIZQUICKIE

Spelling Test—*ie or ei?*

Add *ie* or *ei* to complete the following words. Answers follow.

1. The ch____f's chow m____n was s____zed on the front____r.
2. N____ther my n____ghbor nor my fr____nd is dec____tful.
3. What spec____s of r____ndeer did you see in the f____ld?
4. The sh____k r____gned at the ball.
5. Anc____nt Roman pleb____ans inv____ghed against for____gn fi- nanc____rs.
6. Sc____ntists use a s____smograph to record earthquakes.
7. The v____led queen d____gned to rev____w her tenant's f____fs.
8. H____fers need prot____n to gain w____ght.
9. The w____r across the stream y____lded ____ghty fish.
10. I gave my n____ce an ____derdown quilt when she married the l____utenant.
11. The magician's sl____ght of hand rec____ved careful surv____llance.
12. Bel____ve in your own ability and you will ach____ve the h____gts.
13. A h____nous th____f conc____ved that dastardly crime.
14. The cash____r's rec____pt reflected fr____ght charges.
15. We forf____ted the game in l____u of playing in the f____ry heat.
16. The ruthlessness of the sh____k brought gr____f to his people.
17. The w____rd hermit f____gned qu____t madness.
18. ____ther his consc____nce or his bel____fs made his behavior in- conc____vable.
19. The propr____tor sold counterf____t h____rlooms.
20. The c____ling of the theater was p____rced to add a t____r of seats.

ANSWERS:

1. chIEf's, chow mEIn, sEIzed, frontIEr. 2. nEIther, nEIghbor, frIEnd, decEItful. 3. specIEs, rEIndeer, fIEld. 4. shEIk, rEIgned. 5. ancIEnt, plebEIans, invEIghed, forEIgn, financIErs. 6. scIEntists, sEIsmograph. 7. vEIled, dEIgned, revIEw, fIEfs. 8. hEIfers, protEIn, wEIght. 9. wEIr, yIElded, EIghty. 10. nIEce, EIderdown, lIEutenant. 11. slEIght, recEIved, survEIllance. 12. belIEve, achIEve, hEIghts. 13. hEInous, thIEf, concEIved. 14. cashIEr's, recEIpt, frEIght. 15. forfEIted, lIEu, fIEry. 16. shEIk, grIEf. 17. wEIrd, fEIgned, quIEt. 18. EIther, conscIEnce, belIEfs, inconcEIvable. 19. proprIEtor, counterfEIt, hEIrlooms. 20. cEIling, pIErced, tIEr.

IE AND EI

Choose the definition you believe is closest in meaning to each of the key words below. (As you do this vocabulary test, notice the *ie* and *ei* spellings.) Answers follow.

1. **aggrieved** [ə·grēvd′]—(a) distressed. (b) massed together. (c) aroused. (d) rocky.
2. **cavalier** [kav′ə·lir′]—(a) graceful. (b) supercilious and haughty. (c) expert in horsemanship. (d) stylishly dressed.
3. **inconceivable** [in′kən·sē′və·bəl] —(a) unimportant. (b) unthinkable. (c) improbable. (d) impossible.
4. **obeisance** [ō·bā′səns]—(a) a musical instrument. (b) an Egyptian monument. (c) a large depression. (d) homage.
5. **inveigle** [in·vē′gəl *or* in·vā′gəl] —(a) to lead on by deceit. (b) to flatter. (c) to invite. (d) to steal from.
6. **reprieve** [ri·prēv′]—(a) suspension of a sentence. (b) the death penalty. (c) a repeated musical phrase. (d) to censure.
7. **weir** [wir]—(a) a dam in a stream. (b) a fish net. (c) crazy. (d) a mine entrance.
8. **heinous** [hā′nəs]—(a) extremely wicked. (b) a king or queen. (c) funny. (d) renowned.
9. **nonpareil** [non′pə·rel′]—(a) unaligned. (b) a cable car. (c) misunderstood. (d) unrivaled.
10. **deign** [dān]—(a) to condescend. (b) a Scandinavian king. (c) to exalt. (d) to divert.
11. **specie** [spē′shē]—(a) a category of animals. (b) rare vegetation. (c) a ghost. (d) coined money.
12. **species** [spē′shēz]—(a) museum exhibits. (b) a monocle. (c) a category of animals. (d) coined money.
13. **irretrievable** [ir′i·trē′və·bəl]— (a) extremely valuable. (b) damaged. (c) full of holes. (d) gone forever.
14. **feint** [fānt]—(a) to exhaust. (b) to quarrel loudly. (c) to mislead by a false move. (d) to become unconscious.
15. **plebeian** [pli·bē′ən]—(a) military. (b) common. (c) unusual. (d) an ancient sailor.

ANSWERS:

1. **aggrieved**—(a) distressed. 2. **cavalier**—(b) supercilious and haughty. 3. **inconceivable**—(b) unthinkable. 4. **obeisance**—(d) homage. 5. **inveigle** —(a) to lead on by deceit. 6. **reprieve**—(a) suspension of a sentence. 7. **weir**—(a) a dam in a stream. 8. **heinous**—(a) extremely wicked. 9. **nonpareil**—(d) unrivaled. 10. **deign**—(a) to condescend. 11. **specie**—(d) coined money. 12. **species**—(c) a category of animals. 13. **irretrievable**—(d) gone forever. 14. **feint**—(c) to mislead by a false move. 15. **plebeian**—(b) common.

16 WHICH IS IT: -ISE, -IZE, or -YZE—AdvertISE or AdvertIZE? AnalIZE or AnalYZE?

The question of whether to spell a word with an *-ise*, *-ize*, or *-yze* stumps many people. All three endings are pronounced alike. The problem becomes a lot easier when you realize that the usual suffix is *-ize* and that *-yze* and *-ise* are rather rare exceptions. More than 400 common words end in *-ize*. Here is a list of a few of them:

agonize	emphasize	patronize
Americanize	equalize	philosophize
amortize	familiarize	plagiarize
antagonize	fertilize	pulverize
apologize	generalize	realize
authorize	harmonize	recognize
baptize	hypnotize	reorganize
brutalize	itemize	scandalize
capsize	jeopardize	scrutinize
cauterize	legalize	specialize
characterize	mechanize	subsidize
Christianize	memorize	symbolize
civilize	modernize	sympathize
colonize	monopolize	tantalize
criticize	moralize	terrorize
crystallize	nationalize	utilize
demoralize	neutralize	victimize
disorganize	normalize	visualize
dramatize	ostracize	vocalize
economize	oxidize	vulcanize

REMEMBER: *-ize* is a common American suffix added to words and roots.

Only Two Common Words End in *-yze*

Two common words that end in *-yze* are *analyze* and *paralyze*. There are some less common *-yze* words, to be sure—for example, *catalyze*, *dialyze*, *electrolyze*, and *psychoanalyze*. But if you're in a field where you need to know such technical words, you no doubt already know how to spell them.

Only Thirty-Odd Common Words End in *-ise*

In the United States, a final *-ise* is rare. If you learn to spell the following, you will know all the common *-ise* words you need.

advertise	devise	merchandise
advise	disguise	otherwise
apprise	enfranchise	premise
arise	enterprise	reprise
chastise	excise	revise
circumcise	exercise	rise
clockwise	exorcise	sidewise
comprise	guise	supervise
compromise	improvise	surmise
demise	lengthwise	surprise
despise	likewise	televise

Spelling Test— -yze, -ise, or -ize?

Add *-yze, -ise,* or *-ize* to complete the following words. Answers follow.

1. advert_____
2. apolog_____
3. real_____
4. exerc_____
5. familiar_____
6. Christian_____
7. surpr_____
8. item_____
9. paral_____
10. critic_____
11. lengthw_____
12. patron_____

13. compr_____
14. modern_____
15. special_____
16. psychoanal_____
17. bapt_____
18. comprom_____
19. desp_____
20. superv_____
21. general_____
22. util_____
23. telev_____
24. merchand_____

ANSWERS:

1. advertISE. 2. apologIZE. 3. realIZE. 4. exercISE. 5. familiarIZE 6. ChristianIZE. 7. surprISE. 8. itemIZE. 9. paralYZE. 10. criticIZE. 11. lengthwISE. 12. patronIZE. 13. comprISE. 14. modernIZE. 15. specialIZE. 16. psychoanalYZE. 17. baptIZE. 18. compromISE. 19. despISE. 20. supervISE. 21. generalIZE. 22. utilIZE. 23. televISE. 24. merchandISE.

17 WHICH IS IT: -LY or -ALLY?

A common word-ending is -ly, which is often added to adjectives in order to form adverbs—*greatly, coolly, warmly,* etc. When the original ends in -ic, the adverb-making suffix sometimes is -ally instead of -ly. The extra syllable makes the adverb easier to pronounce.

Adverb Formed by Adding -ALLY

academicALLY	fantasticALLY
artisticALLY	lyricALLY
automaticALLY	systematicALLY

The -ally ending is not always used with adjectives ending in -ic. For instance, one very common -ic word that is made into an adverb by adding only -ly is *public;* the adverb is *publicly.*

Many adverbs that seem to have the -ally suffix do not really have an added syllable. In the following list, each of the basic adjectives ends in -al. So the suffix -ly simply is added to form the adverb.

Adverb Formed by Adding -LY

accidental + ly = accidentally	grammatical + ly = grammatically
critical + ly = critically	incidental + ly = incidentally
final + ly = finally	practical + ly = practically
general + ly = generally	typical + ly = typically

The above adverbs, and dozens similar to them, should be easy to spell. You merely have to remember that you are adding -ly to an adjective that already ends in -al to get the combination -ally.

---

18 WHICH IS IT: -OUS or -US?

Because -ous and -us sound alike, they can cause spelling problems. One easy way exists to tell when to end a word with -ous and when to end it with -us. Adjectives end in -ous and nouns end in -us. Thus, -ous is added to roots and other words to form adjectives: *advantage + ous = advantageous.* The ending -us is found only at the end of nouns. On page 340 are some of the most common -ous and -us words:

QUICKIE QUIZ

-LY OR -ALLY?

Choose the correctly spelled word from each pair below. Answers follow.

1. (a) exceptionally	(b) exceptionly
2. (a) cooly	(b) coolly
3. (a) incidentally	(b) incidently
4. (a) merrily	(b) merrilly
5. (a) criticly	(b) critically
6. (a) generly	(b) generally
7. (a) equaly	(b) equally
8. (a) anxiousally	(b) anxiously
9. (a) thoughtfully	(b) thoughtfuly
10. (a) typicly	(b) typically
11. (a) finally	(b) finly
12. (a) logicly	(b) logically
13. (a) intentionly	(b) intentionally
14. (a) accidentally	(b) accidently
15. (a) publicly	(b) publically
16. (a) scholasticly	(b) scholastically
17. (a) pensivelly	(b) pensively
18. (a) academically	(b) academicly
19. (a) realy	(b) really
20. (a) practically	(b) practicly
21. (a) carefuly	(b) carefully
22. (a) happily	(b) happyly
23. (a) lackadaisicly	(b) lackadaisically
24. (a) usually	(b) usualy
25. (a) lyricly	(b) lyrically
26. (a) basically	(b) basicly
27. (a) elemently	(b) elementally
28. (a) prudentally	(b) prudently
29. (a) intrinsically	(b) intrinsicly
30. (a) demonicly	(b) demonically

ANSWERS:

1. (a) exceptionally. 2. (b) coolly. 3. (a) incidentally. 4. (a) merrily. 5. (b) critically. 6. (b) generally. 7. (b)equally. 8. (b) anxiously. 9. (a) thoughtfully. 10. (b) typically. 11. (a) finally. 12. (b) logically. 13. (b) intentionally. 14. (a) accidentally. 15. (a) publicly. 16. (b) scholastically. 17. (b) pensively. 18. (a) academically. 19. (b) really. 20. (a) practically. 21. (b) carefully. 22. (a) happily. 23. (b) lackadaisically. 24. (a) usually. 25. (b) lyrically. 26. (a) basically. 27. (b) elementally. 28. (b) prudently. 29. (a) intrinsically. 30. (b) demonically.

ADJECTIVES	NOUNS
ambitious	apparatus
callous (meaning "hardened or thickened")	cactus
	calculus
courageous	callus (meaning "a hardened or thickened area of skin")
dangerous	
fictitious	campus
generous	esophagus
humorous	genius
marvelous	hippopotamus
miscellaneous	humus
monstrous	impetus
outrageous	rumpus
pious	sarcophagus
righteous	status
serious	stimulus
wondrous	

19 WHEN IS A FINAL Y CHANGED TO I?

A simple rule tells you when to change a final *y* to an *i* at the end of a word before adding a suffix. Here is that rule:

If a word ends in *y* preceded by a consonant (any letter other than *a, e, i, o,* or *u*), change the *y* to an *i* when you add a suffix. Here are some examples. The dash (—) used in the following list is a substitute for the word "becomes."

accompany	—	accompanied, accompanies, accompaniment
ally	—	allied, allies
angry	—	angrily
beauty	—	beauties, beautified, beautiful (but beautEous)
busy	—	busier, busiest, busily, business
carry	—	carried, carrier, carries
city	—	cities, citified
cry	—	cried, crier, cries
dignify	—	dignified, dignifies
duty	—	duties, dutiful

easy	—	easier, easiest, easily
empty	—	emptier, emptiness
enemy	—	enemies
happy	—	happier, happiest, happily, happiness
heavy	—	heavier, heaviest
lazy	—	lazier, laziest, lazily, laziness
lively	—	livelier, liveliest, livelihood, liveliness
pity	—	pitiful
plenty	—	plentiful (but plentEous)
salary	—	salaried, salaries
steady	—	steadily, steadiness
try	—	tried, tries
worry	—	worrier, worries, worriment

EXCEPTIONS: There are three general exceptions to the above rule:

1. The English language does not like two *i*'s to come together. Thus, even when the final *y* is preceded by a consonant, this *y* does not change to an *i* before a suffix that begins with an *i*. For this reason, words like *babyish, carrying, pitying,* and *trying* have not changed their *y*'s to *i*'s.

2. A number of very simple short words containing a final *y* preceded by a consonant may keep the *y* unchanged before some suffixes. Here are some of the most common such words:

dry	—	dryly, dryness (but drIer)
lady	—	ladylike
shy	—	shyly, shyness (but shIes)
sly	—	slyly, slyness
spry	—	spryly, spryness
wry	—	wryly, wryness

3. The final *y* does not change to *i* before adding a suffix to proper names. Proper names are often exceptions to spelling rules because we respect a person's name and try to preserve its original spelling whenever possible. If a proper name ends in a *y* preceded by a consonant, keep the final *y* intact before adding any suffix—even including the plural -*s*. For example:

Harry	two Harrys	McCarthy	two McCarthys
Larry	two Larrys	O'Reilly	two O'Reillys
Mary	two Marys	Perry	two Perrys

341

WORDS ENDING IN -OUS OR -US

Choose the word or phrase you believe is closest in meaning to each of the key words below. These key words all end in *-ous* or *-us,* and you should also learn their proper spellings. Answers follow.

1. **nebulous** [neb′yə·ləs]—(a) tiny. (b) hazy. (c) foolish. (d) moist.
2. **opprobrious** [ə·prō′brē·əs]—(a) worthy of praise. (b) disgraceful. (c) oily. (d) quick.
3. **ostentatious** [os′tən·tā′shəs]— (a) wealthy. (b) talkative. (c) showy. (d) noisy.
4. **propitious** [prō·pish′əs]—(a) routine or ordinary. (b) impulsive. (c) unfavorable. (d) favorable.
5. **illustrious** [i·lus′trē·əs]—(a) famous. (b) illustrated. (c) wealthy. (d) gallant.
6. **emeritus** [i·mer′ə·təs]—(a) an honorary degree. (b) having seniority. (c) praiseworthy. (d) retired from active service.
7. **devious** [dē′vē·əs]—(a) divided. (b) illegal. (c) varying from a straight course. (d) insane.
8. **meticulous** [mə·tik′yə·ləs]—(a) quick. (b) humorous. (c) very small. (d) careful about details.
9. **portentous** [pôr·ten′təs]—(a) very heavy. (b) ominous. (c) overweight. (d) ridiculous.
10. **impetus** [im′pə·təs]—(a) cunning. (b) disagreeableness. (c) momentum. (d) prejudice.
11. **erroneous** [ə·rō′nē·əs]—(a) foolish. (b) passionate. (c) mistaken. (d) dishonest.
12. **hiatus** [hī·ā′təs]—(a) mobility. (b) a mountain peak. (c) vain pride. (d) a space or gap.
13. **arduous** [är′jōō·əs]—(a) brave. (b) involving great labor. (c) passionate. (d) intense and fervent.
14. **solicitous** [sə·lis′ə·təs]—(a) serene. (b) energetic. (c) bitter. (d) showing care and concern.
15. **ingenuous** [in·jen′yōō·əs]—(a) absolutely true. (b) candid or naive. (c) very wise. (d) native.
16. **onus** [ō′nəs]—(a) burden. (b) Latin word for "one." (c) proof. (d) blame.
17. **indigenous** [in·dij′ə·nəs]—(a) destitute. (b) native. (c) angry. (d) lazy.

ANSWERS:

1. **nebulous**—(b) hazy. 2. **opprobrious**—(b) disgraceful. 3. **ostentatious**—(c) showy. 4. **propitious**—(d) favorable. 5. **illustrious**—(a) famous. 6. **emeritus**—(d) retired from active service. 7. **devious**—(c) varying from a straight course. 8. **meticulous**—(d) careful about details. 9. **portentous**—(b) ominous. 10. **impetus**—(c) momentum. 11. **erroneous**—(c) mistaken. 12. **hiatus** —(d) a space or gap. 13. **arduous**—(b) involving great labor. 14. **solicitous** —(d) showing care and concern. 15. **ingenuous**—(b) candid or naive. 16. **onus**—(a) burden. 17. **indigenous**—(b) native.

When There Is No Consonant

Remember that the rule is: "If a word ends in a *y* preceded by a consonant, change the *y* to an *i* when you add a suffix." What if the final *y* is not preceded by a consonant? Then, obviously, the rule does not apply; the final *y* remains a *y*. Here are some common examples:

allay — allayed, allays
alley — alleys
annoy — annoyance, annoyed
array — arrayed, arrays
bray — brayed, brays
chimney — chimneys
cloy — cloyed, cloys
day — days, daytime
decay — decayed, decays
delay — delayed, delays
destroy — destroyed, destroys
dismay — dismayed, dismays
donkey — donkeys
employ — employed, employer, employment, employs
essay — essayed, essays
foray — forayer, forays
joy — joyous, joys
monkey — monkeys
pay — payment, pays
play — played, playful, plays
portray — portrayal, portrayed, portrays
pray — prayer, prays
stay — stayed, stays
tray — trays

EXCEPTIONS: There are a few common exceptions to the rule that a final *y* preceded by a vowel remains a *y*. All are simple words that most of us learned to spell in elementary school. In the following words the final *y* changes to an *i* even though preceded by a vowel.

day — daily
gay — gaily, gaiety
lay — laid
pay — paid
slay — slain

Spelling Test—*y* or *i?*

Insert *y* or *i* to complete the following words. Answers follow.

1. anno___ed
2. ga___ety
3. ga___ly
4. necessit___es
5. obe___ed
6. sl___ness
7. accompan___ment
8. pr___ed
9. pr___ing
10. emplo___ee
11. traged___es
12. laz___ly
13. laz___ness
14. monke___s
15. compl___ance
16. dut___ful
17. pit___ful
18. jo___ful
19. jo___ous
20. worr___ment
21. beautif___ing

22. beautif___ed
23. dr___ly
24. dr___ness
25. dr___er
26. occup___ed
27. occup___ing
28. portra___al
29. livel___hood
30. wr___ly
31. comed___es
32. merr___ment
33. wear___ness
34. co___ness
35. donke___s
36. certif___ing
37. parod___es
38. penalt___es
39. joll___ty
40. foll___es
41. chimne___s
42. jerse___s

ANSWERS:

1. annoYed. 2. gaIety. 3. gaIly. 4. necessitIes. 5. obeYed. 6. slYness. 7. accompanIment. 8. prIed. 9. prYing. 10. emploYee. 11. tragedIes. 12. lazIly. 13. lazIness. 14. monkeYs. 15. complIance. 16. dutIful. 17. pitIful. 18. joYful. 19. joYous. 20. worrIment. 21. beautifYing. 22. beautifIed. 23. drYly. 24. drYness. 25. drIer. 26. occupIed. 27. occupYing. 28. portraYal. 29. livelIhood. 30. wrYly. 31. comedIes. 32. merrIment. 33. wearIness. 34. coYness. 35. donkeYs. 36. certifYing. 37. parodIes. 38. penaltIes. 39. jollIty. 40. follIes. 41. chimneYs. 42. jerseYs.

Fun With Words

A ROUNDUP

The following sixteen words are among the spelling demons you have already studied. Check the word or phrase you believe is closest in meaning to the key word. Answers follow.

1. **remediable** [ri·mē′dē·ə·bəl]— (a) justifiable. (b) notable. (c) curable. (d) helpful to reading.
2. **severance** [sev′ər·əns]—(a) separation. (b) indignation. (c) deep respect. (d) final.
3. **addle** [ad′l]—(a) to increase. (b) to make strong. (c) to confuse. (d) to stir.
4. **exuberant** [ig·zoo′bər·ənt]—(a) breathless. (b) humorous. (c) striving to please. (d) full of joy and vigor.
5. **rancor** [rang′kər]—(a) tumult. (b) conceit. (c) sourness. (d) malice.
6. **tractable** [trak′tə·bəl]—(a) capable of being lengthened. (b) docile. (c) stubborn. (d) easily angered.
7. **chauvinist** [shō′vən·ist]—(a) a person who makes an extravagant show of patriotism. (b) an overly cautious scientist. (c) a person who finds fault with everything. (d) a musician.
8. **dissidence** [dis′ə·dəns]—(a) disagreement. (b) timidity. (c) nonconformity. (d) a result.

9. **parochial** [pə·rō′kē·əl]—(a) having to do with teaching. (b) ecumenical (c) monastic. (d) provincial.
10. **expedient** [ik·spē′dē·ənt]—(a) suitable and advantageous. (b) moral or ethical. (c) troublesome or costly. (d) a quick solution.
10. **surveillance** [sər·vā′ləns]—(a) slavelike obedience. (b) unusual wisdom. (c) deep respect. (d) close watch.
12. **nucleus** [noo′klē·əs]—(a) a core or central point. (b) a sailfish. (c) a root. (d) an outer part.
13. **somber** [som′bər]—(a) reluctant. (b) gloomy. (c) formal or unfriendly. (d) tranquil.
14. **archeology** [ar′kē·ol′ə·jē]—(a) the study of birds. (b) the study of history through excavations. (c) the study of theology. (d) the science of building.
15. **veritable** [ver′ə·tə·bəl]—(a) real. (b) old and honored. (c) abundant. (d) lively.
16. **flippant** [flip′ənt]—(a) flirtatious. (b) talkative. (c) joyous. (d) pert.

ANSWERS:

1. **remediable**—(c) curable. 2. **severance**—(a) separation. 3. **addle**—(c) to confuse. 4. **exuberant**—(d) full of joy and vigor. 5. **rancor**—(d) malice. 6. **tractable**—(b) docile. 7. **chauvinist**—(a) a person who makes an extravagant show of patriotism. 8. **dissidence**—(a) disagreement. 9. **parochial**— (d) provincial. 10. **expedient**—(a) suitable and advantageous. 11. **surveillance**—(d) close watch. 12. **nucleus**—(a) a core or central point. 13. **somber** —(b) gloomy. 14. **archeology**—(b) the study of history through excavations. 15. **veritable**—(a) real. 16. **flippant**—(d) pert.

Fun With Words

A SECOND ROUNDUP

The following fifteen words are among the spelling demons you have already studied. Check the word or phrase you believe is closest in meaning to the key word. Answers follow.

1. **echelon** [esh′ə·lon]—(a) a series of levels or grades in an organization. (b) a triangular flag. (c) a shade of blue. (d) a series of numbers.

2. **nonchalance** [non′shə·ləns]—(a) superiority. (b) nonconformity. (c) unconcern. (d) insanity.

3. **intermittent** [in′tər·mit′ənt]—(a) occurring at intervals. (b) obvious. (c) fragmented. (d) to come to a decision.

4. **feral** [fir′əl]—(a) manly. (b) containing iron. (c) straight. (d) wild.

5. **prior** [prī′ər]—(a) nearby. (b) just after. (c) just before. (d) higher up.

6. **extraneous** [ik·strā′nē·əs]—(a) unwanted. (b) abundant. (c) extremely loud. (d) external or foreign.

7. **arrogance** [ar′ə·gəns]—(a) boldness. (b) aristocracy. (c) overbearing pride. (d) sarcasm.

8. **gaucherie** [gōsh·rē′]—(a) awkward or tactless action or speech. (b) a South American cowboy.

(c) a small clothing shop for women. (d) ambition.

9. **strident** [strīd′nt]—(a) swaggering. (b) aggressive. (c) shrill. (d) selfish.

10. **Machiavellian** [mak′ē·ə·vel′ē·ən] —(a) politically unscrupulous or crafty. (b) wise. (c) inconsequential. (d) in a robot-like manner.

11. **susceptible** [sə·sep′tə·bəl]—(a) easily influenced. (b) convincing. (c) dignified. (d) contagious.

12. **termagant** [tûr′mə·gənt]—(a) a migratory sea bird. (b) a type of small rodent. (c) a gossipy woman. (d) a scolding woman.

13. **insatiable** [in·sā′shə·bəl]—(a) very tense. (b) flimsy. (c) incapable of being satisfied. (d) incapable of growing.

14. **pivotal** [piv′ə·təl]—(a) serving as a crucial factor. (b) the central core. (c) uplifting. (d) impressive.

15. **viable** [vī′ə·bəl]—(a) easily influenced. (b) powdery. (c) practicable. (d) land that can be plowed.

ANSWERS:

1. **echelon**—(a) a series of levels or grades in an organization. 2. **nonchalance**—(c) unconcern. 3. **intermittent**—(a) occurring at intervals. 4. **feral** —(d) wild. 5. **prior**—(c) just before. 6. **extraneous**—(d) external or foreign. 7. **arrogance**—(c) overbearing pride. 8. **gaucherie**—(a) awkward or tactless action or speech. 9. **strident**—(c) shrill. 10. **Machiavellian**—(a) politically unscrupulous or crafty. 11. **susceptible**—(a) easily influenced. 12. **termagant**—(d) a scolding woman. 13. **insatiable**—(c) incapable of being satisfied. 14. **pivotal**—(a) serving as a crucial factor. 15. **viable**—(c) practicable.

PART THREE

Say It Right

PRONUNCIATION—PART OF YOUR WORD POWER

Good pronunciation goes hand in hand with a good vocabulary. There is little use in learning the meanings of words unless you can pronounce them properly. To learn a new word, you must actually learn three things: its meaning, its spelling, and its pronunciation. That is why vocabulary building, spelling, and pronunciation are taught in the first three sections of this book. Correct pronunciation can be a help to your spelling. If you mispronounce a word, you are likely to misspell it as well. If you pronounce it correctly, you are more likely to spell it correctly. For example, if you pronounce *athlete* without adding an extra *a* sound, you will not be tempted to misspell it as *athalete* by adding that incorrect extra *a*. When you get in the habit of pronouncing all words with care, your spelling is bound to improve.

Your Right to Be Heard

Good pronunciation does not require everyone to speak alike. Regional accents and the tone of one's voice have nothing to do with saying words correctly. You may have a Southern, a Western, a New York, or a Boston accent, and your voice may be full and deep or thin and high. No matter! What does matter is to say every word correctly in your own accent and natural voice.

How to Learn Pronunciation

From childhood on, we learn to say new words by imitating others. In that way, we learn to pronounce most words correctly—but we also repeat the mistakes of our friends and add a few of our own.

As we grow older, we enlarge our vocabulary by reading. Thus, we learn many new words by seeing them in print. The trouble is, however, that we see rather than hear them. The only sure way to learn the pronunciation of new words is to look them up in a good dictionary. And to understand what the dictionary tells us, we must learn how to interpret the symbols in its pronunciation key.

The pronunciation key of the Reader's Digest *Great Encyclopedic Dictionary* is used in this book as your guide to correct pronunciation. It is thoroughly explained on pages 6–7 in the Introduction. Review these pages now, and refer to the key whenever you need to as you study the following chapters.

Those chapters will help to guide you along the path toward good, correct pronunciation. They will help you train yourself to listen to— and to reproduce—the modern accepted pronunciation of words by educated speakers. Good pronunciation, you'll find, is an easy habit to acquire; it is also one of the surest ways to improve your word power.

There are fewer pronunciation demons than spelling demons. If you have serious pronunciation problems, they probably turn up in only one or two sounds or in a few dozen words. In the following chapters we concentrate on the most common pronunciation difficulties chosen from the 2,500 most frequently mispronounced words. Don't spend your time on the many words you already pronounce correctly.

REMEMBER: A poor speaker is often considered a poor thinker. Improve your speech habits, and your words (which reflect your thoughts, feelings, and personality) will get the attention and respect they deserve.

---

1 SPEAK FOR YOURSELF

People judge you not only by what you say, but by how you say it. So it behooves you to give particular care to your pronunciation and how you sound to others.

Fads and fashions come and go in pronunciation; what was once considered cultured and preferred may now sound phony or exaggerated. A hundred years ago, the broad *a* (the *ah* or *ä* sound) was a "must" in good society, and many people pronounced *vase* [vāz *or* vās] as *vahz* [väz]; fifty years ago, the sharp *u* (the yōō sound) was considered the peak of refined pronunciation, and the most careful speakers pronounced *tune* [tōōn] as *tyoon* [tyōōn]. Today some speakers believe that it is more refined to pronounce *either* [ē′thər] as *eyether* [ī′thər] and *been* [bin] as *bean* [bēn]. These are no longer the most frequent pronunciations. Inhabitants of certain regions still say *vahz, tyoon,* and *eyether* naturally, as part of their accepted dialect; and *bean* (bēn) is an accepted British pronunciation of *been* (bin). But if you don't come from New England or the South, you'll be better off sticking to the general American pronunciations found in up-to-date dictionaries.

How Do You Sound to Others?

Pronunciation and speech should be natural, smooth-flowing, and unobtrusive. Don't leave your listeners wondering how long you've lived at Buckingham Palace or how many nights a week you attend Miss Prim's School of Diction. Remember that the purpose of good pronunciation is to speak like a warm, reasonably well-educated human being, to communicate ideas, emotions, and your true personality and beliefs—not to impress people with your superior "refinement." So if you were brought up to say *eyether* and *nyether* as naturally as any other word, continue to say them. They will match the rest of your speech patterns and sound perfectly normal and unaffected. If, however, you've schooled yourself to say *eyether* and *nyether* because you think they sound "high class," drop them fast. These pronunciations repel more people than they attract.

Uh and Thuh or A and Thee?

The words *a* and *the* are two of the simplest words in English; yet many people are confused about how to say them. The letter A is pronounced [ā] as in "He got an A in history" or *A-1*. But the word *a* is normally pronounced *uh* [ə]: *uh book*. Don't try to impress people by saying the letter *a* [ā] when you mean the word *a* [ə].

REMEMBER: The word *a* is pronounced *uh* [ə] in normal conversation. (The exception occurs when you want to stress the word *a*, as in "I didn't say '*the* books,' I said '*a* book.'")

The word *the* is pronounced either *thuh* [thə] or *thee* [thē] depending on its use. Many persons say *thuh* at all times—and this is not incorrect. Thus, you may say "Put thuh apple on thuh table." But most speakers follow an older pronunciation rule—which is good because it makes "the apple" easier, not harder, to say. The rule is that *the* should be pronounced *thuh* before a word beginning with a consonant (*thuh table*) and *thee* before a word beginning with a vowel (*thee apple*). "I ate *thee* apple, *thee* egg, and *thee* onion" is easier to say, you'll find, than "I ate *thuh* apple, *thuh* egg, and *thuh* onion." Here again your local standard pronunciation is what really counts. Don't try to sound fancy and use *thee* all the time. Do not say "Put *thee* apple on *thee* table."

350

NOTE: *A* is an *indefinite article,* and *the* is the *definite article* in English. There are two indefinite articles, *a* and *an. A* is used before a word beginning with a consonant (*a table*) and *an* is used before a word beginning with a vowel (*an apple*). It is never acceptable to speak of *a* apple or *a* egg.

Vayz or Vahz, Tomayto or Tomahto?

If I say *tomayto* and you say *tomahto,* I say *vayz* and you say *vahz,* maybe we'll never get together—because the chances are that you're a hundred years older than I am!

American pronunciation has moved away from the broad *a* until the broad *a* is now associated almost entirely with New England and the South. If you use the broad *a* naturally because you were brought up to say *vase* as *vahz* [väz], *aunt* as *ahnt* [änt], and *laugh* as *lahf* [läf], that's perfectly all right. However, this broad *a* pronunciation is no more proper or more sophisticated than the usual *a* pronunciation in such words. And so, unless it is part of your normal speech patterns, forget it.

	Preferred General Pronunciation
after	af′tər
ásk	ask
aunt	ant
bath	bath
can't	kant
chance	chans
last	last
laugh	laf
pass	pas
patio	pat′ē·ō
plaza	plaz′ə
rather	rath′ər
tomato	tə·mā′tō
vase	vās *or* vāz

EXCEPTIONS: *Lama* (a Tibetan monk) and *llama* (the South American animal) are pronounced exactly alike:

lama	lahma	[lä′mə]
llama	lahma	[lä′mə]

351

QUICKIE QUIZ

DEMONS AND DOUBLE DEMONS

Choose a pronunciation of the following key words. Some will have only one acceptable form; others will have two. A few of the words in this test are new and have been included as a challenge to you.

1. ignoramus	(a) ig′nə·ram′əs	(b) ig′nə·rā′məs
2. sacrifice	(a) sak′rə·fīs	(b) sak′rə·fis
3. radiator	(a) rā′dē·ā′tər	(b) ra′dē·ā′tər
4. tomato	(a) tə·mā′tō	(b) tə·mä′tō
5. Cupid	(a) kyōō′pid	(b) kōō′pid
6. verbatim	(a) vər·ba′tim	(b) vər·bā′tim
7. either	(a) ē′thər	(b) ī′thər
8. appreciate	(a) ə·prē′sē·āt	(b) ə·prē′shē·āt
9. llama	(a) la′mə	(b) lä′mə
10. illustrate	(a) i·lus′trāt	(b) il′ə·strāt
11. Tuesday	(a) tōōz′dē	(b) tyōōz′dē
12. cement	(a) sē′ment	(b) si·ment′
13. patio	(a) pä′tē·ō	(b) pat′ē·ō
14. process	(a) pros′es	(b) prō′ses
15. ultimatum	(a) ul′tə·mä′təm	(b) ul′tə·mä′təm

ANSWERS:

1. **ignoramus**—(a) [ig′nə·ram′əs] *or* (b) [ig′nə·rā′məs] 2. **sacrifice**—(a) [sak′rə·fīs] 3. **radiator**—(a) [rā′dē·ā′tər] 4. **tomato**—(a) [tə·mā′tō] *or* (b) [tə·mä′tō] 5. **Cupid**—(a) [kyōō′pid] 6. **verbatim**—(b) [vər·bā′tim] 7. **either** —(a) [ē′thər] *or* (b) [ī′thər] 8. **appreciate**—(b) [ə·prē′shē·āt] 9. **llama**— (b) [lä′mə] 10. **illustrate**—(a) [i·lus′trāt] *or* (b) [il′ə·strāt] 11. **Tuesday**— (a) [tōōz′dē] *or* (b) [tyōōz′dē] 12. **cement**—(b) [si·ment′] 13. **patio**—(a) [pä′tē·ō] *or* (b) [pat′ē·ō] 14. **process**—(a) [pros′es] *or* (b) [prō′ses] 15. **ultimatum**—(a) [ul′tə·mä′təm] *or* (b) [ul′tə·mä′təm]

Datta or Dayta, Stattus or Staytus?

The long *a* sound [ā], as in *day, ray,* and *stay,* and the flat *a* sound [a] as in *at, cat,* and *rat,* cause some speakers to worry about their pronunciation. Does the sound of the first *a* in *data, aviator,* and *status* agree with the long *a* of *day* or with the flat *a* of *at?* In which of these two series do the *a*'s all sound the same?

day-date-data; ape-ate-aviator; stay-state-status

or

at-bat-data; add-at-aviator; rat-sat-status

The answer is that both pronunciations of the *a* in *data, aviator,* and *status* are correct. Relax! Years ago, speech teachers, actors, and radio commentators used the long *a* so that *day-date-data, ape-ate-aviator,* and *stay-state-status* all sounded alike. Today, however, those concerned with pronunciation agree that the flat *a* is every bit as acceptable. Just stick to your natural pronunciation of *data, aviator,* and *status.*

In the following words either a long *a* or a flat *a* is acceptable:

apparAtus	ap′ə·rā′təs	*or*	ap′ə·rat′əs
Apricot	ā′pri·kot	*or*	ap′ri·kot
dAta	dā′tə	*or*	dat′ə
ignorAmus	ig′nə·rā′məs	*or*	ig′nə·ram′əs
pro rAta	prō rā′tə	*or*	pro rat′ə
stAtus	stā′təs	*or*	stat′əs
sAtrap	sā′trap	*or*	sat′rap

But isn't there a rule for pronouncing these words? Yes. The rule is: Be natural. Pronounce this *a* sound as do others in your locality.

Beware: *Again* [ə·gen′] and *against* [ə·genst′] are almost universally pronounced to rhyme with *end-pen: end-pen-again, end-pen-against.* The long *a* sound of *agayn* [ə·gān′] and *agaynst* [ə·gānst′] is a regional pronunciation. Don't make the vowels in *day-gay-again* or *day-gay-against* sound alike just because you think it sounds better. It doesn't.

Radio and *radiator* have only one acceptable pronunciation: *Raydio* [rā′dē·ō] and *raydiator* [rā′dē·ā′tər]. Their first syllables should sound the same as *day* and *ray: day-ray-radio, day-ray-radiator.* To say them as *bad* and *add (bad-add-radio, bad-add-radiator)* is considered unacceptable pronunciation. The words *fracas* and *verbatim* should also be pronounced with the long *a, fraycas* [frā′kəs] and *verbaytim* [ver · bā′tim].

Note: Another common word that can properly be pronounced in two different ways is *route,* either as *root* [rōōt] or as *rout* [rout]. *Root* is preferred by many careful speakers, but *rout* is acceptable.

Is It Toon or Tyewn, Dooty or Dyewty?

By now, you probably know the answer to the above question. Teachers and careful speakers agree that pronouncing *tune* as *tyewn* or *duty* as *dyewty* is an affectation for most Americans. So unless

353

tyewn and *dyewty* come naturally to you, rhyme *moo-moon-tune* and *moo-too-duty*. Note that this *u* sound may be spelled *-u* (tune), *-ue* (avenue) or *-ew* (dew).

	Preferred General Pronunciation	Less Common Pronunciation
avenue	av′ə·nōō	av′ə·nyōō
duration	dŏŏ·rā′shən	dyŏŏ·rā′shən
duty	dōō′tē	dyōō′tē
stew	stōō	styōō
stupid	stōō′pid	styōō′pid
tube	tōōb	tyōōb
Tuesday	tōōz′dē	tyōōz′dē
tune	tōōn	tyōōn

NOTE: The sharp *u* sound is, of course, still used in many words, such as *beauty* [byōō′tē], *Cupid* [kyōō′pid], and *Hubert* [hyōō′bərt]. And a great many people pronounce *coupon* as [kyōō′pon], even though most authorities prefer [kōō′pon]. If [kyōō′pon] sounds better to you, go ahead and use it.

As we have discussed elsewhere, the way words are spelled changes: everyone once spelled *honor* as *honour* (the British still do), and hundreds of years ago *wife* was written *wif*. Pronunciation also changes. *Appendicitis* [ə·pen′də·sī′tis] used to be pronounced [ə·pen′də·sē′tis]; and *vitamin* [vī′tə·min] used to be pronounced [vit′ə·min], which is still the correct British pronunciation. Other pronunciations are changing today. Your best guide is to say words as do the majority of careful speakers—that is, to follow the pronunciations given in a modern dictionary. Do you pronounce the words listed here in the preferred way? Modern pronunciation does not stress or draw out the final *-or* of the following six words or of similar words ending in *-or*:

	Preferred General Pronunciation		
actor	ak′tər	*not*	ak′tôr
debtor	det′ər	*not*	det′ôr
editor	ed′i·tər	*not*	ed′i·tôr
honor	on′ər	*not*	on′ôr
rumor	rōō′mər	*not*	rōō′môr
senator	sen′ə·tər	*not*	sen′ə·tôr

FOURTEEN PRONUNCIATION DEMONS

This test contains some words that are often mispronounced. Learn their proper meanings and pronunciations. When alternate pronunciations are given, both are acceptable, although the first is preferred. Check the word or phrase you believe is closest in meaning to the key word. Answers follow.

1. **lamentable** [lam′ən·tə·bəl *or* la·ment′ə·bəl]—(a) regrettable. (b) separable. (c) extremely noisy. (d) vicious.
2. **demise** [di·mīz′]—(a) result. (b) death. (c) apprehension. (d) an oath.
3. **tactile** [tak′til]—(a) pertaining to the sense of touch. (b) a satiny material. (c) grasping. (d) silently understood.
4. **contest** [kən·test′]—(a) to ally with. (b) to challenge. (c) to agree to. (d) to strike.
5. **impious** [im′pē·əs]—(a) ape-like. (b) deceptive. (c) irreverent. (d) cruel.
6. **ignominy** [ig′nə·min′ē]—(a) a misconception. (b) a pseudonym. (c) complete ignorance. (d) disgrace.
7. **ignominious** [ig′nə·min′ē·əs]—(a) humiliating. (b) unknown. (c) glorious. (d) breathtaking.
8. **enigma** [i·nig′mə]—(a) a pale yellow color. (b) something that baffles. (c) a disease of the eye. (d) something ancient.
9. **clandestine** [klan·des′tin]—(a) calm. (b) friendly. (c) secret. (d) riotous.
10. **harass** [har′əs *or* hə·ras′]—(a) to torment. (b) to dispute. (c) to haggle. (d) to mimic.
11. **remonstrate** [ri·mon′strāt]—(a) to plead in protest. (b) to beg. (c) to renew. (d) to give up.
12. **incognito** [in·kog′nə·tō *or* in′kog·nē′tō]—(a) at home. (b) an assumed identity. (c) traveling first class. (d) devious.
13. **barrage** [bə·räzh′]—(a) an overwhelming attack. (b) fireworks. (c) a kind of balloon. (d) a deathblow.
14. **potentate** [pōt′n·tāt]—(a) a cure-all. (b) a very strong drink. (c) a person having great power. (d) seeming to be everywhere at once.

ANSWERS:

1. **lamentable**—(a) regrettable. 2. **demise**—(b) death. 3. **tactile**—(a) pertaining to the sense of touch. 4. **contest**—(b) to challenge. 5. **impious**—(c) irreverent. 6. **ignominy**—(d) disgrace. 7. **ignominious**—(a) humiliating. 8. **enigma**—(b) something that baffles. 9. **clandestine**—(c) secret. 10. **harass**—(a) to torment. 11. **remonstrate**—(a) to plead in protest. 12. **incognito**—(b) an assumed identity. 13. **barrage**—(a) an overwhelming attack. 14. **potentate**—(c) a person having great power.

2 "CORRECT PRONUNCIATION"

Just what is "correct pronunciation"? It is any pronunciation used by careful speakers and recorded in dictionaries. Frequently two or more different pronunciations are acceptable, depending on such factors as where people live or how they have learned a given word.

Don't Be a *Yeller Feller*

Some people pronounce words ending in *-ow*, *-o*, or *-a* as if they ended in *-er*; thus *yellow* becomes *yeller*, and *fellow* becomes *feller*. This may sound rustic or "folksy" in the movies, but in real life it is often just plain careless.

bellow	bel'ō	*not*	bel'ər
fellow	fel'ō	*not*	fel'ər
hollow	hol'ō	*not*	hol'ər
potato	pə·tā'tō	*not*	pə·tā'tər
vanilla	və·nil'ə	*not*	və·nel'ər
window	win'dō	*not*	win'dər

Don't Be a *Dese, Dem,* and *Dose* Guy

The voiced *th* [th] sound is common in English, as in *this* and *bathe,* and it is often mispronounced as a *d* by slovenly speakers. You are probably not guilty of this fault, but many persons fall into careless speech patterns unintentionally. So listen to yourself the next time you say one of the following words, and make sure that you hear not even a hint of a *d* where the voiced *th* sound should be.

bother	both'ər
brother	bruth'ər
father	fä'thər
mother	muth'ər
that	that
them	them
these	thēz
this	this
those	thōz

Don't Say *Sawr*

Some speakers pronounce words ending in *-aw* as if they ended in *-awr*. This, too, is careless speech.

crawfish	krô'fish'	*not*	krôr'fish'
draw	drô	*not*	drôr
drawing	drô'ing	*not*	drô'ring
law	lô	*not*	lôr
raw	rô	*not*	rôr
saw	sô	*not*	sôr

Twenty-two other words often pronounced carelessly are given below. Be alert to them.

accept	ak·sept'	*not*	ə·sept'
accessory	ak·ses'ər·ē	*not*	a·ses'rē
audience	ô'dē·əns	*not*	ô'jens
bronchial	brong'kē·əl	*not*	bron'ə·kəl
chic	shēk	*not*	chik
escape	ə·skāp'	*not*	ek·skāp'
figure	fig'yər	*not*	fig'ər
genuine	jen'yoo·in	*not*	jen'yoo·wīn
hearth	härth	*not*	hûrth
human	hyoo'mən	*not*	yoo'mən
Italian	i·tal'yən	*not*	ī·tal'yən
just	just	*not*	jist
larynx	lar'ingks	*not*	lar'niks
manufacture	man'yə·fak'chər	*not*	man'ə·fa'chər
modern	mod'ərn	*not*	mod'rən
perspiration	pûr'spə·rā'shən	*not*	pres'pə·rā'shən
picture	pik'chər	*not*	pit'chər
point	point	*not*	pûrnt
poison	poi'zən	*not*	⌠pī'zən
		not	⌡pûr'zən
something	sum'thing	*not*	⌠sump'ən
		not	⌡sum'thən
spoil	spoil	*not*	spûrl
wrestle	res'əl	*not*	ras'əl

357

Fun With Words

COLORFUL ADJECTIVES

This vocabulary test contains sixteen colorful adjectives that are pronunciation stumblers. Learn both their preferred pronunciations and their meanings. Check the word or phrase you believe is closest in meaning to the key word. Answers follow.

1. **sumptuous** [sum′choō·əs]—(a) luxurious. (b) accuráte. (c) overflowing. (d) serious.
2. **svelte** [svelt]—(a) fashionable. (b) slender. (c) foreign. (d) theatrical.
3. **tacit** [tas′it]—(a) selfish. (b) unspoken. (c) shy. (d) talkative.
4. **piquant** [pē′kənt]—(a) pretty. (b) having a pungent taste. (c) irritated. (d) sweet.
5. **phlegmatic** [fleg·mat′ik]—(a) congested. (b) sluggish. (c) stern. (d) easily irritated.
6. **blasé** [blä·zā′]—(a) scholarly. (b) gracious. (c) bored. (d) brilliant.
7. **grisly** [griz′lē]—(a) white. (b) disheveled. (c) gruesome. (d) sordid.
8. **poignant** [poin′yənt]—(a) painful and distressing to the feelings. (b) poised. (c) repulsive. (d) poisonous.
9. **grandiose** [gran′dē·ōs]—(a) imposing. (b) ominous. (c) greedy. (d) very loud.
10. **flaccid** [flak′sid]—(a) flabby. (b) strict. (c) tart. (d) offensive.
11. **hoary** [hôr′ē]—(a) coarse. (b) cold and frosty. (c) unkempt. (d) gray with age.
12. **maladroit** [mal′ə·droit′]—(a) intentionally insulting. (b) feigning sickness. (c) witty and amusing. (d) clumsy and awkward.
13. **oblique** [ə·blēk′]—(a) complicated. (b) out-of-date. (c) slanting or indirect. (d) sarcastic.
14. **statuesque** [stach′oō·esk′]—(a) graceful and dignified. (b) lavish. (c) secluded. (d) demanding.
15. **posthumous** [pos′choō·məs]—(a) in the rear. (b) rich and fertile. (c) happening after death. (d) decayed.
16. **resilient** [ri·zil′yənt]—(a) elastic. (b) determined. (c) resolvable. (d) highly respected.

ANSWERS:

1. **sumptuous**—(a) luxurious. 2. **svelte**—(b) slender. 3. **tacit**—(b) unspoken. 4. **piquant**—(b) having a pungent taste. 5. **phlegmatic**—(b) sluggish. 6. **blasé**—(c) bored. 7. **grisly**—(c) gruesome. 8. **poignant**—(a) painful and distressing to the feelings. 9. **grandiose**—(a) imposing. 10. **flaccid**—(a) flabby. 11. **hoary**—(d) gray with age. 12. **maladroit**—(d) clumsy and awkward. 13. **oblique**—(c) slanting or indirect. 14. **statuesque**—(a) graceful and dignified. 15. **posthumous**—(c) happening after death. 16. **resilient**—(a) elastic.

3 DON'T LEAVE OUT LETTERS OR SOUNDS

If what you say is false, you may be forced to "eat your words." But don't be careless and swallow your words before you get them out.

Most poor pronunciations are due to the omission of a sound altogether or to the swallowing or slurring of sounds and syllables. Many persons just won't make the effort required to say words distinctly. Most of us, in fact, have "lazy lips."

Poor pronunciation can be corrected easily once you're aware of the problem. Some faults result from omitting or swallowing g, d, t, or r sounds, or the vowel sounds of a, e, i, o, and u. Other errors come from combining simple words into one swallowed mutter, as in *gonna* for *going to.*

Let's go down the following lists and make sure we say all of every word without "eating" a part of it.

Don't Drop Your *G*'s

Don't drop the final g in words ending in *-ing*. If you say the final *-ing* so that it sounds like *-in* or *-en* [ən] you are not pronouncing these words according to generally accepted standards. Pronounce *going* as *going* and not as *goin'*. (On the other hand, don't over-accent the final g—that is, don't close your throat or click the final g.)

Here are ten common *-ing* pronunciation hazards:

beginninG	bi·gin′ing	readinG	rē′ding
cryinG	krī′ing	talkinG	tô′king
doinG	dōō′ing	walkinG	wô′king
eatinG	ē′ting	workinG	wûr′king
lovinG	luv′ing	writinG	rī′ting

Note that although the accent of these words is on the root and not on the *-ing*, the *-ing* must still get a full, unslurred pronunciation. Don't swallow your end-*ings*.

Particularly troublesome for many speakers are the g's in the middle of words. You must not drop the g in the following words if you want to speak well:

lenGth	lengkth	*not*	lenth
recoGnize	rek′əg·nīz	*not*	rek′ə·nīz
strenGth	strengkth	*not*	strenth

Don't Omit the *D*, *K*, or *T* Sound

Careless speakers often omit other letters besides *g*, such as *d*, *k*, or *t*. Here are a few of the most bothersome words:

asKed	askd	*not*	ast
canDidate	kan′də·dāt	*not*	kan′ə·dāt
idenTify	ī·den′tə·fī	*not*	ī·den′ə·fī
kepT	kept	*not*	kep
parTner	pärt′nər	*not*	pär′nər
supposeD	sə·pōzd′	*not*	sə·pōs′
wiDth	width	*not*	with

Poor pronunciation is frequently caused by haste in speaking. Many persons ordinarily drop the final *d* in words like *used* and *told* or the final *t* in words like *compact, contradict, protect,* etc. For this reason, you'll find that one excellent way to improve your pronunciation is to talk less rapidly—hence, less carelessly.

EXCEPTIONS: Some common words have *t*'s that should not be pronounced. Those who try to be overly precise sometimes pronounce these *t*'s. This is as much an error as the omission of a *t* where it should be pronounced. For example:

chestnut	ches′nut′	*not*	chest′nut′
often	ôf′en	*not*	ôf′ten
soften	sôf′en	*not*	sôf′ten

Don't Omit the *R*

Some common words are pronounced carelessly by so many people that the mispronunciations may someday become the preferred pronunciations. Precise speakers today, however, do *not* drop the *r*'s in the following words:

FebRuary	feb′rōō·er′ē	*not*	feb′yōō·er′ē
libRary	lī′brer·ē	*not*	lī′ber·ē

Other words in which the *r* is often—but ought not to be—slurred or dropped are:

formeRly	goveRnment	particulaRly
geogRaphy	itineraRy	secRetary
goveRnor	laboratoRy	similaRly

Don't Omit or Slur the Vowel Sound

Poor speakers tend to leave out or swallow the vowel sounds in a great many words. If you pronounce with care, you give the vowels *a, e, i, o,* and *u* the attention they deserve, even when the sound is a rather weak one. Try saying the following words out loud, and pay attention to the vowels—even though they are usually pronounced merely as a quick *uh* [ə]:

accUrate	ak′yər·it	liAble	lī′ə·bəl
asparAgus	ə·spar′ə·gəs	magAzine	mag′ə·zēn′
authOrize	ô′thə·rīz	memOry	mem′ər·ē
barbArous	bär′bər·əs	motOrist	mō′tər·ist
bElieve	bi·lēv′	opErate	op′ə·rāt
cafEteria	kaf′ə·tir′ē·ə	particUlar	pər·tik′yə·lər
capItal	kap′ə·təl	pecuIIar	pi·kyōōl′yər
cOrrect	kə·rekt′	poEm	pō′əm
crimInal	krim′ə·nəl	poEtry	pō′i·trē
currEnt	kûr′ənt	prepAration	prep′ə·rā′shən
defInite	def′ə·nit	privIlege	priv′ə·lij
equivAlent	i·kwiv′ə·lənt	probAbly	prob′ə·blē
exhIbition	ek′sə·bish′ən	promInent	prom′ə·nənt
factOry	fak′tər·ē	regUlar	reg′yə·lər
favOrable	fā′vər·ə·bəl	restAurant	res′tər·ənt
favOrite	fā′vər·it	simIlar	sim′ə·lər
fedEral	fed′ər·əl	sophOmore	sof′ə·môr
finAlly	fī′nəl·ē	sUppose	sə·pōz′
gEography	jē·og′rə·fē	temperAment	tem′pər·ə·mənt
humOrist	hyōō′mər·ist	temperAture	tem′pər·ə·chər
irOny	ī′rə·nē	usuAlly	yōō′zhōō·əl·ē

EXCEPTIONS: There are two pronunciation demons with *e*'s in the middle that are *not* pronounced. The *e*'s are silent in *pomegranate* [pom′gran·it] and *vineyard* [vin′yərd].

Try Not to Say *Gonna* and *Wanna*

Certain two-word combinations combine so easily that most of us slur them into one word when we speak hastily and without care. Thus, *going to* becomes *gonna* and *want to* becomes *wanna*. Children do it, adults do it, grade-school dropouts do it, and Ph.D.'s do it. Here is a list of the most common two-word combinations that do, nonetheless, sound better when pronounced as two words instead of being jammed together:

can't you	kant yōō	*not*	kan'chə
could you	kŏŏd yōō	*not*	kŏŏd'yə
don't you	dōnt yōō	*not*	dōn'chə
do you	dōō yōō	*not*	dyə
glad to	glad tōō	*not*	glad'tə
going to	gō'ing tōō	*not*	gun'ə
got to	got tōō	*not*	god'ə
has to	haz tōō	*not*	has'tə
kind of	kīnd uv	*not*	kīnd'ə
let her	let hûr	*not*	let'ər
let him	let him	*not*	let'əm
let me	let mē	*not*	lem'ē
ought to	ôt tōō	*not*	ôd'ə
want to	wont tōō	*not*	won'ə
what did	hwot did	*not*	hwot'əd
what you	hwot yōō	*not*	hwot'yə
will he	wil hē	*not*	wil'ē
will you	wil yōō	*not*	wil'yə
would you	wŏŏd yōō	*not*	wŏŏd'yə

These and similar two-word combinations are so often slurred that a few of them together may combine to make sentences that no one understands or really listens to. Don't make a poor first impression on a new acquaintance by saying "Gladdameetcha." He may be tempted to ask "Whatchasay?"

Some Help With Your Aitches

Some Englishmen fail to pronounce the letter *h* at the beginning of words; they say *'elp, 'old, 'appiness,* and so on. This is a tradition that goes back to the beginnings of the English language. In fact, not until the eighteenth century, when scholars and teachers tried to make pronunciation conform more nearly to spelling, was the public advised to sound initial *h*'s. Is the Englishman who still drops his *h*'s guilty of poor pronunciation? Opinions vary. In American English most *h*'s should be pronounced, but a few should never be. Is there a rule as to when you should and should not sound your *h*'s? No. However, to help you solve your *h* problems, here are two useful lists. In the following seven words the initial *h* should always be sounded:

Homage	hom′ij
Huge	hyōoj
Human	hyōo′mən
Humane	hyōo·mān′
Humble	hum′bəl
Humor	hyōo′mər
Humorous	hyōo′mər·əs

In the following ten words the *h* in parentheses is never sounded:

(h)eir	âr	shep(h)erd	shep′ərd
(h)onest	on′ist	T(h)ailand	tī′land
(h)onor	on′ər	t(h)yme	tīm
(h)our	our	ve(h)ement	vē′ə·mənt
pro(h)ibition	prō′ə·bish′ən	ve(h)icle	vē′ə·kəl

QUICKIEQUIZQUICKIEQUIZQUICKIEQUIZQUICKIEQUIZQUICKIEQUIZQUICKIEQUIZQUICKIEQUIZQUICKIE

QUICKIE QUIZ

TEN KEY PUZZLERS

Choose the preferred pronunciation for each of the key words listed below. Answers follow.

1. recognize	(a) rek′ə·nīz	(b) rek′əg·nīz
2. February	(a) feb′yōo·er′ē	(b) feb′rōo·er′ē
3. homage	(a) hom′ij	(b) om′ij
4. candidate	(a) kan′ə·dāt	(b) kan′də·dāt
5. pomegranate	(a) pom′gran·it	(b) pom′ə·gran·it
6. length	(a) lengkth	(b) lenth
7. dirigible	(a) dir′ə·jə·bəl	(b) dir′jə·bəl
8. herb	(a) hûrb	(b) ûrb
9. sophomore	(a) sof′ə·môr	(b) sof′môr
10. chestnut	(a) ches′nut′	(b) chest′nut′

ANSWERS:

1. **recognize**—(b) [rek′əg·nīz] 2. **February**—(b) [feb′rōo·er′ē] 3. **homage** —(a) [hom′ij] 4. **candidate**—(b) [kan′də·dāt] 5. **pomegranate**—(a) [pom′- gran·it] 6. **length**—(a) [lengkth] 7. **dirigible**—(a) [dir′ə·jə·bəl] 8. **herb**— (b) [ûrb] is preferred but (a) [hûrb] is acceptable 9. **sophomore**—(a) [sof′- ə·môr] 10. **chestnut**—(a) [ches′nut′]

QUICKIEQUIZQUICKIEQUIZQUICKIEQUIZQUICKIEQUIZQUICKIEQUIZQUICKIEQUIZQUICKIEQUIZQUICKIE

4 DON'T ADD LETTERS OR SOUNDS

A fault as bad as word-swallowing is its opposite—adding letters or syllables where they don't belong. This is like serving alphabet soup; your listener has to strain out the unrelated letters in order to make sense out of what you say.

The most common alphabet-soup mispronunciations are caused by adding a final -*t* or -*ed* where none belongs or by adding an additional vowel sound where none should be.

Note that many of the most commonly mispronounced words are also spelling demons. If you mispronounce *athlete* as "athalete" you are probably going to misspell the word, too. So learn the words in this chapter; they will improve your spelling as well as your pronunciation.

Don't Add an Extra *T* or -*Ed* Sound

This extra *t* or -*ed* is probably the most substandard speech habit of modern times. To correct it you need to know the proper pronunciation of only seven basic words.

across	ə·krôs′	*not*	ə·krôst′
attack	ə·tak′	*not*	ə·tak′t
attacked	ə·takd′	*not*	ə·tak′təd
drown	droun	*not*	dround
drowned	dround	*not*	droun′dəd
once	wuns	*not*	wunst
twice	twīs	*not*	twīst

Don't Add an Extra Vowel Sound

The following five words are on almost everyone's list of pronunciation demons. None of them has an *a* for a syllable.

athlete	ath′lēt	*not*	ath′ə·lēt
athletic	ath·let′ik	*not*	ath·ə·let′ik
burglar	bûr′glər	*not*	bûr′gə·lər
pamphlet	pam′flit	*not*	pam′fə·lit
translate	trans′lāt	*not*	trans′ə·lāt

The first, fifth, and last words listed below are often mispronounced by children and can make anyone sound a bit childish. Be especially careful of them.

chimney	chim′nē	not	chim′ə·nē or chim′blē
disastrous	di·zas′trəs	not	di·zas′tə·rəs
extraordinary	⎰ik·strôr′də·ner′ē or ⎱eks′trə·ôr′də·ner′ē	not	eks′tər·ôr′də·ner′ē
hindrance	hin′drəns	not	hin′dûr·əns
lightning	līt′ning	not	lī′tə·ning
remembrance	ri·mem′brəns	not	ri·mem′bûr·əns
umbrella	um·brel′ə	not	um·bə·rel′ə

The correct pronunciation of the following four words is one mark of a truly careful speaker. They are mispronounced by many college graduates!

accompanist	ə·kum′pə·nist	not	ə·kum′pə·nē·ist
electoral	i·lek′tər·əl	not	i·lek′tôr′ē·əl
grievous	grē′vəs	not	grē′vē·əs
mischievous	mis′chi·vəs	not	mis′chē·vē·əs

Two words especially bother elementary-school students. If you still pronounce them in a childish way, learn the proper pronunciation now.

elm	elm	*not*	el′əm
film	film	*not*	fil′əm

REVIEW: Note that by adding an extra sound in many of the above words, the speaker also adds an extra syllable. To help you remember the proper pronunciation of these words, keep in mind their correct number of syllables.

One syllable only

elm   film

Two syllables only

athlete	chimney	lightning
attacked	grievous	pamphlet
burglar	hindrance	translate

Three syllables only

athletic   disastrous   mischievous
                  remembrance
                  umbrella

Four syllables only

accompanist

If you learn to pronounce the above words correctly, you will have mastered seventeen of the most commonly mispronounced words in the English language.

Don't Pronounce Silent Consonants

One related danger to that of adding extra sounds is to pronounce silent letters. As you know, many English words have consonants (letters other than *a, e, i, o,* or *u*) that must be written but not pronounced. Examples of such "silent" consonants are the final *b* in words like *lamb* and *crumb;* the silent *d* in *handkerchief;* the silent *g* in *gnat* or *sign.*

Probably no native speaker of English has trouble with most words of this sort; they are too common to give us trouble. Certainly we are so accustomed to the silent letters in such words as *climb, know, pneumonia, psychology, island, whistle,* and *wrench* that there is no danger of our pronouncing the silent letter and thus mispronouncing the word. But there *are* a number of words with troublesome silent consonants. The following list contains some of them. It is best not to pronounce the silent letters within the parentheses in these words.

a(l)mond	ä′mənd	of(t)en	ôf′ən
bla(ck)guard	blag′ərd	poi(g)nant	poin′yənt
ches(t)nut	ches′nut′	(p)seudo	soo′dō
cor(ps)	kôr	s(ch)ism	siz′əm
ex(h)ibition	ek′sə·bish′ən	sof(t)en	sôf′ən
glis(t)en	glis′ən	su(b)tle	sut′l
gun(w)ale	gun′əl	ve(h)ement	vē′ə·mənt
mor(t)gage	môr′gij	ve(h)icle	vē′ə·kəl

The word *parliament* is quite unusual in that its vowel *i* is silent. *Parliament* is pronounced [pär′lə·mənt]. And for good measure, don't forget the fine old nautical word that has five silent letters—*boatswain,* pronounced *bos'n* [bō′sən].

Fun With Words

SILENT LETTERS

These fifteen words contain silent letters. Learn both the meanings and pronunciation of these words. Check the word or phrase you believe is closest in meaning to the key word. Answers follow.

1. **archetype** [är′kə·tīp]—(a) an original pattern or model. (b) a villain. (c) a Greek column. (d) handwriting.
2. **wraith** [rāth]—(a) an apparition. (b) anger. (c) violent pain. (d) a very small creature.
3. **schism** [siz′əm]—(a) a reverberating noise. (b) a joining together. (c) a wearing out. (d) a division into hostile groups.
4. **jeopardize** [jep′ər·dīz]—(a) to mock. (b) to attack. (c) to joke. (d) to risk.
5. **imbroglio** [im·brōl′yō]—(a) complexity of design or structure. (b) a confusion of noises. (c) a kind of embroidery. (d) a troublesome situation.
6. **scintilla** [sin·til′ə]—(a) a spark or trace. (b) part of a flower. (c) a fleet of ships. (d) twinkling.
7. **euphoria** [yoo·fôr′ē·ə]—(a) a pastoral scene. (b) loss of speech. (c) loss of memory. (d) a sense of well-being.

8. **wrest** [rest]—(a) to snatch forcibly. (b) to travel slowly. (c) to slant. (d) to condescend.
9. **sovereign** [sov′rən]—(a) serious. (b) rich. (c) beautiful. (d) supreme.
10. **impugn** [im·pyoon′]—(a) to attack as false or untrustworthy. (b) to take away. (c) to dare. (d) to rub off by friction.
11. **exhortation** [eg′zôr·tā′shən]—(a) the act of obtaining by violence. (b) an expression of joy. (c) an earnest plea. (d) rapture.
12. **eulogistic** [yoo′lə·jis′tik]—(a) clear-minded. (b) laudatory. (c) hopeful. (d) thoughtful.
13. **wreak** [rēk]—(a) to inflict, as vengeance. (b) to smell. (c) to irritate. (d) to dwarf.
14. **vehemence** [vē′ə·məns]—(a) an eager wish. (b) noise. (c) loyalty. (d) great force or violence.
15. **realignment** [rē′ə·līn′mənt]—(a) a new division or grouping. (b) a cure-all. (c) resurgence. (d) an increase.

ANSWERS:

1. **archetype**—(a) an original pattern or model. 2. **wraith**—(a) an apparition. 3. **schism**—(d) a division into hostile groups. 4. **jeopardize**—(d) to risk. 5. **imbroglio**—(d) a troublesome situation. 6. **scintilla**—(a) a spark or trace. 7. **euphoria**—(d) a sense of well-being. 8. **wrest**—(a) to snatch forcibly. 9. **sovereign**—(d) supreme. 10. **impugn**—(a) to attack as false or untrustworthy. 11. **exhortation**—(c) an earnest plea. 12. **eulogistic**—(b) laudatory. 13. **wreak**—(a) to inflict, as vengeance. 14. **vehemence**—(d) great force or violence. 15. **realignment**—(a) a new division or grouping.

5 IS CH PRONOUNCED CH, SH, or K?

The letter combination *ch* can cause problems because it is pronounced in three distinct ways, depending on the word in which it occurs. Thus, *ch* is pronounced "ch" as in *chair* [châr], "sh" as in *champagne* [sham·pān'], and "k" as in *chaos* [kā'os].

The words in which *ch* is pronounced as "ch" (*chest, choose, chop, march*) give few native speakers any trouble. Many are simple words that we have known since childhood. However, some in which *ch* is pronounced as "sh" (*chalet, chaperon, chauffeur*) or as "k" (*archeology, chaos, zucchini*) give many of us trouble. Most of them are from our more complicated adult vocabulary, and probably we first saw them in print rather than hearing them from family or friends. (That is, we may have learned to recognize them without having learned how to say them.)

Is there any rule as to when *ch* is pronounced "ch," "sh," or "k"? No. In simple English words the *ch* often is pronounced as "ch" (*chair, cheese*); in borrowings from the French, the *ch* often is pronounced as "sh" (*champagne, chapeau*); and in words from the Greek or Italian, *ch* is generally pronounced as "k" (*Achilles, Chianti* wine).

Here is a list of the most common *ch* pronunciation demons. Pay special attention to those in which *ch* is properly pronounced as "sh" or as "k."

CH pronounced as "ch"

anchovy	an'chō·vē	chapter	chap'tər
arch	ärch	chard	chärd
chafe	chāf	chattel	chat'l
chaff	chaf	Cherokee	cher'ə·kē
chalice	chal'is	cherub	cher'əb
chancel	chan'səl	chide	chīd

CH pronounced as "sh"

cache	kash	charlatan	shär'lə·tən
chagrin	shə·grin'	chartreuse	shär·trōōz'
chalet	sha·lā'	chateau	sha·tō'
champagne	sham·pān'	chauffeur	shō'fər
chandelier	shan'də·lir'	Cheyenne	shī·en'
chaperon	shap'ə·rōn	chiffon	shi·fon'
charades	shə·rādz'	chivalrous	shiv'əl·rəs

CH pronounced as "k"

Achilles	ə·kil′ēz	chasm	kaz′əm
archaic	är·kā′ik	Chianti	kē·an′tē
archangel	ärk′ān′jəl	chimera	kə·mir′ə
archeology	ar′kē·ol′ə·jē	chiropodist	kə·rop′ə·dist
archetype	är′kə·tīp	chiropractor	kī′rə·prak′tər
archipelago	är′kə·pel′ə·gō	cholera	kol′ər·ə
bronchial	brong′kē·əl	choreographer	kôr′ē·og′rə·fər
Chaldea	kal·dē′ə	hierarchy	hī′ə·rär′kē
chameleon	kə·mēl′ē·ən	hypochondriac	hī′pə·kon′drē·ak
chaos	kā′os	machinations	mak′ə·nā′shənz
charisma	kə·riz′mə	zucchini	zŏŏ·kē′nē

Don't be fooled by the above lists of troublesome *ch* words. There are many more words in which the *ch* sound is pronounced "ch," but they are so common that we all pronounce them properly—for example, *champion, chamber, chance, change, channel, chart, charity, Charleston, checkers, cheek, cherish,* and so on.

---

6 THE HARD G, THE SOFT G, AND SOME OTHER G'S

As everyone who speaks English knows, the letter *c* has two common sounds, the hard *c* [k] sound before *a, o,* and *u* (*cat, canapé, cot, cocoon, cut, custard*); and the soft *c* [s] sound before *e, i,* and *y* (*cent, celebrate, city, cistern, Nancy, cylinder*).

The letter *g* follows the same pattern. The most common *g* sound is the hard *g* (or true *g*) sound usually found before *a, o, u, l, r,* and at the end of words, as in *gas, prodigal, go, asparagus, glow, grass,* and *log.* The less common *g* sound is the soft *g* sound, which is pronounced like a *j* and is usually found before *e, i,* and *y,* as in *gem, engine,* and *clergy.*

The fact that *g* has two distinct sounds usually causes native Americans no problems. We do not stumble when pronouncing *gem* and *get,* even though *gem* follows the general rule—soft *g* [j] sound before an *e*—and *get* does not. We have learned most of the frequently used words as children. However, the soft *g* [j] appears in a number of

369

Fun With Words

C, CH, OR K CHALLENGES

These are fourteen words with a *c, ch,* or *k* sound. Learn the meanings and pronunciations of these words. Check the word or phrase you believe is closest in meaning to the key word. Answers follow.

1. **archaic** [är·kā'ik]—(a) no longer in use. (b) having to do with an archway. (c) a type of suspension bridge. (d) high-ranking.

2. **archives** [är'kīvz]—(a) a place where historical and public documents are kept. (b) ancient temples. (c) small sailing vessels. (d) superior archers.

3. **hierarchy** [hī'ə·rär'kē]—(a) a grouping arranged in successive orders. (b) an archbishop. (c) a presidential cabinet. (d) the upper classes.

4. **chagrin** [shə·grin']—(a) violent anger. (b) pride. (c) vexation. (d) foolishness.

5. **chaotic** [kā·ot'ik]—(a) disordered and confused. (b) calm. (c) a type of horse-drawn carriage. (d) very careful.

6. **debouch** [di·bōōsh' *or* di·bouch']—(a) to issue forth. (b) to humble. (c) to scold. (d) to scoff at.

7. **inchoate** [in·kō'it]—(a) unable to express oneself clearly. (b) in an elementary stage. (c) weak. (d) chaotic.

8. **chicanery** [shi·kā'nər·ē]—(a) petty evasion and trickery. (b) major fraud. (c) candor. (d) a perennial herb.

9. **lachrymose** [lak'rə·mōs]—(a) lazy. (b) tearful. (c) harmful. (d) stupid.

10. **pulchritude** [pul'krə·tōōd]—(a) beauty. (b) overabundance. (c) fighting ability. (d) flattery.

11. **machinations** [mak'ə·nā'shənz]—(a) complexities. (b) mechanical operations. (c) wild cherries. (d) artful schemes.

12. **choreography** [kôr'ē·og'rə·fē]—(a) arrangement of light and shade. (b) the art of arranging dances. (c) the art of making maps. (d) the art of group singing.

13. **pachyderm** [pak'ə·dûrm]—(a) therapeutic heat treatment. (b) something discarded. (c) a giant prehistoric fish. (d) a thick-skinned quadruped, as an elephant.

14. **chary** [châr'ē]—(a) cautious. (b) sticky. (c) cooked to a crisp. (d) aware.

ANSWERS:

1. **archaic**—(a) no longer in use. 2. **archives**—(a) a place where historical and public documents are kept. 3. **hierarchy**—(a) a grouping arranged in successive orders. 4. **chagrin**—(c) vexation. 5. **chaotic**—(a) disordered and confused. 6. **debouch**—(a) to issue forth. 7. **inchoate**—(b) in an elementary stage. 8. **chicanery**—(a) petty evasion and trickery. 9. **lachrymose**—(b) tearful. 10. **pulchritude**—(a) beauty. 11. **machinations**—(d) artful schemes. 12. **choreography**—(b) the art of arranging dances. 13. **pachyderm**—(d) a thick-skinned quadruped, as an elephant. 14. **chary**—(a) cautious.

words that are commonly mispronounced. Learn the following soft *g*
[*j*] pronunciation demons now:

gesticulate	jes·tik′yə·lāt	harbinger	här′bin·jər
gesture	jes′chər	longevity	lon·jev′ə·tē
gibbet	jib′it	manger	mān′jər
gibe	jīb	orgy	ôr′jē
gist	jist	turgid	tûr′jɨd

Words Ending in -*age,*-*ege,* and -*ige*

 Some English words ending in -*age,* -*ege,* and -*ige* have been borrowed from the French; and in these the *g* is neither hard nor soft
but may keep its original French flavor. The French *g* sounds very much
like the *s* in *vision* or *pleasure,* and the common dictionary symbol for it
is *zh.* Here are eight examples where the *g* in -*age,* -*ege,* or -*ige* is preferably pronounced with the French *g* sound of *zh:*

barrage	bə·räzh′	garage	gə·räzh′
camouflage	kam′ə·fläzh	massage	mə·säzh′
corsage	kôr·säzh′	prestige	pres·tēzh′
cortege	kôr·tezh′	sabotage	sab′ə·täzh

NOTE: In several of the above words, the regular soft *g* sound is coming
to be increasingly acceptable: for instance, [kam′ə·fläj] and [pres·tēj′].

The Final -*ng* Sound

 The *g* of a final -*ng* (*ring, long*) always is softened somewhat or
slurred. Do not pronounce this *g* as hard as the *g* in *go* or *dog.* In the
following words do not click your throat shut; don't make a *guh* sound
to end a final -*ng:*

among	among	*not*	among-guh	long	long	*not*	long-guh
bring	bring	*not*	bring-guh	ring	ring	*not*	ring-guh
fling	fling	*not*	fling-guh	sing	sing	*not*	sing-guh
hang	hang	*not*	hang-guh	wrong	wrong	*not*	wrong-guh

 This same softened or slurred *g* sound is usually kept when you add
an -*er* or -*ing* to one of these root words ending in -*ng.* For instance:

371

bringing	bring'ing	*not*	bring-ging
flinging	fling'ing	*not*	fling-ging
hanger	hang'er	*not*	hang-ger
hanging	hang'ing	*not*	hang-ging
nagging	nag'ing	*not*	nag-ging
ringing	ring'ing	*not*	ring-ging
singer	sing'er	*not*	sing-ger
singing	sing'ing	*not*	sing-ging

EXCEPTIONS: There are some exceptions to keeping a final -*ng* soft before adding an -*er*. In *English, finger, longer, stronger,* and *younger,* for example, the *g* is stressed a little more than in *hanger, ringer,* or *singer.* In fact, the proper pronunciations are [ing'glish], [fing'gər], [long'gər], and so forth.

QUICKIEQUIZQUICKIEQUIZQUICKIEQUIZQUICKIEQUIZQUICKIEQUIZQUICKIEQUIZQUICKIEQUIZQUICKIE

QUICKIE QUIZ

GETTING THE GIST OF G'S

In the list below, choose the proper pronunciation for each of the key words. Answers follow.

1. **gist**—(a) jist (b) gist
2. **singer**—(a) sing'gər (b) sing'ər
3. **prodigal**—(a) prod'ə·jəl (b) prod'ə·gəl
4. **gesture**—(a) ges'chər (b) jes'-chər
5. **bringing**—(a) bring'ing (b) bring'ging
6. **sabotage**—(a) sab'ə·täj (b) sab'ə·täzh
7. **longer**—(a) long'gər (b) lông'ər

8. **harbinger**—(a) här'bin·jər (b) här'bin·gər
9. **orgy**—(a) ôr'jē (b) or'gē
10. **asparagus**—(a) ə·spar'ə·gəs (b) ə·spar'gras
11. **stronger**—(a) strong'gər (b) strong'ər
12. **longevity**—(a) lon·gev'ə·tē (b) lon·jev'ə·tē
13. **gesticulate**—(a) ges·tik'yə·lāt (b) jes·tik'yə·lāt
14. **giblet**—(a) jib'lit (b) gib'lit

ANSWERS:

1. **gist**—(a) [jist] 2. **singer**—(b) [sing'ər] 3. **prodigal**—(b) [prod'ə·gəl] 4. **gesture**—(b) [jes'chər] 5. **bringing**—(a) [bring'ing] 6. **sabotage**—(b) [sab'ə·täzh] 7. **longer**—(a) [long'gər] 8. **harbinger**—(a) [här'bin·jər] 9. **orgy**—(a) [ôr'jē] 10. **asparagus**—(a) [ə·spar'ə·gəs] 11. **stronger**—(a) [strong'gər] 12. **longevity**—(b) [lon·jev'ə·tē] 13. **gesticulate**—(b) [jes·tik'yə·lāt] 14. **giblet**—(a) [jib'lit]

QUICKIEQUIZQUICKIEQUIZQUICKIEQUIZQUICKIEQUIZQUICKIEQUIZQUICKIEQUIZQUICKIEQUIZQUICKIE

7 -ATE, -ILE, AND S

If a word of more than one syllable ends in *-ate*, as in *alternate, candidate, estimate, graduate,* etc., is the final *-ate* pronounced [it] or [āt]? Is it grad*uit* or grad*uate,* estim*it* or estim*ate?*

Most such words are pronounced *-ate* [āt]. But, four common nouns that end in *-ate* are exceptions and generally are pronounced *-it* [it].

	[-āt]		[-it]
to alternate	ôl′tər·nāt	an alternate	ôl′tər·nit
to associate	⎧ ə·sō′shē·āt *or*	an associate	⎧ ə·sō′shē·it *or*
	⎩ ə·sō′sē·āt		⎩ ə·sō′sē·it
a candidate	kan′də·dāt		
to concentrate	kon′sən·trāt		
to estimate	es′tə·māt	an estimate	es′tə·mit
to graduate	graj′o͞o·āt	a graduate	graj′o͞o·it
an inmate	in′māt		
a magnate	mag′nāt		

NOTE CAREFULLY: Four common words ending in *-ate* (*alternate, associate, estimate,* and *graduate*), which can be used as either verbs or nouns, should be pronounced *-ate* [āt] as verbs and *-it* [it] as nouns. Thus, these four words are doubly difficult because each has two pronunciations, depending on how it is used.

Is *-ile* Pronounced "isle" or "ill"?

Some words of two or more syllables that end in *-ile* are pronounced [īl] as in *smile, mile,* and *while.* Other words that end in *-ile* are pronounced [il] or even [ēl] or [əl]. Here are twelve words in which· a final *-ile* may cause problems:

	[īl]		[əl *or* il]
Anglophile	ang′glə·fīl	docile	dos′əl
exile	eg′zīl *or* ek′sīl	fertile	fûr′təl
infantile	in′fən·tīl	fragile	fraj′əl
profile	prō′fīl	futile	fyo͞o′təl
reconcile	rek′ən·sīl	hostile	hos′təl
turnstile	tûrn′stīl′	imbecile	im′bə·sil

Some words that end in -*ile* are pronounced properly either as [-īl] or as [-əl], [-il], or [-ēl]. In the following list the more common or slightly preferred pronunciation is given first:

agile	aj'əl	or	aj'īl
domicile	dom'ə·sīl	or	dom'ə·səl
juvenile	jōō'və·nəl	or	jōō'və·nīl
mercantile	mûr'kən·til	or	mûr'kən·tīl
mobile	mō'bəl	or	mō'bēl
puerile	pyōō'ər·il	or	pyōō'rīl
senile	sē'nīl	or	sē'nil
servile	sûr'vīl	or	sûr'vil
textile	teks'til	or	teks'tīl

NOTE: The British tend to pronounce all -*ile* endings as [īl], to rhyme with *smile*. This is not generally accepted American pronunciation. Don't let the English movies or their imitators confuse you. For an American to pronounce all -*ile* endings as if they rhymed with *smile* is at best phony and at worst incorrect.

The S—A Hiss or a Buzz?

The letter *s* has two main sounds, the *hissing s*, as in *see* and *pass*, and the *buzzing s* [z], as in *amuse* and *music*. Most words with *s* are simple to pronounce, but here are several that are not:

Hiss the S		*Buzz the* S	
crease	krēs	abysmal	ə·biz'məl
crisis	krī'sis	demise	di·mīz'
douse	dous	dismal	diz'məl
gasoline	gas'ə·lēn	houses	hou'zəz
grease	grēs	to house (a verb)	houz
house (a noun)	hous	preside	pri·zīd'
mausoleum	mô'sə·lē'əm	reside	ri·zīd'
Vaseline	vas'ə·lēn	resilient	ri·zil'yənt
vise	vīs	surprise	sər·prīz'
		visa	vē'zə

NOTE: *Advice* is a noun (*I will take your advice*) and is pronounced [ad·vīs']. *Advise* is a verb (*to advise a friend*) and is pronounced [ad·vīz']. Remember also that one *house* hisses; two *houses* buzz!

374

In the following words, you may either hiss or buzz it, since either is acceptable:

absorb	ab·sôrb′	or	ab·zôrb′
absorbent	ab·sôr′bənt	or	ab·zôr′bənt
absurd	ab·sûrd′	or	ab·zûrd′
absurdity	ab·sûr′də·tē	or	ab·zûr′də·tē
usurp	yōō·sûrp′	or	yōō·zûrp′
vase	vās	or	vāz, väz
venison	ven′ə·sən	or	ven′ə·zən

QUICKIEQUIZQUICKIEQUIZQUICKIEQUIZQUICKIEQUIZQUICKIEQUIZQUICKIEQUIZQUICKIEQUIZQUICKIE

QUICKIE QUIZ

-ILE AND S SOUNDS

Choose the preferred pronunciation for each of the key words below. Some may properly be pronounced either way; see if you can decide which they are. Answers follow.

1. mobile — (a) mō′bēl — (b) mō′bəl
2. gasoline — (a) gas′ə·lēn — (b) gaz′ə·lēn
3. usurp — (a) yōō·zûrp′ — (b) yōō·sûrp′
4. juvenile — (a) jōō′və·nəl — (b) jōō′və·nīl
5. abysmal — (a) ə·bis′məl — (b) ə·biz′məl
6. textile — (a) teks′til — (b) teks′tīl
7. bibliophile — (a) bib′lē·ə·fil′ — (b) bib′lē·ə·fīl′
8. resilient — (a) ri·sil′yənt — (b) ri·zil′yənt
9. fragile — (a) fraj′īl — (b) fraj′əl
10. Anglophile — (a) ang′glə·fīl — (b) ang′glə·fil
11. mercantile — (a) mûr′kən·til — (b) mûr′kən·tīl
12. Vaseline — (a) vas′ə·lēn — (b) vaz′ə·lēn
13. agile — (a) aj′əl — (b) aj′īl
14. demise — (a) di·mīs′ — (b) di·mīz′
15. virile — (a) vir′əl — (b) vir′īl

ANSWERS:

1. **mobile**—(a) [mō′bēl] *and* (b) [mō′bəl] 2. **gasoline**—(a) [gas′ə·lēn] 3. **usurp**—(a) [yōō·zûrp′] *and* (b) [yōō·sûrp′] 4. **juvenile**—(a) [jōō′və·nəl] *and* (b) [joo′və·nīl] 5. **abysmal**—(b) [ə·biz′məl] 6. **textile**—(a) [teks′til] *and* (b) [teks′tīl] 7. **bibliophile**—(a) [bib′lē·ə·fil′] 8. **resilient**—(b) [ri·zil′-yənt] 9. **fragile**—(b) [fraj′əl] 10. **Anglophile**—(a) [ang′glə·fil] 11. **mercantile**—(a) [mûr′kən·til] *and* (b) [mûr′kən·tīl] 12. **Vaseline**—(a) [vas′ə·lēn] 13. **agile**—(a) [aj′əl] *and* (b) [aj′īl] 14. **demise**—(b) [di·mīz′] 15. **virile**—(a) [vir′əl]

QUICKIEQUIZQUICKIEQUIZQUICKIEQUIZQUICKIEQUIZQUICKIEQUIZQUICKIEQUIZQUICKIEQUIZQUICKIE

375

8 THE SHIFTY ACCENT

Long words have at least one syllable that is pronounced more strongly or more loudly than others. This is called the *accented* or *stressed syllable*. It is indicated in dictionaries by a *primary accent mark* (sometimes called a primary stress mark), usually boldface (′), placed after the syllable. Thus, the word *reader* is pronounced READer and may be shown in your dictionary as [rē′dər]. Some words have two accents. If one of the syllables in such a word is stressed more strongly than the other, the lesser takes a *secondary accent mark*. This secondary accent may be shown in your dictionary as a light-face mark (′) or else with two marks (″). Thus, *realism* is pronounced [rē′əl·iz′əm].

In most words the problem is whether the primary accent falls on the first or second syllable. Of course, the primary accent need not fall either on the first or second syllable but may emphasize the third, fourth, fifth, or even sixth. Very long words are rare in English and cause few pronunciation problems to those who know and use them. The major problem is generally whether to place the primary accent on the first or second syllable.

The following fifteen pronunciation demons should always be accented (stressed) on the first syllable:

AMicable	am′i·kə·bəl	*not*	ə·mik′ə·bəl
COMment	kom′ent	*not*	kə·ment′
COMparable	kom′pər·ə·bəl	*not*	kom·pâr′ə·bəl
DEFicit	def′ə·sit	*not*	def·ə·sit′
FORmidable	fôr′mi·də·bəl	*not*	for·mid′ə·bəl
IMpious	im′pē·əs	*not*	im·pī′əs
IMpotent	im′pə·tent	*not*	im·pō′tənt
INfamous	in′fə·məs	*not*	in·fām′əs
INfluence	in′flōō·əns	*not*	in·flōō′əns
INtricate	in′tri·kit	*not*	in·trik′ət
PREFerable	pref′ər·ə·bəl	*not*	prē·fûr′ə·bəl
REParable	rep′ər·ə·bəl	*not*	rē·pâr′ə·bəl
REPutable	rep′yə·tə·bəl	*not*	rē·pyōōt′ə·bəl
REVocable	rev′ə·kə·bəl	*not*	rē·vōk′ə·bəl
THEater	thē′ə·tər	*not*	thē·ā′tər

Note that careful speakers accent the first syllable of many words ending in *-able:* AMicable, COMparable, FORMidable, PREFerable,

REParable, REPutable, and REVocable. If a prefix such as *in-*, *dis-*, or *ir-* is added to form the negative of such words, the primary accent is still kept on the same syllable as it was without the prefix, as in:

inCOMparable	in·kom'pər·ə·bəl
irREParable	ir·rep'ər·ə·bəl
disREPutable	dis·rep'yə·tə·bəl
irREVocable	i·rev'ə·kə·bəl

Always accent the following words on the second syllable:

clanDEStine	klan·des'tin	*not*	klan'dəs·tin
cruSADE	krōō·sād'	*not*	krōō'sād
deCLINE	di·klīn'	*not*	dē'klīn
disPATCH	dis·pach'	*not*	dis'pach
eLITE	ā·lēt'	*not*	ē'lēt
eNIGma	i·nig'mə	*not*	en'ig·mə
reCRUIT	ri·krōōt'	*not*	rē'krōōt
reMONstrate	ri·mon'strāt	*not*	rem'ən·strāt

This Is Easy—You're Right Either Way

Some words may rightly be accented on either the first or second syllable. No matter which syllable you stress, you are safe; dictionaries accept both pronunciations.

abdomen	ab'də·mən	*or*	ab·dō'mən
acclimate	ak'lə·māt	*or*	ə·klī'mit
adult	ad'ult	*or*	ə·dult'
applicable	ap'li·kə·bəl	*or*	ə·plik'ə·bəl
chauffeur	shō'fər	*or*	shō·fûr'
despicable	des'pi·kə·bəl	*or*	di·spik'ə·bəl
exquisite	eks'kwi·zit	*or*	ik·skwiz'it
gondola	gon'də·lə	*or*	gon·dō'lə
grimace	grim'əs	*or*	gri·mās'
harass	har'əs	*or*	hər·as'
hospitable	hos'pi·tə·bəl	*or*	hos·pit'ə·bəl
inquiry	in'kwər·ē	*or*	in·kwīr'ē
lamentable	lam'ən·tə·bəl	*or*	lə·ment'ə·bəl
perfume	pûr'fyōōm	*or*	pər·fyōōm'
robust	rō'bust	*or*	rō·bust'
romance	rō'mans	*or*	rō·mans'

377

The word *calliope* is a rather special case. It may be accented acceptably on either the first or second syllable, but the pronunciation of the word changes according to your choice of stress: calIIope [kə·lī′ə·pē]; CALLiope [kal′ē·ōp]. Note the final long *e* in the first pronunciation of the word.

Two additional words, *advertisement* and *incognito,* are easy to pronounce because the accent is correct on either the second or the third syllable. You may safely say either adVERtisement [ad·vûr′tis·mənt] or adverTISEment [ad′vər·tīz′mənt] and either inCOGnito [in·kog′nə·tō] or incogNIto [in′kog·nē′tō].

This Is Hard—You May Be Wrong Either Way

In some words the accent changes depending on the use. Thus, a child who conDUCTS himself well has good CONduct. In general, two-syllable words that can be used either as nouns or as verbs have the first syllable accented when they are used as nouns and the second syllable accented when they are used as verbs.

This is not as involved as it sounds. For example, when *conduct* is used as a noun, its first syllable is accented: *The child's CONduct was good.* When *conduct* is used as a verb, its second syllable is accented: *He will conDUCT the orchestra.*

Here are further examples of the shift in stress from noun to verb:

NOUN	VERB
a CONscript [kon′skript] *He is a military CONscript.*	to conSCRIPT [kən·skript′] *He was conSCRIPTed.*
a CONtest [kon′test] *She entered the CONtest.*	to conTEST [kən·test′] *I will conTEST the decision.*
CONverse [kon′vûrs] *The CONverse is true.*	to conVERSE [kən·vûrs′] *Let's conVERSE awhile.*
a CONvict [kon′vikt] *The CONvict escaped from jail.*	to conVICT [kən·vikt′] *He was conVICTed for robbery.*
a DESert [dez′ərt] *He rode through the DESert.*	to deSERT [di·zûrt′] *He deSERTed his family.*
an INsult [in′sult] *I'll stand for no INsults.*	to inSULT [in·sult′] *He inSULTed me.*

an OBject [ob'jikt]	to obJECT [əb·jekt']
What's that OBject?	*Your Honor, I objECT.*
PROGress [prog'res]	to proGRESS [prə·gres']
We're making PROGress.	*You may proGRESS.*
a PROJect [proj'ekt]	to proJECT [prə·jekt']
Our PROJect succeeded.	*Try to proJECT your voice.*
a PROtest [prō'test]	to proTEST [prə·test']
The lawyer filed a PROtest.	*They proTESTed vehemently.*
REFuse [ref'yōōs]	to reFUSE [ri·fyōōz']
Throw your REFuse in that bag.	*I reFUSE to go.*
a SUBject [sub'jikt]	to subJECT [səb·jekt']
Math is a hard SUBject.	*He was subJECTed to insults.*

EXCEPTIONS: Some words are always accented on the first syllable no matter how they are used, others on the second syllable.

Accent the First Syllable		Accent the Second Syllable	
a COMment	[kom'ent]	a deCLINE	[di·klīn']
to COMment		to deCLINE	
a PREFace	[pref'is]	a disPATCH	[dis·pach']
to PREFace		to disPATCH	

A Hint to the Wise

Address is an interesting word. You must always accent the second syllable, adDRESS [ə·dres'], when you use the word as a verb: *The speaker adDRESSed the audience; She adDRESSed the envelope.* Preferably, too, you accent the second syllable when you use the word as a noun meaning a speech or talk: *The speaker delivered the commencement adDRESS.*

You may accent either syllable to mean a person's place of residence —either adDRESS [ə·dres'] or ADdress [ad'res]: *What is Bob Smith's adDRESS?* or *What is Bob Smith's ADdress?*

Since you must say adDRESS in some instances but may say either adDRESS or ADdress in others, when in doubt you will never go wrong if you accent the second syllable: adDRESS.

379

THE SHIFTY ACCENT

Choose the proper pronunciation or pronunciations of the key words given in the list below. This is tricky because some have two acceptable pronunciations; others have shifty accents, depending on whether they are nouns (a CONvict) or verbs (to conVICT). Answers follow.

1. **grimace**—(a) grim'əs (b) gri·mās'
2. **conduct** (*verb*)—(a) kon'dukt (b) kən·dukt'
3. **conduct** (*noun*)—(a) kon'dukt (b) kən·dukt'
4. **infamous**—(a) in'fə·məs (b) in·fām'əs
5. **gondola**—(a) gon'də·lə (b) gon·dō'lə
6. **incognito**—(a) in'kog·nē'tō (b) in·kog'nə·tō
7. **abdomen**—(a) ab'də·mən (b) ab·dō'mən
8. **chauffeur**—(a) shō'fər (b) sho·fûr'
9. **preferable**—(a) pref'ər·ə·bəl (b) pref·ər·a'bəl
10. **incomparable**—(a) in·kom·par'·ə·bəl (b) in·kom'pər·ə·bəl
11. **reparable**—(a) rep'ər·ə·bəl (b) rep'rə·bəl

12. **permit** (*noun*)—(a) pər·mit' (b) pûr'mit
13. **permit** (*verb*)—(a) pûr'mit (b) pər·mit'
14. **romance**—(a) rō·mans' (b) rō'mans
15. **acclimate**—(a) ak'lə·māt (b) ə·klī'mit
16. **irrevocable**—(a) i·rev'ə·kə·bəl (b) ir·rə·vō'kə·bəl
17. **elite**—(a) ā·lēt' (b) ə·lēt'
18. **inhospitable**—(a) in·hos'pi·tə·bəl (b) in'hos·pit'ə·bəl
19. **clandestine**—(a) klan·də·stin' (b) klan·des'tin
20. **crusade** (*noun*)—(a) krōō·sād' (b) krōō'sād
21. **crusade** (*verb*)—(a) krōō·sād' (b) krōō'sād
22. **adult**—(a) ə·dult' (b) ad'ult
23. **contest** (*noun*)—(a) kən·test' (b) kon'test

ANSWERS:

1. **grimace**—(a) [grim'əs] or (b) [gri·mās'] 2. **conduct** (verb)—(b) [kən·dukt'] 3. **conduct** (*noun*)—(a) [kon'dukt] 4. **infamous**—(a) [in'fə·məs] 5. **gondola**—(a) [gon'də·lə] or (b) [gon·dō'lə] 6. **incognito**—(a) [in'kog·nē'tō] or (b) [in·kog'nə·tō] 7. **abdomen**—(a) [ab'də·mən] or (b) [ab·dō'·mən] 8. **chauffeur**—(a) shō'fər] or (b) [shō·fûr'] 9. **preferable**—(a) pref'·ər·ə·bəl] 10. **incomparable**—(b) [in·kom'pər·ə·bəl] 11. **reparable**—(a) rep'·ər·ə·bəl] 12. **permit** (*noun*)—(b) [pûr'mit] 13. **permit** (*verb*)—(b) [pər·mit'] 14. **romance**—(a) [rō·mans'] or (b) [rō'mans] 15. **acclimate**—(a) [ak'lə·māt] or (b) [ə·klī'mit] 16. **irrevocable**—(a) i·rev'ə·kə·bəl] 17. **elite**—(a) [ā·lēt'] 18. **inhospitable**—(a) [in·hos'pi·tə·bəl] or (b) [in'hos·pit'ə·bəl] 19. **clandestine**—(b) [klan·des'tin] 20. **crusade** (*noun*)—(a) [krōō·sād'] 21. **crusade** (*verb*)—(a) [krōō·sād'] 22. **adult**—(a) [ə·dult'] or (b) [ad'ult] 23. **contest** (*noun*)—(b) [kon'test]

9 WHERE ARE YOU?

The pronunciation of the names of countries, cities, rivers, mountains, streets, etc., can cause many problems. Place names may be derived from various American Indian languages, from Chinese, Japanese, Russian, or any of hundreds of other languages that the average person does not know. These may also be pronounced differently in different countries. Thus, the city we know as *Vienna* [vē·en′ə] is *Wien* [vēn] in Germany, and the country we know as *Mexico* [mek′sə·kō] is written *México* in Latin-American countries and pronounced [mä′hē·kō].

Even native American place names can be difficult. *Beaufort* is pronounced [byoō′fərt] when it refers to a town in South Carolina, but [bō′fərt] when the reference is to the town in North Carolina. *Quincy,* Massachusetts, is pronounced [kwin′zē]; the same name in Florida, Illinois, Washington, and California is pronounced [kwin′sē]. The city in central Massachusetts that is spelled *Worcester* is pronounced *Wooster* [woōs′tər], and the Louisiana town of *Natchitoches* is pronounced *Nakitush* [nak′i·tush].

No wonder, then, that an American finds impossible the pronunciation of the capital of Slovenia in Yugoslavia, Ljubljana [lyoō′blyä·nä], or the famous Welsh town with the longest name on record: Llanfairpwllgwyngliigogerychwyrndrobwlllllantysiliogogogoch [hlan·vīr′poōhl·gwin′gahl·gô·ge′roōkh·woōym·droōb′oōhl·hlan·tē·sē′lē·ô′gô·gô·gôkh′].

The only way to pronounce difficult place names properly is to learn the correct pronunciations of the most common ones and to look up others in your dictionary as you encounter them. Here is a list of some of the more frequently used place-name pronunciation demons:

Albuquerque, New Mexico	al′bə·kûr′kē
Ankara, Turkey	äng′kə·rə
Beirut, Lebanon	bā′roōt *or* bā·roōt′
Cairo, Egypt	kī′rō
Cairo, Illinois	kâr′ō
Cannes, France	kan *or* kanz
Champs Élysées, a Paris boulevard	shän′zā·lē·zā′
Des Moines, Iowa	də·moin′
Edinburgh, Scotland	ed′ən·bûr′ə
Eire	âr′ə
Gloucester, Massachusetts	glos′tər *or* glôs′tər
Greenwich	gren′ich

NOTE: Contrary to popular belief [gren′ich] is the proper pronunciation for all the following places: Greenwich Village, a section of New
York City; Greenwich, Connecticut; and Greenwich, England.

Guiana	gē·an′ə
Hawaii	hə·wä′ē *or* hə·wī′yə
Himalayas, the Asian mountain range	him·ē·lā′əz *or* hi·mäl′yəz
Houston, Texas	hyo͞os′tən
La Jolla, California	lə·hoi′yə
Laos	lä′ōs
Mojave Desert	mō·hä′vē
Monaco	mon′ə·kō *or* mə·nä′kō
Moscow, U.S.S.R.	mos′kou *or* mos′kō
Oahu	ō·ä′ho͞o
Okinawa	ō′ki·nä′wä
Palestine	pal′is·tīn
Rio de Janeiro, Brazil	rē′ō də jə·når′ō
Rio Grande river	rē′ō grand′
Salisbury, England	sôlz′bər·ē

NOTE: *Salisbury steak* (a hamburger steak) is pronounced the same
way! Do not pronounce it *Sal-is-bury.*

San Joaquin Valley, California	san′ wô·kēn′ *or* san′ wä·kēn′
San Jose, California	san′ hō·zā′
San Juan, Puerto Rico	sän hwän′
Sault Sainte Marie, Michigan	so͞o′ sänt′ mə·rē′
Schenectady, New York	skə·nek′tə·dē
Thailand	tī′land
Tokyo, Japan	tō′kē·ō
Tucson, Arizona	to͞o·son′ *or* to͞o′son
Versailles	ver·sī′ *or* ver·sälz
Vietnam	vē·et·näm′
Waco, Texas	wā′kō
Worcester, Massachusetts	wo͝os′tər
Worcestershire, a county in England	wo͝os′tər·shir

NOTE: *Worcestershire sauce* is pronounced exactly the same way.

Yosemite National Park   yō·sem′ə·tē

Can you pronounce all these correctly now? If not, practice until
you can.

QUICKIEQUIZQUICKIEQUIZQUICKIEQUIZQUICKIEQUIZQUICKIEQUIZQUICKIEQUIZQUICKIEQUIZQUICKIE

THREE-MINUTE QUICKIE QUIZ

IT'S A GREAT PLACE TO VISIT, BUT . . .

From the choices given below, choose the proper spelling of each place name. Answers follow.

1. (a) Edinburg   (b) Edinburgh   (c) Edinborough
2. (a) Rio de Janero   (b) Rio de Janeiro   (c) Rio de Janiero
3. (a) Tailand   (b) Thiland   (c) Thailand
4. (a) Salisberry   (b) Salisbury   (c) Salesbury
5. (a) Hawaii   (b) Hawai   (c) Hawaai
6. (a) Tucson   (b) Tuscon   (c) Tuscan
7. (a) Alburquerque   (b) Albuquerque   (c) Albuqueque
8. (a) Champs Élysées   (b) Champs de Eylsees   (c) Champs Elyse
9. (a) Canne   (b) Canes   (c) Cannes
10. (a) Himmalayas   (b) Himalayas   (c) Himallayas
11. (a) Worcestershire   (b) Woostershire   (c) Wocestershir
12. (a) Schenectady   (b) Scenecktady   (c) Schenectedy
13. (a) Soo Saint Marie   (b) Salt Sant Marie   (c) Sault Sainte Marie
14. (a) San Wakeen   (b) San Joaquin   (c) San Jacquin
15. (a) Glocester   (b) Gloucster   (c) Gloucester
16. (a) Sioux Falls   (b) Soo Falls   (c) Siox Falls
17. (a) Shillo   (b) Shiloh   (c) Shylo
18. (a) Placamine   (b) Plackmine   (c) Plaquemine
19. (a) Apomattox   (b) Appomattox   (c) Appomatox
20. (a) Berchtesgaden   **(b) Birchtesgarden**   (c) Berktesgaden
21. (a) Galaupagos   **(b) Galápagos**   (c) Gallapagos
22. (a) Wilkes-Barry   **(b) Wilks-Barre**   (c) Wilkes-Barre
23. (a) Seatle   **(b) Seattle**   (c) Settle
24. (a) Guadalahara   **(b) Guadalara**   (c) Guadalajara
25. (a) Torquay   (b) Torkay   (c) Torquey

ANSWERS:

1. (b) Edinburgh. 2. (b) Rio de Janeiro. 3. (c) Thailand. 4. (b) Salisbury. 5. (a) Hawaii. 6. (a) Tucson. 7. (b) Albuquerque. 8. (a) Champs Élysées. 9. (c) Cannes. 10. (b) Himalayas. 11. (a) Worcestershire. 12. (a) Schenectady. 13. (c) Sault Sainte Marie. 14. (b) San Joaquin. 15. (c) Gloucester. 16. (a) Sioux Falls. 17. (b) Shiloh. 18. (c) Plaquemine. 19. (b) Appomattox. 20. (a) Berchtesgaden. 21. (b) Galápagos. 22. (c) Wilkes-Barre. 23. (b) Seattle. 24. (c) Guadalajara. 25. (a) Torquay.

QUICKIEQUIZQUICKIEQUIZQUICKIEQUIZQUICKIEQUIZQUICKIEQUIZQUICKIEQUIZQUICKIEQUIZQUICKIE

10 DON'T LET FOREIGN WORDS CONFUSE YOU

All countries "borrow" words from other countries and languages. We have such foreign expressions as *status quo* (Latin), *hors d'oeuvre* (French), *ersatz* (German), *intermezzo* (Italian), *cabana* (Spanish), *sputnik* (Russian), *hara-kiri* (Japanese), and *aloha* and *ukulele* (Hawaiian).

Others borrow from us, too. In fact, foreign countries now adopt more words from American English than from any other language. The French, Germans, Italians, Latin Americans, Russians, Japanese, etc., have incorporated into their languages such typical American words as *supermarket, cocktail, astronaut,* and *gasoline.* Of course, foreign peoples often spell and pronounce these borrowings in their own way, just as we do when we take from them.

Common foreign imports are bound to cause pronunciation problems for many of us. Who has not been intimidated by French words on a menu? No one is expected to know French, Italian, German, Spanish, Latin, etc., just to be able to pronounce imported "English" properly. Still, it's nice to know the generally accepted Americanized pronunciation of some foreign words that are used widely in the United States. Let's learn a few of those words now.

Parlez-Vous English?

We have borrowed thousands of expressions from the French. Most of them have become so common that we have little trouble saying them. Here are sixty-three words of French origin that retain their French flavor even after they have been somewhat Americanized in sound or spelling. Learn the ones you aren't already sure of.

amour [ə·mŏor']—a love affair; love; a lover.
au courant [ō kōō·rän']—up-to-date.
au gratin [ō grat'ən]—sprinkled with bread crumbs or grated cheese and baked.
au jus [ō zhü']—served with its own natural juice or gravy.
au lait [ō lä']—with milk, as coffee.
au revoir [ō rə·vwär']—good-by.
billet-doux [bil'ē·dōō']—a love letter.
blasé [blä·zā']—bored, as from having seen or done too much.
bourgeois [bŏor'zhwä]—middle-class.

brassiere [brə·zir′]—a woman's undergarment.

buffet [bŏŏ·fā′]—a sideboard; a light meal.

canapé [kan′ə·pā]—an appetizer, usually a cracker topped with caviar, cheese, etc.

cliché [klē·shā′]—a trite expression.

coiffure [kwä·fyŏŏr′]—a style of arranging the hair.

coupe [kōōp or kōō·pā′]—a two-door automobile.

crouton [krōō′ton or krōō·ton′]—a small cube of toast used as a garnish in soups or salads.

cuisine [kwi·zēn′]—a style or quality of cooking.

cul-de-sac [kul′də·sak′]—a blind alley; especially, a trap with only one means of escape.

décolletage [dā·kôl·täzh′]—a garment with a low-cut neckline.

dishabille [dis′ə·bēl′]—the state of being partially or negligently dressed.

dossier [dos′ē·ā]—a collection of documents relating to a particular person or matter.

éclair [ā·klâr′ or i·klâr′]—an oblong pastry filled with custard or whipped cream.

entrée [än′trā]—the principal dish (or main course) at a meal.

faux pas [fō pä′]—a social mistake or breach of etiquette.

fete [fet]—(1) a festival; (2) an outdoor celebration.

fiancé [fē·än′sā]—a man to whom a woman is engaged.

fiancée [fē·än′sā]—a woman to whom a man is engaged.

finesse [fi·nes′]—delicate skill or tact.

gauche [gōsh]—awkward; boorish.

gourmand [gŏŏr′mənd]—a big eater.

gourmet [gŏŏr′mā or gŏŏr·mā′]—a judge or lover of fine food and drink.

habitué [hə·bich′ŏŏ·ā]—a person who frequents a specific place.

hors d'oeuvre [ôr dûrv′]—an appetizer or appetizers.

ingénue [an′zhə·nŏŏ′]—an innocent young girl (chiefly as played by an actress).

liaison [lē′ā·zon′ or lē·ā′zon]—(1) a bond or link; (2) a person who coordinates activities between two groups.

lingerie [län′zhə·rē or län′zhə·rā′]—women's light undergarments.

loge [lōzh]—a box or a balcony section in a theater.

macabre [mə·kä′brə]—gruesome.

mal de mer [mal′ də mâr′]— seasickness.

marquee [mär·kē′]—a canopy over the sidewalk in front of a hotel or theater.

melee [mā′lā *or* mā·lā′]—a brawl or noisy free-for-all.

milieu [mē·lyœ′]—environment; surroundings.

motif [mō·tēf′]—the underlying theme or design in a literary or artistic work.

naive [nä·ēv′]—unsophisticated, artless.

naiveté [nä·ēv′tā]—the quality of being naive.

negligée [neg′li·zhā′]—a dressing gown for women.

nuance [no͞o·äns′ *or* no͞o′äns]—subtle variation in color, tone, or meaning.

passé [pa·sā′]—(1) past the prime; faded; (2) old-fashioned.

patois [pat′wä]—a type of local dialect.

piquant [pē′kənt]—peppery or pungent in taste; agreeably stimulating.

pique [pēk]—a feeling of irritation or resentment.

potpourri [pō·po͞o·rē′ *or* pot·po͝or′ē]—a mixture of incongruous or miscellaneous elements.

ragout [ra·go͞o′]—a meat and vegetable stew.

rendezvous [rän′dä·vo͞o]—a prearranged meeting or the appointed place for a meeting.

repartee [rep′ər·tē′ *or* rep′är·tā]— a witty or quick reply.

résumé [rez′o͝o·mā′]—a summary or recapitulation, as of one's background and job experience.

ricochet [rik′ə·shā′]—to glance from a surface, as a ball or bullet.

roué [ro͞o·ā′ *or* ro͞o′ā]—a man who devotes his time to sensual pleasure.

sachet [sa·shā′]—an ornamental bag of perfumed powder.

salon [sa·lon′]—a drawing room.

savoir-faire [sa·vwär fâr′]—the ability to say and do the right thing; tact.

tête-à-tête [tāt′ə·tāt′]—a private chat; confidential, as between two persons only.

valet [val′ā *or* val′it]—a gentleman's personal servant.

Note that the *i* in many of these French words is pronounced as [ē]: *cliché, fiancé, naive, piquant.*

Most words of several syllables that end in *-et* derive from the French. Many of these words have been Anglicized completely so that the *-et* is pronounced "et," as in *bayonet, cadet, coronet, martinet,* and *tourniquet.* These cause no problems. However, other French borrowings ending in *-et* have not yet been Anglicized completely. The *-et* sound keeps some of its Gallic flavor and is pronounced [ā], as in *bouquet, cabaret, chalet, gourmet,* and *sachet.*

Fun With Words

FROM THE FRENCH

These fifteen words have been taken into English from French. Learn their proper meanings and pronunciations. Check the word or phrase you believe is closest in meaning to the key word. Answers follow.

1. **potpourri** [pō·pŏo·rē′ *or* pot·pŏor′ē]—(a) a Spanish gypsy dance. (b) a dialect. (c) the common people. (d) a medley or mixture.

2. **patois** [pat′wä]—(a) a local dialect. (b) the language of a nation. (c) a foreign accent. (d) a dish in cookery.

3. **ingénue** [an′zhə·nōo′]—(a) a young woman of simplicity and innocence. (b) indifference. (c) a shade of blue. (d) boredom.

4. **gasconade** [gas′kə·nād′]—(a) a coward. (b) a torrent of water. (c) bragging talk. (d) a kind of soufflé.

5. **portmanteau** [pôrt·man′tō]—(a) large overcoat. (b) a cape. (c) a curtain. (d) a suitcase.

6. **milieu** [mē·lyœ′]—(a) grace. (b) environment. (c) softness. (d) one's special occupation.

7. **fete** [fet]—(a) a festival. (b) overflowing. (c) a bouquet. (d) an accomplished deed.

8. **finesse** [fi·nes′]—(a) completion.

(b) slenderness. (c) clumsiness. (d) tact or skill.

9. **macabre** [mə·kä′brə]—(a) a type of corn. (b) a Spanish gypsy dance. (c) envious. (d) gruesome.

10. **métier** [mā·tyā′]—(a) a person's special calling. (b) a measure or norm. (c) a weapon. (d) average.

11. **habiliments** [hə·bil′ə·mənts]—(a) articles of clothing. (b) habits. (c) residences. (d) fortifications.

12. **éclat** [ā·klä′]—(a) abundance. (b) brilliance of action or effect. (c) a kind of pastry. (d) a creamy filling for cakes.

13. **dossier** [dos′ē·ā]—(a) a briefcase. (b) a festival. (c) a collection of papers, documents, etc. (d) a tapestry.

14. **hauteur** [hō·tûr′]—(a) polite anger. (b) style. (c) a well-bred manner. (d) disdainful pride.

15. **esprit** [es·prē′]—(a) lively wit. (b) a group of dancers. (c) a ghost. (d) talkativeness.

ANSWERS:

1. **potpourri**—(d) a medley or mixture. 2. **patois**—(a) a local dialect. 3. **ingénue**—(a) young woman of simplicity and innocence. 4. **gasconade**—(c) bragging talk. 5. **portmanteau**—(d) a suitcase. 6. **milieu**—(b) environment. 7. **fete**—(a) a festival. 8. **finesse**—(d) tact or skill. 9. **macabre**—(d) gruesome. 10. **métier**—(a) a person's special calling. 11. **habiliments**—(a) articles of clothing. 12. **éclat**—(b) brilliance of action or effect. 13. **dossier**—(c) a collection of papers, documents, etc. 14. **hauteur**—(d) disdainful pride. 15. **esprit**—(a) lively wit.

Watch Out for the French *en-*

The French word and syllable *en-* can cause pronunciation problems. In many words it has been Anglicized to our own *en* sound. In others, however, it is pronounced *ahn* or *on*. The following *en-* words and phrases keep the French *ahn* or *on* sound:

en garde [än·gärd']—on guard (a fencing position).
ennui [än'wē]—boredom.
en rapport [än ra·pôr']—in sympathetic agreement.
en route [än rōōt']—on or along the way.
ensemble [än·säm'bəl]—a unified whole, as a matching costume or group of musical performers.
entente [än·tänt']—an understanding or agreement, as between governments.
entourage [än'tōō·räzh']—a group of followers; retinue.
entr'acte [än·trakt']—the interval between the acts of a play, opera, etc.
entrée [än'trā]—(1) the main course of a meal; (2) a means of obtaining entry, as into a special group.
entrepreneur [än'trə·prə·nûr']—a person who starts or conducts a business enterprise.

NOTE: *Envelope* preferably is pronounced with the English *en* sound [en'və·lōp], but the French *en* sound [än'və·lōp] is acceptable.

Sprechen Sie English?

English has also borrowed from the German. The following list includes words that cause pronunciation trouble. Learn the proper American pronunciation of these words now.

blitzkrieg [blits'krēg]—a swift, sudden attack.
ersatz [er·zäts' *or* er'zäts]—a substitute, usually an inferior one.
glockenspiel [glok'ən·spēl]—a musical instrument consisting of tuned metal bars played by striking with a small hammer.
kindergarten [kin'dər·gär'tən]—a school or class for small children.
knockwurst [näk'wûrst]—a highly seasoned sausage.
lieder [lē'dər]—German songs, especially ballads or love poems set to music.
rathskeller [rats'kel·ər]—a beer hall or restaurant.
sauerbraten [sour'brä·tən]—beef marinated in vinegar and cooked.

How About Spanish, Italian, and Latin?

Here are eleven words we have borrowed from Spanish along with a generally accepted American pronunciation for each:

aficionado [ə·fē'syō·nä'dō]—an enthusiast; devotee, as of bull fights.
amontillado [ə·mon'tə·lä'dō]—a pale dry Spanish sherry.
cabana [kə·ban'ə]—literally, a small cabin; a beach bath house.
castanet [kas'tə·net']—one of a pair of wood or ivory disks clapped together in the fingers to accompany a dance or song.
flamenco [flə·meng'kō]—a style of singing and dancing developed by Spanish gypsies.
guava [gwä'və]—a tropical tree, the fruit of which is used in jellies.
hacienda [hä'sē·en'də]—a large ranch, or its main house.
iguana [i·gwä'nə]—a tropical American lizard.
jai alai [hī ə·lī']—a popular Latin-American game somewhat similar to handball but played with a curved wicker basket strapped to the arm.
junta [jun'tə]—(1) a secret political faction; (2) a legislative body.
tortilla [tôr·tē'yä]—a round, flat cornmeal cake used in place of bread in Mexico.

Many imports from Italy are listed below. Note how many of them relate either to music or food. Can you pronounce them all correctly?

alfresco [al·fres'kō]—out of doors.
antipasto [än'tē·päs'tō]—a variety of appetizers.
cadenza [kə·den'zə]—a musical flourish for a solo performer.
Chianti [kē·an'tē]—a dry red wine.
coloratura [kul'ər·ə·tŏor'ə]—(1) a soprano with an unusually wide range and flexibility; (2) runs or trills in vocal music.
crescendo [krə·shen'dō]—a gradual increase in volume in music.
finale [fi·nal'ē]—the last part of a performance.
fortissimo [fôr·tis'ə·mō]—very loud: a musical direction.
grotto [grot'ō]—a cave.
intermezzo [in'tər·met'sō]—a short musical, dramatic, or ballet offering given between the acts of a play or opera.
lasagne [lə·zän'yə]—a dish comprising pasta, ground meat, tomato sauce, and cheese.
obbligato [ob'lə·gä'tō]—an accompanying part of a musical composition.

389

pasta [päs′tə]—any type of spaghetti, macaroni, etc.

pianissimo [pē′ə·nis′i·mō]—very soft: a musical direction.

piazza [pē·äz′ə]—a veranda or porch.

pizza [pēt′sə]—a doughy crust covered with cheese, tomatoes, spices, anchovies, etc., and baked.

pizzicato [pit′sə·kä′tō]—music made by plucking strings rather than by using a bow.

vendetta [ven·det′ə]—a blood feud.

zucchini [zoo·kē′nē]—a green summer squash.

We call Latin a "dead" language, but it lives on in many English expressions, especially scientific, legal, medical, and business terms. The list of Latin terms below includes words that every educated person should be able to pronounce properly and easily.

ad hoc [ad hok′]—a term for any group or committee formed for a specific purpose in a specific situation.

ad hominem [ad hom′ə·nəm]—appealing to one's individual passions or prejudices.

agenda [ə·jen′də]—program of business.

angina [an·jī′nə]—a pain in the chest and arm caused by insufficient coronary circulation.

aurora borealis [ô·rôr′ə bôr′ē·al′is]—the northern lights.

bona fide [bō′nə fīd′]—genuine.

de facto [dē fak′tō]—existing in fact, with or without legal sanction.

erratum [i·rä′təm]—an error.

finis [fin′is or fī′nis]—the end.

ibidem [i·bī′dem]—in the same place.

non sequitur [non sek′wə·tər]—an irrelevant comment or remark.

per se [pûr sā′ or pûr sē′]—by itself.

quasi [kwā′zī or kwā′sī; kwä′zē or kwä′sē]—similar, but not precisely the same.

rara avis [rär′ə ā′vis]—an unusual or rare person or thing.

status quo [stā′təs or stat′əs kwō]—an existing condition or state.

stet [stet]—let it stand: a proofreader's direction.

BEWARE: Many foreign words in this chapter are also spelling and vocabulary demons as well. Many speakers avoid these useful words because they don't know how to pronounce or spell them or exactly how to use them. Don't let such difficulties stand in your way. Study the above lists with care, and consult your dictionary for further help.

PART FOUR

Punctuate It Right

PUNCTUATION MARKS—CLUES TO CLEARER MEANING

Why do we have punctuation? When you talk, you do not depend on words alone to tell your listener what you mean. The tone and stress of your voice affect the meanings of the words you use: You speak calmly or angrily; you whisper or yell. Facial movements and body gestures add meanings: You grin or grimace, nod or shake your head, wiggle a finger, shrug, or raise an eyebrow. The true meaning of conversation is affected by pauses and halts that are as significant as words themselves.

When you write, what you are really doing is "talking" to someone who is not there. That is why your full meaning, pauses, emphases, and emotional states must be suggested by punctuation marks. The primary aim of every punctuation mark is to make unmistakable the meaning of written words. Every mark of punctuation is a road sign set up to help readers grasp what the writer intended to convey. Punctuation is effective if it helps readers to understand; it is ineffective and even harmful if it gets in the way of their understanding.

Punctuation marks serve four general purposes: (1) to terminate; (2) to introduce; (3) to separate; and (4) to enclose. They do more than mark such obvious facts of language as "This is a question." They help group related ideas; they set off words for emphasis; they affect the mood and the tempo of what you write; they indicate which words are to be taken together and which are to be kept separate. Thus, punctuation points up the relationships and the relative importance of words and groups of words.

Words Without End

The right words in the right places will convey our ideas, but only the right punctuation can organize them into meaningful patterns for the eye. We cannot hope to communicate with a reader in this way:

> andsoshesaidtohimyesisupposethatsallrightbutireally
> thinkthatyououghttocheckwithmarty

For clarity, we must separate, punctuate, and organize written words into groups. We do this with some standard devices—actually writing "tricks." Some of these punctuation "tricks" are almost as natural to us as speech itself. Others are more complex and can cause us trouble.

First, we use spaces between words as the initial step in reducing the jumble of letters to an understandable pattern. Even a child just beginning to write does this almost automatically. The space between words is our most basic "punctuation mark"; it takes the place of natural pauses between words in speaking. Spacing in general is used to group written words into understandable patterns.

Thus, we group the elements of a thought, or closely related thoughts, into a series of paragraphs. We also group the smaller elements of single thoughts into sentences. We mark the start of the sentence with a capital letter—or beginning punctuation—and mark the end of it with a period, question mark, or exclamation point, which tells the reader whether our written "voice" is falling, rising, or shouting.

We give the reader further help in understanding the individual parts of an idea and their relationships by using commas, colons, semicolons, dashes, parentheses, and quotation marks. And some of these punctuation marks also help the reader to "hear" our pauses and tone of voice.

In this part of the book you will learn all about these easy devices—the tricks of written communication called *punctuation marks.* Since capitalization and hyphenation are so closely related to punctuation, they will be discussed here, too.

Modern Punctuation

All punctuation in the Western world began with the little dot that we call a *period.* In fact, the very word "punctuation" comes from the Latin word *punctum,* meaning "a point or dot." Gradually, through the centuries, other punctuation marks have been developed in order to signify a variety of changes in mood and tempo within sentences, as well as to clarify the relationships between various elements within a given sentence. Punctuation marks were particularly necessary in the nineteenth century because writers in those days often wrote long, complex sentences, and punctuation helped make them easier to read and to understand.

In our own century, and especially in America, the tendency has been toward simpler, shorter sentences—sentences with just one subject and one predicate and with few qualifying expressions. Thus, there is less need today than there used to be for internal (within a sentence) punctuation—commas, semicolons, and colons—to separate complex clauses and phrases from one another. And since there are more short sentences, the period tends to occur more often than it used to.

The modern tendency toward streamlining has also caused punctuation marks to be dropped from the ends of lines in addresses on letters; and we no longer put periods at the end of newspaper headlines, chapter headings in books, and the like. Today, we think of punctuation and its allies—capitalization and hyphenation—as purely functional rather than as having to conform to hard-and-fast rules. When you finish this part of the book, you should know all you need to know about the reasonable use of punctuation marks in modern writing.

REMEMBER: Without punctuation, written words would be difficult to understand. Punctuation can help you to a more effective use of your vocabulary. It can save you time and effort in writing clearly what you have to say. Much of what follows may be merely a review of what you already know, but the rest of it will help you sharpen your use of punctuation power to a fine point. Do all the tests and quizzes, even if you find them easy.

1 CAPITALIZATION

As in spacing between words and indenting before paragraphs, capitalization is a simple visual trick that helps make our writing intelligible. A capital letter (A, B, C) sticks out because it is bigger than other letters. It is used to direct attention to a new sentence or group of words, or to indicate the proper name of a person, place, or thing.

Capitalization is not difficult. You probably capitalize correctly most of the time without giving it a thought, even if you don't always know the rules. This chapter will tell you some things you need to know in order to capitalize correctly all of the time.

(a) Use a capital letter at the beginning of every sentence or of every word or group of words that has the force of a sentence.

He came to work.
What time did he come to work?
Eight.
That early? Nonsense!

This rule also applies to quoted matter. Every sentence in a direct quotation starts with a capital letter.

> *Bob asked, "What time did he come to work?"*
> *Pete shouted, "Go!"*
> *John said, "No. You can't make me go."*

EXCEPTION: A sentence within a sentence does not start with a capital letter if it is enclosed in parentheses.

> *The meeting will start at noon (please be on time!) and will end at four.*

Remember that the salutation and the complimentary close of a letter have the force of a sentence and therefore must begin with a capital letter.

Dear Mr. Jones:	Dear Mary,
Gentlemen:	Sincerely,

(b) Use a capital letter for the pronoun "I" and for the letter "O" when used as an interjection (generally only in religious contexts).

> *May I go with you?*   *Hear us, O Lord!*

(c) Use a capital letter for proper nouns. A proper noun is the name of a particular person, place, or thing—for instance, Elizabeth, Illinois, Republican Party. A "person" or "place" will probably give you no trouble, but remember that a "thing" is construed very broadly to include monuments (Statue of Liberty), school subjects (Geography, Business Administration), book titles (*Paradise Lost*), and political parties (Republican).

All the major types of proper noun are discussed below. Study them until you are sure that you know when to begin—and when not to begin—a noun with a capital letter.

Proper Nouns That Name Persons or Animals

(1) Capitalize any part or form of a name, including a nickname, epithet, title, initial, or term of address. This rule applies both to real and fictitious names, whether of people or animals.

Robert Brown	Queen Elizabeth	President Lincoln
Bob Brown	the Queen (*but:* a queen)	Senator Taft

Mr. Brown	Your Highness	the Mayor
R. B.	Henry the Eighth	Assemblyman Smith
Battlin' Bob Brown	Sir Walter Raleigh	Professor Jones
Uncle Bob (*but:* He's	Lady Jane Grey	Father Flanagan
my uncle.)	the Prince of Wales	Mr. and Mrs. Brown

EXCEPTIONS: A small, unimportant word in a person's name or title (such as *the, of, and,* etc.) is not capitalized unless it begins a sentence. (Note, above, Henry *the* Eighth and *the* Prince *of* Wales.)

Designations of rank without an accompanying name are capitalized when they stand for a specific person: *the President* (referring to a specific president of the United States, a university, a corporation, etc.). But such words are not capitalized when they simply refer to a class or type of person: *a senator; a president.* Note, too, that titles of rank that follow the name are usually capitalized only when the title is one of very great distinction:

Abraham Lincoln, the President of the United States
H. R. Jones, president of the Highland Bowling Club

Titles of family relationship are capitalized only when used with a name or in place of a name. They are not capitalized when used with a possessive pronoun such as *my* or *your.*

We'll have to ask Mother.
We'll have to ask our mother.

(2) Capitalize the name of a thing or idea when it is treated as though it were a person.

Dame Rumor
Jack Frost
Mother Nature

(3) Capitalize all names for supernatural figures or powers, including pagan deities. Note that words referring to sacred persons, such as epithets or terms of address, are also capitalized. Some pronouns referring to God and Christ (usually *He, Him,* and *His; Thee* and *Thou*) are generally capitalized. But when pagan deities are referred to in general terms, they are known as *gods* with a small g.

God (*but:* a pagan god)	Zeus
Allah	Providence
the Holy Trinity	the Almighty

Proper Nouns That Name Specific Places

(1) Capitalize the standard or accepted name of a geographical place, area, or feature, whether real or fictitious.

Kansas City	the Grand Canyon
Westchester County	the North Pole
Indiana	the Temperate Zone
the West	Lake Huron
the New World	the Promised Land
the Western Hemisphere	Camelot
the Mississippi River	the Happy Hunting Ground
the Pacific Ocean	the Rockies

NOTE: Capitalize *North, South, East,* and *West* only when you are referring to a part of the country. Do not capitalize them when you mean a compass direction, such as *north, south,* or *north by northwest.*

Tucson is in the West. (a section of the country)
Turn right and drive ten miles west. (a compass direction)

West and *East* are also capitalized when you mean a section of the world, referring to the Occident or Orient.

the mystery of the East (the Orient)
the technology of the West (the Occident)

(2) Capitalize the name of a celestial body or system, such as a planet or galaxy, or of any specific place on a celestial body, such as a valley on the moon.

Mars	the Milky Way
the North Star	the Big Dipper
the Great Bear	the Sea of Tranquillity

EXCEPTIONS: The words *sun, moon,* and *solar system* are not capitalized. And *earth* is generally capitalized only when used as a planetary name: *Mars, Jupiter,* and *Earth* revolve around the sun.

(3) Capitalize the name of a specific location, as a street, road, square, or park.

Marymount Road	the Connecticut Turnpike
Route 95	Yellowstone National Park

Proper Nouns That Name Specific Things

The category of "things" is broad enough to include any one-of-a-kind thing with a proper name—for instance, buildings, companies, products, and the like.

(1) Capitalize any one-of-a-kind object with a proper name, as a ship, plane, bridge, tunnel, document, or award.

the Titanic	the Golden Gate Bridge
the Apollo 11	the Declaration of Independence
the White House	the Purple Heart

(2) Capitalize the names of days, months, divisions of history, holidays, and important events.

Monday	World War II	the Depression
September	the Crusades	the Victorian Period
the Fourth of July	the Battle of Midway	the Stone Age

EXCEPTION: Designations of centuries—*the nineteenth century, the twentieth century*—and the names of seasons—*spring, summer,* etc.—are not usually capitalized.

(3) Capitalize all names for religions, sacred writings, religious orders and denominations, and their members.

Christianity	the Old Testament	Catholic
Judaism	the Talmud	Protestant
a Buddhist	the Sermon on the Mount	Methodist
the Bible	Genesis	Franciscan
the Koran	Anglican	Islam

(4) Capitalize all names for peoples, races, tribes, nationalities, etc.

Indian	Eskimo	Spaniard	Hoosier
Anglo-Saxon	Cherokee	New Englander	Neanderthal man
Norwegian	Finn	Italian	Californian

NOTE: Although the words *black* and *white* as designations of skin color are usually not capitalized, there is an increasing tendency toward capitalizing them and using them as racial terms.

(5) Capitalize the names of languages.

English	German	Yiddish	Swahili

(6) Capitalize the names of political parties or movements and their members. Also capitalize the names of executive, legislative, and judicial bodies.

the Agrarian Movement	County Assessor's Office
a Democrat	Detroit Board of Education
the Department of Defense	the U.S. Senate
the Supreme Court	the United Nations

NOTE: Use small letters for terms that refer generally to social ideologies: *fascism, socialism, communism, democracy.* But capitalize such words when referring to specific political systems and their members.

Bill Robinson is a born democrat. (The reference is to his belief in democracy.)
Jack Meredith has been a Democrat since 1960. (The reference is to his party affiliation.)

(7) Capitalize the names of organizations, including their identifying initials, branches, departments, and members.

Roosevelt Square Grade School
Yale University
the Y.M.C.A.
the Boy Scouts of America
a Boy Scout
a Mason

(8) Capitalize the names of companies, trademarks, and brand names.

General Motors	First National Bank
Coca-Cola	the Palace Theater
National Biscuit Company	the Metropolitan Opera

(9) An unimportant word like *a, the, of, and,* etc., should not be capitalized unless it begins a sentence or is the first word of the full title.

Handel's oratorio *The Messiah*
Steinbeck's *Of Mice and Men*

A preposition or conjunction is often capitalized, however, when it is at least four letters long: for example, *Rebel Without a Cause.*

399

(10) Capitalize every important word in the title of a book, chapter, poem, movie, comic strip, painting, musical composition, document, legislative act, treaty, and the like.

Gone With the Wind	the Gettysburg Address,
"Jack and the Beanstalk"	Beethoven's Ninth Symphony
the *Mona Lisa*	the Fifth Amendment
"Terry and the Pirates"	the Treaty of Versailles

NOTE: You've probably noticed that some titles are generally italicized, while others are enclosed in quotation marks. Briefly, titles of full-length works of literature, as well as of most other works of art, are generally italicized; titles of *parts* of books and of such shorter works as short stories and poems (or of comic strips, TV programs, etc.) are usually put in quotation marks. Other kinds of titles—for example, the Bible and its various parts—are neither italicized nor put in quotation marks.

Our class is reading *Robinson Crusoe, Hamlet,* and Kipling's poem "Recessional."

The last book of the New Testament is Revelation.

How do you indicate italics in a handwritten or typewritten manuscript? It's easy! You underline the word or words this way, and the printer will print them *this way.*

(11) Capitalize the name of a specific course in school.

He took Biology, English Composition, and Music last year.

Note that these are specific courses; otherwise, only the word *English* (a language) would be capitalized.

He studied biology, English, and music in school.

Proper Adjectives

Capitalize proper adjectives. A proper adjective is either formed from a proper noun, or is a proper noun used as an adjective. The proper adjectives *American* and *Jeffersonian,* for example, are formed from the proper nouns *America* and *Jefferson.* The proper adjective *Montana* in *a Montana law* is a proper noun used as an adjective.

Paris fashions (proper noun used as adjective)
Parisian glamour (adjective formed from proper noun)

400

EXCEPTIONS: A number of adjectives formed from proper names have become words in their own right and are no longer capitalized.

a platonic relationship (from Plato)
a quixotic outlook (from Don Quixote)

Punctuation Test—Capital Letters

Supply capital letters where needed in the following sentences.

1. john collins was pleased to learn that an ancestor of his had helped to win the american revolutionary war.
2. you were born in the southwest, weren't you? in phoenix?
3. where does the senior republican member of the senate judiciary committee live?
4. the flier, a captain, won a purple heart in vietnam.
5. all points on the map are south of the north pole.
6. this young man, al jenkins, was graduated from lane technical institute.
7. were you in cincinnati when the green bay packers played the bengals?
8. thank you, mr. chairman, for that gracious introduction.
9. to reach fort brown, drive west on u.s. highway 62 and then turn right on state route 19.
10. abraham lincoln was born in kentucky, spent his early years in indiana and several adult years in illinois, and died in washington, d.c.

ANSWERS:

1. John Collins was pleased to learn that an ancestor of his had helped to win the American Revolutionary War.
2. You were born in the Southwest, weren't you? In Phoenix?
3. Where does the senior Republican member of the Senate Judiciary Committee live?
4. The flier, a captain, won a Purple Heart in Vietnam.
5. All points on the map are south of the North Pole.
6. This young man, Al Jenkins, was graduated from Lane Technical Institute.
7. Were you in Cincinnati when the Green Bay Packers played the Bengals?
8. Thank you, Mr. Chairman, for that gracious introduction.
9. To reach Fort Brown, drive west on U.S. Highway 62 and then turn right on State Route 19.
10. Abraham Lincoln was born in Kentucky, spent his early years in Indiana and several adult years in Illinois, and died in Washington, D.C.

2 THE PERIOD

The little dot from which all punctuation grew is still our most common punctuation mark. Its chief function, of course, is as a stop sign: We use it to end a sentence, to bring a single thought to a full stop. Indeed, "full stop" is another name for the period. It can perform a number of functions, but here are its two major uses:

(1) Use a period to end a declarative or an imperative sentence—that is, a sentence that makes a statement or gives a command or request.

> *You left your book on the chair next to your purse and gloves.* (A statement.)
> *Leave your book, please.* (A request.)
> *Good-by. Yes.* (Each of these, even though very short, is a statement.)

Most people think of a sentence as something that must have a subject (such as "I"), a predicate (such as "will buy"), and perhaps an object (such as "an apple"); but this is not always the case. The only true requirement of a sentence is that it must express a complete thought. Therefore, "Yes" and "Good-by" are sentences, for in context they express complete thoughts.

(2) Use a period after initials and most abbreviations.

W. C. Fields	Dr. Edwards	ten ft. wide
Mr. and Mrs. Bolton	William C. Jonas, Ph.D.	Denver, Colo.
the Lessing Co.	Joyce Brown, M.A.	five ft. tall

ONE PROBLEM: Is it U.S.A. or USA, P.M. or PM, F.B.I. or FBI? In many cases either form will do. But since there are hundreds of abbreviations, the best thing to do is to consult your dictionary.

USAGE NOTE: Do not put two periods together. If a sentence ends in an abbreviation with a period, that period suffices to end the sentence; do not add a second period unless a parenthesis intervenes.

> *It took him seven years to earn his Ph.D.*
> *Enclosed are the stamps, coupons, clippings, etc.*
> *I like everything I have (house, family, job, etc.).*
> *The sign read "John Knowles, M.D."*

MORE FOREIGN WORDS

Here are fifteen foreign words to learn or review. Check the word or phrase you believe is closest in meaning to the key word. Answers follow. And while you're at it, be sure that you know the proper pronunciation of these words.

1. **a priori** [ā′ prī·ō′rī]—(a) prior to experience. (b) to the rear. (c) after careful examination. (d) the most important.

2. **ex cathedra** [eks′ kə·thē′drə]— (a) a sermon. (b) highly secret. (c) with authority. (d) contrary to accepted belief.

3. **non sequitur** [non ṣek′wə·tər]— (a) foolishness. (b) an irrelevant remark or conclusion. (c) sound logic. (d) a connected series.

4. **quid pro quo** [kwid′ prō kwō′] —(a) a puzzle. (b) a proposition. (c) something for nothing. (d) one thing in return for another.

5. **in toto** [in tō′tō]—(a) impatiently. (b) strongly. (c) entirely. (d) bluntly.

6. **cadenza** [kə·den′zə]—(a) a musical flourish. (b) a fast dance. (c) a woman soloist. (d) a concert.

7. **vendetta** [ven·det′ə]—(a) a light opera. (b) a feud. (c) a weapon. (d) a cape.

8. **crescendo** [krə·shen′dō]—(a) crisis. (b) an opera score. (c) gossip. (d) increase in volume of sound.

9. **inamorata** [in·am′ə·rä′tə]—(a) a beloved woman. (b) a clandestine affair. (c) immortal. (d) infatuated.

10. **piazza** [pē·az′ə]—(a) a pie. (b) a veranda. (c) a country fair. (d) a fish.

11. **cupola** [kyōō′pə·lə]—(a) a small dome. (b) a bay window. (c) a terrace. (d) trimming.

12. **fiasco** [fē·as′kō]—(a) an altercation. (b) a fistfight. (c) a humiliating failure. (d) a mistake.

13. **libretto** [li·bret′ō]—(a) free and easy. (b) the text or words of an opera. (c) a light opera score. (d) a song.

14. **inferno** [in·fûr′nō]—(a) summer heat. (b) a hot oven. (c) hot-blooded. (d) a hellish place.

15. **flotilla** [flō·til′ə]—(a) a fleet of small ships. (b) a floating dry dock. (c) floating objects. (d) a baking process.

ANSWERS:

1. **a priori**—(a) prior to experience. 2. **ex cathedra**—(c) with authority. 3. **non sequitur**—(b) an irrelevant remark or conclusion. 4. **quid pro quo**— (d) one thing in return for another. 5. **in toto**—(c) entirely. 6. **cadenza**— (a) a musical flourish. 7. **vendetta**—(b) a feud. 8. **crescendo**—(d) increase in volume of sound. 9. **inamorata**—(a) a beloved woman. 10. **piazza**—(b) a veranda. 11. **cupola**—(a) a small dome. 12. **fiasco**—(c) a humiliating failure. 13. **libretto**—(b) the text or words of an opera. 14. **inferno**—(d) a hellish place. 15. **flotilla**—(a) a fleet of small ships.

3 THE QUESTION MARK

The question mark (or interrogation point), the second most common terminal punctuation mark, is used at the end of a word or group of words to indicate that a question is being asked, or, less frequently, to indicate doubt. There are three main ways in which you can make it do its job for you.

(1) Use the question mark to end a direct question.

> *When will you arrive?*
> *Why not?*
> *You left at noon?*

Note that the first two examples above begin with *when* and *why*, which indicate to the reader that the sentence is going to be a question. But the last example depends completely on the question mark to tell the reader that a question is being asked. If you were putting the question to someone in this form, your voice would rise at the word *noon*. It is the question mark that tells the reader how to "think" the sentence correctly.

(2) Use a question mark after each question in a series of questions within a sentence.

> *When will you arrive? on what airline? on what flight?*
> *Can we depend on Bob? on Jim? on Al?*

Question marks used within a sentence in this way call for a series of halts so that extra stress is placed on each element.

(3) Use a question mark to express doubt. Such a question mark is usually put inside parentheses after a date, word, or figure, to show that the writer is not sure that it is correct.

> *Columbus was born in 1446 (?) and died in 1506.* (The date of his death has been firmly established, but the year of his birth is not entirely certain.)
> *At the party, you'll meet the Browns, Bob Pearce (?), and Frank Harrison.* (This means either that the writer is not sure that Bob Pearce will be there or that he is not sure of the correct spelling of Bob's last name.)

WARNING: Such parenthetical question marks are *not* to be used to show the reader that you are too lazy to use your dictionary. In other words, never use a question mark to express doubt over a fact or spelling that you could easily verify if you tried. Don't do this: "Our cruise to the Carribean (?) was wonderful."

TWO MINOR PROBLEMS: First, when is a sentence a statement or request, and when is it a true question? In other words, is a sentence that starts out as a statement but ends up as a question a statement or a question? And, secondly, should you use a period or a question mark after a polite request put in the form of a question or after a rhetorical question (one for which no answer is expected)? The following examples should help solve these problems for you.

> *She asked me how long I'd been away.* (Here the period is required. The question is only an indirect one.)
> *The point at issue is this: Am I right or wrong?* (The question mark is correct because it follows a direct question.)
> *Won't you please come in.*
> *You think you're pretty smart, don't you.*
> *Who knows when the rain will stop.*

The first of these last three sentences is a polite request. The other two are rhetorical questions—that is, they are put in the form of questions, but the speaker does not expect an answer; he is merely giving vent to his feelings. In all three cases most good writers do not use a question mark, but it is not incorrect to use one. The choice is yours.

4 THE EXCLAMATION POINT

The exclamation point is the third and final mark of terminal punctuation, but it appears less often than the period and the question mark.

The exclamation point is used after a word or group of words to indicate that the writer is making some kind of strong exclamation or interjection. In many instances, you can think of this punctuation mark as a shout from the writer or one of his characters. Here are its two main uses:

(1) Use an exclamation point to end a sentence or phrase expressing

strong emotion, shock, surprise, sarcasm, etc., or after an interjection (that is, a single word expressing strong emotion, shock, etc.).

"You'll never catch me alive!" he screamed.
Fancy meeting Jane in Mexico! And she's getting married there!
Hot dogs! Peanuts and popcorn! (These exclamation points merely let the reader know that the vendor is "shouting" his wares.)
Oh! (This exclamation point shows shock, surprise, or delight.)
You're a fine one to tell me how to diet! (Here the exclamation point shows sarcasm.)

(2) Use the exclamation point after some commands.

Column right, march!
Run for your life!

These commands are literally shouted—or, at least, they are so urgent that they'd better be obeyed. Simple commands or polite requests are best followed by either a period or a question mark.

WARNING: Exclamation points lose their effectiveness when overused. Save them for cases of extreme amazement, shock, etc. Too many people try to make up for a dull or uncertain style of writing by using exclamation points to show emotion, as in these two examples:

"I love you, Mary!" he whispered.
"Oh, John!" she replied.

The really competent writer shows feeling in his handling of words, not in the way he punctuates.

A MINOR PROBLEM: Even though you know the common uses of the period, question mark, and exclamation point, there are times when you must rely on your knowledge of the true meaning of the sentence in order to decide which punctuation mark it should end with. At such times ask yourself whether you want the reader to read it as a flat statement, as a question, or as a kind of shout. For example, the short sentence "Sit down" can be punctuated in the following three ways:

Sit down.
Sit down!
Sit down?

The first is a mild command or polite request. The second is an urgent command; it may indicate extreme irritation or anger, or it may be a warning to someone about to fall overboard from a rowboat. The last has a question built into it. It may mean "How can I, since there's no place to sit?" Or perhaps it means "Do you really want me to sit down?"

In any case, as these three examples show, terminal punctuation marks can do a great deal to set the tone or shift the meaning of a sentence.

Punctuation Test—Periods, Exclamation Points, and Question Marks

Supply the punctuation needed in the following sentences. The answers that follow are not necessarily the only possible ones. Can you improve on them?

1. The Brooklyn Bridge can't be a mile long, can it
2. The crash caused me to cry out in horror
3. Ouch that's hot
4. When will your sister arrive I hope she is enjoying her trip
5. That electrician Do you know what he charged Fifty dollars
6. What a shame Mrs. Baker won't be here for the party How disappointed she must be
7. I wonder why the play doesn't begin Oh Now the curtain is rising
8. We should make an early start Can you be ready to leave at 6 A.M.
9. I asked the salesman, "For how long is this article guaranteed " He exclaimed, "Forever"
10. When it's 6 P.M. in Denver, what time is it in Newark, N J

RECOMMENDED PUNCTUATION:

1. The Brooklyn Bridge can't be a mile long, can it?
2. The crash caused me to cry out in horror.
3. Ouch! That's hot!
4. When will your sister arrive? I hope she is enjoying her trip.
5. That electrician! Do you know what he charged? Fifty dollars.
6. What a shame Mrs. Baker won't be here for the party! How disappointed she must be!
7. I wonder why the play doesn't begin. Oh! Now the curtain is rising.
8. We should make an early start. Can you be ready to leave at 6 A.M.?
9. I asked the salesman, "For how long is this article guaranteed?" He exclaimed, "Forever!"
10. When it's 6 P.M. in Denver, what time is it in Newark, N.J.?

5 THE COMMA

Commas are the workhorses of written English and are the punctuation marks used most frequently within sentences. One of the comma's main functions is to keep the meaning of a sentence clear by indicating which of its parts are necessary for the basic sense and which parts are not quite as essential. Another important function of the comma is to show the reader which parts of a sentence belong together, and which should be read as separate, though closely related, elements of the sentence.

More specifically, the comma has the following principal uses:

(1) It may be used to separate the components of a date, of an address, of a large number, or of a series of three or more items, words, or groups of words.

> July 4, 1776
> Thursday, November 12
> Atlanta, Georgia
> 107 Patterson Ave., Tulsa, Oklahoma
> 2,841
> $5,322,476
> *She won the bingo game by covering B3, I4, N2, G1, and O5.*
> *On our vacation we visited friends in Cleveland, Indianapolis, and Denver.*
> *Mr. and Mrs. Snyder, Dr. and Mrs. Brewster, and Mrs. Green were at the party.*

NOTE: In lists or series such as those illustrated in the last three sentences above, many writers omit the last comma (the one that immediately precedes *and*). Both ways of punctuating lists or series are acceptable. Just be sure you are consistent. Do not include the final comma in one instance and drop it in another.

(2) A comma may be used after the salutation (greeting) and after the conventional closing phrase of a letter. A colon (:) is preferred for the salutations in business or other formal letters.

> Dear Jim,
> Dear Mom, (*but* Dear Sir:)
> Best regards,
> Sincerely yours,

(3) A comma is always used to set off the name or title of a person you address directly in writing, or to set off a person's name from his title, academic degree, or the like.

Well, Tom, that's about the end of the story.
I'm very happy to tell you this news, Aunt Jane.
The project chief was Gordon French, Ph.D.

(4) A comma is used to separate the two parts of any sentence that begins as a statement but ends as a question.

He's a devil, isn't he?
That wasn't too much to spend for this dress, was it?

(5) Expressions such as *she said, he wrote,* etc., that either introduce or follow quoted dialogue are usually set off by commas.

George said, "Let's start now."
"Let's start now," said George.
"By tomorrow," Cynthia wrote, "I'll be in Minneapolis again."

(6) A comma is used between each of two or more adjectives that modify the same noun.

We kept up a brisk, steady pace on the hike.
Queechy Lake is a deep, blue, calm body of water.

NOTE: To test whether the modifiers all modify the same noun, substitute the word *and* for the commas: "brisk *and* steady pace"; "deep *and* blue *and* calm body of water." If the word *and* cannot be meaningfully inserted, commas should not be used. Consider, for instance, the sentence "She wore brown leather gloves." Here the gloves are not really brown *and* leather; the two words *brown leather* are a unit that cannot be meaningfully separated. Hence, no comma.

Similarly, if you write "Queechy Lake is a deep blue color," you do not mean that the color is both deep *and* blue; it is *deep blue,* without a comma.

(7) Commas are always used to set off *appositives*—that is, words or phrases that rename, identify, or explain the preceding word or phrase.

I, John Lovell, do make this last will and testament.
The captain of the football team, a senior from Memphis, scored the first touchdown.
Why should this have happened to him, honest fellow that he is?

409

NOTE: Except at the end of a sentence (as in the last of the preceding examples) a pair of commas is always used in such situations, one before and one after the appositive word or words.

(8) Commas may be used to set off an introductory phrase or clause that tells how, when, where, why, etc., the following statement has happened, is happening, or will happen.

> *When the war was over, Jerry returned to Fargo.*
> *In Puerto Rico, it never gets this cold.*
> *Even if it rains cats and dogs tomorrow, we won't call off our picnic.*

NOTE: If the introductory group of words is very short, many writers feel that no comma is needed. It would not be incorrect, for example, to write "In Puerto Rico it never gets this cold." Note, too, that a comma is not generally used to set off a clause or phrase that follows the main statement instead of preceding it:

> *Jerry returned to Fargo when the war was over.*
> *We won't call off our picnic even if it rains cats and dogs tomorrow.*

(9) Commas are often used to separate almost unnecessary words or groups of words (parenthetical expressions) from the rest of the sentence.

> *I appreciate your offer but cannot, however, accept the position.*
> *You are, therefore, the only person who can do the job.*
> *He is, unfortunately, a rather poor sport.*
> *Nancy knew, of course, that the party started at eight.*
> *Yes, you're absolutely right.*
> *You look a little pale, to tell the truth.*

In all the above sentences, the words set off by commas serve mainly as personal emphasis, personal asides, word bridges, or nonessential introductions or conclusions to the major statement. Note that except at the beginning or end of a sentence, the commas are always paired around the parenthetical expression so that it is entirely separated from the essential parts of the sentence.

(10) A comma usually precedes the coordinating conjunction in a compound sentence. A compound sentence is a sentence that is really composed of two or more sentences joined together (that is, coordinated) by a conjunction such as *and, but, for,* or *or.*

410

A boy gave us directions, but they were so complicated we couldn't follow them.

I returned the book to Jane, and she took it right back to the library.

We could hardly hear the speaker, for we sat in the last row of the auditorium.

If the compound sentence is very brief, you may safely omit the comma before the conjunction.

Henry thought he knew his way but he didn't.

At night the children play checkers or I read to them.

(11) Commas should always be used to set off *nonrestrictive clauses.* A nonrestrictive clause is a group of words that describes something or someone without being absolutely necessary for identifying the thing or person. In other words, you can drop a nonrestrictive clause from the sentence without changing the meaning.

Peter's new fishing rod, which is an eleven-footer, cost him a small fortune. (The clause *which is an eleven-footer* is nonrestrictive and must be set off by commas because it merely adds some information about the rod; the rod has already been clearly identified as *Peter's new fishing rod.* Compare this with the following sentence: *The fishing rod that Peter just bought cost him a fortune.* Here the clause *that Peter just bought* is restrictive: It is essential to the meaning of the sentence because it tells the reader which one of Peter's rods the writer is referring to, and so it should not be enclosed in commas.)

My favorite niece, whom I almost never see, lives in Honolulu. (No question about which of my nieces lives in Honolulu, is there? Compare this with the following sentence: *The niece whom I see least often lives in Honolulu.*)

Our house, where three generations have been born and died, stands on a high hill. (Compare *Any house where three generations have been born and died is worth preserving.*)

NOTE: Some writers pepper their sentences too heavily with commas, and others use too few. Remember that the comma is not just a decoration on the page; it has an important job to do in sorting out, separating, and combining the various parts of a sentence. When you are in doubt about whether or not you need a comma at a certain place, try saying the sentence out loud. If it seems natural for you to pause, no matter how briefly, at that spot, a comma may well be in order. If, on the

411

other hand, a pause seems to break into the middle of a tight cluster of words and to make you sound as if you're gasping for breath, do not insert a comma.

Thus, for example, you would not normally say "John and Mary (*pause*) have gone out for a walk." But you would pause for at least an instant at the places where commas are inserted in the following sentence: *John and Mary, who felt they needed a breath of fresh air, have gone out for a walk.*

This is not, of course, a sure-fire way to test your use of commas, but it may often help to resolve your doubts.

6 THE COLON

Once you have learned how to use capital letters, periods, question marks, exclamation points, and commas properly, you have mastered the hardest and most common punctuation marks. Although everyone should understand them, the remaining punctuation marks are used much less frequently.

The colon (:) indicates a division in writing or a pause in speech greater than that of a comma and less than that of a period. It usually separates a general, introductory item from a specific explanation, list, quotation, number, or the like. It often indicates to the reader: "I've told you my overall plan; now look at the details."

The colon has four principal uses:

(1) Use a colon to follow the salutation (greeting) of a formal or business letter, speech, or report.

Dear Dr. Loomis:	To Whom It May Concern:
Gentlemen:	Mr. Chairman, Honored Guests, Ladies and Gentlemen:

When is a letter formal enough to require a colon after the greeting? Usually, when you address the reader by his or her business, professional, or other official title or by an impersonal term of address like *Sir* or *Madam*. The trend, especially in some kinds of business letters, is toward the more informal comma rather than the colon.

(2) Use a colon after a word, phrase, or statement that introduces a list or an item.

> *Grocery list: bread, milk, orange juice, hamburger.*
> *On duty tonight: Jones, Brown, Johnson.*
> *For rent: large 6-room apartment.*
> *Bob excels in the following sports: baseball, basketball, and hockey.*

WARNING: The colon is correctly used after a phrase such as "including the following," "as follows," etc. Do *not* use a colon, however, if the verb in a statement leads directly into a list—that is, if you would *not* pause in saying the sentence. Thus:

> *Bob excels in baseball, basketball, and hockey.*

One simple way to tell when to use the colon and when not to use it is to say the sentence out loud. If you normally take a breath before the list, then use a colon to indicate the pause. If you wouldn't pause when saying the sentence, then don't use a colon.

(3) Use a colon after a statement that introduces a quotation, another statement, or an explanation or amplification of what has just been said.

> *He began the meeting with this warning: "Gentlemen, we're in trouble."*
> *My conclusion is: The dog is not man's best friend.*
> *I have three objections to the plan: It would take too long, it would cost too much, and it would be too risky.*

NOTE: Use the colon in this way only when you want to emphasize the quotation, the second statement, or the amplification by setting it off from the rest of the sentence. If you don't want such strong emphasis, you can link the introductory words and the following statement in some less emphatic fashion.

> *He began the meeting by saying, "Gentlemen, we're in trouble."*
> *My conclusion is that the dog is not man's best friend.*
> *I object to the plan because it would take too long, cost too much, and be too risky.*

(4) A colon is often used to separate the hour from the minutes in a numerical writing of the time of day (12:15), or the volume number from the page number in a citation from a publication (*The Congressional Record* 65:832).

Fun With Words

MORE SHORTIES

Too many vocabulary-building programs concentrate on long, complicated words—the kind few people find useful for everyday business or
conversation. Here's a test of vocabulary shorties, of words having
only three letters. Check the word or phrase you believe is closest in
meaning to the key word. Answers follow.

1. **nib** [nib]—(a) point of a pen.
(b) a fleshy part. (c) cream. (d)
a slight cut.

2. **van** [van]—(a) to excommunicate. (b) forefront. (c) highest
point. (d) background.

3. **yaw** [yô]—(a) an African antelope. (b) to quarrel. (c) to
cast aspersions at. (d) to move
wildly off course.

4. **wan** [won]—(a) pale. (b) a
storage place. (c) ghastly. (d)
to diminish.

5. **wry** [rī]—(a) an incorrect decision. (b) wrong. (c) twisted.
(d) very common.

6. **eke** [ēk]—(a) to piece out or
supplement. (b) to yell or
scream. (c) to trickle forth. (d)
to throw out.

7. **con** [kon]—(a) to end abruptly.
(b) to read with care. (c) to
go with someone. (d) to forfeit.

8. **nub** [nub]—(a) a baby. (b)
the hilt. (c) the gist or point.
(d) the conclusion.

9. **oaf** [ōf]—(a) a dark horse. (b)
a blockhead. (c) a sacrificial
offering. (d) an elf.

10. **vie** [vī]—(a) vigor. (b) to compete with. (c) to consider. (d)
to pledge allegiance.

11. **fen** [fen]—(a) to duel with. (b)
to keep away from. (c) a marsh
or swamp. (d) an oasis.

12. **don** [don]—(a) to put on, as a
garment. (b) a lover. (c)
dance lightly. (d) an infatuation.

13. **dun** [dun]—(a) to annoy. (b)
to chew or bite on. (c) to notify.
(d) to press for payment.

14. **rue** [rōō]—(a) to regret extremely. (b) to wander. (c) to
tint with a red dye. (d) to pine
away.

15. **ebb** [eb]—(a) to fuss over. (b)
to study. (c) to reach a peak.
(d) to wane.

16. **eon** [ē′on]—(a) a vast number.
(b) an atomic particle. (c) an
incalculably long period of time.
(d) several years.

ANSWERS:

1. **nib**—(a) point of a pen. 2. **van**—(b) forefront. 3. **yaw**—(d) to move
wildly off course. 4. **wan**—(a) pale. 5. **wry**—(c) twisted. 6. **eke**—(a) to
piece out or supplement. 7. **con**—(b) to read with care. 8. **nub**—(c) the
gist or point. 9. **oaf**—(b) a blockhead. 10. **vie**—(b) to compete with. 11.
fen—(c) a marsh or swamp. 12. **don**—(a) to put on, as a garment. 13. **dun**
—(d) to press for payment. 14. **rue**—(a) to regret extremely. 15. **ebb**—(d)
to wane. 16. **eon**—(c) an incalculably long period of time.

7 THE SEMICOLON

The semicolon (;) has two basic uses:

(1) The first is to join two or more closely related sentences together into one sentence.

> *The car stopped; Joe got in.*
> *I went to work; I had a quick lunch; I came straight home.*

Notice that *The car stopped* and *Joe got in* as well as *I went to work, I had a quick lunch,* and *I came straight home* are all complete statements by themselves. It would therefore be correct to separate them by means of periods. But in each of the above sentences the complete statements are short and closely related. So it makes sense to tie them together with semicolons. Notice, too, that you could also combine the short independent clauses by means of conjunctions or by means of commas along with conjunctions.

> *The car stopped and Joe got in.*
> *I went to work, had a quick lunch, and came straight home.*

Why not write the sentences this way? You could. But you get a slightly different shade of meaning when you use semicolons instead of conjunctions. The semicolons show that the actions are not quite as closely related to each other as they would seem to be if they were connected by "and."

NOTE: Sometimes the semicolon joins sentence parts that are not complete statements but that would be complete statements if certain words were repeated instead of being left out. The omitted words are, in effect, "carried over" from the first statement in the series and are "understood" in the later statements.

> *In France, we bought perfume; in Ireland, sweaters; in England, shoes.*

It is also correct to use a semicolon before such words and expressions as *nevertheless, accordingly, therefore, however, hence, instead, yet, thus, for example,* and *consequently* when they join two closely related independent clauses. In the following examples a period could be substituted for the semicolon, but the semicolon makes the relationship between the parts more apparent.

We got a late start; nevertheless, we got to the airport on time.
The child was bright; for example, he could do long division.
The weather did not clear; instead, the rain increased.
He was the eldest son; consequently, he inherited everything.

WARNING: In these and similar sentences, either a period or a semicolon may acceptably precede the words *therefore, nevertheless,* and so on. But a comma would not be acceptable. Two independent clauses (complete statements) should not be joined by a comma without the addition of *or, and,* or *but.*

(2) A semicolon may replace a comma when a sentence is very long or already has too many commas. This does not mean that a semicolon may substitute for just any comma. The semicolon may be used to separate the items of a list; or to separate one related group of words from another group of words if there are already commas within the group; or to separate the various self-contained parts of a very long sentence. Study each of the following examples:

Important nutrient groups include: milk, butter, and cheese; meat, poultry, and eggs; green or yellow vegetables; cereals.
You will find references to herb gardens on pages 4, 38, 43, and 72; to wild herbs on pages 18, 37, and 42.
The winning numbers were 1,273; 3,663; 8,462; and 2,370.

Since the numbers already have commas in them, it would confuse the reader if you used more commas instead of semicolons to separate the numbers.

Mr. Green, the plumber; George Crompton, the painter; and Joe Brown were at the party.

Here, too, semicolons are used to help out the reader. If commas were used, we would have *Mr. Green, the plumber, George Crompton, the painter, and Joe Brown were at the party.* The reader would wonder whether five people are mentioned: (1) *Mr. Green,* (2) *a plumber,* (3) *George Crompton,* (4) *a painter,* and (5) *Joe Brown;* or perhaps he would assume that two of the people are *Mr. Green* and *the plumber George Crompton.* Only the use of the semicolon makes it clear who's who at this party.

The bus stop, worse luck, was three blocks away; and Jim, thoroughly drenched by the rain, headed for it at a trot.

416

If there were no internal commas within the two independent clauses, a comma would, of course, be used before *and: The bus stop was three blocks away, and Jim headed for it at a trot.* In this case, only a comma would be needed to organize the sentence into two parts. In the longer sentence, however, commas are already used around *worse luck* and *thoroughly drenched by the rain.* And so we show where the two major parts of the sentence are separated by using a "louder" or "longer" pause at that point: the semicolon.

Punctuation Test—Commas, Semicolons, and Colons

Add commas, semicolons, and colons where necessary to the following letter. Recommended punctuation—though not necessarily the only correct punctuation—follows.

Monday August 30, 1971

Dear Sir

On May 15th I ordered the following from your store 4 chairs your model number 1407-B 1 table your model number M-607 and 2 lamps your model number 1703. These items were to be delivered before 430 P.M. June 25th to me Mr. Charles Bolland 1867 West Street Columbus Ohio. To date the furniture has not been delivered and I have had no word from you. Please let me know when I can expect delivery on the chairs the table and the lamps. I do want them as soon as possible.

Very truly yours

RECOMMENDED PUNCTUATION:

Monday, August 30, 1971

Dear Sir:

On May 15th I ordered the following from your store: 4 chairs, your model number 1407-B; 1 table, your model number M-607; and 2 lamps, your model number 1703. These items were to be delivered before 4:30 P.M., June 25th, to me, Mr. Charles Bolland, 1867 West Street, Columbus, Ohio. To date, the furniture has not been delivered, and I have had no word from you. Please let me know when I can expect delivery on the chairs, the table, and the lamps. I do want them as soon as possible.

Very truly yours,

417

Fun With Words

ONE-SYLLABLE WORDS

Here are some short words to learn. They aren't as short as the three-letter words in an earlier vocabulary test, but they all contain only one syllable. Check the word or phrase you believe is closest in meaning to the key word. Answers follow.

1. **feat** [fēt]—(a) an act of unusual skill or courage. (b) a gala party. (c) a heavy task. (d) a mission of mercy.
2. **rift** [rift]—(a) sediment. (b) a cloud formation. (c) a split or cleft. (d) to manipulate.
3. **filch** [filch]—(a) to strain or filter. (b) to adorn with gold. (c) to cross into enemy lines. (d) to steal small amounts slyly.
4. **harp** [härp]—(a) to dislike violently. (b) to pillage. (c) to dwell on a subject tediously. (d) to argue.
5. **trice** [trīs]—(a) an instant or moment. (b) to bind up. (c) three-fold. (d) a predicament.
6. **curt** [kûrt]—(a) extremely polite. (b) abrupt or brusque. (c) persuasive. (d) coy.
7. **cult** [kult]—(a) to sort or select. (b) a system of zealous devotion to a person or object. (c) to refine. (d) the elite.
8. **staid** [stād]—(a) theatrical. (b) a wide variety. (c) dull. (d) sedate.
9. **crux** [kruks]—(a) the ending. (b) a fork in the road. (c) the pivotal or critical point. (d) a heavy load.
10. **gloss** [glôs]—(a) to give plausible explanations to cover a fault. (b) to act foolishly. (c) to explain thoroughly. (d) to ignore.
11. **flex** [fleks]—(a) to bend, as the arm. (b) to shake. (c) to gather up one's strength. (d) to free from bondage.
12. **waft** [waft]—(a) to relinquish. (b) to sing softly. (c) to wade. (d) to convey by floating, as in air or water.
13. **pent** [pent]—(a) uncooperative. (b) confined; penned up or in. (c) awaiting trial. (d) awaiting approval.
14. **crop** [krop]—(a) to cut or eat off the stems, as of grass. (b) to default. (c) to disappear. (d) to destroy.

ANSWERS:

1. **feat**—(a) an act of unusual skill or courage. 2. **rift**—(c) a split or cleft. 3. **filch**—(d) to steal small amounts slyly. 4. **harp**—(c) to dwell on a subject tediously. 5. **trice**—(a) an instant or moment. 6. **curt**—(b) abrupt or brusque. 7. **cult**—(b) a system of zealous devotion to a person or object. 8. **staid**—(d) sedate. 9. **crux**—(c) the pivotal or critical point. 10. **gloss**—(a) to give plausible explanations to cover a fault. 11. **flex**—(a) to bend, as the arm. 12. **waft**—(d) to convey by floating, as in air or water. 13. **pent**—(b) confined; penned up or in. 14. **crop**—(a) to cut or eat off the stems, as of grass.

8 THE DASH

The dash(—)is both a true punctuation mark and a mark used to indicate an omission of letters or words from a sentence. Since we're learning about the dash in this chapter, we'll take up all its uses.

(1) Use a dash to represent the omission of a word or part of a word, as all or part of a person's name to avoid identifying him, or all or some of the letters of a word that you'd rather not spell out in full.

Mrs. S—, who is suspected of stealing, has left town.
"D—n you, you can go to—!" he shouted.

There is no rule as to which words are considered too blasphemous or obscene to spell out; it depends on your own feelings and on who might read what you write. Modern writers and readers have lost much of their squeamishness about words. Thus, this use of the dash is decreasing.

Similarly, it used to be quite common for the members of certain denominations to avoid spelling out the word *God* by substituting a dash for the letter *o*. This custom stemmed from the belief that the word was too sacred to be written out in anything but a religious work. Here, too, however, modern writers no longer use the dash.

(2) Use a dash between numbers or words to mean "to," "until," or "through," indicating inclusion of all the intervening time, numbers, distances, etc.

Benjamin Franklin (1706–90) was a great American.
Visiting hours are 2:30 P.M.–4 P.M.
For tonight's homework, read chapters 20–25.

There is a danger in this last sentence: Does it mean *from* 20 or *including* 20? *to* 25 or *through* 25? Because the answer is not entirely clear, it is often best to avoid the dash and to write out such words as *to, through, inclusive,* etc.

NOTE: The dashes in the above three examples are only half as long as the others in this chapter. Nonetheless, they are dashes and should not be confused with *hyphens*. (For the use of the hyphen, see page 433.) When you type, you indicate the longer form of the dash by typing two short dashes side by side (--). The short dash (-) and the hyphen do, of course, look somewhat alike.

(3) Use a dash to set off a word or group of words introduced unexpectedly into a sentence, especially a word or phrase that is not structurally related to the rest of the sentence.

That looks like smoke coming from the—help! Fire!
Jerry has a clever idea here—but read his report yourself.
Mountain air is good for you—if, that is, you have strong lungs.

Note that in the first two examples, the dash indicates an abrupt breaking off of one thought and the beginning of another. In the third, there is an added, unexpected thought; the importance of this added thought is emphasized by the use of the dash.

When we see Ann—here she comes now—act as if nothing had happened.
If you like pot roast—you do, don't you?—you'll love this recipe.

Note that in each of these examples a dash is used both before and after an interruption of the normal flow of words; the two dashes set off a thought that only temporarily interrupts the sentence. Note, too, that a question mark may be used before the closing dash to punctuate the interruption. This is equally true of an exclamation point. But a period is never used after declarative interruptions.

(4) Use a dash to separate two identical or almost identical words or expressions when you want to use repetition or to sum something up.

I can do the job—the job you want done.
Lincoln and Wilson—these men were his idols.

These sentences could have been written *I can do the job you want done* and *Lincoln and Wilson were his idols.* But they would have lost the extra force gained through the use of the dash (a pause) followed by repetition or a summing up.

The roar of the surf, the shouts of small children, a woman's laughter—these are the sounds I like best.

(5) Use a dash before a specific list or example that explains in detail some word or phrase in the first part of a sentence.

Two members of the committee called on me—specifically, Gorman and Lewis.
Bring some warm clothes—among other things a sweater and wool socks.

Either a colon or a semicolon could be used in place of the dash in both these sentences. But the recent trend in informal writing is toward the dash in such cases. A colon might be better, perhaps, in a very formal sentence (*This nation finds comfort and support in two great principles: liberty and justice for all*). The semicolon is less formal than the colon, but somewhat more formal than the dash (*After careful deliberation, he decided to plant only perennials; for example, peonies, asters, and delphiniums*). You will not go wrong if you use the punctuation mark that seems most appropriate to you for the type of sentence you are writing.

NOTE: Be careful not to overdo your use of dashes. A mark of the inexperienced, hurried writer is the use of dashes to replace almost all punctuation. We've all read breathless, disorganized writing of this sort:

> *Dear Joe—*
>
> *Just a note—I know I owe you a letter—to say I'll be in Chicago next week—probably Thursday or Friday. Can you meet me at the station—or are you too busy?*

Dash it all, don't dash it all! Write words and sentences and use proper punctuation. The dash is a splendid punctuation mark—but only when it is used properly.

9 QUOTATION MARKS AND ITALICS

There are double quotations marks (" ") and single quotation marks ("). Note that each kind is always used in pairs. Double quotation marks are by far the most frequently used.

Double Quotation Marks

(1) Use double quotation marks to set off a direct quotation—that is, the exact words of a speaker or writer—whether or not your own explanatory words intervene.

421

> *"Mary gave me a bowling ball for Christmas," Ed said.*
> *"Next year," the sales manager continued, "we'll do better."*
> *He finally admitted, "Dan's not such a bad worker."*
> *He wrote "300 red chairs" on his order, and that's what he wants.*

EXCEPTIONS: Long quotations, as from a speech, report, or book, are often typed or printed in a different way: Instead of being set off by quotation marks, they are indented and printed in smaller type. (In typing, you would indent each typed line of the quoted material and indicate the smaller type by single-spacing.) If you prefer to use quotation marks, however, remember that for a quotation that runs into several paragraphs of prose, the marks are placed at the *beginning* of each paragraph and at the end of only the *final* paragraph.

> *Constitutional Amendments VIII and IX read as follows:*

> Excessive bail shall not be required, nor excessive fines imposed, nor cruel and unusual punishments inflicted.
> The enumeration in the Constitution, of certain rights, shall not be construed to deny or disparage others retained by the people.

NOTE: When conversation is quoted, each speaker is given a paragraph of his own, no matter how little he says.

> *"John," Peter called, "do you remember where you put the fishing rods?"*
> *"In the garage, I think," John answered. He entered the room from the kitchen, stretching lazily. "Or maybe it was in the attic." He yawned, then sank into a chair. "Or was it the basement?"*
> *"Well, try to remember," Peter insisted.*
> *"I am trying."*

Notice that descriptive material and additional remarks by the same speaker are included in the same paragraph. But the paragraph changes when the speaker changes.

(2) Use double quotation marks to set off the title of a short or subordinate work, as a book chapter, a newspaper or magazine article, a report, a short story or short poem, a song, a one-act play, and so on. The quotation marks indicate the title of a short work or of part of a longer work or collection. The name of an entire book or other long work and of a newspaper or magazine is generally italicized. (To italicize in typing or writing by hand, you simply underline.)

Read Chapter 2, "Early Childhood," of Thompson's *My Life and Times.*
You should read the editorials in the daily *Globe.*
They sang the song "Oklahoma!" from the musical *Oklahoma!*
I have read Hemingway's short story "The Killers" and his novel *The Old Man and the Sea.*

NOTE: Certain other titles, such as the names of art works or of ships and planes, are usually italicized.

Rembrandt's *Night Watch*
Lindbergh's plane, *The Spirit of St. Louis*

EXCEPTIONS: The Bible and the names of its books, sections, and verses are never put in italics or quotation marks.

John 3:16   the Old Testament   the Apocrypha

(3) Use double quotation marks to set off any word or group of words that you are using in a special way, and to which you want to call attention. There are four classes of terms that can be pointed out in this manner:

(a) Out-of-date or slang expressions, jargon, made-up words, or unusual word combinations. (But use such quotation marks sparingly! They tend to seem affected.)

That restaurant you took us to was "groovy."
I have a cold now—or, more expressly, a "slight catarrh."

(b) Mottoes, clichés, and popular sayings.

Do you believe that "love conquers all"?
I still think we should fight "to make the world safe for democracy."

(c) Nicknames, epithets, or other designations that represent true names or personified objects. (But remember that familiar or common nicknames—such as *Jack* or *Bill* or *Honest Abe* or *Stonewall Jackson*—are *not* set off by quotation marks.)

Robert Johnson—"Big Bob" to his friends—now heads the firm.
Throughout the Southwest he was known as "The Purple Avenger."

NOTE: When a word (or phrase) is pointed out *as* a word, whether it is defined or simply mentioned, it should be written in italics rather than placed within quotation marks.

Your opening paragraph is cluttered with *I believe*'s and *in my opinion*'s.
Bottle has two syllables.

Here the meaning of the italicized words is of no importance; they are quoted simply as words.

A *soft drink* may be defined as a drink that contains no alcohol.

Here the term *soft drink* is being defined, although its meaning is not being used.

Single Quotation Marks

Use single quotation marks to set off a quotation within a quotation.

> *General Granger said, "Remember the words of Colonel Prescott at Bunker Hill: 'Don't fire until you see the whites of their eyes.'"*

This sentence quotes General Granger, who, in turn, is quoting someone else. Note that in this example both quotations end at the same place; so both a single and double closing quotation mark must be used.

> *He reported that "most Englishmen like us 'Yanks.'"*
> *The chairman of the board announced: "Robert Johnson—'Big Bob' to his friends—has been made president of the firm."*

Usage Notes on Quotation Marks

(1) Capitalization: If quoted material begins with a capital letter (because it begins a sentence in the original, or because it is a name or title), keep the capital letter in your quotation.

> *The winning essay was called "How I Overcame Insomnia."*

(2) Punctuation: To separate a quoted remark from the part of the sentence that introduces it, use a comma or—somewhat more formally —a colon.

> *He said, "I'll be glad to vote for you."*
> *The report ends: "We conclude that life cannot exist on Mars."*

When either a comma or a period is needed at the end of a quotation or of any quoted matter, such as a title, the comma or period is *always* placed inside the closing quotation marks.

424

"Next year," said Ed, "we'll do even better."
This statement concludes the report "Is There Life on Mars?": "We
believe that life as we know it cannot exist on Mars."
She said, "I remember that you asked whether my fudge was really
'fudgy.'"

The above examples all illustrate the most important fact about punctuation as it applies to quotation marks: Without exception, commas and periods go inside the closing quotation marks, even when there are single as well as double quotes, or when the comma or period logically applies to the whole sentence rather than to the quoted matter—in other words, always. This is a nice, easy American rule. We're luckier than the British; their rule is more complicated.

But, as the above examples also help to show, our rule for the placement of semicolons, colons, question marks, and exclamation points is the same as the British rule: These punctuation marks are placed inside the closing quotation marks if they belong to the quotation, but outside the quotation marks if they belong to the sentence proper.

Do you believe that "love conquers all"?
Spare us your "sympathy"!
She asked, "Does love conquer all?"
Joe said, "I have the answer"; Jim said, "I'll have it soon"; Bill
said, "I never will!"

Note that no final period is required for the last two sentences above, even though they are declarative statements. The end of the sentence is adequately signaled by the closing quotation marks.

10 PARENTHESES AND BRACKETS

Parentheses, like quotation marks, come in pairs. The beginning or opening parenthesis [(] is placed before the first word of the material to be enclosed, and the ending or closing parenthesis [)] is put after the last enclosed word.

Parentheses are one of three principal ways to separate material in a sentence from the surrounding material: Paired commas make the least separation; paired dashes make a more forceful separation; and parentheses make the greatest separation in thought. They are also useful for separating an extra sentence or two of added, but not entirely essential, comment from the rest of a passage, so that the flow of the central idea is not interrupted.

(1) Use parentheses to set off nonessential—"parenthetical"—material or remarks that explain, question, illustrate, or comment upon the main idea. A parenthetical remark is a remark that is literally "thrown in," often as a helpful aside to the reader.

> *She met her uncle (her mother's brother) at the station.*
> *Eat a green vegetable (spinach, beans, peas, or the like) every day.*
> *You are to call Mr. Olafszyski (spelling?).*
> *The meeting will start at 10 (please be on time!) and end at noon.*

(2) Use parentheses to set off numbers and letters in an outline or list.

> *The company has four main divisions: (1) Research and Development, (2) Production, (3) Sales, (4) Advertising and Promotion.*

USAGE NOTE: When you punctuate a sentence containing parentheses, place commas, semicolons, colons, etc., between the same words or the same parts of the sentence as you would do if there were no parentheses. Remember, however, that the punctuation marks are normally placed after, not before, the parenthesized material.

> *If you like to bake, here is a good recipe.*
> *If you like to bake (I hate to), here is a good recipe.*

EXCEPTION: When parentheses are used simply for setting off numbers or letters in a list, the commas are placed before the parenthesized numbers or letters.

> *He had three interests in life: (a) work, (b) golf, and (c) his son's career.*

If commas, semicolons, colons, etc., are needed within the parentheses, use them.

> *Pick an object from one category (animal, vegetable, or mineral).*

If the parenthetical remark within a sentence is a question or exclamation, put a question mark or exclamation point inside the closing parenthesis. But if the parenthetical remark within a sentence is itself a sentence, do not use a period within the parentheses.

You received a call from Mr. Smith (Smythe?).
The sales meeting will start at noon (we trust that it will begin on time) and end at 4.
That man (I hate the sight of him!) has gone.

Brackets [], which are also used in pairs, are actually squared-off parentheses. They furnish still another way to set off material within a sentence.

(1) Use brackets to enclose parenthetical material that is already within parentheses:

The low-lying region of the eastern United States, the Piedmont (literally, "lying at the foot of mountains" [in this case the Appalachian Range]), extends from New Jersey to Alabama.

(2) Use brackets to enclose explanatory material inserted into a quotation by someone other than the original author:

He told me that his boss said, "You'd better report your symptoms [fatigue and rapid loss of weight] to Dr. Samuels right away."

(3) Use brackets to correct an error in an edited sentence:

July 15 [14], Bastille Day, is a national holiday in France.

As you have no doubt noticed, brackets are used throughout this book and in many dictionaries to set off word pronunciations: **ad·mi·ra·tion** [ad′mə·rā′shən].

---

11 THE APOSTROPHE

The apostrophe (') and the hyphen (-) (which is the next subject discussed) differ from pure punctuation marks in that they do not indicate major divisions of your writing or help to organize your thoughts on paper. These two symbols are often part of a word itself, just as much a part as are any of the word's letters. Sometimes the apostrophe and the hyphen serve to distinguish completely different words, such as *can't* and *cant, we'll* and *well, it's* and *its, girls* and *girl's, old-fashioned* (out-of-date) and *old fashioned* (a cocktail). In such cases, using an apostrophe or hyphen in the wrong place, or leaving one out when it is needed, might just as reasonably be considered a spelling or usage mistake as a punctuation error.

The apostrophe is used in four basic ways:

(1) Use the apostrophe to take the place of an omitted letter or letters when writing a shortened form of a word or phrase. Shortened forms of words or of two-word combinations are called *contractions*.

(a) One-word combinations representing a pronoun (*I, you, he, she, it, they*) joined to a common verb form (such as *am, are, have,* etc.).

I'd	he's
you'll	we've

Here's (here is) and *there's* (there is) are formed in the same way, by adding *here* and *there* to the verb *is*.

(b) One-word combinations representing a common verb form (such as *is, are, could, did,* etc.) joined to *not*.

aren't	doesn't
couldn't	won't

(c) Other standard, familiar, or accepted shortened forms. For example:

o'clock	o(*f the*) clock
'tis	(i)t is

In spelling a contraction, an apostrophe is as important as a letter. Without an apostrophe, *she'll* would be *shell, we'll* would be *well,* and *he'll* would be worse! Every contraction must have an apostrophe—at least until such time as the contraction becomes an accepted full form in its own right, as *plane* for *airplane, phone* for *telephone,* or *cello* for *violoncello.*

> *It's ten o'clock.* (it is)
> *Its tires need air.* (the possessive form of *it*)
> *They're late for work.* (they are)
> *Their house is big.* (the possessive form of *they*)

If you have trouble with such pairs of words—words with similar spellings or sounds—be sure to study the part of this book entitled "Using Your Word Power."

(2) Use the apostrophe to take the place of an omitted figure or figures when writing a shortened form of a number, as a date.

> the class of '88 (1988)
> the flappers of the '20s (1920's)
> the spirit of '76 (1776)

(3) Use the apostrophe to show possession in nouns.

(a) To form the possessive case of a noun that does not end in *s* (or in an *s* or *z* sound), use the apostrophe with *s* (*'s*). This rule applies to all types of nouns, singular and plural.

> Joe's country
> the man's job
> the men's jobs
> Chicago's weather
> Madeline's new coat

(b) To form the possessive case of a plural noun that already ends in *s*, add only an apostrophe (*'*).

> the Joneses' house (two or more people named Jones)
> the bosses' cars (several bosses)
> boys' games (all boys)

(c) To form the possessive case of a singular noun that ends in *s* (or in an *s* or *z* sound), use the apostrophe with *s* (*'s*) if the noun has only one syllable, to show that an extra *s* sound [əz] is pronounced.

> the boss's car   the mouse's cheese
> Jones's job   Yeats's poetry
> the house's value   Marx's teachings

But use the apostrophe alone if the noun has more than one syllable, unless you prefer to think of the extra *s* or *z* sound [əz] as being pronounced.

> Socrates' wisdom   Rodriguez' car
> Moses' people   Thomas's (*or* Thomas') hat
> for goodness' sake   Dickens's (*or* Dickens') works

USAGE NOTES: In cases where more than one possessive word is involved, you may still wonder where to put the apostrophe or the apostrophe and *s*. Here are some helpful hints:

When adding a possessive ending to a compound, add it to the part that is closest to the thing possessed.

his mother-in-law's car
Senator Jones of Texas' speech

When joint possession of something is involved, you may add the possessive ending to the last noun only.

Jack and Jill's pail
a dogs and cats' shelter

When separate possession is involved, add the possessive ending to each noun separately.

Jack's and Jill's injuries (Each one has different injuries.)
England's or France's museums (Each country has its own museums.)

Sometimes a double possessive is acceptable—that is, the preposition *of* plus a possessive ending.

a friend of my brother's
a letter of Carol's

EXCEPTIONS: The apostrophe is often used in certain cases where true possession is not involved but where custom calls for a possessive form.

In certain familiar expressions:
a month's pay
a week's vacation
an hour's drive

With nouns ending in -ing (such as *working, playing, doing, seeing, acting, thinking,* etc.):

Roger's traveling is part of his job. (*not* Roger traveling)
I don't approve of your going. (*not* you going)

REMEMBER: Never use an apostrophe with personal pronouns that are already in the possessive case, such as *his, hers, yours, ours, theirs, its,* and *whose.*

Whose hat is this?
It's hers. It isn't Mary's or yours.
Who's to blame? (a contraction)
The man whose dog barked is a neighbor. (a possessive)

(4) The apostrophe is often used with *s* (*'s*) to form the plural of a figure, a letter, an abbreviation, or a word that is referred to as a word.

Two 12's are 24.
She's at least in her 40's.
He was born in the early '50's. (Here, the first apostrophe indicates the omission of the century numerals. The second apostrophe forms the plural of a figure.)
There are no if's, and's, *or* but's *about it.*
During the blizzard the temperature remained in the 20's.
Do all the instructors have Ph.D.'s?
There are many maybe's *in our vacation plans.*

Punctuation Test—The Apostrophe

1. When (it's, its) eight o'clock, give the dog (it's, its) food.
2. The (Kimberley's, Kimberleys') old car can reach a top speed in the (50s, 50's, 50s').
3. The Ten Commandments are sometimes called (Mose's, Moses', Moses's) laws.
4. The (womens, women's, womens') yoga class will meet at 8 (o'clock. oclock).
5. Write your (s'es, s's, ss') bigger.
6. Yes, (their, there, they're) pleased with (their, there, they're) new house.
7. (Here's, Heres', Hears) to you. Good luck!
8. (There's, Theres, Theirs, Theirs') room for two (2s, 2's, 2s') at a table for 4.
9. Now (you're, your) late for (you're, your) lesson.
10. I like (San Diego's, San Diegos', San Diegoe's, San Diegoes') climate.
11. Three (7s, 7's) equal 21.
12. (Its, It's) true that the dog lost (it's, its) collar.

ANSWERS:

1. it's, its. 2. Kimberleys', 50's. 3. Moses'. 4. women's, o'clock. 5. s's 6. they're, their. 7. Here's. 8. There's, 2's. 9. you're, your. 10. San Diego's. 11. 7's. 12. It's, its.

REVIEW OF PREFIX PRE-

How well do you remember the words beginning with the prefix *pre-* that were taught in the vocabulary-building part of this book? The test below will help you to review the *pre-* words. Check the word or phrase you believe is closest in meaning to the key word. Answers follow.

1. **prerogative** [pri·rog′ə·tiv]—(a) superior power. (b) special privilege. (c) questionable procedure. (d) higher rank.
2. **preempt** [prē·empt′]—(a) to appropriate. (b) to order bluntly. (c) to contradict. (d) to obstruct or block.
3. **predilection** [prē′də·lek′shən]—(a) a preference or predisposition. (b) an extemporaneous speech. (c) a great liking for someone. (d) a slate of candidates for office.
4. **precursor** [pri·kûr′sər]—(a) an attacker. (b) a pursuer. (c) a forerunner. (d) a fugitive.
5. **preferential** [pref′ə·ren′shəl]—(a) favored. (b) of little value. (c) discriminated against. (d) humble.
6. **presentiment** [pri·zen′tə·mənt]—(a) a gift. (b) a premonition. (c) tender sensibility. (d) strangeness.
7. **prevail** [pri·vāl′]—(a) to overthrow. (b) to adhere to. (c) to

be widespread or common. (d) to prevent.
8. **presumptive** [pri·zump′tiv]—(a) affording reasonable grounds for belief. (b) seeking admiration. (c) taking undue liberties. (d) garish.
9. **predictive** [pri·dik′tiv]—(a) commanding. (b) vengeful. (c) pertaining to a grammatical term. (d) foreshadowing the future.
10. **preamble** [prē′am·bəl]—(a) an introductory statement. (b) a constitutional amendment. (c) a short walk. (d) a winding lane.
11. **prefatory** [pref′ə·tôr′ē]—(a) the front of a cathedral. (b) introductory. (c) something more desirable. (d) high esteem.
12. **presumptuous** [pri·zump′chōo·əs]—(a) offensively bold. (b) giving reasonable ground for belief. (c) insincere. (d) luxurious.
13. **presage** [pri·sāj′]—(a) to predict. (b) to guess. (c) to terrify. (d) to brag.

ANSWERS:

1. **prerogative**—(b) special privilege. 2. **preempt**—(a) to appropriate. 3. **predilection**—(a) a preference or predisposition. 4. **precursor**—(c) a forerunner. 5. **preferential**—(a) favored. 6. **presentiment**—(b) a premonition. 7. **prevail**—(c) to be widespread or common. 8. **presumptive**—(a) affording reasonable grounds for belief. 9. **predictive**—(d) foreshadowing the future. 10. **preamble**—(a) an introductory statement. 11. **prefatory**—(b) introductory. 12. **presumptuous**—(a) offensively bold. 13. **presage**—(a) to predict.

12 THE HYPHEN

The hyphen (-) may serve to join several words into one whole word or to divide a single word into separate parts. It is used to connect the parts of certain compound words and phrases, and to show word divisions at the end of a line of type or writing.

If you look for total logic in hyphenation, you are doomed to disappointment. Rules for hyphenation can seem complicated and confusing, but the basic guidelines discussed in this chapter, together with your dictionary, will serve to keep you on the right track.

The Hyphen and Compound Words

A hyphen may be used to join the parts of certain compound words. Some compound words are normally written as two separate words; some are usually joined with hyphens; and some are written "solid" as one word. Many a solid compound was originally written as two words. Then, as the combination grew more common, writers began to recognize it as a unit and to hyphenate it. Finally, the hyphen was dropped, and the two words became one. This happened with *gentleman, bloodthirsty, dressmaker,* and *loudspeaker,* to name but a few.

It is still happening as the language changes and grows. Only a few years ago, *teen-ager* used to be written *teen ager;* now it is generally written *teenager*.

How do you know which words to hyphenate? How do you know whether a term is still written as two words, as a hyphenated compound, or as a solid word? The only way to feel secure is to use an up-to-date dictionary.

Often hyphenation is logical, but sometimes it is not. For example, only your dictionary can tell you that *pre-shrunk* is preferably hyphenated and *preconceived* is never hyphenated; that *snow cloud* is commonly written as two words, *snow-blind* is usually hyphenated, and *snowflake* is always written solid; *stronghearted* is always one word but *strong-armed* is preferably hyphenated. When in doubt, therefore, use your dictionary. But remember that even dictionaries do not always agree on questions of hyphenation. This is an area in which American usage changes very rapidly. So don't be shocked if you pick up a good book and find the words *preshrunk, snowblind,* and *strongarmed* without their prescribed hyphens.

Here are some familiar compound words that are regularly written with hyphens:

a free-for-all	a sit-in
a passer-by	a has-been
a go-between	out-of-date
a know-it-all	first-rate
make-believe	court-martial
to second-guess	know-how

There are a few dependable guides for hyphenating certain types of compound words—guides that can help you to avoid unnecessary trips to the dictionary. Learn these guides and you will save yourself much time and trouble.

(1) Use a hyphen to join written compound numbers from twenty-one to ninety-nine.

forty-eight	eighty-fifth

(2) Use a hyphen to join the two parts of a written fraction.

three-fourths	twenty-five forty-thirds

(3) Use a hyphen to join a number to a noun, a letter to a noun, or a number to a letter in a compound.

a six-cylinder car	an X-ray machine
a 50-foot span	an A-bomb
BU8-8598	a U-turn
a two-base hit	

(4) Use a hyphen to join the words *great* and *in-law* to nouns expressing family relationships.

mother-in-law	son-in-law
stepdaughter-in-law	great-grandson

Note that we do not hyphenate compound words expressing *grand* or *step* family relationships, such as *grandmother, grandson, stepmother.*

(5) Use a hyphen to join the prefixes *ex-* and *self-* or the suffix *-elect* to another word in a compound.

an ex-president	self-reliance
the president-elect	self-employed
his ex-wife	a self-addressed envelope

There are a few exceptions, such as *selfhood, selfless,* and *selfsame.* But almost all the *self-* words are hyphenated: *self-help, self-respect, self-sacrifice,* etc.

(6) Use a hyphen to join together two or more words that combine into a compound adjective. This holds true whether the adjective is a made-up compound (as in *a never-to-be-forgotten day*) or a regularly hyphenated word (as in *a narrow-minded man*).

out-of-town guests
a grin-and-bear-it attitude
a chauffeur-driven limousine

a broad-minded judge
German-American cooking
well-aimed shots

But the hyphen is omitted when an adjective which is made up of *well* combined with another word follows the verb instead of preceding the word it modifies.

What a well-bred child he is!
Yes, he is well bred.
Sandy is a well-dressed girl.
She's always well dressed.

There is a good reason for hyphenating compound adjectives: Without the hyphen there is often a possibility of misunderstanding. For example, the *deep blue sea* can mean either a sea that is both deep and blue or a sea whose color is deep blue. If you mean that the color is deep blue, you make that meaning clear by writing *the deep-blue sea.* But do not hyphenate combinations of an adjective and an adverb ending in *-ly: a happily married couple; a highly successful policy.* Here there is no chance of confusion.

(7) Use a hyphen to connect a compound that is a single unit of measurement.

kilowatt-hour   foot-pound   light-year

(8) Use a hyphen to connect the elements of certain compound titles.

ambassador-at-large   owner-manager   secretary-treasurer

(9) Use a hyphen to separate a prefix from a word that starts with a capital letter.

pro-American
a trans-Canadian highway

a very un-British thing to do
mid-Atlantic

(10) In general, use a hyphen to keep two *i*'s or two *o*'s from coming together when one of them ends a prefix and the other starts a root word.

anti-intellectual	co-occupy
semi-independent	co-owner

In the recent past, the hyphen was commonly used to keep two *e*'s from coming together. Not too long ago, such words as *reentry, reenact, reevaluate, reexamine,* and *preeminent* were spelled with hyphens, the prefixes *re-* and *pre-* being separated from the root words starting with *e.* Although some people still hyphenate such words, modern usage favors the solid form. A hyphen is still generally used, however, with the prefix *de-,* as in *de-emphasize* and *de-escalate.*

Even the rule that two *o*'s should be separated by a hyphen has been greatly modified in recent years. We still hyphenate *co-occupy, co-owner,* and many others; but certain *o-o* words are now preferred in solid form—for instance, *cooperation, coordinate,* and *microorganism.*

(11) Use a hyphen to keep three identical consonants from coming together in compound words.

cross-stitch	shell-like	bell-like	hull-less

(12) Use a hyphen to distinguish a compound from a solid word with a different meaning.

Please re-sign this bill. (Here, the hyphen is necessary to distinguish *re-sign*—to sign again— from *resign*—to give up a job.)

We will re-cover the chair. (Without the hyphen, *re-cover*—to cover again—would look like *recover*—to get well or get something back.)

(13) Use a hyphen to show word division at the end of a line of type or writing. In this instance, the hyphen follows that portion of an incomplete word that ends a line, showing the reader that the word is continued on the next line.

When writing, you may often be faced with the question: "Where can I break a word at the end of a line?" Here is the rule: You can break a word only between syllables. You may not break a one-syllable word at all, no matter how long it is. If you are not certain of the number or correct division of syllables in a word, consult your dictionary. In most dictionaries, each boldface entry word is printed with its syllables separated in some manner—often by dots, like this: **tick·et, fla·vor·ful, Mis·sis·sip·pi.** The dots show you the only points where you may break the word at the end of a line.

Punctuation Test—The Hyphen

In the paragraphs below, combine words or word parts into single, solid words or into hyphenated words when advisable. Recommended hyphenation follows.

Last summer, my sister in law and I took a fly now, pay later, 21 day excursion to our dream city, Paris. Paris was a never to be forgotten, once in a life time experience. We visited the birth place of my great grand mother, bought honest to goodness French wine at ninety five cents a bottle, and ate snails, frog's legs, and a shell like pastry the name of which I can't remember.

I learned some schoolgirl French and can now mispronounce the "Marseillaise"! I sang this national anthem of France for the first time under the Eiffel Tower, to the accompaniment of a one man band. What a self satisfied musician he was!

As we re entered the United States, both my sister in law and I were happy to be home again. However, we vowed to put on our seven league boots and cross the ocean again next year.

ANSWER:

Last summer, my sister-in-law and I took a fly-now, pay-later, 21-day excursion to our dream city, Paris. Paris was a never-to-be-forgotten, once-in-a-lifetime experience. We visited the birthplace of my great-grandmother, bought honest-to-goodness French wine at ninety-five cents a bottle, and ate snails, frog's legs, and a shell-like pastry the name of which I can't remember.

I learned some schoolgirl French and can now mispronounce the "Marseillaise"! I sang this national anthem of France for the first time under the Eiffel Tower, to the accompaniment of a one-man band. What a self-satisfied musician he was!

As we reentered the United States, both my sister-in-law and I were happy to be home again. However, we vowed to put on our seven-league boots and cross the ocean again next year.

A Hard Final Examination on Punctuation

Now that you have completed your study of punctuation, test your punctuation power. Before you begin, you may want to make a quick review of the rules for beginning punctuation (capitalization), end punctuation (the period, question mark, and exclamation point), and internal punctuation (the comma, colon, semicolon, dash, quotation marks, italics, parentheses, apostrophe, and hyphen). If you have studied these punctuation marks, see how high a mark you can make on punctuation! Supply the missing punctuation in the following sentences. Recommended answers follow.

1. the ingredients are as follows eggs celery bread crumbs and parsley
2. tell me i said where will you go from here
3. its about to explode run for your lives
4. the manager was impatient for the new branch office to open but the lobby was not yet ready
5. riding through the peaceful shenandoah valley who i ask could imagine that once cannon roared here and many men died in a single afternoon
6. hes a boor i wont say an out and out liar and i dont know what sally sees in him
7. jerry and i can go now cant we
8. courage patience and hope of these was his resolution compounded
9. youll never learn i guess
10. the games at 830 mary asked
11. jack called harry fatso said bill and thats how the fight started
12. stop the grocer yelled but the man ran out with an armful of canned goods and got away in broad daylight mind you
13. please send a telegram to mr t w brewster pittsburgh pa asking if he can speak at our sales conference and if so on which day
14. on may 6 1970 against the fortune tellers advice she embarked on a long hazardous journey
15. alan bowled 110 george 156 and henry 161
16. captain morton the company commander and major criswell are both west pointers arent they

17. the smiths who had the bungalow next door were related to the smiths who rented the cabin near the creek

18. please send me my red dress in the large closet eddys zippered jacket behind his door and dicks copy of robinson crusoe on his desk

19. dont forget to bring your tennis racket your tennis shoes you forgot them last time and but you know what else youll need here

20. wheres the fire i shouted but the boy kept running

21. according to a book review the presidents girl takes place in 1881 just after the inauguration of americas first bachelor president but the reviewer and perhaps the novel which i havent read is wrong president james buchanan also was a bachelor

22. he may have a soft as silk voice but those muscles

23. dr greenspan when if you had to make a guess would you anticipate a landing on jupiter

24. mary id like you to meet my sister mrs larson

25. the introductions over the girls and the boys retreated to opposite ends of the gymnasium the dance was off to a slow start to put it mildly

26. a philanthropist my nephews not

27. i cant believe that tom asked that joe said knowing how devilishly frighteningly well informed he is but you insist he did eh

28. you say you resent the letter when it came back with postage due

29. shall we go by bus by train by helicopter

30. the antiicer wasnt working and the windshield was freezing up fast

ANSWERS:

1. The ingredients are as follows: eggs, celery, bread crumbs, and parsley.
2. "Tell me," I said, "where will you go from here?"
3. It's about to explode! Run for your lives!
4. The manager was impatient for the new branch office to open, but the lobby was not yet ready.
5. Riding through the peaceful Shenandoah Valley, who, I ask, could imagine that once cannon roared here and many men died in a single afternoon?
6. He's a boor (I won't say an out-and-out liar), and I don't know what Sally sees in him.

7. Jerry and I can go now, can't we?

8. Courage, patience, and hope—of these was his resolution compounded.

9. You'll never learn, I guess.

10. "The game's at 8:30?" Mary asked.

11. "Jack called Harry 'fatso,'" said Bill, "and that's how the fight started."

12. "Stop!" the grocer yelled, but the man ran out with an armful of canned goods and got away—in broad daylight, mind you!

13. Please send a telegram to Mr. T. W. Brewster, Pittsburgh, Pa., asking if he can speak at our sales conference and, if so, on which day.

14. On May 6, 1970, against the fortuneteller's advice, she embarked on a long, hazardous journey.

15. Alan bowled 110; George, 156; and Henry, 161.

16. Captain Morton, the company commander, and Major Criswell are both West Pointers, aren't they?

17. The Smiths who had the bungalow next door were related to the Smiths who rented the cabin near the creek.

18. Please send me my red dress (in the large closet), Eddy's zippered jacket (behind his door), and Dick's copy of *Robinson Crusoe* (on his desk).

19. Don't forget to bring your tennis racket; your tennis shoes (you forgot them last time); and—but you know what else you'll need here.

20. "Where's the fire?" I shouted, but the boy just kept running.

21. According to a book review, *The President's Girl* takes place in 1881, just after the inauguration of America's first bachelor President. But the reviewer (and perhaps the novel, which I haven't read) is wrong: President James Buchanan also was a bachelor.

22. He may have a soft-as-silk voice, but those muscles!

23. Dr. Greenspan, when, if you had to make a guess, would you anticipate a landing on Jupiter?

24. Mary, I'd like you to meet my sister, Mrs. Larson.

25. The introductions over, the girls and boys retreated to opposite ends of the gymnasium; the dance was off to a slow start, to put it mildly.

26. A philanthropist my nephew's not.

27. "I can't believe that Tom asked that," Joe said, "knowing how devilishly, frighteningly well-informed he is, but you insist he did, eh?"

28. You say you re-sent the letter when it came back with postage due?

29. Shall we go by bus? by train? by helicopter?

30. The anti-icer wasn't working, and the windshield was freezing up fast.

PART FIVE

Practical Grammar

PUTTING GRAMMAR TO WORK

If your native tongue is English, you can be certain that you obey the basic rules of English grammar even if you do not know them. Can you imagine yourself saying "I the woman take the saw boy house his from"? Of course not. It makes no grammatical sense; the words do not relate to one another so as to communicate a clear thought. Put the same words together differently—"I saw the woman take the boy from his house"—and you have turned nonsense into grammatical English. Positioning of words in a sentence is the essence of English grammar.

Nobody needs to teach you how to place words in relation to one another in order to make sense. You learned that by yourself, almost miraculously, when you were a small child. What the grammar books and teachers do is this: (1) They analyze and explain how English is built, so that our comprehension of the whys and wherefores is broadened; and (2) they help us to use the language more effectively by pointing out some of its refinements—some of the ways in which we can come closer to expressing our thoughts not just adequately but precisely and attractively.

This section is called "Practical Grammar" because it concentrates mainly on the useful aspects of grammar rather than on rules or ideals. It simply deals with common mistakes—the mistakes that are most often made by careless or uninformed speakers and writers. Some of these errors are particularly serious ones, because they blur the meaning of the statement in which they occur. For example, consider this sentence: "Walter was the first to tell Bill that he had been fired." Do you see why that is bad English, even though it may look right at first? *Who* had been fired? Had Walter been fired? Or had Bill been fired? We cannot answer the question; the sentence is unclear because of a basic flaw in grammar: the writer's failure to provide the pronoun *he* with a single noun to which it directly refers.

Other errors may not necessarily result in confusion. Take, for instance, the sentence we started out with: "I saw the woman take the boy from his house." A fairly common mistake would be to substitute the word *seen* for *saw:* "I *seen* the woman take the boy . . . ." The meaning of the sentence still comes through clearly. Yet *seen* is bad grammar; the past tense of the verb *to see* is *saw,* not *seen.* More important, *seen* in this context is bad usage. No competent speaker or writer would find it acceptable. Anyone who makes such a mistake is advertising his lack of word power.

442

1 WRONG PRONOUNS

Why You Can't Say: *Between you and I, him and me did it.*

This kind of mistake is the result of using the *wrong pronouns*. *I* should be *me; him* and *me* should be *he* and *I*. Why?

Nouns, as you remember, are words that stand for things or people. *Man, books,* and *Chicago* are all nouns. Pronouns are words that stand for nouns. *He, they,* and *it* are all pronouns. And just as all nouns can act either as the subject of a sentence (the person or thing doing something) or the object of a sentence (the person or thing to which something is done), so it is with the pronouns that stand for them. "John gave the book to Mary" is a sentence that contains three nouns. If you used the proper pronouns instead, you would say, "He gave it to her."

In addition to acting as subject or object, some pronouns indicate possession. But practically no one worries about this use; it is obvious that *our* house is not *yours* and that *her* pocketbook is not *mine*.

Many people, however, confuse the subjective and objective forms of pronouns. They say "Pass the ball to John and I," or "John and me were playing football," or "Her daughter looks a lot like she," and they hope that they have used the correct pronouns.

Well, they haven't used the correct pronouns. Here's why: The subjective form of a pronoun (*I, you, he, she, it, we, they*) should always be used as the subject of a verb, and the objective form (*me, you, him, her, it, us, them*) should always be used as the object of a verb or of a preposition (*after, against, before, except, like, to, with,* etc.).

An interesting thing about the above rule is that people seldom break it when they are using just a single pronoun. They may be tempted to use the subjective case after one or two such prepositions as *except* and *like,* but they usually manage to resist the temptation. Most of the time, they know almost by instinct which pronoun to use. For instance, a glance at each of the following sentences will be enough to tell you that it is ungrammatical. Moreover, your immediate reaction—and a correct one—will be disbelief that anyone whose native language is English could speak or write this way:

> *Pass the ball to I.*
> *I'm worried about she.*
> *Me was playing football.*
> *Let's drop in on he tonight.*

Those are ridiculous sentences, are they not? Yet note that when a double pronoun or a noun plus a pronoun is substituted for the obviously ungrammatical single pronoun, the sentences no longer sound so silly.

Incorrect	Correct
Pass the ball to he and I.	*Pass the ball to him and me.*
I'm worried about her family and she.	*I'm worried about her family and her.*
John and me were playing football.	*John and I were playing football.*
Let's drop in on Mary and he tonight.	*Let's drop in on Mary and him tonight.*
The Smiths and them had fun together.	*The Smiths and they had fun together.*

For the most part, then, you do not really have to know what a preposition is, or what the difference is between the objective and the subjective case, in order to get your pronouns right. Since you are most likely to get them wrong when they come doubled up with some other pronoun or a noun, there is an easy way to test your grammar. Simply drop the second word for a moment and see how the sentence looks—or hear how it sounds—with just the single pronoun. *Pass the ball to he? Pass the ball to I?* Nonsense! Only *him* and *me* in those two sentences will satisfy your basic knowledge of grammar. Thus, the correct pronouns when combined must both still be in the objective case (*Pass the ball to him and me*).

Don't let the familiar expression *between you and I* stump you. The word *you* is the same in both the subjective and objective cases —but what about *I?* Does *between I and you* sound right? *Between I?* Of course not. The correct expression is *between you and me.*

NOTE: Correct traditional grammar prescribes the use of the subjective form for a pronoun that follows such verbs as *is, are, was,* and *were* (in other words, most forms of the verb *to be*). Teachers used to insist that their pupils say "It's *I*," or "It was *she,*" and so on. Today, however, almost everybody says "It's *me* (or *her* or *him*)," etc. And so the objective form of the pronoun after *is, are, was,* and *were* has become acceptable. This is a good illustration, however, of how constant usage (so-called "misusage," in fact) wears down the resistance of strict grammarians.

Grammar Test—I or ME? SHE or HER? HE or HIM? WE or US? THEY or THEM?

Choose the word or words from each pair in the parentheses to make a correct sentence. This test is a drill. Repeat it as many times as necessary until you can give the correct answers quickly and automatically. Answers follow.

1. This is a secret between you and (I, me).
2. Will you go shopping with Jane and (I, me)?
3. He gave the gift to my wife and (me, I).
4. What has she got against Walter and (me, I)?
5. You come next, after (I, me).
6. Please buy a book for (she and I, her and me).
7. Stand between Betty and (me, I).
8. He arrived before (me, I).
9. Everyone ate dessert except (I, me).
10. You arrived after (her, she).
11. Mrs. Lanier's daughter looks just like (she, her).
12. That's a personal matter between you and (her, she).
13. Your sister is cute, and I wish you were more like (her, she).
14. Why do you try to dress like (her, she)?
15. Everyone but Sally and (her, she) is waiting on tables.
16. Have you called all the members except (she, her)?
17. Try to talk like (him, he).
18. I gave them to you and (him, he).
19. She asked his name right in front of Bill and (he, him).
20. This should be settled between the lawyer and (we, us).
21. The bus almost left without (us, we) teachers.
22. Everyone was invited to the party but (we, us).
23. Will our children grow up to be like (we, us)?
24. The Smiths couldn't come, but everyone is here except (they, them).
25. All the neighbors but (them, they) grow roses.

ANSWERS:

1. between you and *me*. 2. with Jane and *me*. 3. to my wife and *me*. 4. against Walter and *me*. 5. after *me*. 6. for *her* and *me*. 7. between Betty and *me*. 8. before *me*. 9. except *me*. 10. after *her*. 11. like *her*. 12. between you and *her*. 13. like *her*. 14. like *her*. 15. but Sally and *her*. 16. except *her*. 17. like *him*. 18. to you and *him*. 19. in front of Bill and *him*. 20. between the lawyer and *us*. 21. without *us* teachers. 22. but *us*. 23. to be like *us*. 24. except *them*. 25. but *them*.

445

MORE -ABLE, -IBLE WORDS

Choose the word or phrase which is closest in meaning to each of the key words. As you do this vocabulary test, note the *-able* and *-ible* spellings. Answers follow.

1. **amicable** [am'i·kə·bəl]—(a) amusing. (b) easy to clean. (c) cheerful. (d) friendly.
2. **amenable** [ə·mē'nə·bəl]—(a) unpleasant. (b) capable of being persuaded. (c) praiseworthy. (d) capable of amusing.
3. **feasible** [fē'zə·bəl]—(a) afraid. (b) practicable. (c) understandable. (d) easy to do.
4. **credible** [kred'ə·bəl]—(a) meritorious. (b) bordering on the impossible. (c) financially secure. (d) believable.
5. **creditable** [kred'it·ə·bəl]—(a) financially secure. (b) meritorious. (c) bordering on the impossible. (d) guaranteed.
6. **culpable** [kul'pə·bəl]—(a) perceptible to the senses. (b) conscience-stricken. (c) slanderous. (d) blameworthy.
7. **delectable** [di·lek'tə·bəl]—(a) delightful. (b) fussy. (c) carefully selected. (d) capable of great speed.
8. **equable** [ek'wə·bəl]—(a) steady or even. (b) near the equator.

(c) capable of being compared. (d) fair or just.
9. **estimable** [es'tə·mə·bəl]—(a) careless. (b) popular. (c) worthy of high regard. (d) capable of being counted.
10. **execrable** [ek'sə·krə·bəl]—(a) painful. (b) pugnacious. (c) detestable. (d) responsive.
11. **habitable** [hab'it·ə·bəl]—(a) customary. (b) endurable. (c) well-mannered. (d) capable of being lived in.
12. **impeccable** [im·pek'ə·bəl]—(a) faultless. (b) mysterious. (c) in bad taste. (d) pure.
13. **irreparable** [i·rep'ər·ə·bəl]—(a) that cannot be repaired. (b) damaging or dangerous. (c) that cannot be forgotten. (d) deserving blame.
14. **imponderable** [im·pon'dər·ə·bəl] —(a) soft and light. (b) heavy. (c) that cannot be calculated or valued. (d) thoughtful.
15. **incomparable** [in·kom'pər·ə·bəl] —(a) irrelevant. (b) unworthy. (c) hard to understand. (d) unequaled.

ANSWERS:

1. **amicable**—(d) friendly. 2. **amenable**—(b) capable of being persuaded. 3. **feasible**—(b) practicable. 4. **credible**—(d) believable. 5. **creditable**—(b) meritorious. 6. **culpable**—(d) blameworthy. 7. **delectable**—(a) delightful. 8. **equable**—(a) steady or even. 9. **estimable**—(c) worthy of high regard. 10. **execrable**—(c) detestable. 11. **habitable**—(d) capable of being lived in. 12. **impeccable**—(a) faultless. 13. **irreparable**—(a) that cannot be repaired. 14. **imponderable**—(c) that cannot be calculated or valued. 15. **incomparable**—(d) unequaled.

446

2 SINGULAR AND PLURAL FORMS

WHY YOU CAN'T SAY: *He don't know if everybody is in their proper places.*

This is a mistake because the speaker has mixed up his singular and plural forms.

You will remember that when a singular noun or pronoun (*boy, parrot, it*) is the subject of a sentence, you must also use the singular form of the verb—the action word in the sentence. You say, "The boy *does* his homework; the parrot *flies;* it *grows* bigger." If the noun or pronoun that is the subject of the sentence is a plural (representing more than one person or thing) you must use a plural verb form: "The boys *do* their homework; the parrots *fly;* they *grow* bigger." This matching of singular nouns and pronouns with singular predicates, and plurals with plurals, is what is called "agreement in number."

There are two common errors that cause listeners or readers to wince. The first of these errors is to be found in its simplest form in the expression *he don't. Don't* is, of course, a contraction of *do not.* You would not say "He do not," would you? Then why permit yourself to say "He don't"? You will not make this mistake if you constantly remind yourself that *don't* is a plural verb and that its subject must therefore also be plural.

Wrong	Right
He don't.	*He doesn't.*
She don't.	*She doesn't.*
It don't.	*It doesn't.*

The problem of agreement of subject and predicate becomes more confusing, to be sure, when there is some doubt in your mind whether the subject of a sentence is actually singular or plural. This often happens when the singular subject is separated from its verb by several words that have a plural sound to them. For instance, which is the correct verb form in each of the following sentences?

The smell of garlic and onions (was or were) overpowering.
A touch of money and success (has or have) spoiled her.
Each of the twelve men, not to mention their wives, (is or are) going on a trip.
Everything except the cups (is or are) in the dishwasher.

447

The correct verb for the preceding sentences is the singular one (*was, has, is*). If you are not quite sure how to find the subject so as to determine its number, try saying the sentence without the words (beginning with the preposition *of* or *except*) that intervene between the first noun and the verb:

> *The smell . . . was overpowering.*
> *A touch . . . has spoiled her.*
> *Each . . . is going on a trip.*
> *Everything . . . is in the dishwasher.*

Now it becomes clear, you see, that the real subject is singular and that the verb must also be singular. Remember, too, that intervening phrases like *in addition to* and *together with* do not affect the number of the subject. Here are a few correct sample sentences using *in addition to, together with,* and similar phrases. In each sentence, note the use of the singular verb.

> *Joe, accompanied by Bill, is going fishing.*
> *Mary, along with Jane, has taken on the job.*
> *The cup, in addition to the plate, was broken.*
> *Mr. Hays, together with the whole office staff, is getting a bonus.*

Each and *Everybody* Are Singular

The second common error in the wrong-number category arises from the feeling that many people have that such nouns as *anybody, each, everybody,* and *everyone* are, or ought to be, plural. These words are not plural; each of them refers to one person or thing and should be followed by the singular pronouns *he, his, him; she, her; it, its.* The plural pronouns *them* and *their* are grammatically incorrect in the following sentences.

If anybody calls, tell them I've gone to lunch. (The correct pronoun here would be *him*, which many people still use to refer to one person of either sex.)

Each of the children memorized their telephone numbers. (The correct phrase would be *his telephone number* or *her telephone number.*)

To avoid the generic use of *he,* or the awkward *he or she,* the subject and pronouns can be made plural, or the sentence can be recast to eliminate the need for a pronoun.

If anybody calls, I've gone to lunch.

NOTE: Some nouns may be considered either singular or plural, depending on the context in which they are used. Do not waste your time and energy in worrying about which verb or pronoun to use with such collective nouns as *audience, class, committee, crew, crowd, group, jury, team,* and so on. *The audience were very attentive* is as correct as *The audience was very attentive;* and *The team did its best* is as correct as *The team did their best.* A sensible practice to follow with a collective noun is to treat it as a singular noun if you think of it as a unit, and to treat it as a plural noun if you think of it as composed of a number of individuals. Thus, for example: *The jury has done a good job,* but *The jury have all returned to their homes.*

3 WRONG PRONOUNS

WHY YOU CAN'T SAY: *If your child dislikes spinach, try boiling it in milk.*

The *pro-* in *pronoun* means "in place of." Thus, every pronoun stands in place of a noun; the meaning of a sentence with a pronoun in it is clear only when there is no doubt in the reader's mind about which noun the pronoun stands for. If you use a pronoun that might possibly refer to any one of two or more people, places, or things, you risk being misunderstood by your reader.

This is what was basically wrong with the sentence quoted on the first page of this part of the book: "Walter was the first to tell Bill that he had been fired." Because the order of the words within an English sentence is so important for getting the meaning across, competent writers usually try to place pronouns as close as possible to their antecedents. Similarly, readers tend to assume that the nearest noun preceding a pronoun is the one it refers to. If everything in sentence construction always fitted together tidily, we could take it for granted that the noun represented by *he* in the above sentence is *Bill,* and that Bill is the one who has lost his job. But, any reader may well wonder: Isn't it likely that the writer intends the *he* to refer back to *Walter* rather than to *Bill?*

For the sake of total clarity, the writer should have said "Walter was the first to tell Bill that Bill (*or* Walter) had been fired." It is much better to repeat the noun than to leave the reader in doubt.

The following sentences should also be rewritten to avoid confusion:

> *As soon as their parents bring home the Christmas trees, the children drop everything to attend to them.*
> *If your child does not like spinach, try boiling it in milk.*
> *Margaret went to visit Anne because she was lonely.*
> *Since the cats seem frightened by the dogs, I think we should get rid of them.*

Grammar Test—The Numbers Game

Choose the proper word from each pair in the parentheses below to make a correct sentence. Use this test as a drill to perfect your use of proper verb and pronoun forms. Repeat it as many times as necessary until you can give the correct answer quickly and easily. Answers follow.

1. The aim of the sales manager and his assistant (is, are) to increase sales.
2. The taste of honey, sugar, and chocolate (was, were) too sweet.
3. His job, even with good wages and short hours, (is, are) tedious.
4. The purpose of all these chapters and tests (is, are) to teach you correct grammar.
5. The output of the three clothing factories and their 800 employees (is, are) 200 suits a day.
6. This desk and typewriter, together with the chair, (belong, belongs) to me.
7. Your clothes, including your shirt, (is, are) in the closet.
8. Joe, along with his brother, (run, runs) the family business.
9. The plate, as well as the glass, (was, were) on the table.
10. The teacher and his assistant, along with the principal, (grade, grades) the final exams.
11. Each of the workers must bring (their, his) own lunch.
12. Will any member who has not done so please cast (his, their) vote now?
13. Doesn't anybody have (his, their) driver's license?
14. Every day has (its, their) problems.
15. If somebody lost a wallet, (he, they) should let me know.
16. When someone sneezes, (they, he) should cover (their, his) mouth.
17. None of the children will admit that (they, he) broke the cup.

18. None of the workers will accept the same salary (he, they) made last year.
19. Nobody is going to improve (his, their) computer skills unless (he, they) is willing to practice.
20. Everyone must bring (their, his) own bicycle.

ANSWERS:

1. The aim . . . *is.* 2. The taste . . . *was.* 3. His job . . . *is.* 4. The purpose . . . *is.* 5. The output . . . *is.* 6. This desk and typewriter . . . *belong.* 7. Your clothes . . . *are.* 8. Joe . . . *runs.* 9. The plate . . . *was.* 10. The teacher and his assistant . . . *grade.* 11. Each . . . must bring *his.* 12. Will any member . . . cast *his.* 13. Doesn't anybody have *his.* 14. Every day has *its.* 15. If somebody lost a wallet, *he.* 16. When someone sneezes, *he* . . . *his* mouth. 17. None . . . will admit that *he.* 18. None . . . will accept the same salary *he.* 19. Nobody is going to improve *his* . . . unless *he.* 20. Everyone must bring *his.*

4 MISPLACED MODIFIERS

WHY YOU CAN'T SAY: *When only four, my mother taught me to read.*

The reason is, of course, that you're not saying what you mean to say. Your mother didn't teach you to read when *she* was only four, yet that's what the statement seems to say. These sentences fall into the same trap:

> *The teacher only knows the square root of 81.*
> *The girl who had been kissed quickly left.*
> *While sitting comfortably indoors, a storm blew up.*
> *Lincoln wrote the Gettysburg Address while riding through Pennsylvania on the back of an envelope.*

Just as in our first example, it is unlikely that the teacher knows nothing except the square root of 81, that the girl left because she had been kissed quickly, that the storm was sitting indoors, or that Lincoln rode on an envelope. Yet that is how the sentences can be interpreted. In each case the misinterpretation is due to the fact that an important

451

word or group of words has been put in the wrong place, so that this important word or groups of words seems to describe (or *modify*) the wrong thing. Note how simple it is to rearrange the words, or to add a word or two, so as to resolve all doubts about meanings:

> *Only the teacher knows the square root of 81.*
> *The girl who had been kissed left quickly.*
> *While we were sitting comfortably indoors, a storm blew up.*
> *While riding through Pennsylvania, Lincoln wrote the Gettysburg Address on the back of an envelope.*

It is because the precise placement of words can make or break the meaning of a sentence that the error of misplaced modifiers is so serious. You will not be guilty of such mistakes if you remember the following facts:

(1) A word or phrase that *modifies* something in a sentence changes the meaning of the word or phrase it modifies—usually by describing it in more detail. Thus, an *only* child is not just any child; he is a child who has no brothers or sisters. The modifier must be kept as close as possible to the part of the sentence that it modifies, and it must not be placed in a position where it seems to modify some other word instead of the right one.

It is essential that you place these descriptive words—or modifiers— where they belong. To see just how much difference in meaning results from a different placement, let us look once more at that phrase *an only child*. In it, *only* clearly modifies (changes the meaning of) *child*. But suppose you shift the order of the words so that the phrase reads *only a child*. Instantly, the meaning again changes. Or try shifting the words once more: *a child only*. Here are three sentences containing those three words in the three arrangements. Note the difference in meanings.

> *An only child, having no brothers or sisters, is sometimes spoiled.*
> *Only a child, not a grown person, could enjoy such a show.*
> *In our family, a parent gives orders; a child only listens and obeys.*

Now you know why it is bad grammar to say something such as "I only see my father on Saturdays." Do you really only *see* him, not hear him or talk to him? Or do you see only your *father*, not your mother? Or do you see your father only on *Saturdays?* Unless you put the modifier in the right position, no one can be sure of your intended meaning!

Businesses have been ruined and empires lost because of misplaced, misleading modifiers.

(2) Sometimes modifiers are not merely misplaced; they dangle. A dangling modifier is one that refers to something in the writer's mind— but something that he forgets to include in the sentence. Dangling modifiers are generally groups of words that just float at the beginning of a sentence, with nothing to hang on to, as if the writer starts off to discuss one idea and ends up talking about another. This mistake can make you sound ludicrous, as you can see in the following sentences:

> *After brushing his teeth, the coffee tasted better.*
> *On his first safari, a lion was killed.*
> *When only four, my mother taught me to read.*
> *While asleep in the park, somebody stole her pocketbook.*
> *Walking across the field, a light appeared in the distance.*

Those sentences are all bad boners, because they seem to suggest that coffee brushes teeth, lions go on safaris, mothers can be only four years old, and so on. They can be corrected in a number of ways, depending on the writer's original intention. In one or two of them, as they stand, we can only guess what the writer wanted to say; but here are suggested corrected versions of all five sentences:

> *After he had brushed his teeth, the coffee tasted better.*
> *On his first safari, Peter killed a lion.*
> *When I was only four, my mother taught me to read.*
> *While she was asleep in the park, somebody stole her pocketbook.*
> *As I walked across the field, I saw a light in the distance.*

REMEMBER: When you start a sentence with a phrase that begins with such words as *after, before, on, when,* or *while,* or with a verb form ending in *-ing,* don't forget to provide this modifying phrase with something to modify. Be sure that you (1) state the true subject and (2) place the true subject correctly in order to avoid confusion.

Grammar Test—Just for Fun

Here are some humorously bad examples of misplaced and dangling modifiers. Practice correcting these sentences, each of which may be restated in any of several ways, so that you will never be tempted to say or write such bloopers. Correct the sentences to suit yourself. Just be sure your finished sentences are clear and not ridiculous. No answers are given.

1. While in the bathtub, the telephone rang.
2. After fixing the motor, the car started again.
3. While visiting in Denver, the snowstorm struck.
4. To read well, good light is needed.
5. If your shoes don't fit your feet, get a new pair.
6. When in a hurry to get to Chicago, a jet plane leaves at 9 A.M.
7. Reading the book, the cat sat in her lap.
8. Having been built in 1920, I had to remodel the house.
9. Fighting among themselves, the mothers separated the boys.
10. Waiting impatiently for the mail, the mailman finally came.
11. Walking down the path, the cabin came into view.
12. He watched the parade sitting by the television set.
13. The church was designed by J. T. Smith, whose belfry is full of bats.
14. I spoke to the man with the dog in the blue suit.
15. I heard the bird near the nest that was singing.
16. He waved to me as I left with his right hand.
17. The policeman shot the kidnaper who was fleeing with his gun.
18. The celebrity was escorted by her husband wearing a red gown.
19. Gulping down the food, mother warned us to eat slower.
20. On rereading these sentences, the answers are easy.

5 WRONG VERB FORM

WHY YOU CAN'T SAY: *She had broke it, but I said that I done it.*

This double mistake results from using the wrong forms of the verbs *to break* and *to do* in a sentence.

Every verb has three basic forms, called the "principal parts," and all the *tenses* are built up from these parts. The tenses are the specific forms of the verb that show when the action it describes is taking place: if it is now taking place, has taken place in the past, or will take place in the future. Take the verb *walk:* The present and future tenses are formed from the present infinitive *walk* (you *walk,* he *walks,* they *will walk*); the simple past tense is formed from the past tense *walked* (you *walked,* they *walked*); and the so-called "perfect" tenses are formed from the past participle *walked* (you *have walked,* he *has walked,* they *had walked*). There are several other tenses, of course, to indicate a variety of times before, after, or during an action, but all of them are built in one way or another upon those three basic forms: the present infinitive, the past, and the past participle.

No one is likely to make bad mistakes in tense with such verbs as *walk.* Such verbs are called regular verbs, and they all form both their past tense and past participle simply by adding *-d* or *-ed* to the present infinitive. Thus:

Present Infinitive	Past Tense	Past Participle
walk	walked	walked
hear	heard	heard
vote	voted	voted

Most verbs follow this simple pattern. You learned the pattern and how to form tenses when you were very young. Many people, however, have trouble with the tenses of a different kind of verb: the *irregular* verb. Irregular verbs form their pasts and past participles in a number of different ways, and so their principal parts must be memorized. A child will say "I swim," "I swimmed," and "I have swimmed" because, believe it or not, he knows the language so well that it is second nature to him to form all tenses in the regular, logical way. What he learns as he grows up is that logic does not always work with language. *Swim* is an irregular verb, and its principal parts are *swim, swam, swum.* Grownups who write correct English have memorized those forms, as well as the irregular principal parts of many other common verbs.

Although the great majority of verbs are regular, the most frequently used verbs are not. It is because these verbs are so often used that expressions such as *I done it, I seen it, I have went,* and *I got took* grate upon the ear with such force. The past tense of *do* is *did; done* is its past participle—which means that it may be used only in combination with *have, has, had, was, were,* or (sometimes) *got* or *gotten; I have done it, He has done it, We have done it, They were soon done with their work,* or *The roast got done too fast,* etc. And just as *done* may be used only in tenses formed by adding *have, has,* etc., so *did* may be used only by itself, in the simple past tense: *I did it, He did it, They did it.*

Irregular verbs follow no consistent pattern. Each is irregular in its own way. This means that we must know their principal parts by heart (and, of course, we do know most of them because we have used them constantly all our lives). It also means, though, that we must never forget that the simple past tense is always used alone, whereas the past participle is always combined with a short word like *have* or *had*. Here is a list of seventy-nine of the most common irregular verbs. Learn the ones you are not quite sure of. And remember to use them correctly from now on.

Principal Parts of Irregular Verbs

Present Infinitive	Past Tense	Past Participle
	(*never* used with *have, has, had, was, were,* or *got*)	(*always* used with *have, has, had, was, were,* or *got*)
arise	arose	arisen
awake	awoke	awake *or* awakened
bear	bore	borne
beat	beat	beaten *or* beat
become	became	become
begin	began	begun
bite	bit	bitten *or* bit
bleed	bled	bled
blow	blew	blown
break	broke	broken
bring	brought (not "brang")	brought (not "brung")
build	built	built
burst	burst	burst
catch	caught	caught
choose	chose	chosen
come	came	come
dig	dug	dug
do	did	done
draw	drew	drawn
drink	drank	drunk
drive	drove	driven
eat	ate	eaten
fall	fell	fallen
fight	fought	fought

Present Infinitive	Past Tense	Past Participle
	(*never* used with *have, has, had, was, were,* or *got*)	(*always* used with *have, has, had, was, were,* or *got*)
fly	flew	flown
forbid	forbade	forbidden
forget	forgot	forgotten *or* forgot
forsake	forsook	forsaken
freeze	froze (not "freezed")	frozen
get	got	got *or* gotten
give	gave	given
go	went	gone
grow	grew (not "growed")	grown
hang	hung (for pictures)	hung (for pictures)
	hanged (for men)	hanged (for men)
have	had	had
hide	hid	hidden *or* hid
hurt	hurt	hurt
know	knew (not "knowed")	known
lay (meaning "place" or "put")	laid	laid
lead	led	led
leave	left	left
lend	lent	lent
let	let	let
lie (meaning "recline")	lay	lain
make	made	made
pay	paid	paid
put	put	put
ride	rode	ridden
ring	rang	rung
rise	rose	risen
run	ran	run
say	said	said
see	saw	seen
seek	sought	sought
sell	sold	sold
set	set	set

Present Infinitive	Past Tense (*never* used with *have, has, had, was, were,* or *got*)	Past Participle (*always* used with *have, has, had, was, were,* or *got*)
shake	shook	shaken
shrink	shrank *or* shrunk	shrunk *or* shrunken
sing	sang	sung
sink	sank	sunk
sit	sat	sat
slay	slew (not "slayed")	slain
sling	slung (not "slang")	slung
speak	spoke	spoken
spin	spun	spun
spring	sprang	sprung
steal	stole	stolen
sting	stung (not "stang")	stung
strike	struck	struck
swear	swore	sworn
swim	swam	swum
swing	swung (not "swang")	swung
take	took	taken
teach	taught	taught
tear	tore	torn
think	thought	thought
throw	threw (not "throwed")	thrown
wear	wore	worn
write	wrote	written

NOTE: The most common of all verbs is also the most irregular. Do you know which verb it is? That's right: It is the verb *to be*. Unlike the irregular verbs in the above list, *be* does not have three dependable parts. Its forms change so drastically (for instance, from *am* to *are* to *is* to *was* to *were* to *been*) that no simple rule can cover them. Fortunately, most of us have no trouble with the word, because its many forms are so basic that constant practice has made us perfect. The only error that crops up frequently is the confusion of the singular *was* with the plural *were*. Make sure that you never say "we was," "you was," or "they was." Only the word *were* is correct; it is correct in the expression *you were* even when *you* refers to only one person.

Grammar Test—Correct Verb Forms

In the parentheses below, choose the proper word or words to make a correct sentence. Note that in a few cases either of the two choices is acceptable. This test is a drill. Take it over and over again until you can choose all the right verb forms quickly and easily. Answers follow.

1. I (done, have done) it.
2. They (came, come) yesterday.
3. Mary said she (thunk, thought) of it yesterday.
4. Four sailors (drowned, drownded) in the accident.
5. I (have seen, seen) it.
6. I (have saw, saw) it.
7. We (did, done) it when you told us to.
8. We have (did, done) it before.
9. You (wrote, have wrote) a good letter.
10. They (threw, throwed) out a lot of old magazines.
11. She (has broke, has broken) her promise.
12. The water pipe (burst, bursted) last week.
13. I (knowed, knew) he was right all along.
14. He (drank, drunk) his coffee.
15. He (has drunk, has drank) his coffee.
16. I (brang, brought) a friend along.
17. She has (wrote, written) us a nice note.
18. We have (driven, drove) 300 miles today.
19. The batter (slid, slud) into third base.
20. I'm sorry but I've (forgotten, forgot) his name.
21. You have (gone, went) and done it again!
22. Mrs. Brown has (chosen, chose) not to go.
23. He has been (bitten, bit) by the dog.
24. Just an hour ago she (laid, lay) down for a nap.
25. The farmer (dug, digged) the potatoes before noon.
26. I have (spoken, spoke) to the principal about your behavior.
27. Have you (ate, eaten)?
28. Yesterday a bee (stung, stang) her.
29. The water pipes have (froze, frozen).
30. St. George (slew, slayed) the dragon.
31. My son has (grown, growed) a lot this year.
32. My son (grew, growed) tomatoes in the back yard last summer.
33. Have you (drew, drawn) your pay yet?
34. Have you ever (swum, swam) in the ocean?

35. The birds have all (flown, flew) away.
36. Have you ever (ridden, rode) a horse?
37. She hasn't (drank, drunk) her milk this morning.
38. I'd have (thunk, thought) you knew better than that.
39. He picked up the rock and (slang, slung) it over the fence.
40. Have you (given, gave) him his share?
41. Who (built, builded) this cabin?
42. He (throwed, threw) the snowball at me!
43. We have all (sang, sung) the national anthem.
44. The cut on his finger (bleeded, bled) badly.
45. You have (broke, broken) Mother's favorite vase!
46. She (began, begun) the job yesterday.
47. She (began, has begun) the job already.
48. He (swimmed, swam) the river at its widest point.
49. You have (tore, torn) your dress.
50. Haven't I (seen, saw) you somewhere before?
51. Joe and Tom (begun, began) the job yesterday.
52. Joe and Tom have (begun, began) the job.
53. Have you (worn, wore) that dress before?
54. She (strove, strived) to improve herself.
55. The baseball team got (beat, beaten) badly.
56. Your shirt (shrunk, shrank) in the laundry.
57. Has the whistle (blew, blown)?
58. He had (run, ran) all the way to school.
59. I (done, did) it yesterday.
60. Mother has (hidden, hid) the cooky jar.
61. Have you (learned, learnt) how to fly a plane?
62. Last week he (sprang, sprung) a joke on us.
63. The telephone (rang, rung) while I was in the bathtub.
64. I (knew, knowed) you were going to visit us today!

ANSWERS:

1. have done. 2. came. 3. thought. 4. drowned. 5. have seen. 6. saw. 7. did.
8. done. 9. wrote. 10. threw. 11. has broken. 12. burst. 13. knew. 14. drank.
15. has drunk. 16. brought. 17. written. 18. driven. 19. slid. 20. forgotten *or*
forgot. 21. gone. 22. chosen. 23. bitten *or* bit. 24. lay. 25. dug. 26. spoken.
27. eaten. 28. stung. 29. frozen. 30. slew. 31. grown. 32. grew. 33. drawn. 34.
swum. 35. flown. 36. ridden. 37. drunk. 38. thought. 39. slung. 40. given.
41. built. 42. threw. 43. sung. 44. bled. 45. broken. 46. began. 47. has begun.
48. swam. 49. torn. 50. seen. 51. began. 52. begun. 53. worn. 54. strove *or*
strived. 55. beaten *or* beat. 56. shrank *or* shrunk. 57. blown. 58. run. 59. did.
60. hidden *or* hid. 61. learned *or* learnt. 62. sprang. 63. rang. 64. knew.

Fun With Words
INTERESTING VERBS

The following sixteen words are interesting verbs that you should know. Check the word or phrase you believe is closest in meaning to the key word. Answers follow.

1. **ravage** [rav'ij]—(a) to enrage. (b) to plunder. (c) to devour. (d) to wear away.
2. **edify** [ed'ə·fī]—(a) to scold. (b) to praise. (c) to improve and enlighten. (d) to have exceptional pleasure from.
3. **haggle** [hag'əl]—(a) to wrangle or dispute. (b) to scold. (c) to lie. (d) to beg.
4. **curtail** [kər·tāl']—(a) to curl or intertwine. (b) to deprive of. (c) to confuse. (d) to cut short.
5. **supplicate** [sup'lə·kāt]—(a) to strangle. (b) to grow weak. (c) to beg humbly. (d) to curse.
6. **extol** [ik·stōl']—(a) to announce. (b) to collect. (c) to scold or harass. (d) to praise.
7. **facilitate** [fə·sil'ə·tāt]—(a) to tease. (b) to make easy. (c) to pretend. (d) to congratulate.
8. **cavort** [kə·vôrt']—(a) to prance around. (b) to fling. (c) to find fault with. (d) to enjoy in a carefree manner.
9. **sully** [sul'ē]—(a) to keep hidden; make secret. (b) to hinder.

(c) to defile; soil. (d) to put the blame on someone.
10. **usurp** [yōō·zûrp']—(a) to charge high interest rates. (b) to intrude upon. (c) to disturb. (d) to seize power or position.
11. **goad** [gōd]—(a) to annoy. (b) to incite or spur. (c) to argue. (d) to beg.
12. **augment** [ôg·ment']—(a) to urge. (b) to dispute. (c) to promise. (d) to increase; add to.
13. **inundate** [in'un·dāt]—(a) to flood; deluge. (b) to break down. (c) to retreat. (d) to enter into an agreement.
14. **waive** [wāv]—(a) to forgo. (b) to demand. (c) to look for. (d) to be irresolute.
15. **confound** [kon·found']—(a) to impress. (b) to bring together. (c) to frustrate. (d) to confuse; perplex.
16. **heed** [hēd]—(a) to agree to; accept. (b) to dispute. (c) to pay attention to; consider carefully. (d) to prepare for.

ANSWERS:

1. **ravage**—(b) to plunder. 2. **edify**—(c) to improve and enlighten. 3. **haggle**—(a) to wrangle or dispute. 4. **curtail**—(d) to cut short. 5. **supplicate** —(c) to beg humbly. 6. **extol**—(d) to praise. 7. **facilitate**—(b) to make easy. 8. **cavort**—(a) to prance around. 9. **sully**—(c) to defile; soil. 10. **usurp** —(d) to seize power or position. 11. **goad**—(b) to incite or spur. 12. **augment**—(d) to increase; add to. 13. **inundate**—(a) to flood; deluge. 14. **waive**—(a) to forgo. 15. **confound**—(d) to confuse; perplex. 16. **heed**— (c) to pay attention to; consider carefully.

6 CONFUSION OF ADJECTIVES AND ADVERBS

WHY YOU CAN'T SAY: *My mother treats me real cruel when I shout too loud.*

This sentence is wrong because the writer has confused his adjectives and his adverbs. Both adjectives and adverbs are modifiers—that is, they are both words that help to describe other words and thus change or modify the other words' meanings.

The rule is simple: Adjectives modify nouns or pronouns; adverbs modify verbs, adjectives, or other adverbs. In most cases, too, the rule is easy to follow. We all say "John is a *brave* man" or "Mary is a *happy* woman" without thinking twice. *Brave* and *happy* describe the nouns *man* and *woman*. They are adjectives. We also say correctly "John fought *bravely*" or "Mary smiled *happily*." *Bravely* and *happily* describe the verbs *fought* and *smiled*. They are adverbs.

Those are the most basic forms, uses, and placements of adjectives and adverbs, and they should cause little trouble. There are several common situations, however, in which mistakes are often made. The mistake is always the same—that is, an adjective is used where an adverb belongs, or an adverb is used instead of an adjective. This confusion generally happens for one of four different reasons:

(1) The sentence is phrased in such a way that the adverb is placed closer to a noun or a pronoun than to the verb it modifies; as a result, the writer is misled into substituting an adjective for the adverb.

> *Al treated his wife cruel.*
> *I saw the snake clear before it slithered away.*

In those sentences, the words *cruel* and *clear* explain how Al treated his wife and how I saw the snake. They do not describe the wife and the snake. You won't make this type of error if you remember that adverbs answer the questions *how?*, *when?*, *where?*, and *how much?* even when they follow a noun instead of a verb. The above sentences should read this way:

> *Al treated his wife cruelly.*
> *I saw the snake clearly before it slithered away.*

(2) Many people tend to forget that adverbs modify *adjectives* as well as verbs. Thus, sentences like the following are wrong:

Al is real cruel to his wife.
You have to be awful brave to handle poisonous snakes.
It was plain thoughtless of him to forget his umbrella.

Really cruel, awfully brave, and *plainly thoughtless* would be the correct expressions in the above sentences. It is bad grammar to modify an adjective with an adjective. No one who is in command of the language would do so.

(3) A third, extremely frequent reason for confusion stems from the fact that there is one kind of verb that should usually be followed by an adjective rather than an adverb. Not realizing this, many speakers and writers use adverbs instead of adjectives with these verbs (thus advertising their lack of word power). Consider the following sentences. Are they right or wrong?

Velvet feels smoothly to the touch.
Cindy looks gorgeously in her new dress.
These roses smell well.
That orchestra sounded too loudly for my ears.
The eggs tasted rottenly this morning.

Note that the verbs in these sentences are descriptive of the action of the five senses—sight, hearing, smell, taste, and touch. Such verbs are generally followed by adjectives, because it is not the verb that is being described; it is the subject. Thus, it is *velvet* that feels *smooth,* *Cindy* who looks *gorgeous,* the *roses* that smell *good,* and so on. The adverbial form instead of the adjectival is wrong in every one of the five sentences.

To clarify this distinction, think for a moment about the difference between *The dog smells bad* and *The dog smells badly.* In the first sentence, the dog has a bad odor, whereas in the second sentence his sense of smell is poor. In other words, the adjective *bad* modifies (that is, describes) the noun *dog,* but the adverb *badly* modifies the verb *smells.* Only if you want to say that the dog has a poor sense of smell can you say that he smells *badly.* Eggs have no sense of taste; therefore they can only taste *rotten.* Roses have no sense of smell; therefore they can smell only *good* or *bad,* not *well* or *badly.*

NOTE: Here is a good way to test your grammar in this type of sentence: The verb *to be* never takes an adverb; and so you can decide whether or not to use an adverb after a verb like *feel, look, smell,* etc., by substituting some form of *to be* for it. If the sentence sounds peculiar with *is, are, was,* or *were,* you should be using an adjective, not an adverb. Let's try this test on just two of the above five sentences:

Cindy looks (is?) gorgeously in her new dress.
That orchestra sounded (was?) too loudly for my ears.

It immediately becomes obvious that the adverbs are wrong and should be changed to adjectives. Remember the *to be* test, and you will have no further trouble with verbs relating to the five senses.

(4) People are sometimes confused by the fact that while most adverbs end in *-ly,* some do not. A good example of such an adverb is *hard.* As an adjective, *hard* may mean "violent," as in *a hard punch.* The adverbial form of this adjective, however, is not *hardly.* The word *hardly* means "scarcely or barely." The adverb meaning "violently or with great energy" is *hard,* without the *-ly:* "The boxer punched his opponent hard."

Some adverbs even have two forms, one with and one without the *-ly.* It is a common mistake of people who think they know more about grammar than they actually do to criticize highway signs that read "Drive Slow!" They insist that the only correct adverbial form is *slowly* —but they are wrong. Here is a list of some common adverbs that have two acceptable forms. The illustrative sentences are all correct.

Adverbs Without *-ly*		Adverbs With *-ly*	
bright	(*The sun shone bright this morning.*)	brightly	(*The sun shone brightly this morning.*)
deep	(*Drink deep.*)	deeply	(*She felt the loss deeply.*)
fair	(*Play fair.*)	fairly	(*We must deal fairly with him.*)
high	(*Aim high in life.*)	highly	(*He thinks highly of you.*)
loose	(*This collar fits too loose.*)	loosely	(*Tie the rope loosely to the post.*)
quick	(*Come quick!*)	quickly	(*He asked me to come quickly.*)
slow	(*Drive slow.*)	slowly	(*He drove slowly off.*)
soft	(*Speak soft, please.*)	softly	(*To speak softly is to speak well.*)
tight	(*Tie the rope tight.*)	tightly	(*He held her tightly by the hand.*)

If both *bright* and *brightly, deep* and *deeply, slow* and *slowly,* and so on are adverbs, how do you know which to use? It's simple. The *-ly* forms are generally best for formal speech or writing. The shorter forms without the *-ly* are used in less formal speech or writing, and especially in commands, requests, or instructions: *drink deep, play fair, aim high, come quick,* etc.

REMEMBER: Do not force the suffix *-ly* onto adverbs that should not or need not have it. When in doubt, consult your dictionary.

Grammar Test—WELL or GOOD? BAD or BADLY? SLOW or SLOWLY?

Choose the proper word from each pair in the parentheses below. Use this test as a drill to help you perfect your use of adverbs and adjectives. Repeat it until you can give all the correct answers quickly and easily. Answers follow.

1. You did (well, good) on your test.
2. The new quarterback passes the ball (well, good).
3. He did very (badly, bad) on the final exam.
4. He feels (sad, sadly) about the loss of his dog.
5. The shoes feel (badly, bad) on my feet.
6. The green chair looked (good, well) in the living room.
7. This stew tastes (horribly, horrible).
8. Even though I burned my tongue, I can still taste (well, good).
9. My chances for a raise look (slimly, slim).
10. The water feels (cold, coldly).
11. The doctor said her chances for a full recovery look (well, good).
12. The new quarterback looks (good, well) in practice.
13. The flowers look (beautiful, beautifully) in the yard.
14. This silk feels so nice and (softly, soft).
15. Her voice sounded very (harshly, harsh) to me.
16. That perfume smells (divine, divinely).
17. I did my homework (easily, easy).
18. He writes his papers more (legible, legibly) than I do.
19. This horse runs very (fastly, fast).
20. She takes everything too (serious, seriously).
21. I can see your mistake (plainly, plain) enough.
22. He plays chess (wonderful, wonderfully) well.

465

23. She treated him very (cruel, cruelly).
24. Let's do the job (different, differently) the next time.
25. You must go (straight, straightly) to bed.
26. You must play (fair, fairly).
27. Breathe (deep, deeply) and say "ah."
28. You must work (hardly, hard).
29. She sees (well, good) with her new glasses.
30. My sore hand feels (awfully, awful).

ANSWERS:

1. well. 2. well. 3. badly. 4. sad. 5. bad. 6. good. 7. horrible. 8. well. (Remember, you might taste *good* to a cannibal, but when you taste something yourself, you taste it *well*.) 9. slim. 10. cold. 11. good. 12. good. 13. beautiful. 14. soft. 15. harsh. 16. divine. 17. easily. 18. legibly. 19. fast. (There is no such word as *fastly*.) 20. seriously. 21. plainly. 22. wonderfully. 23. cruelly. 24. differently. 25. straight. 26. fair *or* fairly. 27. deep *or* deeply. 28. hard. 29. well. 30. awful.

7 THE DOUBLE NEGATIVE

WHY YOU CAN'T SAY: *I can't hardly wait until Christmas.*

Almost everybody knows that *I don't want none* is bad grammar. And almost everybody knows that this use of two negatives (*do not* and *none*) in a single statement is called a *double negative.* Many people believe, too, that a double negative is wrong because two *no's* add up to a *yes;* in other words, *I do not want none* means *I do want some.* This is only partly true, however. The trouble with double negatives is not that they cancel each other out and may therefore lead to misunderstandings, for nobody assumes that the person who says "I don't want none" means anything but an emphatic *no.* The real trouble with double negatives is that they are never permitted to creep into the English of good speakers and writers. To use them is to display unmistakably your lack of word power.

Obvious double negatives cause little trouble for most people who try to speak and write correctly; but there are several words that can be used in a negative sense without being recognized as negatives, and these are often combined with other words to form what might be called "subtle" double negatives. Below is a list of several such words. Note that the list does not include immediately recognizable negatives *never, not, no,* and such obviously negative contractions as *can't, don't, shouldn't,* etc. If you combine any of the following words with an obvious negative, you may be guilty of creating a double negative of the subtle kind that good writers are especially careful to avoid:

barely	neither
but (meaning "only")	nothing
ever	nowhere
except	only
hardly	rarely
just	scarcely
merely	seldom
nearly	

Here are some samples of sentences containing subtle double negatives:

Bad Grammar	Good Grammar
They aren't barely old enough to vote.	*They're barely old enough to vote.*
I can't hardly wait until Christmas.	*I can hardly wait until Christmas.*
You can't go neither.	*You can't go either.*
We didn't scarcely have money enough.	*We had scarcely money enough.*
I haven't ever got time to read.	*I never have time to read.*
He isn't but ten years old.	*He is only ten years old.*
She just merely weighs ninety pounds.	*She weighs merely ninety pounds.*
He hasn't worked here except six months.	*He has worked here only six months.*
The curtains wouldn't barely cover the windows.	*The curtains would barely cover the windows.*
We seldom ever come here.	*We seldom come here.*

A Final Word About Grammar

The seven kinds of mistake we have talked about in the foregoing pages are not the only grammatical errors that people are likely to make. They are, however, the most frequent mistakes—the ones that modern writers are most careful to avoid. If you feel that your grammar

467

needs improvement in certain areas that require a study of the basic rules and regulations, you can find those rules set forth in detail in any modern grammar book.

There are dozens of books available. They will provide answers for your questions about such intricate matters as, for example, the active and passive voices, the inflection of adjectives and adverbs, and the correct use of the subjunctive mood. Remember, however, that grammar and good usage can change from one generation to the next. So if you decide to study grammar, make sure that you get a *modern* textbook.

Grammar is a living thing; like all living things, it never stops changing. Old-fashioned grammarians used to lay down the law as if English were a dead (and therefore unchanging) language. There are many laws, to be sure, but the modern grammar book does more than just spell them out: it helps you to interpret them and to understand why some of them are no longer fully in effect.

The more you increase your word power, including your knowledge of usage, punctuation, and grammar, the more you will realize that it is *you* who have power over *words*, not the other way around. By now you should be in command of your native language as never before. Your dictionary and your grammar book are helpful aids. They are guides to growth, not slave drivers. Use them wisely, and they will serve you well.

Always remember that language is a tool to be used. The better you can use this tool to express your ideas, thoughts, feelings, and emotions, the more successful you will be and the more complete and fulfilled a human being you will be. But language, including grammar, is merely a tool, not a religion or a way of life. It is better to make mistakes than to put this most powerful tool aside. You will improve your word power only by constant and careful use.

If you are not in the habit of writing, assign yourself the task of writing a letter every week, or of keeping a diary, taking notes for your club or business conferences, etc. As you listen to radio and TV newscasters, as you read magazines, newspapers, and books, note carefully how others use word power. Copy down new words you hear or see and learn how to spell, pronounce, and use them. Note how professional speakers and writers use words, punctuate their sentences, use or avoid split infinitives and double negatives, handle tricky sentences. Try to read at least one magazine a week and one book a month to keep alert to how professional writers use word power.

PART SIX

PART SIX

Using Your Word Power

USE YOUR WORD POWER RIGHT

English, like all other languages, has several levels of usage, ranging from *standard* to *informal* to *dialect* to *slang* to *nonstandard.*

Standard usage refers to the words and expressions accepted as correct by authorities on the language as it is spoken and written today. *Standard* is the only level that is thoroughly acceptable in every situation—at a formal or informal gathering, in a carefully worded business report, or in a personal letter. It is always "good" usage.

Informal usage refers to words and expressions that are quite all right in casual talk and writing, but are not appropriate for formal social and business occasions. For example, "How do you do" and "Hello" are standard and may be used anywhere at any time. But "Hi" is acceptable only on an informal level; you wouldn't greet the President of the United States or a new employer with a "Hi."

Dialect refers to local words, expressions, pronunciations, and speech patterns of a specific region. It is most noticeable as a pronunciation or accent. We have all heard Southern accents, Brooklyn accents, Boston accents, etc. Many expressions are unique to one area—*sowbelly* for *salt pork,* for instance—which may not be fully understood elsewhere. Dialect isn't "wrong." It simply isn't meaningful from coast to coast.

Slang is the vocabulary of special occupational, age, ethnic, or interest groups that has gained some popularity with the general public. *Cool* meaning "excellent" is a recent example. The difficulty of slang is that often its meaning is clear only to special groups, and it can quickly become out of date. Some years ago people were calling things they liked *hot stuff.* By the time you read these words, a new slang term may have forced *cool* back to its old, standard usage.

Nonstandard usage is at the bottom of the scale, and includes certain written and spoken forms—*should of, ain't, didn't ought to,* for example—that are totally unacceptable. It is so far removed from standard usage that it seems to say, "I ain't never been to school."

Who Determines Standard Usage?

Standard usage is determined by what the majority of highly regarded writers and speakers use. Dictionary makers and grammarians in America consider themselves reporters, not judges. They report what is being written and said by the experts. Thus, when your dictionary

USING YOUR WORD POWER

defines a word, or indicates a preference for one particular spelling, or labels a word "nonstandard," you are not bound by some old-fashioned pedantic decree. You are being told what standard usage actually is in America today.

In this section we will discuss usage as if *standard* were the only "correct" usage. This is not always true, of course. Many informal, dialect, and slang terms may be used "correctly" at some time or place. Once you have mastered standard usage, you will know when and how to deviate from it.

What Is Correct Usage?

What is wrong with the sentence "I ain't going"? *Ain't* is not a standard word. It is nonstandard usage. The standard, accepted way to say this is "I am not going." Such bad usages will be discussed later.

What is wrong with the sentence "The witness raised his right handle and swore to tell the truth"? Obviously the word *handle* is used instead of the word *hand*. The speaker or writer (clearly a foreigner) has not yet learned the difference between *handle* and *hand* because they sound and look somewhat alike. Of course, you would not make such a mistake, but you might say or write *accede* for *exceed, emigrant* for *immigrant, principal* for *principle,* and *there* or *their* for *they're*. In this part of the book you will learn to distinguish between such pairs or groups of words that sound alike or look alike.

What is wrong with the sentence "He drove from here at Chicago yesterday"? Obviously, the word *at* should be *to*. Correct usage links *from* and *to* together—we say that one goes *from* somewhere *to* somewhere else. Certain words are always linked together to achieve specific meanings. No one whose native tongue is English will fail to link *from* and *to*. But some people do sometimes forget to link *either* with *or* and *neither* with *nor;* and they don't know whether to link *accompanied* with *by* or *with,* and *wait* with *on* or *for*. This part of the book will help you to learn what words are linked correctly together.

Thus, a discussion of usage may be divided into four categories: (1) bad usage that you should avoid; (2) sound-alike, look-alike word pairs that may snare you; (3) words whose meanings are confused even though they do not look or sound alike; and (4) words that must be linked together properly if the writer wants to use them in a standard, fully acceptable way. Learn the proper meanings and forms of all the usage hurdles in this section.

1 WRONG USAGE

Usage that is glaringly wrong includes nonstandard words such as *ain't* and *disremember,* incorrect forms such as *nowheres* for *nowhere,* and faulty combinations such as *the reason is because, where at,* and *hadn't ought.*

In this chapter you will find the most grossly incorrect usages in modern English listed alphabetically. Most of these are not fine points or niceties; they are the worst usage demons in the language—the most damaging to anyone's speech or writing. By all means, learn them well, and remember not to use them.

ain't This word, of course, is popular but incorrect. Educated speakers sometimes use *ain't* in humorous contexts, as when mimicking uneducated speakers. But most of us will do well never to use the word, even in fun.

> WRONG   *I ain't going.*   RIGHT   *I'm not going*
>   *He ain't got any.*   *He hasn't any.*

alongside of *Alongside* is complete by itself and the *of* is incorrect.

> WRONG   *The black car pulled up alongside of Harry.*
> RIGHT   *The black car pulled up alongside Harry.*

alright The correct expression is *all right*—two words.

REMEMBER: You would not write *alwrong;* so don't write *alright.*

altho, tho These shortened forms for *although* and *though* are being used more and more often, but they are still not accepted as standard English.

> WRONG   *Altho the hour was late, I finished the work.*
> RIGHT   *Although the hour was late, I finished the work.*

and etc. *Etc.* is the abbreviation of *et cetera,* Latin for *and so forth.* Since the *and* is already there in *etc.,* don't add another *and* before it. If you do, you are actually saying *and and so forth.*

> WRONG   *We played cards, checkers, and etc.*
> RIGHT   *We played cards, checkers, etc.*

anyplace, everyplace, noplace, someplace These words are frequently used by modern writers and speakers and are not horribly bad usage. But they are most at home in informal contexts. The words *any-*

where, everywhere, nowhere, and *somewhere* are preferred in formal writing.

INFORMAL *I can't find it anyplace.*
Well, it must be someplace!

STANDARD *I can't find it anywhere.*
Well, it must be somewhere!

anyways, someways. These words do not exist in standard speech. Use *anyway* and *some way* or *somehow.*

WRONG *I never liked that job anyways.*
We'll have to convince him someways.

RIGHT *I never liked that job anyway.*
We'll have to convince him somehow

anywheres, everywheres, nowheres, somewheres These words do not exist in standard speech. Use *anywhere, everywhere, nowhere,* and *somewhere.*

WRONG *Anywheres you want to go is all right with me.*
There's nowheres I'd rather go than Hawaii.

RIGHT *Anywhere you want to go is all right with me.*
There's nowhere I'd rather go than Hawaii.

as how This is an awkward substitute for *that.* It should be avoided.

WRONG *Knowing as how you don't like to swim, let's just fish.*

RIGHT *Knowing that you don't like to swim, let's just fish.*

awful Despite what pedants may say, *awful* is no longer restricted to meaning "awesome" or "majestic." A common, accepted, now standard meaning of *awful* is "unpleasant"—*an awful party, an awful movie.* However, *awful* should not be used as an adverb; that is, it should not be used to mean *very* or *really.* The correct form for such use would be *awfully.*

WRONG *Mrs. Glenn is an awful good worker.*
Yet Mrs. Glenn is awful poor.

RIGHT *Mrs. Glenn is an awfully (or very) good worker.*
Yet Mrs. Glenn is awfully (or very) poor.

being as, being that These two word combinations should not be used as substitutes for *because, since,* or *as.*

WRONG *Being as she's going, so will I.*
Being that it rained, we did not go.

RIGHT *Since she's going, so will I.*
Because it rained, we did not go.

could of, should of, would of These are corruptions of *could have,
should have,* and *would have.* Although the two words sound alike,
never write *of* for *have.*

    WRONG   *That was a job he should of taken.*
                 Cora would of phoned if she had known the number.
    RIGHT   *That was a job he should have taken.*
                 Cora would have phoned if she had known the number.

didn't ought See *hadn't ought.*

disregardless, irregardless These two words don't exist in standard
usage. They have the dubious distinction of being one-word double
negatives. *Regardless* already means "heedless, having no regard
for or consideration of"—so what else could *disregardless* or *irregardless* mean?

    WRONG   *Irregardless of the weather, I'm still going.*
    RIGHT   *Regardless of the weather, I'm still going.*

disremember This word does not exist in standard usage. Do not use
it to mean *forget.*

    WRONG   *I disremember what Jerry said.*
    RIGHT   *I forget what Jerry said.*

enthuse This is a comparatively new verb, based on the standard
noun *enthusiasm* and the standard adjective *enthusiastic.* It is used
informally to mean "to be enthusiastic." But most good writers dislike the word, whether or not they consider it nonstandard.

    DUBIOUS   *He enthused about the project.*
    STANDARD *He was enthusiastic about the project.*

equally as good This is an awkward blend of *equal to* and *as good as.*
One or the other is better than a sloppy mixture of both.

    WRONG   *A picture is equally as good as a thousand words.*
    RIGHT   *A picture is equal to (or as good as) a thousand words.*

everyplace See *anyplace.*

everywheres See *anywheres.*

graduate A school *graduates* a student, but a student must *graduate
from* a school.

    WRONG   *Frances graduated high school last month.*
    RIGHT   *Frances graduated (or was graduated) from high school
                 last month.*

hadn't ought, didn't ought, had ought These are substandard; *ought not* or *ought* alone will say the same thing.

WRONG   *You hadn't ought to do that.*
          You didn't ought to say that.
          He had ought to take the job.

RIGHT   *You ought not to do that.*
          You ought not to have said that.
          He ought to have taken the job.

half a, a half, a half a *A half* is formal; *half a* is less formal but thoroughly acceptable. *A half a* is unnecessary.

WRONG   *He bought a half a watermelon.*
RIGHT   *He bought half a watermelon.*
          He bought a half watermelon.

individual See *party.*

in back of This wordy phrase meaning "behind" may not be bad usage, but competent writers consider it awkward.

AWKWARD   *In back of the fence was an apple tree.*
BETTER   *Behind the fence was an apple tree.*

irregardless See *disregardless.*

is when, is where These expressions may be used correctly to indicate time or place, but they should never be used to define a word or idea.

WRONG   *Monotheism is when there is only one God.*
          Monotheism is where there is only one God.

RIGHT   *Monotheism is the belief that there is only one God.*
          The time to be silent is when you have nothing to say.
          This is where I work.

kind of, sort of; kind of a, sort of a The expressions *kind of* and *sort of* to mean *rather* or *somewhat* are entirely acceptable. But most people consider *kind of a* and *sort of a* as bad usage.

INFORMAL   *She looked kind of tired.*
          I was sort of disappointed.

FORMAL   *She looked rather tired.*
          I was somewhat disappointed.

WRONG   *What kind of a camera is that?*
          What sort of a man was Woodrow Wilson?

RIGHT   *What kind of camera is that?*
          What sort of man was Woodrow Wilson?

like to have, liked to These are not acceptable as substitutes for *almost* or *nearly*. They are among the worst usages still frequently heard.

WRONG *I like to have died in the accident.*

  He liked to bought that house.

RIGHT *I nearly died in the accident.*

  He almost bought that house.

most *Most* means "more than half." It may not be used as a substitute for *almost*.

WRONG *Most everyone came to the party.*

RIGHT *Almost everyone came to the party.*

noplace See *anyplace*.

no sooner . . . when This combination is nonstandard; do not use it. The correct expression is *no sooner . . . than*.

WRONG *He had no sooner sat down when the phone began to ring.*

RIGHT *He had no sooner sat down than the phone began to ring.*

nowheres See *anywheres*.

off of This phrase is considered very careless usage by precise speakers and writers. *Off* is all that is needed; the *of* is unnecessary.

WRONG *Get off of that bicycle.*

  He jumped off of the dock and swam to the boat.

RIGHT *Get off that bicycle.*

  He jumped off the dock and swam to the boat.

NOTE: *Off* and *off of* do not mean "from." Never use *off of*. But don't use *off* either when you mean "from."

WRONG *I got this sweater off of my father.*

  The thief stole $10 off Mr. Clark.

RIGHT *I got this sweater from my father.*

  The thief stole $10 from Mr. Clark.

party, individual, person A *party* means "a group of persons" (*The Coast Guard sent out a search party. We reserved a table for a party of four*). *Party* means "one person" only in the legal sense of "a person involved in a transaction" (*the party of the first part*) or in the unique telephone-operator use "Your party does not answer." Don't use *party* to mean "one person," "a stranger," "a human being," or to avoid naming a specific person in referring to him. *Individual* means "one person as distinguished from a group" (*This job doesn't need a* *committee; it needs one hard-working individual. He doesn't follow the crowd; he's a true individual*). Don't use *individual* to mean "a human being." *Person*, however, does mean "a human being" (*A person who likes history will like this book*).

WRONG   *Then this strange party asked me for a match.*
Who is the party who opened the door for us?
A certain party asked me for a date last night!
Any individual who likes football should watch tonight's game.

RIGHT   *Then the stranger asked me for a match.*
Who is the person who opened the door for us?
A certain person asked me for a date last night!
Anybody who likes football should watch tonight's game.
Another party has reserved this row of seats.
The party of the first part must sign the contract.
One individual can change the history of a nation.
I don't like him as a teacher, but he's a nice person.
There wasn't another person in the entire park.

real This word is an adjective. It is not an adverb meaning "really or very." Don't use it as a substitute for these words.

WRONG   *Yesterday was a real nice day.*
RIGHT   *Yesterday was a really nice day.*

the reason is because Precise speakers and writers object strongly to this expression. *Because* means "for this reason." Thus, when you say "the reason is because," you're actually saying "the reason is for this reason," which is redundant (that is, you are saying the same thing twice). Standard usage calls for *the reason is that*.

WRONG   *The reason we're late is because the car wouldn't start.*
RIGHT   *The reason we're late is that the car wouldn't start.*

should of See *could of.*

someplace See *anyplace.*

someways See *anyways.*

somewheres See *anywheres.*

sort of, sort of a See *kind of.*

sure This word does not mean *surely*. *Sure* is an adjective and *surely* is an adverb. Do not use *sure* when you mean *surely*.

> WRONG   *That sure is a good product.*
> RIGHT   *That surely is a good product.*
> *There's no sure way to make a profit in business.*

these here, those there; this here, that there These four expressions are considered nonstandard. *These, those, this,* and *that* are adequate alone; *here* and *there* are neither needed nor wanted.

> WRONG   *These here pies are good compared with those there.*
> *This here pie is tastier than that there one.*
> RIGHT   *These pies are good compared with those.*
> *This pie is tastier than that one.*

tho See *altho*.

thusly This does not exist in standard speech. The word is *thus* and only *thus*. *Thus* is an adverb and does not need the added adverbial ending *-ly*.

> WRONG   *The pump is primed thusly.*
> RIGHT   *The pump is primed thus* (or, better, *this way*).

ways The only standard use of this word is as a plural of *way*, meaning "method, plan, or manner." Do not use it as a substitute for *way* or to mean "distance."

> WRONG   *It's a long ways from here to Tulsa.*
> RIGHT   *It's a long way from here to Tulsa.*

where . . . at Don't use *at* after *where*. *Where* means "at a place" and is complete by itself. The *where . . . at* combination is redundant.

> WRONG   *Where are you staying at?*
> RIGHT   *Where are you staying?*

would of See *could of*.

Usage Test—Avoiding Poor Usage

In the sentences below, choose the words or phrases in parentheses that are correct or preferred usage. Answers follow.

1. A certain (party, person) whom I won't mention says she likes you.
2. She (ought not, hadn't ought) to go.
3. (Being as, Because, Being that) it's late, I cannot go.

478

4. I'm not going (anywhere, anywheres).
5. (Regardless, Irregardless, Disregardless) of the price, I'll buy it.
6. Is everything (alright, all right)?
7. He worked only (a half, half a, a half a) day.
8. You should (of, have) voted for me.
9. Knowing (as how, that) you like cake, I've baked one for you.
10. When did your brother (graduate from, graduate) college?
11. I left the mower (in back of, behind) the garage.
12. He is (most, almost) always in a good mood.
13. He made an (awful, awfully) bad mistake.
14. Can you get the lid (off, off of) this jar?
15. Is she (enthused, enthusiastic) about the party?
16. Yes, I'm angry, and the reason (why is, is because, is that) you are late.
17. I (sure, surely) appreciate all you've done for us.
18. She prefers (this, this here) chair.
19. Put the blueprint (alongside, alongside of) the scale model.
20. (Most, Almost) anyone could have done better.

ANSWERS:

1. person. 2. ought not. 3. Because. 4. anywhere. 5. Regardless. 6. all right. 7. a half *or* half a. 8. have. 9. that. 10. graduate from. 11. behind. 12. almost. 13. awfully. 14. off. 15. enthusiastic. 16. is that. 17. surely. 18. this. 19. alongside. 20. Almost.

2 PAIRS THAT SNARE

Some words sound and look nearly alike, but have different meanings. Words that look or sound alike are often called *homonyms*, and we are so used to such pairs that most of them do not trouble us. Thus, few people confuse *ate* and *eight; know* and *no; pore* and *pour; wait* and *weight;* or *bark* (of a dog) and *bark* (of a tree). Where problems of usage do occur is with pairs or groups of words that are both similar enough and different enough to be confused with one another.

Someone has described such usage problems as "pairs that snare" —and we are using that phrase for the title of this chapter. The word pairs or groups listed in alphabetical order are truly traps for the unwary. A good speaker or writer must distinguish between these sound-alike, look-alike words. Learn exactly what each word means in the following list and how to spell and use it exactly:

accede (1) to consent or agree; (2) to come into office.
> *I will accede to your plan.*
> *The prince acceded to the throne.*

exceed to surpass; to go beyond the limit of.
> *For safety's sake, don't exceed the speed limit.*
> *This year's profits exceeded last year's.*

accept to take something offered.
> *I accept your invitation.*
> *Did you accept his resignation?*

except to exclude or leave out; with the exception of.
> *When I say I like fruit, I except plums.*
> *No one is going except Kenneth.*

access a way of getting to something or someone.
Some people have access to the F.B.I.'s files.

excess surplus; overabundance.
> *This year there is an excess of eggs on the market.*
> *The bill was in excess of $400.*

adapt to adjust; to fit or make fit.
> *Eskimos learn how to adapt to the cold.*

adopt to take as one's own.
> *We are going to adopt a child.*
> *The club adopted a new set of rules.*

REMEMBER: You go to an *adoption* agency to *adopt* a child, and the child will learn to *adapt* to your way of life.

advice rhymes with *ice* and has a hissing *s* sound [ad·vīs']. It is a noun and means "counsel, suggestion, or information."
> *People who give unsolicited advice are very tiresome.*
> *Consider this advice carefully before you take it.*

advise rhymes with *eyes* and has a buzzing *z* sound [ad·vīz']. It is a verb and means "to give advice to; counsel."
> *I advise you to try to stay in school.*

REMEMBER: One seeks adv*ice* about pr*ice*. The w*ise* have a right to adv*ise*.

affect to influence.

Government decisions affect the future of us all.

Your insults don't affect me in the slightest.

effect (1) to bring about a result; to produce or accomplish something; (2) a result or consequence.

The doctor will try to effect a cure.

His medicine had a good effect on me.

Saunders effected a total reorganization of the sales department.

REMEMBER: To *affect* is merely to influence, but to *effect* is to produce a result.

aisle a passageway.

The bride and groom walked up the aisle.

isle an island.

They vacationed on the Isle of Wight.

all ready means that *all* or everything is *ready* or prepared.

The house is all ready for us to move in.

I'm all ready for bed.

already means "previously, earlier; by this time."

We had already left when the accident happened.

It's already 10 o'clock.

all together means that *all* or everything is *together,* in the same place or at the same time.

The guests arrived all together.

altogether means "completely; absolutely."

You are altogether wrong.

allusion a reference or mention.

The preacher made an allusion to Homer.

illusion a false impression; something that seems to be something else or that actually does not exist.

The white walls create the illusion that the room is very large.

altar a platform or raised area, as in a church.

The bride and groom stood before the altar.

alter to change.

The tailor altered Debbie's dress.

If it rains, we must alter our plans.

anecdote a short narrative.
He told an anecdote about his childhood.
antidote something that counteracts a poison, disease, or bad mood.
What's the antidote for arsenic?
Laughter is the best antidote to disappointment.
REMEMBER: *Anti-* means "against." An *anti*dote acts *against* a poison, disease, etc.

angel a heavenly being; an extremely beautiful or sweet person.
Hark! The herald angels sing.
Thanks; you're an angel.
angle (1) a geometric figure formed by two straight lines meeting; (2) a projecting corner; (3) a point of view.
a 90-degree angle
The dog disappeared around an angle of the house.
The problem must be studied from all angles.

assure to guarantee; state with confidence.
I assure you that his intentions are good.
ensure to make certain.
These measures will ensure the success of our program.
insure to guard against loss or harm.
When you mail this package, please insure it.

baited containing or holding bait, as a trap or a fishhook.
My poor dog fell into a baited trap.
bated held in.
He waited with bated breath.

beside at the side of, next to.
Walk beside me.
He lives in a house beside an enormous tree.
besides in addition to; moreover.
It was snowing; besides, it was below zero.

blond (1) a fair-haired person of either sex; (2) a golden color.
The brother and sister are both blonds.
Is the table made of blond wood?
blonde a blond woman or girl.
The sisters are blondes.
REMEMBER: A blonde is a girl, like Ella, Eva, and Elinore.

brake (1) a device that stops or slows down; (2) to reduce the speed of.
> *The car needs new brakes.*
> *The boy braked his bicycle to a stop.*

break (1) to smash; (2) an opening.
> *Don't break the window.*
> *There is a break in the clouds.*

breath air from or in the lungs.
> *The air is so cold you can see your breath.*
> *Asthmatics are often short of breath.*

breathe to inhale and exhale.
> *Now that the danger is over, I can breathe easily.*

breadth width; the opposite of length.
> *What are the length and breadth of your property?*

bridal of or pertaining to a bride.
> *Her bridal gown was trimmed with lace.*

bridle (1) headgear attached to the reins to control a horse; (2) of or pertaining to horseback riding; (3) to draw in the chin through anger, pride, etc.
> *Put on the bridle and saddle.*
> *We galloped along the bridle path.*
> *Our probing questions made him bridle.*

brunet a dark-haired man, or the color of his hair.
> *My brother is a brunet.*

brunette a dark-haired girl or woman, or the color of her hair.
> *My sister is a brunette.*

canon a rule or law, especially of religious faith; sacred books.
> *This canon has been enacted by the church council.*

cannon a large gun, often mounted on wheels.
> *An old cannon stood at the entrance to the fort.*

canvas a sturdy cloth.
> *The tent is made of canvas.*

canvass to solicit votes, sales, opinions, etc., especially by going from house to house.
> *We canvassed the neighborhood selling magazines.*

QUICKIE QUIZ
PAIRS THAT SNARE

In the sentences below, choose the words in parentheses that are correct or preferred usage. Answers follow.

1. The surfer had sun-streaked (blond, blonde) hair.
2. His warning to drive carefully had no (affect, effect) at all.
3. I hoped the prescribed (anecdote, antidote) would (affect, effect) a cure.
4. Can we (adapt, adopt) this filing system to fit our files?
5. Now then, (all together, altogether), let's sing.
6. If I had the (capital, capitol), I'd go into business for myself.
7. There are no tickets available for two on the (aisle, isle).
8. We hope to (accede, exceed) last year's sales.
9. The Senate's duty is to (advice, advise) and consent.
10. Do you have (access, excess) to a good library?
11. It's (all ready, already) time to leave.
12. He has (allusions, illusions) of becoming famous.
13. I would (accept, except) the job (accept, except) for the late hours.
14. What is your (advice, advise)?
15. It's (all together, altogether) impossible!
16. The painting shows an (angel, angle) (beside, besides) the right hand of God.
17. Paris is the (capital, capitol) of France, and also its foremost—or (capital, capitol)—city.
18. According to the old joke, the cat put a piece of cheese in his mouth and waited by the mouse hole with (baited, bated) (breathe, breath).
19. Don't (accept, except) the package. Send it back.
20. The left rear tire blew out, and he (braked, breaked) the car to a stop.

ANSWERS:

1. blonde (also acceptable: blond). 2. effect. 3. antidote; effect. 4. adapt.
5. all together. 6. capital. 7. aisle. 8. exceed. 9. advise. 10. access. 11. already
12. illusions. 13. accept; except. 14. advice. 15. altogether. 16. angel; beside.
17. capital; capital. 18. baited; breath. (*Baited* here is, of course, a pun on *bated*.) 19. accept. 20. braked.

capital (1) major or most important; (2) the city that is the seat of a central government; (3) money for investment; (4) a large letter, such as *A, B, C,* etc.
The Wright brothers began by having a capital idea.
Springfield is the capital of Illinois.
My capital brings in only a small income.
capitol the main building of a government.
In Washington, the Smiths visited the Lincoln Memorial and the Capitol.
REMEMBER: A capitol building often has a dome. All other capitals are spelled with an *a*.

cede to grant; give up something.
Germany ceded territory to Poland in 1945.
seed that from which something is grown.
We planted watermelon seeds.

censer a vessel for burning incense, as in religious ceremonies.
The priest swung the censer.
censor (a) a person who examines books, plays, letters, etc., to prohibit what seems objectionable; (2) to prohibit, suppress, or remove allegedly objectionable material.
The censor cut a scene from the movie.
Every dictator censors the newspapers in his country.
The military censor examined mail from the war zone.
censure to reprimand, blame, or denounce.
The principal censured the students for their rude behavior.
REMEMBER: A censor decides what to leave in *or* take out.

chafe to irritate or make sore by rubbing.
The tight collar chafed my neck.
chaff (1) to tease or make fun of; (2) the husks of grain.
It is impolite to chaff a stranger.
Separate the wheat from the chaff.

chord (1) a combination of three or more musical tones; (2) a string or strings of a guitar, violin, etc.; (3) an emotional response; (4) in geometry, a straight line intersecting a curve or arc.
The opening chords of the symphony were very loud.
The chords of the guitar are made of nylon.

485

His sad words struck a responsive chord in her, and she began to cry.

Chord AB connects the ends of the arc AB of circle C.

cord (1) a string, rope, etc., used to tie something; (2) an insulated electric wire with a plug at one end; (3) a cubic measure for firewood; (4) a rib, as in fabric (a short form of the word *corduroy*); (5) a cordlike part of the body.

Tie the box with this cord.

The toaster needs a new electric cord.

We bought two cords of firewood.

Wear your cord jacket.

Shouting strains the vocal cords.

cite to quote or refer to.

I would like to cite Genesis 2:2.

sight (1) something seen; (2) vision; (3) an aiming device; (4) to see.

The Grand Canyon is one of the sights of Arizona.

He lost the sight in one eye.

The sight of that gun needs adjusting.

We sighted land on Tuesday, May 7, at 3 P.M.

site a place where something is located.

The tool company has found a new plant site.

The site of the Grand Canyon is Arizona.

clench to close tightly.

The angry boy clenched his fists.

The pain caused me to clench my teeth.

clinch (1) to secure firmly by bending down a protruding point, as of a nail or staple; (2) to make sure of; (3) the act of grasping.

Sam clinched the nails of the bookcase he was building.

He tried hard to clinch the sale.

The fighters went into a clinch.

coarse (1) composed of large particles; (2) vulgar.

Use coarse-grained sugar, not confectioner's sugar.

He made a coarse remark.

course (1) direction; (2) passage or duration of time; (3) progress; (4) a series of actions or events making up a unit.; (5) ground passed over; (6) a series of classes, or a curriculum of studies; (7) a portion of a meal; (8) a line of conduct.

Our course was due north.

In the course of a week he completed the job.

The disease must run its course.

My uncle is taking a course of treatments for arthritis.

John liked walking on the golf course.

He took a chemistry course in high school.

The main course was veal and potatoes.

You are following a wise course.

complement (1) to complete or perfect; (2) that which completes; (3) a complete number or amount.

A red scarf complemented her outfit.

A good dessert is always a complement to a fine meal.

The ship had a full complement of crewmen.

complementary (1) serving to complete; (2) referring to one of two colors that when mixed produce a third color.

Husbands and wives often make complementary remarks: One finishes what the other begins to say.

Blue and yellow are complementary colors.

compliment (1) an expression of praise or admiration; (2) to express praise or admiration.

Larry heaped compliments on the chef's cooking.

I would like to compliment you on your cooking.

complimentary (1) conveying or using praise; (2) given free.

To tell someone they're ugly is hardly a complimentary remark.

The new shop handed out complimentary packs of chewing gum.

consul a foreign-based government official below the rank of ambassador.

Is there a Swedish consul in Omaha?

council (1) a group of people organized to deliberate or rule; (2) a meeting.

The city council meets on October 1.

The Council of Trent was held in Italy in the sixteenth century.

counsel (1) to advise; (2) advice; (3) a lawyer or adviser.

Will you listen to my counsel?

His guardian counseled him well.

Is the plaintiff's counsel in court?

487

core the center, especially of fruit.
Jane threw an apple core into the wastebasket.
corps an organized unit of people.
He joined the Peace Corps.

currant a small black or red berry.
Try spreading currant jelly on your currant bun.
current (1) a continuous onward flowing, as of water or electricity;
(2) belonging to the present.
Tides and currents affect ships.
Phil's electric razor works only on alternating current.
Current events sometimes scare me.

dairy (1) a farm or barn where milk cows are kept; (2) a place where
milk and milk products are prepared and sold.
The Hopkinses run a dairy farm.
We bought milk and ice cream at the local dairy.
diary a daily record or journal.
I keep a diary of daily happenings.

decent suitable; respectable.
Please wear a decent suit to the party.
She was a decent woman of modest means.
descent the act of coming down.
Our descent from the mountain was painfully slow.
dissent (1) to differ; disagree; (2) difference of opinion; disagreement.
Three justices dissented from the Supreme Court's decision.
Justice Holmes filed many notable dissents in the Supreme Court.

desert (1) an arid region [dez'ərt]; (2) to abandon or forsake [di·
zûrt'].
Lawrence rode a camel across the desert.
He intended to desert his wife and children.
dessert [di·zûrt'] a sweet course at the end of a meal.
Strawberry pie is my favorite dessert.

device [di·vīs'] a contrivance, as a tool or aid.
He invented a device for cracking ice.
devise [di·vīz'] to invent or construct.
He devised a new way to make bread rise.

die (1) to perish; (2) to stop or diminish.
The grapes will die on the vine.
The sound died away.
dye (1) to color by a chemical process; (2) the coloring matter used.
She dyed her hair red.

dual double.
My sports car has a dual carburetor.
duel (1) a prearranged combat between two people, usually with swords or pistols; (2) any contest between two people.
Burr killed Hamilton in a duel.
Chess is a duel of wits.

effect—affect See *affect—effect.*

emigrant a person who leaves one country to move to another.
The Italian emigrants got on the boat at Naples.
immigrant a person who enters one country from another.
The immigrants to America got off the boat in New York.

eminent well-known; distinguished; highly respected.
Watson is an eminent biologist.
imminent about to happen; impending.
He predicted that an earthquake was imminent.

envelop [in·vel′əp] to wrap or enclose.
Fog often envelops the local airport.
envelope [en′və·lōp] a paper wrapper, as for a letter.
He addressed the envelope.

exceed—accede See *accede—exceed.*

except—accept See *accept—except.*

excess—access See *access—excess.*

faint (1) timid, feeble; (2) to lose consciousness briefly.
Alice felt faint with hunger.
Victorian ladies often fainted at the sight of a mouse.
feint a mock attack or blow; to make a mock attack in order to divert attention from a real one.
He feinted with his left and hit me with his right.

farther This word may be used interchangeably with *further*, but precise writers prefer to restrict its use to mean "at a greater distance."
I can see farther than you can.

further This word may be used interchangeably with *farther*, but precise writers prefer to restrict its use to mean "more."
I have nothing further to report.

fiancé a man who is engaged to be married.
He is Helen's fiancé.

fiancée a woman who is engaged to be married.
Helen is his fiancée.

flaunt to make a gaudy display; to show off something.
Some people like to flaunt their wealth.

flout to defy.
He flouts all the rules, but he'll get caught someday.

formally in a formal way.
Have you two been formally introduced?

formerly some time ago; previously.
West Virginia was formerly part of Virginia.

foul (1) disgusting; evil; (2) out-of-bounds; (3) something that is out-of-bounds or against the rules.
A foul smell arose from the swamp.
"Foul ball!" shouted the umpire.
The boxer was disqualified for committing a foul.

fowl a chicken, duck, turkey, or pheasant.
Jack has never eaten any kind of fowl.

idle not active.
The plant was idle during the strike.

idol an object or image of a god; a person who is greatly admired.
Pagan people's often set up idols to worship.
Daniel Boone is every boy's idol.

idyl *or* **idyll** [īd'l] (1) a poem or prose work that concentrates on simple, pastoral scenes; (2) any very attractive, simple scene or event.
Tennyson's Idylls of the King *is a very moving poem.*
Our summer in Nantucket was an idyl.

illusion—allusion See *allusion—illusion.*

QUICKIE QUIZ
REVIEW OF PAIRS THAT SNARE

In the sentences below, choose the words in parentheses that are correct usage. Answers follow.

1. It's hard to swim against the (currant, current).
2. One of my favorite songs is "The Lost (Chord, Cord)."
3. I hope we can (clench, clinch) the contract tonight.
4. He (deserted, desserted) from the army and hid out in the (desert, dessert).
5. She painted the room in (complementary, complimentary) colors.
6. To illustrate my point, I will (cite, sight, site) a line from Shakespeare.
7. The murder suspect refused to answer the questions on the advice of (consul, council, counsel).
8. This is a (dual-purpose, duel-purpose) tool, a combined screwdriver and wrench.
9. I want to (complement, compliment) you on your fine work.
10. Do you believe (censership, censorship, censureship) endangers freedom of speech?

ANSWERS:

1. current. 2. Chord. 3. clinch. 4. deserted; desert. 5. complementary. 6. cite.
7. counsel. 8. dual-purpose. 9. compliment. 10. censorship.

immigrant—emigrant See *emigrant—immigrant.*

imminent—eminent See *eminent—imminent.*

ingenious clever; imaginative.
　　Ingenious minds dream up ingenious plans.
ingenuous naive; frank and open.
　　Gloria has an ingenuous way of believing everything she hears.

isle—aisle See *aisle—isle.*

its the possessive form of *it.*
　　Give the dog its food.
it's the contraction of "it is."
　　It's time to go.

491

later [lā′tər] more late; after some time.
  It's later than you think.
  My father got home later than I did.
latter [lat′ər] the second of two.
  I like both apples and pears but prefer the latter.
ladder [lad′ər] parallel steps for climbing.
  Come down off that ladder!

lead (1) a metal (rhymes with *head*); (2) to be first or to conduct (rhymes with *need*).
  He picked up a section of lead pipe.
  Who's leading in the race?
  Oliver wants to lead an orchestra when he grows up.
led This word also rhymes with *head*. It is the past tense of the verb *lead* (to be first or to conduct).
  At first, he led in the race, but somebody passed him.
NOTE: The verb *lead* [lēd] becomes *led* [led] in the past tense. We *lead* to the *east*; we *led* to the *west*.

loose This word has a hissing *s* sound. It means "not tight; untied or free."
  This shirt collar is too loose.
  Let the dog loose.
lose This word rhymes with *ooze*; it has a buzzing *z* sound. It means (1) to misplace; to suffer the loss of; (2) to be beaten.
  Did you lose your wrist watch in addition to losing the race yesterday?

material anything of which something can be made; fabric.
  Building materials are expensive.
  The dress was made of synthetic material.
materiel [mə·tir′ē·el′] supplies, especially military supplies.
  The general needs more troops and materiel.

miner a person who works in a mine.
  Lewis began as a coal miner.
minor (1) a person who is under age; (2) of little importance.
  In this state, you're a minor until you're 18.
  Even minor inconveniences infuriate Jane.

moral (1) adhering to the laws of God and man; (2) a point or lesson.
George Washington was a moral and just person.
The moral of the story is "Beware of flattery."
morale [mə·ral'] a state of mind in terms of confidence and courage.
The morale of our troops is high.

naval referring to a navy or ships.
Naval battles helped win World War II.
navel the sunken indentation in the abdomen, or any similar indentation.
I think a swimming suit should cover the navel.
She ate a navel orange for lunch.

passed This is the past tense of the verb *pass*. Hence, *pass + ed*. It means (1) to have gone by, got by, or moved through; (2) to have handed something to someone.
Beth passed the exam easily.
We passed the gate without seeing it.
Davie passed the salt to his aunt.
past having already happened; time gone by.
This past week was very warm.
The past is over, so don't worry about it.

peace freedom from war or disturbance.
Let us pray for peace in our time.
piece a part or portion.
I'll have a piece of pie.

pedal a foot-operated lever.
A pedal of the bicycle fell off.
peddle to sell at retail; to hawk.
Where do you plan to peddle these items?

personal of, for, or belonging to a particular person.
A man's letters are his personal property.
personnel [pûr'sə·nel'] (1) the people employed on a job; (2) of or having to do with workers.
The U. S. Air Force takes good care of its personnel.
Apply for a job in the company's personnel office.

precede (1) to go in advance of; (2) to come first.
The usher preceded us down the aisle.
A precedes B in the alphabet.
proceed to go on or go forward.
If there are no further questions, I will proceed with the lecture.

prescribe to recommend or set down a rule to be followed.
The doctor prescribed absolute rest for the patient.
proscribe to ban something, as by decree.
Cannibalism is proscribed in most societies.

principal (1) major; (2) a person who takes a leading part; (3) capital as opposed to interest.
Carelessness is a principal cause of highway accidents.
The principal of the school attended our concert.
The principal was $10,000 and the interest 10 percent a year.
principle a general rule or truth, as in ethics or morality.
It's not the money but the principle of the thing that matters.

quiet calm; still; silent.
This quiet, moonlit night fits my mood.
quit to stop doing something.
You can't fire me. I quit!
quite (1) entirely; (2) really; (3) noticeably.
That is, I assure you, quite true.
Mary felt quite ill during dinner.

rain liquid precipitation.
The forecast is for rain today.
rein a device used to guide a horse.
Adjust the saddle and reins.
reign (1) to rule, as a sovereign; (2) the rule of a sovereign.
Cromwell reigned over England like a king.
It happened in the reign of Queen Wilhelmina.

raise (1) to lift something; (2) to grow or breed something.
Raise your right hand.
He raises chickens.
raze to demolish.
The wreckers began to raze the building.

494

rise (1) to get up; (2) to grow higher.
I often rise when the sun rises.
When the snows melt, the river will rise in its banks.
NOTE: *Raise* is a transitive verb, which means that it must have an object: *Raise the table. Rise* is an intransitive verb, which means that it cannot take an object: *I rise at six.* Note this difference: *Melinda raised her hand; Melinda has risen from her chair.*

respectably in a worthy or proper manner.
The man seemed poor, but he was respectably dressed.
respectfully in a respectful or polite way.
Children should speak respectfully to their elders.
respectively in a specified order.
"Auf Wiedersehen," "au revoir," and "good-by" are, respectively, German, French, and English farewells.

stationary in a fixed position; standing still.
The population of France remained stationary for a century.
stationery writing paper and related materials.
Herbert bought a notebook at the stationery store.

straight not curved or crooked.
A straight line is the shortest distance between two points.
strait (1) a narrow passage of water connecting two larger bodies of water; (2) (plural) a restricted or distressing situation.
We passed through the Strait of Magellan.
That family next door is in dire financial straits.

suit [so͞ot] (1) A coat with matching trousers or skirt; (2) a series of playing cards; (3) a proceeding in a law court; (4) the courting of a woman.
Grandfather still wears a blue suit every Sunday.
If hearts are trumps, why didn't you lead another suit?
Robert's lawyer argued his suit eloquently.
After the briefest of suits, Juliet said yes to Romeo.
suite [swēt] a set of rooms, of matching furniture, or related musical compositions, etc.
They reserved the bridal suite at the Ritz.
My cousin has a new living-room suite.
Everybody loves Tchaikovsky's "Nutcracker Suite."

than when compared with; except; but.

   I am taller than you.

   I refer to none other than our president, Hugh Smith!

then at that time; in that case; for that reason; also.

   Life was easy in 1875; there were no cars then.

   If you won't go, then I will, and then you'll be sorry.

their, theirs the possessive forms of *they*.

   It is their house.

   The house is theirs.

there at that place.

   Put the box over there.

there's the contraction of *there is*.

   There's no reason to worry.

they're the contraction of *they are*.

   They're ready to start.

REMEMBER: *There* is the opposite of *here*, and the two words are spelled almost alike. The apostrophe in *they're* stands for the missing *a* in *they are*. *Their* and *theirs* are possessive forms of the pronoun *they*, and possessive pronouns never include apostrophes. (See, for a similar snaring pair, *its* and *it's*.)

thorough complete.

   Mrs. Curtis gave the room a thorough cleaning.

threw the past tense of *to throw*.

   Mrs. Grover threw another blanket on her sleeping child.

through from one side or one end to the other.

   Let's walk all the way through the woods.

to toward; in the direction of.

   He drove from Chicago to Indianapolis.

too (1) also; (2) more than enough.

   I, too, can solve hard problems.

   This candy is too sweet.

two the number after one; two is 2.

   Two and two are four.

REMEMBER: *I, too, took the two twins to Tom's.* In this sentence, *too*, *two*, and *to* are used properly and are immediately followed by the identical letters that spell them correctly.

496

vain (1) conceited; (2) useless
That model is unusually vain.
Several vain attempts to find a job discouraged Charlie.

vane a direction pointer.
The weekend farmers bought a new weather vane for the barn.

vein a blood vessel.
The lumberman cut a vein, not an artery.

waist the narrow part of the body above the hips, or the corresponding part of a garment.
Exercise can produce a slimmer waist.

waste (1) needless consumption or destruction; (2) refuse.
I think golf is a waste of time.
The waste from the factory polluted the river.

weather day-to-day climate.
What's the weather forecast for today?

whether if it be the case that; in case.
I shall go whether or not you do.

whose the possessive of the pronoun *who.*
Whose book is this?

who's the contraction of *who is.*
Who's going to go with me?

REMEMBER: The apostrophe in *who's* stands for the missing *i* in *who is.* There is no apostrophe in *whose* because possessive pronouns never have apostrophes.

your the possessive of the pronoun *you.*
Is this your book?

you're the contraction of *you are.*
You're late for work.

Tests given to 15,000 college freshmen from more than 300 colleges show that one in every six still misuses *their–there–they're;* one in eight still has trouble with *to–too–two;* one in twenty still confuses *its–it's* and *than–then;* one in forty still confuses *principal–principle;* and one in fifty still confuses *accept–except, affect–effect,* and *quiet–quit–quite.* How do you compare with these college students? Review your personal usage demons over and over until they are no longer troublesome. You will enjoy the extra word power that this will give you.

QUICKIE QUIZ

MORE PAIRS THAT SNARE

In the sentences below, choose the words in parentheses that are correct usage. Answers follow.

1. What you don't eat goes to (waist, waste), but what you do eat goes to your (waist, waste)!
2. This country was founded on the (principal, principle) of individual freedom for all.
3. The secretary (proceeded, preceded) to take the minutes of the meeting.
4. How did your fiancé (propose, purpose) to you?
5. (You're, Your) late for (you're, your) appointment.
6. Have you read Tolstoy's novel *War and* (*Peace, Piece*)?
7. We sailed through the (Straight, Strait) of Gibraltar.
8. The sun will (rise, raise) at 5:45 tomorrow morning.
9. Please don't make (personal, personnel) phone calls during office hours.
10. (Who's, Whose) going to pay for all this?
11. He gave her a box of (stationary, stationery) for Christmas.
12. Give those (to, too, two) books (to, too, two) me (to, too, two).
13. It's already half (passed, past) eight.
14. We won even though the first three runs were (their's, theirs).
15. Name the three (principal, principle) cities in Canada.
16. I was hired by the (personal, personnel) manager.
17. We ate dinner and (than, then) saw a movie.
18. We will have the picnic (whether, weather) the (whether, weather) is good or bad.
19. Please be (quiet, quit, quite).
20. Put (their, there, they're) books over (their, there, they're).

ANSWERS:

1. waste; waist. 2. principle. 3. proceeded. 4. propose. 5. You're; your. 6. *Peace.* 7. Strait. 8. rise. 9. personal. 10. Who's. 11. stationery. 12. two; to; too. 13. past. 14. theirs. 15. principal. 16. personnel. 17. then. 18. whether; weather. 19. quiet. 20. their; there.

3 CONFUSED WORDS

Here begins an alphabetical list of "confused words." These are different from Pairs that Snare. Confused Words are usage problems because their meanings are related in some way. Thus, *allude* and *refer*, *flotsam* and *jetsam*, and *imply* and *infer* do not sound or look alike; yet many people confuse them because their meanings or uses are related.

To speak and write well you must keep these words straight in your mind. Many of these pairs are among the most interesting in our language. Once you are truly at home with them, you can have fun helping to settle the debates of those of your friends who are still unsure about the distinctions between these words.

WARNING: Not all definitions are given for every word in the following list. Many have several different meanings; we deal here only with meanings that might be confusing.

a use *a* before words beginning with a consonant sound (all sounds except *a, e, i, o, u*).
> *He drew up a chair and sat down.*
> *I ate a peach.*
> *He is not a union member.* (Even though *union* begins with a *u*, the sound is that of the consonant *y*.)

an use *an* before words beginning with a vowel sound (*a, e, i, o, u*).
> *I ate an orange.*
> *A policeman stopped Ernest at the bridge.*
> *Ms. Adams has an M.A. in history.* (Even though *m* is a consonant, the sound is that of a vowel, *em*.)

aggravate to make worse.
> *His discomfort was aggravated by a toothache.*

irritate to annoy or vex.
> *Their constant nagging irritated their parents.* (As a result, their little misunderstanding was enormously *aggravated*.)

allude to mention indirectly or in passing.
> *He alluded to his past job but didn't go into the details.*

refer to mention directly or in detail.
> *He referred bitterly to his most recent clash with the foreman.*

alumnus a male graduate.

Eisenhower was an alumnus of West Point.

alumni [ə·lum′nī] graduates, whether male or both male and female.

The West Point alumni were from the class of 1970.

My son and my daughter are both alumni of Ohio State.

alumna a female graduate.

She is an alumna of Cliffbriar Women's College.

alumnae [ə·lum′nē] the plural of *alumna.*

Both my daughters are alumnae of Cliffbriar Women's College.

REMEMBER: *-us* is very often an ending of masculine names and words, such as G*us*, Cassi*us*, and alumn*us*. *-a* is very often an ending of feminine names and words, such as Alm*a*, Ann*a*, and alumn*a*.

among (1) refers to three or more things having some sort of loose relationship to one another; (2) in the midst of; amid.

He found the textbook he wanted among (or amongst) the many others on the shelf.

Steven relaxes only when he's among his friends.

between refers to two related things, or to more than two when each is being compared to or related to each of the others.

Susan sat down between her brother and his friend.

There was a bond between the members that held our whole group together.

NOTE: The old distinction between *among* or *amongst* (for more than two) and *between* (for only two) has become increasingly blurred. *Between* is now considered generally acceptable except in cases where *among* really means "in the midst of; amid."

amoral See *immoral—amoral—unmoral—immortal.*

amount quantity in mass or bulk.

He spent a small amount of money.

Charlie ate a large amount of mashed potatoes.

number quantity in terms of separate items or units.

The tenants filed a number of complaints against the landlord.

George owns a small number of books.

There is a large number of baked potatoes in the oven.

NOTE: *Number* always tells how many, 1, 2, 3, or 4, etc. *Amount* tells how much. See also the usage discussion of *fewer–less* later on in this chapter.

anxious distressed with worry.

The mother was anxious about her missing child.

eager happily expectant.

The mother was eager to visit her married daughter.

NOTE: *Anxious* may also be used to mean *eager;* but this has not yet become entirely standard usage.

apt (1) inclined to as a matter of course; usually expected to; (2) quick to learn.

It's apt to be hot in summer.

Henry is an apt student of the practical sciences.

likely probable; expected but not as a matter of course.

The weather report says it's likely to be hot tomorrow.

liable (1) responsible for the consequences; (2) in danger of experiencing something disagreeable.

He was held personally liable for his firm's debt.

If you play tennis at high noon, you're liable to get a heat stroke.

NOTE: Many precise writers still differentiate between these three words, but more and more people are using them interchangeably.

as introduces a group of words containing a verb (in other words, a *clause*).

Taffy tastes sweet, as candy should.

My son eats as I ate when I was his age—rapidly.

as if introduces (1) contrary-to-fact or untrue comparisons; (2) non-comparative conjectures.

My son eats as if he were starving. (This is contrary to fact; he isn't starving.)

Molly insists on singing as if she were Barbra Streisand. (This, too, is obviously contrary to fact.)

It looks as if we'll all be fired. (This makes no comparison; it is a conjecture.)

like introduces a group of words without a verb (in other words, a *phrase*).

My son eats like a horse. (But: *My horse eats hay, as a horse should.*)

He sings like an Irish tenor—with his heart in every note.

NOTE: Vast numbers of persons use *like* where standard usage prescribes *as* or *as if.* Careful writers and speakers avoid this misuse of *like,* however. They remember that *like* is a preposition and that prepositions introduce phrases, whereas conjunctions introduce clauses. If you wish to write and speak proper English, whether formal or informal, you will learn the above distinctions and respect them.

avocation—vocation *See vocation— avocation.*

bad—badly *See well—good—bad—badly.*

because of by reason of; on account of.
>   *Because of my errors, we lost the match.*

due to has the same meaning as *because of,* but is preferably used only when you can substitute *caused by.*
>   *My absence was due to (caused by) illness.*

REMEMBER: When in doubt whether to use *because of* or *due to,* say the sentence to yourself and see if it continues to make perfect sense when you substitute *caused by.* If *caused by* sounds all right, *due to* is all right. If *caused by* sounds awkward—as it would in the sentence that begins "Because of my errors"—*due to* is not good usage in that context.

can to be able to.
>   *Frank, who is only thirteen, can drive a car.*

may to have permission to.
>   *Because of his youth, Frank may not drive a car even though he knows how.*

NOTE: The distinction between *can* and *may* is rapidly disappearing. Except in very formal English, you may (and can) correctly use *can* for both meanings.

compare One compares *like* things, things that are of the same class or kind.
>   *How does your new car compare with the old one?*

contrast One contrasts *unlike* things, things that are of different kinds or classes.
>   *Contrast a horse and buggy with a modern car.*

connotation what a word suggests or implies.
>   *The word "snake" has unpleasant connotations for most people.*

denotation the specific meaning of a word.
>   *The denotation of "snake" is simply this: a legless reptile with a long, thin body.*

contemptible deserving of contempt.
Hitler was a contemptible person.
contemptuous showing or feeling contempt.
Churchill was always contemptuous of Hitler.

continual over and over again; regular but interrupted.
We had a continual series of hot spells last summer.
continuous nonstop; constant and not interrupted.
Many plants and animals thrive in the continuous jungle heat.

credible believable.
His story, though unusual, is credible.
creditable praiseworthy; to one's credit.
Roger's grades in school are very creditable.
credulous gullible; too much inclined to believe.
Only a credulous person would fall for that old trick.

disinterested impartial; unbiased.
An umpire must be an entirely disinterested but keen observer.
uninterested not interested; uncaring.
I am uninterested in any TV program that lacks comedy.

egoist a self-centered, selfish person.
An egoist lives only for his own pleasure.
egotist a person who boasts about himself.
Marian is such an egotist that she talks about herself all the time.
NOTE: These two words may be used interchangeably. But precise writers appreciate the distinction in meaning between the talkative egotist and the I-centered egoist.

elder, eldest Careful writers once used these synonyms for *older* and *oldest* in comparing ages, as of brothers and sisters. However, most people now use *older* and *oldest* exclusively, except in the expression "elder statesman."
older, oldest the comparative and superlative of *old.*
Jim's older brother is the oldest child in a family of six.

explicit specifically said or written.
When we discussed your debt, you made me the explicit promise of repayment by January.
implicit implied or understood but not directly stated.
Though we never discussed it openly, there was an implicit understanding between us that you'd return the money.

fewer applies to number, to separate items, units, parts, or portions that can be counted. It tells how many.

Louise has fewer books than Marilyn.

He found fewer bargains at the sale than he had hoped for.

less applies to amount or quantity of nonseparable things.

Apples cost less money than lemons.

During a drought there is less water in the pond.

NOTE: One has a *fewer number* of things and a *less amount* of a thing than someone else. See the definitions of *amount* and *number* in this chapter and note how they correspond to *fewer* and *less.*

flotsam a ship's goods or parts found floating in the water.

jetsam a ship's goods or parts thrown overboard (jettisoned) in order to lighten a ship that is in danger of sinking.

NOTE: The literal distinction between these words is important only to marine lawyers and nautical writers. The rather hackneyed expression *flotsam and jetsam,* which derives from the literal meanings, generally refers to any worthless trifles found "floating" around on sea or land.

hanged put to death by hanging.

The spy was hanged at noon.

hung suspended or caused to be suspended from a wall, ceiling, etc.

We hung our reproduction of the "Mona Lisa" above the side-board.

NOTE: People are, unfortunately, sometimes *hanged.* Pictures are *hung.*

historic famous in history.

The Constitutional Convention was a historic occasion.

historical concerned with history.

I read historical novels and often visit our local historical society.

if introduces a cause-and-effect relationship, or suggests doubt.

If it rains, we won't go to the races.

I wonder if it's raining in St. Louis.

whether introduces an indirect question or an alternative.

He asked whether we would go if it rained.

We'll go whether or not it rains.

NOTE: The distinction between *if* and *whether* is becoming increasingly blurred. Use the one that sounds right to you in a given context, and it will probably be right.

QUICKIE QUIZ
CONFUSED WORDS

In each of the sentences below, choose the word in parentheses that is correct or preferred usage. Answers follow.

1. The weather forecast says it is (apt, likely, liable) to rain today.
2. Her mother said that she (can, may) go.
3. She is an (alumnus, alumni, alumna, alumnae) of the local college.
4. Did you (compare, contrast) the price of meat at the two stores?
5. This salad is good but it needs (a, an) onion.
6. The word *red* has an unpleasant (connotation, denotation) for many people.
7. (Because of, Due to) the bad weather, we arrived late.
8. One could say that all cats are (egoists, egotists).
9. Milk that is kept in the sun is (apt, likely, liable) to turn sour.
10. Your story of catching a thirty-pound trout is (incredible, incredulous).
11. Let's keep this a secret (between, among) the three of us.
12. The whistle blew one long (continual, continuous) blast.
13. Who has the (fewest, less) chores to do?
14. The audience yawned and seemed (disinterested, uninterested) in the speech.
15. It looks (as if, like) it's going to rain.
16. Can sin and (immorality, immortality) be forgiven?
17. My small son is (anxiously, eagerly) looking forward to Christmas.
18. I don't fully understand the problem; please be more (explicit, implicit).
19. Do you and your wife belong to the (alumnus, alumni, alumna, alumnae) association?
20. He has a (contemptible, contemptuous) attitude toward sloppy work.
21. We expect a large (amount, number) of people at the dance.
22. (Can, May) you really do a hundred push-ups?
23. This painting is beautiful, (as, like) a painting should be.
24. This painting looks (as, like) a photograph.
25. My pocketbook tells me we (can, may) have steak for dinner if we want to.

ANSWERS:

1. likely (preferred). 2. may (preferred). 3. alumna. 4. compare. 5. an. 6. connotation. 7. Because of. 8. egoists (preferred). 9. apt (preferred). 10. incredible. 11. between *or* among. 12. continuous. 13. fewest. 14. uninterested. 15. as if. 16. immorality. 17. eagerly (preferred). 18. explicit. 19. alumni. 20. contemptuous. 21. number. 22. Can. 23. as. 24. like. 25. can.

immoral violating morality; sinful.
> *It is immoral to steal another man's wife.*

amoral not subject to moral judgment; lacking a knowledge of right and wrong.
> *Cats are amoral; they can't be censured for killing birds.*

unmoral not pertaining to morality; neither moral nor immoral.
> *Most scientists believe their research to be unmoral, no matter what the results.*

immortal never dying; eternal or remembered forever.
> *Christians believe in the immortal soul.*
> *Beethoven wrote nine immortal symphonies.*

imply to suggest or hint.
> *He implied that my friend John had stolen a necklace.*

infer to conclude or derive from.
> *From what he said, I inferred that he believed John had stolen a necklace.*

NOTE: You will often hear people use *infer* as an exact synonym for *imply* in the above sense. This is incorrect usage. Someone *implies* (hints or suggests) something, from which you *infer* (conclude) something. In other words, an inference correctly follows from an implication.

in indicates location, situation, or position.
> *I walked in the park for an hour.*
> *She held a child in her arms.*
> *The doctor is in his office.*

into indicates direction or motion to or toward a location or situation.
> *I walked into the park at 9:30.*
> *The doctor just went into his office.*

REMEMBER: *In* means you are there; *into* means you are on your way or have just arrived.

incomparable—uncomparable See *uncomparable—incomparable.*

incredible hard to believe.
> *It's incredible that you could have made such a mistake!*

incredulous skeptical; hard to convince.
> *I was incredulous when I heard that you—you, of all people!—had made such a mistake.*

learn to acquire knowledge or skills.
    Students learn.
teach to impart knowledge or skills.
    Teachers teach.

leave to go away from; to depart.
    When does the next plane leave for Los Angeles?
let to permit.
    Will you let me go to Los Angeles?
NOTE: *Leave* does not mean *let* or *permit*. Wrong: *Leave me go. Leave me do it.* Right: *Let me go. Let me do it.* There is one case, however, in which *leave* may be correctly substituted for *let:* when the verb is followed by an object plus the word *alone. Leave me alone* and *Leave Gerald and his sister alone* are as good usage as *Let me alone* and *Let Gerald and his sister alone.*

less—fewer See *fewer—less.*

liable—apt—likely See *apt—likely—liable.*

libel—slander See *slander—libel.*

lie to recline.
    Lie down on the couch.
lay to put something down.
    Lay the plate on the table.
NOTE: Confusion occurs because the past tense of *lie* is *lay.*
The present tense of *lie* is *lie: Lie down on the couch.*
The present tense of *lay* is *lay: Lay the plate on the table.*
The past tense of *lie* is *lay: He lay down on the couch yesterday.*
The past tense of *lay* is *laid: He laid the plate on the table.*
Note, moreover, that *lie* is an intransitive verb—which means that it does not have a direct object: *Lie down. Lay* is a *transitive* verb—which means that it must have an object: *Lay the plate down.* Study the difference between these two sentences, both of which are correct: (1) *Now I lie down to sleep;* (2) *Now I lay me down to sleep.*

like—as—as if See *as—as if—like.*

likely—apt—liable See *apt—likely—liable.*

luxurious characterized by luxury.
The governor lives in a luxurious mansion.
luxuriant growing lushly; abundant.
The grass on the front lawn is luxuriant.

majority more than half.
He won the election by a clear majority: 60 of the 102 votes cast.
plurality more than any other, but not more than half the total.
Smith won by a plurality: forty votes against thirty for each of his two opponents.

mania a compulsive craving, enthusiasm, or love for something.
Some people have a mania for mountain climbing.
phobia a compulsive fear of something.
Alex has only one real phobia: Spiders terrify him.

may—can See *can—may.*

number—amount See *amount—number.*

oldest—eldest See *eldest—oldest.*

ophthalmologist a physician (M.D.) who specializes in diseases of the eye.
oculist an older word for *ophthalmologist.*
optician any person who makes or sells eyeglasses or other optical goods.
optometrist a technician who measures visual ability and provides lenses for eyeglasses.
NOTE: *Ophthalmologist* is a more complicated word than *optometrist,* and an ophthalmologist also has a more complicated medical education.

oral—verbal See *verbal—oral*

persecute to oppress; to harass persistently.
The Romans persecuted the early Christians.
prosecute to try by law.
The engineer of the wrecked train was prosecuted for criminal negligence.
NOTE: A *pro*fessional lawyer *pro*secutes a person in court.

qualitative refers to *quality,* to the nature or value of something. *Qualitative analysis shows that water is made up of hydrogen and oxygen.*

quantitative refers to quantity, to the amount or size of something. *When you say that your state is "greater" than mine because of its high per-capita income, that's a purely quantitative judgment. Quantitative analysis shows that water has two atoms of hydrogen to one of oxygen.*

refer—allude See *allude—refer.*

shall This word is used with *I* and *we* (the "first person") to express the future tense of verbs. The correct combination is usually *I shall, we shall.*

  I shall be in Chicago next week.

  We shall be in Chicago next week.

will This word is used with *you* (the "second person") and with *he, she, it,* and *they* (the "third person") to express the future tense of verbs. The correct combination is usually *you will, he will, she will, it will, they will.*

  You will be in Chicago next week.

NOTE: It makes no difference if *you* refers to one person, two people, or three hundred people; the combination is still *you will.*

  He (or *she, it, they*) *will be in Chicago next week.*

EXCEPTIONS: The above rules are reversed in expressing determination or command.

  I will go despite your disapproval.

  We will go despite your disapproval.

  You shall do as I say!

  He (or *she, it,* or *they*) *shall do what the king orders!*

NOTE: The preceding rules for *shall* and *will* are still observed by formal writers and speakers. In ordinary use, however, more and more people accept the use of *will* almost all the time, and *shall* is relegated to a few specific uses in questions involving the first person, such as *shall we go?*

sit to seat oneself; to be seated.

  Sit on the couch.

set to put something down.

  Set the plate on the table.

slander a spoken defamation or unjustified attack on a person's reputation.

Three people heard him slander me by saying I can't hold down a job.

libel a published written (or broadcast) defamation or unjustified attack on a person's reputation.

A newspaper or TV commentator can be sued for libel.

stalagmite a tapering formation growing upward from the floor of a cave.

stalactite a tapering formation hanging down from the roof of a cave.

strategy an overall campaign or plan.

Our World War II strategy was to concentrate on Europe before turning our attention to the Asian theater of war.

tactics specific techniques and ploys.

Our sales tactics include daily newspaper advertising and 20 percent discount offers.

teach—learn See *learn—teach.*

uncomparable not open to comparison, so different that comparison is impossible.

Horses and airplanes are uncomparable (or, better, not comparable).

incomparable unique; in a class by itself or himself.

Bessie Smith was an incomparable singer.

unconscious (1) not conscious, as a person who has fainted; (2) totally unaware; (3) that part of the mind not in the field of awareness.

Edna was unconscious for two hours after the accident.

No psychiatrist can probe the unconscious.

subconscious mental activity of which one is not aware, but which can sometimes be brought to the level of consciousness.

Oswald may have had a subconscious desire to injure his father.

A psychiatrist can help some people to understand their subconscious urges.

uninterested—disinterested See *disinterested—uninterested.*

unorganized without any plan or order.
An unorganized mob can accomplish nothing but chaos.
disorganized having a bad, misused, or abandoned plan or order.
The office, where everything had worked so smoothly, became completely disorganized after Mr. Avery resigned.

verbal communication in words, whether spoken or written.
These children rate very high in verbal skills.
oral spoken as opposed to written communication.
John chose to give his teacher an oral rather than a written report.
REMEMBER: *Verbal* does not distinguish between speech and writing; *oral* does.

vocation a person's main work.
Carpentry was Mr. Egan's vocation.
avocation a person's hobby or diversion.
Stamp collecting was Mr. Egan's favorite avocation.

warp the yarn that runs lengthwise in a loom.
woof the yarn that runs crosswise in a loom.

well (1) in a satisfactory or excellent manner; (2) in good health.
Mark plays soccer well, but he does badly at tennis.
Kevin looks well in spite of his long illness.
good satisfactory or excellent.
My grandmother's hearing is still good.
bad (1) in poor health; (2) sorry; (3) unpleasant; spoiled.
After two sleepless nights, I feel pretty bad.
I feel bad about having forgotten my wife's birthday.
The eggs taste bad.
badly not in a satisfactory manner.
Even when Mark feels good, he plays tennis badly.
The child behaved badly in school.
NOTE: Many people say "I feel badly" when they mean "I feel bad." This is not yet standard usage, however, and should be avoided. "I feel badly" actually means "My sense of touch is not good."

whether—if See *if—whether.*

will—shall See *shall—will.*

QUICKIE QUIZ
REVIEW OF CONFUSED WORDS

In each of these sentences choose the word in parentheses that is correct or preferred usage. Answers follow.

1. (Sit, Set) the teapot on the table before you (sit, set) down.
2. The Grand Canyon is of (incomparable, uncomparable) beauty.
3. My (ophthalmologist, optometrist) will soon be operating on the cataract in my left eye.
4. Golf is the (vocation, avocation) of a professional golfer.
5. (Shall, Will) it rain today?
6. A good judge should be somewhat (incredible, incredulous).
7. I taught the dog to (lay, lie) down and roll over.
8. I didn't mean to (infer, imply) that you're not a good worker.
9. I felt (badly, bad) when she thought I'd insulted her.
10. I don't know why you don't (leave, let) Diane go downtown by herself at her age.
11. He didn't put it in writing, but I had his (oral, verbal) approval.
12. Well, it's better to be (disorganized, unorganized) than not organized at all!
13. How did we get (in, into) this argument?
14. It's impossible to trip over a (stalactite, stalagmite).
15. The yard has a (luxuriant, luxurious) growth of weeds.
16. Your work for the committee has been most (credible, creditable, credulous).
17. This is the most (historic, historical) building in the town.
18. Cheating on a test is (contemptible, contemptuous).
19. I can't stand your (continual, continuous) interruptions.
20. Did he say (if, whether) he liked the plan or not?

ANSWERS:

1. Set; sit. 2. incomparable. 3. ophthalmologist. 4. vocation. 5. Will. 6. incredulous. 7. lie. 8. imply. 9. bad. 10. let. 11. oral. 12. disorganized. 13. into. 14. stalactite. 15. luxuriant. 16. creditable. 17. historic. 18. contemptible. 19. continual. 20. whether (preferred).

4 LINKED WORDS

In good usage, certain words go together in order to convey the right meaning. For example, certain verbs are usually followed by specific prepositions in standard speech and writing. *Wait on* and *wait for* are both correct, but in different situations. In some instances, *differ from* is correct; others, *differ with* sounds better. Know when to link *differ* with *from* or *with* if you are to master the fine points of usage. This section takes up the most common linked words that are used together.

accompanied by People are accompanied *by* other people or living creatures.

accompanied with Things are accompanied *with* other things.

Elston was accompanied by his wife and his youngest son.

He accompanied his words with angry gestures.

agree to People agree *to* a thing, a plan, a scheme, etc.

agree with Someone or something agrees *with* a person or people.

I agree to your terms.

I agree with you.

The climate seems to agree with you.

NOTE: We may also use *agree on* in connection with a plan: *Our team agreed on a plan of action.*

compare to to liken one thing to another; to point out similarities.

compare with to examine and point out differences and similarities.

He compared her eyes to the blue Mediterranean.

The doctor compared Irene's left eye with her right.

Gretchen compared her answers with those in the book.

correspond to to resemble in function or character.

correspond with to exchange letters.

QUESTIONABLE USAGE   *Part A in the diagram corresponds with this red and blue plastic part.*

Man's hair corresponds with the fur of animals.

GOOD USAGE   *Part A in the diagram corresponds to this red and blue plastic part.*

Man's hair corresponds to the fur of animals.

Carol and I have corresponded with Amanda.

QUICKIE QUIZ
LINKED WORDS

In each of the sentences below, choose the word in parentheses that is correct or preferred usage. Answers follow.

1. Please try (and, to) be on time.
2. If you have a cough accompanied (by, with) a fever, see a doctor.
3. How do this year's sales correspond (to, with) last year's?
4. He asked me to compare this year's sales (to, with) last year's.
5. We find that this year's sales are vastly different (from, than) last year's.
6. I am accusing neither Ronald (or, nor) Kate.
7. Oh, my love, shall I compare thee (to, with) a summer's day?
8. The president was accompanied (by, with) his son.
9. Do you agree (to, with) the plan or not?
10. How long did you have to wait (on, for) her at the airport?

ANSWERS:

1. to (preferred). 2. with. 3. to (preferred). 4. with. 5. from (preferred).
6. nor. 7. to. 8. by. 9. to. 10. for.

differ from to be different from, to be unlike.
differ with to disagree with in opinion.
> *This brand differs from that in price, if nothing else.*
> *When it comes to politics, I differ with him completely.*
> *Whether you differ with his ideas or not, you must work together.*

different from This is the standard two-word combination.
different than Though still considered unacceptable by some purists, this combination has gained wide currency. It can no longer be labeled as "substandard."

> PREFERRED   *The outcome was different from what I had expected.*

> ACCEPTABLE   *The outcome was different than I had expected.*

either . . . or These two words must go together.
neither . . . nor These two words must go together.

> WRONG   *Neither you or your brother may go.*

> RIGHT   *Neither you nor your brother may go.*
> *Either you or your brother may go.*
> *Neither the boy next door nor his friend can go with us.*

514

try and acceptable in speech and informal writing.
try to the formal, standard usage.

INFORMAL   *Try and open this desk drawer.*

PREFERRED   *Try to open this desk drawer.*

wait on to serve.
wait for to await.

WRONG   *I'll be very late, so don't wait on me.*

RIGHT   *Please ask the man who waited on us to bring us the check.*
I'll be very late, so don't wait for me.

5 SIX KEY QUESTIONS ABOUT USAGE AND GRAMMAR

Most people are vague about the difference between good usage and good grammar. In fact, even grammarians and authorities on English usage disagree as to where usage ends and grammar begins—or vice versa. The simplest (and perhaps the most realistic) way to distinguish between usage and grammar is to say that grammar deals with the way words are put together in order to achieve *clear* communication, whereas usage is often a question of using the proper word and sometimes is only a matter of *polish* and *manners* rather than of *clarity*.

This is not a sharp distinction, however. Very often, a mistake in grammar does not obscure the meaning of a sentence; very often, too, what was once considered an ugly mistake becomes standard usage if it gains currency among well-informed speakers and writers. Thus, our great-grandparents would have rebuked anyone who said "Who are you looking for?" Most modern authorities, on the other hand, find that expression preferable to "For whom are you looking?" even though the latter is grammatically "correct."

In this final chapter of our discussion of usage and grammar, let us try to answer six questions that many people find puzzling. One particularly troublesome thing about some of these problems is that they show how good usage does not always coincide with good grammar in the traditional sense of the word *grammar*. Read each of the following questions carefully, and consider your own reaction to it before studying the answer.

QUESTION: How can you tell when to use *who* or *whom* (*whoever* or *whomever*) in a sentence?

ANSWER: You cannot go wrong by dropping the words *whom* and *whomever* from your vocabulary. Grammatically, *whom* is the objective form of *who; who* or *whoever* is correctly the subject of a verb, and *whom or whomever* is correctly the object of a verb or preposition. In modern English, however, *who* and *whoever* are acceptably used in both cases. Thus, only the most fastidious teachers and writers would consider the following sentences incorrect:

> *Who do you want to see?*
> *I did not know who I was talking to.*
> *I don't know who you mean.*
> *My office hires whoever our supervisor recommends.*

This use of the subjective *who* or *whoever* where grammarians prescribe the objective *whom* or *whomever* has become acceptable in informal writing. And this is increasingly true even in the more formal style that some people consider best for such things as sermons, commencement addresses, and business reports.

If you want to be thoroughly correct do use *whom* and *whomever*— but just be sure you use them correctly. Where many people go wrong is in assuming that *whom* is somehow more "highbrow" than *who;* as a result they often use *whom* where *who* is the only correct grammatical form. This misuse of *whom* is bad usage and must be avoided. The following sentences are all incorrect:

> *Whom shall I say is calling?*
> *Sally was a woman whom we thought could be trusted.*
> *A teacher whom I know is very fair flunked my son in math.*
> *Give the reward to whomever deserves it.*

Only *who* or *whoever* is grammatically justifiable in the above four sentences. *Whom* and *whomever* are wrong.

REMEMBER: *Who* and *whoever* are almost always acceptable in modern informed usage. *Whom* and *whomever* can be safely used only by those who know their grammar well.

QUESTION: Is it always wrong to split an infinitive?

ANSWER: No. Most modern teachers, writers, and speakers agree that it is far better to do so than to rephrase a sentence into a self-conscious, awkward construction in order to avoid splitting an infinitive.

As you know, an infinitive is the verb form preceded by *to:* for instance, *to win, to eat, to understand.* You "split" the infinitive when you insert a word or group of words between *to* and the verb. Sometimes such insertions are unpleasant because they leave the listener or reader caught in midair waiting for the infinitive to be completed—as if waiting for the other shoe to drop. Here is an example of such a bad split infinitive:

> *We intend to, despite rain, sleet, hail, or snow, deliver the mail on time.*

This sentence is certainly improved by removing the "split" in some such fashion as this:

> *Despite rain, sleet, hail, or snow, we intend to deliver the mail on time.*

Most people naturally avoid long, awkward splits. What they are more likely to say is something like this:

> *I don't expect you to completely understand what I've been trying to tell you.*

How would you avoid splitting the infinitive in such a sentence? You could say "completely to understand" or "to understand completely," but either of those changes might weaken your point. In this case, therefore, the split infinitive is preferable to any alternative.

REMEMBER: If a split infinitive makes a sentence unclear or hard to read, rewrite the sentence. If the clearest, most forceful way of stating your idea seems to require a split infinitive, go ahead and split it.

QUESTION: Is it always wrong to end a sentence with a preposition?

ANSWER: No. The rule about not ending sentences with prepositions (*at, for, from, in, with,* etc.) was never really obeyed even in the days when schoolmarms tried to enforce it. A famous grammar book of a century or so ago facetiously stated the rule this way: "Never use a preposition to end a sentence with."

Modern writers believe that the natural order of words is the right order. Therefore the following sentences are all correct:

517

Fame is a goal worth working for.
Love is a force that we must reckon with.
Patsy tries to never do anything she'll be ashamed of.

Compare that last sentence with a rewritten version that avoids both the split infinitive and the final preposition: "Patsy tries never to do anything of which she'll be ashamed." This version, which might have been considered "better" fifty or sixty years ago, sounds stilted to modern ears.

QUESTION: May the possessive pronoun *whose* be used in place of *of which* to refer to things?
ANSWER: Yes. *Whose* may refer either to people or to things. Consider the following sentences:

Correct but Awkward	Preferable
This is the bicycle of which the chain is broken.	*This is the bicycle whose chain is broken.*
The one book of which the contents never grow stale is the Bible.	*The one book whose contents never grow stale is the Bible.*

Certainly the *whose* construction in the above sentences reads more smoothly than the *of which* construction. Therefore, since both are acceptable, the less awkward one is preferable.

QUESTION: In an adjective clause (a group of words that modify a noun or pronoun), when should the introductory relative pronoun be *which* rather than *that*—and vice versa?
ANSWER: Many careful writers prefer to use *which* to introduce a nonrestrictive clause, which can be omitted from the sentence without changing its basic meaning; and *that* to introduce a clause that is essential to the meaning. Thus:

San Francisco, which I visited last year, is my favorite city.
Our summer cottage, which is an hour's drive from Detroit, is right on the water.
The city that I like best is San Francisco.
Only a cottage that is right on the water will suit my family.

In the first two of those sentences, the central idea would remain unchanged (*San Francisco is my favorite city* and *Our summer cottage is right on the water*) if the adjective clause were omitted. In the third and fourth sentences, the basic meaning is either lost or changed if the clauses are dropped (*The city is San Francisco* and *Only a cottage will suit my family*).

NOTE: Substituting *which* for *that* in a restrictive clause is not acceptable. Remember: When there is doubt as to which of the two words is correct, a phrase with *which* can be dropped without changing the meaning of the sentence.

QUESTION: Is it permissible to begin a sentence with *and* or *but?*

ANSWER: Yes. *And* and *but* are coordinating conjunctions (which means that they are used to join closely related ideas to each other). If the ideas that they coordinate are briefly expressed or tightly linked, it is often best to combine these ideas into a single sentence by means of either a comma or a semicolon. Thus:

> *Jane took a walk, and Sally accompanied her.*
> *Jane, who felt she needed a breath of fresh air, took a walk; and because the weather was so unusually warm, Sally accompanied her.*

Sometimes, though, for the sake of emphasis or contrast or because the coordinated ideas are less closely connected than they are in the examples above, the second idea may seem to deserve a sentence of its own. It is not wrong to start such a sentence with *and* or *but*. The greatest writers in our language have often done so. But here is a word of warning (and note that this very sentence begins with *but*): A loose, uninteresting style of writing or speaking can result from the careless habit of beginning too many sentences with coordinating conjunctions. Don't permit yourself to write like this:

> *Jane took a walk, and Sally accompanied her. But I stayed home to mow the lawn. But I didn't do much, because of the heat. And so I sat down and picked up a magazine. And it was fun just doing nothing for a change. But soon I began to feel guilty. And so I went out to the kitchen to start supper. But the groceries hadn't been delivered and I had to wait. And so I . . .*

REMEMBER: The reason some teachers advise against starting sentences with *and* or *but* is that they know how monotonous such loose structuring can become. *But* if you don't make a careless habit of starting sentences that way, don't be afraid to do it sometimes. *And,* even more important, don't think of it as a grammatical "mistake."

REVIEWING THE SPECIALISTS

Here are eight words having to do with specialists in medicine and related fields. Choose the answer you believe is closest in meaning to each of the key words below. Answers follow.

1. **pediatrician** [pē′dē·ə·trish′ən]— (a) a specialist in foot diseases. (b) a physician specializing in the diseases and care of babies and small children. (c) a bone specialist. (d) a surgeon specializing in bone fractures.

2. **chiropractor** [kī′rə·prak′tər]—(a) a specialist in foot diseases. (b) a therapist who attempts to relieve pain and cure disease by manipulation of the spinal column. (c) a specialist in the diseases and care of children. (d) a heart specialist.

3. **physiotherapist** [fiz′ē·ō·ther′ə· pist]—(a) one who treats brain diseases. (b) one who treats injury and disability by external means such as massage, heat, exercise, etc. (c) a specialist in nerve diseases and psychic disorders. (d) one who treats kidney and liver diseases.

4. **cardiologist** [kär′dē·ol′ə·jist]— (a) a specialist in interpreting brain waves. (b) a doctor who treats stomach disorders. (c) a bone surgeon. (d) a doctor who specializes in the function and diseases of the heart.

5. **biologist** [bī·ol′ə·jist]—(a) a specialist in the study of plant and animal life. (b) a specialist in the treatment of diseases caused by bacteria. (c) a doctor of internal disorders. (d) a two-man surgical team.

6. **optometrist** [op·tom′ə·trist]—(a) a scientist who studies stars. (b) a technician who fits your eyes with glasses. (c) a doctor who examines your eyes. (d) a physician who treats diseases of the eye.

7. **ophthalmologist** [of′thal·mol′ə· jist]—(a) a technician who fits and prescribes eyeglasses. (b) a merchant who sells glasses. (c) a specialist in ear, nose, and throat diseases. (d) a medical doctor who treats eye disorders.

8. **podiatrist** [pə·dī′ə·trist]—(a) a bone doctor. (b) a children's doctor. (c) a therapist who treats foot ailments. (d) a nerve specialist.

ANSWERS:

1. **pediatrician**—(b) a physician specializing in the diseases and care of babies and small children. 2. **chiropractor**—(b) a therapist who attempts to relieve pain and cure disease by manipulation of the spinal column. 3. **physiotherapist**—(b) one who treats injury and disability by external means such as massage, heat, exercise, etc. 4. **cardiologist**—(d) a doctor who specializes in the function and diseases of the heart. 5. **biologist**—(a) a specialist in the study of plant and animal life. 6. **optometrist**—(b) a technician who fits your eyes with glasses. 7. **ophthalmologist**—(d) a medical doctor who treats eye disorders. 8. **podiatrist**—(c) a therapist who treats foot ailments.

INDEX

All the words, roots, prefixes, and suffixes defined in How To INCREASE YOUR WORD POWER are indexed by page number. This index includes words that appear in *Fun With Words, Quickie Quiz,* and *Exploring Words* features as well as those discussed in the text.

a, 350–51, 499
a–, 171, 179, 195
a/an, 499
ab–, 180, 185–89
abate, 195
abbreviate, 192
adbicate, 191
abdomen, 377, 380
abduct, 185
abductor, 191
aberrant, 305
aberration, 191
abeyance, 195, 306
abhor, 185
abhorrent, 185
abject, 187
abjure, 185, 191
able, 213
–able, 18, 37, 143, 277, 294–96, 297, 325, 376–77
–ably, 294, 295
abnegation, 191
abnormal, 186
abnormality, 186
abort, 186
abortion, 186
abortive, 186, 191
abrade, 187
abrasive, 191
abridge, 27
abrogate, 187
abs–, 185, 186, 188, 189
abscess, 53, 187, 319
abscond, 187, 189
absent, 186
absenteeism, 186
absent-minded, 186
absolute, 187
absolution, 187
absolve, 186, 187
absorb, 187–88, 375
absorbent, 188, 375
absorption, 188
abstain, 188
abstemious, 187
abstention, 188

abstinence, 188, 191
abstract, 117, 187
abstracted, 187
abstruse, 187
absurd, 375
abuse, 188
abusive, 188
abut, 195
abysmal, 374, 375
ac–, 35, 54, 58, 145
academic, 275
academically, 338
accede, 53, 322
accede/exceed, 480
accentuate, 27
accept, 53, 357
accept/except, 480, 497
acceptance, 267
access, 53
access/excess, 480
accessory, 53, 357
accident, 35
accidentally, 292, 338
acclimate, 377, 380
accompanied by/ accompanied with, 513
accompanist, 365, 366
accord, 54, 192
accordance, 54
according, 54, 192
accordingly, 54, 192
accredit, 47, 58–59
accreditation, 59
accurate, 361
Achilles, 369
–acious. 161, 277
–acity, 266
acoustics, 47
acquire, 145, 194
acquirement. 145
acquisition, 145, 195
acquisitive, 145

acr–, 13-14
acrid, 13
acrimonious, 13
acrimony, 13
across, 364
act, 14
act–, 14, 15–16, 260
action, 14
activate, 15, 16
active, 15
activity, 15–16
actor, 16, 354
actual, 16
actuality, 16
actually, 16
acu–, 13–14, 140
acuity, 13, 33
acumen, 13, 33
acute, 13-14
–acy, 267
ad–, 35, 54, 72, 79, 82, 94, 98, 99, 100, 102, 103, 104, 113, 115, 129, 145, 163, 168, 177, 189–90, 192–94, 195
adage, 195
adapt, 189
adapt/adopt, 480
adaptation. 27
addict, 190
addle, 191, 345
address, 190, 379
adduce, 47
adequate, 72, 276
adhere, 99, 190
adherence, 99, 100
adherent, 99–100
adhesion, 99-100
adhesive, 99, 100
ad hoc, 225, 390
ad hominem, 390
adipose, 191
adjacent, 102, 103. 190
adjoin, 103
adjoining, 103
adjunct, 104

administer, 190
admire, 190
admissible, 111, 112
admission, 111, 112
admit, 111–12
admittance, 111, 112
admonish, 115, 274
admonition, 115
admonitory, 27
adolescent, 319
Adonis, 29
adopt, 189
adopt/adapt, 480
adore, 190
adroit, 195, 229
adult, 377, 380
advantageous, 338
advent, 195
adventure, 168
adventurer, 168
adventurous, 168
advertisement, 378
advice, 190. 374
advice/advise, 480
advise, 374
advise/advice, 480
advocate, 177
aesthete, 135
af–, 79, 82, 192
affability, 195
affair, 192–93
affect, 75–76
affect/effect, 481, 497
affinity, 27
affirm, 79
affirmation, 79, 195
affirmative, 79
affix, 27
affluence, 82
affluent, 82
affront, 195
afghan, 61
aficionado, 225, 389
after, 351

ag–, 14, 15, 94, 98, 140
again, 353
against, 353
agency, 14
agenda, 14, 390
agent, 14
aggravate, 98, 193
  aggravate/ irritate, 499
aggression, 94
aggressive, 94
aggressor, 94
aggrieved, 335
agile, 15, 277, 374, 375
agility, 15
agitator, 271
agrarian, 191
agreeable, 296
agree to/agree with, 513
agronomist, 151
aisle, 293
  aisle/isle, 481
–al, 16, 19, 21, 22, 35, 72, 94, 122, 200, 267, 275, 299–300, 301, 325
à la carte, 225
à la mode, 225
albatross, 191
Albuquerque, 381
alcoholism, 267
alfresco, 389
align, 27
allay, 17
all ready/already, 481
all together/ altogether, 481
allude/refer, 499
allusion, 27
  allusion/ illusion, 481
–ally, 338, 339
almond, 292, 366
already/all ready, 481
altar/alter, 481
alter ego, 225
alternate, 373
altogether/all together, 481
altruist, 135
alumnus/alumni/ alumna/ alumnae, 500
am–, 18–19, 81
amalgamate, 191
amanuensis, 158
amateur, 18, 81
amateurish, 18
amateurishly, 18
amatory, 18, 19

ambi–, 71, 184, 196
ambidextrous, 71, 73, 184, 196
ambience, 196
ambiguous, 71, 196
ambitious, 196
ambivalence, 196
ambulate, 202, 236
amenable, 446
American, 270
ami–, 296
amiability, 18
amiable, 18, 296
amicability, 19
amicable, 19, 376, 446
amicably, 19
amity, 47
amnesia, 268
among, 371
  among/ between, 500
amontillado, 389
amoral/immoral/ unmoral/ immortal, 506
amorous, 19
amount/number, 500
amour, 384
amphibian, 23
an/a, 499
–an, 270, 277–78
anachronism, 66
analysis, 268
analyze, 336
–ance, 267, 300, 302, 304, 306, 343
anchovy, 368
–ancy, 267, 302, 304
and, 515, 519
–ane, 270, 277
anecdote/antidote, 482
anesthetist, 85
angel, 25
  angel/angle, 482
angina, 390
angle/angel, 482
Anglophile, 373, 375
Anglophobe, 47
anim–, 19–21, 124
animal, 19–20
animalistic, 20
animality, 20
animate, 20, 47
animated, 20
animation, 20
animosity, 20
Ankara, 381
annals, 21–22
annex, 193

annu–, 21–22
annual, 22, 200
annuity, 22, 47
annulment, 195
–ant, 160, 270, 278, 300, 302, 303–5
antagonism, 47
ante–, 42, 183, 198, 200
antebellum, 198
antecede, 198
antecedent, 42, 47, 198
antechamber, 183, 198
antedate, 198
anthrop–, 24, 230
anthropo–, 24, 71, 96
anthropologist, 24, 151
anthropology, 24, 66, 71, 271
anti–, 184, 198, 199–200, 245, 482
antiaircraft, 199
antibiotic, 199
anticlimax, 199
antidote, 47, 199
  antidote/ anecdote, 482
antipasto, 389
antipathetic, 199
antipathy, 47, 199
antiquary, 151
antiseptic, 199
antisocial, 184
antithesis, 47
antitrust, 200
anxious/eager, 501
ap–, 127
aperture, 268
apostasy, 324
apostle, 292
apparatus, 353
apparent, 193
apparition, 193
appear, 193
appearance, 193
append, 27
appendicitis, 354
appetite, 127–28
appetizer, 128
appetizing, 128
applicable, 377
appreciable, 27
appreciate, 352
apprehension, 27
apprehensive, 319
appropriate, 27
appurtenance, 27, 306
apricot, 353
a priori, 403
apt/likely/liable, 501

apt–, 189
aquatic, 23
aquiline, 269
–ar, 270, 275, 307, 309, 311–12
arable, 301
arbitrary, 317
arboreal, 23
arch, 17, 368
arch–, 25, 26
–arch, 25
archaic, 369, 370
archangel, 25, 369
archbishop, 25
archenemy, 25
archeo–, 25, 96
archeological, 25
archeologist, 151
archeology, 25, 96, 345, 369
archetype, 367, 369
archi–, 25
archipelago, 369
architect, 26
architecture, 26
archives, 370
–archy, 25, 26
arctic, 292
ardor, 268
arduous, 342
Argyle, 61
aristocrat, 272
Armageddon, 197
arrive, 194
arrogance, 346
artistically, 338
–ary, 32, 178, 270, 275, 314–16
as/as if/like, 501
ascendancy, 324
ascetic, 135
ascribe, 182, 195
ask, 351
asked, 360
asparagus, 292, 361, 372
aspect, 195
aspersion, 195
aspirant, 195
aspiration, 27
assignment, 195
associate, 194, 373
association, 194
assure/ensure/ insure, 482
astronomy, 272
at–, 165
–ate, 20, 60, 65, 72, 93, 95, 133, 178, 251, 252, 258, 273, 276, 373
athlete, 292, 293, 348, 364, 365

athletic, 364, 366
-ation, 179, 294–95
attack, 364
attacked, 364, 365
attend, 194
attention, 195
attentive, 195
attract, 163
attraction, 163
attractive, 163, 277
au courant, 384
aud-, 28–29, 30, 124
audacity, 266
audibility, 28
audible, 28, 277
audience, 28, 357
audio, 28–29
audit, 28
audit-, 28–29, 30, 124
audition, 29, 267
auditor, 30
auditorium, 30
auf Wiedersehen, 225
augment, 461
au gratin, 384
August, 41
au jus, 384
au lait, 384
aunt, 351
aura, 17
aural, 47
au revoir, 384
aurora borealis, 390
aut-, 30–31
authorize, 361
auto-, 30–31, 71
autobiography, 34
autocracy, 30
autocrat, 30
autograph, 30–31, 272
autography, 31
automat, 31
automatic, 31
automatically, 338
automation, 31
automobile, 31, 71
autopsy, 268
avenue, 354
aver, 17
averse, 17
aversion, 171, 191
avert, 171
aviator, 352–53
avid, 17
avocation, 179, 189, 191
avocation/vocation, 511
avow, 17
awful, 473
azure, 56

bad/badly, 502, 511
bailiwick, 158
baited/bated, 482
baker, 270, 314
bakery, 314
band-, 209
banter, 313
bar, 210
barbarous, 361
bark, 210
barrage, 355, 371
bask, 17
bas-relief, 117
bated/baited, 482
bath, 351
bayonet, 386
Beaufort, 381
beauty, 354
because, 477
    because of/due to, 502
bedlam, 61
been, 349
beggar, 270, 307
beginning, 359
behemoth, 108, 109
Beirut, 381
bel-, 247
believe, 361
belli-, 94
belligerent, 92–93, 94
bellow, 356
bene-, 31–32, 183
benediction, 32, 229
benefactor, 31, 183
beneficial, 32
beneficiary, 32
benefit, 32
benevolent, 32
benign, 32, 230
benign-, 31, 32
benignant, 305
beside/besides, 482
betrayal, 267
between/among, 500
bi-, 71, 87, 184, 200–201, 265
biannual, 200
bibelot, 158
bibliophile, 375
bicameral, 200
bicuspid, 184
bicycle, 200–201, 265, 318
biennial, 66, 200
bigamy, 71, 87, 201, 265
bilateral, 201
bilingual, 66, 201
billet-doux, 384
bin-, 201

binoculars, 201
bio-, 34, 124, 201
biochemist, 34
biochemistry, 34
biographer, 34
biographical, 34
biography, 34
biological, 34
biologist, 34, 520
biology, 34, 271
biped, 23
biscuit, 243
bisect, 38
bivouac, 318
blackguard, 366
blasé, 358, 384
blatant, 305
blitzkrieg, 388
blond/blonde, 482
bloomers, 41
boatswain, 366
bobby, 41
bologna, 61
bona fide, 225, 390
bonnet, 243
booklet, 280
boot, 243
bother, 356
bouquet, 386
bourgeois, 384
bovine, 276
bowdlerize, 41
boycott, 41
boyish, 276
brac-, 222
bracelet, 222
braces, 243
braggadocio, 108, 109
brake/break, 483
brassiere, 385
break/brake, 482
breath/breathe/breadth, 483
brewery, 314
bridal/bridle, 483
bring, 371
bringing, 372
bronchial, 357, 369
brother, 356
brunet/brunette, 483
buffet, 385
burglar, 364, 365
but, 519
by, 513

cabalistic, 158
cabana, 389
cabaret, 386
cab rank, 243
cache, 368
cad-, 35
cadenza, 389, 403
cadet, 386

cafeteria, 361
Cairo, 381
calico, 61
calliope, 378
callous, 269, 340
callus, 340
calvary, 197
camera, 200
camouflage, 371
can/may, 502
canapé, 225, 385
candidate, 360, 363, 373
canine, 276
Cannes, 381
canon,/cannon, 483
can't, 351
cantaloupe, 61
can't you, 362
canvas/canvass, 483
cap-, 37, 40, 233, 296
capability, 37
capable, 37, 296
capably, 37
capacity, 266
caper, 313
capital, 361
    capital/capitol, 485
capricious, 319
capsule, 280
capt-, 37–38, 40
captivate, 39
captive, 39
captivity, 39
captor, 39
capture, 37–38, 39
caravansary, 158
cardiologist, 85, 520
carnivora, 66
carnivorous, 23
carp, 17
carte blanche, 225
cas-, 35, 36–37
castanet, 389
casual, 35
casualty, 35
cat, 318
catalogue, 272
caudate, 276
cavalier, 29, 335
cavort, 461
ced-, 42, 204, 250
cedar, 318
cede-, 42, 43, 44, 45, 198, 321–22
cede/seed, 485
ceed-, 42, 43–44, 45, 244, 321
ceiv-, 37, 39, 40
celibacy, 267
cement, 352
censer/censor/

523

censure, 485
cent–, 22, 45–46, 237
centennial, 22, 45–46
centi–, 46
centipede, 46
century, 46
cept–, 37, 39, 40
cerise, 56
cern–, 48
cerulean, 56
cess–, 42, 43, 44–45
chafe, 368
chafe/chaff, 485
chaff, 368
chagrin, 368, 370
Chaldea, 369
chalet, 368, 386
chalice, 368
chamber, 369
chameleon, 369
champagne, 61, 368
Champs Élysées, 381
chance, 351, 369
chancel, 368
chandelier, 368
change, 369
changeable, 296
channel, 369
chaos, 369
chaotic, 370
chaperon, 368
chapter, 368
charades, 368
chard, 368
charisma, 369
charity, 369
charlatan, 368
Charleston, 369
chart, 369
chartreuse, 56, 368
chary, 370
chasm, 369
chateau, 368
chattel, 368
chauffeur, 368, 377, 380
chauvinism, 41, 108, 109
chauvinist, 345
checkers, 369
cheek, 369
chemist, 243
cherish, 369
Cherokee, 368
cherub, 368
chestnut, 292, 360, 363, 366
Cheyenne, 368
Chianti, 369, 389
chiaroscuro, 117
chic, 17, 357

chicanery, 370
chide, 17, 368
chiffon, 368
chimera, 369
chimney, 365
chips, 243
chiropodist, 85, 369
chiropractor, 520
chivalrous, 368
cholera, 369
chord/cord, 485–86
choreographer, 151, 369
choreography, 370
Christianize, 274
chrom–, 275
chron–, 258
chronically, 66
churlish, 108, 109
cid–, 35, 36
cigarette, 280
cip–, 37, 40
circum–, 168, 183, 202–3
circumambulate, 202
circumference, 202
circumflex, 202
circumlocution, 66, 202
circumnavigate, 202
circumscribe, 182, 202
circumspect, 203
circumstance, 203
circumstantial, 66
circumvent, 168, 183, 203
circus, 243
cite/sight/site, 486
city, 318
claim–, 49–50
clairvoyance, 306
clam–, 49
clandestine, 355, 377, 380
clar–, 210
–cle, 55, 59, 280
clench/clinch, 486
cliché, 385, 386
clinch/clench, 486
clos–, 51, 222–23
clud–, 51, 52, 217
clus–, 51
co–, 100, 203, 204
coarse/course, 486–87
codicil, 280
coequal, 204
coerce, 204
coeval, 204
coexist, 204
cognizant, 305

cognomen, 130
cohere, 100, 204
coherence, 100
coherent, 100, 305
cohesion, 100
cohesive, 100
cohort, 204
coiffure, 385
col–, 105, 110, 184, 203
coldness, 269
colic, 318
colicky, 318
collaborate, 204
collapsible, 296
colleague, 204
collect, 105
collective, 105
collector, 105, 307
collide, 204
colloquial, 110
colloquialism, 110
cologne, 61
coloratura, 389
column, 292
com–, 110, 112, 122–23, 128, 131, 132, 133, 136, 137, 183, 184, 203–7
combat, 203
combine, 183, 205
commendable, 205
comment, 376, 379
commentary, 317, 322
commerce, 205
commission, 112
commit, 112, 205
committee, 112
commotion, 205
communist, 270
community, 205–6
compact, 206
comparable, 296, 376
compare/contrast, 502
compare to/ compare with, 513
compassion, 206
compatible, 206, 296
compatriot, 203
compel, 122, 206
compelling, 122
compensate, 144
compete, 128, 206
competence, 129, 319
competent, 128–29
competition, 128
competitive, 128

competitor, 128, 271
compile, 205
complacent, 205
complaisant, 205
complement/ compliment, 487
complementary/ complimentary, 487
completely, 131
completion, 131
complex, 132–33, 206
complexion, 133
complexity, 133
compliance, 205
complicate, 133
complicated, 133
complication, 133
compliment/ complement, 487
complimentary/ complementary, 487
component, 136
compose, 136
composite, 136
composition, 206–7
composure, 136
compound, 137
comprehensive, 319
compress, 207
comptroller, 308
compulsion, 122, 123
compulsive, 122–23
compulsory, 122, 123, 276
con, 414
con–, 42, 48, 51, 57, 62, 69, 76, 79, 86, 97, 104, 146, 153,156,159, 163,168,169, 171,203,245
concave, 207
concede, 42, 203–4, 322
conceive, 53
concentrate, 373
concept, 53
conception, 53
concern, 48
concerning, 48
concession, 42
conclave, 208
conclude, 51
conclusion, 51
conclusive, 51
concomitant, 208
concordant, 208
concourse, 62

concrete, 57
concur, 62
concurrent, 62, 208
cond–, 189
condemn, 292
conducive, 69
conduct, 69, 378, 380
confectionery, 314
confederacy, 267
confer, 76
conference, 76
confide, 207
confirm, 79
confirmation, 79
confound, 86, 461
Confucian, 278
confuse, 86
confusion, 86
congenial, 89
congenital, 89, 208
conglomerate, 208
congratulate, 97
congratulation, 97
congregate, 207
conjoin, 104, 208
conjunction, 104
conjunctive, 104
connect, 213
connotation, 208
connotation/ denotation, 502
consanguinity, 208
conscience, 319
conscious, 319
conscript, 378
conservative, 135
consonant, 305
conspicuous, 153–54
constancy, 324
consul/council/ counsel, 487
contain, 159
container, 159
containment, 159
contemptible/ contemptuous, 503
content, 159
contest, 355, 378, 380
continent, 159
continental, 159
contingency, 156, 305, 324
contingent, 156
continual/ continuous, 503
continue, 213
continuous/ continual, 503

contra–, 64, 209, 210
contraband, 209
contraceptive, 209
contract, 163
contraction, 164
contractor, 164
contractual, 164
contradict, 64, 209
contradiction, 64
contradictory, 64
contrast/compare, 502
contrite, 208
convalescent, 319
convene, 168–69
convenience, 169
convenient, 169
convent, 168, 169
convention, 168, 169
conventional, 168–69
conversant, 172, 305
conversation, 172
conversational, 172
conversationalist, 172
converse, 172, 378
conversion, 172, 295
convert, 171–72
converter, 172
convertible, 172, 295
convex, 207
convict, 378
conviviality, 208
convocation, 208
cool, 318
cop–, 258
coquette, 15
cor–, 146, 203
cord/chord, 485–86
cord–, 54–55, 192
cordial, 54
cordiality, 54
core/corps, 488
corollary, 322
coronet, 386
corp–, 55, 140
corpor–, 55, 56
corporate, 56
corporation, 56
corps, 292, 366
corps/core, 488
corpse, 55
corpulence, 55
corpulent, 55
corpuscle, 55
correct, 361
correctable, 295
correction, 295

correspond, 207
correspond to/ correspond with, 513
corrupt, 146–47
corruption, 147
corsage, 371
cortege, 371
cosmo–, 71
cosmopolitan, 71
cotton wool, 243
could you, 362
council/counsel, 487
counter–, 209–10
counterattack, 209
counterbalance, 209
counterclockwise, 209
counterespionage, 209
counterfeit, 209
counterpart, 209
counterpoise, 210
countersign, 210
counterstatement, 210
countless, 278
coup d'état, 225
coupe, 385
coupon, 354
cours–, 62, 63
course/coarse, 486–87
couth, 264
covenant, 305
coy, 17
–cracy, 272
crass, 17
–crat, 30, 272
crawfish, 357
cre–, 57
crease, 374
creation, 267
cred–, 58, 78, 140, 296
credence, 66
credentials, 59
credible, 78, 296, 446
credible/ creditable/ credulous, 503
credit, 58–59
creditable, 58, 446
creditable/ credible/ credulous, 503
creditor, 58
credo, 66
credulous, 66, 78, 277
credulous/ credible/

creditable, 503
cresc–, 57, 106
crescendo, 78, 389, 403
crescent, 57
cret–, 48, 49, 57
criminal, 361
crisis, 374
critically, 338
criticize, 274
crop, 418
crouton, 385
cruc–, 296
crucible, 296
crumpet, 243
crusade, 377, 380
crustacean, 270
crux, 17, 418
crying, 359
cub–, 59–60
cubicle, 59–60
cuisine, 385
cul-de-sac, 225, 385
–cule, 280
cull, 17
culpable, 446
cult, 418
cumb–, 59, 60, 106
Cupid, 352, 354
cupola, 403
–cupy, 233
cur–, 62–63, 250
curmudgeon, 29
currant/current, 488
currency, 62
current, 62, 361
current/currant, 488
curs–, 62, 63, 241
curt, 418
curtail, 461
curvature, 268
cut, 318
cutlery, 317
–cy, 323

dahlia, 41
dairy/diary, 488
damask, 61
darling, 280
data, 352–53
de–, 35, 39, 49, 63–64, 80, 125, 133, 137, 142, 148, 160, 164, 210–12, 213, 232
debar, 210
debark, 210
debase, 212
debit, 58
debonair, 29

debouch, 370
debtor, 355
dec–, 265
deca–, 265
decadent, 35,
    212, 305
decant, 212
decay, 35
deceit, 39
deceitful, 39
deceive, 39
decent/descent/
    dissent, 488
decentralize, 211
deception, 39
deceptive, 39
deci–, 265,
decimate, 73, 273
decipher, 211
declaim, 49, 211
declamation, 49
declamatory, 49
declare, 210
decline, 211, 377,
    379
declivity, 212
decolletage, 385
decrease, 211
deduce, 78, 212
de facto, 225,
    390
defend, 211
defer, 211
deferential, 90
deficient, 319
deficit, 376
defile, 212
definite, 361
deflect, 80, 211
deform, 211
defray, 212
defunct, 212
dehumidify, 210
deification, 63
deify, 63
deign, 335
deity, 64
dejection, 120
del–, 296
delectable, 446
delegate, 212
deliver, 211
demagogic, 73
demeanor, 313
demi–, 265
demise, 212, 355,
    374, 375
democracy, 272
democrat, 272
demolish, 274
demote, 211
demure, 15
denial, 267
denim, 61
denotation/
    connotation,
    502
depend, 125
dependable, 125

dependence, 125
dependent, 125
deplete, 131, 211
depletion, 131
deplorable, 296
depopulate, 211
deport, 142–43
deportation, 143
deportment, 143
depose, 137
deposit, 137
deposition, 137
depository, 137
depreciate, 211
depredate, 212
derision, 212
derm–, 71, 221
dermatologist, 71,
    85, 261
dermatology, 73
descend, 211
descendant/
    descendent,
    302
descent/dissent
    /decent, 488
describe, 148
description, 148
descriptive, 148
desert, 378
    desert/dessert,
    488
desirable, 296
Des Moines, 381
despic–, 296
despicable, 296,
    377
despotic, 275
dessert/desert,
    488
detain, 160
detectable, 295
detection, 295
detention, 160
deterrent, 212
detract, 164, 211
detraction, 164,
    212
detractor, 164
device/devise,
    488
devious, 342
devise/device,
    488
dexterity, 73
dexterous, 196
dextro–, 71
dextrous, 196
di–, 93, 172, 213,
    214, 265
dialogue, 272
diameter, 273
diary/dairy, 488
dic–, 32
dicho–, 265
dict–, 64–65,
    140, 229
dictate, 65
dictation, 65

dictator, 65
dictatorial, 65
diction, 65
dictionary, 65,
    270
dictum, 73
die/dye, 489
dif–, 76, 213
difference, 76
different from/
    different
    than, 514
differ from/differ
    with, 514
diffidence, 306
diffuse, 213
digest, 92
digestion, 93
digestive, 93
digress, 120
dire, 17
dirigible, 363
dis–, 48, 51, 59,
    76,112, 125,
    137, 147,
    164, 172,
    183, 213–16,
    232, 295,
    376
disable, 213
disarm, 214
disastrous, 366
disavow, 216
discern, 48
discernible, 48
discerning, 48
discernment, 48
disclaim, 216
disclose, 51
disclosure, 51
discomfit, 214
disconnect, 213
disconsolate, 216
discontinue, 213
discredit, 59
discreet, 48–49
discrete, 48–49
discriminate, 214
discursive, 78
disdain, 216
disease, 183
disfigure, 214
dishabille, 385
dishearten, 214
disingenuous, 216
disintegrate, 214
disinter, 216
disinterested/
    uninterested,
    503
dislocate, 213
disloyal, 214
dismal, 374
dismantle, 214–
    15, 216
dismiss, 112–13
dismissal, 113
disorganized/
    unorganized,

511
disorient, 215
disown, 215
disparate, 216
disparity, 216
dispatch, 377, 379
dispel, 144
dispensable, 126
dispensary, 126
dispensation, 144,
    216
dispense, 125,
    216
disposal, 138
dispose, 137–38
disposition, 138
disreputable, 377
disrupt, 147
disruption, 147
disruptive, 147
dissect, 215
dissemble, 216
disseminate, 215
dissent/descent
    /decent, 488
dissidence, 345
dissipate, 215
dissonance, 216,
    306
dissuade, 215
distend, 216
distillery, 314
distract, 164
distracted, 164,
    165
distraction, 164
distraught, 165,
    216
diurnal, 23
div–, 63, 64
diverse, 172, 173
diversion, 172,
    173
diversity, 172,
    173
divert, 172, 214
divine, 64
divinely, 64
divinity, 64
doc–, 67, 68
docile, 67, 277,
    373
docility, 67
doct–, 67–68,
    106
doctor, 67–68
doctoral, 67, 68
doctorate, 67
doctrinal, 68
doctrine, 68
document, 68
documentary, 68
documentation, 68
doing, 359
dolorous, 269
domicile, 374
don, 414
Don Juan, 29
donor, 271

don't you, 362
dormant, 278,
    305
dormitory, 271
dossier, 385, 387
dot–, 199
douse, 374
do you, 362
dramatics, 271
draper's, 243
draw, 357
drawing, 357
drom–, 258
dromedary, 317
drown, 364
drowned, 364
druggist, 270
du–, 265
dual/duel, 489
duc–, 69, 70, 71,
    244, 250
duckling, 280
duct–, 69, 71,
    185
duel/dual, 488
due to/because
    of, 502
dun, 414
duo–, 265
duration, 354
dustbin, 243
duty, 353–54
dye/die, 489

e–, 105, 106,
    110, 113,
    118, 147,
    169, 174,
    178, 180,
    217, 219
eager/anxious,
    501
–eal, 267
–ean, 270, 277
eating, 359
eau de cologne, 61
ebb, 414
echelon, 346
éclair, 385
éclat, 387
economy, 272
ecru, 56
ed–, 296
–ed, 19, 266,
    274, 279,
    340, 341,
    343
Eden, 197
edible, 296
edict, 73, 78
edify, 461
Edinburgh, 381
editor, 307, 354
ef–, 74, 217, 219
efface, 219
effect, 75–76
    effect/affect, 480

effeminate, 219
effervesce, 217
efficiency, 75
efficient, 74–75
effluence, 90
effrontery, 317
–efy, 329
egg whisk, 243
egoist/egotist,
    503
egregious, 219
Eire, 381
either, 349, 352
    either/neither,
    514
eject, 120
eke, 414
–el, 281, 299,
    300, 301
elder/eldest, 503
elect, 105, 106
election, 106
elector, 106
electoral, 365
electorate, 106
electrician, 270
electrify, 274
elide, 219
elig–, 296
eligibility, 106
eligible, 106, 296
elite, 377, 380
elm, 365
elocution, 110
eloquence, 110
eloquent, 110
em–, 222
emanate, 219
embrace, 222
emeritus, 342
emigrant/
    immigrant,
    489
eminent/
    imminent,
    489
emission, 113
emit, 113, 219
emotion, 118
emotional, 118
en–, 16, 19, 51,
    223
enact, 16, 33
enactment, 16
enamored, 19, 33,
    73
–ence, 267, 301–3
    304, 306
enclose, 51,
    222–23
–ency, 82, 267,
    300, 302,
    304
endemic, 73
enforceable, 296
en garde, 388
engender, 313
enigma, 355, 377
enjoin, 120

enni–, 21, 22
–ennial, 45
ennui, 388
en rapport, 225,
    388
en route, 388
ensemble, 388
ensure/insure, 482
–ent, 14, 35, 36,
    40, 42, 57,
    59, 60, 74,
    82, 102,
    110, 121,
    128, 136,
    156, 157,
    159, 190,
    270, 278,
    300, 302,
    304, 305
entente, 388
entomology, 271
entourage, 388
entr'acte, 388
entrée, 385, 388
entrepreneur, 158,
    388
envelop/envelope,
    489
envelope, 388
enviable, 296
environment, 292
eon, 414
epicure, 41
e pluribus unum,
    225
equ–, 20–21, 72,
    81
equable, 446
equal, 275
equanimity, 20–21
equanimous, 21
equi–, 71
equilibrium, 71,
    72, 73, 81
equivalent, 361
equivocal, 72
equivocate, 72
–er, 270, 279,
    307–8,
    309–10,
    311–12, 325,
    340, 341,
    343, 371–72
errant, 305
erratum, 390
erroneous, 342
error, 268
ersatz, 388
erupt, 147
eruption, 147
–ery, 314, 315–16
–es, 273
escape, 292, 357
esprit, 387
esprit de corps,
    –est, 279, 340,
    341
estimable, 446
estimate, 373

estuary, 317
et, 281
etc., 472
et cetera, 472
ethno–, 71
ethnology, 71
–ette, 281
–ety, 268
etymologist, 151
eulogistic, 367
euphoria, 367
European, 278
evade, 217
evasive, 219
event, 169–70
eventful, 169
eventual, 169–70
eventuality, 170
eventually, 170
evidence, 176,
    319
evident, 174
evince, 219
evocation, 177
evocative, 177
evoke, 177
evolution, 180
evolve, 181, 219
ex–, 39, 42, 43,
    49–50, 52,
    76, 105,
    106, 110,
    113, 118,
    126, 133,
    138, 139,
    143, 147,
    154, 165,
    169, 174,
    177, 180,
    217–19
exacerbate, 219
exaction, 219
ex cathedra, 403
excavate, 217
exceed, 42, 321
    exceed/accede,
    480
exceedingly, 42
except, 39
    except/accept,
    480
exception, 39
exceptional, 39
exceptionally, 39
excerpt, 218
excess, 43
    excess/access,
    480
excessive, 43
excitement, 267
exclaim, 49
exclamation, 50
exclamatory, 50
excludable, 52
exclude, 52, 217
exclusion, 52
exclusive, 52
exclusively, 52
exclusiveness, 52

excommunicate, 218
excoriate, 219
excrescence, 106
excruciate, 217
excusable, 296
execrable, 446
exemplary, 317, 322
exhale, 218
exhibition, 292, 361, 366
exhortation, 367
exhume, 217
exigency, 324
exile, 373
exodus, 197
exonerate, 219
expect, 154
expectancy, 154
expectant, 154
expectation, 154
expediency, 324
expedient, 345
expedite, 218
expel, 144
expend, 126
expendable, 126
expenditure, 126
expense, 126
expenses, 126
expensive, 126
expire, 218
explicit, 133
    explicit/
    implicit, 503
export, 143
expose, 138
exposé, 138
exposition, 139
expository, 139
exposure, 138–39
expound, 139
expulsion, 144
exquisite, 377
extant, 305
extenuate, 219
exterminate, 218
extinguish, 218, 274
extirpate, 219
extol, 461
extort, 218
extra–, 184, 220
extract, 165
extraction, 165
extraneous, 346
extraordinary, 220, 365
extrasensory, 220
extricate, 218
exuberant, 345

fabricate, 241
fac–, 32, 74, 75, 192
facile, 74

facilitate, 461
facility, 74
fact–, 74, 75, 81
factor, 31
factory, 361
faint/feint, 489
fall–, 296
fallacy, 267, 324
fallible, 296
fan–, 244
fantastically, 338
farcical, 301
farmer, 307
farther/further, 490
father, 356
faux pas, 385
favorable, 361
favorite, 361
feasible, 296, 446
feat, 418
feathery, 277
February, 292, 293, 360, 363
fect–, 75, 76, 237
federal, 361
feint, 335
    feint/faint, 489
feline, 73, 276
fellow, 356
fen, 414
fend–, 234
fer–, 76–77, 81, 260
feral, 346
fertile, 373
fess–, 244
fete, 385, 387
fettle, 301
fewer/less, 504
fiancé, 385, 386
    fiancé/fiancée, 490
fiancée, 385
    fiancée/fiancé, 490
fiasco, 403
fic–, 74–75, 255
–fic, 276
fiction, 74
fictional, 74
fictitious, 74
figure, 357
filch, 418
filial, 73, 275
film, 365
finale, 389
finally, 338, 361
finesse, 385, 387
finger, 372
finis, 390
firm–, 79–80
–fit, 32
flaccid, 358
flamboyant, 305
flamenco, 389
flat, 243
flaunt/flout, 490

flect–, 80–81
flex, 418
flex–, 80
flexibility, 80
flexible, 80, 295
fling, 371
flinging, 372
flippant, 345
flotilla, 403
flotsam/jetsam, 504
flout/flaunt, 490
flu–, 82–83
fluctuation, 90
fluency, 82
fluent, 82
flux–, 82, 83, 96
for, 515
formally/
    formerly, 490
formerly, 360
    formerly/
    formally, 490
formidable, 296, 376
fortissimo, 389
foul/fowl, 490
found–, 86
foundry, 86
fowl/foul, 490
fracas, 353
fract–, 83, 84, 96
fraction, 83, 96
fractional, 83
frag–, 83–84
fragile, 83–84, 373, 375
fragility, 84
fragment, 84
fragmentary, 84
frang–, 83
frankfurter, 61
fresco, 117
frieze, 117
fring–, 83, 84
frolic, 318
frolicked, 318
frolicking, 318
from/than, 514
from/with, 514
fuchsia, 56
–ful, 97, 326, 340, 343
fund–, 86, 87, 184
furbelow, 158
further/farther, 490
fus–, 86–87, 96, 213
fuse, 86–87
fusion, 86, 96
futile, 373
–fy, 273, 340

gam–, 87–88,

124, 167, 201
garage, 371
garner, 313
gasconade, 387
gasoline, 374, 375
gauche, 385
gaucherie, 346
Gehenna, 197
gen–, 32, 88–89
genealogist, 270
genealogy, 101
generally, 338
genesis, 88
genial, 88–89
genit–, 88, 89
genital, 89
genius, 88
genocide, 101
genuine, 89, 357
geo–, 91–92, 96
geographer, 91
geographic, 91
geographical, 91
geography, 91, 360, 361
geologic, 91
geological, 91
geologist, 91
geology, 91, 96, 271
geometric, 92
geometry, 91–92, 273
ger–, 92–94
gest–, 92, 93–94
gestate, 93
gestation, 93
gesticulate, 371, 372
gesture, 371, 372
gibbet, 371
gibe, 371
giblet, 372
gist, 371, 372
glad to, 362
glisten, 366
globule, 280
glockenspiel, 388
glorious, 276
gloss, 418
Gloucester, 381
goad, 461
going to, 361, 362
golden calf, 197
golfer, 270
gondola, 377, 380
good/well, 511
goodness, 268
gosling, 280
got to, 362
gouache, 117
gourmand, 385
gourmet, 385, 386
government, 292, 360
governor, 360

grad–, 94–96, 106
gradation, 106
gradual, 94–95, 96
gradualism, 95
graduate, 95, 373
graduation, 95
grammatically, 338
grandiose, 276, 358
–graph, 29, 272
–graphy, 34, 93, 167, 272
grat–, 96, 97–98
grateful, 97
gratification, 97
gratify, 97, 274
gratis, 120
gratitude, 96, 97
gratuitous, 98
gratuity, 98
grav–, 98–99, 124, 193
grave, 98
gravid, 275
gravitate, 99
gravitation, 99
gravitational, 99
gravity, 99
grease, 374
Grecian, 278
greengrocer, 243
greenish, 276
Greenwich, 381–82
greg–, 251
gress–, 94. 95–96
grievous, 365
grimace. 377, 380
grisly, 358
gristle, 292
grotto, 389
guava, 389
Guiana, 381
guillotine, 41
gunwale. 292, 366
gyn–, 167
gynecologist, 85, 167, 261

habiliments, 387
habitable. 446
habitué. 385
hacienda, 389
haggle, 461
hallmark, 108, 109
handkerchief, 292
hang, 371
hanged/hung, 504
hanger, 372
hanging. 372
harass, 355, 377
harbinger, 371, 372

hard, 464
harp, 418
has to, 362
hatter, 309
hauteur, 387
Hawaii, 382
hearth, 357
heed, 461
hegira, 108, 109
heinous, 335
heir, 363
hemi–, 71, 265
hemisphere, 71, 265
hepta–, 265
her–, 99–100
herb, 363
herbivorous, 23
heresy, 324
heroism, 267
hes–, 99–100
heterogeneous, 101
hexa–, 265
hiatus, 342
hierarchy, 369, 370
Himalayas, 382
hindrance, 365
historic/historical, 504
hoary, 358
hoi polloi, 158
hollow, 356
homage, 363
homogeneity, 101
homonym, 101
honest, 363
honor, 354, 363
honorary, 275
horrible, 296
hors d'oeuvre, 385
hospitable, 377
hostile. 373
hour, 363
house, 374
houses, 374
Houston, 382
hoyden. 15
huge, 363
human. 277, 357, 363
humane, 363
humble, 363
humid, 275
humidify, 210
humor, 363
humorist, 361
humorous, 363
hung/hanged, 504
hurtle, 301
hydro–. 167
hydroelectric, 167
hyper–, 184, 220
hyperacidity, 220
hypercorrect, 220–221

hypercritical, 184
hypersensitive, 221
hypno–, 167
hypnosis, 167
hypo–, 184, 221–22
hypochondria, 221
hypochondriac, 135, 369
hypocrisy, 324
hypodermic, 221
hypotenuse, 221
hypothesis, 222
hypothetical, 222
hypothyroidism, 184

–ial, 32, 54, 110, 255, 267, 275
–ian, 270, 277
ibidem, 390
–ible, 28, 80, 106, 107, 157, 277, 294–96, 297, 325
–ibly, 294, 295
–ic, 221, 275
ichthyologist, 151
–ician, 270
icon–, 167
iconoclast, 101, 167
–ics, 271
–id, 13, 275–76
identify, 360
idiosyncrasy, 324
idle/idol/idyl, 490
–ience, 28
if/whether, 504
–ify, 63, 97, 329–30
ignominious, 355
ignominy, 355
ignoramus, 352, 353
iguana, 389
il–, 222, 223–24, 280
–ile, 15, 67, 74, 83, 113, 275, 277, 373
illegible, 107
illiterate, 223–24
illusion/allusion, 481
illustrate, 352
illustrious, 342
im–, 123, 131, 133, 134, 139, 143, 222, 224, 295

imbalance, 224
imbecile, 373
imbroglio, 367
immigrant/emigrant, 489
imminent/eminent, 489
immoral/amoral/unmoral/immortal, 506
impasto, 117
impeccable, 446
impel, 123
impending, 144
impertinent, 160
impetus, 342
impious, 355, 376
implacable, 298
implement, 131–32
implementation, 132
implicate, 133–34
implication, 134
implicit, 134
implicit/explicit, 503
imply, 134
imply/infer, 506
imponderable, 446
import, 143
impose, 139
imposing, 139
imposition, 139
impotent, 376
impressionism, 117
impugn, 367
impulse, 123
impulsion, 123
impulsive. 123
in/into, 506
in–, 36, 40, 52, 57, 60, 75, 79. 82, 84, 100, 102, 104, 133, 134, 145, 149, 154, 156, 170, 177, 180, 183, 222–23, 224, 227, 232, 262-63, 295, 377
inactive, 33
inadmissible, 111, 112
inalienable, 298
inamorata, 403
inapproachable, 263
inarticulate, 224
inaudible, 28
incapable, 37, 183

incarcerate, 227
incarnate, 224, 227
incendiary, 317
incense, 319
inception, 40
incessant, 223
inchoate, 370
incidence, 36, 306
incident, 36
incidental, 36
incidentally, 36, 338
incipience, 40
incipient, 40, 227
includable, 52
include, 52
inclusion, 52
inclusive, 52
incognito, 355, 378, 380
incoherent, 120
incomparable, 377, 380, 446
    incomparable/
    uncompar-
    able, 510
incompetent, 129
incomplete, 131
inconceivable, 335
incongruous, 223
inconsequential, 224
inconspicuous, 154
inconvenient, 169
incorporate, 56
increase, 57
incredible/
    incredulous, 506
increment, 57
incubate, 60
incubator, 60
incumbency, 227
incumbent, 60, 278
incur, 78
incursion, 227
indefensible, 296
indelible, 296
indemnity, 223
indescribable, 182
indigenous, 342
indigestible, 93
indigestion, 93
indigo, 56
indispensable, 126
individual, 476–77
indoctrinate, 78, 106
indomitable, 223
–ine, 64, 275
inequitable, 224

inestimable, 298
inexorable, 223
infamous, 224, 380
infantile, 373
infect, 75
infection, 75
infectious, 75
infer, 506
inference, 306
inferno, 403
infirm, 79–80
infirmary, 80
inflection, 90, 295
influence, 82–83, 267, 376
influential, 83
influx, 96
infraction, 90
infringe, 84, 227
infringement, 84
infuse, 86
–ing, 274–75, 278, 318, 325, 328, 359, 371–72
ingenious, 89
ingénue, 385, 387
ingenuous, 89, 342
ingratiate, 227
ingratitude, 97
inhabitant, 270
inherent, 120, 227
inhibit, 227
inhospitable, 380
inject, 102
injection, 102
injunction, 104
inmate, 373
innate, 226
innocuous, 269
inquire, 145
inquiry, 145, 268, 377
inquisition, 145
inquisitive, 145, 146
insatiable, 223, 224, 346
inscribe, 149
inscription, 149
inscrutable, 298
insoluble, 301
inspect, 154
inspection, 154
inspector, 154
insufferable, 223
insular, 313
insult, 378
insuperable, 224
insure/ensure, 482
intact, 156
intelligible, 296
intangible, 157

inter–, 45, 111, 147, 226, 227–28
interact, 33
interbreed, 226
intercept, 226
intercession, 45
intercollegiate, 227
interdenomina-
    tional, 227
interdependent, 227
interfere, 226
interject, 226
interjection, 120
interlocutor. 111
interlude, 226
intermezzo, 227–28, 389
intermittent, 346
intern, 85
internecine, 227
internist, 85
interrupt, 147
interruption, 147–48
intestate, 223
into/in, 506
in toto, 403
intra–, 183, 228
intramural, 183, 228
intravenous, 228
intricacy, 324
intricate, 376
intro–, 69
introduce, 69
introduction, 69
introductory, 69, 276
inundate, 461
invalidate, 223
inveigle, 335
invent, 170
invention, 170
inventive, 170
inventor, 170
invincible, 296
inviolate, 223
invisible, 176
invocation, 178
invoke, 177–78
involve, 180
involved, 180
involvement, 180
–ion, 29, 32, 65, 83, 86, 94, 104, 121, 129, 133, 139, 153, 166, 176, 250, 267, 294–95, 325
ir–, 222. 224. 295, 377
iridescent, 319
irony, 361
irreducible, 70

irrefutable, 298
irrelevance, 306
irreparable, 377, 446
irresistible, 224, 296
irretrievable, 335
irrevocable, 178, 298, 377, 380
irritate/
    aggravate, 499
–ise, 336, 337
–ish, 117, 273, 275, 341
isle/aisle, 481
islet, 280
–ism, 267
–ist, 270
it–, 196, 250
Italian, 357
–ite, 127, 271
itinerary, 360
its/it's, 491, 497
–ity, 13, 18, 19, 20, 21, 22, 64, 98, 99, 268
–ive, 15, 121, 141, 173, 277
–ize, 258, 273, 337, 338

jac–, 102, 103, 190
jai alai, 389
ject–, 102–3, 233
jeopardize, 367
jeremiad, 197
jetsam/flotsam, 504
jeweler, 309
Jezebel, 197
join–, 103–4
joint–, 103
joyous, 277
Judas, 197
July, 162
junct–, 103, 104
junction, 104
juncture, 120
junta, 389
jur–, 237
just, 357
juvenile, 276, 374. 375
juxtaposition, 101

kept, 360
kindergarten, 388
kind of, 362
kleptomaniac, 135
knockwurst, 388

lab–, 257
laboratory, 360
lachrymose, 370
ladder/later/
  latter, 492
laid, 507
La Jolla, 382
lama, 351
lamasery, 317
lamentable, 355,
  377
Laos, 382
lapidary, 317
larynx, 357
lasagne, 389
lascivious, 319
last, 351
later/latter/
  ladder, 492
laudatory, 276
laugh, 351
lavatory, 271
law, 357
lay/lie, 507
–le, 299–300,
  301
lead/led, 492
leaflet, 280
learn/teach, 507
leave/let, 507
lect–, 105–6, 107,
  124, 251
lecture, 107
led/lead, 492
leg–, 105, 106,
  107, 296
legerdemain, 158
legible, 107, 296
length, 359, 363
leprechaun, 158
less/fewer, 504
–less, 278, 326
let/leave, 507
–let, 280
lethal, 301
let her, 362
let him, 362
let me, 362
lexicographer, 151
liable, 361
  liable/apt/
  likely, 501
liaison, 385
libel/slander, 510
library, 270, 292,
  360
libretto, 403
license, 319
lie/lay, 507
lieder, 388
lieu, 303
lieutenant, 160,
  303
lifeless, 278
lift, 243
lig–, 105
lightning, 365
like/as/as if,
  501–2

likely/apt/liable,
  501
linage, 328
lineage, 328
ling–, 201
–ling, 280
lingerie, 385
linguistics, 101,
  271
literacy, 324
literate, 223
livable, 296
Ljubljana, 381
llama, 351, 352
Llanfairpwllgwy-
  ngllgo-
  gerych-
  wyrndrobw-
  llllantysilio-
  gogogoch,
  381
locate, 213
locut–, 110–11
locution, 202
loge, 385
logician, 270
–logue, 271
–logy, 24, 25, 34,
  91, 271
long, 371
longer, 372
longevity, 371,
  372
longitude, 268
loose/lose, 492
loqu–, 110
loque–, 124
lorry, 243
lose/loose, 492
lout, 29
loving, 359
lucid, 276
luminary, 101
lurid, 269
luscious, 319
luxuriant/
  luxurious,
  508
–ly, 279, 326,
  338, 339,
  461–65
lyrically, 338

macabre, 385,
  387
macadamize, 162
Machiavellian,
  346
machinations, 369,
  370
magazine, 361
magdalene, 197
magistracy, 324
magn–, 21
magnanimity, 21
magnanimous, 21
magnate, 373
magnification, 130

majority/
  plurality,
  508
mal–, 183,
  229–30, 231
maladroit, 229,
  358
malaise, 231
malcontent, 229,
  231
mal de mer, 385
male–, 229, 231
malediction, 229,
  231
malefactor, 130,
  231
malevolent, 231
malfeasance, 231
malfunction,
  183–84
malicious, 319
malignant, ·
  229–30
malleable, 298
malodorous, 231
mammalian, 23
manger, 371
manipulate, 130
mansard, 162
manu–, 75, 81
manual, 275
manufacture, 75,
  81, 357
marine, 252
marriageable, 296
marsupial, 23
martinet, 162,
  386
massage, 371
massive, 277
material/
  materiel,
  492
matri–, 26, 167
matriarch, 26,
  130
matriarchy, 26,
  33, 167
matriculate, 130
matrimony, 267
maudlin, 162
mausoleum, 108,
  109, 162,
  374
mauve, 56
maverick, 108,
  109, 162
may/can, 502
meander, 108,
  109
mecca, 108, 109
mega–, 167
megalomaniac,
  135
megaphone, 167
melee, 386

memorable, 296
memory, 361
–men, 267
–ment, 68, 84,
  115, 153,
  267
mercantile, 374,
  375
mercenary, 322
mercurial, 301
merg–, 184
meridian, 238–39
meteorology, 271
–meter, 273
meticulous, 342
métier, 387
–metry, 91, 273
mettle, 301
Mexico/
  México, 381
microscope, 273
milieu, 386, 387
millinery, 314
mimic, 318
mimicked, 318
mimicking, 318
miner/minor,
  492
minx, 15
mir–, 190
mis–, 24, 184,
  229, 230,
  231
misanthrope, 24,
  230
misanthropic, 24,
  66
misanthropist, 24
misanthropy, 24
misapprehension,
  231
mischievous, 365,
  366
misconception,
  231
misconstrue, 231
miscreant, 231
misdemeanor, 231
mishap, 231
misinform, 184
misnomer, 231
misogamy, 101
misogyny, 101
misrepresent, 230
miss–, 111–14
missile, 113
misspell, 230
mistake, 230
mit–, 111–15,
  252, 260
mobile, 31, 117,
  144, 374,
  375
modern, 357
Mojave, 382
molecule, 280
mon–, 26, 115–16
Monaco, 382
monarch, 26

monarchy, 26
monetary, 322
monit-, 115, 116
monitor, 116
monitory, 116
mono-, 87, 167, 265
monocle, 167
monogamous, 101, 265
monogamy, 87, 167
monologue, 265, 272
monotreme, 23
monument, 115-16, 267
monumental, 116
-mony, 13, 267-68
moral/morale, 493
morsel, 280
mortgage, 292, 293, 366
mosaic, 318
mosaicked, 318
mosaicking, 318
Moscow, 382
mot-, 118-19
mother, 356
motif, 386
motivation, 144
motive, 144
motorist, 361
mountebank, 158
mov-, 118, 119
multitude, 268
mundane, 269
mural, 117, 228
mute, 243

nagging, 372
naive, 386
naiveté, 386
nappy, 243
nasc-, 121
nascent, 121
nat-, 121-22, 124
natal, 144
Natchitoches, 381
nation, 121
national, 121
nationalism, 121
native, 121-22
nativity, 122
naval/navel, 493
nebulous, 342
neglig-, 296
negligence, 319
negligible, 296 298
neither/either, 514
nemesis, 108, 109
-ness, 268, 326, 340, 341

neurologist, 85
New Yorker, 409
nex-, 193
nib, 414
nicotine, 162
niggardly, 269
nimrod, 158
nocturnal, 23
nomenclature, 130
nominal, 130
nominate, 274
-nomy, 272
non-, 184, 232, 265, 293
nonbelligerent, 93
nonchalance, 346
nonchalant, 232
noncomformist, 232
nonentity, 232
nonflammable, 184
nonpareil, 335
nonsense, 232
non sequitur, 390, 403
nontransference, 77
nor/or, 514
norm-, 186
nostalgic, 269
noticeable, 296
notoriety, 268
noun, 245
nov-, 265
novelty, 268
nuance, 386
nub, 414
nucleus, 345
number/amount, 500

o-, 113
oaf, 414
Oahu, 382
ob-, 76, 113, 139, 233, 234
obbligato, 389
obeisance, 335
obese, 233
obfuscate, 234
object, 233, 379
obligate, 234
oblique, 234, 358
oblong, 234
obnoxious, 234
obsession, 182
obsolete, 234
obstacle, 234
obstetrician, 85
obstetrics, 234
obstreperous, 234, 269
obtrude, 233
obtuse, 234
oc-, 36, 62, 233, 234

occasion, 36-37
occasional, 37
occident, 36
occidental, 36
occult, 235
occupy, 233
occur, 62-63
occurrence, 63
ocher, 56
oct-, 265
ocular-, 201
oculist/
  ophthal-
  mologist/
  optician/
  optometrist, 508
of-, 76-77, 233, 234
offend, 234
offer, 76-77
offering, 77
offertory, 77
often, 360, 366
of which, 518
-oid, 275, 276
Okinawa, 382
older/oldest, 503
-olent, 276, 277
-ology, 271
omission, 113
omit, 113
omni-, 167
omnipotent, 167
omniscience, 130
omniscient, 319
omnivorous, 130
on, 515
on-, 235
once, 364
onset, 235
onslaught, 235
onus, 342
op-, 139, 233, 234, 235
operate, 361
ophthalmologist, 85, 261, 520
ophthalmologist/
  oculist/
  optician/
  optometrist, 508
opponent, 140
opportune, 234
oppose, 139-40
opposite, 140-41
opposition, 140-41
oppress, 234
opprobrious, 343
opprobrium, 235
opt-, 189
optician/
  optometrist/
  ophthal-
  mologist/
  oculist, 508
optimist, 135
optometrist, 520

optometrist/
  optician/
  ophthal-
  mologist/
  oculist
  508
opulent, 277
or/nor, 514
-or, 16, 30, 89, 111, 116, 167, 241, 268, 271, 307, 308-9, 310, 311-12
oral/verbal, 511
orbital, 252
ordin-, 252
ordinance, 306
orgy, 371, 372
orifice, 130
-orium, 30
orn-, 253
ort-, 186
orthodontist, 85
orthopedist, 85
-ory, 18, 271, 275
-ose, 276
ostensible, 296, 298
ostentatious, 342
ought to, 362
-our, 307, 311-12
-ous, 19, 21, 196, 276-77, 325, 338, 340, 342
out-, 235, 236
outermost, 235
outset, 236
outside, 236
over-, 184, 235, 236
oversight, 236
overweight, 236
overwrought, 236
oviparous, 23
ovoid, 276

pachyderm, 23,
pacify, 274
Palestine, 382
palette, 117
pallid, 269
pamphlet, 364
panacea, 240
pandemonium, 240
panic, 318
panicked, 318
panicking, 318
panicky, 318
panoply, 240
panorama, 240
par-, 193
paragon, 240
paralyze, 336
paranoia, 240
paranoid, 135

paraphernalia, 240
pariah, 108, 109
parliament, 292, 293, 366
parochial, 345
parsimony, 268
particle, 280
particular, 361
particularly, 360
partner, 360
party, 476–77
pass, 351
passé, 386
passed/past, 493
pasta, 390
pastel, 117
pasteurize, 162
path–, 199, 257
patio, 351, 352
patois, 386, 387
patri–, 26, 38
patriarch, 38
patriarchy, 33
peace/piece, 493
peaceable, 277, 296
peculiar, 361
pecuniary, 275
pedal/peddle, 493
–pede, 46
pediatrician, 85, 261, 520
pel–, 122–24
pell–, 122–24
pend–, 125–27, 140
pending, 144
pens–, 125–27
pent, 418
penta–, 265
per–, 22, 113, 160, 236–38
perambulate, 236
percent, 46, 237
perceptible, 298
percolate, 237
percussion, 237
perdition, 237
perennial, 22
perfect, 237
perfidious, 237
perfume, 377
perfunctory, 322
perimeter, 240
peripatetic, 240
periphery, 240
perjure, 237
perjury, 268
permeate, 237
permissible, 114
permission, 114
permissive, 114, 130
permit, 113–14, 380
pernicious, 237
perpendicular, 237
perpetrator, 313

perpetual, 237
perplexity, 238
per se, 390
persecute, 508
persevere, 238
persist, 238
person, 477
personable, 298
personal/ personnel, 493
perspective, 238
perspiration, 292, 357
pertain, 160, 238
pertinacious, 160
pertinent, 160
pervade, 238
pessimist, 135
pet–, 127–29
petit–, 127–29
petite, 15
petition, 129
petrol, 243
Pharisee, 197
phil–, 24
philanderer, 29
philanthropist, 24
philanthropy, 24
philologist, 151
phlegmatic, 358
phobia/mania, 508
phon–, 257
phonetics, 130
phono–, 38
phonograph, 38, 272
photography, 167
physiotherapist, 520
pianissimo, 390
piazza, 390, 403
picaresque, 269
picnic, 318
picnicked, 318
picnicking, 318
picture, 357
piece/peace, 493
pinnate, 276
piquant, 358, 386
pique, 386
pittance, 306
pivotal, 346
pizza, 390
pizzicato, 390
plausible, 296, 298
plaza, 351
pleasurable, 296
plebeian, 335
plet–, 131–32
plex–, 132–34, 140
plic–, 132–34
plicit–, 132–34
plurality/majority, 508
plutocracy, 272

plutocrat, 272
ply–, 132–34
pod–, 38
podiatrist, 85, 261, 520
podium, 38
poem, 361
poetry, 361
poignant, 292, 358, 366
point, 359
politic, 318
politicking, 318
poly–, 87
polygamy, 87–88
pomegranate, 361, 363
pon–, 136, 140, 141, 142, 239
popular, 275
populous, 276
port–, 142–43
portable, 143
portentous, 342
portmanteau, 387
pose–, 136, 137–42
posit–, 136, 137, 139, 140–41
positive, 141
post, 239
post–, 141, 238–39, 242
postal, 275
postcard, 239
poster, 239
posterior, 239
posterity, 239
postgraduate, 238
posthumous, 239, 358
postmeridian, 238–39
post-mortem, 239
postpone, 141, 239
postponement, 141
postprandial, 239
postscript, 182, 239
potable, 298
potato, 356
potency, 324
potentate, 355
potpourri, 386, 387
pound–, 136, 137
practically, 338
pragmatist, 135
pram, 243
pre–, 43, 44, 52, 65, 116, 122, 149, 152, 170, 241–42, 246
preamble, 432
precaution, 240

precede, 43, 44
precede/ proceed, 494
precedence, 43
precedent, 43
precept, 241
precinct, 241
precipice, 241
precipitate, 242
precipitation, 242
precise, 242
preclude, 52
precocious, 242, 269
precocity, 246
precursor, 78, 240, 432
predict, 65
predictable, 65, 295
prediction, 65, 295
predictive, 432
predilection, 246, 432
preempt, 432
prefabricate, 241
preface, 242, 379
prefatory, 432
preferable, 376, 380
preference, 90
preferential, 432
prehensile, 23
prelate, 242
preliminary, 242
premeditate, 242
premolar, 241
premonition, 116
premonitory, 116, 246
prenatal, 122
preparation, 361
preponderance, 306
preposterous, 242
prerequisite, 242
prerogative, 242, 432
presage, 242, 432
prescient, 246
prescribe, 149, 150
prescribe/ proscribe, 494
prescription, 149, 292
prescriptive, 149
presentiment, 432
preside, 152, 374
presidency, 152
president, 152
presidential, 152
pressure, 268
prestige, 246, 371
presume, 242
presumptive, 432
presumptuous, 432

pretense, 319
pretext, 246
prevail, 432
prevaricator, 242
prevent, 170
prevention, 170, 171
preventive, 170–71
priceless, 278
prim–, 265
prima donna, 15
principal/ principle, 494, 497
prior, 346
pristine, 269
privilege, 361
pro–, 43, 44, 50, 70, 89, 95, 102, 118, 124, 141, 149, 165, 174, 178, 244–45, 246
probably, 361
procedural, 43–44
procedure, 43–44, 321
proceed, 43, 44, 244, 321
proceed/ precede, 494
proceeding, 43
proceedings, 43–44
proceeds, 43–44
process, 44, 352
procession, 44
processional, 44
proclaim, 50
proclamation, 50
proclivity, 245
procure, 245
prodigal, 245, 372
produce, 70, 244
product, 70
productive, 70
productivity, 70
profane, 244
profanity, 244
profess, 244–45, 246
profession, 245
professor, 245
proffer, 313
profile, 373
progenitor, 89
prognostication, 246
progress, 95, 379
progression, 95
progressive, 95
prohibition, 363
project, 102, 379
projectile, 102–3
projection, 102–3
projectionist, 102–

103
projector, 102–3
prominent, 361
promiscuous, 245
promote, 118
promotion, 118
promulgate, 245, 246
pronoun, 245
propaganda, 245
propel, 124
propeller, 124, 307
propensity, 246
propitiate, 246
propitious, 342
proposal, 141
propose, 141
proposition, 141
proprietary, 317
propulsion, 124
pro rata, 353
proscribe, 149, 150
proscribe/ prescribe, 494
proscription, 149
prosecute, 508
protest, 379
proto–, 265
protract, 165
protraction, 165
protractor, 165
provender, 313
provide, 174–75
provided, 175
providence, 175
provident, 175
provider, 175
provision, 175
provisional, 175
provisions, 175
proviso, 246
provocation, 178, 246
provocative, 178
provoke, 178
pseudo–, 38, 366
pseudonym, 38
psycho–, 38
psychoanalysis, 38
ptomaine, 292
pub, 243
publicly, 338
puerile, 374
pulchritude, 370
puls–, 122–24
punctuation, 393
punctum, 393
purchaser, 307
pyro–, 38
pyromaniac, 38
Pyrrhic victory, 108, 109

quadr–, 265

qualitative/ quantitative, 509
quart–, 265
quasi, 390
quest–, 145–46
quid pro quo, 403
quiet/quit/quite, 494, 497
Quincy, 381
quint–, 265
quir–, 145–46
quisit–, 145–46
quisling, 162
quit/quite/quiet, 494

radiator, 352, 353
radio, 353
ragout, 386
raillery, 317
rain/rein/reign, 494
raise/raze/rise, 494–95
rampant, 305
rancor, 345
rankle, 301
rara avis, 390
rather, 351
rathskeller, 388
rational, 301
raucous, 269
ravage, 461
raw, 357
raze/raise/rise, 494–95
re–, 40, 44, 50, 54, 63, 70, 80, 87, 118–19, 123, 129, 132, 146, 152, 154, 161, 168, 173, 178, 181, 184, 247–49
–re, 307, 310–11
react, 33
reader, 376
reading, 359
realignment, 367
realism, 376
realist, 135
rebel, 247
rebuff, 247
recalcitrant, 248
recall, 247
recede, 44, 322
receding, 44
receipt, 40, 292
receivable, 296
receive, 40
receiver, 40
receptacle, 40
reception, 40
receptionist, 40
receptive, 40

recess, 44–45
recession, 45
recessional, 45
recessive, 249
reciprocal, 248
reclaim, 50
recognize, 359, 363
recompense, 249
reconcile, 373
reconnaissance, 248
reconnoiter, 248
record, 54–55
recoup, 248
recourse, 78
recriminate, 248
recruit, 377
recumbent, 78, 106
recuperate, 248
recur, 63
recurrence, 63
recurrent, 63
redolent, 277
redress, 249
reduce, 70
reducible, 293
reduction, 70
refer/allude, 499
reference, 90
referendum, 90
refinery, 314
reflect, 80–81
reflection, 81
reflective, 81
reflex, 90
refresh, 247
refrigerate, 247
refund, 87, 184
refusal, 267
refuse, 379
regardless, 474
regress, 120
regular, 361
reign, 292
reign/rein/rain, 494
reiterate, 248
relapse, 248
relegate, 248
reliable, 296
relinquish, 248
remediable, 345
remembrance, 365, 366
reminiscence, 248
remiss, 249
remonstrate, 355, 377
remote, 118–19
removal, 119
remove, 119
remunerate, 248
render, 313
rendezvous, 386
reparable, 376, 380
repartee, 386

repel, 123
repellent, 123
repetition, 129
repetitious, 129
repetitive, 129
replaceable, 296
replete, 132, 322
repletion, 132,
    249
reprehensible, 319
represent, 230
reprieve, 248,
    335
repulsion, 123
repulsive, 123
reputable, 376
require, 146
requirement, 146
requisite, 146
rescind, 248
reside, 152, 374
residence, 152
resident, 152,
    270–71
residential, 152
resilience, 306
resilient, 358,
    374, 375
respect, 154–55
respectable, 155
respectably/
    respectfully/
    respectively,
    495
respectful, 155
respectfully/
    respectably/
    respectively,
    495
resplendent, 305
responsible, 296
restaurant, 361
résumé, 386
resuscitate, 319
retain, 161
retainer, 161
retention, 161
retentive, 161
retract, 166
retractable, 166
retraction, 166
retrenchment, 249
reverberate, 249
reversal, 173
reverse, 173
reversible, 173
reversion, 173
revert, 173
revile, 248
revise, 248
revival, 12
revive, 11, 12
revocable, 296,
    376
revocation, 178
revoke, 178
revolt, 181
revolution, 181
revolutionary, 181

revolve, 182
revolver, 181
rhapsody, 292
rheumatism, 292
rhinoceros, 292
rhubarb, 292
rhyme, 292
rhythm, 292
ribald, 269
ricochet, 386
rift, 418
ring, 371
ringing, 372
Rio de Janeiro,
    382
Rio Grande, 382
ripa, 194
rise/raze/raise,
    494–95
risky, 277
–rive, 194
robust, 377
roister, 313
romance, 377,
    380
romantic, 135
roué, 386
route, 353
rudimentary, 322
rue, 414
rumor, 354
runner, 307
rupt–, 146–48
rupture, 148

–s, 266, 273,
    274, 340,
    341, 343
sabotage, 371,
    372
sachet, 386
sacrifice, 352
Salisbury, 382
sallow, 269
salon, 386
San Joaquin, 382
San José, 382
San Juan, 382
satrap, 353
sauerbraten, 388
Sault Sainte
    Marie, 382
savoir-faire, 386
saw, 357
Schenectady, 382
schism, 366, 367
scholar, 270, 307
scintilla, 367
–scope, 273
scrib–, 148–50,
    260
script–, 148–50
se–, 49, 107,
    250–51
secede, 33, 250
secondary, 275
secret, 49
secretarial, 49

secretary, 49,
    270, 360
secretive, 49, 277
–sect, 38
secular, 313
secure, 250
sed–, 152–53,
    250
sedate, 182
sedative, 182
–sede, 321
sedentary, 182,
    317
sediment, 153
sedition, 250
seduce, 250–51
seed/cede, 485
segregate, 251
select, 107, 251
selection, 107
selective, 107
self–evident, 174
semi–, 265
senator, 354
senile, 374
sensation, 295
sensible, 295
sensory, 220
sept–, 265
sequel, 301
sergeant, 303
serve, 303
serviceable, 296
servile, 374
sess–, 152, 153
session, 153
set/sit, 509
severance, 345
sex–, 265
shall/will, 509
shambles, 108,
    109
shanghai, 108,
    109
shellac, 318
shellacked, 318
shellacking, 318
shepherd, 363
shibboleth, 197
shrapnel, 162
shrew, 15
–sia, 268
sid–, 152, 153
sideburns, 162
sidle, 301
sight/site/cite,
    486
similar, 275, 361
similarly, 360
sing, 371
singer, 372
singing, 372
sinister, 313
–sis, 268
sit/set, 509
site/sight/cite,
    486
skepticism, 267
slander/libel, 510

sleepless, 278
sleeplessness, 268
socialite, 271
sociat–, 194
socio–, 38
sociology, 38
soften, 360, 366
solecism, 108,
    109
solicitous, 342
solvere, 186
somber, 345
something, 357
somni–, 38
somniferous, 38
sophomore, 292,
    361, 363
soporific, 276
sorbere, 187–88
sorrel, 56
sound, 185
sovereign, 367
spec–, 153
specie, 335
species, 335
specimen, 267
spect–, 153, 154–
    55
spectacle, 155
spectacles, 155
spectacular, 155
spheroid, 276
spic–, 153
spoil, 357
squalor, 313
staid, 418
stainless, 278
stalactite/
    stalagmite,
    510
staple, 301
stationary/
    stationery,
    314, 495
stationer, 314
statuesque, 358
status, 352–53
status quo, 390
stentorian, 108,
    109
stet, 390
stethoscope, 273
stew, 354
straight/strait,
    495
strategy/tactics,
    510
strength, 359
strident, 346
stringent, 278
stronger, 372
study, 117
stupid, 354
suave, 29
sub–, 60, 126,
    142, 150,
    166, 173,
    183, 184,
    251–53

subconscious, 252, 254
subconscious/ unconscious, 510
subcutaneous, 253
subject, 379
subjugate, 254
sublimate, 254
subliminal, 253, 254
submarine, 252
submerge, 184, 254
submit, 252
suborbital, 252
subordinate, 252–53, 254
suborn, 253, 254
subscribe, 150, 254
subscriber, 150
subscription, 150
subservient, 253, 254
subside, 254
subsidiary, 253, 254
subsidy, 253
substandard, 183
substantiate, 253, 254
substitute, 253
subterranean, 253
subtle, 254, 366
subtract, 166
subtraction, 166
suburbanite, 271
subversion, 173–74
subversive, 173, 254
subvert, 174
subway, 243
suc–, 60, 251
succeed, 53, 321
succumb, 60
suckling, 280
suf–, 251
sug–, 184, 251
suit/suite, 495
sully, 461
sum–, 251
sumptuous, 358
sup–, 142, 251
super–, 183, 255–57
superannuated, 255
supercilious, 255, 256
superficial, 255
superfluous, 256
superhighway, 255
superimpose, 256
superintendent, 256

superiority, 268
superlative, 256
supernatural, 255
supernumerary, 256, 317
supersede, 256, 321, 322
supersensitive, 256
supersonic, 256
superstition, 257
superstructure, 183
supervene, 256
supervise, 257
supplicate, 461
suppose, 142, 360, 361
supposed, 142
supposition, 142
sur–, 251
surprise, 374
surveillance, 345
sus–, 126, 251
suscept–, .296
susceptible, 296, 346
suspend, 126–27
suspenders, 127
suspense, 127, 319
suspension, 127
suspicion, 319
sustenance, 306
svelte, 15, 358
–sy, 268, 323
syl–, 257
syllable, 257
sym–, 257
sympathy, 257
symphony, 257–58
syn–, 257–59
synagogue, 259
synchronize, 258
syncopate, 258
syndicate, 259
syndrome, 258
synod, 259
synonym, 258
synopsis, 259
syntax, 258–59
synthesis, 259
sys–, 257
systematically, 338

tacit, 358
tact, 157
tact–, 156–57
tactful, 157
tactics/strategy, 510
tactile, 355
tactless, 157
tain–, 159, 160, 161
–tain, 188

talking, 359
tang–, 156, 157, 296
tangent, 157
tangential, 157
tangible, 157, 296, 301
tantalize, 108, 109
tax–, 258–59
teach/learn, 507
tekt–, 26
tele–, 175
telegraph, 272
telescope, 273
televise, 175
television, 175
tempera, 117
temperament, 292, 361
temperature, 292, 361
temporal, 301
ten–, 159, 160, 161
tenacious, 160, 161, 277
tenacity, 161, 267
tenant, 303
tend–, 194
tent–, 159, 160, 161
ter–, 265
termagant, 346
terminate, 274
terrible, 277, 296
terrific, 276
terrorize, 274
tête-à-tête, 386
tetra–, 265
textile, 374, 375
Thailand, 363, 382
than/from, 514
than/then, 496, 497
that, 356
that/which, 518–19
the, 350–51
theater, 376
their/there/ they're, 496, 497
theirs/there's, 496
them, 356
then/than, 496
theology, 271
thermometer, 273
Thespian, 108, 109
this, 356
thorough/threw/ through, 496
those, 356
threw/through/ thorough, 496

thyme, 363
–tics, 271
tin, 243
tin–, 159
ting–, 156
–tion, 76
titan, 108, 109
titular, 313
to/too/two, 496, 497
Tokyo, 382
tomato, 351
too/to/two, 496
toothless, 278
tortilla, 389
tourniquet, 386
toxico–, 38
toxicology, 38
traceable, 296
tract, 166
tract–, 163–67
tractable, 345
traction, 166
tractor, 167
traffic, 318
trafficked, 318
trafficking, 318
trans–, 114, 150, 259–60, 261
transact, 33, 259–60
transatlantic, 260
transcend, 261
transcribe, 150, 182, 260
transcript, 150
transfer, 77, 81, 260
transferable, 77
transferal, 90
transference, 77
transform, 260
transfusion, 261
transgress, 120, 261
translate, 364
transmission, 114
transmit, 114, 260
transmitter, 114
transparent, 261
transpose, 261
traveler, 270
treacle, 243
tri–, 265
trice, 418
trigonometry, 273
trivial, 301
trud–, 233
trumpery, 322
try and/ try to, 515
tube, 354
Tucson, 382
–tude, 268
Tuesday, 352, 354
tune, 349, 353–54
turbulence, 306

turgid, 371
turnstile, 373
twice, 364
two/to/too, 496
–ty, 268, 326
tycoon, 29
typically, 338

–ule, 280
–ulent, 55, 276, 277
–ulous, 276
ulterior, 313
ultra–, 183, 263
ultraconservative, 262
ultramodern, 183, 262
ultraviolet, 262
umbrella, 365, 366
un–, 21, 184, 185, 232, 262–64, 295
unanimity, 21
unanimous, 21
unapproachable, 262–63
unbend, 184, 264
unbroken, 263-264
uncivilized, 263
uncomparable/incom–parable, 510
uncompromising, 263
unconscious/subconscious, 510
unconventional, 168–69
uncouth, 264
under–, 184, 235, 236
underground, 243
underhanded, 236
underwear, 236
underweight, 236
–une, 325
uni–, 265
unintelligible, 263
uninterested/distinter–ested, 503
union, 267
unkempt, 263
unmitigated, 263
unmoral/immoral/amoral, 506
unorganized, 511

unorganized/disorganized, 511
unparalleled, 263
unsavory, 322
unscathed, 263
unsound, 185
untenable, 298
untoward, 263
unwieldy, 263
unwonted, 263
–uous, 153
urbane, 278
–ure, 38, 75, 106, 148, 168, 268
us–, 188
–us, 338, 340, 342
usually, 361
usurp, 375, 461

vad–, 217
vagary, 322
vain/vane/vein, 497
valet, 386
van, 414
vane/vain/vein, 497
vanilla, 356
vase, 349, 351, 375
vaseline, 374, 375
vehemence, 367
vehement, 363, 366
vehicle, 363, 366
vein/vain/vane, 497
ven–, 168–69
vendetta, 390, 403
venison, 375
venous, 228
vent–, 168, 169–71
verbal/oral, 511
verbatim, 352, 353
verbose, 276
veritable, 345
vernal, 301
vers–, 171, 173
Versailles, 382
vert–, 171–72, 214
vest, 243
viable, 346
victory, 268

vid–, 174–75, 176
video, 175–76
vie, 414
Vienna, 381
Vietnam, 382
villager, 309
vineyard, 361
violence, 319
violent, 277
virago, 15
virile, 375
vis–, 174, 176
visa, 374
viscera, 319
viscount, 292
vise, 374
visible, 176
vision, 175, 176
visionary, 176
visual, 176
visualize, 176
vital, 11
vitality, 12
vitamin, 11, 354
vivacious, 11
vivid, 11
viviparous, 12
voc–, 72, 177, 178–79
vocabulary, 178–79
vocation, 179, 188
vocation/avocation, 511
vocational, 179
vok–, 177–78
volatile, 276
volt–, 181
volut–, 181
volv–, 180
voracious, 277
votary, 322

Waco, 382
waft, 418
waist/waste, 497
waistcoat, 243
wait on/wait for, 513, 515
waive, 461
walking, 359
wan, 414
want to, 361, 362
warp/woof, 511
waste/waist, 497
wastrel, 29
water color, 117

weather/whether, 497
Wednesday, 292
weir, 335
well/good, 511
welter, 313
Westerner, 309
what did, 362
where, 478
whether/if, 504
whether/weather, 497
which/that, 518–19
who/whom, 516
whoever/whomever, 516
who's/whose, 497
whose, 518
widow's mite, 197
width, 360
Wien (Vienna), 381
wife, 354
will/shall, 509
will he, 362
will you, 362
window, 356
windscreen, 243
winsome, 15
with/by, 513
with/from, 514
with/to, 513
woof/warp, 511
Worcester, 381, 382
Worcestershire, 382
working, 359
would you, 362
wraith, 367
wreak, 367
wrest, 367
wrestle, 299, 357
wretch, 292
writing, 359
wrong, 293, 371
wry, 414

–y, 257, 268, 276, 277, 340–41
yaw, 414
Yosemite, 382
younger, 372
your/you're, 497
–yze, 336, 337

zoologist, 151
zucchini, 369, 390